Justiciability of Human Rights Law in Domestic Jurisdictions

Alice Diver • Jacinta Miller
Editors

Justiciability of Human Rights Law in Domestic Jurisdictions

Springer

Editors
Alice Diver
Dept. of Law and Criminology
Edge Hill University
Ormskirk, Lancs, UK

Jacinta Miller
School of Law
Northumbria University
Newcastle, UK

ISBN 978-3-319-24014-5 ISBN 978-3-319-24016-9 (eBook)
DOI 10.1007/978-3-319-24016-9

Library of Congress Control Number: 2015958718

Springer Cham Heidelberg New York Dordrecht London

Printed on acid-free paper

Springer International Publishing AG Switzerland is part of Springer Science+Business Media (www.springer.com)

Foreword

The timing of this book with its eclectic and impressive range of essays could not have been published at a better or more opportune moment. Human rights, in all their guises, are often the subject of high-level and vociferous debate in both national and international circles. It seems that not a day passes without some call to either abolish or modify human rights legislation or perhaps even to introduce new laws on humanitarian grounds. In compiling this edited volume, Alice Diver and Jacinta Miller have undoubtedly filled a real gap within the current literature.

This book presents a wide range of topics across an extensive geographical spread. In so doing, it considers some of the major tensions that exist in developing and developed jurisdictions, from a myriad range of perspectives. The essays present a diverse collection of themes all unified by a single golden thread—that of the interpretation given to human rights protection, and if indeed such rights are to be given true substance, the extent to which these can, or even should, be enforced by the courts. The potential tensions in the relationship between human rights and the rule of law are also called into question by another central and unifying theme: that of human dignity. A fundamental question concerns the extent to which the right to dignity can be promoted and protected by law. Similar issues are apparent in the context of protection of other human rights that engage social, political or economic considerations. While these arguments are framed principally in terms of 'rights', the message that emerges ultimately is that such rights may, in fact, be non-justiciable.

The global perspective of the current collection of articles is to be commended highly as an exemplar for demonstrating the superficiality with which some societies and cultures may address similar tensions. Although details and contexts may differ, the potential impact of human rights, in its widest interpretation, is based upon commonalities rather than differences. After all, human rights law affects us all.

This book is a welcome contribution to the polemic discussion of the challenges of human rights in a global context. The careful and nuanced analyses offered by the contributors will be of value to scholars, decision-makers, as well as those responsible for shaping evolving policy balanced within a framework of competing interests. There is no doubt that readers of this treatise will be compelled to reflect carefully and fully upon what it tells us about human rights law and the extent to which these rights are truly amenable to adjudication by the courts.

Jo Samanta

Preface

This collection of 16 essays, by 19 authors, is the result of an open call for contributions sent out in the summer of 2014. The general theme was intended to be something along the lines of 'Human Rights? Humans Wronged!'[1] and the invitation to submit a chapter proposal encouraged prospective contributors to look critically at current human rights issues and to evaluate whether the domestic justiciability of certain 'rights' was at times essentially fictive in nature. Several authors sought further clarification: 'Are we looking for gaps in implementation, enforcement, or monitoring?' 'What issues or countries in particular are you hoping to hear about?' The answering brief was, 'Everything and anything that makes you angry, bewildered or upset about the fate of your fellow humans, irrespective of topic or jurisdiction. Success stories are equally welcome however.' As the proposals began to arrive, several colleagues remarked upon the clear lack of 'success stories' amongst them. Generally, contributors were concerned with highlighting in some detail exactly how the limitations or failings of human rights law were continuing to impact significantly upon the rights of some of the most vulnerable members of society. The need to promote and protect human dignity was a common theme, across a wide geographical range (Africa, Europe, South America, the Middle East) and somewhat diverse topics, such as health-relevant rights issues (first chapter to seventh chapter), aspects of transitional justice (eighth chapter to tenth chapter), issues in criminal justice (11th chapter and 12th chapter) and matters falling within the remit of property rights (13th chapter to 16th chapter). The question of whether or not domestic judges and legislators are best placed to embed or ensure greater consistency in relation to domestic justiciability is often

[1] I am very grateful to my patient editor, Anke Seyfried, for suggesting the book's current title instead and for indulging my request for the collection to be as wide-rangingly inclusive as possible, in terms of its subject matter, geographic scope and authorship: early career researchers are well represented here, as are a good number of more established academics, in a bid to gather in a wide range of perspectives, arguments and approaches to the various issues surrounding the domestic justiciability of human rights.

asked within these essays; there are also useful discussions on how the concepts of equality, non-discrimination, fairness and equity might serve—or indeed at times fail—to remind domestic decision-makers of their obligations towards those who lack the means to make their voices heard.

The first chapter is by Jo Samanta (Reader in Medical Law, De Montfort University, Leicester, UK) and is entitled 'Enforcing Human Rights at End of Life: Is There a Better Approach?' It focuses on questions that surround the end, and the ending, of life, from the perspective of lawyers, clinicians and wider society. UK politicians and the media frequently view high-profile cases as comprising either a 'right-to-die' or a 'right-to-live'. Legal challenges relevant to end-of-life decision-making have prompted calls for law reform and led to adjudication before domestic and European courts. The common thread between such cases is the assertion of human rights violations: despite their promise, human rights sometimes fail to deliver, often on the basis of a wide margin of appreciation. This chapter reviews some of the dilemmas that have involved end-of-life decisions for adults with, and without, capacity. It considers a range of domestic and European decisions that have involved a breach, or an alleged breach, of the human rights protected by the European Convention. On the basis of recent jurisprudence, it argues that enforcement of legal rights through the court system should be the last, rather than first, resort.

The second chapter is jointly authored by Jacinta Miller (Senior Lecturer in Law, Northumbria University) and Alice Diver (Senior Lecturer, School of Law and Criminology, Edge Hill University) and is entitled 'Can Rights Be Ring-Fenced in Times of Austerity? Equality, Equity and Judicial 'Trusteeship' over the UK's Fairness Agenda'. It seeks to argue that although the state has a general duty to preserve finite public resources during times of 'austerity', it must also seek to promote just and 'equitable outcomes' via its decision-making processes. Equitable concepts may prove to be more useful than basic equality principles when seeking to define adequacy of living standards; this is especially so given how budgetary limitations have impacted significantly upon the lives of the most vulnerable members of society, not least in respect of such 'fragile' socio-economic rights as adequate housing or access to health care. The promotion and protection of such rights tend to require considerable levels of financial and political bolstering, in the absence of which they are often at risk of being forever framed as merely aspirational in nature, suitable only for some gently progressive form of eventual realisation. Litigation in domestic courts remains key to the promotion of such rights and interests: a rights template tied to the notion of 'socio-economic equity' could perhaps persuade domestic judges to avoid indulging in 'over-deference' and instead perhaps see themselves as the 'trustees' of public budgets, and indeed of those fundamental socio-economic rights that such funds are meant to protect. Arguably, domestic judges are best placed to keep reminding legislators and policymakers of their duties to identify, outline and avoid dipping below basic rights norms and standards and to prevent, or at least clearly denounce, egregious lapses in the preservation of human dignity.

The third chapter is a joint contribution by David Hand (PhD Candidate), Chantal Davies (Solicitor, Senior Lecturer in Human Rights Law and Discrimination Law) and Ruth Healey (Senior Lecturer in Human Geography), University of Chester, UK. Entitled 'The Right to Healthcare: A Critical Examination of the Human Right of Irregular Migrants to Access State-Funded HIV/AIDS Treatment in the UK', it looks at how health care legislation within the United Kingdom has, together with immigration policies, progressively restricted the rights of 'irregular migrants' to access free medical treatment (referred to disparagingly by some as 'health tourism') in spite of the existence of the right to the 'highest attainable standard of health' having been outlined clearly in international human rights law. Policy discussions concerning the allocation of health resources have typically been led by the perception that overseas patients must be actively discouraged from "taking advantage" of the UK's National Health Service, particularly in the context of treatments for HIV/AIDS. The jurisprudence of the European Court of Human Rights is also significant, as are the socio-legal implications of the failure by decision-makers to distinguish between HIV and AIDS.

The fourth chapter by Jacinta Miller (Senior Lecturer in Law, Northumbria University) also examines issues surrounding the right to health, not least that of human dignity. Entitled 'Dignity: A Relevant Normative Value in 'Access to Health and Social Care' Litigation in the United Kingdom?' it considers the extent to which greater recognition might be given to the value of dignity within cases involving 'access to care' difficulties. Particular reference is made to the recent Strasbourg case of *Mc Donald v United Kingdom*. The approach taken in this case raised a number of thorny questions as to how 'dignity' might be better understood and indeed protected during and after assessments of the health and social care needs of older persons, against a backdrop of economic recession and finite resources. The chapter asks whether the concept of a right to dignity as outlined in the *McDonald* litigation is compatible with the current understanding of dignity as it exists in health law generally, not least in relation to the 'right to health' approaches set out in Article 12 ICESCR and CESCR General Comment 14. It argues that dignity is not simply a negotiable interest to be crudely balanced against other individual and collective rights: rather, it offers a clear, baseline standard against which any meaningful forms of implementation and monitoring of a meaningful right to access health or social care must be assessed.

The fifth chapter, written by Emmanuel Kolawole Oke (PhD Candidate, Faculty of Law, University College Cork, Ireland), is entitled 'Patent Rights, Access to Medicines, and the Justiciability of the Right to Health in Kenya, South Africa and India'. It examines how the national courts in these three developing countries have respectively addressed the tensions between patent rights and the right to health, via litigation. As a result of the WTO's Agreement on Trade Related Aspects of Intellectual Property Rights, developing countries that are members of the WTO are required to provide patent protection for pharmaceutical products. These patent rights create conflicts, however, between the intellectual property rights of pharmaceutical companies and the right to health of those patients who cannot afford to pay for patented medicines. The chapter examines the nature of the clash between patent rights and the right to health, before considering the issue of justiciability of the right to health in Kenya, South Africa and India. It concludes with an analysis of how the domestic courts have adjudicated upon some of the key pharmaceutical patent cases involving the right to health.

The sixth chapter is authored by Eghosa O. Ekhator and Rhuks Ako (both of the University of Hull Law School, UK) and Ngozi Stewart (Faculty of Law, University of Benin, Nigeria). It is entitled 'Overcoming the (Non)justiciable Conundrum: The Doctrine of Harmonious Construction and the Interpretation of the Right to a Healthy Environment in Nigeria'. Its main argument is that the legal framework regulating socio-economic rights in Nigeria is essentially ambiguous. Such rights, listed under Section II of the Constitution (Fundamental Objectives and Directive Principles), remain non-justiciable by virtue of section 6(6)(c) of the Constitution. Nigeria, as a dualist state, has however ratified and incorporated into national law the African Charter on Human and People's Rights in accordance with relevant constitutional provisions. As such, socio-economic rights must be essentially justiciable. This chapter aims to provide a critical examination of the status of such socio-economic rights in Nigeria, using the right to a healthy environment as a case study and taking a holistic approach to both sides of the argument. Premised on the doctrine of harmonious construction, the authors suggest a means of resolving the debate that currently surrounds the existence and nature of the (non)juridical 'right' to a healthy environment.

The seventh chapter is by Deborah Magill (Research Assistant, Transitional Justice Institute, Ulster University, Northern Ireland) and is entitled 'Justiciable Disability Rights and Social Change: A Northern Ireland Case Study'. Disability discrimination legislation within the UK has for several decades provided justiciable rights for people with disability; these justiciable rights have also been utilised by organisations to bring about significant social changes for disabled people, both individually and collectively. This chapter examines the strategic use of domestically justiciable individual rights by organisations in the area of disability rights in the workplace. In particular, it analyses the differing perspectives on the utility of justiciable rights in securing social change, of two key organisations: Disability Action and the Equality Commission for Northern Ireland. An introduction to the origins and objectives of each organisation is followed by a detailed look at Disability Action's involvement in referring and supporting claimants seeking to litigate their rights and how the Equality Commission for Northern Ireland has engaged in a litigation strategy throughout the decade 2001–2011. The chapter then explores the role played by litigation and its significance for the Equality Commission and Disability Action in their pursuit of achieving meaningful social change for disabled workers. It analyses the reasoning behind each of the organisations' engagement with Industrial Tribunals in Northern Ireland. The empirical data used in this analysis has been drawn from seven case files held by the Equality Commission for Northern Ireland on completed cases that were examined in considerable detail, with interview transcripts from semi-structured interviews with four staff from Disability Action and eight staff from the Equality Commission for Northern Ireland, Disability Action and Equality Commission for Northern Ireland publications. The analysis also looks to insights drawn from the current literature on law and social change.

The eighth chapter is by Katie Boyle (Anna Lindh Fellow, Lecturer and ESRC Researcher, University of Limerick/University of Edinburgh). Entitled 'Economic, Social and Cultural Rights in Northern Ireland: Legitimate and Viable Justiciability Mechanisms for a Conflicted Democracy', it proposes justiciability mechanisms for economic, social and cultural rights in Northern Ireland. The research builds on an examination of the particular circumstances of Northern Ireland: a transitional 'conflicted democracy' within a wider liberal state, which is a member of the EU and Council of Europe, committed to the operation of international human rights law. The most vulnerable and marginalised persons in society, especially during times of conflict, are often exposed to ESC rights violation on a number of indicators, and transitional justice mechanisms tend to focus mainly upon civil and political rights, meaning that an economic, social and cultural rights deficit is left largely unaddressed. Northern Ireland falls within such a category, and as a result rights violations can undermine its fragile peace. This chapter explores those mechanisms that could assist in addressing the rights deficit in Northern Ireland in accordance with the particular constitutional framework of the UK and with the rule of law. These justiciable mechanisms are applicable beyond the Northern Ireland context, holding wider relevance for the rest of the UK and beyond.

The ninth chapter is by Francesca Capone (Research Fellow in Public International Law and Didactic Co-ordinator of the Master Programme in Human Rights and Conflict Management, Scuola Superiore Sant'Anna, Pisa, Italy). Entitled 'Children in Colombia: Discussing the Current Transitional Justice Process Against the Backdrop of the CRC Key Principles', it outlines why Colombia is at present widely regarded as one of the most interesting case studies in the fields of human rights and transitional justice. The five-decade long civil war has resulted in a countless number of victims, disproportionately affecting the most vulnerable sectors of the population, not least, children. Over the past few years, the Colombian government has sought to achieve a twofold aim: passing laws and regulations to enhance its compliance with international human rights law standards and establishing measures, legal and non-legal, to promote a comprehensive transitional justice process, based upon achieving reconciliation, justice and reparations for the victims of the ongoing armed conflict. Both sets of actions have had an impact on children. Domestic laws aimed at embedding the tenets of the Convention on the Rights of the Child and its Optional Protocols, together with legislation arising out of the transitional justice process, have forged a unique framework: this merits analysis, particularly as it relates to promoting and protecting the best interests of the child principle and to the child's right to participate in all decisions and processes affecting them.

The tenth chapter is by Hilmi Zawati (Chair of the International Centre for Legal Accountability and Justice). Entitled 'Prosecuting International Core Crimes Under Libya's Transitional Justice: The Case of Saif Al-Islam Gaddafi and Abdullah Al-Senussi', it looks to the aftermath of the widespread and systematic violence directed by former Libyan government forces and paramilitaries against peaceful demonstrations in Benghazi and other Libyan cities in mid-February 2011 and to the UN Security Council's unanimous adoption of Resolution 1970, referring the situation in Libya to the Prosecutor of the International Criminal Court under Chapter VII of the Charter of the United Nations (pursuant to Article 13(b) of the Rome Statute of the International Criminal Court). Consequently, the Pre-Trial Chamber I (PTCI) of the Court issued three warrants of arrest for Muammar Qaddafi and his son Saif Al-Islam, as well as for Abdullah Al-Senussi, Gaddafi's intelligence chief. After the killing of Muammar Qaddafi on 20 October 2011, and following the capture of Saif Al-Islam and Al-Senussi, Libya challenged the admissibility of the cases against them. While the PTCI has determined that the case against Al-Senussi is inadmissible before the Court, it rejected Libya's challenge of the admissibility of the case against Saif Al-Islam and requested that the Libyan government meet its obligations under the UN Security Council's Resolution 1970 (2011) and surrender the suspect to ICC custody in The Hague. After examining the ICC's complementarity regime and its inconsistent decisions on the admissibility of the above cases, and also considering the challenges involved in prosecuting international core crimes under Libya's transitional justice system, this chapter explores whether or not the latter is equipped to undertake the prosecution of Saif Al-Islam and Al-Senussi for international core crimes—particularly those widespread and systematic attacks—allegedly committed by Libyan government agents against the civilian population during the February 2011 uprising. After an extensive analysis of the above cases, this chapter argues that the post-Gaddafi Libyan courts are not the proper judicial bodies to undertake such prosecutions, and reaches the conclusion that, unless Libya restores its justice system and establishes effective judicial mechanisms and democratic institutions, the country will continue to suffer instability for a considerable period of time.

The 11th chapter is by Michelle-Thérèse Stevenson (PhD Candidate, Centre for Criminal Justice, School of Law, University of Limerick). It is entitled 'DNA Evidence Under the Microscope: Why the Presumption of Innocence Is Under Threat in Ireland' and highlights how DNA provides a formidable type of evidence which is becoming increasingly relied upon by the prosecution in Ireland, to the point perhaps where 'fair hearing' rights (under Article 6 of the European Convention) may be compromised. In many jurisdictions, courts and criminal investigators have been quick to seize upon its probative power, yet apparently slow to acknowledge the potential for fallibility. Yet despite DNA evidence's clear advantages, research demonstrates that the interpretation of certain DNA mixtures may be subject to bias. What is more, the scientific community continues to warn that there is still no definitive frame of reference for interpreting certain mixed DNA profiles. There are two additional problems running parallel to this in Ireland. First, the presumption of innocence is marginalised in the jurisdiction. Second, the Criminal Justice (Forensic Evidence and Database System) Act 2014 raises a number of human dignity and rights concerns which present the ancient legal precept of presumed innocence with even further challenges in Ireland. The purpose of this chapter is therefore to investigate the extent to which DNA evidence imperils the presumption of innocence in Ireland.

The 12th chapter is by Maria Helen Murphy, (School of Law, Maynooth University, Ireland.) It is entitled 'Surveillance and the Right to Privacy: Is an 'Effective Remedy' Possible?' and argues that privacy—the right most directly implicated in any discussion of surveillance—is often identified solely as being of benefit to the individual, weighing against general social goods such as security. The imperceptibility of both the concept of privacy and the value of 'national security' favours the security side of the equation, as threats from terrorism and organised crime loom large, and as omnipresent fears in our security conscious society. Recognising these challenges, recourse to an external—yet legitimate—source of privacy protection is an attractive option. Accordingly, the European Convention on Human Rights (ECHR) is a crucial instrument of human rights protection in the area of surveillance. Ireland has avoided direct scrutiny of its surveillance regime from the ECtHR, although the jurisprudence of the Strasbourg Court has played a clear role in the formulation of Irish surveillance legislation. In spite of this influence, there is cause to suspect that legislative reforms may not add up to effective protection of the right to respect for private life as guaranteed by Article 8 of the European Convention. While Article 8 is the substantive article most relevant in the surveillance context, the right to an effective remedy, as provided for in Article 13, must also be considered. The specific function of Article 13 is to ensure the 'availability at national level of a remedy to enforce the substance of the Convention rights and freedoms'. The inherently secretive nature of surveillance presents a considerable obstacle to the justiciability of Article 8 rights in the surveillance context. This chapter considers how the challenges to providing an effective remedy in the surveillance context can be resolved in Ireland and uses the Criminal Justice (Surveillance) Act 2009 (Surveillance Act) as a case study in order to evaluate how the Oireachtas has attempted to meet the standard for an effective remedy.

The 13th chapter is by Roberto Cippitani (Università degli Studi di Perugia, Perugia, Italy). Entitled 'The 'Contractual Enforcement' of Human Rights in Europe', it argues that the sphere of private law can adapt to new and unforeseen social and economic events and circumstances: its traditional function was to provide logical, legal tools (such as contracts, wills and trusts) to solve those difficult problems that tend to arise within the realm of 'human relationships'. Just as private law matters are no longer beyond the reach of human rights law, such too might certain private law concepts (e.g. good faith, fiduciary obligation, fairness, liability and the need for redress) provide a useful means of embedding meaningful rights protections into domestic legal systems. The concept of the contract is particularly significant however, for example, in respect of implementing public policies that are ostensibly aimed at protecting personal and collective rights. Given that 'the contract' arose from a need to protect property interests, and guide exchanges of key rights between individuals and organisations in a manner that aimed to promote some level of fairness and equality between the contracting parties, it is not surprising that much domestic case law and legislation on private law matters increasingly reflect the influence of human rights principles, as do a number of Constitutional provisions. Examples are drawn from domestic constitutions, case law and statutes on the areas of social service provision, consent to health treatments or research activities, the capacity to provide such consent and the protection of privacy and human dignity. Put simply, the chapter argues that the increasingly blurred distinctions between the spheres of public and private laws seem to be gradually allowing for a more active embedding of fundamental rights protections at the level of domestic implementation.

The 14th chapter is by Alice Diver (Senior Lecturer, Edge Hill University) and is entitled 'Putting Dignity to Bed? The Taxing Question of the UK's Housing Rights Relapse'. It argues that the UK's recent statutory cap on Housing Benefit (known generally as the 'bedroom tax') has given rise to a small but significant spate of domestic cases examining such issues as legally justified discrimination, equality and the impacts of public purse decision-making on the realisation of resource-dependent socio-economic rights. Taken together, these decisions provide useful, if depressing, guidance for anyone keen to challenge the introduction of similar austerity measures: a meaningfully juridical right to adequate housing seems unlikely to be fully embedded into domestic law, or indeed usefully defined, any time soon. The question of whether some form of adequate housing baseline rights standard can be identified (i.e. in respect of preventing indignity, squalor or homelessness) remains unanswered; instances of unequal treatment and discrimination may be framed as both lawful and justified on the basis of finite state resources. Arguably, if public funds are needed for the realisation of such basic entitlements as adequate housing or social security, then these rights might be more accurately described as social privileges. If a 'duty' to preserve finite state resources provides an acceptable 'get out clause' for jurists and legislators (to legally infringe basic rights), then there is no guarantee that similar reasoning might not yet be applied to cases involving civil or political rights issues. Economic austerities should not bring to mind political atrocities: where benefit caps have led directly to food banks, evictions and squalor, it can be argued that the concept of a human dignity baseline has been ill-served by those tasked with ensuring meaningful protection for human rights.

The 15th chapter is by Khanyisela Moyo (Lecturer, Transitional Justice Institute and School of Law, Ulster University) and is entitled 'Justiciable Property Rights and Post-colonial Land Reform: A Case Study of Zimbabwe'. It argues that land reform is an intrinsic component of the right to an adequate standard of living, in that landlessness amounts to an abrogation of the obligation to fulfil this right as outlined in the International Covenant on Economic, Social, and Cultural Rights (ICESR) and the Universal Declaration of Human Rights (UDHR). Access to land is a basic component of the right to adequate food. Further, the World Bank has stated that the emphasis of land reform in developing countries ought to be on improving property rights. Yet land reform programmes also involve the modification of prevailing property rights in a manner that can be construed as infringing upon the right to property. This chapter scrutinises the tension between a justiciable right to property and a state-led agrarian land reform programme in a post-colonial context by examining Zimbabwean constitutional law. Land reform was a crucial component in Zimbabwe's transition from the racist colonial past to majority rule and justice. The major aims of this reform were to transfer land from whites to blacks so as to foster peace, empower the landless and war veterans, reduce overpopulation in communal areas, maintain and if possible increase existing levels of agricultural production and improve standards of living. Cognisant of the economic importance of the white farmers and also of the experience of Mozambique, where their departure resulted in economic collapse, the country's independence negotiations struck a balance between two competing policy objectives, namely to redress historical economic inequalities and to promote economic growth. These concerns were reflected in the declaration of rights enshrined in the country's independence Constitution, which incorporated a right to property clause that provided the basis for state action. This chapter is divided into three sections. Section 1 outlines the conceptual framework that underlines the nexus between land reform, the right to property and justiciability. Section 2 is a discussion of the various land reform policies adopted by the government of Zimbabwe from 1980 to 2013, focusing on the relevant constitutional and legislative arrangements. Section 3 concludes by analysing these constitutional and legislative frameworks and outlines the implications for human rights justiciability.

The final chapter is by Vinodh Jaichand (Dean and Head of the School of Law, University of the Witwatersrand, Johannesburg, South Africa). It is entitled 'Women's Land Rights and Customary Law Reform in South Africa: Towards a Gendered Perspective'. It argues that the implementation of land rights for women has proven difficult in traditional areas in South Africa, with the use of customary law proving problematic. Arguably, customary law appears quite discriminatory; the Traditional Courts Bill, withdrawn three times from the legislative agenda, has sparked significant controversy. Changes in traditional societal notions on the limitations of the rights of women to access to land have been noted; the constitution provides however for the recognition of customary law, to the extent that it accords with the values of that constitution. As a result, the jurisprudence of the Constitutional Court alludes to "living customary law" rather than "traditional customary law" and the principles of gender balance and equality should be consciously factored in and integrated into customary law as part of the process of social change occurring in communities since the inception of the Constitution. Rather than looking at points of difference between traditional systems of justice and constitutional law, an attempt is made here to reconcile them.

The editors are very grateful to Jo Samanta for kindly agreeing to write the Foreword for this collection; thanks are due also to all of the authors who gave of their time to contribute, and to all who assisted in the circulation of the original call for chapters just over a year ago. Professors Rory O'Connell and Fionnuala Ní Aoláin of the Transitional Justice Institute and Dr Eugene McNamee, Head of the Law School, Ulster University, also merit thanks, for their advice, insight and support. Thanks are also due to Julia Bieler (Editorial Assistant, Springer), for all her kind help and assistance, and not least to Anke Seyfried, Law Editor with Springer, for all of her wisdom and patience and for her willingness to take a chance on this book project.

Londonderry, UK Alice Diver
Londonderry, UK Jacinta Miller

Contents

Biographies

Rhuks Temitope Ako teaches at the School of Law, University of Hull, United Kingdom. He qualified as a Barrister and Solicitor of the Supreme Court of Nigeria in 1999. He obtained his PhD from the University of Kent at Canterbury, UK, following the awards of LLM and MPhil from the Obafemi Awolowo University, Ile-Ife, Nigeria. His research interests include environmental justice, environmental human rights (both of which he teaches at the post-graduate level), corporate social responsibility (CSR) minority rights and public participation law usually in relation to, but not exclusively to, Nigeria's oil industry. Other interests include human security and public private partnership (PPP) in Africa. Dr. Ako has won a number of international awards and fellowships, including the 2010 Volkswagen-Stiftung 'Our Common Future' Fellowship and the 'Limits to Growth' Fellowship in 2012.

Katie Boyle PhD, is a constitutional lawyer specialising in the domestic implementation and justiciability of economic, social and cultural (ESC) rights. Her doctoral research identified routes to a justiciable remedy for violations of ESC rights in Northern Ireland as a conflicted transitional justice democracy (University of Limerick 2014). She has previously worked as a legal advisor and litigator for the Government Legal Service in the UK and Scotland. Her work has featured in submissions to the UN Universal Periodic Review (2012) and to the United Nations Committee on Economic, Social and Cultural Rights (2015). Dr Boyle is currently working as a post-doctoral Research Fellow at the Crucible Centre for Human Rights Research at the University of Roehampton in London, where she has compiled the UK Equality and Human Rights Commission 'Populating the United Nations Measurement Framework' project identifying where gaps in human rights protection exist within the UK. She has also previously worked as a Research Consultant with the Scottish Human Rights Commission in connection with Scotland's National Action Plan for human rights and the domestic implementation of ESC rights in Scotland. She was previously appointed as Economic and Social Research Council Fellow at the University of Edinburgh in connection with the Scottish independence referendum and is the previous sole recipient of the

Department of Foreign Affairs Anna Lindh Fellowship, in Ireland, awarded in connection with her work on ESC rights in Northern Ireland. She has lectured in the Comparative International Protection of Human Rights at post-graduate level at the University of Limerick, Ireland. Her research interests primarily focus on ESC rights, deliberative transitional justice mechanisms, constitutional/sub-constitutional transitions and post-conflict reconciliation.

Francesca Capone PhD (Scuola Superiore Sant'Anna and Tilburg University), is a Research Fellow at Scuola Superiore Sant'Anna and Didactic Coordinator of the Masters in Human Rights and Conflict Management Scuola Superiore Sant'Anna, Masters and Training Programmes Division. She was previously a guest lecturer for the MA in Human Rights at the School of Advanced Study, University of London, and also served as a Research Fellow at the British Institute of International and Comparative Law.

Roberto Cippitani has been a Jean Monnet Chair holder at the Università degli Studi di Perugia since 2011 (project TeKla—The European Knowledge Legal Area) and Co-ordinator of Jean Monnet Research project: Individual Rights & Regional Integration. His teaching and research activity are devoted to EU private law, especially on the interpretation and general theory of EU law, contracts within and between EU institutions, legal aspects of EU policies of research, innovation and education, as well as EU and international integration processes. He gives lectures in EU legal matters in several universities within Europe and abroad, in particular in Latin America and Asia. He teaches on courses at all levels: under-graduates, post-graduates, masters, PhD and training vocational courses. He has published a number of monographs and articles (in Italian, English and Spanish) concerning EU legal topics and another five books or articles concerning Civil Law and General Theory of Law. He is responsible for several projects funded under EU programmes (e.g. Jean Monnet, Erasmus, Tempus, ESF, FP of RTD).

Chantal Davies PhD (Chester), MA (Oxon), MA (Chester), LPC (Solicitor), PGCE, FHEA. After graduating with a law degree from Oxford University, Chantal qualified as a Solicitor with Eversheds in Cardiff specialising in employment, human rights and discrimination laws. She then moved on to practice as a Senior Solicitor in Davies Wallis Foyster in Manchester. In 1998, she moved to work as a Solicitor for the Equal Opportunities Commission (EOC) in Manchester, heading up a unit tackling strategic and wider enforcement of the gender equality legislation. Whilst working as a Solicitor for the EOC, apart from undertaking a number of major legal test cases, including to the Court of Appeal and the European Court of Justice, she also sat on several European and national bodies and gave several keynote lectures to leading national organisations. Chantal has been a qualified solicitor for 17 years and her practice has specifically focused on areas of equality law and human rights. Chantal is now a Senior Lecturer in Human Rights Law and Discrimination Law in the Law School at the University of Chester. Chantal has recently completed a 12-month funded project considering the experiences of BME undergraduate students and is currently undertaking follow-up research in relation to the perceptions of BME students towards employability. Chantal is also the Director of the Forum for Research into Equality and Diversity.

Alice Diver (LLB, LLM, Solicitor, PGCHEP, FHEA, PhD), Senior Lecturer, Edge Hill University, England, has been a Lecturer in Law since 1993 (at the NWRC and Ulster University, Northern Ireland) and was course director for the LLB degrees at the School of Law (Magee) Ulster University from 2009 to 2014, having joined their teaching team in 2004. She was external examiner for the Law degrees at LYIT, Ireland (2010–2014), and IPAV, Dublin (1999–2002). Prior to becoming a lecturer, she worked as a Solicitor in private practice in both Belfast and Derry, Northern Ireland (1989–1995). She teaches in the areas of equity & trusts, land law, social and economic rights and dissertation research methods. Her publications focus largely upon the areas of human rights, property law, adoption and cultural heritage. She has recently published 'A Law of Blood-Ties: The 'Right' to Access Genetic Ancestry' (2013, Springer Int'l) and currently serves as a board member/trustee for several charitable organisations in Northern Ireland (Apex Housing, Kinship Care, Londonderry Inner City Trust, the Buildings Preservation Trust).

Eghosa Osa Ekhator is a recent graduate from the Law School, University of Hull, where he completed a PhD. His PhD research focused on the roles of civil society organisations (CSOs) in regulating the activities of multinational corporations in the oil and gas sector in Nigeria. He is also a Senior Counsel with Bwala & Co, a law firm based in Abuja, Nigeria. Eghosa is also a Barrister and Solicitor of the Supreme Court of Nigeria. He holds an LLB from the University of Benin, Nigeria; an LLM in International Business Law from the University of Hull; and an MSc in Public Sector Management from the University of Hull. His research areas include human rights, socio-economic rights, environmental justice, public sector management and international trade law, amongst others.

David Hand (BA, Chester), LLM (Irish Centre for Human Rights), is a PhD Candidate at the University of Chester Law School. His research explores the human right to health for irregular migrants in the UK with HIV/AIDS. In particular, his research focuses on the attitudes of policymakers towards immigration and how the perceived threat of health tourism shapes health care legislation in the UK. David obtained a BA in Law with Psychology from the University of Chester before pursuing an LLM in International Human Rights Law at the Irish Centre for Human Rights. In 2013, he worked as an intern for the Legal Resources Centre, a non-profit law clinic in South Africa, before returning to Chester to embark on further study. In March 2015, he presented his research to date at the Annual Student Human Rights Conference at the University of Nottingham.

Ruth Healey (BSc, MA, PhD, PGCE, FHEA) is a Senior Lecturer in Human Geography at the University of Chester. Her research explores asylum seeker and refugee experiences in host countries with a particular focus on integration policies and notions of belonging. Her PhD explored the employment experiences of Tamil refugees living in London, UK.

Vinodh Jaichand is Professor and Head of the School of Law at the University of the Witwatersrand, Johannesburg. He was the recipient of the National University of Ireland Galway President's Award for Teaching Excellence (2010–2011) and has been involved in human rights education for more than 22 years with experience in the NGO world. He is the former National Director of Lawyers for Human Rights in South Africa and has taught and examined on the Mediterranean Masters on Human Rights and Democratisation in Malta and acted as an examiner for the European Masters in Human Rights and Democratisation in Venice. As Deputy Director at the Irish Centre for Human Rights, he was the architect of the LLM in Economic, Social and Cultural Rights (launched in September 2009). He has participated in the training of police, lawyers, prosecutors and judges in China, South Africa, Slovenia, Slovakia, Hungary, Ireland, Ethiopia, Nepal and India. He holds membership in the Editorial Review Board Human Rights Series of the Republic of Letters Publishing, in the Editorial Review Board of Human Rights & Human Welfare, in the Advisory Board of the Sur-International Journal on Human Rights, in the International Advisory Board of Diakonia, Jerusalem. He was the first Chairman of the Board of Integrating Ireland, a member of Consulting Editorial Board of the University of Ghana Law Journal and reader for the International Journal for Transitional Justice. He holds a doctorate (summa cum laude) and LLM (magna cum laude) in International Human Rights Law from the Centre for Civil and Human Rights University of Notre Dame Law School, with other degrees from the University of Miami, University of Natal and University of Durban-Westville.

Deborah Magill (PhD) is a Researcher at the Transitional Justice Institute at Ulster University, where she has lectured for 4 years. After graduating first in her year from Ulster University (Magee) with a First-Class Honours degree in Law with Accounting, she completed a PhD in Employment Law and Discrimination. During her undergraduate and post-graduate studies, she has been the recipient of numerous awards, including the Faculty of Social Sciences Academic Excellence Award and the University College Dublin Law Review/A & L Goodbody award for the most outstanding article. Her current research project for the TJI examines how socio-economic rights might be embedded in transitional justice processes in post-conflict states. She is also the editor of the undergraduate research yearbook and co-ordinator of Ulster University's Street Law project.

Jacinta Miller (LLB, MSc, PGCHEP, FHEA, PhD) has been a Lecturer at the School of Law, University of Ulster, since 2003, and an Associate Researcher at the Transitional Justice Institute since 2013. She graduated in 2002 with an LLB in Law and Business Studies (1st Class Honours) from the University of Ulster (Magee) and completed her PhD on the 'right to health' in 2009. She completed her Postgraduate Certificate in Higher Education Practice in 2007 and has been a Fellow of the Higher Education Academy since 2008. Prior to studying and teaching in the area of law, she worked in health care. She qualified as a Registered General Nurse in 1987 at the North Down College of Nursing (Ulster Hospital), maintaining her registration until 2000. She completed an MSc in Community Health at the University of Edinburgh in 1994. She has worked in both hospital and community settings in Northern Ireland and also worked with Concern Worldwide and Oxfam in East Africa (Sudan, Ethiopia and the Great Lakes Region). Her teaching and research interests are in the areas of health law, human rights, European Union law, evidence and criminal law.

Khanyisela Moyo is a Law Lecturer at the Transitional Justice Institute (TJI), Ulster University, Northern Ireland. She holds an LLB (Hons) from the University of Zimbabwe; a Masters in International Human Rights Law from Oslo, Norway; an LLM in Public International Law from Nottingham University, United Kingdom; and a PhD in Transitional Justice from Ulster University. She teaches on the LLM in Human Rights programme and delivers the Jurisprudence module for the LLB degree. She has published widely in refereed journals on a wide variety of issues. In addition to transitional justice, her research interests include post-colonial legal theory, feminist legal theory, minority rights, land rights, law of international organisations, issues of collective security and economic, social and cultural rights.

Maria Helen Murphy (PhD) is a Lecturer in Law at Maynooth University. Maria's primary research interests include privacy law, surveillance and human rights. Maria holds a PhD from the University College Cork, a magna cum laude LLM from Temple University (Philadelphia) and a First-Class Honours BCL (International) degree from UCC.

Emmanuel Kolawole Oke is a PhD Candidate at the Faculty of Law, University College Cork. He obtained his LLB from the University of Lagos in 2007. He further obtained a Master's degree in Intellectual Property and Technology Law from the National University of Singapore in 2011. Emmanuel is equally a qualified legal practitioner in Nigeria. He is interested in international patent law and policy, and he is particularly interested in how developing countries can optimally utilise patent laws to stimulate innovation and technological development. His PhD thesis seeks to examine how developing countries can effectively balance their patent laws to encourage innovation as well as address public health challenges. This will be done by using a comparative approach to highlight how different developing countries have adjusted their patent laws and come up with unique ways of balancing patent laws with public health concerns. In addition, the thesis seeks to examine avenues through which state actors (developing countries) and non-state actors (pharmaceutical companies) can collaborate and cooperate in addressing the public health issues that emanate from the enforcement of patent laws. The objective of the thesis is to come up with a patent law model for developing countries that complies with international trade obligations and equally contains appropriate safeguards for the health of the citizens.

Jo Samanta LLM, BA (Hons), PGCE, is a Principal Lecturer in Law at **De Montfort University, Leicester**. She is a non-practising solicitor, nurse and midwife. Her teaching and research interests lie in the field of medical law and ethics. She is Chair of the Business and Law Faculty Human Research Ethics Committee and sits on several University and Faculty Committees. She has a particular research interest in end-of-life decision-making and has published widely on the interface between law and clinical practice.

Michelle-Thérèse Stevenson Centre for Criminal Justice, School of Law, University of Limerick, Ireland, started her PhD thesis in January 2014 under the supervision of Dr Andrea Ryan after being awarded a School of Law scholarship. Her research focus is the effect of DNA evidence on the presumption of innocence. She completed her primary degree in 2012 at Mary Immaculate College, where she achieved First-Class Honours in French and Philosophy and was awarded the college medal for Philosophy. In 2014, she graduated with a First-Class Honours Master's degree in Human Rights in Criminal Justice at the University of Limerick, following the grant of a UL 40 Scholarship. Previously, Michelle worked as a full-time journalist with Benn Publications, IPC Magazines, Independent News and Media Group and the science journals division of Reed Elsevier academic publishers, for whom she last worked in 2009.

Ngozi Finette Stewart LLB (Benin), LLM (Benin), Dip IEL (Geneva), PhD (Leicester), BL (Lagos), is a specialist in Environmental Law and Ethics. Her core areas include biodiversity conservation, environmental regulation, coastal management, sustainability issues in aviation, food security and climate change, and ecological integrity. She has been a key participant in United Nations working groups on Human Rights and the Environment, as well as a member of the technical review committee under the IUCN. She is a member of a number of professional bodies, including the IUCN (Ethics Specialist Committee) and the Earth Law Alliance. Dr Stewart is currently a Researcher and Senior Lecturer at the University of Benin, Nigeria, where she lectures in administrative law, environmental law, international protection of human rights and air and space law.

Hilmi M. Zawati is an international criminal law jurist and human rights advocate, currently Chair of the International Centre for Legal Accountability and Justice (ICLAJ). He has studied law at different American, Canadian, Middle Eastern and African universities and earned several law degrees, including the prestigious Doctor of Civil Law (DCL) in International Comparative Law (McGill), MA in Comparative Law (McGill), PhD in International Energy Political Economics (CPU), MA in Islamic Law of Nations (Punjab), Post-Graduate Diploma in Public Law (Khartoum) and LLB (Alexandria-Beirut campus). Before Joining ICLAJ, Dr. Zawati served as the President of the International Legal Advocacy Forum (ILAF) for two consecutive terms. Over the past 30 years, he has taught numerous subjects at both Kuwait University and Bishop's University and been a prominent speaker and author on a number of hotly debated legal issues. During the past decade or so, he organised, co-chaired and participated in several international conferences and addressed major academic and professional gatherings in a number of Middle Eastern countries, Africa, Europe and at home in Canada. Dr. Zawati has an accomplished body of trans-disciplinary scholarship. Over the past 40 years, he published 24 books and tens of articles in both Arabic and English. His present primary research and teaching areas are public international law, international criminal law, international humanitarian and human rights law, international gender justice system, international environmental law of armed conflict and Islamic law of nations (siyar). He has been a committed human rights activist over the last three decades and has actively advocated the human rights of wartime rape victims throughout the world ever since the first reports of war crimes during the Yugoslav dissolution war of 1992–1995. He is also the author of several prize-winning books on international humanitarian and human rights law, including his recent book *The Triumph of Ethnic Hatred and the Failure of International Political Will: Gendered Violence and Genocide in the Former Yugoslavia and Rwanda* (Edwin Mellen Press, 2010). Dr. Zawati's most recent work is his book *Fair Labelling and the Dilemma of Prosecuting Gender-Based Crimes at the International Criminal Tribunals* (Oxford University Press, 2014).

Enforcing Human Rights at End of Life: Is There a Better Approach?

Jo Samanta

1 Introduction

Questions about the end, and ending, of life are of concern to lawyers, clinicians and society more generally. High profile 'right-to-die' and 'right-to-live' cases are a frequent focus of media and political attention. In the United Kingdom the recent profusion of challenges that have concerned end of life decision-making has extended from proposals for law reform to adjudication of disputes before domestic and European courts. Tragic and heartrending circumstances typically underscore the complex disputes and challenges that are brought before these courts. The common thread between them is the assertion of human rights violations.

In end of life cases whilst appeals to human rights might seem to be a logical call, all too often that promise fails to deliver. The Human Rights Act 1998, which gives effect to the European Convention for the Protection of Human Rights and Fundamental Freedoms,[1] consists mainly of negative prohibitions but also imposes a range of positive obligations. To some extent, the legislation has effectively revolutionised many aspects of public health care delivery by way of legally enforceable duties on public bodies such as the National Health Service. These duties also extend, in certain circumstances, to private providers of healthcare as well as health practitioners themselves. Nevertheless, the Human Rights Act is not a panacea for all disgruntled litigants. Constitutional protections such as Convention rights are designed traditionally to safeguard the person's fundamental rights and freedoms against state interference. The extent of positive duties imposed upon member states tends to be limited although in certain circumstances it does impose obligations to act. More negatively, enforceable positive rights are seldom

[1] Hereinafter referred to as "the Convention".

J. Samanta (✉)
De Montfort University, Leicester, UK
e-mail: JSamanta@dmu.ac.uk

A. Diver, J. Miller (eds.), *Justiciability of Human Rights Law in Domestic Jurisdictions*, DOI 10.1007/978-3-319-24016-9_1

conferred where resource allocation decisions are involved. The Act safeguards human rights in two ways: first, by requiring that domestic legislation is compatible with the Convention and second, by mandating that public authorities act in compliance with Convention rights.

It is trite law that any person who claims that a public authority has acted, or proposes to act, in a way that is incompatible with Convention rights can bring proceedings against that authority[2] if he or she is a 'victim.'[3] Claimants may also bring an action if they are likely to be a victim, in order to prevent an actual or threatened violation of a Convention right from taking place. Victims can also be family members or those who are connected closely to the person whose rights have allegedly been infringed.[4] Nevertheless, in the area of healthcare and, in particular, at end of life these ostensible rights may be difficult to realise.[5]

This chapter reviews some of the seemingly intractable dilemmas and conflicts that have involved end-of-life decisions for adults with, and without, capacity. It considers a range of domestic and European decisions that have involved breach, or alleged breach, of rights protected by the Convention. These decisions have typically engaged three provisions: the right to life, as protected by Article 2, Article 3 which protects the right not to be subject to inhuman or degrading treatment and Article 8, namely respect for private and family life. Less commonly Articles 9, 6 and 14 have also been engaged. On the basis of the outcomes of recent jurisprudence it concludes that enforcement of legal rights through the court system should be the *last*, rather than first, resort. Whilst the courts are perhaps uniquely qualified for dispute resolution with authority to impose binding decisions on litigants, its adversarial approach is not ideal for the inevitable poignancy of this stage of life. The rule of the court is that one party will win, and that winner takes all. Juridical enforcement of rights against a backdrop of tragic circumstances, professional reputations and ethical beliefs, high emotion and often acute media interest is perhaps not in the best interests of any of the parties concerned. Alternatives means of resolution are proposed as a positive approach for conflict resolution at end of life.

---

[2] Human Rights Act 1998, section 7(1)(a).

[3] Within the meaning of the Human Rights Act 1998, section 7(7).

[4] This has been a key characteristic of cases brought following the death of the primary victim (e.g. *Nicklinson*).

[5] Samanta (2012), pp. 382–391.

2 Withholding and Withdrawal of Life-Sustaining Treatment

Decisions that concern withholding or withdrawing life-sustaining treatment from patients will inevitably engage consideration of the right to life, although the extent to which this right is infringed will be fact and circumstance dependent. Decisions such as these may also brush with the criminal law. At its most fundamental, Article 2 imposes a negative obligation on the state, to refrain from taking life, as well as a positive obligation to safeguard the life of all persons within its jurisdiction, irrespective of their decision-making capabilities.

The positive obligation on the state to preserve life by providing timely and adequate medical care and "take appropriate steps to safeguard the lives of those within its jurisdiction"[6] is a significant aspect of the right to life. Although the negative right not to be 'intentionally deprived of life' is essentially absolute and without exception, withholding life-prolonging treatment in a patient's best interests will not constitute a deprivation of life.[7] The common law suggests that, as far as treatment provision is concerned, the right to have one's life sustained by medical treatment is far more compelling where the individual has been detained, rather than in healthcare related situations.[8]

Medical treatment decisions for adults who lack decision-making capacity are made in their best interests, in accordance with the Mental Capacity 2005.[9] For purposes such as these it is a well-established principle that there is no duty to provide life-sustaining treatment where this is futile.[10] This principle is reflected similarly in the Mental Capacity Code of Practice[11] and contemporary professional guidance.[12]

3 Prolonged Disorders of Consciousness

The concept of 'prolonged disorder of consciousness' comprises a range of conditions caused by brain injury that spans from patients who are in a coma (unconscious), vegetative state (VS), through to the minimally conscious state (MCS).

[6] *LCB* v *UK* (1998) 27 EHRR 212.

[7] *Airedale Trust v Bland* [1993] 1 All ER 831.

[8] *R (Application of Mrs Dianne Pretty) v Director of Public Prosecutions and Secretary of State for the Home Department* [2002] 1 AC 800.

[9] Unless the previously competent person had made a valid and applicable advance decision that pertains to the decision to be taken.

[10] *Airedale Trust v Bland* [1993] AC 789 at 868.

[11] Paragraph 5.31.

[12] General Medical Council (2010), p. 80.

Vegetative state and the MCS can be temporary or permanent conditions and patients may alternate between these. Characteristic sleep/wake cycles are often apparent and diagnosis depends upon persistent lack of evidence that patients can communicate, or interact meaningfully, with their environment. Patients in VS and MCS invariably lack decision making capacity and their care and management presents a complex array of legal and ethical challenges.

In the paradigmatic and controversial decision of *Airedale Trust v Bland*,[13] the House of Lords considered the legality of withdrawing life-sustaining treatment, including clinically assisted nutrition and hydration (CANH) from a patient who had been left in a permanent vegetative state (PVS) following injuries sustained in the Hillsborough disaster. Although the case preceded the implementation of the Human Rights Act, the right to life was recognised as a founding principle protected by law as well as a natural right rooted in antiquity.[14]

The heart of the issue concerned whether withdrawal of life-sustaining treatment was in the best interests of a man who would never regain capacity. The House of Lords held that life-sustaining treatment can, and should, be withheld when starting or continuing treatment is not a patient's best interests. Determining whether life-sustaining treatment would be in a person's best interests was to be determined by responsible clinicians according to a *Bolam* justifiable standard (meaning that the decision of whether to withdraw or continue life-sustaining treatment was supported by a responsible body of medical opinion).[15] According to Lord Keith the decision whether continued treatment of a PVS patient was one essentially for clinicians although Lord Browne-Wilkinson recognised that a doctor's perspective might well be influenced by that doctor's own approach to the sanctity of life.[16] On this point Lord Mustill was alone in his reservations about the use of *Bolam* for decisions that concern withdrawal of life-sustaining treatment,[17] a stance reflected recently by the Supreme Court.[18] The presumption in *Bland* was that people in PVS have no enduring interests of any kind, in being kept alive or allowed to die,[19] and that on this basis continuation of treatment would not be in their best interests. The inference that can be drawn here is that consciousness is a necessary condition for recognition of interests.[20] Hoffmann LJ was largely alone in his forthright rejection of the argument that patients in PVS had no interests at all since it was "demeaning to the human spirit" to suggest that unconscious individuals had no interest in their personal privacy and dignity or in how they lived or

---

[13] *Airedale Trust v Bland* [1993] 1 All ER 831.

[14] *Airedale NHS Trust v Bland* [1993] AC 789 at 826 C-E.

[15] *Bland*, p. 862 *per* Lord Keith.

[16] *Bland per* Lord Browne-Wilkinson, p. 883.

[17] *Bland*, p. 895.

[18] *Aintree University Hospitals v James* [2013] UKSC 67.

[19] *Bland*, p. 861.

[20] *Bland*, p. 897 *per* Lord Mustill.

died.[21] For Wicks, the overriding approach in *Bland* was to deny the possibility of any enduring benefit of the inherent value of human life,[22] even though individuals in PVS are undoubtedly 'persons in being'.

The right to life, in its guise of the sanctity of life, was referred to only briefly in the *Bland* judgments and then only to remind us of its fundamental, though not absolute, nature.[23] Nevertheless, the court expressed its reverence for human life for its own sake and as a fundamental and shared value of humanity. According to Hoffmann LJ, "there is an intrinsic value in human life, irrespective of whether it is valuable to the person concerned or indeed to anyone else. Those who adhere to religious faiths which believe in the sanctity of all God's creation and in particular that human life was created in the image of God himself will have no difficulty with the concept of the intrinsic value of human life. But even those without any religious belief think in the same way .... What matters is that, in one form or another, they form part of almost everyone's intuitive values."[24] Recognition and respect for the value of the person aligns closely with that of Finnis who claims that there are no human individuals who are not persons. Anthony Bland in a PVS was a profoundly disabled and vulnerable person. Although he had lost his ability to think and feel he nonetheless retained "the humanity, the *human* life, which until his death goes on shaping, informing, and organising his existence *towards* the feeling and thinking which are natural to human life".[25] Finnis's notion of the sanctity of life is linked to the 'essence of being a human being', which is itself rooted in biological, rather than conscious, criteria. Ohlin instead maintains that personhood is, in effect, a 'cluster concept' and that without being 'unpacked' it offers little useful normative guidance as regards human rights.[26] He argues further that it is unnecessary to have regard to personhood *per se*, but that the individual components of a personhood assessment, are the essential factors that go to determine whether an individual possesses human rights.

In principle, the right to life (in line with other Convention rights) applies to all living persons regardless of their cognitive state. In fact, this is emphasised in that almost all of the Convention rights are preceded by the word 'everyone'. The extent to which this is reflected in *Bland* or subsequent decisions involving patients in PVS, is nevertheless moot, following consideration of more recent developments and contemporary trends in approaches to policy.

The first opportunity to consider the compatibility of *Bland* with Convention rights, following implementation of the Human Rights Act, was the Court of

[21] *Bland*, pp. 853–854.

[22] Wicks (2013), pp. 75–97.

[23] *Bland*, p. 866.

[24] *Airedale NHS Trust v Bland* [1993] AC 789 at 826 C-E.

[25] Finnis (1995) (*emphasis in the original.*)

[26] Ohlin (2005), pp. 209–249.

Appeal decision of *NHS Trust A v M; NHS Trust B v H*.[27] This concerned applications for declarations that discontinuation of CANH from two patients in PVS would be lawful and in their best interests. Unfortunately the Court failed to grapple fully with the opportunity to consider the potential protection of Convention rights and the Court provided disappointingly little analysis of the rights to life of the patients concerned. For Butler-Sloss P the point of commencement was, albeit uncontroversially, that patients in PVS were alive and were therefore entitled to a right to life. Nevertheless, withdrawal of life-sustaining treatment would not amount to an "intentional deprivation of life" within the meaning of Article 2, provided that withdrawal was in accordance with a respected body of medical opinion.[28] Although Article 2 imposes positive obligations to provide treatment where this was in the best interests of the person this duty did not extend to situations of medical futility where therapeutic treatment would not deliver a benefit. This approach, which aligns fully with that of *Bland*, reduces the assessment of futility to a matter of good faith in professional opinion, rather than a matter of principle, for purposes of human rights considerations. Previously, in *Bland*, it had ultimately been the futility of CANH that had justified its termination.[29] Nevertheless, it is difficult to reconcile the concept of futility for the purposes since CANH as a treatment will invariably achieve its physiological aim of providing nutrition.[30] To some extent this tension has been clarified recently by *Aintree*.[31] Although assessments of physiological futility, are likely to be exclusively clinical evaluations, those assessments that require appraisal of goals of treatment and quality of life will be governed by wider considerations. It seems apparent that the notion of 'futility' is used, at times, by judges and by clinicians to obscure and ultimately curtail those difficult conversations.

For the purposes of the appeal in *NHS Trust A v M; NHS Trust B v H*, Butler-Sloss P cautioned that unless treatment withdrawal could be sanctioned by the court "there would be a duty in every case to take steps to keep a terminally ill patient alive by all means possible, and to continue those steps indefinitely."[32] In these situations because patients would not be consciously aware of treatment withdrawal there was no breach of the right to be free of inhuman or degrading treatment as protected by Article 3. This particular perspective might need to be reconsidered in light of recent evidence that withdrawal of CANH from patients in PVS or MCS often presents 'challenges' for clinical management as the process of dying can be prolonged. Following treatment withdrawal people in PVS may exhibit clear indications of 'physiological distress.' Of even more concern is that people in

[27] *NHS Trust A v M; NHS Trust B v H* [2001] Fam 348.

[28] [2001] Fam 348, p. 30.

[29] *Airedale Trust v Bland* [1993] AC 789 at 805 *per* Lord Goff.

[30] Maclean (2001), p. 785.

[31] *Aintree University Hospitals v James* [2013] UKSC 67.

[32] *NHS Trust A v M; NHS Trust B v H* [2001] Fam 348, p. 29.

MCS may experience pain and distress and yet have no means of communicating their plight.[33] Since Article 3 rights might well engage here, clinical management will require judicious assessment followed by prophylactic use of pain relief, and possibly even sedation.

Although an anticipatory declaration of best interests from the Court of Protection is required prior to withdrawal or withholding CANH from persons in PVS (or MCS)[34] once the diagnosis of PVS has been confirmed the conclusion follows that withdrawal of life sustaining treatment will be in that patient's best interests.[35] For patients in definitive PVS, therefore, the 'safeguard' of obtaining court sanction appears to offer little more than a rubber stamping procedure. It also reflects the lack of effect of Convention rights for people in PVS, who nevertheless, are still 'alive' for the purposes of the law. However, to put things into perspective not every patient in PVS is made subject to an application for a Court of Protection declaration of best interests. In fact, in over 20 years since *Bland* only around 40 applications have been made to withdraw CANH from patients in PVS.[36] To date all of these applications have been driven by interested parties: whether hospital trusts, commissioners of care or close friends or family members. This means that many patients will live out their natural life span in long-term care.

Following the acute stage of brain injury and possibly specialist neuro-rehabilitation, most patients receive long-term care in their own homes, or at least in residential or specialist care homes. The extent to which Convention rights are formally protected in these environments is an important consideration. All public bodies which carry out functions that are 'public in nature' must act in compliance with the Convention. Although the term 'public body' has not been defined categorically by the Act, for these purposes a 'generously wide scope' is to be given to the expression of 'public function'.[37] Nevertheless, despite this wide interpretation not all private care homes fall within the definition of a public authority.[38] Whether a body is a 'public authority' depends ultimately on its functions, rather than its status: if its function is private then section 6(5) HRA will not apply. This could have important implications for the purposes of

[33] Royal College of Physicians (2013), p. 79.

[34] Practice Direction 9E—applications relating to serious medical treatment.

[35] *W (by her litigation friend B) v M (by her litigation friend, the Official Solicitor) and Others* [2011] EWHC 2443 *per* Baker J.

[36] Royal College of Physicians (2013), p. 63 (although, of course, not all cases are reported).

[37] *Aston Cantlow and Wilmcote with Billesley Parochial Church Council v Wallbank* [2003] UKHL 37.

[38] *YL (by her litigation friend The Official Solicitor) v Birmingham City Council* [2007] UKHL 27 and *R (on the application of Heather) v Leonard Cheshire Foundation* [2002] EWCA Civ 366 both concluded that private care homes were not public authorities for the purposes of the Convention. This is unfortunate in that these decisions impede the development of a positive culture of human rights.

safeguarding all Convention rights of this class of patients including qualified rights such as Article 9: the right to freedom of thought, conscience and religion.

In the context of patients in PVS and Article 9 rights the High Court decision of *Ahsan v University Hospitals of Leicester NHS Trust*[39] provides some indication of the possible approach of the domestic courts notwithstanding the fact that this decision concerned the quantification of damages in a settled case of clinical negligence. In this case the court held that the former religious views of a devout Muslim woman who had sustained severe brain injuries had to be taken into account when determining whether she should be cared for at a nursing home, or within the family home where her religious views could be better respected. For the purpose of awarding damages care in a nursing home was a considerably cheaper option. The court held that even though the patient was definitively in a PVS, for the purposes of ascertaining her best interests it was necessary to consider intangible factors such as familial, religious and spiritual benefits even though "no tangible benefits, whether physical or emotional [were] likely to flow from a recognition of those wishes and beliefs in view of her profound mental incapacity and lack of awareness."[40] This decision provides an important demonstration of the court's recognition that people with prolonged disorders of consciousness retain enduring interests in how they are cared for, irrespective of their lack of awareness since they remain 'persons in being.' Nevertheless, there are important caveats. The case concerned the award of damages as compensation for a settled clinical negligence action. It was also a decision at first instance. For these reasons it is questionable as to whether this decision sets a valuable precedent for the assessment of best interests in the context of Article 9 for the purposes of best interests determinations and particularly for decisions with implications for public provision of healthcare.

For the provision of long-term care for patients with prolonged disorders of consciousness (in non-negligence situations) the extent to which their qualified rights will be respected (such as those decisions that carry resource implications) is uncertain. For the provision of acute healthcare following the initial injury the primary duty of compliance with the Convention is likely to be shared between the commissioners of care, health practitioners and hospital trusts, as care providers. All of these are undoubtedly public bodies for the purposes of the Human Rights Act. Nevertheless, the situation is less clear when it comes to service delivery by non-NHS providers of care. In order to secure compliance with Convention rights for long-term care the inclusion of express contractual terms in service agreements might provide a more effective way to ensure compliance by providers of healthcare, as well as a more effective means of enforcing claims. This is likely to be even more important if contracting with providers of healthcare from jurisdictions outside member states of the Council of Europe.

---

[39] *Ahsan v University Hospitals of Leicester NHS Trust* [2007] PIQR, p. 19.

[40] *Ahsan*, para 56.

4 Minimally Conscious Patients

The condition referred to as the MCS became recognised as a definitive diagnosis only in 2002.[41] It is a spectrum of conditions that extends from just above VS to patients who border on full consciousness. Prior to its clinical recognition it seems likely that patients with MCS were categorised as being in PVS or at least in a 'PVS-like' condition. The case of *W (by her litigation friend B)* v *M (by her litigation friend, the Official Solicitor) and Others* [2011][42] was the first reported case to consider whether withdrawal of CANH would be in the best interests of a patient in MCS. The case concerned a woman who had been left in a MCS after contracting viral encephalitis. Her condition was described as being in a state of awareness somewhat above that of vegetative state. After some years, and with the support of her family, her doctors applied for a declaration that withdrawal of CANH would be in her best interests. Although there was evidence from her sister that M would not have wished to have her life sustained in the condition that she was in Baker J held that since there was no valid and applicable advance decision these former views were not determinative, even though the Mental Capacity Act 2005 requires that these factors are taken into account in determining the best interests of an adult who lacks capacity.[43] A balance sheet was used to weigh the advantages and disadvantages of granting the declaration. For Baker J the factor that carried the most significant weight was the preservation of life. Without further consideration it was stated that the test of best interests was wide enough to encompass all rights conferred by Articles 2, 3 and 8 of the Convention. Although the court was invited to consider the application of the Convention rights in greater detail Baker J cautioned that the court should resist the temptation to "stray beyond the issues that arise in this specific case".[44] Although one can appreciate the logic of this stance, the centrality of human rights considerations surely called for at least some deliberation. Ultimately, in referring to Article 2 as the most fundamental human right Baker J concluded that the declaration should not be granted on the basis that "M does experience pain and discomfort, and her disability severely restricts what she can do. Having considered all the evidence, however, I find that she does have some positive experiences and importantly that there is a reasonable prospect that those experiences can be extended by a planned programme of increased stimulation".[45] Because of the unique nature of the case and also because it was reasonable to think that there are several-fold more patients in MCS than PVS, Baker J offered guidance for future applications for the withdrawal of CANH. It is apparent that human rights was at the forefront of Baker J's mind in

[41] Giancino et al. (2002), pp. 349–353.

[42] [2011] EWHC 2443: hereinafter referred to as *Re M*.

[43] Mental Capacity Act 20015, section 4(6).

[44] [2011] EWHC 2443, p. 57.

[45] [2011] EWHC 2443, p. 251.

that a chief concern was the lack of public funding for family members to assist them in bringing, or defending, an application which could infringe their Article 6 rights. Since non-means tested funding is available to parents whose children are the subject of care proceedings under the Children Act 1989 (justified on the basis of the fundamental and life-changing consequences which flow from a care order) the same arguments were applied to applications for the withdrawal of CANH. Perhaps unsurprisingly, the decision in *Re M* has attracted considerable academic debate.[46] However, until more recently the bottom line appeared to be that although cases and situations were likely to be fact dependent, the direction of policy was that unless PVS was confirmed the sanctity of life would prevail, albeit subject to a 'ceiling of care'.[47]

Re M was followed by *Aintree v James*[48] which was the first Mental Capacity Act 2005 decision to be heard by the Supreme Court. The facts were that following successful treatment for cancer Mr James was hospitalised for a blocked stoma. Whilst in hospital he developed a serious infection and major organ failure which led to a stroke. Following resuscitation following a cardiac arrest he was diagnosed as being in a MCS. There was no issue that Mr James lacked decision-making capacity. The decision for the court was whether, in the event of further clinical deterioration, that withholding certain potentially life-saving treatment would be in his best interests. The treatments were: invasive circulatory support, renal dialysis and cardiopulmonary resuscitation. It was accepted evidence that despite Mr James' altered consciousness his care and treatment caused him discomfort and pain. It was also recognised that his prospects of leaving hospital were virtually nil. And yet he took pleasure in seeing his wife and his children during their visits and he enjoyed watching videos on his son's phone. The dispute arose since the family believed sincerely that Mr James should be given every opportunity to survive his condition in the event of clinical deterioration. At first instance a balance sheet was used and Jackson J concluded that it would be inappropriate to grant the declarations sought at that time,[49] since "the assessment of best interests . . .encompasses factors of all kinds, and not medical factors alone, and reaches into areas where doctors are not experts."[50]

In the interim Mr James' condition deteriorated and the trust's subsequent appeal was allowed. Mr James died shortly thereafter. However, due to the importance of the issues and the differences in approach taken by the trial judge and the Court of Appeal permission was given to appeal to the Supreme Court. The Supreme Court considered the different interpretations given to best interests by the trial judge and the Court of Appeal: at trial the judge had found that the treatments in question

---

[46] Jackson (2013), pp. 559–561; Kitzinger and Kitzinger (2014).

[47] (Representing a limit on interventions that will not be in the clinical best interests of the patient).

[48] *Aintree University Hospitals v James* [2013] UKSC 67.

[49] *An NHS Trust v DJ and others* [2012] EWHC 3524.

[50] *Ibid.*, p. 82.

could not be considered futile based on their previous efficacy. Equally they were not futile in the sense that they could only return Mr James to a quality of life not worth living. The evidence suggested that Mr James, despite his low state of awareness, appreciated the quality of life that he had. Although the burdens of treatment were considerable these had to be balanced by the benefits of continued existence. Neither could it be said that there was no chance of recovery since recovery could mean resumption of a quality of life that Mr James himself would regard as worthwhile.[51]

This compares with the Court of Appeal which held that the trial judge had applied the wrong test in law. Although the starting point was the person's wishes that person would need to recognise the futility of treatment, its burdensome nature and the fact that he would never be discharged home. Overall, Mr James' wishes had to yield to what was in his medical interests. Lady Justice Arden believed that where there was any doubt the court should proceed on the basis that an individual would act as a reasonable person would act—meaning that an objective test should be applied. Since treatment would be burdensome a reasonable person would reject it. Hence treatment would not be in his best interests.

In a diplomatic judgment the Supreme Court held that at the time the decision had been made the trial judge had been correct in his approach. It had indeed been too early to say that in the event that the treatments were needed it was too early to say that withholding these would be in Mr James best interests. The purpose of the best interests test was to consider matters from the patient's perspective rather than the perspective of the reasonable person. Its conclusion was that (at the time that it had considered the issue) the Court of Appeal had indeed reached the right result, albeit for the wrong reasons.

Consideration of Mr James' Convention rights was notable in its absence. Although Jackson J stated that he had balanced the various rights enjoyed by Mr James and his family in reaching his conclusions this point was not reconsidered, at least expressly, by the appellate courts.[52] Nevertheless, it is apparent that Mr James' Convention rights under Articles 2, 3 and 8 were central, albeit unspoken, aspects of this best interests application.

Aside from these central Convention rights the Supreme Court indirectly considered Mr James Article 6 rights, the right to a fair trial, in its caution against bringing applications for declarations of best interests too early. This was because the court would be unlikely to determine whether or not treatments would, or would not be, in the best interests of a patient in some hypothetical situation in the future. Although no guidance was given as to when these applications should be brought the court did state that the framing of declarations needed to be precise.

[51] *Ibid.*, p. 84(1)(d).

[52] *An NHS Trust v DJ and others* [2012] EWHC 3524, p. 84(4).

To some degree this gap was addressed recently in *Sandwell and West Birmingham Hospitals NHS Trust v CD and Others*,[53] when Theis J set out guidance for out of hours applications for declarations of best interests in medical treatment situations. The case concerned AB, a 20 year old woman with multiple disabilities that included severe learning disability and cerebral palsy. She had been admitted to hospital on the 12th June 2014 with a condition such that her doctors wished to apply for a declaration that in the event of further clinical deterioration it would not be in her best interests to receive certain life-sustaining treatments. An application was made eventually to Theis J, who sat as the out of hours judge at around 5.15 p.m. on Friday 20 June 2014. The only information provided was the application, some medical notes and a two page document from Dr Y, the lead critical care clinician at the hospital. Because the application had been brought out of hours the Official Solicitor had not been represented. The patient's mother, who had not had sufficient time to arrange for representation, had participated in the hearing by telephone in a public area of the hospital. Following subsequent meetings with the multidisciplinary team all parties and the family agreed with the ceiling of care suggestions and therefore at a later hearing, the declaration was granted that it would not be in ABs best interests to be given certain life-sustaining treatment.

Following this case the judge was sufficiently concerned about the timing and practical arrangements that she provided guidance for out-of-hours hearings. In recognising the difficult judgments involved in making applications for best interests,[54] she suggested that these ought to be made earlier, rather than later, so as to allow the necessary safeguards to be put in place to permit an effective hearing in compliance with Article 6. These included involvement of the Official Solicitor, ensuring that all parties had relevant documentation and to ensure that parties could participate in private. Efforts to seek resolution of matters should run parallel to the issuing of an application.[55] Proper and effective contingency plans for a hearing should be put in place at the earliest opportunity,[56] together with information about the patient's history and quality of life. Theis J recognised the inherent difficulties in these situations and also that she had the benefit of hindsight.

It seems difficult to argue with the pragmatic approach of Theis J. Nevertheless in the acute hospital sector where the competing rights of others are concerned this is surely an area where the Article 6 derogation will come into play. Pre-emptive preparation of cases that might proceed to a court hearing would certainly have implications for service providers, as public bodies. Anticipatory preparation of evidence and obtaining expert witness statements requires considerable investment of time and resources. Taken in the context of the multitude of pressing constraints

[53] *Sandwell and West Birmingham Hospitals NHS Trust v CD and Others* [2014] EWCOP 23.
[54] *Ibid.*, p. 35.
[55] *Ibid.*, p. 39(1).
[56] *Ibid.*, p. 39(3).

upon the National Health Service, and more particularly in the acute sector, one cannot help wondering whether resources might be better invested in trying to resolve disputes by focused communication and alternative dispute resolution. In fact, it is perhaps salutary to note that this seemingly intractable dispute was, in fact, settled by a meeting of ABs parents and the multidisciplinary team. It was not settled by the court.

5 Requests for Treatment

In end of life decision-making, situations will arise when a competent patient's wishes, even for seemingly routine treatment, will conflict with the doctor's clinical opinion (or the administrator's budget). In these situations it has been asserted repeatedly that the courts will not order a doctor to treat a patient. Balcombe LJ went so far as to say that he could conceive of no situation where it would be proper for the court to "order a doctor, whether directly or indirectly, to treat a child in a manner contrary to his or her clinical judgement."[57] And the same applies to adults. The doctor's duty to provide treatment was the central issue in *R (on the application of Burke) v General Medical Council* [2005][58] which concerned a man with degenerative cerebellar ataxia who wished for reassurance that CANH would *not* be withdrawn from him when it became necessary to sustain his life. Due to the nature of his condition it was apparent that, ultimately, he would be unable to communicate his wishes even though he would retain mental capacity. On this basis Mr Burke sought to challenge guidance from the General Medical Council that withholding or withdrawing CANH would be within the bounds of good medical practice at the time that his prognosis became so poor, and his condition so severe that continued CANH would no longer be in his medical best interests. He claimed that withdrawal of CANH would be incompatible with his Convention rights under Articles 2, 3, 8 and 14. For these purposes the guidelines were amenable to judicial review since the General Medical Council is a public authority for the purposes of the Human Rights Act.[59]

In a highly controversial decision the court found in his favour and made a series of pervasive declarations. Munby J ruled that the guidance concentrated principally on the rights of competent patients to refuse, rather than receive, treatment. The guidance did not concede the heavy presumption in favour of life-prolonging treatment in its failure to require trusts to obtain declarations of best interests prior to withdrawal of CANH circumstances other than PVS and MCS. Supporting his analysis on rights-based discourse, he concluded that the

[57] *Re J (A Minor) (Child in Care: Medical Treatment)* [1993] Fam 15.

[58] *R (on the application of Burke) v General Medical Council* [2005] EWCA 1003.

[59] Human Rights Act 1998, section 6.

guidance of the General Medical Council could be in violation of Convention rights.[60] The Court of Appeal endorsed the High Court's view that withdrawal of life-prolonging treatment, which satisfies the common law and in a manner compatible with the patient's Article 3 and 8 rights, would not breach Article 2. However, deliberately bringing about the death of a competent patient by withdrawing life-prolonging treatment contrary to the patient's wishes would infringe Article 2. The Court of Appeal also held that the High Court had been mistaken in equating the patient's best interests with the wishes of a competent patient since the two might well be in conflict. As in *Re J* the Court of Appeal emphasised that patients may not demand any treatment that is not considered to be clinically indicated by the clinicians, although the General Medical Council conceded that a second opinion ought to be offered these situations. In the event that doctors and patients disagree fundamentally about a clinical assessment or a patient's request for treatment, attempts to enforce Convention rights are likely to be less effective that attempts to find another doctor who may be prepared to treat the patient.

Resource issues can be an underlying, although often unspoken, additional factor in refusals of requests for treatment situations. The case of *Osman*[61], although not a medical case, considered the extent of the state's positive obligation to preserve life and established that it was not absolute in a world of finite resources. The court recognised the obligation to "refrain from the intentional and unlawful taking of life, but also to take appropriate steps to safeguard the lives of those within its jurisdiction"[62] this positive obligation was to be moderated by significant limitations. These included recognition that difficult choices often have to be made. For reasons such as these it is difficult to establish positive rights to receive medical treatment in the context of a publicly funded health service. A further limitation will involve the need to balance the right to life with the negative obligations imposed by the other rights that will be owed to that individual.[63] In the context of end of life care this could involve the right to be free from degrading treatment (such as repeated cardio-pulmonary resuscitation or invasive life supporting measures that offer relatively little benefit) as well as the right to make autonomous choice about the dying process as protected by Article 8 rights to respect for private life.[64] Ultimately, Convention rights are not concerned with distributive justice (whether of social or economic resources[65]) if thc problem involves resource constraints the only recourse might be to self-fund or alternatively to find another commissioner who is willing to pay.

---

[60] The guidance has since been revoked and replaced by General Medical Council (2010).

[61] *Osman v United Kingdom* [1998] 29 EHRR 245.

[62] *Osman ibid.*, p. 115.

[63] Wicks (2013), p. 87.

[64] *Pretty v United Kingdom* [2002] 35 EHRR 1, p. 67.

[65] *Matthews v Ministry of Defence* [2003] UKHL, p. 26 *per* Lord Hoffmann.

6 *'Do Not Attempt Cardiopulmonary Resuscitation'* Notices

Cardiopulmonary resuscitation (CPR) is an intervention whereby attempts are made to re-start the circulation following cardiac or respiratory arrest. Perceptions of resuscitation are influenced frequently by media portrayal where resuscitation is almost always successful and patients recover swiftly back to their former good health. For reasons such as these anticipatory decisions not to make resuscitative efforts [Do not attempt cardiopulmonary resuscitation notices (DNACPR)], are considered controversial and somewhat emotive. Nonetheless, DNACPR notices are an important aspect of healthcare and are likely to affect most individuals, directly or indirectly, at some point during their lives.[66] According to recent statistics 68 % of people will die in hospital and around 80 % of these will die with a DNACPR notice in place.[67] DNACPR decisions will engage Article 8 rights because they concern how a person chooses to pass the closing days and moments of life and the management of their death.[68] Despite their ubiquity it is noteworthy that very few disputes have reached the courts, although some have been settled. Perhaps the key reason is because in English law doctors cannot be compelled to give particular treatment to a patient which they believe is not in that patient's clinical best interests.[69]

DNACPR decisions are somewhat unique compared with other end-of-life decisions in that they are anticipatory and therefore provide an opportunity for discussion with the patient and their relatives. Because of their significance in that they potentially deprive patients of the chance of lifesaving treatment the presumption is in favour of patient involvement.

The case of *R (David Tracey) v Cambridge University Hospitals NHS Foundation Trust and Others* [2014] concerned a dispute regarding a DNACPR notice. The dispute did not concern the substantive decision to withhold CPR but rather the process and underlying policy by which the decision was reached. Since a DNACPR decision concerns a person's autonomy, integrity, dignity and quality of life, issues that all engage Article 8, the decision-making process must be fair, proportionate and afford due respect to the interests safeguarded by that right.

Following a diagnosis of terminal lung cancer Mrs Tracey was informed that she had around 9 months to live. To make matters worse she was subsequently involved in a serious road traffic accident, 2 weeks later. She sustained a cervical spine fracture and was admitted to the critical care unit at Addenbrookes. Following admission she become seriously ill and developed pneumonia. Although she was ventilated she retained decision-making capacity and could communicate by

[66] *R (David Tracey) v Cambridge University Hospitals NHS Foundation Trust and Others* [2014] EWCA Civ 33, p. 2.

[67] *R (David Tracey) v Cambridge University Hospitals NHS Foundation Trust and Others* [2014] EWCA Civ 33 *per* Lord Dyson.

[68] *Pretty v UK* (2002) 35 EHRR 1, pp. 61, 64, 67.

[69] *Re J (a minor) (wardship: medical treatment)* [1991] 1 FLR 366.

whispering and writing. It was recorded in her medical records that she had expressed a "clear wish" to be involved in all decisions that affected her care. After her condition had been stabilised a decision was taken to remove her from the ventilator although it was recognised that this intervention could precipitate a cardiac arrest. At that point a DNACPR notice was completed. On the evidence it was apparent that neither Mrs Tracey nor her family had been involved in this decision. Several days later, when her condition had improved, the notice was discovered and subsequently removed by doctors on the basis of Mrs Tracey's and her daughter's strong objections. Unfortunately, a few days later Mrs Tracey's health deteriorated and she informed the staff that she did not wish to discuss resuscitation. A second DNACPR notice was completed following consultation with her family. Mrs Tracey died shortly thereafter.

The main issues of the subsequent dispute concerned the circumstances by which the first notice had been imposed: did the placing of the DNACPR decision in her medical record engage Article 8 and second, did failure to discuss the notice with Mrs Tracey and her family breach her Article 8 rights. In relation to the first issue the court unanimously accepted that Article 8 rights were engaged. With respect to the second issue the court held that there was a strong presumption in favour of patient involvement. Furthermore, doctors are obliged to tell patients if they believe that CPR would be futile in order to ensure that patients could arrange to receive a second opinion if they so wished. Nevertheless, an important caveat was added. The court held that it would be inappropriate (and therefore not a breach of Article 8 rights) to involve the patient or the family if doctors considered that this would cause physical or psychological harm. Article 8 did not mandate the arrangement for a second opinion.[70] Whilst this case appears to be a victory for human rights and disclosure of information several questions remain unanswered. It is apparent that a large number of DNACPR notices are already in place. The court did not address itself to the issue of whether the decision was to have retrospective effect. Furthermore, if (as with Mrs Tracey) a competent person refuses to discuss resuscitation, do doctors have a duty to involve family members and if so, how will this duty be aligned with the duty of confidentiality (also protected by Article 8).

7 The Pervasive Nature of Article 8

The Article 8 right to respect for private and family life is engaged invariably in end of life decision making since "A decision as to how to pass the closing days and moments of one's life and how one manages one's death touches in the most immediate and obvious way a patient's personal autonomy, integrity, dignity and

[70] *R (David Tracey) v Cambridge University Hospitals NHS Foundation Trust and Others* [2014] EWCA Civ 33.

quality of life."[71] The right also protects bodily integrity to the extent that adults with capacity may refuse even lifesaving medical treatment, whether at the end of their lives or otherwise. It has also been engaged with any decision which concerns a patient's personal autonomy, integrity, dignity and quality of life.

As a qualified right any interference with Article 8 must be 'in accordance with the law', have a legitimate aim and be necessary in a democratic society. To ascertain whether the interference accords with the law requires careful scrutiny. The law must be accessible and provide sufficient, rather than absolute, clarity[72] sufficient for the consequences of an action to be reasonably foreseen.[73] The second requirement is that any interference must meet the test of legitimate aim, which in the context of end of life care is likely to include protection of health, protection of morals or protection of the rights of others. A paramount factor concerns whether the interference is 'necessary in a democratic society' and requires evidence of some pressing social need,[74] that the reasons for the interference are both relevant and sufficient and a test of proportionality: whether the association between the action taken and the aim of the intervention is acceptable. Since the assessment of proportionality involves a value judgment to be made at the juncture at which a balance must be struck between the importance of the objective pursued and the value of the right encroached upon, the European Court has recognised that it might be less appropriate than a national court to decide whether an appropriate balance has been struck in any national context. It is for this reason that the principle of proportionality has been linked to the concept of the margin of appreciation which provides considerable discretion to public authorities. Disputes regarding the compass of protection provided by Article 8 rights have arisen most acutely in challenges that concern rights to assisted dying.

8 Assisted Dying

Although the Suicide Act 1961 abrogated the rule of law whereby it was a crime for a person to commit (or attempt to commit) suicide, the Act failed to confer a right to commit suicide.[75] Section 2 of the Suicide Act provides that it is a substantive offence to assist the suicide of another. The central justification for the blanket ban on assisted suicide is the perceived risk to the lives of vulnerable people who might perceive themselves to be a burden to their family, friends and society.

[71] *Ibid.*, p. 32.

[72] *Olsson v Sweden* (No 1) A 130 (1988), p. 62.

[73] A useful illustration is provided by *R (Purdy) v Director of Public Prosecutions* [2009] UKHL 45.

[74] *Dudgeon v United Kingdom* (1981) A 45, pp. 51 and 53.

[75] *R (Pretty) v DPP* [2002] 1 AC 800 *per* Lord Bingham at 35.

The offence of assisted suicide has precipitated several trans-jurisdictional challenges, argued on the basis of Convention rights. This is perhaps not unexpected in that 36 of the 45 member states of the Council of Europe prohibit any form of assisted suicide and a future consensus appears to be remote. Between 1998 and 2011 a total of 215 people from the United Kingdom had utilised the services of Dignitas in Switzerland and that no one providing assistance in these circumstances had been prosecuted.[76] Nevertheless, some evidence suggests that because of current law some people with progressive degenerative conditions might feel compelled to end their lives whilst they are still physically able rather than wait until they require assistance from others in order to do so. From this perspective the prohibition could be conceived as an impetus to prematurely curtail some people's lives.[77] In English jurisdiction the expression 'mercy killing' is reserved for the killing of a person for motives which, from the perspective of the perpetrator, are for the victim's benefit and often at the victim's request. Even if that person wished to die and the killing was carried out purely on compassionate grounds, that killing will amount to murder.[78]

In Pretty v UK[79] the applicant, Mrs Pretty, suffered from motor neurone disease. She alleged that the Director of Public Prosecution's (DPP) refusal to grant her husband prospective immunity from prosecution if he assisted her suicide and second that the blanket prohibition on assisted suicide in section 2 of the Suicide Act 1961 violated her Article 2, 3, 8, 9 and 14 Convention rights. Article 9 was argued on the basis that it protects the freedom to manifest one's beliefs although it was held that this did not extend to protect the right to manifest one's belief in assisted suicide. Although the House of Lords had held previously that Mrs Pretty's desire to end her life did not engage her Convention rights, the European Court held that her Article 8(1) rights were engaged in that the right to family and private life encompassed the right to decide how and when to die and in particular, the right to avoid a distressing and undignified death.[80] The court expressed that dignity and respect for autonomy are core and pervasive values of the Convention.[81] It is also apparent that spouses or partners in close relations with people who wish to die can invoke an Article 8 right of their own.[82] It is apparent that the majority of member states attach greater weight to protection of human life than to rights to end life.[83] Nevertheless, despite this clear line of judicial authority that Article 8 rights are engaged, and interfered with, these breaches have often been justified, with insufficient analysis, by the 'margin of appreciation' enjoyed by member states.

---

[76] *R (Nicklinson) v Ministry of Justice* [2014] UKSC 38, p. 48.

[77] *Ibid.*, p. 96.

[78] *Airedale Trust v Bland* [1993] AC 789 at 885.

[79] *Pretty v UK* [2002] 35 EHRR 1.

[80] *Haas v Switzerland* (2011) 53 EHRR 33, p. 51; *Gross v Switzerland* (2014) 58 EHRR 7, p. 60.

[81] *Pretty v United Kingdom* (2000) 35 EHRR 1, p. 65.

[82] *Koch v Germany* (2013) 56 EHRR 6, pp. 46 and 51.

[83] *Haas v Switzerland* (2011) 53 EHRR 33, p. 55.

The subsequent case of *R (Purdy) v Director of Public Prosecutions* [2010][84] concerned a woman with multiple sclerosis. In view of the progressive nature of her condition she believed that the time would come when she would wish to take her own life. Since she would need her husband's assistance to do so she sought to ensure, as far as possible, that he would not be prosecuted on his return after accompanying her to the Suicide Clinic, Dignitas, in Switzerland. Although she accepted that the DPP could not provide her husband with a guarantee of immunity from prosecution she argued that she was entitled to expect the law to be foreseeable, in advance. The House of Lords upheld her contention that the DPP's refusal to publish guidance infringed her Article 8 rights. Mrs Purdy was entitled to expect that the law would be accessible and foreseeable in the exercise of the scope of its exercise of discretion. The House of Lords called for the DPP to identify those factors which would distinguish between cases in which prosecution would be disproportionate and those situations where it did not.[85] Under the doctrine of the rule of law, the law should be capable of being known, understood and obeyed by its subjects and should be applied publicly and consistently by impartial courts acting as arbiters. This permits citizens to plan their lives and to know, in advance, whether an activity they are planning is lawful or not. The DPP has since published a policy document which lists the public interest factors that are likely to balance in favour of prosecution against those that will tend to weigh against.[86] This was in response to the call in *Purdy* for the DPP to "to clarify what his position is as to the factors that he regards as relevant for and against prosecution" in cases of encouraging and assisting suicide.[87]

In R (*Nicklinson*) *v Ministry of Justice*; *R (AM) v Director of Public Prosecutions*[88] the Supreme Court considered the extent to which the blanket prohibition against assisted suicide was a disproportionate and unjustifiable interference with the Article 8 rights of individuals who had made a clear, settled and informed decision to commit suicide but who were unable, because of their physical circumstances, to take their own lives without assistance from others. This issue was one of constitutional relevance: did section 2 of the Suicide Act fall within the United Kingdom's margin of appreciation within Article 8(2) and more fundamentally, whether it was appropriate for the court to consider this issue (rather than Parliament). The court held that it was open to a domestic court to consider whether section 2 infringes Article 8.[89] The extent to which the prohibition in section 2 interfered with the Article 8 rights of citizens in determining how and when they should die could not be construed compatibly with Article 8. Nevertheless, the

[84] *R (Purdy) v Director of Public Prosecutions* [2009] UKHL 45.

[85] *Ibid.*, p. 64.

[86] Crown Prosecution Service (2010).

[87] *R (Purdy) v Director of Public Prosecutions* [2009] UKHL 45, p. 55.

[88] *R (Nicklinson) v Ministry of Justice*; *R (AM) v Director of Public Prosecutions* [2014] UKSC 38.

[89] *Ibid.*, p. 76.

majority in *Nicklinson* declined to make a declaration of incompatibility[90] in order to allow Parliament an opportunity to consider the matter.[91] For Lord Neuberger "Parliament now has the opportunity to address the issue of whether section 2 should be relaxed or modified, and if so how, in the knowledge that, if it is not satisfactorily addressed, there is a real prospect that a further, and successful, application for a declaration of incompatibility may be made".[92] This is perhaps the strongest indication to date that the court is prepared to make a declaration of incompatibility should the matter arise again.

Article 8(2) provides that state interference with the right to family and private life will be lawful if this is necessary in a democratic society. Martin, a co-applicant in the Nicklinson case, argued that the DPP's policy document was insufficiently clear in respect of the likelihood of prosecution of individuals, such as health professionals and carers, who were prepared on the basis of compassionate motives, to assist a person to commit suicide. The current policy of the DPP means that cases are assessed *ex post facto* and by reference to their own unique facts. Evidence put before the court suggests that health practitioners will almost invariably refuse to provide information regarding suicide in order to avoid contravening the law.[93] The purpose of the DPP's Code of Policy is, however, not to forecast the likelihood of prosecution but rather to ensure its public availability so that the public is aware of its scope and to ascertain whether it is applied consistently.

The Supreme Court held that the question of whether current law was incompatible with Article 8 lay within the margin of appreciation and was therefore a decision for the Parliament. Five Justices[94] held that court had constitutional authority to make a declaration that the general prohibition on assisted suicide was incompatible with Article 8. Of those, Lords Neuberger, Mance and Wilson declined to grant a declaration of incompatibility in this case but in their dissent Lady Hale and Lord Kerr would have done so. Four judges[95] concluded that the question whether the law was compatible with Article 8 required consideration by Parliament, which was inherently better qualified than the courts to consider. For the purposes of recognising and respecting the Convention rights of applicants with strong and arguable positions it is arguable that this case has achieved little else than perpetuating the supremacy of Parliament.

---

[90] In accordance with the Human Rights Act 1998, section 4.

[91] *R (Nicklinson) v Ministry of Justice*; *R (AM) v Director of Public Prosecutions* [2014] UKSC 38, p. 114.

[92] *Ibid.*, p. 118.

[93] *R (Nicklinson) v Ministry of Justice*; *R (AM) v Director of Public Prosecutions* [2014] UKSC 38, p. 137.

[94] Lords Neuberger, Mance and Kerr and Baroness Hale.

[95] Lords Clarke, Sumption, Reed and Hughes.

9 Conclusion

The European Convention on Human Rights circumscribes very considerable promise for healthcare and end of life decision making and healthcare more generally. It is also apparent that most end of life challenges and disputes will engage Convention rights, irrespective of whether these are considered expressly by the courts or not and it is apparent that in some situations mere brief nods to relevant rights are given, rather than any meaningful consideration. Whether this would make a difference to the ultimate decision is more uncertain, particularly in the context of applications for declarations of best interests.

Decision-making at end of life, or otherwise, simply means making a choice. It requires identification of the range of possible choices and considering each in the context of their implications. For the purposes of best interests declarations whether the courts are best placed to adjudicate, at least in the first instance, is a difficult and contentious call.

End-of-life dilemmas and challenges present a complex interplay of law, morals and public policy; the courts remind us often that they are courts of law and not of morals.[96] Nevertheless, in end of life decision-making, the courts often stand perilously close to acting as moral arbiters. In *Bland* Lord Browne Wilkinson asked:

> Should judges seek to develop new law to meet a wholly new situation? Or is this a matter which lies outside the area of legitimate development of the law by judges and requires society, through the democratic expression of its views in Parliament, to reach its decisions on the underlying moral and practical problems and then reflect those decisions in legislation?[97]

This seems to be what the court in *Nicklinson* were alluding to in their reticence to make a declaration of incompatibility. Nevertheless, for situations that involve sensitive handling and in the context of seeking relationships of trust, many of these issues might be better resolved, at least in the first instance, by skilled and sensitive communication, mediation, or referral to a Clinical Ethics Committee. Although the courts are best placed for enforcing a decision where relationships have broken down, often irretrievably, the involvement of a clinical ethics committee might offer a more positive way forward for the benefit of all parties concerned, and far more within the ethos of the recognition of natural human rights.

References

Crown Prosecution Service. (2010). *Policy for prosecutors in respect of cases of encouraging or assisting suicide*. London: UK Gov. Available at http://www.cps.gov.uk.

[96] For example in *Re A (Children) (conjoined twins)* [2000] 4 All ER 961 at 969 *per* Ward LJ.

[97] *Airedale Trust v Bland* [1993] AC 789, p. 878.

Finnis, J. (1995). Misunderstanding the case against Euthanasia: Response to Harris's first reply. In J. Keown (Ed.), *Euthanasia examined: Ethical, clinical and legal perspectives* (pp. 62–71). Cambridge: Cambridge University Press.

General Medical Council. (2010). *Treatment and care towards the end of life: Good practice in decision-making*. London: GMC.

Giancino, J. T., Ashwal, S., Childs, N., Cranford, R., Jennett, B., Katz, D. I., et al. (2002). The minimally conscious state: Definition and diagnostic criteria. *Neurology, 58*(3), 349–353.

Jackson, E. (2013). The minimally conscious state and treatment withdrawal: *W v M. Journal of Medical Ethics, 39*, 559–561.

Kitzinger, C., & Kitzinger, J. (2014). Withholding artificial nutrition and hydration from minimally conscious and vegetative state patients: Family perspectives. *JME Online*. http://jme.bmj.com/content/early/2014/01/03/medethics-2013-101799.full.pdf.

Maclean, A. R. (2001). Crossing the Rubicon on the Human Rights Ferry. *The Modern Law Review, 64*(5), 775–794.

Ohlin, J. (2005). Is the concept of the person necessary for human rights? *Columbia Law Review, 105*, 209–249.

Royal College of Physicians. (2013). *Prolonged disorders of consciousness: National clinical guidelines*. London.

Samanta, J. (2012). Equality for followers of South Asian religions in end-of-life care. *Nursing Ethics, 20*(4), 382–391.

Wicks, E. (2013). When is life not in our own best interests? The best interests test as an unsatisfactory exception to the right to life in the context of permanent vegetative state cases. *Medical Law International, 13*(1), 75–97.

Case Law (UK)

Ahsan v University Hospitals of Leicester NHS Trust [2007] PIQR

Aintree University Hospitals v James [2013] UKSC 67

Airedale Trust v Bland [1993] 1 All ER 831

An NHS Trust v DJ and others [2012] EWHC 3524

Aston Cantlow and Wilmcote with Billesley Parochial Church Council v Wallbank [2003] UKHL 37

Matthews v Ministry of Defence [2003] UKHL

NHS Trust A v M; NHS Trust B v H [2001] Fam 348

R (Application of Mrs Dianne Pretty) v Director of Public Prosecutions and Secretary of State for the Home Department [2002] 1 AC 800

R (David Tracey) v Cambridge University Hospitals NHS Foundation Trust and Others [2014] EWCA Civ 33

R (Nicklinson) v Ministry of Justice; R (AM) v Director of Public Prosecutions [2014] UKSC 38

R (on the application of Burke) v General Medical Council [2005] EWCA 1003

R (on the application of Heather) v Leonard Cheshire Foundation [2002] EWCA Civ 366

R (Purdy) v Director of Public Prosecutions [2009] UKHL 45

Re A (Children) (conjoined twins) [2000] 4 All ER 961 at 969

Re J (A Minor) (Child in Care: Medical Treatment) [1993] Fam 15

Re J (a minor) (Wardship: medical treatment) [1991] 1 FLR 366

Re M [2011] EWHC 2443

Sandwell and West Birmingham Hospitals NHS Trust v CD and Others [2014] EWCOP 23

W (by her litigation friend B) v M (by her litigation friend, the Official Solicitor) and Others [2011] EWHC 2443

YL (by her litigation friend The Official Solicitor) v Birmingham City Council [2007] UKHL 27

Case Law (Strasbourg)

Dudgeon v United Kingdom (1981) A 45
Gross v Switzerland (2014) 58 EHRR 7
Haas v Switzerland (2011) 53 EHRR 33
Haas v Switzerland (2011) 53 EHRR 33
Koch v Germany (2013) 56 EHRR 6
LCB v UK (1998) 27 EHRR 212
Olsson v Sweden (No 1) A 130 (1988)
Osman v United Kingdom [1998] 29 EHRR 245
Pretty v United Kingdom [2002] 35 EHRR 1

Legislation

Human Rights Act 1998
Mental Capacity Act 2015

Can Rights Be Ring-Fenced in Times of Austerity? Equality, Equity and Judicial 'Trusteeship' over the UK's Fairness Agenda

Jacinta Miller and Alice Diver

1 Introduction

The need for some form of 'fairness agenda' has been cited on several occasions in connection with the UK's ongoing programmes of welfare reform.[1] That the state has an over-arching duty to preserve finite resources, whilst also promoting just and 'equitable outcomes' via its decision-making processes, has also been noted in a number of recent cases arising out of the introduction of 'austerity measures.'[2] Whether equitable concepts are set to expand upon basic equality principles in cases involving adequate living standards remains to be seen. What does seem fairly clear is that budgetary limitations have the potential to impact significantly upon the lives of the most vulnerable members of society, particularly in respect of such particularly 'fragile rights' as housing or health care provision. This is especially so where certain socio-economic rights have tended to require considerable levels of financial and political bolstering, in the absence of which they risk

[1] See http://www.theguardian.com/politics/2010/oct/06/david-cameron-fairness-people-deserve (accessed 30.04.15); http://www.telegraph.co.uk/news/politics/david-cameron/9000249/David-Cameron-my-vision-for-a-fair-Britain.html (accessed 10.10.15).

[2] See for example *MA and others* v *The Secretary Of State For Work And Pensions* [2014] EWCA Civ 13; *R (D) v Worcestershire County Council* [2013] EWHC 2490 (Admin); *R (Hardy) v Sandwell Metropolitan Borough Council* [2015] EWHC 890 (Admin); *R (Rutherford) v SSWP* [2014] EWHC 1631 (Admin).

J. Miller (✉)
School of Law, Northumbria University, Newcastle, UK
e-mail: j.miller@ulster.ac.uk

A. Diver
Transitional Justice Institute, School of Law, University of Ulster, Londonderry, UK

Dept. of Law and Criminology, Edge Hill University, Ormskirk, Lancs, UK
e-mail: divera@edgehill.ac.uk

A. Diver, J. Miller (eds.), *Justiciability of Human Rights Law in Domestic Jurisdictions*, DOI 10.1007/978-3-319-24016-9_2

being forever framed as merely aspirational in nature, suitable only for some gently progressive form of realization. Litigation in domestic courts remains key: as Harris argued, 'non-justiciability may be revealed as the reason for there being no legally enforceable rights.'[3] Equally, the notion of a justiciable right to an adequate standard of living is perhaps still a little too 'malleable,' to be considered on a 'justiciability-par' with weightier civil or political rights.[4] This chapter will argue that a rights-template tied to the notion of 'socio-economic equity' (rather than equality) could frame domestic judges as the 'trustees' of public budgets, and indeed of the socio-economic rights that such funds are meant to protect and promote. This could in turn potentially serve to challenge at least some of the increasingly profound 'cycles of poverty that can only be broken through structural reforms.'[5] The role of domestic courts is a fundamental, and essentially fiduciary one: judges are best placed to keep reminding legislators and policy-makers of the need to identify (and avoid dipping below) clearly articulated rights standards which should in themselves be firmly grounded upon such key rights concepts as human dignity and 'bodily integrity.'[6]

2 Justiciability?

> [n]either morality nor justice... requires considerable sacrifices of some persons for the sake of trifling gains to others, even if the ideal of equality may seem initially to point in that direction.[7]

In the absence of meaningful definitional standards, many socio-economic rights essentially become fictive: as Harris has observed, 'consistent with the rule of law, the determinative factor in judicial review should be whether an applicant has established enforceable legal rights.'[8] By the same token, to be meaningfully juridical, human rights must at least be 'subject to the scrutiny of a court of law

[3] Harris (2003), p. 633. Harris uses the terms 'judicial review' and 'justiciability' almost interchangeably when he argues that 'the courts have struggled to determine whether the exercise of the prerogative of mercy is vulnerable to judicial review, that is, whether or not it is justiciable' (p. 636).

[4] See Finkelstein (1924), p. 341. See also Hunt (1996), p. 66. Hunt acknowledges that both legal and non-legal processes are necessary to achieve fuller implementation of human rights; Farmer (2003) on the contribution of legal processes to the implementation of human rights generally and how alternative strategies for realisation are often needed.

[5] Muvingi (2009), p. 163.

[6] Waldorf (2012), p. 173. Waldorf then analyses the difficulties and limitations associated with addressing socio-economic rights violations, albeit in respect of transitional justice: 'Socio-economic factors were mostly relegated to historical background, where they could be more easily ignored' (p. 176).

[7] Rakowski (1993), p. 2.

[8] Harris (2003), p. 632.

or another judicial or quasi-judicial process.'[9] Whilst it is now generally accepted that most, if not all, socio-economic rights are essentially justiciable[10] (at least in the sense of having some chance of being successfully litigated at the level of domestic courts and tribunals) it can also be argued that many such rights still tend to become particularly 'flimsy' at particular points in their implementation and subsequent monitoring stages.[11] As Hoffman LJ observed,

> Human rights include the right to a minimum standard of living, without which many of the other rights would be a mockery. But they certainly do not include the right to a fair distribution of resources or fair treatment in economic terms – in other words, distributive justice. Of course distributive justice is a good thing but it is not a fundamental right.[12]

Domestic enforcement can thus be quite 'frustrating'[13] for rights advocates, not least when it comes to identifying some form of useful minimum standards or rights-thresholds. With entitlements to social security having been recognized however as a juridical form of property right, national courts are clearly obliged to protect vulnerable 'rights beneficiaries' who may be at risk of suffering harm. Although judges cannot force domestic decision-makers to always act equitably, they can at least identify and, if needs must, loudly condemn clear instances of inequity and degradation as they arise or seem likely to occur. Repeatedly reminding those who hold the public purse-strings of their moral duty to actively protect basic levels of subsistence, might eventually enable some level of budget 'ring-fencing,' aimed specifically at preventing violations of human dignity. Where law-making boundaries clearly exist however between the judiciary and the executive, it may be argued that calls for judicial oversight run the risk of falling prey to 'judicial self-limitation' with some jurists' desire for change perhaps being too easily stymied by some 'fear of the consequences that might ensue if courts were to interfere in such matters.'[14]

---

[9] Arambulo (1999), p. 55. This is traditionally viewed in the context of individual litigation through domestic courts or via individual complaint mechanisms. See also Sepulveda (2003) on how the work of quasi-judicial organisations (such as the UN Treaty monitoring bodies) can also be taken as evidence of justiciability.

[10] See further Nolan (2009); See however O'Connell (2011), pp. 532–554 on how courts in Canada, India, and South Africa have moved away from protecting socio-economic rights in favour of tacitly endorsing the 'neo-liberal policy prescriptions' of legislators.

[11] See further Donnelly (2007); Itzcovich (2013), pp. 287–308.

[12] *Matthews v Ministry of Defence* [2003] UKHL 4 per Hoffman LJ, para 26.

[13] Collingsworth (2002), p. 185.

[14] Finkelstein (1924), p. 341; see also Jackson (1992); Jowell (2003), p. 593 on how UK courts have adopted this approach.

3 Judicial (Over)Deference or Judges as 'Rights-Trustees'?

> Providing that the court limits itself to an investigation of the legal issues raised, there is no constitutional impropriety in such review. To the contrary, it is precisely the proper role of the court.[15]

Factors which might affect rights-enforcement at the level of domestic law and policy-making include socio-political resistance to international monitoring mechanisms, as occurred in the UK recently over the UN's criticism of its 'bedroom tax' welfare reforms.[16] Similarly, if certain types of rights are found to exist only where they have firstly been clearly defined in enshrining domestic statutes or judicially endorsed via case law, and underpinned by adequately earmarked state resources, then this perhaps calls into question the very nature of such 'rights.' Arguably, they may be better framed as state-sanctioned social privileges, especially given that access to such entitlements may be almost entirely dependent upon favourable social contexts: a legacy of political conflict or financial recession may easily serve to freeze or reverse progressive implementation, or hinder intended impacts. Basic principles of non-discrimination and equality (of treatment, or of opportunity) may fall short where there is instead a need for fairness-led, equitable outcomes, not least in cases involving resource-dependent decision-making.[17] Again, the ideals and language of 'equity' (e.g. 'trusteeship', fairness, justice, fiduciary obligations towards vulnerable beneficiaries) might prove useful in overcoming some of the difficulties that tend to attach to the implementation of such economically fragile rights. There seems to be increasing judicial reluctance however to comment upon the unfairness of certain resource allocations, highlight systemic welfare failings, or denounce the harshness of some fiscal policies. Arguably, if judges were framed as the moral 'trustees' of the fragile, dignity-based entitlements of the vulnerable, then perhaps legislators might be encouraged to allocate and earmark sufficient resources to protect such fundamental rights.

Courts would not be usurping elected legislators in their role as budget administrators; rather they would be calling upon them to be mindful of their 'fiduciary duty' to equitably care-take scarce public funds, without harming those social beneficiaries most in need of protection. Arguably, such an approach might enable a useful measure of rights 'ring-fencing' on the basis that it must be possible to

[15] Finn (2002) on the proper role of the courts, the need for judicial review, the abuse of political power as an 'exercise in bad faith or for improper purposes with no possibility of legal remedy' and how this 'is contrary to the rule of law, and should not be countenanced without compelling reason.' (available at http://www.austlii.edu.au/au/journals/FedLRev/2002/9.html. Accessed 01.02.15).

[16] See for example Rolnik (2009); http://www.theguardian.com/society/2013/sep/11/bedroom-tax-should-be-axed-says-un-investigator (accessed 31.01.15). Responses were fairly predictable: See for example http://www.theguardian.com/society/2014/feb/03/ministers-savage-un-report-abolition-bedroom-tax (accessed 30.01.15).

[17] See further Turk (1992), Craven (1995), Cranston (1973), Orwin and Pangle (1984), and Vierdag (1978).

identify a point at which basic standards of human dignity have been allowed to fall below an acceptable rights-threshold. Ensuring that such situations are rectified as a matter of urgency, rather than political expediency, is a key task. Democratically mandated 'austerity measures' might otherwise remain forever problematic; decisions which appear overtly discriminatory might well be challenged in court, but ultimately deemed rights-compliant on the basis that they were made both lawfully and rationally, and are therefore entirely 'justified' in political or economic terms. This is especially so where the 'greater good' has traditionally tended to demand preservation of scarce public funds by rationing allocations on the basis of 'merit' i.e. the most urgent need. Similarly, if domestic law and policy-makers have demonstrated sufficiently high levels of 'due regard' for the rights of those likely to be adversely affected (via, say, political debate or public consultation) then this too might serve to 'court-proof' many controversial policy decisions which might otherwise have been framed as sorely testing the limits of rights compliance and good conscience.[18]

Domestic courts dealing with such contentious issues as social security payments, health care or adequate housing, remain well placed however to make significant contributions to human rights jurisprudence, irrespective of whether these matters are viewed as value-based, moral dilemmas or as grounded in clear legal entitlements.[19] As Farmer has observed,

> ...human rights discussions are excessively legal and theoretical in focus. They seek to define rights, mandate punishment by appropriate authorities for the violators, enforce international treaties, and so on.[20]

Given that signatory states must view all individuals as 'equal in human dignity'[21] some meaningfully workable degree of government accountability should arise where this basic principle has been side-lined.[22] Focusing on the presence or absence of domestic legal remedies should allow for some discussion of 'what it actually takes to enable people to be secure against the standard, predictable threats to their rights.'[23] Non-discrimination at least provides a useful starting point: as Freeman pointed out, basic principles of 'natural justice' might be invoked even

---

[18] See further Le Sueur (1995), p. 240.

[19] See however Nolan et al. (2013), p. 1 on how elected legislators (and public administrations) 'have the primary responsibility, and the greatest capacity, for giving effect to such rights.'

[20] Farmer (2003), p. 19. Farmer also cites Henkin (1981) on how remedies in international law are similarly limited. See also Collingsworth (2002) who suggests that remedies must lie in domestic law.

[21] See the Preambles to the UDHR, the ICCPR and the ICESCR for example.

[22] See The UN General Assembly Resolution 60/147 (December 2005); although no article within The ICESCR establishes such a right, General Comment No. 14 (2000) para 59 states that 'any person or group victim of a violation of the right to health should have access to effective judicial or other appropriate remedies at both national and international levels.'

[23] Shue (1996), p. 160.

where no other obvious norms or legal rules are evident.[24] The procedural or administrative aspects of a claim may allow for some useful level of judicial oversight even if the core grievances of a plaintiff cannot be litigated.[25] As Toebes argued in respect of the Netherlands, 'justiciability does not always refer to rights as such but, rather to elements'[26] within those rights. Litigating significant aspects of the right to health care (rather than searching for some workably specific domestic definition of a right to health) can thus serve to create significant precedent.[27] As McLean has further stressed, 'even where rights are not formally provided for in constitutions, where a remedy is provided it can reasonably be concluded that the right is taken to exist.'[28] On this point Toebbes conceded however that

> In spite of the fact that the Dutch courts are said to have paid considerable attention to economic and social rights, there are very few judgements in which the Dutch courts have granted direct effect to economic, social and cultural rights.[29]

That said, as a basic starting point 'the equality principle is a dominant and recurring theme of international human rights law.'[30] National equality laws have in turn essentially been 'legitimated on the grounds that they further the liberal goals of State neutrality, individualism and the promotion of autonomy'.[31] The notions of equality of opportunity and equal treatment in theory should provide considerable scope for enabling a greater indivisibility of human rights,[32] and creating an underpinning philosophy of allocating scarce resources in the most equitable ways possible.[33] Historical and socio-political context clearly also

---

[24] Freeman (2001), p. 1379 on the principle of natural justice (as applied in cases such as *National Bank of Greece and Athens v Metliss* [1958] AC 509 (see para 525, per Viscount Simonds).

[25] See also McCrudden (2000) on how judges may 'refer extensively to the decisions of foreign courts when interpreting human rights guarantees.'

[26] Toebes (1999), p. 168.

[27] See for example *Soobramoney v Minister of Health, KwaZulu-Natal* (CCT32/97) [1997] ZACC 17; 1998 (1) SA 765 (CC); 1997 (12) BCLR 1696 (27 November 1997). See also Bilchitz (2003) on how the approach may be administrative rather than substantive; See also *R v Cambridgeshire Health Authority ex p. B* [1995] 1 WLR 898 and *Rodgers v Swindon Primary Health Care Trust and the Secretary of State for* Health [2006] EWCA Civ 392 as examples of judicial reviews taken in relation to Health Authority decisions to not provide particular medicines. See further McTeer (1995); Elias-Jones and Samanta (2005), p. 823 argue that until a better system exists (based perhaps on medical ethics committees) the courts are likely to remain as the 'arbiters of the child's best interests' in such contexts.

[28] McLean (1999), p. 59, who suggests that a legal right truly exists only where an actual legal remedy is present.

[29] Toebes (1999) who differentiates between direct effect and the 'internal effect' of Treaties via domestic law.

[30] Bayefsky (1990), p. 2. See also McCrudden (2003), p. xiii on how the grounds of discrimination have expanded and how new concepts of equality have developed; Kolm (2002) on how 'justice, fairness, or equity' can underpin global 'codes' of justice.

[31] Fredman (2001), p. 154.

[32] Turk (1992).

[33] See for example the CESCR Committee's '*Concluding Observations of the Committee on Economic, Social and Cultural Rights: Algeria*' (28/12/1995) UN Document E/C.12/1995/17

matters: the South African Constitution for example admitted that a fresh focus on non-discrimination was unlikely to correct entrenched inequalities which had resulted from decades of unfair laws and policies. As its Preamble states, 'the People of South Africa recognize the injustices of the past,' whilst Article 1 (a) underscores the importance of 'human dignity, the achievement of equality and the advancement of human rights and freedoms.'[34] Legally embedding equality principles could prevent blatantly unlawful forms of discrimination, removing any 'arbitrary, invidious or unjustified distinction or differentiation unwarranted by those made subject to them.'[35] Preventing indirect discrimination, especially as it relates to accessing or using essential services, also has clear ties to the promotion of human dignity and to poverty avoidance,[36] as Farmer's work on 'structural violence'[37] made very plain.[38]

And yet, 'equal treatment can perpetuate inequalities'[39] not least where decision-makers are free to cite an over-arching need to protect the 'public good'[40] or promote a notion of higher 'state necessity.'[41] Ensuring a decent standard of living is not merely about achieving broad-brush social or economic equalities: if everyone is equally ill, impoverished, or living in a similar state of degrading squalor, then it can hardly be said that principles of equal treatment have served either to define, or ring-fence the funds to protect, meaningful rights standards. The concept of 'adequacy' might be more clearly articulated via equitable principles of justice or fairness: these in turn could point perhaps to some discernible minimum rights thresholds of provision, which might then be used to embed positive state obligations, or at least to highlight (or prevent a repeat of) abject failings of law and policy. Where however rights are repeatedly defined as being dependent upon a state's 'maximum available resources,' or couched in the language of perpetually progressive aspiration, domestic jurists are perhaps left with few options. They must either frame inadequate domestic legal frameworks as being essentially compliant with human rights obligations, or quietly classify them as inevitable contraventions, justified on the basis that decision-makers (i.e. budget

para 16 which cited deep concern over 'the fact that the philosophy of the Covenant, based on the principle of non-discrimination and on the idea of the universality of human rights, has not fully taken root.'

[34] See The South African Constitution available at http://www.constitutionalcourt.org.za/site/theconstitution/thetext.htm (accessed 10.10.14).

[35] McKean (1983), p. 185.

[36] See Oppenheimer et al. (2002) on Villerme's nineteenth century study of mortality rates and living conditions in France, Chadwick's report on English sanitary conditions and Virchow's study of the Prussian typhus epidemic.

[37] Farmer (2001, 2003).

[38] See also however Leary (1994) on how there may be no automatic link between resources and health status.

[39] Fredman (2001), p. 2.

[40] Lee (1998), p. 40.

[41] See further Price-Smith (2001), p. 10.

holders) must protect the 'greater good.' In other words, national laws or policies on funding allocations which engage socio-economic rights may be profoundly *unfair* in terms of individual impacts and compromises to human dignity, but will remain essentially justifiable on the basis that public funds must be directed towards other, higher-priority rights issues. Judges face a difficult task in attempting to overturn decisions arising from such reasoning. It can be argued however that,

> The greater the legal content of any issue, the greater the potential role of the court, because under our constitution and subject to the sovereign power of Parliament it is the function of the courts and not of political bodies to resolve legal questions.[42]

In doing so, domestic courts can surely look to the various 'ethical concept[s], grounded in principles of distributive justice.'[43] As Whitehead and Dahlgren argued, 'health inequality' is not completely removed from 'health inequity' given how both concepts have the potential to create 'systematic, socially produced (and therefore modifiable) and unfair' outcomes.[44] The two concepts can still however be differentiated: health inequalities may arise from justified instances of discrimination (for example, an unavoidable targeting of resources during times of disaster, war or political transition) while health inequities might be better challenged on the basis that unnecessarily harsh, unfair decisions have been made.[45] Domestic law and policy-makers seem however to prefer the more clearly defined parameters of equality principles on the basis that these

> can be assessed with respect to specified measurable outcomes, whereas judging whether a process is equitable or not is more open to interpretation.[46]

In respect of defining 'health justice,' two approaches to equitable fairness (direct and indirect) seem possible.[47] The direct approach could simply see 'equity as an end in itself' and perhaps involve a meaningful nod to distributive justice: an indirect approach could however be aimed instead at having 'equity embedded within the concept of social justice' which might encourage greater judicial scrutiny of the various underlying processes which permit (and at times seem to endorse) inequalities.[48] The idea of inherent human dignity remains relevant, despite its often subjective nature.[49] Used objectively however, human dignity can reveal

---

[42] *A v Secretary of State for the Home Department* [2004] UKHL 56 per Lord Bingham of Cornhill, para 29.

[43] Braveman and Gruskin (2003).

[44] See Whitehead and Dahlgren (2006a, b).

[45] Braveman and Gruskin (2003), p. 256.

[46] *Ibid.*

[47] Peter (2000) (available at http://www.hsph.harvard.edu/hcpds/wpweb/foundations/peter.html. Accessed 28.02.14).

[48] *Ibid.*

[49] Feldman (1999), p. 685; Feldman (2000); See further *Pretty v United Kingdom* (Application no. 2346/02) (2002) 35 EHHR 1. Both sides used arguments based upon human dignity and indignity, respectively.

underlying policy 'attitudes to an individual or group...[and] social norms or expectations.'[50] As Feldman has further argued, a focus upon

> "*the inherent dignity of the human person*" as a foundation for rights is different from conferring a right to dignity...on the other hand, one clearly has an interest in having one's human dignity respected, and this may support more specific rights.[51]

Arguably, a truly juridical, enshrined right to avoid indignity, underpinned by such key equitable principles as fairness, would make it more difficult for budget-holders to simply dismiss or explain incidents of poverty, squalor and avoidable ill-health as inevitable, austerity-led events.

4 Identifying Baselines: (In)equality or (In)equity?

> The "very simple tripartite typology of duties"...was not supposed to become a new frozen abstraction to occupy the same rigid conceptual space previously held by "negative rights" and "positive rights"... The constructive point was: look at what it actually takes to enable people to be secure against the standard, predictable threats to their rights.[52]

The task of differentiating between rights-bearing legal issues and socio-political complaints over resource-allocations often falls to domestic judges; they must then decide whether the matter in question is one of fundamental principle (involving moral rights or legal notions of justice) or one of higher state policy, requiring utilitarian calculations on the use of finite resources, and the nature of the 'public good'.[53] As Allan suggested,

> when the modern welfare–regulatory state confers extensive discretionary powers on public agencies, enabling them to perform wide-ranging and perhaps loosely defined public functions, the clear cut distinction between law and administration, or law and public policy, dissolves.[54]

Although individuals cannot require (or perhaps even reasonably expect) domestic courts to overturn allocations of scarce or finite resources, or to create social welfare entitlements where none have previously existed in national law, certain state actions on 'distributive justice' can at least be subject to some manner of judicial overview, not least in relation to preventing instances of overt bias or discrimination. As King has argued, judicial deference should not necessarily

---

[50] *Ibid.*, p. 686.

[51] *Ibid.*, p. 689.

[52] Shue (1996), p. 160.

[53] See Jowell (2003) who suggests that this has been the approach developed by the courts within the UK (p. 593).

[54] Allan (2003), p. 433.

preclude judicial intervention, particularly where fundamental human rights protections are at stake.[55] In respect of the United Kingdom, domestic courts have, post-Human Rights Act, 'gone much further in reviewing resource allocation decisions on human rights grounds than under administrative law.'[56] The question for human rights advocates is perhaps not *whether* domestic courts should discuss resource distribution but one of gauging *when* exactly judicial intervention or critique will actually be precluded by domestic law.[57] Arguably, court decisions on the use of scarce resources could be viewed either as examples of 'discretionary allocative decision making'[58] (long regarded as an area where judges ought 'not to trespass'[59]) or as providing useful guidance which may eventually translate into 'allocative impact.'[60] If some 'legitimate expectation' or target-based duties can be identified then judicial involvement seems entirely legitimate.[61] Where an inability to access resources directly impacts upon the ability to subsist,[62] domestic litigation becomes less about examining the remit of certain rights, and much more aligned with the less easily ignored concepts of welfare, charity and 'powerlessness.' As Frankovits has argued,

> Policies and programs which rest primarily on a perception of need and powerlessness subtly reinforce the powerlessness of the recipients who are seen as being given justice rather than as receiving their rights. The recognition of entitlement is in itself an act of empowerment.[63]

Where individual entitlements arise by virtue of innate humanity, they should have the potential to withstand changes of government and to address at least some of the problems associated with resource scarcity. Where there is a clear distinction between actual, available levels of resources and those which *should* be made available under principles of equality and non-discrimination,[64] it may be argued

[55] King (2007), p. 198.

[56] *Ibid.*, p. 222.

[57] *Ibid.*

[58] *Ibid.*, p. 198.

[59] *Ibid.*, p. 221 (citing *R (Douglas)* v *North Tyneside Metropolitan Borough Council and (2) Secretary of State for Education and Skills* [2003] EWCA Civ 1847, [2004] 1 WLR 2363, per Scott LJ on how judges are '*not to trespass into the discretionary area of resource allocation. That is an area that is not justiciable.*' (at para 62).

[60] *Ibid.*, p. 109. King defines decisions of allocative impact as being 'those in which the effect of the decision is to impose a financial burden upon public resources.'

[61] On distributive justice as 'the appropriate distribution of goods' see further Freeman (2001); Rawls (1971); See also Nozick (1974) who suggests that 'economic goods arise already encumbered with rightful claims'); Dworkin (1981a), p. 185; Dworkin (1981b), p. 283 on equality being more about resources than welfare.

[62] See Shue (1996) on the relationship between basic human rights and subsistence rights.

[63] Frankovits (1996) citing Dodson (1995).

[64] See for example *R v Cambridgeshire Health Authority ex p. B* [1995] 1 WLR 898; *Rodgers v Swindon Primary Health Care Trust and the Secretary of State for* Health [2006] EWCA Civ 392. See further McKeever and Ní Aoláin (2004) on the rights 'mainstreaming' approach which looks beyond courts to such bodies as Human Rights and Equality Commissions.

that some sort of 'minimum rights threshold' (rather than a domestically defined, economic austerity-led benchmarking) is needed. This could serve as a 'practical minimal floor of well-being as a standard for distributive analysis.'[65] Alston's view of the Millennium Development Goals as targets to be achieved ('a ceiling') rather than basic levels below which standards should not fall ('a floor')[66] seems particularly apt: domestic judgments perhaps represent the best opportunity for identifying—if not actually raising—those rights-benchmarks which have failed to ring-fence funds to enable meaningful standards of living, or embed a culture of dignity-led human rights.[67] As the World Health Organisation ('WHO') has made very plain: '[t]here is a health baseline below which no individual in any country should find themselves.'[68] A clear danger with having rights-vague minimum thresholds is that frequently 'the floor will become the ceiling.'[69] As Chapman has further argued, there is a clear need to focus upon the actual content of such rights, and to assess how these might be tied to core state obligations which might then be cited as underpinning, legal duties.[70] If domestic courts are unable to frame certain rights as fully juridical (on the basis of too-scarce resources for example) then they might at least be able to provide some useful level of guidance on where equitable baseline standards might be found to exist.

The notion of fairness ought not to be tied to resource allocations but to rights-impact: where state decisions have served to strip individuals of their dignity, then either no clearly discernible rights baseline exists or it has been effectively disregarded by law and policy-makers. If 'the extent of policy freedom inherent to progressive realisation' affords domestic decision-makers considerable scope in relation to pleading a scarcity of resources,[71] then gauging whether a juridical human rights violation has occurred requires a fairly substantive analysis of state conduct. Failure to recognise that key decisions on resource allocations tend to impact most profoundly upon the vulnerable, can easily create structurally embedded forms of poverty, homelessness and chronic ill-health.[72] A 'rescue approach' to

---

[65] Arambulo (1999), p. 136. See also Eide (1989) and Black et al. (2003).

[66] Alston (2005).

[67] See for example the Somalia famine, where although steady rises in mortality rates had been documented since 1987 it was not until 1992 that the situation reached crisis point and drew public attention. See Persson et al. (1993) and Flanagin (1993) on how in one town, over a 2 week period, 2300 bodies were collected, with a death toll of 40 times the crude mortality rate identified by the World Health Organisation as an emergency indicator.

[68] World Health Organisation (1981), p. 30 available at http://whqlibdoc.who.int/publications/9241800038.pdf (accessed 10.02.15).

[69] Chapman and Russel (2002), p. 9.

[70] *Ibid.*; See also Arambulo (1999) who describes the minimum core content of a right as a universal concept, based on 'a theoretical legal perspective' but also underpinned by a clear minimum threshold. This she suggests is a relative concept, even though it may still provide for a practical approach.

[71] Den Exter and Hermans (1999), p. 4. See further Sen (2003), p. 31.

[72] *Ibid.*, p. 32.

situations which have arisen directly from inequitable policy decisions does not seem particularly inappropriate,[73] especially if decision-makers are framed as the 'trustees' of scarce resources, tasked with safeguarding the basic rights of those who would be most affected by any down-shifting of baseline standards.[74] Difficulties in implementation remain likely, given how 'inequalities combine, interact, and are reproduced through interlinked economic, political, and socio-cultural processes.'[75] There is therefore a need for states to more clearly identify and target the intended 'beneficiaries' of finite resources on the basis of equitable distributions rather than via a blunt equality of treatment. As Le Franc *et al.* have noted, making judgements upon the basis of equality of opportunity remains a complex process requiring a complicated formula which might

> …consist of the determinants that should not lead, other things equal, to differences in outcome; luck, which comprises the determinants that are seen as a fair source of inequality provided that they are even-handed, with respect to circumstances.[76]

McCrudden has also stressed the importance of 'preventing status harm,'[77] with its focus on actively requiring public authorities to be aware of the fundamental needs of those groups which clearly experience inequality and then actively work towards *remedying* shortcomings. Thus domestic equality laws and wider international law principles may amount to 'an adjunct to the protection of particularly prized public goods'[78] focussing perhaps upon a fiduciary duty of just 'distribution …rather than on the characteristics of the recipient'.[79] As Farmer has further suggested in respect of the right to health, 'any distinguishing characteristic, whether social or biological can serve as a pretext for discrimination and thus as a cause of suffering.'[80] Inequalities in the context of health rights have been documented in relation to issues of gender, race, religion, age and socio-economic status.[81] Although socio-economic status is not one of the traditional comparators within health law, its relevance has been flagged up via international law's focus on

---

[73] *Ibid.*, p. 42.

[74] Roemer (2002), p. 457. Roemer has further suggested that equality of opportunity differs from equality of outcome insofar as 'equal opportunity policy must create a level playing field, after which each individual is on his own.'

[75] See World Bank (2006), p. 28 (available at http://www-wds.worldbank.org/external/default/WDSContentServer/IW3P/IB/2005/09/20/000112742_20050920110826/Rendered/PDF/322040World0Development0Report02006.pdf. Accessed 17.03.14).

[76] Le Franc et al. (2006), p. 3 (available at http://www.gsoep.de/documents/dokumentenarchiv/17/60141/papertrannoy_lefranc_pistolesi.pdf. Accessed 12.05.14).

[77] McCrudden (2000), p. 514.

[78] *Ibid.* See also Lee (1998), p. 40 on how health may be viewed as a 'hybrid economic good,' with both public and private benefit.

[79] McCrudden (2000), p. 513. As such, 'equals should be treated as equals, except where differences can be justified.'

[80] Farmer (2003), p. 46.

[81] See Adler et al. (1999), p. 180. This is 'a composite measure that typically incorporates economic status measured by income; social status measured by education, and work status

the concept of vulnerable groups. As Braveman and Gruskin also point out, 'social justice or fairness ...is an ethical concept, grounded in principles of distributive justice.'[82] There are a number of extra difficulties attaching to the 'operationalisation' of a 'health equity' agenda (as opposed to a basic equality of opportunity rights template) in this context, especially where social disadvantage was a pre-existing or immutable factor. If health is regarded more as a 'social advantage,' then a 'right' to health may be better defined or described in fairly 'relative terms.'[83] Arguably, equitable notions could be used here to at least underscore the importance of such key concepts as human dignity. That said, relying on "the inherent dignity of the human person" as a foundation for embedding fragile rights is different from finding 'a right to dignity...'[84] despite the fact 'dignity is often linked to autonomy or the freedom of the individual.'[85] Where social inequalities are perhaps inevitable (on the basis of perpetually scarce resources, for example) then legally justifiable forms of discrimination may arise as unavoidable outcomes.

As Fabre has observed, issues of economic, social and cultural rights seem to represent a sort of crossroads for the concepts of democracy and distributive justice.[86] Particularly during times of economic crisis, it may well be the case that 'people oppose constitutional social rights on the grounds that they give unacceptable powers of interference to the judiciary.'[87] And yet judicial enforcement remains central to the embedding of human rights as meaningful concepts in domestic law. As McKeever and Ní Aoláin have further argued, there are two main models of judicial enforcement in respect of economic, social and cultural rights: a minimum level of enforcement related only to procedural aspects and the more substantive mode of enforcement reflecting a clearly 'constitutionalised' right.[88] The substantive enforcement model would seek to 'define and enforce a set of social and economic rights protections' whose 'entrenchment can be achieved either by constitutional or legislative means.'[89] They also suggest a third model which would not be utterly dependent upon judicial enforcement however and which would look also to the 'mainstreaming' of human rights provisions, for example national Human Rights Commissions or the use of equality impact

measured by occupation.' See also Navarro (1990) on gauging health inequality via social status rather than by way of race or gender.

[82] Braveman and Gruskin (2003).

[83] *Ibid.*, p. 254.

[84] Feldman (1999), p. 689.

[85] Fredman (2001), p. 155.

[86] Fabre (2000), p. 2.

[87] *Ibid.*

[88] McKeever and Ní Aoláin (2004), p. 58. The minimum enforcement model protects those 'due process rights' associated with economic, social and cultural rights. This amounts to procedural review of how a decision has been taken. Principles of equality (as they relate to logic and rationality) provide a useful basis for such a review, but do not necessarily create much scope for overturning decisions that might have led to inequitable outcomes.

[89] Fredman (2001), p. 163.

assessments. In this sense 'mainstreaming means that equality is not just an add-on or after thought but is a factor taken into account in every decision and policy.'[90] However, because basic 'procedural justice does not require any particular outcome,'[91] non-discrimination remains significant to the equality rights template; even in the wake of the *Thlimmenos v Greece* decision, there is little guidance on how to provide rights protection for those who are different in terms of requiring meaningful equity of outcome rather than basic equality of allocation, opportunity or treatment.[92] As *Burnip* confirmed, there is clearly a state obligation to actively 'make provision to cater for the significant difference.'[93] Such a substantive approach to the issue of specific entitlements might require domestic jurists to at least consider questions of distributive justice.

5 Conclusion

Where public funds are involved, certain rights issues may be seen as beyond the remit of domestic judiciaries. In times of economic austerity, this may create a sort of amnesty for 'widespread ignorance of the ICESCR not only among judges but also among governments and the community.'[94] Given however the vast amount of legal and political discourse generated by the various human rights bodies and by domestic litigation, it is clear that 'we will not be able to say in hindsight, "*if only we had known*."'[95] If the task of protecting resource-dependent, fragile socio-economic rights is to be almost always left exclusively to elected politicians rather than shared with the courts, then this perhaps also challenges the concept of rights-indivisibility.[96] Similarly, where the most fundamental socio-economic rights are entirely dependent upon adequate resources being made available, it may be more appropriate to refer to them as mere parcels of privilege, very easily prone to being set aside or to suffering open-ended implementational delays. As such, they may still be described as dishearteningly 'opaque'[97] concepts in terms of both their

[90] *Ibid.*, p. 165.

[91] See further Barnard and Hepple (2000), p. 563 on Fredman's approach to substantive equality, which draws upon four major concepts: equality of results, equality of opportunity, equality as 'auxiliary to human rights' and equality based on a central value such as 'dignity.'

[92] *Thlimmenos v Greece* (2001) 31 EHRR 44 (see para 44) established that indirect discrimination may occur via non-differential treatment: 'the right not to be discriminated against ...is also violated when States without an objective and reasonable justification fail to treat differently persons whose situations are significantly different.'

[93] *Burnip v Birmingham City Council and Anor* [2012] EWCA Civ 629 (15 May 2012), para 15.

[94] The International Commission of Jurists (2002) (available at http://www.icj.org/IMG/pdf/doc-61.pdf. Accessed 03.12.13).

[95] Abbott (2002), p. 505.

[96] Spano (2014), p. 2.

[97] Arambulo (1999), p. 55.

scope and content. That said, some measure of increased coherence is gradually emerging, especially where the various UN Committees have continued to stress their disquiet over the lack of embedded meaningful monitoring at domestic level. The key to protecting such rights in domestic law, it seems, is via a consistent, close scrutiny (judicial or otherwise) of relevant domestic laws, policies, customs and impacts. Unfortunately, if domestic jurists seem at times to be 'less than involved in the pursuit of the attainment of economic, social and cultural rights'[98] then these rights are unlikely to crystallize into a legally enforceable kind of entitlement any time soon. As such, the concept of domestic non-justiciability can be used to both categorise and gauge the limitations of human rights law. Requiring domestic decision-makers to focus particularly upon such basic concepts as human dignity, fairness, and equitable outcomes, could yet provide a means of overcoming at least some of the barriers that tend to arise during times of financial austerity.[99] Policy reforms and budgetary decisions which result in profound human rights infringements should not simply be dismissed as an inevitable consequence of economic downturn. Domestic lawyers and elected legislators must seek to identify and promote clear baseline rights-thresholds, below which many of the signs of human dignity cease to be evident, and human degradation and indignity perhaps become near-normative. Arguably, with public purse-strings being increasingly tightened on the basis of targeting finite resources at those most 'deserving' of state help, it may be argued that human rights protections during times of austerity have much more in common with charitable dispositions than they do with automatic, inherent entitlements.

Depressing though this thought may be, it does at least provide some basis for the argument that elected law-makers have been politically mandated to act as 'rights settlors.' This obliges them to not only clearly define socio-economic rights (by setting clearly articulated, dignity-based minimum standards and thresholds) but to also allocate equitable levels of resources, which must then be ring-fenced as budget priorities.[100] The courts could in turn be framed as 'trustees' of the rights in question, and tasked with determining whether or not just and equitable resource allocations have been made. For them to do otherwise (through fear of overstepping their remit, or of 'puncturing' margins of appreciation) is clearly a derogation of their responsibilities to protect the most vulnerable 'rights beneficiaries.' The state's continuing 'fairness agenda' of socio-economic rights austerity, seems set at times on almost mirroring the horrors of civil or political rights violations, in terms of

[98] The International Commission of Jurists (2002), p. 11.

[99] See further Chetty (2002), p. 24. As Chetty has stressed however (in respect of South Africa), the 'public finance implications of socioeconomic rights' cannot simply be overlooked. There may be an 'immense magnitude of ...backlogs' to contend with, in addition to a significant 'inequity in socio-economic rights that must be realised with relatively limited resources in a transitionary environment.'

[100] Such a strategy might encourage a re-direction of public funds towards poverty alleviation, away from other expenses. See for example: http://www.theguardian.com/uk-news/2015/apr/09/tory-labour-renew-trident-threat-reality-nuclear-election (accessed 01.05.15).

embedding widespread hunger, poverty, homelessness, and degradingly inadequate health care provision. Domestic judges must not permit a traditional deference towards Parliament to enable and perpetuate socio-economic injustices: to do so is to tacitly endorse not only a domestic level erosion of human rights law, but the gradual forfeiture of human dignity thresholds.

References

Abbott, F. M. (2002). The Doha Declaration on the TRIPS Agreement and public health: Lighting a dark corner at the WTO. *Journal of International Economic Law, 5*(2), 469–505.

Adler, N., Boyce, T., Chesney, M., Cohen, S., Folkman, S., Kahn, R., et al. (1999). Socio economic status: The challenge of the gradient. In J. Mann, S. Gruskin, M. Grodin, & G. Annas (Eds.), *Health and human rights: A reader*. London: Routledge.

Allan, T. R. S. (2003). Doctrine and theory in administrative law: An elusive quests for the limits of jurisdiction. *Public Law, 29*, 429–454.

Alston, P. (2005). Ships passing in the night: The current state of the human rights and development debate seen through the lens of the millennium development goals. *Human Rights Quarterly, 27*, 755.

Arambulo, K. (1999). *Strengthening the supervision of the International Covenant on Economic, Social and Cultural Rights: Theoretical and procedural aspects*. Oxford, England: Hart.

Barnard, C., & Hepple, B. (2000). Substantive equality. *Cambridge Law Journal, 59*, 562.

Bayefsky, A. (1990). The principle of equality or non-discrimination in international law. *Human Rights Quarterly, 11*, 1.

Bilchitz, D. (2003). Placing basic needs at the center of socio economic rights jurisprudence. *ESR Review, 4*, 1.

Black, R., Morris, S., & Bryce, J. (2003). Where and why are 10 million children dying every year. *The Lancet, 361*, 2226.

Braveman, P., & Gruskin, S. (2003). Theory and methods defining equity in health. *Journal of Epidemiology and Community Health, 57*, 254.

Chapman, A., & Russel, S. (2002). *Core obligations: Building a framework for economic, social and cultural rights*. Antwerp, Belgium: Intersentia.

Chetty, K. (2002). The public finance implications of recent socio-economic rights judgments. *Law Democracy & Development, 6*, 231.

Collingsworth, T. (2002). The key human rights challenge: Developing enforcement mechanisms. *Harvard Human Rights Journal, 15*, 183.

Cranston, M. (1973). *What are human rights?* London: Bodley Head.

Craven, M. (1995). *The International Covenant on Economic, Social and Cultural Rights: A perspective on its development*. Oxford, England: Clarendon.

Den Exter, A., & Hermans, H. (Eds.). (1999). *The right to health care in several European countries: Expert meeting, held in Rotterdam, the Netherlands. April 27–28 1998*. The Hague: Kluwer Law International.

Dodson, M. (1995). *Social Justice Report 1995, Human Rights and Equal Opportunity Commission*. http://www.humanrights.gov.au/word/social_justice/sj_report_95.doc. Accessed 14.12.10.

Donnelly, J. (2007). The relative universality of human rights. *Human Rights Quarterly, 29*(2), 81.

Dworkin, R. (1981a). What is equality? Part 1: Equality of resources. *Philosophy and Public Affairs, 10*, 185.

Dworkin, R. (1981b). What is equality? Part 2: Equality of welfare. *Philosophy and Public Affairs, 10*, 283.

Eide, A. (1989). Realisation of economic, social and cultural rights and the minimum threshold approach. *Human Rights Law Journal, 10*, 35.

Elias-Jones, A. C., & Samanta, J. (2005). The implications of the David Glass Case for future clinical practice in the UK. *Archives of Disease in Childhood, 90*, 822.
Fabre, C. (2000). *Social rights under the constitution: Government and decent life*. Oxford, England: Oxford University Press.
Farmer, P. (2001). *Infections and inequalities: The modern plagues*. Berkeley, CA: University of California Press.
Farmer, P. (2003). *Pathologies of power: Health, human rights and the new war on the poor*. Berkeley, CA: University of California Press.
Feldman, D. (1999). Human dignity as a legal value – Part I. *Public Law*, 682–702.
Feldman, D. (2000). Human dignity as a legal value – Part II. *Public Law*, 61–71.
Finkelstein, M. (1924). Judicial self-limitation. *Harvard Law Review, 37*, 338–364.
Finn, C. (2002). The justiciability of administrative decisions: A redundant concept? *Federal Law Review, 30*, 239.
Flanagin, A. (1993). Somalia's death toll underlines challenges of a post-cold war world. *JAMA, 268*, 1985–1987.
Frankovits, A. (1996). Rejoinder: The rights way to development: A national human rights NGO speaks on donor aid. *Food Policy, 21*, 123.
Fredman, S. (2001). Equality: A new generation. *Industrial Law Journal, 30*, 145.
Freeman, M. D. A. (2001). *Lloyd's introduction to jurisprudence*. London: Sweet & Maxwell.
Harris, B. V. (2003). Judicial review justiciability and the prerogative of mercy. *Cambridge Law Journal, 62*, 631–660.
Henkin, L. (1981). *The international bill of rights*. New York: Columbia University Press.
Hunt, P. (1996). *Reclaiming social rights*. Aldershot, England: Ashgate.
The International Commission of Jurists. (2002, September 26–27). *Report of the expert's round-table concerning issues to the proposed optional protocol to the international covenant of economic, social and cultural rights*.
Itzcovich, G. (2013). One, none and one hundred thousand margins of appreciations: The *Lautsi* case. *Human Rights Law Review, 13*(2), 287–308.
Jackson, J. H. (1992). Status of treaties in domestic legal systems: A policy analysis. *American Journal of International Law, 86*, 310.
Jowell, J. (2003). Judicial deference: Servility, civility or institutional capacity. *Public Law*, 592.
King, J. A. (2007). The justiciability of resource allocation. *Modern Law Review, 70*, 197.
Kolm, S. C. (2002). *Justice and equity*. Cambridge, MA: MIT Press.
Le Franc, A., Pistolesi, N., & Trannoy, A. (2006). Equality of opportunity: Definitions and testable conditions, with an application to income in France. *Journal of Public Economics, 93*, 1189–1207.
Le Sueur, P. (1995). Justifying judicial caution: Jurisdiction, justiciability and policy. In B. Hadfield (Ed.), *Judicial review: A thematic approach*. Dublin, Ireland: Gill & Macmillan.
Leary, V. (1994). The right to health in international human rights law. *Health and Human Rights, 1*, 28.
Lee, B. (1998). Judicial review and access to health care. In T. Buck (Ed.), *Judicial review and social welfare: Citizenship and law series*. London: Pinter.
McCrudden, C. (2000). A common law of human rights?: Transnational judicial conversations on constitutional rights. *Oxford Journal of Legal Studies, 4*, 499.
McCrudden, C. (Ed.). (2003). *Anti-discrimination law: The International Library of Essays in Law and Legal Theory, Second Series*. Aldershot, England: Dartmouth Publishing Company.
McKean, T. (1983). *Equality and discrimination under international law*. Oxford, England: Clarendon.
McKeever, G., & Ní Aoláin, F. (2004). Thinking globally, acting locally: Enforcing socio-economic rights in Northern Ireland. *European Human Rights Law Review, 2*, 158.
McLean, S. (1999). A UK perspective in health care restraints. In A. den Exter & H. Hermans (Eds.), *The right to health care in several European countries: Expert meeting, held in*

Rotterdam, the Netherlands. April 27–28, 1998. The Hague, the Netherlands: Kluwer law International.
McTeer, M. A. (1995). A role for law in matters of morality. *McGill Law Journal, 40*, 893.
Muvingi, I. (2009). Sitting on powder kegs: socioeconomic rights in transitional societies. *International Journal of Transitional Justice, 3*, 163–182.
Navarro, V. (1990). Race or class versus race and class: Mortality differentials in the US. *The Lancet, 356*, 1238.
Nolan, A. (2009). Addressing economic and social rights violations by non-state actors through the role of the state: A comparison of regional approaches to the 'Obligation to Protect'. *Human Rights Law Review, 9*(2), 225–255.
Nolan, A., O'Connell, R., & Harvey, C. (Eds.). (2013). *Human rights and public finance: Budgets and the promotion of economic and social rights*. London: Hart.
Nozick, R. (1974). *Anarchy, state and Utopia*. New York: Basic Books.
O'Connell, P. (2011). The death of socio-economic rights. *Modern Law Review, 74*, 532–554.
Oppenheimer, G., Bayer, R., & Colgrove, J. (2002). Health and human rights: Old wine in new bottles? *Journal of Law Medicine and Ethics, 30*, 522.
Orwin, C., & Pangle, T. (1984). The philosophical foundations of human rights. In M. Platter (Ed.), *Human rights in our time – Essays in memory of Victor Baras*. London: Westview Press.
Persson, L. A., Aden, A. S., Ibrahim, M., Omar, M., & Wall, S. (1993). Letter: Famine in Somalia. *The Lancet, 341*, 1478.
Peter, F. (2000, January). *Health equity and social justice: Harvard Center for Population and Development studies working paper series* (10) (2).
Price-Smith, A. T. (2001). *The health of nations: Infectious disease, environmental change and their effects on national security and development*. Cambridge, MA: MIT Press.
Rakowski, E. (1993). *Equal justice*. London: Clarendon.
Rawls, J. (1971). *A theory of justice*. Boston: Harvard University Press.
Roemer, J. (2002). Equality of opportunity: A progress report. *Social Choice and Welfare, 19*(2), 455.
Sen, A. (2003). *Inequality re-examined*. Oxford, England: Oxford University Press.
Sepulveda, M. (2003). *The nature of the obligations under the International Covenant on Economic, Social and Cultural Rights*. School of Human Rights Research Series 18. Antwerp, Belgium: Intersentia.
Shue, H. (1996). *Basic rights: Subsistence, affluence and U.S. Foreign Policy*. Princeton, NJ: Princeton University Press.
Spano, R. (2014). Universality or diversity of human rights? Strasbourg in the age of subsidiarity. *Human Rights Law Review*, 1–16.
Toebes, B. (1999). *The right to health as a human right in international law*. Oxford, England: Intersentia.
Vierdag, E. (1978). The nature of the rights granted by The International Covenant on Economic, Social and Cultural Rights. *Netherlands Yearbook of International Law, 9*, 69.
Waldorf, L. (2012). Anticipating the past: Transitional justice and socio-economic wrongs. *Social and Legal Studies, 21*, 171–186.
Whitehead, M., & Dahlgren, G. (2006a). *Levelling up (Part 1): A discussion paper on concepts and principles for tackling social inequities in health*. WHO Collaborating Centre for Policy Research on Social Determinants of Health: University of Liverpool.
Whitehead, M., & Dahlgren, G. (2006b). *Levelling up (Part 2): A discussion paper on European strategies for tackling social inequities in health*. WHO Collaborating Centre for Policy Research on Social Determinants of Health: University of Liverpool.
World Bank. (2006). *World Bank world development report: Equity and development*. World Bank: OUP.
World Health Organisation. (1981). *Global strategy for health for all by the year 2000*. Geneva, Switzerland: WHO.

UK Case Law

A v Secretary of State for the Home Department [2004] UKHL 56
Burnip v Birmingham City Council & Anor [2012] EWCA Civ 629 (15 May 2012)
MA and others v The Secretary Of State For Work And Pensions [2014] EWCA Civ 13
Matthews v Ministry of Defence [2003] UKHL 4
National Bank of Greece and Athens v Metliss [1958] AC 509
R (D) v Worcestershire County Council [2013] EWHC 2490 (Admin)
R (Douglas) v North Tyneside Metropolitan Borough Council; Secretary of State for Education and Skills [2003] EWCA Civ 1847, [2004] 1 WLR 2363
R (Hardy) v Sandwell Metropolitan Borough Council [2015] EWHC 890 (Admin)
R (Rutherford) v SSWP [2014] EWHC 1631 (Admin)
R v Cambridgeshire Health Authority ex p. B [1995] 1 WLR 898
Rodgers v Swindon Primary Health Care Trust and the Secretary of State for Health [2006] EWCA Civ 392

Strasbourg Case Law

Pretty v United Kingdom (Application no. 2346/02) (2002) 35 EHHR 1
Thlimmenos v Greece (2001) 31 EHRR 44

South African Case Law

Soobramoney v Minister of Health, KwaZulu-Natal (CCT32/97) [1997] ZACC 17; 1998 (1) SA 765 (CC); 1997 (12) BCLR 1696 (27 November 1997)

UN Documents

CESCR 'Concluding Observations: Algeria' (28/12/1995) UN Document E/C.12/1995/17
CESCR General Comment No. 14 '*The Right To The Highest Attainable Standard Of Health* (Article 12)' E/C.12/2000/4
Rolnik R '*The Promotion And Protection Of All Human Rights, Civil, Political, Economic, Social And Cultural Rights, Including The Right To Development: Report Of The Special Rapporteur On Adequate Housing As A Component Of The Right To An Adequate Standard Of Living, And On The Right To Non-Discrimination In This Context*' (Distr. GENERAL A/HRC/10/7 4 February 2009)
Turk D '*The Realization of Economic, Social and Cultural Rights: Final Report*' (1992) E/CN.4/Sub.2/1992/16
UN General Assembly Resolution 60/147 '*Basic Principles and Guidelines on the Right to a Remedy and Reparation for Victims of Gross Violations of International Human Rights Law and Serious Violations of International Humanitarian Law*' (16 December 2005) A/RES/60/147

Websites

http://www.telegraph.co.uk/news/politics/david-cameron/9000249/David-Cameron-my-vision-for-a-fair-Britain.html
http://www.theguardian.com/politics/2010/oct/06/david-cameron-fairness-people-deserve
http://www.theguardian.com/society/2013/sep/11/bedroom-tax-should-be-axed-says-un-investigator
http://www.theguardian.com/society/2014/feb/03/ministers-savage-un-report-abolition-bedroom-tax
http://www.theguardian.com/uk-news/2015/apr/09/tory-labour-renew-trident-threat-reality-nuclear-election

The Right to Healthcare: A Critical Examination of the Human Right of Irregular Migrants to Access State-Funded HIV/AIDS Treatment in the UK

David Hand, Chantal Davies, and Ruth Healey

1 Introduction

The United Kingdom's National Health Service ('NHS') emerged in the post-war era as part of a joint European effort to consolidate key social rights such as the right to health.[1] To this end, the NHS pledged to provide a 'comprehensive health service' imparting health services free of charge at the point of delivery.[2] It is true that, for the most part, the NHS has fulfilled its intended role and has offered its valuable services free of charge irrespective of the patient's background. On the other hand legislation has always permitted 'the making and recovery of charges [for health services]' where 'expressly provided for' in the Act in question.[3] Irregular migrants are 'foreign nationals who do not comply with immigration law requirements.'[4] They carry the more familiar label of 'illegal immigrants' in everyday parlance. That term is avoided here partly because of its (largely erroneous) associations with criminality, but primarily because of the stigmatising and dehumanising effects that such epithets bear on the individual concerned.[5] For these reasons the more neutral term 'irregular migrant' is preferred by some authors and is used throughout this chapter.[6] Irregular migrants include clandestine entrants into

[1] Romero-Ortuño (2004).

[2] National Health Service Act (1946), p. 1.

[3] Health and Social Care Act (2012), Article 1 (4), p. 2.

[4] da Lomba (2011), p. 357.

[5] Platform for International Cooperation on Undocumented Migrants, *PICUM's Comments on the Communication from the Commission on 'Policy priorities in the fight against illegal immigration of third-country nationals'* COM (2006) 402 final.

[6] See for example da Lomba (2011).

D. Hand (✉) • C. Davies • R. Healey
University of Chester, Chester, UK
e-mail: d.hand@chester.ac.uk; Chantal.davies@chester.ac.uk; r.healey@chester.ac.uk

A. Diver, J. Miller (eds.), *Justiciability of Human Rights Law in Domestic Jurisdictions*, DOI 10.1007/978-3-319-24016-9_3

the country, those in possession of falsified travel documents such as passports, those who have overstayed their visas or who are in employment contrary to their conditions of residence, and refused asylum seekers.[7]

The early 2000s witnessed an increased presence of irregular migrants across the member states of the European Union,[8] an unfortunate development given that the UK was already wary of increased numbers of asylum seekers over the previous 20 years.[9] The UK's expanding immigrant population has fuelled negative stereotypes of 'foreigners' in the public imagination. Often these have been sustained by inflammatory language used by politicians and tabloid newspapers.[10] With asylum seekers commonly depicted as opportunists with an in-depth knowledge of the country's social support system, many UK citizens believe that their rights as citizens are being subverted in order to accommodate these 'newcomers.'[11] Indeed Labour MP Margaret Hodge wrote that a change in policy was needed which placed 'the legitimate sense of entitlement felt by the indigenous family' before even the 'legitimate need demonstrated by the new migrants.'[12]

The NHS Constitution published by the Department of Health is an open endorsement of universal access to health care services. The section titled *Principles that guide the NHS* is uncompromisingly inclusive and reads as follows:

> The NHS provides a comprehensive service, available to all irrespective of gender, race, disability, age, sexual orientation, religion, belief, gender reassignment, pregnancy and maternity or material or civil partnership status . . . it has a duty to each and every individual it serves and must respect their human rights. At the same time, it has a wider duty to promote equality through the services it provides and to pay particular attention to groups or sections of society where improvements in health care and life expectancy are not keeping pace with the rest of the population.[13]

The subsequent paragraph states that access to NHS services 'is based on clinical need, not an individual's ability to pay. NHS services are free of charge except in limited circumstances sanctioned by Parliament.'[14] Despite the optimism engendered by the above passages, immigration policy has often been entangled with NHS regulations, and the perceived costs associated with maintaining a comprehensive health service in a time of globalisation and increased migration has justified restrictions on access to certain health services for overseas patients.[15] Section 121(b) of the National Health Services Act 1977, for example, provided for

---

[7] Ibid.

[8] Romero-Ortuño (2004).

[9] Stevens (2010), p. 363.

[10] Hargreaves 2000.

[11] Stevens (2010).

[12] Margaret Hodge (2007), para 10.

[13] NHS Constitution – *The NHS Belongs To Us All* (26 March 2013) London: Department of Health, p. 3.

[14] Ibid.

[15] Pobjoy and Spencer (2012).

the 'making and recovery . . . of such charges as the Secretary of State may determine . . . in respect of such persons not ordinarily resident in Great Britain as may be prescribed.' However the notion of 'ordinary residence' was not accorded much attention until the case of *R v. Barnet London Borough Council, ex parte Shah,*[16] in which the House of Lords determined that the term referred to an individual's lawful presence in the UK, undertaken 'voluntarily and for settled purposes as part of the regular order of life.'[17]

Although it was not concerned with the provision of health services *per se*, the *Barnet* ruling had a direct impact on NHS service users from overseas. The immediate conclusion one might have drawn from the House of Lords' definition of 'ordinary residence' was that irregular migrants were, by definition, eligible for statutory charges in respect of health care services, their unlawful presence in the UK disqualifying them from 'ordinary residence' status.[18] Indeed the National Health Service (Charges to Overseas Visitors) Regulations 1989 were subsequently enacted in order to expand upon the powers contained in section 121 of the National Health Services Act 1977. Crucially, the 1989 regulations included the new definition of 'ordinary residence'. Thereafter any patient who could not for legal purposes be considered ordinarily resident in the UK was liable for recovery of statutory charges for secondary care, or treatment received in hospital.[19] It is however notable that general practitioner services, or primary care, remained free for all patients.[20] Equally, a number of secondary treatment services remained exempt from the making and recovery of charges, among them treatment of infectious diseases. HIV/AIDS, however, was not covered by this exemption (Charges to Overseas Regulations 1989: reg. 3).

The Charges to Overseas Visitors Regulations were updated in 2011 so that statutory charges would not be recoverable from anyone who had been granted temporary asylum or humanitarian protection, or was awaiting a decision in respect thereof (reg. 11). In the case of HIV/AIDS treatment however, regulation 6 stipulated that only initial diagnostic services and any follow-up counselling required by infected patients would be exempt from statutory charges. Therefore, overseas patients testing positive for the HIV virus would incur significant personal costs if they chose to undergo the course of highly active antiretroviral therapy (HAART) required to curb the onset of AIDS in the body.[21] Inspired though it may have been by the desire to minimise health care expenditure, regulation 6 arguably amounted to little more than a false economy when one weighed the costs of providing drug

[16] [1983] WLR 16.

[17] Ibid., para 343.

[18] da Lomba (2011).

[19] Pobjoy and Spencer (2012).

[20] Stevens (2010).

[21] Taylor (2009).

therapy to all NHS patients against the destructive effects (both personal and societal) of the virus when simply left to thrive in the individual.[22]

2 The Emerging Mythology Around 'Health Tourism'

Since 1989 asylum seekers denied or pending decisions on their applications have been the recurring subject of Department of Health policy guidelines (e.g. Charges to Overseas Visitors Regulations 1989), while the national media has worked to 'expose' those NHS trusts imparting expensive AIDS treatment to asylum seekers free of charge.[23] Amid the economic challenges beleaguering the country in recent years, there is an apparently stronger case than ever for arguing that visitors who do not pay taxes in the UK should not enjoy the fruits of a health service funded by the public.[24] Compounding matters is the fact that the UK of today is altogether more globalised, and a far cry from the homogenous society of 1946 when the NHS was founded. The Department of Health's (2010) consultation paper drew an express link between implementing restrictions on public services and deterring migration in accordance with wider government policy. Although ostensibly willing to recognise a duty towards overseas patients 'whose life or long-term health is at immediate risk' the paper was at pains to prevent the NHS from being treated as an 'international health service.'[25]

Arguably, these developments were emblematic of tacit fears over the prospect of free health-care becoming a 'pull factor' for asylum seekers to come to the UK, depleting finite state resources in the process.[26] These fears were sustained by a barrage of anecdotal reports doing the rounds which suggested that foreigners from outside the EU were entering the country in order to obtain free medical treatment before unceremoniously departing for their homelands (Refugee Council, 2006). Anecdotal though they may have been, these allegations of 'health tourism' prompted a former Minister for Health to declare 'there is absolutely no doubt in my mind . . . that there is a significant amount of abuse going on.'[27] The Select Committee on Health (2005), however, conceded a lack of evidence to suggest that the NHS faced a legitimate financial threat from health tourism, including in relation to HIV/AIDS treatment. Indeed, when invited to expand on his allegations

[22] Fowler et al. (2006).

[23] Sawyer (2004).

[24] Department of Health, *Review of access to the NHS by foreign nationals – Consultation on proposals* (February 2010).

[25] Ibid., p. 1.

[26] Stevens (2010), p. 369.

[27] BBC News, *Are Health Tourists Draining the NHS?* 14 May 2004 http://news.bbc.co.uk/1/hi/health/3356255.stm, para 20 (accessed 07.01.2015).

the same health minister admitted that accurate figures on the number of migrants coming to the UK solely to benefit from health services could not be furnished.[28]

On the contrary, there is a body of evidence which would appear to contradict the belief that the UK is a potential 'magnet' for HIV positive individuals from other countries.[29] A study has shown, for example, that many migrants with HIV do not actively seek treatment until the onset of physical symptoms, which in many cases are not manifest until several months after their arrival in the UK.[30] A House of Commons Health Committee (2005) report recognised that this behaviour calls into question the widely held belief that overseas recipients of HIV drug therapy are health tourists.[31] A second point is that the stigma associated with HIV infection in some cultures prevents many from availing of testing services in their homelands; thus many arrive in the UK unaware of their HIV status.[32] Moreover, it is recognised that there are alternative grounds, such as the threat of violence, on which an asylum seeker is more likely to base their application.[33]

Notwithstanding a lack of evidence to support the perceived threat of health tourism, its mere utterance has invited a reaction in legislative and policy-making circles. Addressing the House of Lords, Baroness Boothroyd perfectly captured the prevailing mood with the remark that 'it would be a great pity if the goodwill of this nation were stretched to breaking point.'[34] The conclusion to which one is inescapably drawn is that barriers to health services (and post-diagnostic HIV treatment in particular) for irregular migrants appear firmly couched in government apprehension towards the perceived ill-effects of uncontrolled immigration.

3 Health Care as a 'Human Right'

The counter side to this discussion is the concept of health care as a human right, a tenet of civilised society, which should be available to everyone whatever their residence status.[35] According to this argument a public-funded health service is fundamental to the successful realisation of the right to health care.[36] The NHS is revered by medical practitioners for its upstanding values, not least of which is its assertion that health care is a basic human right that should be available to all patients based on clinical need rather than their ability to pay for the health services

[28] *Ibid.*

[29] Secretary of State for Health (2005), p. 19.

[30] Erwin and Peters (1999).

[31] Bettinson and Jones (2007).

[32] Ibid.

[33] Ibid.

[34] Hansards, House of Lords debates (2004) vol. 658, col. 950.

[35] Stevens (2010).

[36] da Lomba (2011).

provided.[37] The uncomfortable truth is that medical practitioners have been compelled to adhere to rules, such as the Charges to Overseas Visitors Regulations, drafted with a view to discouraging undesirable patients from seeking health services otherwise available to the general public. From a medical standpoint this would appear ethically dubious.[38] If one sets aside this question of medical ethics, however, there are also fundamental legal implications of barring access to health services for a proscribed class of patients. The principle of equality of access to health care has long been recognised under international law. Indeed the 1948 Universal Declaration of Human Rights set out a basic framework for the right to health, article 25 stating that '[e]veryone has a right to a standard of living adequate for the health and well-being of himself and of his family, including . . . medical care and necessary social services . . .' [gendered language in original]. Access to health care is also recognised as an important prerequisite for the realisation of the *right to the highest attainable standard of health* provided by article 12 of the International Covenant on Economic, Social and Cultural Rights (ICESCR)· The ICESCR was ratified by the UK in 1976, though it has not yet been incorporated into domestic legislation.[39] States who have signed the ICESCR must take 'appropriate measures' to realise the right to the highest attainable standard of health. According to the Committee on Economic, Social and Cultural Rights (CESCR), which oversees the implementation of the ICESCR, full realisation of the right to health includes the *prevention, treatment and control of epidemic diseases*[40] and requires that article 12 be accorded an 'inclusive' interpretation.[41] Signatory states are therefore called upon to provide health facilities for everyone without discrimination.[42] In General Comment 14, the CESCR has addressed some of the more pressing challenges affecting access to health care in the high contracting states.[43] In doing so it has emphasised the importance of 'economic accessibility' of health services and high contracting states are expected to ensure that services are affordable for 'socially disadvantaged groups'.[44]

If we accept the empirical evidence, 'socially disadvantaged' is a term befitting many irregular migrants.[45] Adding to the traumatic past experiences impacting upon their mental and physical health, many are forced to endure extreme poverty, substandard accommodation, social isolation and austere state support.[46]

---

[37] Hall (2006).

[38] Ibid.

[39] Ibid.

[40] ICESCR Article 12 (2).

[41] CESCR *General Comment No 14: The Right to Health (Article 12)* (11 August 2000). E/C.12/2000/4, para 11.

[42] ICESCR, Article 2(2).

[43] General Comment 14 (2000) *op cit.* n 41, para 12.

[44] Ibid., para 33.

[45] Taylor (2009).

[46] Connelly and Schweiger (2000).

Cumulatively these factors have been shown to impact negatively on the physical and mental wellbeing of irregular migrants, while strong positive correlations have been demonstrated between HIV/AIDS prevalence and negative social factors such as poverty and inequality. Migrants who are not infected on arrival in the UK are therefore at increased risk of infection.[47]

The situation is a great deal harsher for certain classes of irregular migrants such as refused asylum seekers; in other words, those who have been unsuccessful in their asylum applications and have exhausted all opportunities to appeal the Home Office's decision. Through no fault of their own, refused asylum seekers are often prevented from returning to their homelands: some find themselves stateless, others are denied the requisite travel documents by their governments and many more are too sick to travel.[48] To revert to the point made above, it would be disingenuous to suggest that 'health tourism' is the default position at play in these scenarios (which are not uncommon in themselves) since the practice implies that the refused asylum seeker is capable of returning to their homeland unhindered once they have received the treatment they need (Refugee Council, 2006). In spite of this, policy trends would suggest that the individual's right to health is increasingly linked to their legal right to be in the UK.[49]

Irregular migrants are identified as being outside of the national community by virtue of having fallen into dis-accord with the immigration laws of the UK. As such, they are systematically excluded from services that are deemed the exclusive domain of the national community.[50] Health legislation that deals with irregular migration is heavily informed by this rationale: consider the Charges to Overseas Regulations 2004 which were enacted in order to 'protect finite NHS resources by closing up loopholes where it has been identified that certain regulations may be open to abuse' (Department of Health, 2003: para. 1). Despite this distorted logic, the CESCR (2002) noted in its concluding observations that it had not identified any factors which could prevent the UK from fully implementing the ICESCR in its entirety. It is suggested that the active barring of overseas patients from potentially life-saving drug therapy means that the UK cannot give full effect to its international obligations pursuant to article 12 ICESCR.[51] A supposedly comprehensive health care model that distinguishes between national and overseas patients, and imparts services accordingly, cannot be said to be offering the highest attainable standard of health to its patients.[52]

---

[47] Cherfas (2006).

[48] 'Still Human Still Here – The campaign to end destitution of refused asylum seekers' *Information for the Committee on Economic, Social and Cultural Rights' (CESCR) review of the United Kingdom, 42nd session, 4–22 May* 2009.

[49] da Lomba (2011).

[50] *Ibid.*

[51] *Ibid.*

[52] Romero-Ortuño (2004).

4 Applicability of European Human Rights Law

Having considered some of the more broad-brush international mechanisms theoretically capable of protecting irregular migrants with HIV/AIDS, it is fitting to explore what, if any, protection is offered under European supra-national law. A useful starting point is the European Convention on Human Rights and Biomedicine (1997), drafted by the Council of Europe and not to be confused with the similarly titled (but altogether more familiar) European Convention on Human Rights, which is discussed below. Article 3 of the Convention on Biomedicine provides for the right to 'equitable access to health care.' It calls for signatory states 'to take appropriate measures with view to providing, within their jurisdiction equitable access to health care of appropriate quality' taking medical needs into account. It is, however, an expressly qualified right and its scope is limited by 'available resources.' In the absence of supplementary guidelines on how article 3 is supposed to apply to those who do not have a legal right to reside in a Council of Europe state, member states are free to determine the entitlement of irregular migrants to access the same medical treatment as nationals. Similarly there is no mechanism under article 3 of the Convention on Biomedicine to prevent a member state from expelling an irregular migrant who is HIV-positive, even where treatment would be cut off as a result.[53] For these reasons the Convention on Biomedicine is not discussed further in this chapter.

Whilst the more familiar European Convention on Human Rights (ECHR, 1949) does not provide for a right to health *per se*, it has birthed potentially the most elaborate human rights jurisprudence in the world, its provisions often taking on meanings that go far beyond the original intent. Indeed many of the ECHR's provisions have been used as a basis for arguing for a human right to health care, the most relevant being articles 2 (the right to life), 3 (the right to freedom from torture, inhuman and degrading treatment or punishment), 8 (the right to respect for home, family and private life) and 14 (the right to freedom from discrimination). These provisions have typically been invoked to resist the expulsion of irregular migrants where it is believed that their health will be compromised as a result of the cessation of treatment, or due to the same treatment being unavailable, or prohibitively expensive in the expellee's homeland.[54] Such factors are highly relevant for HIV/AIDS patients for whom the withdrawal of drug therapy causes impairment of the immune system, leaving the individual vulnerable to deadly opportunistic infections. Given the obvious indignity that this entails, it is not difficult to imagine why the absolute nature of article 3 ECHR has proven a popular choice for those seeking to resist deportation on health grounds and it is this which will provide the focus for the remainder of this chapter.

The European Court of Human Rights ('ECtHR'), the judicial arm of the ECHR charged with implementing its provisions, has emphasised on a number of

[53] Derckx (2006).

[54] Ibid. See also Stevens (2010).

occasions that signatory states have a prerogative in international law to control the entry, movement and expulsion of aliens who are present in their territory (e.g. *Chahal v UK* [1997][55]). Moreover European human rights law does not confer onto aliens a right to resist removal 'in order to continue to benefit from medical, social or other forms of assistance provided by the expelling state.'[56] However, the ECtHR's jurisprudence *does* recognise that article 3 ECHR may apply in this regard in exceptional circumstances, particularly where the unavailability of medical treatment in the applicant's home country would give rise to suffering so serious that it could be classed as *inhuman and degrading treatment*. It is to these examples that we now turn.

5 Domestic and European Jurisprudence

While it may be recognised under ECtHR jurisprudence that article 3 ECHR could potentially be interpreted to prevent the expulsion of a patient suffering from AIDS who would otherwise be unable to access treatment in his home country, there is only one instance of such a decision ever being made by Strasbourg. The judgement issued by the ECtHR in *D v UK* ('the D case') is thus the defining case in this area. The court in the D case recognised an exceptional right for an AIDS patient to remain in a host country in order to have access to medical treatment. The applicant's circumstances were found to be sufficiently exceptional to satisfy the threshold for inhuman and degrading treatment set by the ECtHR for medical *refoulement* (the act of expelling, returning or extraditing a person to another state 'where there are substantial grounds for believing that he would be in danger of being subjected to torture' as per the Convention against Torture and Other Cruel, Inhuman or Degrading Treatment of Punishment, 1987: art 3).

The applicant himself, D, was a convicted drug trafficker from St Kitts who, by the time of his release on license from HM Prison Wayland in 1996, was in the advanced stages of AIDS and terminally ill. In spite of his being reliant on a charitable organisation for accommodation and food, and a counsellor who prepared him emotionally for death, the immigration authorities directed that D be deported back to St Kitts. D did not have any close family in St Kitts who would have been able to care for him and expert evidence indicated that the island nation lacked the facilities to cater for his palliative needs. The European Commission on Human Rights declared D's petition admissible on the grounds that his removal would expose the applicant to a real risk of inhuman and degrading treatment, and so would breach article 3 ECHR.[57] D had argued that his removal to St Kitts would condemn him to living out his remaining months in squalid poverty and isolation,

[55] App. no. 22414/93 [1997] 23 EHRR 423.

[56] *D v UK* App. no. 30240/96 [1997] 24 EHRR 423, para 54.

[57] Ibid., para 37.

his health drastically compromised by the unsanitary conditions on the island. With local hospitals ill-equipped to thwart the onset of disease and infection induced by his living conditions, D claimed he would endure a painful and lonely death. The Commission agreed, by majority, that these factors cumulatively amounted to inhuman and degrading treatment within the meaning of article 3 ECHR.[58] Meanwhile, the UK government had argued that the supposed risk of inhuman and degrading treatment stemmed entirely from the applicant's illness and St Kitts' infrastructural problems, meaning that D's circumstances would be no different to those of any other AIDS sufferer on the island. In any case, the applicant would not have found himself in his unfortunate position had he not attempted entry into the UK in possession of controlled narcotics in the first place.[59]

Although the Commission was indeed mindful of the UK's right to control the entry, movement and expulsion of aliens, as well as the right to take action to curb the passage of controlled substances through its borders, it observed that article 3 'enshrines one of the fundamental values of democratic societies' and could not simply be withheld from an individual on account of their past conduct, no matter how reprehensible.[60] Regardless of whether or not the applicant had entered the UK in accordance with its immigration laws, he was still physically present in the territory itself. Thus, as far as article 1 ECHR was concerned he was within the jurisdiction of a signatory state and subject to convention protection.[61] Moreover, article 3 ECHR, by virtue of its fundamental standing in human rights law, demanded 'sufficient flexibility' for manoeuvre in situations where anticipatory ill-treatment stemmed from the effects of a naturally occurring illness, rather than, say, the deliberate acts of a state or non-state actor.[62] The Commission considered how D's last few months of life would be if the applicant were to remain in the UK, alleviated by a combination of modern drugs and palliative care, against what, according to the expert evidence, awaited him in St Kitts. It was thus moved to conclude that the applicant, if returned, would endure 'acute mental and physical suffering' brought about by a string of 'exceptional circumstances.'[63] These exceptional circumstances would have inflicted treatment on the applicant that was both inhuman and degrading.[64] 'Exceptional circumstances' were thus the operative words in the D case and the Commission felt compelled to attach a final caveat to its judgment: that aliens who are subject to expulsion cannot in principle invoke the ECHR to assert entitlement to medical assistance from the signatory state. Ultimately, the decision to uphold D's application turned upon what the Commission identified as 'compelling humanitarian considerations.'[65] Thus there was little

[58] Ibid., para 40.

[59] Ibid., para 42.

[60] Ibid., paras 46–47.

[61] Ibid., para 48.

[62] Ibid., para 49.

[63] Ibid., para 52.

[64] Ibid., para 53.

[65] Ibid., para 54.

cause to believe that subsequent medical cases would entail circumstances sufficiently serious to warrant article 3 intervention.

In spite of the potential positive implications of the D case for irregular migrants with HIV in the UK, a later case, ostensibly similar to *D v UK* on its facts, *N v Secretary of State for the Home Department* (2005)[66] stands in stark contrast on the basis of its resoundingly negative judgment. The appellant, a Mrs N, unsuccessfully petitioned the Court of Appeal,[67] the House of Lords, and later the ECtHR whose judgment is discussed in detail below.[68] Mrs N arrived in the UK in 1998 under a false passport. She claimed asylum on the grounds that she had been held captive and subjected to mistreatment, including rape, at the hands of 'rogue elements' of the National Resistance Movement in Uganda. It subsequently emerged that she was very ill and she was admitted to Guy's Hospital in London whereupon she was diagnosed HIV-positive with disseminated tuberculosis. She later developed *Kaposi's sarcoma*, an aggressive form of cancer typically affecting individuals whose immune systems have been compromised. Asylum applications being as drawn out as they are, it was not until 2001 that the Home Office rejected Mrs N's application. By this point her condition had stabilised and she appealed before the Immigration Appeals Tribunal (IAT) which cited 'overwhelming' evidence that returning Mrs N to Uganda would violate article 3 ECHR as set out in schedule 1 of the Human Rights Act 1998 (an instrument which at the date of the D case had not yet been introduced into the UK). Medical evidence reported Mrs N's condition as 'stable' and opined that she was 'likely to remain well for decades' if granted leave to remain in the UK. By contrast the report warned that she would not enjoy the benefits of the full treatment she required in Uganda, an unacceptable state of affairs likely to result in 'ill-health, pain, discomfort and an early death'. The evidence suggested that the treatment Mrs N required was available only in sporadic supply and at considerable expense in Uganda. Moreover none of her relatives seemed willing or able to provide her with accommodation and care once returned. A consultant physician concluded that she would live for another 2 years at best if removed from the UK.

In 2003 the IAT ([2002] UK Immigration Appeal Tribunal (06707—HX05310-02) allowed an appeal by the Secretary of State and the matter was brought before the Court of Appeal, the majority finding that the respondent's circumstances fell short of the 'extreme' kinds of cases reserved for article 3 ECHR.[69] Indeed, Mrs N's predicament was 'similar to that of many who suffer from HIV/AIDS' in the UK, for whom withdrawal of treatment inevitably entails a reduction in life expectancy.[70] Carnwath LJ dissented on the basis that he felt that it was for the fact-finding tribunal to determine whether the appellant's circumstances were

[66] *N v SSHD* [2005] UKHL 31.

[67] *N v SSHD* [2003] EWCA CD 1369.

[68] *N v UK* App. no. 26565/05 [2008] 47 EHRR 39.

[69] *Op cit.* n 67, para 43.

[70] Ibid., para 49.

'sufficiently serious' to fall under article 3 ECHR.[71] Nevertheless, the Court of Appeal rejected this on the basis that, without a 'special feature' giving rise to the same sort of compelling humanitarian considerations seen in the D case, it would be inappropriate to open the 'article 3' door to aliens seeking to establish a right to medical treatment.[72]

The House of Lords reached the same conclusion in 2005, though its assessment of the scope of article 3 was an altogether more clinical affair, rejecting the humanitarian approach that the Court of Appeal had adopted.[73] Lord Hope was not satisfied that Mrs N's circumstances were sufficiently exceptional in nature and that any finding to the contrary would have the unwanted effect of extending the 'exceptional category of case' exemplified by the D case.[74] In the core text of his judgement, Lord Hope made the following telling remark, that any such extension of the scope of article 3:

> would risk drawing into the United Kingdom large numbers of people already suffering from HIV in the hope that they too could remain here indefinitely so that they could take the benefit of the medical resources that are available in this country.[75]

For Lord Hope, the fallout of a ruling in favour of Mrs N would have been 'a great and no doubt unquantifiable commitment of resources' which the parties to the ECHR would never have intended to include.[76] Although the ECHR is considered a 'living instrument' and allows for the development of its provisions beyond the normal meaning of their express wording, it was opined that any extension of the scope of a provision would bind *all* of the signatory states, not merely the UK.[77] The pivotal question, as Lord Hope saw it, was whether the signatory states would have agreed to be bound by such an extension.[78] Baroness Hale was sympathetic to the fact that Mrs N had not come to the UK in order to receive HIV treatment, but to escape harassment in her native Uganda. It was not disputed that she had been unaware of her HIV status until her diagnosis in the UK.[79] Both Baroness Hale and Lord Hope consulted the concurring opinion of Judge Pettiti, who in the D case had emphasised that the Commission was not concerned with unequal healthcare standards between states, nor, by extension, the existence of an obligation to provide treatment to aliens where such treatment was unavailable in their homelands. Rather, the Commission had been influenced by the very exceptional circumstances of D's case: the humanitarian implications of removing an individual

[71] Ibid., para 54.

[72] Ibid., para 49.

[73] Bettinson and Jones (2006).

[74] *N v SSHD* (2005) *op cit.* n 66, paras 51–52.

[75] Ibid., para 53.

[76] Ibid.

[77] Ibid., para 21.

[78] Ibid.

[79] Ibid., para 57.

whose life was coming to an end as a result of terminal illness.[80] It was these humanitarian considerations alone in the D case that had qualified the general principle that aliens subject to expulsion cannot 'claim any entitlement to remain in the territory of a contracting state in order to continue to benefit from medical, social or other forms of assistance provided by the expelling state.'[81]

Lord Hope determined that, as a result of the D case, the appellant's *present* condition was the deciding factor when examining whether the claim activated article 3 ECHR.[82] Unlike D, Mrs N was not in a critical condition. As Lord Nicholls observed, the treatment she was undergoing in the UK promised decades of good health, her immune system supported by drugs which mitigated the risk of opportunistic infection, albeit, without actually restoring her to her former state of health.[83] Indeed, Mrs N owed her present stability to the sophisticated course of antiretroviral treatment at her disposal in the UK. Lord Hope observed that the treatment imparted to the appellant was akin to a life support machine. He even admitted that it was 'somewhat disingenuous' for the House of Lords to concentrate on Mrs N's present state of health where that was indisputably linked to the very treatment she risked losing if returned to Uganda.[84]

Nevertheless, any negative health effects suffered by Mrs N as a consequence of her expulsion could not be 'sensibly detached' from the implications of upholding her article 3 claim.[85] Lord Hope's judgement considered a number of negative article 3 decisions in HIV/AIDS cases following D, noting that in each instance the ECtHR had focused on the applicant's *present* state of health before weighing it against the article 3 ECHR claim.[86] Apparently, the fact that significant advancements in HIV/AIDS treatment had taken place since the 1997 D ruling did not factor into the Court's decision in each case.[87] Indeed, the cases indicated strongly that the D case was the paradigm for 'very exceptional circumstances.' This was irrespective of the fact that N's present state of health was purely the reflection of a sophisticated drug regime; it did not mirror the compelling humanitarian considerations of the D case. Because of this, the House of Lords could not have accepted Mrs N's claim without adding to the exceptional circumstances list, something the Commission had been most adamant should not happen.[88]

[80] Ibid., paras 34–35 and 68.

[81] *D v UK* (1997) *op cit.* n 56, para 54.

[82] *N v SSHD* (2005) *op cit.* n 66, paras 36 and 43.

[83] *Ibid.*, para 3.

[84] *Ibid.*, para 49.

[85] *Ibid.*, para 21.

[86] See *BB v France* (1998) (App. no. 47/1998/950/1165) as cited in *SSHD*, para 38; *Karara v Finland* (App. no. 40900/98, 29 May 1998), para 39; *SCC v Sweden* (App. no. 46553/99, 15 February 2000), para 41; *Henao v The Netherlands* (App. no. 13669/03, 24 June 2003), para 45; *Ndangoya v Sweden* (App. no. 17868/03, 22 June 2004), para 46; *Amegnigan v The Netherlands* (App. no. 25629/04, 25 November 2004), para 47.

[87] *Ibid.*, para 50.

[88] *Ibid.*, para 48.

Her appeal having been unanimously dismissed by the House of Lords, Mrs N petitioned the Grand Chamber of the ECtHR in a final bid to challenge her removal from the UK.[89] However, the majority similarly held that her removal would not breach article 3 ECHR, and that it was not necessary to examine an adjoining claim under article 8 ECHR. The Court highlighted the 'minimum level of severity' threshold which had to be reached before ill-treatment could fall under article 3 ECHR, stressing that the threshold is *relative* and moulds to fit 'all of the circumstances of the case.' The ECtHR would therefore consider such factors as the nature and duration of the anticipated ill-treatment, the mental and physical effects of the treatment, and (where required) the age, sex and state of health of the victim.[90] While maintaining its position that suffering emanating from the effects of a naturally occurring illness (as opposed to 'intentional acts or omissions of public authorities or non-State bodies') could fall within the scope of article 3 ill-treatment, the Court deemed it appropriate to observe the high threshold set in the D case as binding in all subsequent cases.[91]

Again, this high threshold is a result of the principle in the D case that aliens who are pending removal from a sovereign state cannot claim any entitlement to remain in order to continue to benefit from social assistance (including medical treatment) provided by the expelling state.[92] With this rule in mind, the ECtHR were moved to the conclusion that the applicant's circumstances, notwithstanding her expected loss of life expectancy in Uganda, were not sufficiently serious to engage the UK's responsibility under the ECHR.[93]

The ECtHR also saw fit to point out that even though the rights contained in the ECHR may have 'implications of a social or economic nature' they were drafted primarily with a view to protecting *civil and political rights.*[94] Thus, even though article 3 demands sufficient flexibility to interfere in expulsion cases, this does not mean that signatory states are under an obligation to alleviate socio-economic deficiencies in other jurisdictions. It stressed, above all, that inherent to the whole of the ECHR is '*a search for a fair balance*' between the general interests of the community and the protection of the fundamental rights of the individual. Notwithstanding medical progress in the treatment of HIV/AIDS, it would have placed too great a burden on the signatory states to require them to provide unlimited health care to all aliens who do not have a right to remain in the state's territory.[95]

Interestingly, there was a robust dissenting opinion from Judges Tulkens, Bonello and Spielmann who argued that there were 'substantial grounds' to support

[89] *N v UK* (2008) *op cit.* n 68.
[90] *Ibid.*, para 29.
[91] *Ibid.*, para 43.
[92] *Ibid.*, para 54.
[93] *Ibid.*, para 42.
[94] *Ibid.*, para 44.
[95] *Ibid.*

the belief that N's application was one of 'exceptional gravity.'[96] The joint dissenting opinion invoked the ECtHR's past definition of *degrading treatment* within the meaning of article 3 ECHR,[97] calling attention to the fact that ill-treatment could be classed as 'degrading' where it 'humiliates or debases an individual, showing a lack of respect for, or diminishing, his or her human dignity, or arouses feelings of fear, anguish or inferiority capable of breaking an individual's moral and physical resistance.'[98] The dissenting judges pointed out the 'Pretty threshold' (from *Pretty v UK*, 2002), which recognises that 'intense physical or mental suffering' which 'flows from naturally occurring illnesses, physical or mental, may be covered by article 3.'[99] This rationale had been bolstered by the D case, in which the ECtHR had recognised that state responsibility could be engaged amid a risk of a serious illness being exacerbated by treatment connected to the conditions of expulsion. Provided that the minimum level of severity was reached, the dissenting three considered it appropriate to apply the ECtHR's definition of degrading treatment, equally, in situations where suffering arises from the absence of facilities required to treat a naturally occurring illness in a second state.[100]

6 An 'Integrated Approach'

The joint dissenting opinion in *N v UK* expressed disappointment that the majority of the Grand Chamber had deviated from the 'integrated approach'[101] to socio-economic and civil-political rights espoused in *Airey v Ireland* (1979–80).[102] Central to the *Airey* case was the acceptance by the ECtHR that *social and economic* interests could, where necessary, be protected by rights which are inherently *civil and political* in nature.[103] According to the *substantive integrated approach* both aspects of human rights are intrinsically linked, since the enjoyment of civil-political rights is often meaningless without their socio-economic counterparts.[104] Consider, by way of illustration, the *travaux préparatoires* of the ECHR which queries: 'What indeed does freedom mean, what does the inviolability of the home mean for a man [or woman] who has got no home?'[105] For judges, the substantive integrated approach is a holistic examination of the boundaries of

[96] *Ibid.*, para O-13.

[97] *Ibid.*, para O-I5.

[98] See *Pretty v UK* App. no. 2346/02 [2002] 35 EHRR 1, para 52.

[99] *Ibid.*

[100] *N v UK* (2008) *op cit.* n 68, para O-15.

[101] *Ibid.*, para O-16.

[102] 2 EHRR 305.

[103] Bettinson and Jones (2009).

[104] Mantouvalou (2005).

[105] *Ibid.* (citing the Council of Europe).

Convention rights as they apply to the unique circumstances of the applicant, rather than being bound by an unqualified rule that the Convention rights are purely civil and political.[106] Hence, in *Sidabras v Lithuania* (2006)[107] the ECtHR cited with approval the rule adopted in *Airey* (1979–80).[108] In doing so it held that the effect of a law prohibiting two former KGB officers from seeking employment in the private sector was to breach their right to a 'private life' under article 8 ECHR.[109] The House of Lords were even willing to recognise socio-economic rights under article 3 ECHR in *R (Adam, Limbuela and Tesema) v Secretary of State for the Home Department* (2005).[110] This case concerned article 3's compatibility with section 55 of the Nationality, Immigration and Asylum Act 2002, providing for the withdrawal of state support from delayed asylum applicants, who, being already forbidden from seeking work (Asylum and Immigration Act 1996: s. 8) would have been pushed into destitution.[111]

7 The 'Exclusion Approach'

In light of the above it is curious that the majority of the Strasbourg judges presiding in *N v UK* rejected, in no uncertain terms, any consideration of welfare rights connected to the applicant's article 3 claim.[112] Instead they adopted what can be called 'the exclusion approach'[113] essentially the antithesis of the integration approach, and determined that article 3 ECHR could not be used as a vehicle to enforce a right to medical treatment. The rationale in the main judgement was conservative: 'Although many of the rights it contains have implications of a social or economic nature, the Convention is essentially directed at the protection of civil and political rights.' Given that the standard of medical care from one state to another is subject to considerable variance, the resounding conclusion held by the majority (*N v UK*, 2008)[114] was that article 3 'does not place an obligation on the contracting state to alleviate such disparities through the provision of free and unlimited health care to all aliens without a right to stay within its jurisdiction.' Although article 3 is capable of intervening in situations where *refoulement* is a risk (*Soering v UK*, 1989[115]) the ECtHR did not treat Mrs N's application as an anti-

[106] Bettinson and Jones (2009).

[107] App. nos. 55480/00; 59330/00 [2006] 42 EHRR 6.

[108] *Op cit.* n 96, para 47.

[109] *Ibid.*, para 50.

[110] UKHL 56, 1 AC 396.

[111] Mantouvalou (2005).

[112] *N v UK* (2008) *op cit.* n 68, para 24.

[113] Bettinson and Jones (2009), p. 84.

[114] *N v UK* (2008) *op cit.* n 68, para 44.

[115] *Soering v UK* (App. no. 14038/88) [1989] 11 EHRR 439.

refoulement claim. Rather, it was treated as an attempt by a refused asylum seeker to continue receiving expensive drug therapy unavailable in her home town and, thus, 'smuggle' social and economic interests into article 3 jurisprudence.[116] The House of Lords had adopted the same position in *N v SSHD*, Lord Brown observing that central to the appellant's submission was that the UK was under a *positive obligation* to refrain from expelling her so that her treatment could continue unhindered. Accordingly, there was an 'unbreakable link'[117] between the alleged obligation not to return and the consequential duty to provide treatment since '[t] here would simply be no point in not deporting her unless her treatment were to continue.'[118]

Thus, the House of Lords and the ECtHR adopted the position that the circumstances surrounding 'the N cases' were distinguishable from the D case in that the latter had involved a negative obligation not to deport an individual who would have inevitably suffered an undignified death.[119] Conversely, N sought to remain in the UK indefinitely, supported by treatment which had not even existed when the judgement in the D case was delivered. It is therefore to be understood that, whereas D was asserting a right to remain in the UK to die, Mrs N, by invoking the same principle, wanted to remain in order to enjoy an enhanced quality of life.[120] The lapse in time between the D ruling in 1997 and *N v UK* in 2005 brought about vast improvements in medical treatment for AIDS sufferers, meaning that a decision in favour of Mrs N would have implicitly resulted in increased costs to the state as other aliens in her position sought to assert the same right to long-term sophisticated medical treatment.[121]

The humanitarian implications of cutting off an AIDS patient from her treatment and leaving her to an uncertain fate were glaringly obvious from the onset. Nevertheless, the unhappy task facing both courts was to delimit the scope of the signatory states' article 3 obligations where a naturally occurring illness was concerned.[122] Referring to the D case in *N v SSHD*, Baroness Hale noted that the article 3 'test' lay in determining whether the appellant's illness had 'reached such a critical stage (i.e. he was dying) that it would be inhuman to deprive him of the care which he is currently receiving.'[123] It is to be remembered that the D judgement was itself an extension of article 3 ECHR, and so to find for Mrs N, whose illness was curtailed and had not been permitted to reach a critical stage, would have imposed a particularly onerous obligation on the UK (and indeed the rest of the ECHR

[116] Bettinson and Jones (2009).

[117] Ibid., p. 73.

[118] *N v SSHD* (2005) *op cit.* n 66, para 88.

[119] *N v SSHD* (2005) *op cit.* n 66, para 93.

[120] Mantouvalou (2005).

[121] Bettinson and Jones (2009).

[122] Ibid.

[123] *N v SSHD* (2005) *op cit.* n 66, para 69.

signatories) to provide treatment to aliens in the regrettably common situation in which Mrs N found herself.[124]

8 The Policy Dilemma

Although not articulated in explicit terms in *N v UK*, the joint dissenting opinion suggested that policy considerations lay at the heart of the main judgement. In other words the real reason behind the majority's decision to reject Mrs N's application was the unspoken fear that the UK's resources (and potentially that of the Council of Europe member states) would be stretched to capacity if the state were obliged to offer medical services to all overseas patients suffering from serious illnesses.[125] It will, no doubt, be familiar that the shared conclusion of 14 of the Grand Chamber judges was that no obligation exists under article 3 ECHR to provide 'free and unlimited health care' to aliens who do not have a right to remain in the jurisdiction of signatory states, who would otherwise be laden with 'too great a burden.'[126] This was reminiscent of Lord Hope's concerns in *N v SSHD* over the 'very great and no doubt unquantifiable commitment of resources' resulting from the creation of such an obligation.[127]

Mantouvalou has argued that the judgements delivered by the House of Lords and the ECtHR in the N cases were couched in a the rhetoric of a 'floodgate argument'[128] or the fear of causing signatory states to be overwhelmed by aliens with serious illnesses, each asserting an irrevocable right to free health care. If Lords Brown's estimation was to be believed, the expected annual cost incurred by the state to provide N with antiretroviral therapy would be £7000, a conservative figure given the likely inclusion of additional social welfare and immigration control costs if more AIDS sufferers were drawn to the UK in the hope of qualifying for the same treatment.[129] However, the joint dissenting opinion in *N v UK* dismissed the floodgate argument on the grounds that it was 'misconceived.' The three dissenting judges cited Rule 39 statistics (ECtHR, 2014) illustrating the total number of petitions the ECtHR had received from the UK each year compared to the relatively paltry number of HIV/AIDS cases dealt with.[130]

It would appear that thc dissenting three are not the only ones dissatisfied with the outcome of the N cases. Commentators like Bettinson and Jones (2009) are, equally, unable to accept the floodgate argument in *N v UK*. They have proposed

[124] Bettinson and Jones (2009).

[125] Mantouvalou (2009).

[126] *N v UK* (2008) *op cit.* n 68, para 44.

[127] *N v SSHD* (2005) *op cit.* n 66, para 53.

[128] Mantouvalou (2009), pp. 815–816.

[129] *N v SSHD* (2005) *op cit.* n 66, para 92.

[130] *N v UK* (2008) *op cit.* n 68, para O-I8.

that repercussions would have been minimal had the Court simply applied and stuck to the two-stage test used in the D case: (1) 'has the applicant's illness attained an advanced or terminal stage?' (2) If so, would their return leave them bereft of medical treatment and family support, subjecting them to 'acute mental and physical suffering?'[131] The authors highlighted that not since the D case had the Court observed that the removal of an alien suffering from a serious illness could give rise to an article 3 breach, a point which they maintained neutralised any concerns over the floodgates opening if N's application were upheld. In any case, it will be recalled from above that many HIV-positive migrants in the UK are unaware of their condition on arrival; indeed that had been the case with Mrs N herself.[132] Perhaps it was then rash to presume that this trend should abruptly reverse itself just because the Court had found in favour of a HIV-positive applicant for a second time.

Mantouvalou expressed similar criticism of the floodgate arguments scattered throughout the N cases, noting that there was 'great scepticism' on the matter in other jurisdictions.[133] For perspective, let us consider the case of *Chan v Canada (Minister of Employment and Immigration)* [1995][134] in which the appellant, a Chinese national, sought asylum in Canada amid fears of being forcibly sterilised upon his return to China for having violated its one-child birth control laws. The Supreme Court of Canada, while 'mindful that the possibility of a flood of refugees may be a legitimate political concern' conceded that it was not an 'appropriate legal consideration'. To weigh such concerns in its decision making process, it reasoned, would be to 'unduly distort the judicial-political relationship,' while debasing an institution primarily concerned with the protection of fundamental freedoms.[135] In a similar vein, the joint dissenting opinion in *N v UK* considered it inappropriate to attempt to qualify the scope of article 3 ECHR in the face of the applicant's circumstances. It argued that policy considerations such as budgetary constraints served only to undermine the absolute character of article 3, just as they undermined the integrity of all of the rights and fundamental freedoms set out in the ECHR.[136] The crux of the dissenting judgement was that the ECHR rights could not be divorced from 'prevailing practical realities.'[137] As Lord Hope had remarked in *N v SSHD*, any decision taken by those tasked with implementing the provisions of the ECHR guaranteed 'profound consequences' for the applicant.[138]

The N cases exposed an uncomfortable juxtaposition between the preservation of finite state resources and the duty to observe basic principles of human rights and

[131] *D v UK* (1997) *op cit.* n 56, para 52.

[132] Bettinson and Jones (2009).

[133] Ibid., p. 826.

[134] [1995] 3 SCR 593.

[135] Ibid., para 151.

[136] *N v UK* (2008) *op cit.* n 68, para O-I8.

[137] *Ibid.*, para O-I10.

[138] *N v SSHD* (2005) *op cit.* n 66, para 20.

dignity. The absence of a right to health care for failed asylum seekers who are HIV/AIDS sufferers brings this issue into sharp focus, and the resultant moral and legal questions are not easily resolved. It is a given, for instance, that the protection of human rights itself exerts a toll on state resources. At what point then can it be reasonably determined that the anticipated implications of enforcing an individual's rights are so profound, so destructive, as to release the state from an otherwise absolute obligation?[139] *N v UK* brought this conundrum to the forefront, the three dissenting judges endorsing a somewhat purist approach to article 3 as it ought to apply in situations such as Mrs N's.[140] One might argue that *N v UK* was more complex, perhaps more emotive, than other medical cases heard by the ECtHR since it related to AIDS, a disease which (presently) has no cure and which disproportionately affects the poorest regions of the world. Its strong ties with poverty intensifies perceptions of global inequality and social injustice, and the joint dissenting opinion perfectly illustrated the controversy surrounding the sadly necessary task of setting limits to the state's article 3 obligations towards aliens with HIV/AIDS.

Then again, Mantouvalou points out that scarcity of resources has not so easily deterred the ECtHR from finding a breach of the ECHR in the past, particularly where article 3 is concerned.[141] In *Aliev v Ukraine* (1997)[142] one of a few cases concerning the alleged substandard condition of Ukrainian prisons, the Court remarked that a 'lack of resources cannot in principle justify prison conditions which are so poor as to reach the threshold of treatment contrary to article 3 of the Convention.'[143] In this instance the ECtHR were prepared to enforce an article 3 obligation irrespective of the respondent state's financial position. What *N v UK* suggests, however, is that even if the ECtHR had found that the UK owed an obligation towards Mrs N under article 3, the respondent state could be relieved of that obligation if the evidence indicated that aliens, spurred on by the positive judgement, would arrive *en masse* in the signatory states lured by the prospect of free medical treatment.[144]

Notwithstanding the above, let us recall that the joint dissenting opinion had objected to the *implicit* use of a floodgates argument in the main judgement. If the majority of the Grand Chamber were genuinely worried that the Council of Europe member states would become the 'sick-bay of the world' as a result of Mrs N's petition, this was not explicitly clarified in the main judgement. Indeed the matter was something of an elephant in the room throughout the proceedings.[145] One would assume that such a portentous claim would be substantiated with carefully

[139] Mantouvalou (2009).

[140] *N v UK* (2008) *op cit.* n 68, para O-I1.

[141] Mantouvalou (2009).

[142] App. no. 41220/97, as cited by Mantouvalou (2009).

[143] Ibid., p. 826.

[144] Ibid.

[145] *N v UK* (2008) *op cit.* n 68, para O-I8.

weighed evidence, especially since it informed the ECtHR's decision to reject the applicant's petition.[146] This is somewhat unsatisfactory in light of evidence which suggests that most asylum seekers are not drawn to the UK for treatment, and certainly not those who are harbouring the HIV virus.[147] What is more, Sawyer argues that it cannot be held that the ECHR applies *universally* in the jurisdiction of signatory states if there is no absolute principle guaranteeing state protection for aliens who are subject to expulsion.[148] On the contrary, this would suggest something of a double standard, with one's immigration status ultimately trumping the inalienability of human rights and fundamental freedoms. At the very least it appears counter-intuitive to the understanding that human rights are grounded in rudimentary notions of fair treatment.[149]

9 Conclusion

This chapter has attempted to illustrate how health care rules in the UK, spurred by the apparent threat of health tourism, have sought to restrict access to HIV treatment for those who are perceived as 'not belonging' in the country. This trend has led many commentators to the conclusion that the right to health care in the UK is contingent on one's legal right to reside in accordance with immigration law. It has also been argued that this is problematic in terms of the UK's commitment to uphold article 12 ICESCR (the right to the highest attainable standard of health). Despite this, European law grants states a wide discretionary margin of appreciation in their enforcement of immigration policy domestically. With the notable exception of the D case, this also applies to the provision of HIV treatment to irregular migrants. Although in the D case the ECtHR appeared willing to support a right to treatment for irregular migrants with HIV/AIDS in exceptional circumstances, the right appears to have been in retreat ever since.

The *N* cases were important in terms of highlighting the current legal standing (with relevance to human rights legislation) of HIV/AIDS sufferers who are not entitled to remain in the UK. It was shown that national legislation (including the HRA and relevant health legislation) has progressively tightened executive control over the imparting of health services to irregular migrants. A prominent theme in discussions concerning the allocation of health resources has been the perceived need to discourage hordes of immigrants from 'taking advantage' of the NHS, especially when it comes to antiretroviral drug therapy. In its haste to obstruct pathways to HIV/AIDS treatment for vulnerable migrants, the UK bears the risk of neglecting its duty to ensure that socially disadvantaged groups enjoy the highest

[146] Mantouvalou (2009).

[147] Erwin and Peters (1999).

[148] Sawyer (2004).

[149] Ibid.

attainable standard of health. On the other hand, the ECtHR entrusts signatory states with considerable power to determine the entry, movement and expulsion of aliens while the right to 'equitable access to health care' is qualified by the availability of resources. Even article 3 ECHR jurisprudence does not recognise a duty to alleviate suffering endured as a result of harsh socio-economic conditions in a second state.

It is not disputed that there is a need to apply boundaries to the scope of article 3 ECHR, since any obligation arising from the prohibition of ill-treatment becomes an absolute one. Nevertheless, the authors are in agreement with the dissenting judges in *N v UK* that the main judgement in that case was permeated by a covert 'floodgate argument'. Given the apparent lack of evidence to justify this fear of 'health tourism,' it was unfortunate for the applicant that both the House of Lords and the ECtHR were so preoccupied by such concerns. Perhaps there is something to be taken from the dictum of Mahoney JA in *Chan v Canada*: that immigration policy belongs in the political sphere and merely serves as a distraction from the 'practical realities' (i.e., the suffering of the applicant) in the judicial sphere.

References

Bettinson, V., & Jones, A. (2006). Is inadequate medical care insufficient to resist removal? The return of foreign nationals with HIV/AIDS and article 3 ECHR. *Journal of Social Welfare and Family Law, 28*(1), 70–80.

Bettinson, V., & Jones, A. (2007). The future of claims to resist removal by non-nationals suffering from HIV/AIDS. *Liverpool Law Review, 28*(2), 182–213.

Bettinson, V., & Jones, A. (2009). The integration or exclusion of welfare rights in the European Convention on Human Rights: The removal of foreign nationals with HIV after *N v UK* (Application No. 26565/05; decision of the Grand Chamber of the European Court of Human Rights, 27 May 2008). *Journal of Social Welfare and Family Law, 31*(1), 83–94.

Cherfas, L. (2006, October). *Negotiating access and culture: Organizational responses to the healthcare needs of refugees and asylum seekers living with HIV in the United Kingdom.* University of Oxford Refugees Study Centre Working Paper No. 33.

Connelly, J., & Schweiger, M. (2000). The health risks of the United Kingdom's new asylum act: The health of asylum seekers must be closely monitored by service providers. *British Medical Journal, 321*(7252), 5–6.

da Lomba, S. (2011). Irregular migrants and the human right to health care: A case-study of health-care provision for irregular migrants in France and the United Kingdom. *International Journal of Law in Context, 7*(3), 357–374.

Department of Health. (2010, February). *Review of access to the NHS by foreign nationals – Consultation on proposals.*

Derckx, V. (2006). Expulsion of illegal residents (aliens) with medical problems and Article 3 of the European Convention on Human Rights. *European Journal of Health Law, 13*(4), 313–319.

Erwin, J., & Peters, B. (1999). Treatment issues for HIV+ Africans in London. *Social Science and Medicine, 49*(11), 1519–1528.

European Court of Human Rights. *Rules of Court (1 July 2014).* http://www.echr.coe.int/Documents/Rules_Court_ENG.pdf

Fowler, A., Collins, L., Larbalestier, N., Kulasegaram, R., de Ruiter, A., & Micunovic, V. (2006). HIV, HAART, and overseas visitors. *Sexually Transmitted Infections, 82*, 516.

Hall, P. (2006). Failed asylum seekers and health care: Current regulations flout international law. *British Medical Journal, 333*, 109–110.

Hargreaves, I. (2000, April 24). How the newspapers nourish racial intolerance. *New Statesman.*
Health Select Committee. *Third report of the session 2004/5 on new developments in sexual health and HIV/AIDS policy.*
House of Commons Health Committee. (2005). *New developments in HIV/AIDS and sexual health policy* – Third report of session 2004–05, 8 March 2005.
House of Lords Hansard Debates. (2004, March 5). http://hansard.millbanksystems.com/lords/2004/mar/05/national-health-service-and-overseas
Kelley, N., & Stevenson, J. (2006). *First do no harm: Denying healthcare to people whose asylum claims have failed.* London: Refugee Council.
Mantouvalou, V. (2005). Work and private life: Sidabras and Dziautas v Lithuania. *European Law Review, 30*(4), 573–585.
Mantouvalou, V. (2009). *N v. UK*: No duty to rescue the nearby needy? *Modern Law Review, 72* (5), 815–828.
Margaret Hodge MP. (2007, May 20). A message to my fellow immigrants. *The Observer.*
NHS Constitution – the NHS belongs to us all, 26 March 2013 (London: Department of Health, 2013).
Platform for International Cooperation on Undocumented Migrants, *PICUM's Comments on the Communication from the Commission on 'Policy priorities in the fight against illegal immigration of third-country nationals' COM* (2006) 402 final.
Pobjoy, J., & Spencer, S. (2012). Equality for all? The relationship between immigration status and the allocation of rights in the United Kingdom. *European Human Rights Law Review, 2*, 160–175.
'Proposed Amendments to National Health Service (Charges to Overseas Visitors) Regulations 1989: A Consultation' (28 July 2003).
Romero-Ortuño, R. (2004). Access to health care for illegal immigrants in the EU: Should we be concerned? *European Journal of Health Law, 11*, 245–272.
Sawyer, C. (2004). Insufficiently inhuman: Removal AIDS patients from the United Kingdom. N v. Secretary of State for the Home Department (Terence Higgins Trust intervening) [2003] EWCA Civ 1369. *Journal of Social Welfare and Family Law, 26*(3), 281–288.
Secretary of State for Health. (2005). *Government response to the Health Select Committee's third report of session 2004–2005 on new developments in sexual health and HIV/AIDS policy.* Norwich, England: Crown Copyright.
Stevens, D. (2010). Asylum seekers and the right to access health care. *Northern Ireland Legal Quarterly, 61*(4), 363–390.
'Still Human Still Here – The campaign to end destitution of refused asylum seekers' Information for the Committee on Economic, Social and Cultural Rights' (CESCR) review of the United Kingdom, 42nd session, 4–22 May 2009.
Taylor, K. (2009). Asylum seekers, refugees, and the politics of access to health care: A United Kingdom perspective. *British Journal of General Practice, 59*(1), 765–772.

Case Law

Strasbourg

Airey v. Ireland (Application No. 6289/73) (1979–80) 2 EHRR 305
Amegnigan v The Netherlands (App no 25629/04, 25 November 2004)
Arcila Henao v. The Netherlands (Application No. 13669/03), 24 June 2003
BB v. France (Application No. 30930/96), 7 September 1998, (European Commission)
Bensaid v. United Kingdom (Application No. 44599/98) [2001] 33 EHHR 10
Chahal v. United Kingdom (Application No. 22414/93), [1997] 23 EHHR 423
D v. United Kingdom (Application No. 30240/96) (1997) 24 EHRR 423

Henao v The Netherlands (App no 13669/03, 24 June 2003)
Ireland v. United Kingdom (Series A, No. 25) (1979–80) 2 EHRR 25
Karara v Finland (App no 40900/98, 29 May 1998)
N v. United Kingdom (Application No. 26565/05) (2008) 47 EHRR 39
Ndangoya v Sweden (App no 17868/03, 22 June 2004)
Pretty v. United Kingdom (Application No. 2346.02) (2002) 35 EHRR 1
Saadi v. Italy (Application No. 37201/06) [2009] 49 EHRR 30
SCC v Sweden (App no 46553/99, 15 February 2000)
Sidabras v. Lithuania (Application Nos. 55480/00; 59330/00) (2006) 42 EHRR 6
Soering v. United Kingdom (Application No. 14038/88) [1989] 11 EHRR 439

Canada

Chan v. Canada (Minister of Employment and Immigration) [1995] 3 Supreme Court Reports 593

UK

N v. Secretary of State for the Home Department [2002] United Kingdom Immigration Appeal Tribunal 06707 – HX05310-02
N v. Secretary of State for the Home Department (Terence Higgins Trust Intervening) [2003] EWCA CD 1369
N v. Secretary of State for the Home Department [2005] UKHL 31
R v. Barnet London Borough Council, ex parte Shah (Nilish) [1983] 2 WLR 16
R (on the application of Adam, Limbuela and Tesema) v. Secretary of State for the Home Department [2005] UKHL 56, 1 AC396
R (Adam, Limbuela and Tesema) v Secretary of State for the Home Department (2005) UKHL 56; 1 AC 396

Legislation

Asylum and Immigration Act 1996
Health and Social Care Act 2012
Human Rights Act 1998
Immigration Act, Rules of the Supreme Court, 1985 [Canada]
National Health Service (Charges to Overseas Visitors) Regulations 1989, SI 1989/406
National Health Service (Charges to Overseas Visitors) Charging (Amendment) Regulations 2004, SI 2004/614
National Health Service (Charges to Overseas Visitors) Regulations 2011, SI 2011/1556
Nationality, Immigration and Asylum Act 2002

Websites

BBC News, *Are Health Tourists Draining the NHS?* 14 May 2004 http://news.bbc.co.uk/1/hi/health/3356255.stm

UN Documents

Committee on Economic, Social and Cultural Rights, General Comment No. 14: The Right to the Highest Attainable Standard of Health (Art. 12) (Document E/C.12/2000/4), 11 August 2000

Convention against Torture and Other Cruel, Inhuman or Degrading Treatment or Punishment (New York: 1987)

Convention for the Protection of Human Rights and Dignity of the Human Being with regard to the Application of Biology and Medicine: Convention on Human Rights and Biomedicine (Oviedo: 1997)

Convention for the Protection of Human Rights and Fundamental Freedoms (Strasbourg: 1949)

International Covenant on Economic, Social and Cultural Rights (New York: 1966)

United Nations, *Concluding Observations of the Committee on Economic, Social and Cultural Rights: United Kingdom of Great Britain and Northern Ireland, United Kingdom of Great Britain and Northern Ireland – Dependant Territories. 05/06/2002. E/C.12/1/Add.79.* (Geneva: UN, 2002)

Universal Declaration of Human Rights (Paris: 1948)

Dignity: A Relevant Normative Value in 'Access to Health and Social Care' Litigation in the United Kingdom?

Jacinta Miller

1 Introduction

The 'rationing' of health and social care within the Kingdom (UK) is an accepted reality today.[1] As such, a growing body of case law has developed giving clear guidance on the legal principles and rights that the UK Courts look to when questions of availability and access to health and social care are brought before them.[2] The case of *McDonald v UK*[3] however highlights how limited the approach to justiciability on rationing issues is within the courts, particularly in the context of a growing elderly population and finite resources.[4] While the courts in the *McDonald* litigation[5] were prepared to review the procedural aspects associated with the decision making on the care provided, they were reluctant to assess in substantive terms the impact of the decision on the individual.[6] Although dignity

[1] The case of *McDonald v United Kingdom* 4241/12 (2014) 60 E.H.R.R. 1 is in itself evidence of this; See also Callahan (2012), pp. 12–13 who suggests that rationing within the NHS is no longer covert but overt. He highlights the use of tools such as Quality-Adjusted Life Years in decisions involving questions over 'which types of treatment should be made available?' as an example of this.

[2] Newdick (2004).

[3] *McDonald v United Kingdom* (2014), *op cit.* n 1.

[4] For discussion on the limitations of the current approach to litigating a right of access to health and social care see Clough and Brazier (2014); Clements (2011); O'Cinneide (2013), pp. 385–410.

[5] *McDonald v United Kingdom* (2014), *op cit.* n 1; R *(On the Application of McDonald) v Royal Borough of Chelsea and Kensington* [2011] UKSC 33; R *(On the Application of McDonald) v Royal Borough of Chelsea and Kensington* (2010) EWCA 1109; R *(On the Application of McDonald) v Royal Borough of Chelsea and Kensington* (2009) EWHC 1582 (admin).

[6] Clough and Brazier (2014), p. 141.

J. Miller (✉)
School of Law, Northumbria University, Newcastle, UK
e-mail: j.miller@ulster.ac.uk

A. Diver, J. Miller (eds.), *Justiciability of Human Rights Law in Domestic Jurisdictions*, DOI 10.1007/978-3-319-24016-9_4

was acknowledged as being relevant throughout the various stages of the litigation, there was limited discussion of the concept. This chapter questions whether fuller consideration could have been given to the concept of dignity as understood within the disciplines of health and law,[7] including Article 12 of the International Covenant on Economic, Social and Cultural Rights (ICESCR). In spite of the relationship between health and dignity being clearly acknowledged within the international law on a right to health, there is limited guidance on what dignity means within the jurisprudence on Article 12 ICESCR.[8] However, empirical research on both health and law has the potential to develop the concept as a standard in law. The concept has been increasingly referred to within professional guidance,[9] empirical research[10] and within a growing body of literature[11] and case law.[12] This represents a body of evidence which the courts could refer to in the context of access to health and social care litigation, and which they can in turn contribute to by embedding dignity as a value that ought to be considered in decision-making on access to social and health care entitlements.

2 The *McDonald* Litigation

McDonald v United Kingdom involved a challenge[13] against the decision (and care plan) made by a local borough council under their statutory duties.[14] The local council had a duty to assess the client's needs, make provision for those needs 'and in doing so [they could] take account of their resources.'[15] As a result of a stroke,

[7] Foster (2011) highlights examples of primary research on health care (which focused on trying to understand the meaning of dignity and the factors which impact upon it) and reviews of case law looking at how the courts have approached 'dignity.'

[8] Jacobson (2007), p. 292.

[9] See for example Department of Health (2001) which refers to the concepts of 'respect and dignity'; Royal College of Nursing (2008a).

[10] See for example Cairns et al. (2013).

[11] Jacobson (2007); Foster (2011); see also McCrudden (2008); Moon (2006); Moon and Allen (2006); O'Connell (2008).

[12] See for example McCrudden *ibid* who reviews human rights treaty law and jurisprudence to question the understanding of dignity in the context of human rights law and O'Connell *ibid* who examines the concept in the context of equality law.

[13] The challenge at the Supreme Court R *(McDonald)* [2011] UKSC, para 5 gave rise to four issues for appeal. These included whether the care plan reviews were a re-assessment of needs, whether due regard was given to the nature of needs within the requirement of disability legislation, whether Article 8 ECHR had been infringed and whether that interference was lawful.

[14] The relevant statutory provisions which placed duties upon the Royal Borough of Chelsea and Kensington in respect of Ms McDonald's care included: The National Health Service and Community Care Act (2009), S 47; National Assistance Act (1948) S 29(1); Chronically Sick and Disabled Persons Act (1947) S 2(1); Local Authority Social Services Act (1970) S 7(1).

[15] *R (McDonald)* [2011], opt cit. n 5, para 8.

Ms McDonald suffered from limited mobility and frequency of urination: this contributed to her being at risk of falling.[16] She needed assistance to access the toilet both during the day and the night. Her request for night-time assistance was rejected by the council, and alternative care was eventually put in place, which was the provision of incontinence pads for her to use. The use of incontinence pads was viewed as 'a practical and appropriate solution to Ms McDonald's night-time toileting needs...,'[17] in the context of available resources and given the rejection by Ms McDonald of the other care alternatives offered to her. Her needs and wishes in the context of the care plan were considered to be 'elimination of risk of injury' and 'a desire for independence and privacy', both of which could be met, it was argued, with the provision of incontinence pads.[18] Lord Brown found that there was no interference with Article 8 ECHR rights, but stated that even if an interference with the right to home, family and private life was identified, it could be justified under Article 8(2) ECHR.[19] The ECtHR did find that there was an interference with Article 8, however save in respect of a violation between November 2008 and 2009 (based on procedural aspects), that interference was lawful.[20]

The ECtHR in the case reaffirms that health and social care interests are justiciable on the basis of Article 8 ECHR, including "complaints about public funding to facilitate the mobility and quality of life of disabled applicants."[21] The ECtHR also reaffirmed its view that Article 8 in principle gives rise to positive obligations, even in the context of access to health and social care.[22] However it viewed this case as giving rise to a negative obligation in respect of the right: the issue was not one of "a lack of action [as] the state had not refused assistance to Ms McDonald" rather it was in relation to a "decision of the local authority to reduce the care package that it had hitherto been making available to her".[23] Any interference with Ms McDonald's Article 8 ECHR rights, after November 2009, was considered to be lawful and proportionate in the context of the legitimate aim of the "economic well-being of the state and the interests of other care-users".[24] The state's decision was viewed in the context of a wide margin of appreciation as it involved issues of general policy and the Court stated that the "... margin is

[16] *Ibid.*, para 1.

[17] *Ibid.*, para 11 referring to the 2010 Care Plan Review for Ms McDonald.

[18] *Ibid.*, para 12 citing Rix LJ in *R (McDonald)* (2010) EWCA, para 53.

[19] *Ibid. per* Brown LJ, para 9. Walker LJ, Kerr LJ and Dyson LJ all agreed with Brown LJ's judgment and dismissed the appeal. Lade Hale provided the only dissenting judgment.

[20] *McDonald V UK* (2014), *op cit.* n 1, para 59. A violation was found to have occurred in the period between 21 November 2008 and November 2009. Within that time, care was not provided in line with the assessment made. No violation was found to have occurred after November 2009.

[21] *Ibid.*

[22] *Ibid.*, para 48.

[23] *Ibid.*, para 48.

[24] *Ibid.*, para 53.

particularly wide when the issues involve an assessment of the priorities in the context of the allocation of limited State resources."[25]

While the case provides evidence of the justiciability of access to health and social care claims, it also supports the view that the approach of both the UK courts and the ECtHR to justiciability of economic, social and cultural rights is limited. Clough and Brazier suggest the case provides an example of the failure of Article 8 ECHR to protect the elderly, with its narrow focus on 'procedural issues' rather than on the "impact of the decisions on the substantive rights or dignity"[26] of the individual. Clements goes further in his criticism stating that it is worrying that "parts of the judiciary do not consider that such distressing circumstances engage fundamental human rights at all".[27] Pritchard-Jones suggests that there is as much to learn from the case in respect of what is not said, as there is in terms of what *is* said, given the "ECtHR's disinclination to engage with substantive discussions of dignity and autonomy".[28]

The criticisms of a focus on procedure, a reluctance to consider 'normative values' or minimum standards and judicial deference in the context of resource allocation questions are part of the wider debate on the extent to which courts should be involved in challenges relevant to social justice.[29] O'Cinneide suggests that even though there are times when it appears that courts look to some substantive aspects (for example non-discrimination and equality) of economic, social and cultural rights, they continue to limit the review of these rights by tying these aspects to the process of decision-making rather than looking to the impact of the decision on the individual.[30] This is an approach which he describes as 'ethically aimless'.[31] He highlights *McDonald v UK* as an example of this, with the core issues of 'rationality' and 'dignity' being relegated to side issues while the court focused on procedural matters.[32] Whilst acknowledging the arguments for limited judicial intervention and the dangers of judicial intervention in the context of finite resources, O'Cinneide suggests that there is a need for the courts to view decisions in the context of social justice. Lady Hale's approach in the *McDonald* case also seems to suggest that a standard related to the impact on the individual is necessary in the context of access to care decisions within finite resources:

---

[25] *Ibid.*, para 55.

[26] Clough and Brazier (2014), p. 141.

[27] Clements (2011), p. 684.

[28] Pritchard-Jones (2015), p. 111.

[29] O'Cinneide (2013), pp. 395–396.

[30] *Ibid.* One example of this is found in *Eisai Limited v. The National Institute for Health and Clinical Excellence (NICE), The Alzheimer's Society, Shire Pharmaceuticals Limited* [2007] EWHC 1941 (Admin) QBD (Admin). One factor considered by the court in this case was the discriminatory effect of one aspect of the process of evaluation of the treatment.

[31] O'Cinneide (2013), p. 403 who further notes that 'ethical aimlessness' was a term first used by Anthony Lester in association with the common law before the 'modern rule of law' and human rights.

[32] *Ibid.*, p. 403.

> As Lord Lloyd put it in *Barry* 'in every case, simple or complex, the need of the individual will be assessed against the standards of civilized society as we know them in the United Kingdom' (p598F). In the United Kingdom we do not oblige people who can control their bodily functions to behave as if they cannot do so, unless they themselves find this the more convenient course. We are, I still believe, a civilized society. I would have allowed the appeal.[33]

If the CESCR General Comment (which elaborates on the meaning of Article 12 ICESCR in stating that '[e]very human being is entitled to the enjoyment of the highest attainable standard of health conducive to living a life in dignity'[34]) is considered, then the standard of a civilized society requires that individuals are treated with dignity. In the original High Court case, the only references made to dignity (or rather, 'indignity') were by the applicant, in her claim that the withdrawal of night-time care exposed her to 'risk and indignity.'[35] In the Court of Appeal the applicant's lawyers continued to view the withdrawal of care as an 'affront to her dignity,'[36] argued that dignity was at the heart of Article 8 ECHR[37] and that the impact upon 'Ms McDonald's core right of dignity' was not proportionate to the aim of 'equitable allocation of resources' nor to the aim of saving money in the decision on what care to provide.[38] In contrast the council viewed the provision of incontinence sheets as a way to protect dignity and privacy, supporting this argument by highlighting the experience of others: that is, that 'most people were willing to accept them' and were happy with this form of care.[39] As such, within the High Court and Court of Appeal no issue of dignity was associated with the nature of the care. In the context of the earlier care plan failing to meet the needs of Ms McDonald, which could allow for a finding of a violation of Article 8 ECHR, the courts suggested that this "was not born out of any disrespect" for the applicant's dignity but out of a concern for the council's "responsibilities to all its clients within the limited resources available to it within its budget".[40]

Within the Supreme Court Judgment, Lord Brown provided some insight as to why he considered that there was no disrespect for the dignity of the applicant: his view was that the council had "sought to respect as far as possible her personal feelings and desires, at the same time taking account of her safety, her independence and their own responsibilities towards all their other clients."[41] Evidence of

[33] *McDonald* [2011] UKSC, *op cit.* n 5, para 79 citing *R v Gloucestershire County Council ex parte Barry* [1997] AC 584 at 589F.

[34] CESCR *General Comment No 14: The Right to Health (Article 12)* (11 August 2000). E/C.12/2000/4, para 1.

[35] *Ibid.*, paras 1 and 4.

[36] *McDonald* (2010) EWCA, *op cit.* n 5, para 2.

[37] *Ibid.*, para 63.

[38] *Ibid.*, para 70.

[39] *Ibid.*, paras 24 and 26–27. The evidence appears anecdotal and not based upon any formal evaluation.

[40] *Ibid.*, para 66.

[41] *Mc Donald* [2011] UKSC, *op cit.* n 5, para 19.

this included offering alternative choices and aspects of support such as direct payments. In essence, he viewed autonomy as being closely associated with the notion of dignity. The decision to provide 'incontinence sheets' was also considered to be an 'acceptable practice': this seems to suggest that if dignity were relevant here, evidence of 'acceptable practice' was a sufficient indicator of it having been met. Lady Hale was critical of this approach, highlighting that no evidence had been submitted to support this acceptable practice: in fact she suggested that the evidence would tend to disagree with that approach.[42] The range of literature and guidance on caring for individuals who suffer incontinence would suggest that dignity is a key aspect of their care.[43] Although the applicant was continent, she was being treated as if she was not, and as such it would seem that the guidance on incontinence care could be a starting point in evaluating the care. The difference between 'accepted practice' and 'expected practice' in health care is one which has also been discussed in the context of negligence by Samanta.[44]

Within the ECtHR dicta there is also limited reference to the concept of dignity, although the Court concurred with Lady Hale and stated that dignity was engaged in this case as the applicant "was faced with the possibility of living in a manner which 'conflicted with her strongly held ideas of self and personal identity'."[45] The Court associated the concept of dignity with the feelings of the applicant and not with any moral standard of conduct associated with the approach of the state. The Court went on to conclude that the 'applicant's personal feelings and desires had properly been balanced against the local authority's concern for her safety, independence and respect for other care users.'[46] As such, dignity appears to have been viewed as an interest of no greater value than safety or independence.

Throughout the *McDonald* litigation the focus was on procedural aspects of decision-making within finite resources, including a broad definition of needs as safety and privacy, with the standard of care being assessed as 'acceptable practice'. Ms McDonald's feelings of humiliation were acknowledged but the view appeared to be that her negative feelings towards the care would be temporary, as 'acceptable practice' suggested this feeling would change once she had tried the incontinence sheets. Dignity was also associated with the efforts to involve the applicant in the

[42] *Ibid.*, para 75 Lady Hales states 'Such Department of Health Guidance as there is, points the other way.' Although Lady Hale does not identify the specific guidance, see para 31 where Lord Walker identifies a statement in the Department of Health Document (2000) in support of the proposition that incontinence sheets could be provided: 'incontinence sheets should not be offered prematurely.'

[43] See for example Centre for Health Service Studies University of Kent & Royal College of Physicians (2009) *Privacy and Dignity in Continence Care Project* (2009) (available at https://kar.kent.ac.uk/24800/1/Phase_1_Privacy_and_Dignity_in_Continence_Care_Report_November_2009.pdf accessed 20/5/2015).

[44] Samanta and Samanta (2003).

[45] *McDonald v UK* [2014], *op cit.* n 1, para 47, citing *Pretty v United Kingdom* 2346/02 (2002) 35 EHRR 1.

[46] *Ibid.*, para 56.

decision-making process. Rather than being viewed as a core value to which the courts should look, it was viewed as an interest or right in the same way as autonomy and safety were regarded, and as such it seems it could be limited for the wider good in the context of finite resources. Lady Hale in her dissent does look to care standards in the context of a hospital or care home setting to identify whether the approach is acceptable, although she acknowledges that the same care is not always possible in a community setting as it would be in a hospital setting.[47] The approach to both justiciability and dignity in the case is limited: it avoids questions as to what dignity ought to mean, as well as questions as to the approach that should be taken in law, towards dignity.

3 Dignity: What Does It Mean?

Foster, although describing the concept of dignity as a 'slippery one,' argues that it is an important and useful concept, despite the criticism of it being vague.[48] In recent years debates over the meaning of dignity have increased, in the context of both law and health care discourses.[49] Often, understanding of that concept begins with reference to end of life choices and palliative care. For example, Jacobson highlights that in bioethics, debates on dignity were embedded in the controversies related to aspects of care of the dying.[50] In law, Foster highlights that courts tend to look to the concept in 'hard cases', and argues that if the concept is applicable in such cases it can also have wider relevance.[51] Foster thus views dignity 'as the transaction that constitutes the whole bioethical encounter.'[52] It is an approach which acknowledges that the concept arises from the interaction between individuals and groups; the individual is 'seen' as a person by those with whom they are interacting.[53]

The 'transaction' approach taken by Foster is appealing in that it allows for the recognition of both subjective and objective aspects of the concept of dignity. The subjective aspect can be described in terms of impacts upon the individual including feelings of humiliation, invisibility, or exclusion, while the objective aspects

---

[47] *Ibid.*, para 78 "*The Care Quality Commission's Guidance, Essential Standards of Quality and Safety*" (2010), p. 117 requires that people who use services have access to toilets, baths and showers which will enable them to maintain privacy and dignity, in close proximity to their living areas. The Commission's recent *Review of Compliance* at Ipswich Hospital NHS Trust found that dignity was not always sufficiently considered because people were not taken to a toilet away from their bed-space and commodes were used all the time", p. 8.

[48] Foster (2011), p. 4.

[49] *Ibid.*, Chapters 5–7.

[50] See Jacobson (2007), pp. 297–299.

[51] Foster (2011), p. 3.

[52] *Ibid.*, p. 15.

[53] Pleschburger (2007).

can be viewed in the conduct towards the individual, and the standard of conduct expected by society, of all individuals. The subjective aspect of dignity appears to equate to what in health has been described as 'personal or basic dignity' and in law as 'dignity as quality'.[54] When an individual is treated without dignity, the term 'objectification' has been used to describe the approach to their care: that is, the patient is not seen as an individual, and is lost amongst the processes of tasks and budgets.[55] That focus on the elements of care, rather than looking to the individual being cared for, has been one of the criticisms made in respect of the separation of social and health care, leading to calls for increasingly multi-disciplinary approaches to ensure that the holistic needs of the individual are both recognized and met.[56] The recognition of such an integrated, person-centred approach has also been called for at governance level.[57] Given these factors, it is interesting that only limited references to health have been made in the *McDonald* case,[58] with no real consideration of the long term impacts upon maintaining and improving 'functional capacities' such as continence.[59]

The objective aspect of dignity appears to equate to a 'moral standard' or what has been described in law as a 'status' concept: in other words it appears to be associated with the value placed upon the individual by society.[60] As such, it is unsurprising that dignity in law is closely associated with concepts of equality, whether generally or in the context of human rights law. This approach of splitting dignity into two major categories is supported by qualitative research in health care.[61]

In spite of the difficulties in defining dignity, there have been attempts by the professional regulatory bodies and unions for health and social care practitioners to explain the concept. The more detailed attempts, Foster suggests, are found in the context of nursing,[62] although he highlights that all the definitions are subject to criticism. The need for these professions to explain the concept is telling as to the importance which they place on its value in health and social care.[63] Thus, there is a growing body of health care research which seeks to understand what dignity means from the perspective of those receiving care or providing care, on how dignity

[54] See Foster (2011) and Jacobson (2007).

[55] Band-Winterstein (2015), pp. 1–15.

[56] Department of Health (2014), para 5.20.

[57] Newdick (2014).

[58] *McDonald v UK* (2014), *op cit.* n 1, paras 30–34. The relevant international law referred to was the UN Convention on The Rights of Persons with Disabilities and the European Union Charter of Fundamental Rights.

[59] See General Comment 14, *op cit.* n 34 (which will be discussed further in this essay, in the context of the International Right to Health.) Although a referral was offered in relation to incontinence care, this was refused as she was in fact continent.

[60] Oosterveld-Vlug et al. (2014).

[61] See Foster (2011), p. 75 citing Pleschburger (2007).

[62] *Ibid.*

[63] *Ibid.*

should be measured, and the factors influencing subjective and objective concepts of dignity.[64] One study, based upon a small sample, suggests that patients recognise that quality of life and dignity are not necessarily synonymous concepts, although the likelihood of violations of dignity does increase for those requiring support from others, such as occurs for persons living in care homes.[65] This emphasizes that when there is some aspect of dependence, the potential for dignity to be compromised increases.[66] The studies, much as Foster's theoretical examples in relation to dignity also do, highlight that dignity is not solely about autonomy or independence, or about the way we are made to feel, but also about how the individual is treated: that treatment provides an indication also of how wider society views that individual.[67] The studies, in their attempts to identify factors which 'maintain or retain dignity,' give rise to a common theme of dignity as an 'evaluation of oneself in close relation to others.'[68] Arguably this still leaves some sense of vagueness associated with the concept, which requires greater clarification within the context of the law.

The concept of dignity in law has traditionally been considered in challenges related to 'end of life' decisions[69]; individual integrity and autonomy[70]; equality[71] and human rights.[72] There is also a need to consider the concept in the context of health and social care law, and in particular in respect of access to treatment cases. As with the understanding of dignity in health, understanding of the concept in law seems however to have been discussed to a large extent within end of life contexts, namely those cases which Foster describes as 'hard cases'. In the context of the *McDonald* case, the ECtHR referred to *Pretty v UK*[73] to discuss one aspect of dignity, which is 'self-identity' and the right to choose. Other aspects which the Courts have recognized include 'physical integrity' and equality.[74] McCrudden suggests that there are three aspects to the 'minimum core' of dignity in human rights law which include: (1) 'the intrinsic worth of the human being,' (2) respect for the intrinsic worth of the human being and (3) that "...the state should be seen to exist for the sake of the individual human being, and not vice versa (the 'limited-

---

[64] See for example Pleschburger (2007); Royal College of Nursing (2008b). Cairns et al. (2013); Oosterveld-Vlug et al. (2014).

[65] Ibid., p. 26.

[66] Ibid. See also Pleschburger (2007).

[67] Foster (2011); chapter 1 provides hypothetical examples to highlight this point.

[68] Oosterveld-Vlug et al. (2014), p. 26.

[69] See for example *Airedale N.H.S. Trust v Bland* [1993] A.C. 789; *Pretty v. United Kingdom* (2002) 2346/02 (2002) 35 EHRR 1.

[70] See for example *Tyrer v United Kingdom* [1978] ECHR 2; *Pretty v. United Kingdom* (2002) *ibid.*

[71] See Moon (2006); Moon and Allen (2006) in relation to Canadian law; O'Connell (2008) in respect of the European Convention on Human Rights.

[72] See McCrudden (2008) on the approach to dignity within Human Rights law.

[73] *Pretty v. United Kingdom, op cit.* n 69.

[74] McCrudden (2008), p. 723.

state' claim)."[75] He goes on to consider the nature of dignity, and questions whether it is a right which can be enforced or a principle from which rights can be derived, and which underpins judicial interpretation.[76] He suggests that dignity is best viewed as a notion 'underpinning' other rights.[77] This would suggest that it is a value within the law of this jurisdiction. This was the perspective put forward by Lord Justice Munby in *Burke v General Medical Council*[78] when he said that dignity

> is a core value of the common law, long pre-dating the Convention...the invocation of dignity of the patient in the form of declaration habitually used when the court is exercising its inherent declaratory jurisdiction in relation to the gravely ill or dying is not some meaningless incantation...it is a solemn affirmation of the law's and society's recognition of our humanity and of human dignity as something fundamental.[79]

Although the Court of Appeal was critical of Lord Justice Munby in this case, his comments on dignity were 'not disapproved'.[80] One criticism by Foster of the approach of Munby J in the *Burke* case, is over his view that autonomy and dignity have equivalence in law. Foster suggests that 'dignity is a deeper concept than autonomy,'[81] and although he describes both concepts as rights he refers to 'dignity as the parent right'.[82] Arguably dignity is more than a right (if McCrudden's description of the minimum core is accepted; it is a value which underpins rights, and is the standard by which rights implementation is assessed. It should not be subject to limitation in the way that autonomy would be when assessed against other rights. Yet despite dignity being the 'parent right', in the *McDonald* litigation it is trumped by the need for safety in the context of finite resources. Contrast this with the approach of the ECtHR in respect of autonomy and safety in deprivation of liberty challenges and the requirement for safeguards.[83] An approach where dignity is balanced against interests or rights such as autonomy or safety, contradicts the description of it as being fundamental, or as being a value which underpins rights.

If dignity is a value within the context of human rights and equality law, it ought to be the context in which rights protection is considered (whether that is described as the 'standard of a civilized society', the 'expected practice' or a 'measure of humanity').[84] Such a standard would have imposed a positive obligation upon the council in *McDonald v UK* to ensure that care met that standard. It would have

[75] *Ibid.*, p. 679.

[76] *Ibid.*, pp. 680–681.

[77] *Ibid.*, p. 683 (citing *Pretty v. United Kingdom, op cit.* n 69).

[78] *R (On the Application of Burke) v General Medical Council* [2005] QB 424.

[79] *Ibid.*, para 57.

[80] Foster (2011), p. 101.

[81] *Ibid.*, p. 110. He goes on to say that autonomy is a manifestation of dignity.

[82] *Ibid.*

[83] *HL v UK* 45508/99 (2004) ECHR 471.

[84] *Burke v General Medical Council* [2005], *op cit.* n 78, para 71, citing, para 72, Baroness Hale (2004), p. 22.

required the Court to question how the needs of the individual were to be met, in a way that was consistent with dignity. To date, as Foster has highlighted, the adoption and development of dignity as a standard, or what he has called a 'lodestone,' has not been taken up by the Courts. Fabre also suggests that dignity can contribute to '. . .a common metric by which to judge the relative importance of conflicting interests.'[85] That common metric can be described in terms of a 'minimal decent life' and equality.[86] In the context of health care, as previously argued in this chapter, there is empirical evidence to suggest that 'expected practice', with reference to dignity, can be defined. In the particular facts of the *McDonald* case it would require looking to the NHS values, professional codes of conduct and the existing research in relation to incontinence (the outcome in this case would have similar implications for the applicant as for those who actually are incontinent) and the approach to dignity and health within those standards.[87] Foster highlights the relevance of *Bolam v Friern Hospital Management Committee*[88] and the requirement in negligence cases for a practice to be 'endorsed by a responsible body of opinion in the relevant specialty' as a useful approach to look at standards of care, an approach which Samanta suggests involves looking to 'expected' and not 'accepted' practice.[89] A right to health approach requires that care should be based upon need, and that the care in question is 'scientifically and medically appropriate'.[90]

Réaume suggests that a failure to respect human dignity is associated with 'prejudice, stereotyping and exclusion from benefits or opportunities.'[91] Given the acknowledgment that ageism exists in health care provision it is unsurprising that failure to respect dignity is a recurring theme in reports and inquiries on health care provision involving older people.[92] It ultimately comes back to the value which society places upon the individual:

> the more important a particular benefit is to one's ability to participate fully in society, or the more it is a marker of true belonging in society, the more one should worry that exclusion from it will carry the connotation that members of the excluded group deserve less respect.[93]

[85] Fabre (2000), p. 2.

[86] Fredman (2006), p. 60; Moon (2006); Moon and Allen (2006).

[87] In particular see the Centre for Health Service Studies University of Kent & Royal College of Physicians (2009).

[88] [1957] 1 WLR 583; See also Samanta and Samanta (2003) on the impact of *Bolitho v City and Hackney Health Authority* [1998] AC 232 on *Bolam.*

[89] Foster (2011), p. 7.

[90] CESCR General Comment 14 (2000), para 12 (d).

[91] Moon (2006), p. 705, citing Réaume (2003), p. 672.

[92] See Harris and Regmi (2012), pp. 263–266; Parliamentary and Health Service Ombudsman (2011). See also Northern Ireland Human Rights Commission (2015).

[93] Moon (2006) citing Réaume (2003), p. 695.

Strikingly, in contrast to a developing advocacy and a large body of evidence of ageism and the rights of older people, there is a limited body of case law relating to older people and health care.[94] The reaction to the evidence of ageism and the issue of dignity within health care, has seen an upsurge in research on the meaning of dignity in health and social care, as well as campaigns to ensure greater respect for individual dignity. This would suggest that in respect of litigation on health and social care access, the courts ought to give more consideration to this normative legal value. A starting point in developing a more meaningful, rights-led approach to dignity in this particular context could be via the international right to health.

4 Dignity and the Right to Health

The argument that Article 12 ICESCR is an important starting point in developing greater understanding of dignity is made despite the UK's view that the Covenant does not give rise to justiciable rights, but to principles that guide policy.[95] The UK state reports to the Committee on Economic, Social and Cultural Rights (CESCR), the Treaty monitoring body of the ICESCR, suggest that policy and action on health (not least in relation to older people) is compliant with right to health requirements.[96] As such, there is an acknowledgement by the UK of the right to health, irrespective of their view of the right as a non-justiciable one.[97] Whether the right is viewed as a set of principles to guide policy or as a justiciable right, the starting point to understanding it is found in General Comment 14 of the Committee on Economic, Social and Cultural Rights.[98]

General Comment 14 describes the right as comprising of those freedoms and entitlements which are necessary in order that an individual can attain 'the highest attainable standard of health conducive to a life in dignity' possible for them.[99] Two important caveats exist in relation to this standard; (1) there are aspects beyond the

[94] Rodriquez-Pinzon and Martin (2003).

[95] United Kingdom's 5th Periodic Report on Implementation of the International United Nations Covenant on Economic, Social and Cultural Rights (31 January 2008) E/C.12/GBR/5, paras 51 and 74.

[96] *Ibid.*, paras 296–325.

[97] Department of Health NHS Constitution for England (2013) (available at https://www.gov.uk/government/uploads/system/uploads/attachment_data/file/170656/NHS_Constitution.pdf accessed 19/5/2015). Although the phrase 'right to health' is not specifically used within the Constitution, many of the rights associated with it are identifiable, e.g. non-discrimination; See also Department of Health, Social Services and Public Safety for Northern Ireland (June 2014) *Making Life Better: A Whole System Strategic Framework for Public Health* 2013–2023 (available at http://www.dhsspsni.gov.uk/mlb-strategic-framework-2013-2023.pdf accessed 18/5/2015), p. 8 in which the 'right to the highest attainable standard of health' is acknowledged as an underpinning value.

[98] General Comment 14 (2000), *op cit.* n 34.

[99] *Ibid.*, para 1 The definition in Article 12(1) is developed with reference to dignity.

control of the state in respect of what health level can be achieved by an individual[100] and (2) the individual right to those freedoms and entitlements which are within the control of the state can be lawfully limited. Lawful limitation of the right is allowed on the same grounds as civil and political rights, and in addition, state discretion is afforded in implementation of the right within the context of available resources and the point from which progress in implementation of the right to health starts.[101] Two overlapping approaches have been developed to explain the obligations imposed upon the state, which are subject to limitation; both can be identified within General Comment 14.[102]

The first of the frameworks to explain state obligations revolves around a traditional obligations approach to human rights, and is associated with civil and political rights as much as with economic, social and cultural rights. That framework is the tri-partite obligations of 'respect, protect, and fulfill'.[103] The second framework has been described as a useful tool to examine state policy,[104] and involves viewing state conduct in the context of questioning *what* should be made available and *who* has access. The literature also speaks of acceptability and quality, and sometimes affordability, in relation to entitlements. However, this chapter focuses on availability and accessibility, viewing the facets of acceptability, affordability and quality as aspects of that broader categorization. The overlap of these characteristics with the concepts of availability and accessibility can be seen in the context of the *McDonald* case. The care she wanted, namely, the provision of carers to assist her in accessing toilet facilities during the night, was not provided; instead, an alternate care package was provided, which was the supply of 'incontinence sheets'. The state view, and indeed the ECtHR view, was that acceptable care was provided within the available resources: the alternative view would be that there was no access to the necessary care, given that the care plan gave rise to questions of acceptability on the part of Ms McDonald. In assessing the right of access to care, including the quality of care, the court looked largely to affordability, and viewed the acceptability of the care from the perspective of the care provider only.

The framework of availability and accessibility allows questions to be asked on how decisions are made as well as in respect of the impact of those decisions. General Comment 14 provides guidance on what should be considered in looking at those decisions. Procedural aspects to be considered include: whether decisions are based on scientific evidence and assessed needs, whilst the impact of those

[100] *Ibid.*, paras 8 and 9.

[101] *Ibid.*, para 31.

[102] *Ibid.*, paras 34–37; See also United Nations Commission on Human Rights, *Report of the Special Rapporteur on the Right of Everyone to the Enjoyment of the Highest Attainable Standard of Physical and Mental Health, Paul Hunt* (11 February 2005) E/CN.4/2005/51 who discusses these frameworks, paras 46–50.

[103] See Sepulveda (2003) for an overview of the development of the recognition of these obligations.

[104] Hunt (2005), para 46.

decisions is considered in the context of whether they are discriminatory, provide for equality of opportunity, and are 'conducive to a life in dignity.' The scope of what should be made available (freedoms and entitlements) can be considered with reference to Article 12(2), which outlines broad programmatic areas of the right to health. However given the breadth of the programmatic area, and the acknowledgement in General Comment 14 of the broad definition of health, the scope of the right is arguably determined by the impact on health. Three references are made to the concept of dignity in the main text of General Comment 14.[105] The right is described as the right to 'the highest attainable standard of health conducive to living a life in dignity'[106] suggesting that dignity is part of the definition of the right as well as a standard to be met. It also seems to be a pre-requisite for realisation of the right, when the right to health is described as being dependent upon other human rights 'as contained in the International Bill of Rights', one of which is stated as 'human dignity'.[107] The third reference to dignity is found in the context of care for older people. The concept is associated with care which should 'maintain the functional capacities' of older people through preventive care as well as via curative care.[108] It is not clear given the formulation of the statement if this is a general principle to be applied in respect of the right to health or one associated with the care of the terminally ill only. The rationale for an approach which focuses on supporting the 'maintenance of functional capacities,' appears to be associated with resources: the argument made is that over a longer time care will be less resource intensive.[109] Reference is also made to General Comment 6 on the economic, social and cultural rights of older persons, which in turn emphasizes the importance of the United Nations Principles on Older Persons (1991)[110] which states that

> older persons should be able to live in dignity and security and be free of exploitation and physical or mental abuse, should be treated fairly, regardless of age, gender, racial or ethnic background, disability, financial situation or any other status, and be valued independently of their economic contribution.[111]

General Comment 14 seems to suggest that dignity ought to be part of any rights approach, including a right to health approach. However, given the limited references to the concept it is difficult to identify what exactly that means within any

[105] General Comment 14 (2000), paras 1, 3 and 25. A further reference is made in footnote 13 of the General Comment to 'healthy, natural and workplace environments'.

[106] *Ibid.*, para 1.

[107] *Ibid.*, para 3.

[108] *Ibid.*, para 25.

[109] *Ibid.* See also CESCR (1993) General Day of Discussion on the Rights of the Ageing and Elderly with Respect to Rights recognized in the Covenant, 20 December 1993, E/C.12/1993/SR.12. The concept of dignity was mentioned in the context of independence and involvement with the community.

[110] United Nations Principles for Older Persons, 16 December 1991, General Assembly resolution 46/91.

[111] *Ibid.* Article 17 as cited in CESCR *General Comment No 6: The Economic, Social and Cultural Rights of Older Persons* (8 December 1995). Contained in E/1996/22, para 5.

right to health approach. One aspect is that dignity appears to be a part of the definition of a right to health ('the highest attainable standard of health conducive to living a life in dignity').[112] A second aspect, raised in respect of older persons, is that 'functional capacities' should be supported, although here it appears to be about supporting and maintaining independence. The final three aspects of the concept in General Comment 14, are, it is suggested, more in keeping with the traditional perspectives of dignity in law: (1) dignity as associated with individual integrity (freedom from inhumane and degrading treatment and torture),[113] (2) dignity as associated with non-discrimination and equality law[114] and (3) dignity as associated with care for the terminally ill.[115]

The concluding observations of the Committee on Economic Social and Cultural Rights, responsible for monitoring the implementation of the ICESCR, appear to offer limited further guidance on the meaning of dignity in the context of the right to health. A review of the concluding observations in 2014, and a search within the Bayefsky database of concluding observations until 2005, highlights few references to the term 'dignity' in association with health.[116] As with General Comment 14, when dignity is explicitly used, it is referred to as a standard with which legislation should be consistent.[117] One factor of that standard is found in the concept of 'inhumane conditions',[118] although this linkage of dignity to inhumane conditions is found in a discussion report between the Committee and the State, in respect of the State report and not the concluding observations.[119] In the discussion report, concerns related to state-run nursing homes were acknowledged by the state

[112] *Ibid.*, para 1.

[113] General comment 14 (2000).

[114] *Ibid.*

[115] *Ibid.*, para 25.

[116] In a review of the 2014 Concluding Observations of the CESCR there are only two references to the concept of dignity. See CESCR *Concluding Observations regarding El Salvador* (19 June 2014). E/C.12/SLV/CO/3-5, para 22, CESCR; CESCR *Concluding Observations regarding China, including Hong Kong, China and Macao* (13 June 2014) E/c.12/CHN/CO/2, para 30. The issue of forced evictions in the context of city renewal sees the state urged to ensure '...free, prior and informed consent and with full respect for their safety and dignity.' A thematic search of the Bayefsky.com site also highlights limited references to the concept, with only 6 references made to the concept up until 2001 and 3 references between 2001 and 2005.

[117] *Ibid.* Concluding Observations regarding El Salvador, para 22 "The Committee urges the State party to revise its legislation on the total prohibition of abortion to make it compatible with other fundamental rights such as the woman's right to health and life, and consistent with the dignity of women."

[118] CESCR *Concluding Observations regarding Germany* (24 September 2001) E/C.12/1/Add/68, paras 24 and 42. The observations refer to a grave concern about 'inhumane conditions' in nursing homes for older people.

[119] Economic and Social Council *Summary Record of the 49th Meeting Regarding Germany* (30 August 2001). E/C.12/2001/SR.49, para 67 (a statement by Mr Willers, a representative of the State).

representative, including the fact that care "quality was poor, and many, instead of providing active nursing care, resorted to passive treatment in the form of sedation, with a resulting high incidence of incontinence, malnutrition and dehydration."[120] It was an acknowledgment of the need for change, particularly when the state believed that "living standards were governed by a series of laws and that the aim of social welfare was to enhance human dignity".[121] However in the concluding observations it was concerns in respect of conditions that were raised, with no mention of dignity.

In 2011 the Special Rapporteur on the Right to Health provided a 'thematic report' on the right to health of older people which expands on some aspects of dignity.[122] In that report there are eight references to the term 'dignity' in the context of older people which includes the perception of dignity as (1) part of a right to health approach,[123] (2) an aim or standard for care in life[124] and in terminal illness,[125] (3) related to the security or integrity of the individual[126] and (4) as an aspect of autonomy. In relation to autonomy two references are interesting and include firstly, as per General Comment 14, the need to maintain the functional capacities of older people,[127] (although again this is a very broad concept and in this instance appears to relate to contribution to society as much as to physical capacity) and secondly the Special Rapporteur makes mention of "the impact of institutionalization on the autonomy of older persons and its often harmful effect on their dignity."[128] A further aspect of indignity was also highlighted, namely the linkage to 'humiliation' in the statement "[l]oss of full independence, restricted freedom of movement and lack of access to basic functions would cause feelings of deep frustration and humiliation to any individual. Older persons are no exception to this."[129] The last comment has particular resonance in the *McDonald* litigation. A further comment by the Special Rapporteur on dignity, which is worth stating in full, is that "older persons must be treated with as much dignity during the process of dying as they should have been in the early phases of their life course."[130] The statement highlights the development of the concept in approaches to end of life

[120] *Ibid.*

[121] *Ibid.*, para 68 (a statement by Ms Kuck-Schneelmelcher, a representative of the State). Despite this the issue was raised again in the CESCR *Concluding Observations regarding Germany* (12 July 2011) E/C.12/DEU/CO/5, para 27 where the Committee on ESCR observed that the state had not taken sufficient measures to deal with the difficulties in state nursing homes.

[122] Grover (2011).

[123] *Ibid.*, para 10.

[124] *Ibid.*, para 11.

[125] *Ibid.*, paras 21, 54, 59–60.

[126] *Ibid.*, para 61.

[127] *Ibid.*, para 21.

[128] *Ibid.*, paras 49 and 61 where dignity and autonomy are also associated together.

[129] *Ibid.*, para 49.

[130] Grover (2011), para 60.

care. Although dignity seems to be acknowledged as a key standard within the right to health, there is a need to develop understanding of that concept further not only in relation to care of the dying but also in respect of all aspects of care to enable a standard of health which is conducive to living a life in dignity.

The centrality of the concept of dignity to the right to health is reflected in a recent 'right to health assessment' of emergency health care by the Northern Ireland Human Rights Commission.[131] Within the report the concept of dignity is frequently referred to, and is equated with a 'person-centred approach' to care,[132] although the report suggests there is more to do to understand dignity when it states that:

> There are, however, a number of gaps in the referencing of human rights in domestic law. The operational meaning of "dignity" is often lacking within both the Quality Standards and the PCE Standards. It is therefore difficult to ascertain how "dignity," including dignity in death, can be put into effect, especially in the challenging environment of an [emergency department][133]

The research to develop the operationalization of the concept already exists if reference is made to existing case law and empirical research on health care practice, although it is accepted that more needs to be done on this. Both research and case law can contribute to the understanding of the notion of dignity within 'a right to health' approach to health and social care.

5 Conclusion

If "...policies in respect of the elderly reflect the ethical principles of society"[134] then there is a need to question which ethical principles have relevance in decisions on access to health and social care for the elderly. The evidence that would suggest that dignity ought to be a central value which requires greater consideration includes: (1) it is a recurring theme where failures of care have been identified, (2) there is a growing body of literature and empirical work on the concept of dignity in health and in law which courts can look to, to question the application of dignity in the context of particular legal questions and (3) dignity is a central value which informs human rights protections. If the access to health and social care litigation were to be considered in the context of a right to health approach, then a fourth factor can be identified: it is part of the core standard of the right. The central

---

[131] NIHRC (2015), p. 92.

[132] Ibid., p. 17. 'Dignity' was referred to 107 times. The inquiry found no systemic evidence of violations.

[133] Ibid., p. 21.

[134] General Day of Discussion on the Rights of the Ageing and Elderly (1993), *op cit*. n 110, para 29.

argument against using dignity as a core standard lies in the criticism that it remains a too vague, unclear concept, a criticism which is less true today. In recent years there has been an increase in empirical research on the concept, which provides some guidance as to what dignity means in respect of health and social care practice, (and in the context of particular types of care) which can in turn contribute to the development of dignity as a norm within the current narrow approach to justiciability of access to care challenges. This research provides guidance on how dignity is perceived and maintained in care settings. A consideration of empirical evidence as to what dignity means in relation to continence care, including the requirement to 'maintain functional capacities,' ought to have been relevant to the discourses throughout the *McDonald* litigation. However if dignity is to become a meaningful standard in access to health care litigation (and provide what O'Cinneide describes as a 'normative steer'[135]) in a way that would not create 'judicial overreach,'[136] then greater consideration needs to be given to its meaning and its application, both within the international right to health jurisprudence and in the approaches of the ECtHR and the domestic courts respectively.

References

Band-Winterstein, T. (2015). Health care provision for older persons: The interplay between ageism and elder neglect. *Journal of Applied Gerontology, 34*, NP113–27.

Cairns, D., Williams, V., Victor, C., Richards, S., Le May, A., Martin, W., et al. (2013). The meaning and importance of dignified care: Findings from a survey of health and social care professionals. *BMC Geriatrics, 13*, 28. doi:10.1186/1471-2318-13-28.

Callahan, D. (2012). Must we ration health care for the elderly. *Journal of Law Medicine and Ethics, 40*, 10–16.

Clements, L. (2011). Disability, dignity and the *cri de coeur*. *European Human Rights Law Review, 6*, 675–685.

Clough, B., & Brazier, M. (2014). Never too old for health and human rights. *Medical Law International, 14*(3), 133–156.

Department of Health. (2001). NHS constitution for England and Wales. http://www.nhs.uk/NHSEngland/thenhs/about/Pages/nhscoreprinciples.aspx. 18/5/2015.

Department of Health. (2014, January) The hard truth: The journey to putting people first. Volume One of the Government Response to the Mid Staffordshire NHS Foundation Trust Public Inquiry. Cm 8777. https://www.gov.uk/government/uploads/system/uploads/attachment_data/file/270368/34658_Cm_8777_Vol_1_accessible.pdf. 2/6/2015.

Fabre, C. (2000). *Social rights under the constitution: Government and decent life*. Oxford, England: Oxford University Press.

Foster, C. (2011). *Human dignity in bioethics and law*. Oxford, England: Hart.

[135] O'Cinneide (2013), p. 403. In the context of the discussion on accountability, the 'normative steer' is being suggested in relation to social justice.

[136] *Ibid.*, p. 408. In particular O'Cinneide (2013) suggests that judicial review should only be available where a 'sufficiently grave situation' arises and that social justice is an important aspect of legal accountability.

Fredman, S. (2006). From deference to democracy: The role of equality under the Human Rights Act 1998. *Law Quarterly Review, 122*, 53–81.
Grover, A. (2011, July 4). *Thematic study on the realization of the right to health of older persons by the special rapporteur on the right to everyone to the enjoyment of the highest attainable standard of physical and mental health, Arnand Grover*. A/HRC/18/37.
Harris, J., & Regmi, S. (2012). Ageism and equality. *Journal of Medical Ethics, 38*(5), 263–266.
Jacobson, N. (2007). Dignity and health: A review. *Social Science and Medicine, 64*, 292–302.
McCrudden, C. (2008). Human dignity and judicial interpretation of human rights. *European Journal of International Law, 19*(4), 655–724.
Moon, G., & Allen, R. (2006). Dignity discourse in discrimination law: A better route to equality? *European Human Rights Law Review, 6*, 610–642.
Moon, G. (2006). From equal treatment to appropriate treatment: What lessons can Canadian equality law on dignity and on reasonable accommodation teach the United Kingdom? *European Human Rights Law Review, 6*, 695–721.
Newdick, C. (2004). *Who should we treat? Rights, rationing, and resources in the NHS* (2nd ed.). Oxford, England: Oxford University Press.
Newdick, C. (2014). From hippocrates to commodities: Three models of NHS governance. *Medical Law Review, 22*(4), 162–184.
Northern Ireland Human Rights Commission. (2015). Emergency health care. http://www.nihrc.org/uploads/publications/NIHRC_Emergency_Healthcare_Report.pdf. 3/05/2015.
O'Cinneide, C. (2013). Legal accountability and social justice. In N. Bamforth & P. Leyland (Eds.), *Accountability in the contemporary constitution* (pp. 385–410). Oxford, England: Oxford University Press.
O'Connell, R. (2008). The role of dignity in equality law: Lessons from South Africa and Canada. *International Journal of Constitutional Law, 6*(2), 267–286.
Oosterveld-Vlug, M., Pasman, H., van Gennip, I., de Vet, C., & Onwuteaka-Philipsen, B. (2014). Assessing the validity and intra-observer agreement of the MIDAM-LTC; An instrument measuring factors that influence personal dignity in long-term care facilities. *Quality of Life and Health Outcomes, 12*, 17. doi:10.1186/1477-7525-12-17.
Parliamentary and Health Service Ombudsman. (2011). Care and compassion? Report of Health Service Ombudsman on ten investigations into NHS care of older people. http://www.ombudsman.org.uk/__data/assets/pdf_file/0016/7216/Care-and-Compassion-PHSO-0114web.pdf. 28/05/2015.
Pleschburger, S. (2007). Dignity and dying in nursing homes: The residents' views. *Age and Dying, 36*(2), 197–202.
Pritchard-Jones, L. (2015). Night-time care, Article 8 and the European Court of Human Rights: A missed opportunity. *Journal of Social Welfare and Family Law, 37*, 108–110.
Réaume, D. (2003). Discrimination and dignity. *Louisiana Law Review, 63*, 645–695.
Rodriquez-Pinzon, D., & Martin, C. (2003). The International Human Rights status of elderly person. *American University International Law Review, 18*(4), 915–1008.
Royal College of Nursing. (2008a). Dignity campaign. http://www.rcn.org.uk/development/practice/dignity/story_of_the_rcn_dignity_campaign. 18/5/2015.
Royal College of Nursing. (2008b). Defending dignity. Challenges and opportunities for nursing. Royal College of Nursing. http://www.rcn.org.uk/__data/assets/pdf_file/0011/166655/003257.pdf. 20/5/2015.
Samanta, A., & Samanta, S. (2003). Legal standard of care: A shift from the traditional Bolam Test. *Clinical Medicine, 3*(5), 443–446.
Sepulveda, M. (2003). *The nature of the obligations under the International Covenant on Economic, Social and Cultural Rights' School of Human Rights Research Series 18*. Antwerp, Belgium: Intersentia.
United Kingdom 5th Periodic Report on Implementation of the International United Nations Covenant on Economic, Social and Cultural Rights (31 January 2008) E/C.12/GBR/5.

United Nations Material

International Covenant on Economic, Social and Cultural Rights (adopted 16 December 1966, entered into force 3 January 1976), 993 United Nations Treaty Series 3 (ICESCR).
CESCR *Concluding Observations regarding Germany* (24 September 2001) E/C.12/1/Add/68.
CESCR *Concluding Observations regarding Germany* (12 July 2011) E/C.12/DEU/CO/5.
CESCR *Concluding Observations regarding El Salvador* (19 June 2014). E/C.12/SLV/CO/3-5.
CESCR *Concluding Observations regarding China, including Hong Kong, China and Macao* (13 June 2014) E/c.12/CHN/CO/2.
CESCR *Concluding Observations regarding El Salvador* (19 June 2014) E/C.12/SLV/CO/3-5.
CESCR *General Day of Discussion on the Rights of the Ageing and Elderly in Respect to Rights recognized in the Covenant* (20 December 1993). E/C.12/1993/SR.12.
CESCR *General Comment No 6: The Economic, Social and Cultural Rights of Older Persons* (8 December 1995). Contained in E/1996/22.
CESCR *General Comment No 14: The Right to Health (Article 12)* (11 August 2000). E/C.12/2000/4.
Economic and Social Council *Summary Record of the 49th Meeting Regarding Germany* (30 August 2001). E/C.12/2001/SR.49.
United Nations Commission on Human Rights, *Report of the Special Rapporteur on the Right of Everyone to the Enjoyment of the Highest Attainable Standard of Physical and Mental Health, Paul Hunt* (11 February 2005) E/CN.4/2005/51.
United Nations Principles for Older Persons, 16 December 1991, General Assembly resolution 46/91.

Cases

Airedale N.H.S. Trust v Bland [1993] A.C. 789
Bolam v Friern Hospital Management Committee [1957] 1 WLR 583
Eisai Limited v. The National Institute for Health and Clinical Excellence (NICE), The Alzheimer's Society, Shire Pharmaceuticals Limited [2007] EWHC 1941 (Admin) QBD
HL v UK 45508/99 (2004) ECHR 471
McDonald v United Kingdom – 4241/12 (2014) 60 E.H.R.R. 1
Pretty v United Kingdom 2346/02 (2002) 35 EHRR 1
R (On the Application of Burke) v General Medical Council [2005] QB 424
R *(On the Application of McDonald) v Royal Borough of Chelsea and Kensington* [2011] UKSC 33
R *(On the Application of McDonald) v Royal Borough of Chelsea and Kensington* (2010) EWCA 1109
R *(On the Application of McDonald) v Royal Borough of Chelsea and Kensington* (2009) EWHC 1582 (admin)
R (on the Application of McDonald) v Royal Borough of Kensington and Chelsea [2011] UKSC 33
Tyrer v United Kingdom [1978] ECHR 2

Patent Rights, Access to Medicines, and the Justiciability of the Right to Health in Kenya, South Africa and India

Emmanuel Kolawole Oke

1 Introduction

The human right to health is accorded recognition in a number of international legal instruments and in the basic law of several countries across the world. The recognition of the right to health in legal instruments, however, is not a guarantee that it is being enjoyed on an equal basis in every country in the world. There are several reasons why certain people, particularly poor patients living in developing countries, do not enjoy the right to health. One contributory factor in this regard is the current global structure for the protection of intellectual property rights as embodied in the World Trade Organization's Agreement on Trade-Related Aspects of Intellectual Property Rights ('TRIPS Agreement'). Patent rights have a direct impact on the right to health, especially in developing countries where patented pharmaceutical products are usually priced beyond the reach of poor patients. One of the international agreements that provides for the right to health is the International Covenant on Economic, Social and Cultural Rights ('ICESCR').[1] Article 12 (1) of the ICESCR mandates the states parties to the Covenant to 'recognize the right of everyone to the enjoyment of the highest attainable standard of physical and mental health'. In 2000, the UN Committee on Economic, Social and Cultural Rights ('CESCR') adopted General Comment No. 14 in an attempt to provide further definition for Article 12 of the ICESCR.[2] Paragraph 12 of General Comment

[1] International Covenant on Economic, Social and Cultural Rights, G.A. Res. 2200A (XXI), (1996) http://www.ohchr.org/EN/ProfessionalInterest/Pages/CESCR.aspx.

[2] United Nations Committee on Economic, Social and Cultural Rights. (2000). General Comment No. 14 on the right to the highest attainable standard of health, article 12 of the International Covenant on Economic, Social and Cultural Rights. U.N. Doc. E/C.12/2000/4.

E.K. Oke (✉)
Faculty of Law, University College Cork, Corcaigh, Ireland
e-mail: e.oke@umail.ucc.ie

A. Diver, J. Miller (eds.), *Justiciability of Human Rights Law in Domestic Jurisdictions*, DOI 10.1007/978-3-319-24016-9_5

No. 14 is very relevant to the question of access to medicines. It enumerates four essential, interrelated components of the right to health: availability, accessibility, acceptability, and quality. In particular, it provides that essential drugs must be available in a country.[3]

According to the World Health Organization ('WHO'), essential drugs are drugs that 'satisfy the priority health care needs of the population' and 'are intended to be available within the context of functioning health systems at all times in adequate amounts ... and at a price the individual and the community can afford.'[4] In addition, General Comment No. 14 states that health care services must be economically accessible to everyone, suggesting that the prices of essential drugs should not be so expensive as to be unaffordable for poor patients.[5] This makes access to essential medicines at an affordable price an integral component of the right to health.[6] States have an obligation to respect, protect and fulfil the right to health.[7] The obligation to *respect* the right to health demands that states should not interfere directly or indirectly with the enjoyment of the right to health.[8] Essentially, the obligation to *respect* the right to health requires that states should, *inter alia*, 'refrain from denying or limiting equal access for all persons ... to preventive, curative and palliative health services.'[9] The obligation to *protect* the right to health requires states to, *inter alia*, 'adopt legislation or to take other measures ensuring equal access to health care and health-related services provided by third parties.'[10] The obligation to *fulfil* the right to health demands that states should, *inter alia*, 'give sufficient recognition to the right to health in the national political and legal systems, preferably by way of legislative implementation, and to adopt a national health policy with a detailed plan for realizing the right to health.'[11]

The obligation of states to respect, protect and fulfil the right to health has implications for the design, implementation, interpretation and enforcement of their national patent laws. The obligation to *respect* the right to health requires that when designing, implementing, or interpreting patent laws, the various arms and organs of government (including the courts) should not adopt an approach that interferes directly or indirectly with the enjoyment of the right to health. In order to effectively *protect* the right to health, states should ensure that the patent rights owned by third parties such as pharmaceutical companies are not permitted to be exercised

---

[3] As defined by the World Health Organization Action Programme on Essential Drugs http://apps.who.int/medicinedocs/pdf/s2237e/s2237e.pdf.

[4] World Health Organization (2015) (available http://www.who.int/topics/essential_medicines/en/ accessed 22.01.15).

[5] UN CESCR 2000, para 12(b).

[6] Hristova (2011), p. 356; United Nations Human Rights Council (2013) A/HRC/23/L.10/Rev.1.

[7] UN CESCR (2000), para 33.

[8] Ibid.

[9] Ibid., para 34.

[10] Ibid., para 35.

[11] Ibid., para 36.

and enforced in a manner that makes it more difficult for poor citizens to have access to affordable generic drugs. The obligation to *fulfil* the right to health demands that, when designing or amending their national patent laws, states should not ignore or overlook the possible implications such legislative proposals can have on the realization of the right to health. States equally have core obligations with regard to the right to health. One of the core obligations of states is to 'provide essential drugs, as from time to time defined under the WHO Action Programme on Essential Drugs.'[12] It must be stressed that this core obligation is one from which no derogation is permissible.[13]

The objective of this chapter is to examine how the national courts in three developing countries (Kenya, South Africa, and India) have addressed the tension between patent rights on pharmaceutical products and the right to health. The chapter is structured into three main sections. Section 2 examines the nature of the relationship between patent rights and the right to health while Sect. 3 deals with the justiciability of the right to health in Kenya, South Africa, and India. Section 4 provides an analysis of how the national courts of these three developing countries have adjudicated some of the pharmaceutical patent cases involving tensions between the right to health and patent rights.

2 The Nature of the Relationship Between Patent Rights and the Right to Health

There is a divergence of opinion with regard to how the relationship between patent rights and human rights should be conceptualized.[14] In his review of the literature, Gold identifies three broad approaches to the conceptualization of the relationship between patent rights and human rights:

1. The 'subjugation approach,' which states that when patent rights and human rights conflict, human rights considerations should trump patent rights;
2. The 'integrated approach,' which views patents as a human right; and
3. The 'co-existence approach,' which asserts that patent law and human rights law are distinct but share a basic concern in defining the optimal amount of patent protection required to incentivize and practice socially useful innovation.[15]

[12] Ibid., para 43(d).

[13] Ibid., para 47.

[14] See for example Drahos (1999); Helfer (2003); Yu (2007a) pp. 1039–1114; Yu (2007b), pp. 709–753; Torremans (2008); Grosheide (2010); Helfer and Austin (2011); Gold (2013); Plomer (2013).

[15] Gold (2013), pp. 186–187.

In his description of the 'subjugation approach' Helfer notes that this approach 'views human rights and intellectual property as being in fundamental conflict' and it considers

> strong intellectual property protection as undermining – and therefore as incompatible with – a broad spectrum of human rights obligations, especially in the area of economic, social, and cultural rights.[16]

He further notes that the 'prescription that proponents of this approach advocate for resolving this conflict is to recognize the normative primacy of human rights law over intellectual property law in areas where specific treaty obligations conflict.'[17] Plomer suggests that this approach 'might arguably be more accurately described as the "primacy of human rights" view.'[18] Gold describes the 'integrated approach' as an approach that assimilates 'patent rights into human rights analyses' instead of 'introducing human rights considerations into patent policy as advocated by some adherents of the subjugation approach'. The 'integrated approach' does not consider patents and human rights as distinct, rather it views 'patents as part of human rights law.'[19] However, as will be demonstrated below, advocates of the 'integrated approach' typically misconstrue the provisions of international human rights instruments such as Article 15(1)(c) of the ICESCR which provides for the protection of the moral and material interests of authors and inventors. They build their arguments on the false premise that provisions such as Article 15(1)(c) show that intellectual property rights (including patent rights) are human rights.[20] Helfer provides a description of the 'coexistence approach' as an approach that sees both human rights and intellectual property rights 'as concerned with the same fundamental question: defining the appropriate scope of private monopoly power that gives authors and inventors a sufficient incentive to create and innovate, while ensuring that the consuming public has adequate access to the fruit of their efforts.'[21] Helfer further notes that this approach

> views human rights law and intellectual property law as essentially compatible, although often disagreeing over where to strike the balance between incentives on the one hand and access on the other.[22]

Before identifying the correct one among the three approaches, it is essential to first determine the status of intellectual property rights (including patent rights) under international human rights law. Article 15(1)(c) of the ICESCR recognizes the right of everyone to 'benefit from the protection of the moral and material interests resulting from any scientific, literary or artistic production of which he is

[16] Helfer (2003), p. 48.

[17] Ibid.

[18] Plomer (2013), p. 151.

[19] Gold (2013), p. 188.

[20] Ibid.

[21] Helfer (2003), p. 48.

[22] Ibid.

the author'. A similar provision is also contained in Article 27(2) of the Universal Declaration of Human Rights (UDHR). Article 27(2) of the UDHR provides that 'Everyone has the right to the protection of the moral and material interests resulting from any scientific, literary or artistic production of which he is the author'. At first reading, these two provisions appear to equate intellectual property rights (IPRs) with other types of human rights and this has led some authors such as Millum (2008) and Marks (2009) to conclude that they provide a human rights basis for patent rights and other forms of IPRs.[23]

However, the CESCR, in its General Comment No. 17, has made it clear that human rights and IPRs are not on the same level, and it would be erroneous to rely on Article 15(1)(c) to equate intellectual property rights with human rights.[24] According to the CESCR, Article 15(1)(c) solely 'safeguards the personal link between authors and their creations ... as well as their basic material interests which are necessary to enable authors to enjoy an adequate standard of living' while 'intellectual property regimes primarily protect business and corporate interests and investments.'[25] In essence, the human right contained in Article 15(1)(c) is not coterminous with intellectual property rights. The approach adopted by the CESCR is equally supported by the drafting history of both Article 27(2) of the UDHR and Article 15(1)(c) of the ICESCR. It has been noted that the provisions were included in both instruments after considerable debate and controversy.[26] According to Chapman the drafting history of both the UDHR and ICESCR supports 'relatively weak claims of intellectual property as a human right.'[27]

Strictly speaking, the human right contained in both Article 15(1)(c) of the ICESCR and Article 27(2) of the UDHR is a right to the protection of the 'moral and material interests' of authors and inventors in their creative works. This right is separate from, and should never be confused with, intellectual property rights. The CESCR, in General Comment No. 17, stresses the point that the protection of the moral and material interests of authors and inventors does not necessarily coincide with what is currently regarded as intellectual property rights in national laws and international agreements.[28] While the right to the protection of the moral interests and material interests of authors and inventors in their creative works is a fundamental entitlement, intellectual property rights are not fundamental entitlements as they can be limited, traded, amended or even forfeited.[29] With regard to the scope

[23] Millum (2008); Marks (2009), pp. 80–99.

[24] UN CESCR (2005) General Comment No. 17 on the right of everyone to benefit from the protection of the moral and material interests resulting from any scientific, literary or artistic production of which he or she is the author, article 15(1)(c) of the ICESCR (2005), paras 1 and 3.

[25] Ibid., para 2.

[26] Yu (2007a), p. 1073.

[27] Chapman (2001).

[28] UN CESCR (2005), para 2.

[29] Ibid.

of the right to the protection of the *moral* interests of authors and inventors in their works, the CESCR notes that it includes

> the right of authors to be recognized as the creators of their scientific, literary and artistic productions and to object to any distortion, mutilation or other modification of, or other derogatory action in relation to, such productions, which would be prejudicial to their honour and reputation.[30]

In other words, the right to the protection of the *moral* interests of authors and inventors is akin to the protection of moral rights contained in the copyright laws of countries such as Germany and France.[31] The moral rights of authors should however not be confused with copyright.[32] One can thus infer from this that moral rights (as distinct from copyright) enjoy the status of human rights.

In distinguishing between the 'moral interests' of authors and inventors, and the 'material interests' of authors and inventors, the CESCR in General Comment No. 17 notes that 'Unlike other human rights, the material interests of authors are not directly linked to the personality of the creator, but contribute to the enjoyment of the right to an adequate standard of living'.[33] In other words, while the protection of the *moral interests* in intellectual creations deal with the personal connection between creators and their creations, the protection of the *material interests* in intellectual creations deal with the pecuniary connection between creators and their creations.

In an effort to distinguish between the protection of *material interests* on the one hand and the protection of intellectual property rights on the other hand, the CESCR notes that

> the purpose of enabling authors to enjoy an adequate standard of living can also be achieved through one-time payments or by vesting an author, for a limited period of time, with the exclusive right to exploit his scientific, literary or artistic production.[34]

In other words, it is not mandatory to grant patent rights or copyright in order to protect the *material interests* of intellectual workers. The right of intellectual creators to an adequate standard of living, i.e. their *material interests*, can equally be protected through other means such as one-time payments, prizes, or monetary awards.[35]

The CESCR admits that Article 15(1)(c) of the ICESCR does not specify the method or procedure for the protection of the *moral* and *material* interests of authors and inventors.[36] Nevertheless, the CESCR notes that the protection under Article 15(1)(c) 'need not necessarily reflect the level and means of protection

---

[30] Ibid., para 13.

[31] Yu (2007a), pp. 1081–1082.

[32] Drahos (1999), 14, pp. 13–14.

[33] UN CESCR (2005), para 15.

[34] Ibid., para 16.

[35] Yu (2007a), p. 1089.

[36] UN CESCR (2005), para 10.

found in present copyright, patent and other intellectual property regimes, as long as the protection available is suited to secure for authors the moral and material interests resulting from their productions.'[37]

One other factor that distinguishes the protection of *moral* and *material* interests from the protection of intellectual property rights is the fact that the former, being human rights, are inalienable rights unlike intellectual property rights. As the CESCR points out,

> intellectual property rights are generally of a temporary nature, and can be revoked, licensed or assigned to someone else. While under most intellectual property systems, intellectual property rights, often with the exception of moral rights, may be allocated, limited in time and scope, amended and even forfeited, human rights [such as the moral and material interests of authors and inventors] are timeless expressions of fundamental entitlements of the human person.[38]

The analysis provided above of the real meaning of the phrase 'moral and material interests' should be enough to dispel any notion that patent rights or any other forms of intellectual property rights are human rights as canvassed by proponents of the 'integrated approach.' Furthermore, in relation to the human rights status of intellectual property rights, it is also important to note the decision of the Constitutional Court of South Africa in *Re Certification of the Constitution of the Republic of South Africa* (1996) where with regard to the objection lodged against the failure of the new text of the South African Constitution to recognize a right to intellectual property, based on the grounds that it was a 'universally accepted fundamental right' the court held that the recognition of a right to intellectual property 'cannot be characterised as a trend which is universally accepted.'[39]

With regards to the 'coexistence approach' Gold provides a very good critique:

> ...while proponents of the coexistence approach view human rights law and patent protection as essentially compatible in theory, disagreement often arises in practice over exactly where to strike the balance between incentives for innovation on the one hand and access on the other ... little exists by way of concrete examples of just how this "coexistence" plays out in practice. At best, the coexistence asserted by the proponents of this theory is more properly viewed as a *need* for coexistence, a need that recognises that neither intellectual property rights nor human rights are likely to disappear as concepts or institutions anytime soon.[40]

In practice, it is quite difficult to foresee how human rights and intellectual property rights (including patent rights) can co-exist in all aspects. There are aspects of patent rights, particularly patent rights on pharmaceutical products and processes, that negatively impact upon the human right to health and when such conflicts occur, a practical choice has to be made between patent rights or human

---

[37] Ibid.

[38] Ibid., para 2.

[39] Re *Certification of the Constitution of the Republic of South Africa, 1996*. (1996, September 6). Case CCT 23/96, decision of the South African Constitutional Court, para 75.

[40] Gold (2013), p. 189.

rights. More importantly, any notion that patent rights and human rights can 'peacefully co-exist' is swiftly dispelled by the recent trend of incorporating TRIPS-plus standards into the bilateral and plurilateral free trade agreements negotiated (or currently being negotiated) between developed and developing countries outside the multilateral framework provided by the World Trade Organization.[41] These TRIPS-plus standards can exacerbate the negative impact that patent rights have on the enjoyment of the right to health in developing countries.

The typical TRIPS-plus standards that are included in these bilateral and plurilateral free trade agreements include: the extension of patent terms to compensate for delays in the examination of patent applications or in obtaining marketing approval for a drug; patent linkage requirements that prevent the grant of marketing approval to producers of generic drugs when there is an existing patent on the brand name drug; the grant of patents on new forms or new uses of known drugs; periods of exclusivity for clinical test data; and border enforcement measures that permit customs authorities to seize goods suspected to have infringed patent rights.[42] These TRIPS-plus standards can limit the ability of a country to use the flexibilities in the TRIPS Agreement, delay the production of cheaper generic drugs, and consequently hinder access to affordable drugs (Ibid.). There is therefore no better time than now for developing countries to insist on the primacy of human rights obligations.

The 'subjugation approach' therefore appears to be the preferable way to conceptualize the relationship between patent rights and human rights. Properly construed, the 'subjugation approach' does not suggest that patent rights should be discarded or abolished. It rather recognizes the essential distinction between the fundamental nature of human rights and the regulatory nature of patent rights. The intellectual property system (including the patent system) is best construed, according to Shubha Ghosh, as a system of rights and obligations that regulates creative activity.[43]

Thus, if patent rights are not human rights under international human rights law, there is no justifiable reason why a country should allow its patent system to trump the enjoyment of the human right to health. This does not necessarily mean that patent rights should no longer be protected, but it means that states should not permit patent rights to be exercised in ways that impede the enjoyment of the human right to health. Patent rights should be made to serve the interests protected by human rights.[44]

[41] Sell (2007), p. 59.

[42] Correa and Matthews (2011), p. 21 (available http://www.undp.org/content/dam/undp/library/hivaids/Discussion_Paper_Doha_Declaration_Public_Health.pdf.accessed. 23.01.51).

[43] Ghosh (2008), p. 106.

[44] Drahos (1998), p. 367.

3 The Right to Health in Kenya, South Africa and India

3.1 *Kenya and South Africa*

The jurisprudence on the right to health in South Africa is more robust than that of Kenya. This can be explained by the fact that the right to health was introduced into the South African Constitution in 1996, while it was only recently introduced into the Kenyan Constitution in 2010. Nevertheless, the right to health is a justiciable right in Kenya pursuant to Article 43(1)(a) of the Kenyan Constitution of 2010 which provides that everyone has the right to 'the highest attainable standard of health, which includes the right to health care services, including reproductive health care.' Thus, Kenyans can institute legal proceedings to challenge any governmental action (including legislative enactments on patent rights and other IPRs) that potentially or actually infringes their right to health.

Section 27(1)(a) of the South African Constitution of 1996 provides that everyone has the right to have access to 'health care services, including reproductive health care'. Section 27(2) further mandates the South African government to take 'reasonable legislative and other measures, within its available resources, to achieve the progressive realisation of each of these rights.' Section 27(3) provides that no one may be refused emergency medical treatment. The South African Constitutional Court has, in a line of cases, made pronouncements on the meaning and effect of these provisions on the right to health.

In *Soobramoney v. Minister of Health,* the South African Constitutional Court held that the appellant's demand to receive dialysis treatment at a state hospital must be determined in accordance with sections 27(1) & (2) which provides for access to health care services provided by the state 'within its available resources.'

> The provincial administration which is responsible for health services in KwaZulu-Natal has to make decisions about the funding that should be made available for health care and how such funds should be spent. These choices involve difficult decisions to be taken at the political level in fixing the health budget, and at the functional level in deciding upon the priorities to be met. A court will be slow to interfere with rational decisions taken in good faith by the political organs and medical authorities whose responsibility it is to deal with such matters.[45]

The court in this case adopted what Ferraz calls the 'reasonableness approach' and, as Ferraz points out, the court confined its role 'to an assessment of the rationality and good faith of the decisions taken at the political and technical branches of the state.'[46]

The 'reasonableness approach' to the right to access health care was also followed in the decision of the same court in the latter case of *Minister of Health*

[45] *Soobramoney v. Minister of Health.* (1997, November 27). Case CCT 32/97, decision of the South African Constitutional Court, para 29).

[46] Ferraz (2013), p. 385.

& Ors v. Treatment Action Campaign & Ors (No. 2) (*Minister of Health*, 2002).[47] There are however crucial differences between the facts of *Soobramoney* and those of the *Treatment Action Campaign ('TAC') case*. In the *TAC case*, TAC (an NGO involved in HIV/AIDS Advocacy) challenged the restrictions imposed by the South African government upon the availability of nevirapine (a drug that can be used to prevent mother-to-child transmission of HIV) in the public health sector.[48] The government had confined the administration of the drug to research and training sites. TAC contended that these restrictions were unreasonable vis-à-vis the provisions of the Constitution. According to TAC,

> the measures adopted by government to provide access to health care services to HIV-positive pregnant women were deficient in two material respects: first, because they prohibited the administration of nevirapine at public hospitals and clinics outside the research and training sites; and second, because they failed to implement a comprehensive programme for the prevention of mother-to-child transmission of HIV.[49]

One of the key issues the court had to consider was whether, in the light of provisions such as section 27 of the Constitution, the government was constitutionally obliged and had to be ordered to plan and implement an effective, comprehensive and progressive programme for the prevention of mother-to-child transmission of HIV throughout the country.[50] The court in applying its 'reasonableness approach' held that the

> policy of confining nevirapine to research and training sites fails to address the needs of mothers and their newborn children who do not have access to these sites. It fails to distinguish between the evaluation of programmes for reducing mother-to-child transmission and the need to provide access to health care required by those who do not have access to the sites.[51]

Unlike its attitude towards the government's policy in *Soobramoney*, in this case the court was willing to question the government's policy with regards to the administration of nevirapine and it held that 'the policy of government in so far as it confines the use of nevirapine to hospitals and clinics which are research and training sites constitutes a breach of the state's obligations under section 27(2) read with section 27(1)(a) of the Constitution.'[52] The policy was held to be unreasonable. According to the court, 'a policy of waiting for a protracted period before taking a decision on the use of nevirapine beyond the research and training sites is also not reasonable within the meaning of section 27(2) of the Constitution.'[53] The court ordered the government to, *inter alia*, remove without delay,

---

[47] *Minister of Health v. Treatment Action Campaign* (No. 2). (2002, July 5). CCT 8/02, decision of the South African Constitutional Court.

[48] Ibid., para 4.

[49] Ibid., para 44.

[50] Ibid., para 50.

[51] Ibid., para 67.

[52] Ibid., para 80.

[53] Ibid., para 81.

> the restrictions that prevent nevirapine from being made available for the purpose of reducing the risk of mother-to-child transmission of HIV at public hospitals and clinics that are not research and training sites.[54]

The implication of the *TAC* case is that, even though the South African Constitutional Court prefers to adopt a 'reasonableness approach' in its evaluation of government policies that affect socio-economic rights and despite the fact that the court equally respects the doctrine of separation of powers, where the government adopts a policy that is unreasonable and inconsistent with the provisions of the Constitution, the court can actually give an order that has an impact on policy making.

It should also be noted that in the *TAC* case, the government's policies with regard to the administration of nevirapine were not based on resource constraints as in the *Soobramoney* case. As Ferraz notes, the 'cost of providing the drug was virtually none, given a pledge by the pharmaceutical suppliers to give it for free.'[55] Even the court acknowledged the fact that the 'cost of nevirapine for preventing mother-to-child transmission is not an issue in the present proceedings' and that it was 'admittedly within the resources of the state.'[56] The government policies on nevirapine were based on what Ferraz calls 'dubious (not to say completely ungrounded) assertions that the drug in question (Nevirapine) was not scientifically proven to work.'[57]

In *Minister of Health v. New Clicks,* (*Minister of Health*, 2005),[58] the South African Constitutional Court held that the right to health also includes the right to have access to affordable medicines and that the state has an obligation to 'promote access to medicines that are affordable.'[59] According to Sachs J. in this case, 'preventing excessive profit-taking from the manufacturing, distribution and sale of medicines is more than an option for government. It is a constitutional obligation flowing from its duties under section 27(2).'[60] In the same case, Moseneke J. stated that,

> It seems self-evident that there can be no adequate access to medicines if they are not within one's means. Prohibitive pricing of medicine ... would in effect equate to a denial of the right of access to health care. Equally true is that the state bears the obligation to everyone to facilitate equity in the access to essential drugs which in turn affect the quality of care.[61]

A combined reading of section 27 of the South African Constitution and the decisions in *Soobramoney, TAC,* and *New Clicks* leads one to conclude that the right to health care in South Africa, which includes the right to have access to

[54] Ibid., para 135(3)(a).

[55] Ferraz (2013), p. 388.

[56] *Minister of Health v. Treatment Action Campaign (No. 2).* (2002, July 5). *Op cit.* n 47, para 71.

[57] Ferraz (2013), p. 388.

[58] *Minister of Health v. New Clicks.* (2005, September 30). CCT 59/2004.

[59] Ibid., para 514.

[60] Ibid., para 659.

[61] Ibid., para 706.

affordable medicines, imposes an obligation on the government to facilitate access to affordable medicines through the adoption of reasonable measures though this obligation can only be fulfilled within the limits of available resources. Furthermore, where the government adopts a policy that is inconsistent with the Constitution and which also violates the right to health, the court can demand that the government should change its policy.

3.2 *India*

The Indian Constitution, which came into force in 1950, incorporates civil and political rights as fundamental rights in Part III of the Constitution while socio-economic rights are contained in Part IV of the Constitution which deals with the Directive Principles of State Policy. In relation to health, Article 39(e), contained in Part IV of the Constitution, provides that the state shall, in particular, direct its policy towards securing 'that the health and strength of workers, men and women, and the tender age of children are not abused'. Another provision in Part IV of the Constitution that touches on health is Article 41 which provides *inter alia* that the state 'shall, within the limits of its economic capacity and development, make effective provision for securing the right to ... public assistance in cases of ... sickness and disablement'. Furthermore, Article 47, also contained in Part IV of the Constitution, provides *inter alia* that the state 'shall regard the raising of the level of nutrition and the standard of living of its people and the improvement of public health as among its primary duties.'

However, the provisions of Part IV of the Indian Constitution are non-justiciable. According to Article 37 of the Constitution, the provisions of Part IV of the Constitution 'shall not be enforceable by any court' though 'the principles therein laid are nevertheless fundamental in the governance of the country' and the state has the duty 'to apply these principle in making laws.' Initially, the Indian Supreme Court adopted a strict approach towards the interpretation of this prohibition against the justiciability of the Directive Principles of State Policy. As Dhanda points out,

> In the early years, this prohibition of justiciability was strictly interpreted by the Supreme Court. Thus, the Court ruled that legislation was required for the implementation of the Directives. The [Directive Principles of State Policy] without more did not create a justiciable right in favour of individuals. Consequently, courts could not compel the state to carry out any of the [Directive Principles of State Policy]. Further, due to the prohibition on justiciability, no law could be declared void on the ground that it infringed the [Directive Principles of State Policy].[62]

In subsequent years, however, the Indian Supreme Court began to adopt an 'expanded reading' of the justiciable provisions on civil and political rights and

[62] Dhanda (2013), p. 406.

they 'started to pronounce upon matters of health which were by the text of the Constitution included in the [Directive Principles of State Policy].'[63] Essentially, the court found a way of 'settling the contours of the right to health' through the adoption of an expansive reading of the fundamental right to life contained in Article 21 of the Indian Constitution. According to Article 21 of the Indian Constitution, 'No person shall be deprived of his life or personal liberty except according to procedure established by law.'

Dhanda notes that the Indian Supreme Court 'started with a very formal and legalistic interpretation' of the right to life by ruling 'that the deprivation of life and liberty was permissible provided it was done by a duly enacted parliamentary legislation.'[64] The Supreme Court moved progressively from this formal and legalistic interpretation and it started to expand the ambit of the right to life by first enhancing 'the fairness requirements of the right to life and liberty depriving procedure' and then the court later pronounced on 'the quality of life guaranteed by the Constitution.'[65] The court ruled that the right to life 'was not a right to bare physical existence but a right to a full and meaningful life. And a full and meaningful life includes the right to health within its purview.'[66] Some of the cases where the Indian Supreme Court has made pronouncements on the right to health are examined below.

In Consumer Education & Research Centre and others v. Union of India and others,[67] the Indian Supreme Court held that the

> expression "life" assured in Art. 21 of the Constitution does not connote mere animal existence or continued drudgery through life. It has a much wider meaning which includes right to livelihood, better standard of life, hygienic conditions in [the] work place and leisure.[68]

In the same case, the Supreme Court held that 'the right to health and medical care is a fundamental right under Article 21.'[69] In *Paschim Banga Khet Samity v. State of West Bengal,*[70] which involved the failure of government medical hospitals to provide timely emergency medical treatment to an individual who fell off a train and who suffered serious head injuries and brain haemorrhage, the Indian Supreme Court held that,

> Article 21 imposes an obligation on the State to safeguard the right to life of every person. Preservation of human life is thus of paramount importance. The Government hospitals run by the State and the Medical Officers employed therein are duty bound to extend medical

---

[63] Ibid.

[64] Ibid.

[65] Ibid.

[66] Ibid., pp. 406–407.

[67] *Consumer Education & Research Centre and others. v. Union of India and others.* (1995) SCC (3) 42.

[68] Para 24.

[69] Ibid., para 26.

[70] *Paschim Banga Khet Samity v. State of West Bengal.* (1996) 4 SCC 37.

> assistance for preserving human life. Failure on the part of a Government hospital to provide timely medical treatment to a person in need of such treatment results in [a] violation of his right to life guaranteed under Article 21.[71]

The court further noted that the limitation of financial resources cannot justify the failure of the state to discharge its constitutional obligations with regard to the provision of adequate medical services.[72] However, arguments relating to the limitation of financial resources in the context of the right to health and the provision of medical facilities by the state are not entirely foreclosed by the Indian Supreme Court. Where, due to the limitation of financial resources, the government has adopted a particular policy with regards to the provision of medical services, the Indian Supreme Court assesses the particular policy by adopting an approach akin to the 'reasonableness approach' adopted by the South African Constitutional Court in the *Soobramoney* case.

For instance, in *State of Punjab and others v. Ram Lubhaya Bagga* (1998)[73] the Indian Supreme Court had to determine whether the State of Punjab was justified in adopting a policy of not reimbursing an employee for his full medical expenses if such expenses were incurred in any hospital in India that was not a government-owned hospital in Punjab. In this case, the Supreme Court held that,

> [S]o far as questioning the validity of governmental policy is concerned, in our view it is not normally within the domain of any court, to weigh the pros and cons of the policy or to scrutinize it and test the degree of its beneficial or equitable disposition for the purpose of varying or modifying it, based on however sound and good reasoning, except where it is arbitrary or violative of any constitutional, statutory or any other provision of law. When Government forms its policy, it is based on [a] number of circumstances ... including constraints based on its resources ... it would be dangerous if [the] court is asked to test the utility, beneficial effect of the policy or its appraisal based on facts set out on affidavits. The Court would dissuade itself from entering into this realm which belongs to the executive. It is within this matrix that it is to be seen whether the new policy violates Article 21 when it restricts reimbursement on account of ... financial constraints.[74]

In other words, once the government has already adopted a policy relating to the provision of a medical facility, unless the said policy is arbitrary or unreasonable, the court will not interfere in accordance with the doctrine of separation of powers. The implication of this is that the government cannot rely upon the argument that it has financial constraints to justify its failure to provide a medical facility. As the court held in the *Samity case*, the state cannot avoid its obligation on account of financial constraints. The state has to take steps to establish a policy on the provision of medical facilities, and limited financial resources will not excuse the government's failure to establish a policy in this regard. But once the government has adopted a particular policy with regard to the provision of a medical facility, the

[71] Ibid., para 9.

[72] Ibid., para 16.

[73] *State of Punjab v. Ram Lubhaya Bagga* (1998) 4 SCC 117.

[74] Ibid.

court will only interfere where that policy is unreasonable or in violative of the Constitution.

Thus in the *Lubhaya Bagga* case, the court held that, 'the State can neither urge nor say that it has no obligation to provide [a] medical facility. If that were so it would be ex facie violative of Article 21.'[75] The court then noted that under the policy adopted by the State of Punjab, 'medical facility continues to be given and ... an employee is given [the] free choice to get treatment in any private hospital in India but the amount of payment towards reimbursement is regulated.'[76] The court held that this policy was not in violation of Articles 21 or 47 of the Constitution. The approach adopted by the court in the *Lubhaya Bagga* case was followed in the later Supreme Court case of *Confederation of Ex-Servicemen Associations and others v. Union of India and others* (2006).[77]

In *Mohd. Ahmed (Minor) v. Union of India and others*, (2014)[78] the Delhi High Court made some landmark pronouncements on the right to health in the context of access to medicines as it affects a patient suffering from a rare disease. The central issue before the court was whether a child born to poor parents and who is suffering from Gaucher's disease (a chronic and rare disease) is entitled to free medical treatment. especially where the treatment for the disease is known of, the prognosis is good, and there is every likelihood that the child can lead a normal life. It was argued on behalf of the child that, since the drugs needed for the treatment of the child were available in India, both the Central Government and the Government of Delhi had an obligation under Article 21 of the Constitution to provide free treatment to the child and other patients in the same situation.[79] The child's counsel argued that the government could not raise the plea of financial constraint.[80] The plea of financial constraint however formed the kernel of the submissions made by the Central Government and the Government of Delhi. They contended that because of their limited resources they were unable to fund the treatment of the child as the disease is a lifelong one and the condition of the child is chronic.[81]

Anand Grover, the former UN Special Rapporteur on the Right to Health, made legal submissions in this case. Grover argued that, as India had signed and ratified the International Covenant on Economic, Social and Cultural Rights (ICESCR), India is duty bound to fulfil its international legal obligations.[82] According to Grover,

---

[75] Ibid.

[76] Ibid.

[77] *Confederation of Ex-Servicemen Associations and others v. Union of India and others*. (2006, August 22). SCC Writ Petition (civil) 210 of 1999.

[78] *Mohd. Ahmed (Minor) v. Union of India and others*. (2014, April 17). W.P.(C) 7279/2013, decision of the High Court of Delhi.

[79] Ibid., para 11.

[80] Ibid., para 14.

[81] Ibid., para 27.

[82] Ibid., para 34.

> States are required to adopt and implement a public health strategy and plan of action that reflects the epidemiological burden of disease that not only addresses major disease burdens but also the health concerns of the whole population. Therefore ... even if a small percentage of the population had a life-threatening condition there should be [a] public health strategy and plan to address their treatment needs. In other words, the Government can be directed to have a plan in place to make medicines available for rare diseases, like Gaucher disease etc.[83]

Grover's argument brings into focus the central problem with the government's argument in this case. Essentially, the Indian government had failed to put in place a policy or adopt a public health strategy to provide medicines to those suffering from rare diseases such as Gaucher's disease. This is a violation of the government's obligation with regard to the right to health. It is true that the government has limited resources, but as the Indian Supreme Court held in the *Samity* case, the state cannot avoid its constitutional obligation with regard to the right to health on account of financial constraints. Even in the *Lubhaya Bagga* case where the Indian Supreme Court recognized the fact that the financial resources of the state are not unlimited, the court still made it clear that the failure to adopt a policy with regard to the provision of a medical facility is ex facie violative of the Constitution.

In this case, neither the Central Government nor the Delhi Government had adopted any policy or public health strategy for the provision of drugs to those suffering from rare diseases. As the Delhi High Court pointed out,

> Unfortunately, the Government of India does not have any policy measure in place to address rare diseases, particularly those of a chronic nature. All the Central and State schemes at the highest provide for a one-time grant for life-saving procedures and do not contemplate continuous financial assistance for a chronic disease such as [Gaucher's disease], which involves lifelong expenditure.[84]

The court however stated that, in accordance with the doctrine of separation of powers, it could not direct parliament to enact legislation on the right to public health or with regard to rare diseases or orphan drugs, even though this may be eminently desirable.[85] According to the court, as the 'formulation of a policy is within the exclusive domain of the Executive,' it will refrain from issuing directives for the formulation of a policy.[86]

In its decision in this case, the court referred to the UN CESCR's General Comment No. 14 on the right to health. The court quoted paragraph 43(d) of General Comment No. 14 which states that one of the core obligations with regard to the right to health (from which no derogation is permissible) is the provision of essential drugs. Furthermore, the court quoted paragraph 52 of General Comment No. 14 which provides that a state violates its obligation to fulfil the right to health when it fails to, *inter alia*, 'adopt or implement a national health policy designed to

[83] Ibid., para 35.

[84] Ibid., para 42.

[85] Ibid., para 44.

[86] Ibid., para 45.

ensure the right to health for everyone'. The court admitted that the state does not have unlimited financial resources. Nevertheless, the court held that 'no Government can say that it will not treat patients with chronic and rare diseases due to financial constraint[s].'[87] The court adopted the view that 'core obligations under the right to health are non-derogable' and that though 'this minimum core is not easy to define,' it 'includes at least the minimum decencies of life consistent with human dignity.'[88]

Invariably, the court came to the conclusion that the state has an obligation to provide access to medicines, including medicines for rare diseases. According to the court,

> Article 21 of the Constitution clearly imposes a duty on the Government to take whatever steps are necessary to ensure that everyone has access to health facilities, goods and services, so that they can enjoy, as soon as possible, the highest attainable standard of physical and mental health ... Government must at the bare minimum ensure that individuals have access to essential medicines even for rare diseases like enzyme replacement for Gaucher disease ... Government cannot cite financial crunch as a reason not to fulfil its obligation to ensure access to medicines or to adopt a plan of action to treat rare diseases ... no government can wriggle out of its core obligation of ensuring the right of access to health facilities for [the] vulnerable and marginalized section of society [such as] the petitioner by stating that it cannot afford to provide treatment for rare and chronic diseases.[89]

Thus, by failing to adopt a policy for the provision of medicines for the treatment of rare diseases such as Gaucher's disease, the government had violated its constitutional obligation with regard to the right to health.[90] As health is a subject matter within the jurisdiction of the state government in India, the court ordered the Government of Delhi to 'discharge its constitutional obligation and provide the petitioner with enzyme replacement therapy ... free of charge as and when he requires it.'[91] The ruling of the court with regard to the non-derogable core obligation of the state to provide access to essential medicines at affordable prices irrespective of resource constraints, has enormous implications for the tension between patent rights and the right to health in India. Even though the court in this case did not consider the tension between patent rights and the right to health, the court has confirmed by its ruling that the Indian government has a non-derogable core obligation to facilitate access to essential medicines at affordable prices.

This ruling implies that in any case where the exercise or enforcement of patent rights on pharmaceutical products granted by the government hinders poor patients from having access to essential medicines, there is a violation of the government's obligation to provide access to essential medicines at affordable prices. If this

[87] Ibid., para 64.

[88] Ibid., para 67.

[89] Ibid., paras 68 and 69.

[90] Ibid., paras 85 and 86.

[91] Ibid., para 89.

approach is incorporated into the decisions of the Indian courts whenever they are adjudicating disputes involving the interpretation or enforcement of patent rights, it will ensure that owners of patent rights on pharmaceutical products are not allowed to exercise their patent rights in a manner that impedes the enjoyment of the right to health.

Thus, three clear principles are discernible from the decisions of the Indian courts on the right to health. One, the state cannot justify its failure to provide medical facilities by arguing that it has limited financial resources. The state is obliged to at least adopt a policy with regard to the provision of medical facilities. Two, once a policy has been adopted by the state, the court will only interfere with such a policy if it is unconstitutional, unreasonable or arbitrary. As long as the policy itself is not unreasonable, the measures contained in the policy need not be adequate. Three, the state has a core obligation to provide access to essential medicines at affordable prices. There can be no derogation from this core obligation irrespective of financial constraints.

4 Incorporating the Right to Health into the Adjudication of Disputes Involving Pharmaceutical Patents

4.1 Kenya

In the 2008 case of *Pfizer Inc. v. Cosmos Limited*, Pfizer alleged that Cosmos had infringed its patent on a medicinal product known as 'azithromycin dehydrate.'[92] Cosmos argued, *inter alia*, that it was entitled to import, manufacture, sell, and export the patented product without the authority of Pfizer by virtue of section 58 (2) of the Industrial Property Act which allows parallel importation. Section 58 (2) provides that 'the rights under the patent shall not extend to acts in respect of articles which have been put on the market in Kenya or in any other country or imported into Kenya'. Cosmos presented evidence to the tribunal establishing that the medicines containing the patented product were available in Kenya having been imported from India, Bangladesh, and China.[93] In other words, the patent rights of Pfizer, with respect to those products which were readily available in Kenya, had been exhausted. Cosmos was attempting to rely on the principle of international exhaustion of patent rights as reflected in section 58(2), and though this principle might not give Cosmos the right to manufacture the patented product, it would entitle Cosmos to import those patented products from India, Bangladesh, and China and to resell them in Kenya.

[92] *Pfizer Inc. v. Cosmos Limited.* (2008, April 25). Case No. 49 of 2006, decision of the Kenyan Industrial Property Tribunal at Nairobi, p. 1.
[93] Ibid., pp. 3–4.

However, in a rather curious and confusing manner, the tribunal conflated parallel importation with compulsory licenses and voluntary licenses. According to the tribunal,

> parallel importation ... is applicable for instance where the government has allowed a third party to exploit the patent, and that party imports the product from other countries where it is legitimately put on the market ... This could also be with the authority of the patent holder by way of a contractual or voluntary license.[94]

The tribunal could not comprehend a situation where a third party could engage in the parallel importation of a patented product without the authorization of the patentee or the government, and its definition of parallel importation clearly contradicts what is contained in section 58(2). Section 58(2) does not actually require a person or a company to obtain government authorization or a compulsory/voluntary license before engaging in parallel importation.

Cosmos equally argued that the patented product was used for the treatment of opportunistic infections in HIV/AIDS patients and that the WHO listed the product as an essential medicine for the treatment of genital chlamydia trachomatis and trachoma.[95] By raising this argument, Cosmos had highlighted a tension between the enforcement of Pfizer's patent rights on one hand and the need to facilitate access to this essential medicine for Kenyan patients on the other hand. The resolution of this tension therefore required a proper appreciation of the fact that patent rights ought to serve the needs and interests of fundamental rights such as the right to have access to essential medicines at affordable prices. If the tension had been approached from this dimension, it would have enabled the tribunal to interpret the patent law with the objective of ensuring that it does not impede access to medicines. However, in this particular case, the Kenyan tribunal took the view that the product was not a first-line treatment for HIV/AIDS patients and that even if this were the case, it would not entitle the respondents to exploit the patent without authorization.[96]

By interpreting the provisions of section 58(2) in this manner and ignoring the impact this could have on access to anti-retroviral drugs in Kenya, the tribunal overlooked the rationale behind the introduction of parallel importation into the Kenyan Industrial Property Act of 2001 via the provisions of section 58(2). During the parliamentary debates on the 2001 Act, it was stated by the Kenyan Minister for Trade and Industry that the provision on parallel importation was specifically introduced to permit the importation into Kenya of 'medicines which are required for human life, especially [for the treatment of] HIV/AIDS and [other] opportunistic diseases, as well as malaria.'[97] The tribunal thus failed to appreciate the essential distinction between the regulatory nature of patent rights and the fundamental nature of the right to have access to essential medicines. It could be argued that

[94] Ibid., p. 13.
[95] Ibid., p. 16.
[96] Ibid., p. 17.
[97] Kenyan National Assembly Official Record (Hansard) (2001, June 12), p. 1043.

the tribunal failed to appreciate this essential distinction because Article 43(1)(a), which made the right to health a justiciable right in Kenya, was only introduced into the Kenyan Constitution in 2010 i.e. two years after the tribunal's judgment. However, even without invoking a constitutional right to health, a tribunal that is mindful of the fundamental importance of securing access to medicines would have examined the rationale behind the inclusion of section 58(2) in the Kenyan patent law. As noted above, section 58(2) was introduced in order to facilitate the importation of medicines for the treatment of HIV/AIDS and opportunistic ailments. A tribunal that is mindful of the fundamental importance of facilitating access to affordable medicines would have construed section 58(2) in accordance with the objective of ensuring that the enforcement of a patent right does not defeat the aims of the drafters of the patent law.

In the more recent case of *Patricia Asero Ochieng et al. v. Attorney General*, (2012) the Kenyan High Court had an opportunity to consider the relationship between intellectual property rights and the right to health.[98] In this case, the petitioners were HIV/AIDS patients, and they alleged that certain sections of the Kenyan Anti-Counterfeit Act of 2008 threatened their access to essential drugs thereby infringing their right to life, dignity, and health.[99] The petitioners argued that the government failed to specifically exempt generic drugs from the definition of counterfeit goods in the Act.[100] Specifically, section 2 of the Act defined counterfeiting in relation to medicine as meaning 'the deliberate and fraudulent mislabelling of medicine with respect to identity or source, whether or not such products have correct ingredients, wrong ingredients, have sufficient active ingredients or have fake packaging'. The respondents, however, argued that the Anti-Counterfeit Act was enacted to prohibit trade in counterfeit goods in Kenya and was not intended to prohibit generic drugs.[101] The respondents argued that the Act was intended to 'protect the public from the harm of using counterfeit goods and that extra care needs to be taken to ensure that the medicine in the market meets the required standard.'[102]

Contrary to the arguments of the respondents in this case, it appears that the real intent behind the Kenyan Anti-Counterfeit Act was not really the protection of the public from harm, but rather the Act was designed to secure, amongst other things, the intellectual property rights of pharmaceutical companies. Von Braun and Munyi point out that, because the two bills preceding the enactment of the Anti-Counterfeit Act were not backed by any public policy decision, it is 'difficult to discern the real motive or motivations behind the enactment of the legislation' but 'during the legislative process, there was a lot of public debate, at least as demonstrated by

[98] *Patricia Asero Ochieng et al. v. Attorney General.* (2012, April 20). Petition No. 409 of 2009, decision of the Kenyan High Court.

[99] Ibid., para 1.

[100] Ibid., para 14.

[101] Ibid., para 39.

[102] Ibid., para 42.

numerous media reports on the effect counterfeiting has had on the local manufacturing sector' and the 'Kenya Association of Manufacturers ... was leading in the lobbying towards legislation on anti-counterfeiting.'[103] Harrington and O'Hare equally note that the Kenya Association of Manufacturers played a key role in securing the passage of the Act.[104] According to Harrington and O'Hare, the Kenya Association of Manufacturers 'represents over 700 members, both domestic and foreign-owned firms, among whom are major pharmaceutical concerns marketing and manufacturing their products in Kenya.'[105] They note that the Association established an Anti-Counterfeit Committee and 'engaged closely in the legislative process itself' while also 'frequently briefing key parliamentary committees.'[106]

The former UN Special Rapporteur on the Right to Health, Anand Grover, filed an *amicus* brief in the *Ochieng* case. According to the former Special Rapporteur,

> the definition of "counterfeiting" within the Act effectively conflates generic medicines with medicines which are produced in violation of private intellectual property rights, and this conflation of legitimately produced generic medicines with those that possibly violate intellectual property rights is likely to have a serious adverse impact on the availability, affordability and accessibility of low-cost, high-quality medicines.[107]

Grover agreed with the contention of the petitioners that the Act could endanger the right to health because it does not exclude generic drugs.[108] Grover also provided a definition of generic medicines (which was quoted in the court's judgment) as drugs that

> have the same composition and contain the same substances as patented formulations of the same drugs, and are essentially identical copies [that] can be used for the same purposes as their non-generic counterparts.[109]

In its analysis of the meaning and implication of the right to health, the High Court referred to Article 43(1)(a) of the Kenyan Constitution which guarantees the right to health, Article 12 of the ICESCR, and the UN CESCR's General Comment No. 14 on the right to health. The High Court proceeded to delineate the nature of the state's obligation with regard to the right to health. The court held that the state's obligation entails both a positive and a negative duty. The state has a positive duty to ensure that its citizens have access to health care services and medicines; it equally has a negative duty to refrain from taking actions that would affect access to these health care services and medicines. Thus, any legislative enactment that

[103] Von Braun and Munyi (2010), p. 243.

[104] Harrington and O'Hare (2014), p. 22.

[105] Ibid.

[106] Ibid.

[107] *Patricia Asero Ochieng et al. v. Attorney General.* (2012, April 20). *Op cit.* n 98, para 35.

[108] Ibid., para 34.

[109] Ibid., para 76.

would make medicines too expensive for citizens would be in violation of the state's obligation.[110]

The court equally highlighted the danger inherent in conflating the definition of counterfeit drugs and generic drugs by referring to cases where generic drugs in transit were seized on the basis of being counterfeit.[111] Though the court did not mention any particular country, it is obvious that the court was referring to instances like the seizure by Dutch Customs authorities in 2008 and 2009 of multiple shipments of drugs that were in-transit from India to developing countries in Africa and Latin America.[112] The court agreed with the petitioners and the Special Rapporteur that the 'definition of "counterfeit" in section 2 of the Act is likely to be read as including generic medication' and quoting from the Special Rapporteur's *amicus* brief, it stated that 'this would affect the availability of generic drugs and pose a real threat to the petitioners' right to life, dignity and health.'[113] The court disagreed with the respondent's argument that the Act was primarily intended to protect consumers from counterfeit medicines. According to the court 'the tenor and object of the Act is to protect the intellectual property rights of individuals.'[114]

The court was of the view that the rights to life, dignity, and health must take priority over intellectual property rights. The court noted that if the Act is implemented as originally written,

> the danger that it poses to the right of the petitioners to access essential medicine ... is far greater and more critical than the protection of the intellectual property rights that the Act seeks to protect. The right to life, dignity and health of the petitioners must take precedence over the intellectual property rights of patent holders.[115]

The court thus adopted and applied the 'subjugation approach' by upholding the primacy of human rights over intellectual property rights. The High Court further held that,

> It is incumbent on the state to reconsider the provisions of section 2 of the Anti-Counterfeit Act alongside its constitutional obligation to ensure that its citizens have access to the highest attainable standard of health and make appropriate amendments to ensure that the rights of petitioners and others dependent on generic medicines are not put in jeopardy.[116]

However, unfortunately the Kenyan government failed to incorporate the court's ruling in this case into the recent amendments made to the Anti-Counterfeit Act in 2014 despite the demands of health activists in this regard.[117] Unlike the approach

[110] Ibid., para 66.

[111] Ibid., para 75.

[112] Micara (2012).

[113] *Patricia Asero Ochieng et al. v. Attorney General*. (2012, April 20). *Op cit*. n 98, para 75.

[114] Ibid., para 82.

[115] Para 85.

[116] Ibid., para 88.

[117] Nzomo (2014) (available https://ipkenya.wordpress.com/2014/12/17/president-assents-to-anti-counterfeit-amendment-act-2014/ accessed 24 January 2015).

adopted by the tribunal in the *Pfizer v. Cosmos* case, the decision of the Kenyan High Court in this case demonstrates the court's recognition of the tension between the enforcement of intellectual property rights and the protection of the right to health. The court refused to be misguided into overlooking the fact that the Anti-Counterfeit Act was enacted to enhance the protection of intellectual property rights in Kenya. With the recognition that there was a tension to be resolved, the court equally demonstrated an implicit understanding of the essential distinction between the fundamental nature of the right to health and the regulatory nature of IPRs. This can be seen from the court's statement that the danger posed by the Anti-Counterfeit Act to the petitioner's right to access essential medicines was far greater and more critical than the protection of IPRs. It is therefore not surprising that the court, while not disparaging IPRs, held that the right to health must take priority over IPRs.

These two cases from Kenya illustrate the important role that courts can play in enhancing access to medicines in developing countries. In a situation where most courts adopt the approach of the tribunal in the *Pfizer* case, there is no doubt that patent rights will almost always trump the right to health. However, if courts adopt the more robust approach that was applied by the Kenyan High Court in the *Ochieng* case, it will lead to two things: one, states will be careful in implementing legislation (especially legislation on patent rights) that can significantly impede access to medicines; and, two, pharmaceutical companies that own patents on pharmaceutical products will ensure that they do not exercise their patent rights in ways that negatively affect the enjoyment of the right to health.

4.2 South Africa

In *Pfizer Ltd. v. Cipla Medpro (Pty) Ltd* (2005),[118] Cipla Medpro had initiated revocation proceedings against Pfizer in 2004 with regards to one of Pfizer's pharmaceutical patents. Cipla had alleged that the patent was unclear and obvious. The patent in question concerned a 'besylate salt of amlodipine, a drug used for hypertension and reduction of blood pressure.'[119] Pfizer markets a product called Norvasc which contains the patented chemical, while Cipla had already started to market its own generic version called Nortwin in South Africa even before Pfizer's patent expired or was revoked. In response to Cipla's application for the revocation of its patent (which was set to expire in 2007), Pfizer brought this action for an interim interdict against Cipla to prevent the infringement of its patent pending the

[118] *Pfizer Ltd. v. Cipla Medpro (Pty) Ltd.* (2005, March 24). Case No.: 87/2439, (2005) BIP 1; [2005] ZACCP 1, decision of the Court of the Commissioner of Patents for the Republic of South Africa.

[119] Ibid., p. 2.

final determination of the revocation proceedings. In granting Pfizer's application for an interim interdict, Botha J., sitting as the Commissioner of Patents, held that:

> If one looks at the broad picture: the respondents have hardly entered the market. The applicants have only two years of their patent left. In two years the respondents will be at liberty to sell Nortwin in any event. The applicant is a manufacturer that relies on patent protection to recoup the cost of research and development. The respondent is a manufacturer of generic products that are manufactured without the expense of original research. For that reason it is wrong to argue, as the respondents have done endlessly, that the applicants can retain their market share by reducing their prices. The regime of an open market is only something to which they have to submit on the expiry of the patent.[120]

It is rather surprising that the only characters that featured in the court's 'broad picture' were the applicant and the respondent—Pfizer and Cipla. The court appears to have been more concerned about the importance of ensuring that Pfizer is able to recoup the money it spent on research and development. While it is fair for pharmaceutical companies to seek to recoup their investment in producing new drugs, the approach adopted by the court completely ignores other important characters like poorer patients who might not be able to afford to pay for Norvasc sold by Pfizer but who might be able to afford Nortwin sold by Cipla. In other words, the court should have considered the potential impact that Pfizer's patent rights could have on the enjoyment of the right to health by poorer patients in South Africa.

In a later case, *Aventis v. Cipla*,[121] the dispute involved a patent for 'New Taxoid-Based Compositions' that belonged to Aventis and which covered claims for compositions containing 'Taxane' derivatives including the Taxane derivative known as 'docetaxel.'[122] Taxane derivatives such as docetaxel are used as chemotherapy treatments for a number of cancers. Aventis was seeking an interim interdict against Cipla because, in March 2011, Aventis discovered that Cipla was about to import into South Africa two products made in India, namely, 'Cipla Docetaxel' and 'Cipla Docetaxel solvent' which when mixed with the relevant product would constitute an infringement of the patent belonging to Aventis. Aventis therefore brought an application for an interdict to prohibit the respondents from mixing the Cipla products and an interdict to prohibit the respondents from selling the products to any person who would mix the products in accordance with the patent.[123] The interim interdict was refused because the Commissioner of Patents was of the view that the applicants' prospect of success at a full trial was slender.[124]

---

[120] Ibid., p. 22.

[121] *Aventis v. Cipla*. (2011, October 20). Unreported Case No.: P93/8936, decision of the Court of the Commissioner of Patents for the Republic of South Africa.

[122] Ibid., para 2.

[123] Ibid., para 3.

[124] Ibid., para 26.

Aventis however appealed to the South African Supreme Court of Appeal and the decision of the Commissioner of Patents was overruled by the Supreme Court of Appeal.[125] With regard to Aventis' request for an interim interdict, the appellate court agreed with the arguments of the *amicus curiae*, Treatment Action Campaign, that the public interest cannot be ignored when deciding whether or not to issue an interim interdict.[126] The NGO based its opposition to the grant of an interim interdict on the right to health guaranteed in section 27(1) of the South African Constitution and urged the appellate court to construe the Patents Act 'through the prism of the Constitution' and in a way that appropriately balances the rights of a patentee against the constitutional rights of others.[127]

The appellate court was however of the view that construing the Patents Act through the prism of the Constitution does not necessarily mean that Aventis should be denied the right to enforce its patent.[128] In its consideration of the balance of convenience and the public interest, the court noted that there was no suggestion that Aventis was not able to meet the demand for the patented drug nor could it be said that Cipla's version of the drug offered superior medicinal benefits.[129] The court further noted that there would be no material disruption to patients if an interdict was granted. The court was not swayed by the argument that an interdict would adversely affect patients that could not afford Cipla's drug. According to the court,

> [w]here the public is denied access to a generic [drug] during the lifetime of a patent, that is the ordinary consequence of patent protection and it applies as much in all cases. To refuse an interdict only so as to frustrate the patentee's lawful monopoly seems to ... be an abuse of the discretionary powers of a court.[130]

What can be deduced from this approach is that, while the court was willing to consider the public interest and the rights of patients, it was equally reluctant to allow these interests and rights to trump the monopoly rights of patentees. In essence, the court was willing to hold that the denial of access to generic drugs should be considered as part of the price society pays for securing monopoly rights through the grant of patents. The court did not however attempt to consider whether the right to health could take precedence over patent rights in certain cases. This is probably because it was unnecessary to do so in this particular case. Based on the facts presented before the court, there would be no material prejudice to poorer patients if an interim interdict was granted to Aventis. It was established before the court that Aventis was already marketing its own generic version of the patented drug and, more importantly, the patented drug itself was already being sold to the

---

[125] *Aventis v. Cipla*. (2012, July 26). Case Nos.: 139/2012 & 138/2012; [2012] ZASCA 108, decision of the South African Supreme Court of Appeal.

[126] Ibid., para 46.

[127] Ibid., para 44.

[128] Ibid., para 45.

[129] Ibid., para 55.

[130] Ibid., para 56.

government at a rate which was cheaper than the price of Cipla's generic version.[131] The court therefore held that Aventis' patented drug was 'considerably more accessible' to patients dependent on public health care than Cipla's generic version and that 'there will be no prejudice at all to those patients, or to the state, if an interdict were to be granted.'[132]

4.3 India

In the case of *Hoffmann-La Roche Ltd. v. Cipla Ltd.*, (2008)[133] the Delhi High Court refused to grant an injunction sought by Roche against Cipla for the latter's production of 'Erloticip' (a generic version of Roche's patented anti-cancer drug known as 'Erlotinib'). The Delhi High Court noted that:

> [T]he Court cannot be unmindful of the right of the general public to access life saving drugs which are available and for which such access would be denied if the injunction were granted . . . The degree of harm in such eventuality is absolute; the chances of improvement of life expectancy; even chances of recovery in some cases would be snuffed out altogether, if [an] injunction [were to be] granted . . . Another way of viewing it is that if the injunction in the case of a life saving drug were to be granted, the Court would in effect be stifling Article 21 [of the Indian Constitution] so far as those [who] would have or could have access to Erloticip are concerned.[134]

According to the Delhi High Court,

> as between the two competing public interests, that is, the public interest in granting an injunction to affirm a patent during the pendency of an infringement action, as opposed to the public interest in access for people to a life-saving drug, the balance has to be tilted in favour of the latter.[135]

The court observed that the damage that would be suffered by Roche (the patent owner) in this case can be assessed in monetary terms but that the

> injury to the public which would be deprived of the defendants product, which may lead to shortening of lives of several unknown persons, who are not parties to the suit, and which damage cannot be restituted in monetary terms, is not only uncompensatable, it is irreparable.[136]

---

[131] Ibid., para 57.

[132] Ibid., para 58.

[133] *Hoffmann-La Roche v. Cipla Ltd.* (2008, March 19). I.A. 642/2008 in CS(OS) 89/2008, decision of the High Court of Delhi.

[134] Ibid., para 85.

[135] Ibid., para 86.

[136] Ibid.

The decision of the Delhi High Court in this case was upheld on appeal by the Division Bench of the Delhi High Court in *Hoffmann-La Roche v Cipla Ltd* (2009).[137] In concurring with the trial court, the Division Bench held that,

> [I]n a country like India where [the] question of general public access to life saving drugs assumes great significance, the adverse impact on such access which the grant of [an] injunction in a case like the instant one is likely to have, would have to be accounted for. [Erloticip] is the Indian equivalent produced by the defendant in India as a generic drug manufacturer. It is priced at Rs. 1600 per tablet. Even if this does not make it inexpensive, the question of [the] greater availability of such [a] drug in the market assumes significance.[138]

However, the Delhi High Court has also held in *Novartis v. Cipla Ltd* (2015)[139] that a generic drug company cannot rely on the right to life contained in Article 21 of the Indian Constitution to justify the infringement of a valid patent.[140] In this case, the court granted an injunction restraining Cipla from infringing Novartis' patent on Indacaterol (a drug used in the treatment of chronic obstructive pulmonary disease). The court stated that Novartis had established a prima facie case for the validity of its patent and that Cipla had merely urged grounds of invalidity by relying on documents which, according to Cipla, constituted prior art 'without explaining to the court and to the other side ... how these documents can be categorized as [prior art].'[141] The court further stated that Novartis, on the other hand, provided the points of distinction between the earlier patents relied upon as prior art and its own patent. The court held that, 'if [a] patent is valid, the defendant has failed to establish [a] prima facie credible defence and the case of infringement is made out by the patentee, the patentee may be entitled [to an] injunction.'[142]

The court distinguished this case from that of *Hoffmann-La Roche Ltd. v. Cipla Ltd* where a credible challenge was raised to the validity of Roche's patent by Cipla and it stated that 'Article 21 cannot be pressed into service by an infringer seeking to justify the infringement of a valid patent and the statutory rights conferred by the statute.'[143] The court further stated that if Cipla was 'so very much concerned about the welfare of [the] public ... and its grounds are genuine and correct, it could have filed [an] application for [the] grant of [a] Compulsory Licence.'[144] The implication of the court's ruling in this case is that a generic drug company cannot rely on the right to health to justify the infringement of a valid pharmaceutical patent. If a

---

[137] *Hoffmann-La Roche v. Cipla Ltd.* (2009, April 24). FAO (OS) 188/2008, decision of the Division Bench of the High Court of Delhi).

[138] Ibid., para 81.

[139] *Novartis v. Cipla Ltd.* (2015, January 9). I.A. No. 24863/2014 in CS(OS) 3812/2014, decision of the High Court of Delhi.

[140] Ibid., para 89.

[141] Ibid., para 83.

[142] Ibid., para 87.

[143] Ibid., para 89.

[144] Ibid., para 91.

generic drug company believes that the demand for a patented drug is not being met by the patentee or that the patentee is selling its drug at a price that is not reasonably affordable, the generic company can apply for a compulsory licence.

The case of *Natco v. Bayer* (2012)[145] is the first case in India in the post-TRIPS Agreement era where an applicant invoked the relevant provisions of the Indian Patents Act to seek the grant of a compulsory licence. The patentee in this case, Bayer, invented a drug called 'Sorafenib' and obtained an Indian patent for the drug in 2008. The drug is sold under the trade name 'Nexavar' and it is used for the treatment of kidney cancer and liver cancer. The applicant, Natco, an Indian generic drug manufacturer, had initially requested for a voluntary licence from Bayer to sell the drug at a cheaper price. Bayer did not grant this request and Natco subsequently applied for a compulsory licence. In granting Natco's request for a compulsory licence, one of the issues considered by the Indian Controller of Patents was the price at which the drug was being sold in India. According to section 84(1)(b) of the Indian Patents Act of 2005, one of the grounds for the grant of a compulsory licence is that 'the patented invention is not available to the public at a reasonably affordable price'.

Natco argued that the price of the drug was 'too high and simply unaffordable by the common man making the product inaccessible and out of reach.'[146] According to Natco, a drug that costs Rs. 280,000 per month 'will push a large proportion of the population into poverty.'[147] In response, Bayer argued, *inter alia*, that 'reasonable' price must mean 'reasonable' to the public and the patentee as well, and that 'the cost of R&D and the cost of manufacture, both have to be taken into account while determining "reasonable affordable price".'[148]

In deciding to grant the compulsory licence, the Controller agreed that the drug, being sold at a price of Rs. 280,000 per month, was not reasonably affordable to members of the public. The Controller disagreed with Bayer's argument that 'reasonable affordable price' should be construed with reference to both the public and the patentee, and held that it has to be construed predominantly with reference to the public. According to the terms of the compulsory licence granted to Natco by the Controller, Natco is meant to sell the drug at the price of Rs. 8880 per month.[149]

Bayer subsequently lodged an appeal against the decision of the Controller at the Indian Intellectual Property Appellate Board (IPAB). In March 2013, IPAB issued its final judgment and it dismissed Bayer's appeal against the grant of the compulsory licence.[150] IPAB upheld the order of the Controller of Patents though it

---

[145] *Natco v. Bayer*. (2012, March 9). Compulsory Licence Application No. 1 of 2011, decision of the Indian Controller of Patents.

[146] Ibid., para 11.

[147] Ibid.

[148] Ibid.

[149] Ibid., para 15.

[150] *Bayer v. Union of India and others*. (2013, March 4). OA/35/2012/PT/MUM, decision of the Indian Intellectual Property Appellate Board.

increased the rate of royalty to be paid by Natco to Bayer from 6 to 7 % (Ibid., para 54). In its final judgment, IPAB referred to section 83 of the Indian Patents Act which contains the general principles applicable to the working of patented inventions in India. Specifically, section 83(d) provides that patents should not impede the protection of public health. Section 83(g) further states that patents are granted to make the benefit of the patented invention available at reasonably affordable prices to the public. IPAB noted that it could not 'ignore these markers' in its decision.[151]

IPAB's final decision in this case indicates that it was mindful of the need to protect the right to health and the right to have access to medicines. In its judgment, reference was made to the Doha Declaration on the TRIPS Agreement and Public Health of 2001.[152] The Doha Declaration provides, *inter alia*, that the TRIPS Agreement 'does not and should not prevent members from taking measures to protect public health . . . [and] that the Agreement can and should be interpreted and implemented in a manner supportive of WTO members' right to protect public health and, in particular, to promote access to medicines for all.'[153] Importantly, IPAB noted that, under the Doha Declaration, countries 'affirmed their full right to use the TRIPS flexibilities . . . especially in connection with [their] right to protect public health and in particular, to promote access to medicines for all.'[154] This led IPAB to the conclusion that the running theme is 'public health and access to medicine, a facet of [the] right to life.'[155] IPAB's statement, that public health and access to medicine is a facet of the right to life, definitely implies an awareness on the part of IPAB that it was dealing with a matter that involved the right to health.

IPAB further held that 'the Controller was right in holding that the sales of the drug by the appellant at the price of about [Rs.] 280,000 ... considering the purchasing capacity of the public ... was not reasonably affordable to the public.'[156] IPAB's decision was affirmed by the Bombay High Court in July 2014[157] and Bayer's subsequent petition to the Indian Supreme Court for a special leave to appeal against the judgment of the Bombay High Court was dismissed by the Supreme Court in December 2014.[158]

[151] Ibid., para 22.

[152] World Trade Organization (2001).

[153] Ibid., para 4.

[154] *Bayer* (2013), para 20.

[155] Ibid.

[156] Ibid., para 44.

[157] *Bayer v. Union of India and others*. (2014, July 15). Writ Petition No. 1323 of 2013, decision of the Bombay High Court.

[158] *Bayer v. Union of India and others*. (2014, December 12). Petition(s) for Special Leave to Appeal (C) NO(S). 30145/2014, decision of the Supreme Court of India.

5 Conclusion

This chapter has shown that the courts in Kenya, South Africa, and India have interpreted the right to health to include an obligation on the state's part to provide/ facilitate access to medicines. By incorporating the right to health into the adjudication of patent disputes, national courts in developing countries can play a crucial role in improving access to medicines at affordable prices. The incorporation of the right to health into the adjudication of disputes involving pharmaceutical patents does not necessarily imply that patent rights will no longer be recognized and respected, it only means that courts should not permit patent rights to be exercised and enforced in a manner that impedes access to medicines and the enjoyment of the right to health.

References

Chapman, A. (2001). Approaching intellectual property as a human right: Obligations related to article 15(1)(c). *Copyright Bulletin, 35*(3), 4–36.

Correa, C., & Matthews, D. (2011). *The Doha Declaration ten years on and its impact on access to medicines and the right to health.* Discussion paper. United Nations Development Programme. http://www.undp.org/content/dam/undp/library/hivaids/Discussion_Paper_Doha_Declaration_Public_Health.pdf. Accessed 23 Jan 2015.

Dhanda, A. (2013). Realising the right to health through co-operative judicial review: An analysis of the role of the Indian Supreme Court. In O. Vilhena, U. Baxi, & F. Viljoen (Eds.), *Transformative constitutionalism: Comparing the apex courts of Brazil, India and South Africa* (pp. 405–413). Pretoria, South Africa: Pretoria University Law Press.

Drahos, P. (1998). The universality of intellectual property rights: Origin and development. In: *Intellectual property and human rights.* Proceedings of a panel discussion held by the World Intellectual Property Organization in collaboration with the Office of the UN High Commissioner for Human Rights, World Intellectual Property Organization, Geneva, 9 November 1998.

Drahos, P. (1999). Intellectual property and human rights. *Intellectual Property Quarterly, 3*, 349–371.

Ferraz, O. L. M. (2013). Between usurpation and abdication? The right to health in the courts of Brazil and South Africa. In O. Vilhena, U. Baxi, & F. Viljoen (Eds.), *Transformative constitutionalism: Comparing the apex courts of Brazil, India and South Africa* (pp. 375–404). Pretoria, South Africa: Pretoria University Law Press.

Ghosh, S. (2008). When property is something else: Understanding intellectual property through the lens of regulatory justice. In A. Gosseries, A. Marciano, & A. Strowel (Eds.), *Intellectual property and theories of justice* (pp. 106–121). Basingstoke, England: Palgrave Macmillan.

Gold, E. R. (2013). Patents and human rights: A heterodox analysis. *The Journal of Law, Medicine and Ethics, 41*(1), 185–198.

Grosheide, W. (Ed.). (2010). *Intellectual property and human rights: A paradox.* Cheltenham, England/Northampton, MA: Edward Elgar.

Harrington, J., & O'Hare, A. (2014). Framing the national interest: Debating intellectual property and access to essential medicines in Kenya. *The Journal of World Intellectual Property, 17* (1–2), 16–33. doi:10.1002/jwip.12020.

Helfer, L. (2003). Human rights and intellectual property: Conflict or coexistence? *Minnesota Intellectual Property Review, 5*(1), 47–61.

Helfer, L., & Austin, G. (2011). *Human rights and intellectual property: Mapping the global interface*. New York: Cambridge University Press.

Hristova, M. (2011). Are intellectual property rights human rights? Patent protection and the right to health. *Journal of the Patent and Trademark Office Society, 93*(3), 339–361.

International Covenant on Economic, Social and Cultural Rights, G.A. Res. 2200A (XXI), (1996).

Kenyan National Assembly Official Record (Hansard). (2001, June 12).

Marks, S. (2009). Access to essential medicines as a component of the right to health. In A. Clapham & M. Robinson (Eds.), *Realizing the right to health* (Swiss human rights book series, Vol. 3, pp. 80–99). Zurich, Switzerland: Ruffer & Rub.

Micara, A.G. (2012). TRIPS-plus border measures and access to medicines. *The Journal of World Intellectual Property, 15*(1), 73–101. doi:10.1111/j.1747-1796.2011.00431.x.

Millum, J. (2008). Are pharmaceutical patents protected by human rights? *Journal of Medical Ethics, 34*, e25. doi:10.1136/jme.2007.022483.

Nzomo, V. (2014). President assents to Anti-Counterfeit (Amendment) Act 2014. IP Kenya. https://ipkenya.wordpress.com/2014/12/17/president-assents-to-anti-counterfeit-amendment-act-2014/. Accessed 24 Jan 2015.

Plomer, A. (2013). The human rights paradox: Intellectual property rights and rights of access to science. *Human Rights Quarterly, 35*(1), 143–175.

Sell, S. K. (2007). TRIPS-Plus free trade agreements and access to medicines. *Liverpool Law Review, 28*(1), 41–75. doi:10.1007/s10991-007-9011-8.

Torremans, P. (Ed.). (2008). *Intellectual property and human rights*. The Hague, the Netherlands: Kluwer Law International.

United Nations Committee on Economic, Social and Cultural Rights. (2000). General Comment No. 14 on the right to the highest attainable standard of health, article 12 of the International Covenant on Economic, Social and Cultural Rights. U.N. Doc. E/C.12/2000/4.

United Nations Committee on Economic, Social and Cultural Rights. (2005). General Comment No. 17 on the right of everyone to benefit from the protection of the moral and material interests resulting from any scientific, literary or artistic production of which he or she is the author, article 15(1)(c) of the International Covenant on Economic, Social and Cultural Rights. U.N. Doc. E/C.12/GC/17.

United Nations Human Rights Council. (2013). Access to medicines in the context of the right of everyone to the enjoyment of the highest attainable standard of physical and mental health. A/HRC/23/L.10/Rev.1.

Universal Declaration of Human Rights, G.A. Res. 217A (III), (1948).

Von Braun, J., & Munyi, P. (2010). New enforcement mechanisms challenge the legality of generics in the name of public health: The emergence of anti-counterfeiting legislation in East Africa. *African Journal of International and Comparative Law, 18*(2), 238–253.

World Health Organization. (2015). Essential medicines. http://www.who.int/topics/essential_medicines/en/. Accessed 22 Jan 2015.

World Trade Organization Ministerial Conference. (2001, November 14). Declaration on the TRIPS Agreement and public health. WT/MIN(01)/DEC/2.

Yu, P. K. (2007a). Reconceptualizing intellectual property interests in a human rights framework. *UC Davis Law Review, 40*(3), 1039–1149.

Yu, P. K. (2007b). Ten common questions about intellectual property and human rights. *Georgia State University Law Review, 23*(4), 709–753.

Case Law

Aventis v. Cipla. (2011, October 20). Unreported Case No.: P93/8936, decision of the Court of the Commissioner of Patents for the Republic of South Africa.
Aventis v. Cipla. (2012, July 26). Case Nos.: 139/2012 & 138/2012; [2012] ZASCA 108, decision of the South African Supreme Court of Appeal.
Bayer v. Union of India and others. (2013, March 4). OA/35/2012/PT/MUM, decision of the Indian Intellectual Property Appellate Board.
Bayer v. Union of India and others. (2014, July 15). Writ Petition No. 1323 of 2013, decision of the Bombay High Court.
Bayer v. Union of India and others. (2014, December 12). Petition(s) for Special Leave to Appeal (C) NO(S). 30145/2014, decision of the Supreme Court of India.
Confederation of Ex-Servicemen Associations and others v. Union of India and others. (2006, August 22). Writ Petition (civil) 210 of 1999, decision of the Indian Supreme Court.
Consumer Education & Research Centre and others. v. Union of India and others. (1995, January 27). 1995 SCC (3) 42, decision of the Indian Supreme Court.
Hoffmann-La Roche v. Cipla Ltd. (2008, March 19). I.A. 642/2008 in CS(OS) 89/2008, decision of the High Court of Delhi.
Hoffmann-La Roche v. Cipla Ltd. (2009, April 24). FAO (OS) 188/2008, decision of the Division Bench of the High Court of Delhi.
Minister of Health v. New Clicks. (2005, September 30). CCT 59/2004, decision of the South African Constitutional Court.
Minister of Health v. Treatment Action Campaign (No. 2). (2002, July 5). CCT 8/02, decision of the South African Constitutional Court.
Mohd. Ahmed (Minor) v. Union of India and others. (2014, April 17). W.P.(C) 7279/2013, decision of the High Court of Delhi.
Natco v. Bayer. (2012, March 9). Compulsory Licence Application No. 1 of 2011, decision of the Indian Controller of Patents.
Novartis v. Cipla Ltd. (2015, January 9). I.A. No. 24863/2014 in CS(OS) 3812/2014, decision of the High Court of Delhi.
Paschim Banga Khet Samity v. State of West Bengal. (1996, May 6). (1996) 4 SCC 37, decision of the Indian Supreme Court.
Patricia Asero Ochieng et al. v. Attorney General. (2012, April 20). Petition No. 409 of 2009, decision of the Kenyan High Court.
Pfizer Ltd. v. Cipla Medpro (Pty) Ltd. (2005, March 24). Case No.: 87/2439, (2005) BIP 1; [2005] ZACCP 1, decision of the Court of the Commissioner of Patents for the Republic of South Africa.
Pfizer Inc. v. Cosmos Limited. (2008, April 25). Case No. 49 of 2006, decision of the Kenyan Industrial Property Tribunal at Nairobi.
Re Certification of the Constitution of the Republic of South Africa, 1996. (1996, September 6). Case CCT 23/96, decision of the South African Constitutional Court.
Soobramoney v. Minister of Health. (1997, November 27). Case CCT 32/97, decision of the South African Constitutional Court.
State of Punjab v. Ram Lubhaya Bagga. (1998, February 26). (1998) 4 SCC 117, decision of the Indian Supreme Court.

Overcoming the (Non)justiciable Conundrum: The Doctrine of Harmonious Construction and the Interpretation of the Right to a Healthy Environment in Nigeria

Rhuks Ako, Ngozi Stewart, and Eghosa O. Ekhator

1 Introduction

There was a proliferation of written constitutions globally in the twentieth century following the Second World War. The extensive suffering and loss of lives during the years of this conflict prompted multilateral efforts to ensure the protection and promotion of human rights.[1] This was the genesis of the United Nations (UN) system, and the concerns with the protection of individual rights that came to be articulated in the form of Universal Declaration of Human Rights (UDHR). Furthermore, the liberation of many colonies was catalysed by nationalist movements all over Asia and Africa which espoused the cause of individual civil-political rights as well as socio-economic entitlements.[2] Most of these newly independent nations chose to adopt written constitutions as the basis for the organization of their governments. In the Post-Colonial setting, countries increasingly opted for constitutional texts that sought to internalize the practice of democracy while also guaranteeing a set of substantive rights to their citizens.[3] Many of such texts borrowed from constitutional provisions from foreign jurisdictions with established democracies as well as the provisions of international instruments such as the International Covenant on Civil and Political Rights (ICCPR) and the International Covenant on Economic, Social and Cultural rights. These rights

[1] Belz (1972), pp. 640–669.

[2] Ackerman (1997), pp. 771–797.

[3] Ibid.

R. Ako • E.O. Ekhator (✉)
University of Hull Law School, Hull, UK
e-mail: r.ako@hull.ac.uk; E.O.Ekhator@2005.hull.ac.uk; eghosaekhator@gmail.com

N. Stewart
Faculty of Law, University of Benin, Benin, Nigeria
e-mail: ngozi.stewart@uniben.edu

A. Diver, J. Miller (eds.), *Justiciability of Human Rights Law in Domestic Jurisdictions*, DOI 10.1007/978-3-319-24016-9_6

have been (problematically) differentiated as enforceable (or Fundamental Rights) or non-enforceable (Fundamental Objectives) in various Constitutions, including Nigeria.

Nigeria's operative Constitution of the Federal Republic of Nigeria (CFRN) 1999 permits the enforceability of fundamental rights (civil and political rights) while rendering provisions that express fundamental objectives (economic, social and cultural rights) non-justiciable. The latter category includes section 20 that implicates the 'right' to a healthy environment. While this presents a situation wherein the 'right' to a healthy environment is non-justiciable, there are cogent arguments that the right to a healthy environment is justiciable, mainly as a result of the ratification and adoption of the African Charter on Human and Peoples' Rights (African Charter). This chapter contributes to this debate by critically analysing the legal provisions that implicate the existence (or otherwise) of the right to a healthy environment in Nigeria to determine if, and the extent, to which they are justiciable. It also draws on the Indian experience as India shares both a political history and similar constitutional provisions *vis-à-vis* the 'right' to a healthy environment. Particularly, it highlights and draws on the manner the Indian judiciary has interpreted its relevant constitutional provision based on the doctrine of harmonious construction.

In view of this, the chapter is divided into six sections including this introduction. The second part of this chapter highlights the background to constitutionalism in Nigeria. This section provides the basis to understanding the relevant constitutional provisions that have initiated the debate on the existence and justiciable nature (or otherwise) of the 'right' to a healthy environment in Nigeria. The third section discusses the relevant provisions that implicate the 'right' to a healthy environment in the CFRN 1999 and their enforcement. This section critically analyses the enforcement of the 'right' to a healthy environment in Nigeria, specifically the role of the African Charter and the Fundamental Rights (Enforcement Procedure) (FREP) Rules 2009. Section 4 discusses the Indian experience where the doctrine of harmonious construction has been used by the judiciary to interpret its constitutional provisions that are similar to Nigeria's. Thereafter, the fifth section critically examines why and how the Nigerian uncertainty may be resolved by drawing on the harmonious construction doctrine. The sixth section concludes the chapter.

2 Constitutionalism in Nigeria

A constitution is a code of norms that aspires to regulate the allocation of powers, functions, and duties among the various agencies and officers of government, and to define the relationship between these and the public.[4] A constitution has also been

[4] Finer et al. (1995).

defined as the 'whole system of government of a state, the collection of rules which establish and regulate or govern the government'.[5] The term is also used more narrowly, in the sense of a specific legal document, often entitled *The Constitution*.[6] In this regard, the constitution may be defined as the set of fundamental principles that together describe the organizational framework of the state and the nature, the scope of, and the limitations on the exercise of state authority.[7] It also defines the relationship among different kinds of laws (establishing their relative priority and clarifying how conflicts among them are to be resolved) as well as describing how the "primary" or constitutional rules themselves can be created or changed.[8]

From the above definitions, it can be argued that what a constitution *is* can hardly be distinguished from what a constitution *does*. In very broad terms therefore, a constitution "constitutes a political entity, establishes its fundamental structure, and defines limits within which these three functions cannot easily be distinguished, so that it is often distinct to associate them with separate parts of a constitution."[9] There are three standard elements for inclusion in a Constitution: basic governmental structures and the relations between the main powers and functions of government; basic values and commitments; and *fundamental* rights.[10]

Nigeria's constitutional history dates back to 1914 with her emergence as a nation via the efforts of the British to mould the Northern and Southern Protectorates into a united entity by virtue of the amalgamation proclamations of 1914.[11] The first attempt at a constitutional government for Nigeria was the Clifford Constitution of 1922 and till date none of the constitutions (both colonial and post-colonial) provided for the justiciability and enforceability of socio economic rights.[12]

The origin of the inclusion of human rights within Nigeria's constitution may be traced to the movement of minorities to be recognized given the changing political landscape. As the realities of attaining political independence from the British Colonial Government became palpable, ethnic minorities began to challenge what they felt would be the political dominance by the three major ethnic groups in national affairs. In an attempt to secure their political relevance, ethnic minorities increasingly and persistently demanded for the creation of more states along ethnic divides. The traction gained by ethnic minorities in this regards could not be ignored and was considered in the Constitutional Conference of 1957–1958.

[5] Wheare (1966), p. 1.

[6] Hyndman (2000), pp. 95–112.

[7] Mohanan (1997).

[8] Ibid.

[9] Bellamy and Castiglione (1996), pp. 10–11.

[10] Gavison (2002), pp. 89–105.

[11] Diala (2013), pp. 135–162.

[12] Till date, Nigeria has had nine constitutions and there are: the Clifford Constitution of 1922; the Richards Constitution of 1946; the Macpherson Constitution of 1951; the Lyttelton Constitution of 1954; the Independence Constitution of 1960; the Republican Constitution of 1963; the 1979 Constitution; the 1989 Constitution; and the extant 1999 Constitution. See Okafor and Ngwaba (2013), pp. 688–726.

However, rather than concede to the ethnic minorities' demands for the creation of more states or regions, the British Colonial Government entrenched some fundamental human rights in the constitution in accordance with the recommendation of Sir Henry Willinks Commission. These 'fundamental' rights were immediately incorporated and entrenched in the Independence Constitution of 1960, via sections 18–32.[13]

In essence, the two salient factors that accounted for the inclusion of the Fundamental Human Rights (FHR) in Nigeria's 1960 Constitution were the demands by the early nationalists and the recommendation of the Willinks Commission on Minorities.[14] Though the Commission believed that the inclusion of a chapter on human rights would allay the fears of the minorities, it acknowledged the inherent limitation of such rights. It observed that '…while provisions of this kind are difficult to enforce and sometimes difficult to interpret they should be inserted in the constitution because they define beliefs widespread among democratic countries and provide a standard to which appeal may be made by those whose rights are infringed.[15]

Indeed, Nigeria's human rights regime has become difficult to interpret primarily because of the demarcation between fundamental human rights and fundamental objectives (which implicate state duties to protect certain non-fundamental rights). The CFRN lists the fundamental human rights in Chapter IV and these include the civil and political rights such as the rights to life, freedom of association, human dignity etc. The fundamental objectives are contained in Chapter II with section 20 implicating the right to a healthy environment. While these will be discussed in more detail in the following section, it is suffice to note that this distinction in rights emanates from the ideological rivalry between east and west during the drafting of the International Bill of Rights.[16] Nigeria adopting the western conception of human rights as "fundamental" also included socio-economic in its non-justiciable parts of the constitution.

As a result of Nigeria's political heritage, the country adopted the western conception of fundamental human rights as "civil" and "political" in nature, excluding "socio-economic" rights. Nonetheless, the CFRN recognizes the existence of socio-economic 'rights', even if not as justiciable rights via its "Fundamental Objectives and Directive Principles of State Policy" (FODP) provisions expressed in Chapter II. The Constitutional Drafting Committee (CDC) offered reasons for the delineation of rights in the constitution. According to the committee, unlike first generation rights that impose restraints on the state, socio-economic rights require positive action on the part of the state to effectuate them. In essence, if socio-economic rights were made justiciable, the courts would be choked with a multiplicity of cases, a situation that will not augur well for Nigeria as an

[13] Diala (2013).

[14] Nwabueze (1982), p. 151.

[15] Ojo (1977–1980).

[16] Craven (1995).

underdeveloped nation that lacks the material wherewithal to actualise probable judicial pronouncements. The CDC expressed their view thus:

> ...all fundamental rights are, in the final analysis, rights which impose limitations on executive government and are accordingly easily justiciable. By contrast, economic and social "rights" are different. They do not impose any limitations on governmental powers. They impose obligations of a kind which are not justiciable. To insist that the right to freedom of expression is the same kind of "right" as the "right" to free medical facilities and can be treated alike in a constitutional document is basically unsound.[17]

The CDC's reason for excluding economic and social rights from being justiciable is questionable. Indeed, economic, social and cultural rights are complementary to civil and political rights, thereby making the later unachievable without the former.[18] Tamraker emphasizes the foregoing assertion as follows:

> Political and civil rights are the source of freedom while economic, social and cultural rights describe all matters mainly freedom, equality and progress. Civil rights advocate about individual development and, economic, social and cultural rights advocate for the holistic interest of marginalized class, ethnicity and those with different cultural identity. Therefore, there requires proper homework for institutional development of such rights. Both of these rights are said to be supplementary to one another, therefore achievement of one right can be possible only with the existence of another. Following, human rights are presented as fundamental rights in totality.[19]

Further validation of the above view can be found in the example of the European Court of Human Rights (ECHR). Protocol 1 to the Convention for the Protection of Human Rights and Fundamental Freedoms contains the right to education that is considered in conjunction, with civil and political rights rather than with economic and social rights. Therefore, 'the argument that economic, social and cultural rights are not real rights, and the tendency to dismiss them as such, is thus both misguided and counterproductive.'[20]

It is trite to note that the CDC rejected the recommendation of its sub-committee during the deliberations for a limited justiciability of these Objectives and Principles, including the possibility of obtaining mere declaratory judgments from the courts. Two main reasons were advanced in support of the CDC's rejection of this proposal. Firstly, cognizance by the courts would lead to constant confrontation between the executive and/or the legislature on the one hand and the judiciary on the other. Secondly, these Fundamental Objectives and Directive Principles relate to policy goals or directions rather than to the existence or extent of legal rights vested in any individual or group normally subject to the jurisdiction of courts of law.[21]

The first of the above reasons advanced by the CDC cogent because the anticipated conflicts may be avoided by making the language of such provisions

---

[17] Craven (1995), p. 6.

[18] Agbakwa (2002).

[19] See Oloka-Onyango (1995–1996).

[20] Mapulanga-Hulston (2002).

[21] CDC Report, Vol 1, p. vii 1976.

as unambiguous as possible. With the benefit of hindsight, in cases where the courts have interpreted fundamental rights to contemplate certain non-justiciable rights under Chapter II of the Constitution, there have been no "conflicts" between any of the governmental arms. For example, the decision in case of *Gbemre v. SPDC* which was decided in 2005 that interpreted the fundamental human right to life to include the 'right' to a healthy environment has not presented grounds for conflict between and/or among the various arms of government.

On the issue of the FODP being simply goals and principles: does this portend that these guidelines cannot give rise to legal claims where the need arises? Could it be that being guidelines, they represent such vital interests, generally of a politico-economic nature, that their cognizance by the courts is forbidden in veiled application of the principles of *de maximis praetor non curat?*[22] This is implicit in the objection that "it is a field in which professional lawyers who preside over courts of law are not necessarily the most competent judges."[23] If provisions (like environmental protection) under the FODP Chapter are regarded as so fundamental that they cannot be adjudicated upon, or better put, that an individual has no right to enforce an action for environmental degradation, then the reason behind 'fundamentalism' is flawed. The value of such a 'fundamental directive' becomes eroded.

The foregoing legislative loophole is what fundamentally affects the justiciable nature of environmental matters in Nigeria. This is because environmental rights are extensions of socio-economic rights because, arguably, environmental claims, whether they focus on matters like health or on species diversity, seem to import certain substantive values that are rooted in the precepts of a modern welfare state.[24] The next section will examine environmental matters under the 1999 Constitution of Nigeria and their (non) justiciable character as extensions of socio-economic and cultural rights.

3 Doctrine of 'Harmonious Construction' in India

3.1 The 1999 CFRN and the 'Right' to a Healthy Environment and Debates on Justiciability

This section aims to highlight the provisions of the CFRN that implicate the 'right' to a healthy environment. The CFRN contains provisions that implicate environmental protection. While section 16(2) provides that the state shall direct its policy towards ensuring the promotion of a planned and balanced economic development,

---

[22] A rule expressive of the view that international law is too weak to take cognizance of questions involving important issues; it is to reserve to states freedom of action in disputes of importance. Generally see Harris (2008); Boer (2005), pp. 134–137.

[23] CDC Report, Vol. 1, p. vii 1976.

[24] Sax (1990), pp. 93–105. Also see Miller (1976) and Lucas (1972).

section 17(2)(d) provides that 'in furtherance of the social order – exploitation of human or natural resources in any form whatsoever for reasons other than the good of the community shall be prevented.' Section 17(3) provides that the state shall direct its policy towards providing adequate opportunities for securing the means of livelihood and employment; providing adequate medical and health facilities; protection of children and aged and promotion of family life. However, it is section 20 that appears to explicitly highlight the state's responsibility with regards environmental protection. It provides that: 'the state shall protect and improve the environment and safeguard the water, air, land, forest and wildlife of Nigeria.'

Notably, all the provisions highlighted above are contained in Chapter II of the CFRN, that is, the Chapter on FODP thus non-justiciable by virtue of section 6(6)(c) of the Constitution. The non-justiciable nature of these provisions may relate to the definition of the terms "Fundamental Objectives" and "Directive Principles" of state policy. While the former refers to the identification of the ultimate objectives of the nation, the latter indicates the path which leads to those objectives.[25] In other words, FODPs are tantamount to moral, rather than legal, precepts. While Okon[26] describes them as mere guiding principles, Ojo[27] likens them to a cheque on a bank payable whenever the resources of the bank permit. In essence, all the matters under Chapter II on the face of it do not have the force of law.

The classic case on the effect of section 6(6)(c) of the CFRN that renders Chapter II non-justiciable is *Bishop Okogie (Trustee of Roman Catholic Schools)* & Ors *v. Attorney – General of Lagos State.*[28] In that case, Maman Nasir, President of the Court of Appeal (as he then was), held that while section 13 of the Constitution makes it a duty and responsibility of the judiciary, among other organs of government, to conform to, observe and apply the provisions of Chapter II, section 6(6)(c) of the same Constitution makes it clear that no court has jurisdiction to pronounce on any decision as to whether any organ of government has acted or is acting in conformity with the FODP.[29]

However, there are three main arguments that underscore the position that FODP provisions, particularly section 20 that implicates the right to a healthy environment, are justiciable. First is the broad interpretation of the right to life to include the right to a healthy environment; second, the impacts of the African Charter which expressly provides for the existence of the rights; and thirdly, the impact of the FREP Rules. These are considered in turn.

[25] Wiles (2006–2007). Also see CDC Report vol 1, v.

[26] Okon (2003).

[27] Ojo (1977–1980), p. 42. Also cited in Okon (2003), p. 264.

[28] [1980] FNR 445.

[29] Ibid., p. 445.

3.2 The Broad Interpretation of the Right to Life

The broad (judicial) interpretation of the fundamental human right to life to include the right to a healthy environment is increasingly gaining grounds internationally. Countries with similar political and constitutional backgrounds and economic standing such as Pakistan, India and Bangladesh routinely adopt this broad conception of the right to life to give recognition to and enforce the right to a healthy environment. A Federal High Court (sitting in Benin City) in *Gbemre v. SPDC*[30] interpreted the fundamental right to life under section 33 of the 1999 Constitution to contemplate the right to a clean and healthy environment. The applicant in that case, suing in a representative capacity, alleged that the oil production activities of the respondents (Shell Petroleum Development Company of Nigeria (SPDC) and the Nigerian National Petroleum Corporation (NNPC)—specifically gas flaring—violated his constitutional rights to life and the dignity of the human person (sections 33(1) and 34(1) CFRN) in that they adversely affected his life and health as well as his immediate natural environment. The court granted all the reliefs sought by the appellant and held (in a declaratory judgment) that gas flaring is a threat to the life of human beings, and as a result, ruled that the respondents should take immediate steps to stop further flaring of gas in the applicant's community.

Following this decision, Egede[31] has argued that with the broad interpretation adopted by the court, it should be possible for courts to order compensation to victims of environmental destruction; cessation of the environmentally harmful activity; or, even order legislation to prohibit polluting activities. However, it is premature to expect such developments given for several reasons. First, as noted above, the court made a declaratory order; in other words, it merely proclaimed the existence of a legal relationship, but did not contain any specific orders to be carried out by, or enforced against the defendant. In essence, it merely ascertains the rights and duties of the litigants.[32]

Secondly, SPDC filed an appeal to the Court of Appeal, a move that technically puts the decision of the High Court on hold pending the decision of the higher court. Notably, the appeal appears to have fizzled out without any hearing on the substantive issue thus leaving the High Court's decision technically of less value. While refusing to comply with the High Court's order, Shell's appeal is hinged on the argument among others, that the court failed to apply proper judicial procedure and Shell lacked adequate resources to liquefy gas flares.[33] Thirdly, the outcome of a single case, particularly when it is being appealed, is barely enough grounds to make these assertions. This is more so because in *Ikechukwu Opara &*

[30] [2005] 6 AHRLR 152.

[31] Egede (2007), pp. 249–284.

[32] See *Akunnia v. The Attorney General of Anambra State* (1977) SCR 161.

[33] Black (2005) Contempt Case for Shell Over Gas (BBC News, 24 December 2005). http://news.bbc.co.uk/1/hi/sci/tech/4556662.stm.

Others v. Shell Petroleum Development Company Nig. Ltd. and 5 others,[34] a case with facts similar to the *Gbemre case*, a Federal High Court sitting in Port-Harcourt held that the fundamental right to life could not be interpreted to include the right to a healthy environment.[35]

3.3 Impact of the African Charter

The second main means or pathway of advancing the right to a healthy environment in Nigeria is the African Charter. The argument here is simply that since Nigeria has ratified and adopted the treaty into her body of laws, the provisions of the Charter—which include the express right to a healthy environment—are applicable in its entirety. Briefly, Nigeria operates a dualist system wherein treaties are not applied domestically unless incorporated through domestic legislation.[36] Thus, where an international treaty has been signed and legislature has passed a law in accordance with section 12(1) CFRN adopting such a treaty, it becomes part of the country's laws. Section 12(1) states: "No treaty between the federation and any other country shall have the force of law except to the extent to which any such treaty has been enacted into law by the National Assembly".

Nigeria has domesticated the African Charter by ratifying it and domesticating it via the African Charter on Human and Peoples' Rights (Ratification and Enforcement) Act.[37] As the title of the law suggests, its purpose is to localize the African Charter which establishes the system for the promotion and protection of human rights in Africa within the framework of the AU (and the OAU before it) into Nigeria. The Charter recognizes, promotes and protects a wide range of human rights, traversing civil and political, socio-economic and cultural, individual and collective rights[38] including the right to a healthy and clean environment articulated in article 24. In essence, the right to a healthy environment exists in Nigeria via the incorporation of the African Charter in accordance with section 12(1) of the CFRN hence enforceable by the courts.[39]

The *locus classicus* on the status of the African Charter in Nigeria is the case of *General Sani Abacha and others v. Chief Gani Fawehinmi* where the defendant challenged his arrest and detention by the military government as illegal and unconstitutional on the basis that it contravened (amongst other constitutional provisions) Articles 4, 5, 6 and 12 of the African Charter (Ratification and Enforcement) Act. The Supreme Court held that the African Charter is part of Nigerian Law

[34] Suit No. FHC/PH/CS/518/2005.

[35] The case is discussed subsequently in the sub-section on FREP Rules.

[36] Egede (2007), pp. 249–284. Enabulele (2009); Ekhator (2014), pp. 63–79.

[37] Cap A9 Laws of the Federation of Nigeria 2004.

[38] Ssenyonjo (2012).

[39] See *General Sani Abacha v. Chief Gani Fawehinmi* (2000) SC No. 45/1997.

and enforceable by courts in Nigeria. According to the court, where the National Assembly enacts a treaty into law, as was the case with the African Charter, it becomes binding and Nigerian Courts must give effect to it like all other laws falling within the judicial power of the Courts. The court stated further that the Charter gives to citizens of member states of the Organisation of African Unity (now the African Union) rights and obligations, which are to be enforced by our Courts, if they must have any meaning. In other words, if the substantive right to a healthy environment is to have any meaning, it must be judicially enforceable nationally.[40]

The court described the status of the African Charter in Nigeria as a statute with international flavor thus where there is a conflict between it and another statute, its (the Charter) provisions will prevail. The presumption is that the legislature does not intend to breach an international obligation. Notably, the Supreme Court expressed its opinion that even though the Charter possesses "a greater vigor and strength" than any other domestic statue, it remained subject to the Constitution.[41] Defining the limits of the Charter's vigor and strength, the Supreme Court opined that the National Assembly or the Federal Government could not be prevented from removing the Charter from the body of municipal laws by simply repealing the enabling Act.

The Supreme Court's decision in the above case suggests that barring the revocation of the African Charter by the Legislature or the Executive, the substantive right to enjoy a healthy environment subsists and remains enforceable before Nigerian courts.[42] This position has received judicial acknowledgement from the regional judicial authorities, specifically the African Commission on Human and Peoples' Rights in *Social and Economic Rights Action Centre and the Centre for Economic and Social Rights v. Nigeria*[43] involving the alleged infringement of Ogoni peoples' rights guaranteed by the African Charter, including Article 24, during oil exploration and production activities, the African Commission observed that the incorporation of the African Charter into Nigeria's municipal laws meant all the rights contained therein can be invoked in Nigerian courts. The Commission also observed that Article 24 imposes an obligation on the State to take reasonable and other measures to prevent pollution and ecological degradation, to promote conservation, and to secure an ecologically sustainable development and use of natural resources (Paragraph 46).

Atsegbua et al.[44] present a counter-argument to the existence of an enforceable right to a healthy environment based on both the provisions of the African Charter

---

[40] Ako (2013), p. 25.

[41] See *Muhammed Garuba and Others v. Attorney-General of Lagos State* Unreported suit no. ID559M/90.

[42] Ako (2014), p. 7. A Paper presented at the 3rd UNITAR-Yale Conference on Environmental Governance and Democracy, available at: http://conference.unitar.org/yale2014/sites/conference.unitar.org.yale2014/files/2014%20UNITAR-Yale%20Conference-Ako_0.pdf. Also see Ako (2013), p. 25.

[43] Communication 155/96.

[44] Atsegbua et al. (2004).

itself and its domestication into Nigeria law by an Act of the National Assembly. They posit that flowing from the *Abacha case*, whenever there is "any conflict between section 20 of the Constitution and article 24 of the African Charter, it will be resolved in favour of the Constitution. In this regard, they aver that it is doubtful if the Charter can be used to elevate environmental rights from non-justiciable rights to justiciable rights."[45] With regards the domestication Act, they argue that since the African Charter (Ratification and Enforcement) Act is inferior to the Constitution and the former is subject to amendment, or, even repeal—as noted in the *Abacha* case[46]—the constitutional provisions on the non-justiciable nature of the 'right' to a healthy environment is superior.

The arguments made are noted but may be rebutted by the assertion that the provisions of a subsidiary law are only unenforceable to the extent that they are not in consonance with the words or spirit of the constitution. While in fact the provision of section 20 of the CFRN has been the basis that the argument for the existence of a human right to a healthy environment has been advanced, clearly, it really does not expressly provide for the 'right'. In other words, section 6(6)(c) of the CFRN provides expressly that the state duty to "protect and improve the environment and safeguard the water, air, land, forest and wildlife of Nigeria" is not enforceable. Strictly speaking, it renders the state duty to section 20 non-justiciable but does not prevent citizens from claiming their rights that are expressly provided for in subsidiary legislation and/or international treaties from being enforced against the state. This is more so that Nigeria has carried out her international obligation as stipulated in article 1 of the African Charter to recognize the rights, duties and freedoms an enshrined in the Charter and undertaken to responsibility to give effect thereto. The direction which recognition of the right to a healthy environment has taken in Nigeria, such as the "new" FREP Rules of 2009 and the recommendations of the National Conference enunciates the above argument.

3.4 The FREP Rules and the Right to a Healthy Environment

The 2009 FREP Rules made by the Chief Justice of Nigeria pursuant to section 46 (3) of the CFRN provides the broad framework for initiating human rights related suits in Nigeria.[47] The 2009 FREP Rules (an update to the 1979 Rules) create a special (fast-track) legal procedure intended for use to enforce the fundamental human rights provisions of the Constitution pursuant to section 46 of the CFRN. The updated version provisions directly relates to the recognition of legal rights in

[45] Ibid., p. 143.

[46] Page 586 (f)–(g).

[47] Ako (2014).

the field of the environment that implicate the existence of the right to a healthy environment in Nigeria.[48]

Preamble 3 lists the fundamental objectives of the Rules to include improving access to justice for all classes of litigants especially the poor, the illiterate, the uninformed, the vulnerable, the incarcerated, and the unrepresented by respecting municipal, regional and international bills of rights. While municipal bills of rights refer to the CFRN, regional ones will refer to the African Charter and international to treaties such as the International Covenant on Civil and Political Rights (ICCPR) and the International Covenant on Economic, Social and Cultural Rights (ICESCR). Order 1(2) of the FREP Rules defines "human rights" to include "fundamental rights" with the latter defined as rights provided for in Chapter IV of the Constitution, and those stipulated in the African Charter on Human and Peoples' Rights (Ratification and Enforcement) Act.

Clearly, the intention of the FREP Rules is to ensure that the broadest conception and protection of human rights is afforded to Nigerians. Thus, the African Charter has added value to the human rights regime operative in Nigeria as the FREP Rules concede to its wide conception of human rights. Furthermore, as Amechi[49] notes, the FREP Rules have laid to rest any lingering doubt regarding the justiciable nature of the socio-economic provisions of the Act including the right to a healthy environment, by expressly defining fundamental rights as including "any of the rights stipulated in the African Charter on Human and People's Rights (Ratification and Enforcement) Act".

The decision in *Ikechukwu Opara & Others v. Shell Petroleum Development Company Nig. Ltd. and 5 others*[50] does not tally with Amechi's averment. In that case, the Federal High Court adopted a restrictive interpretation of the FREP Rules. The court struck out a suit (with facts similar to *Gbemre's case*) on the grounds that it had procedural defects. Amongst other issues, the court held that the rights created by the African Charter were beyond the definition ascribed to "fundamental rights" as contemplated by section 46 CFRN and so cannot be enforced by means of FREP Rules.

With the *Opara case* and *Gbemre case* having opposite outcomes and on appeal as well as conflicting academic opinions, clearly the legal determination of the interpretation and practical implications of the FREP Rules vis-à-vis the right to a healthy environment remains uncertain. For example, while Ebeku (2007)[51] was of the opinion that the adoption of the FREP Rules procedure in the *Gbemre case* may (amongst other issues) provide the basis for a successful appeal, Ako[52] averred that

[48] Ako (2013).

[49] Amechi (2010), p. 329.

[50] Suit No. FHC/PH/CS/518/2005.

[51] Ebeku (2007).

[52] Ako (2013), p. 33. Also see Oluduro (2014), p. 404 who made a similar assertion stated thus "an individual whose socio-economic rights have been or are likely to be violated can rely on the provisions of the African Charter, including the right to a satisfactory under Article 24 of the Charter to advance the protection of such rights."

the court's reasoning in the *Opara case* would have been decided differently if the FREP Rules of 2009 were in existence at that material time. Based on this uncertainty, the Indian experience is suggested as a means to end the debate by adopting the doctrine of harmonious construction. This suggestion is made based on the development in Nigeria that indicate a preference for the recognition of the right to benefit from a healthy environment as well as the international shift towards the recognition of the 'right'.

Before discussing the doctrine of harmonious construction, it is important to note that the National Conference that concluded sitting in August 2014 presents a positive indication of the future of legal rights in environmental matters in Nigeria.[53] They include the requirement of *locus standi* should be abolished in Public Interest Litigation; the capacity of courts be enhanced in environmental right cases; and environmental rights be constitutionally recognized in Nigeria, amongst others.[54] It is significant that some provisions of the FREP Rules resonate in these recommendations. While there is a long way still for these recommendations to become a reality—they have to be approved by the executive and sent through as proposals for constitutional amendment—there is a clear indication of the rising recognition that citizens' environmental rights should progress beyond being mere state "fundamental objectives". In other words, these recommendations read alongside the domestication of the African Charter, the "new" provisions of the FREP Rules are indicative of the intention that the body of rights in Nigeria should include that to enjoy a healthy environment. To stretch the argument even further, one may claim that these subsidiary laws are made to further the objectives of the CFRN. After all, subsidiary laws are intended to flesh out constitutional provisions.

4 Moving Beyond the Quagmire: Recourse to the Doctrine of 'Harmonious Construction'

The doctrine of harmonious construction is an interpretation tool that the Indian courts have relied upon extensively to resolve inconsistencies in the same Act. An apt description of the doctrine was provided in *Venkataramana Devaru v. State of Mysore*[55] where the court observed: "The rule of construction is well-settled that when there are in an enactment two provisions which cannot be reconciled with each other, they should be so interpreted that, if possible, effect should be given to both. This is what is known as the rule of harmonious construction." Similarly, in *Krishan Kumar v. State of Rajasthan and Ors*,[56] the Supreme Court of India opined, "It is settled principle of interpretation that where there appears to be inconsistency

[53] Etemire (2014).

[54] Draft Report of the National Conference, 2014.

[55] 1958 SCR 895.

[56] 1992 AIR 1789.

in two sections of the same Act, the principle of harmonious construction should be followed in avoiding a head on clash." The court further observed: "It should not be lightly assumed that what the Parliament has given with one hand, it took away with the other. The provisions of one section of statute cannot be used to defeat those of another unless it is impossible to reconcile the same."

In essence, where it appears that two provisions of a law may be construed to have different (conflicting) meanings, or where one appears to derogate the allusions of the other, the courts nonetheless have to give effect to both provisions.[57] Notably, adopting an interpretation of the legislation that reduces one of the provisions to a "dead letter" is not a harmonious construction as one part is being destroyed and consequently court should avoid such a construction.[58] The practical consequence of implementing "harmonious construction" was adequately presented in *M/s. British Airways Plc. v. Union of India and Others*[59] where the Supreme Court held:

> While interpreting a statute the Court should try to sustain its validity and give such meaning to the provisions which advance the object sought to be achieved by the enactment. The Court cannot approach the enactment with a view to pick holes or to search for defects of drafting which make its working impossible. It is a cardinal principle of construction of a statute that effort should be made in construing the different provisions so that each provision will have its play and in the event of any conflict a harmonious construction should be given. The well-known principle of harmonious construction is that effect shall be given to all the provisions and for that any provision of the statute should be construed with reference to the other provisions so as to make it workable. A particular provision cannot be picked up and interpreted to defeat another provision made in that behalf under the statute. It is the duty of the Court to make such construction of a statute which shall suppress the mischief and advance the remedy. While interpreting a statute the Courts are required to keep in mind the consequences which are likely to flow upon the intended interpretation.

The Indian courts have been progressive with the utilization of the doctrine of harmonious construction to enforce socio-economic rights in the country. There are two main steps by which this has been achieved. First is by taking advantage of elaborating the links between civil and political rights to cover some economic, social and cultural rights. For example, the right to life has been broadly defined to include the right to a healthy environment based on the argument that the lack of a healthy environment leads dissipates the essence of the right to life. Arguably, living in 'unhealthy' environment(s) leads to death (denial of the right to life) through illnesses traceable to living in the polluted environments. These links have been drawn at the international level at theoretical, academic and practical levels (Article 10 of the Rio Declaration 1992; Basel Convention on the Control of the Transboundary Movement of Hazardous Wastes and Their Disposal 1992; and

[57] *Jagdish Singh v. Lt. Governor, Delhi and Ors.* Case No.: Appeal (civil) 1866 of 1997 at the Supreme Court of India.

[58] Ibid.

[59] AIR 2002 SC 391.

Aarhus Convention on Access to Information, Public Participation and Access to Justice in Environmental Matters 1998) have developed substantially that it is now accepted that by encouraging environmental protection, for instance, environmental rights "may be cast as a means to the end of fulfilling human rights standards."[60] Furthermore, the entrenchment of the sustainable development paradigm that promotes an integral appreciation and consideration of economic, environment and social imperatives has contributed to the acceptance of the intrinsic linkages between human rights and the environment.

Secondly, by recognizing that the right to a healthy environment is an integral aspect of the right to life, the question of the former being non-justiciable presents a conflict with the latter that is a 'fundamental' right. This conflict thus presents the basis upon which the two constitutional provisions are open to harmonious construction. The courts seizing on this opportunity have interpreted the right to life broadly to include the right to a healthy environment and to breathe life to the latter 'right' that is one of the FODPs and expressed in a hitherto non-justiciable part of the constitution. Regarding the first point, in *Subhash Kumar v. State of Bihar*[61] the Supreme Court interpreted the right to life guaranteed by Article 21 of the Indian Constitution to include the right to a wholesome environment with the latter comprising the right of enjoyment of pollution-free water and air for full enjoyment of life. With regards the latter position, in *Sheikh Bishmillah v. State of Madhya Pradesh and Ors*,[62] it was held that "It is the Court's duty to give a harmonious construction to the directive principles and duties vice versa the fundamental rights."

Recent decisions from the Indian Supreme Court indicate the evolution of a new brand of jurisprudence with the development of a new form of legal action, variously termed as public interest litigation (PIL) and social action litigation. PIL is characterized by a non-adversarial approach, the participation of *amicus curiae*, the appointment of expert and monitoring committees by the court, and the issue of detailed interim orders issued by the Supreme Court of India and the High Courts under Articles 32 and 226 respectively. This expanded notion of the right to life enabled the courts, in its Public Interest Litigation jurisdiction, to overcome objections on grounds of justiciability to its adjudicating the enforceability of Economic Social and Cultural Rights. In fact, the recent trend of case law suggests that it is difficult to have a clear-cut division between human rights cases and environmental cases.

---

[60] Anderson (1996).

[61] 1991 1 SCC 598.

[62] 1994 (0) MPLJ 224.

5 Harmonious Construction Doctrine and Right to the Environment in Nigeria

The central question here then is to determine why and how the doctrine of harmonious construction may benefit Nigeria, particularly in overcoming the judicial conundrum with regards the status of the right to a healthy environment. As noted previously, Nigeria and India share a common political history having been colonized by British hence, their legal heritages are similar just as there constitutional provisions are. With both countries having a list of enforceable fundamental human rights and a list of FODPs deemed non-justiciable by a constitutional provision, they are in the proverbial "same-boat" situation. Undoubtedly, there is need to have a certain degree of predictability in a legal systems otherwise, it will fail to serve the citizens it is meant to safeguard. Indeed, this is the situation in Nigeria where many matters are not pursued through the legal system for fear of the unknown. The 'unknown' refers to the uncertainty in the manner laws/regulations will be applied, especially where there is a prominent opponent; the period of time it will take to reach a judicial resolution; potential abuse of legal rules and processes; lack of proper enforcement mechanism, amongst others.[63]

Thus the Nigerian judiciary can learn from the Indian experience to resolve the uncertainty surrounding the justiciable character (or otherwise) of the right to a healthy environment in Nigeria. The key question to ask regarding the adoption of the harmonious construction doctrine in Nigeria is—paraphrasing the decision in *M/s. British Airways Plc. v. Union of India and Others*—what are the consequences to flow upon the intended interpretation which the (Nigerian) courts should keep in mind. The main consequence is that the citizens will be able to enforce a right to a healthy environment, a situation that augurs well for the citizens, the environment, the economy and the movement towards achieving benchmarks of the contemporary (sustainable) development paradigm.

The recognition of the right does not necessary have to impose the burden of financial compensation from the government (that can ill afford it) as some are wont to suggest. Even if the courts initially make declaratory judgments, this will ensure that future government policies and laws take cognizance of the importance of the environment and related human rights. Also, in a country where corporate activities have resulted in environmental degradation leading to violent conflicts and negative consequences including economic, social, environmental and human rights violations, recognition of the right will promote a higher level of *modus operandi*.

Furthermore, to avoid both inherent and potential ambiguities in the legal interpretation of constitutional provisions, as with other laws, Nigerian judges may emulate the Indian judiciary that refer back to the doctrine of harmonious construction in their judgments. Arguably, the *Gbemre's* case is a practical manifestation of the doctrine harmonious construction. However, many of the decisions

[63] Ako (2013), pp. 33–39.

of Judges in Nigeria on socio-economic rights (including right to the environment) are not premised on any theoretical doctrine or framework, thus such judgements should be premised on the doctrine of harmonious construction. Also, in the right to environment in Nigeria is neither justiciable nor enforceable, however, it can be made implicit via other justiciable sections of the constitution (especially right to life). Thus, Nigerian judges through the prism of harmonious construction can provide the necessary constitutional linkages or connections between the civil and political rights and socio-economic provisions in the constitution.

6 Conclusion

This chapter has undertaken a critical analysis of the justiciable nature of socio-economic rights in Nigeria with emphasis on the right to a healthy environment. Following an exposition of both sides of the argument, it argued, based on similarity on the Indian constitutional provisions, that recourse may be had to the doctrine of harmonious construction to resolve ambiguities in the constitution. The reliance on the doctrine not only presents framework upon which judgments may be based, it also ensures that such decisions are cogent and devoid of the 'consistent ambiguity' that characterizes both judicial and academic opinion.

References

Ako, R. (2013). *Environmental justice in developing countries: Perspectives from Africa and the Asia-Pacific*. Abingdon, England: Routledge.

Ako, R. (2014). Environmental justice in Nigeria's oil industry: Recognizing and embracing contemporary legal developments. In R. V. Percival, J. Lin, & W. Piermattei (Eds.), *Global environmental law at a crossroads*. Cheltenham, England: Edward Elgar.

Anderson, M. R. (1996). Human rights approaches to environmental protection: An overview. In A. E. Boyle & M. R. Anderson (Eds.), *Human rights approaches to environmental protection*. Oxford, England: OUP.

Atsegbua, L. A., Dimowo, F., & Akpotaire, V. (2004). *Environmental law in Nigeria: Theory and practice*. Lagos, Portugal: Ababa Press.

Belz, H. (1972). Changing conceptions of constitutionalism in the era of World War II and the Cold War. *The Journal of American History, 59*(3), 640–669.

Bellamy, D., & Castiglione, D. (Eds.). (1996). *Constitutionalism transformation; European and theoretical perspectives*. Oxford, England: Blackwell.

Boer, R. (2005). Fundamentalism. In T. Benenett, M. M. Grossberg, & R. Williams (Eds.), *New keywords: A revised vocabulary of culture and society* (pp. 134–137). London: Blackwell.

Craven, M. (1995). *The International Covenant on Economic, Social and Cultural Rights: A perspective on its development*. Oxford, England: Clarendon.

Diala, A. C. (2013). The dawn of constitutional governance in Nigeria. In M. K. Mbondenyi & T. Ojienda (Eds.), *Constitutionalism, constitution making and the constitutional reform in Africa: Cotemporary perspectives from sub-Saharan Africa* (pp. 135–162). Cape Town, South Africa: PULP.

Finer, S. E., Bogdanor, V., & Rudden, B. (Eds.). (1995). *Comparing constitutions*. Oxford, England: Clarendon.
Harris, H. (2008). *Fundamentalism and evangelicals*. Oxford, England: Oxford University Press.
Miller, D. (1976). *Social justice*. Oxford, England: Clarendon.
Mohanan, P. (1997). *Constitutional law*. Toronto, Ontario, Canada: Irwin Law.
Nwabueze, B. (1982). *A constitutional history of Nigeria*. Lagos, Portugal: Longman.
Okafor, O. O., & Ngwaba, U. (2013). Economic and social rights: A century of constitutional subordination. In E. Azinge & J. Adediran (Eds.), *Nigeria: A century of constitutional evolution* (pp. 688–726). Lagos, Portugal: Nigerian Institute of Advanced Legal Studies.
Ssenyonjo, M. (Ed.). (2012). *The African Regional Human Rights System: 30 years after the African Charter on Human and Peoples' Rights*. Leiden, the Netherlands: Martinus Nijhoff.
Oluduro, O. (2014). *Oil exploitation and human rights violations in Nigeria's oil producing communities*. Cambridge, England: Intersentia.
Wheare, K. (1966). *Modern constitutions*. Oxfordshire, England: OUP.

Articles

Ackerman, B. (1997). The rise of world constitutionalism. *Virginia Law Review, 83*(4), 771–797.
Agbakwa, S. (2002). Reclaiming humanity: Economic social and cultural rights as the corner stone of African Human Rights. *The Yale Human Rights and Development Journal, 5*, 177–216.
Amechi, E. (2010). Litigating right to healthy environment in Nigeria: An examination of the impacts of the fundamental rights (enforcement procedure) rules 2009, in ensuring access to justice for victims of environmental degradation. *Law, Environment and Development Journal, 6*(3), 320–334.
Ebeku, K. (2007). Constitutional right to a healthy environment and human rights approaches to environmental protection in Nigeria: *Gbemre v. Shell* Revisited. *Review of European Community & International Environmental Law, 16*(3), 319.
Egede, E. (2007). Bringing human rights home: An examination of the domestication of human rights treaties in Nigeria. *Journal of African Law, 51*(2), 249–284.
Ekhator, E. O. (2014). Improving access to environmental justice under the African charter: The roles of NGOs in Nigeria. *African Journal of International and Comparative Law, 22*(1), 63–79.
Enabulele, A. (2009). Implementation of treaties in Nigeria and the status question: Whither Nigerian courts. *African Journal of International and Comparative Law, 17*(2), 326–341.
Etemire, U. (2014). The 2014 Nigerian national conference and the development of environmental law and governance. *Law and Politics in Africa, Asia and Latin America, 4*, 482–490.
Gavison, R. (2002). What belongs in a constitution. *Constitutional Political Economy, 13*(1), 89–105.
Hyndman, P. (2000). Constitutions, constitutionalism and the effective implementation of the International Standards of Human Rights. *The Australian Year Book of International Law, 21*, 95–112.
Lucas, J. R. (1972). Justice. XLVII 237.
Mapulanga-Hulston, J. K. (2002). Examining the justiciability of economic, social and cultural rights. *The International Journal of Human Rights, 6*(4), 29–48.
Ojo, A. (1977–1980). Fundamental human rights in Nigeria: The 1963 and 1979 Constitutional provisions. *NJCL*, 118.
Okon, E. (2003). The environmental perspective in the 1999 Nigerian constitution. *Environmental Law Review, 5*(4), 256–278.
Oloka-Onyango, J. (1995–1996). Beyond the rhetoric: Reinvigorating the struggle for economic and social rights in Africa. *California Western International Law Journal, 26*, 1–73.

Sax, J. (1990). The search for environmental rights. *The Journal of Land Use & Environmental Law, 6*(1), 93–105.
Wiles, E. (2006–2007). Aspirational principles or enforceable rights? The future for socio-economic rights in national law. *The American University Law Review, 22*, 35–64.

Cases

Akunnia v. The Attorney General of Anambra State (1977) SCR 161
Bishop Okogie (Trustee of Roman Catholic Schools) & Ors *v. Attorney – General of Lagos State* [1980] FNR 445
Jagdish Singh v. Lt. Governor, Delhi and Ors. Case No.: Appeal (civil) 1866 of 1997 at the Supreme Court of India
General Sani Abacha v. Chief Gani Fawehinmi (2000) SC No. 45/1997
Ikechukwu Opara & Others v. Shell Petroleum Development Company Nig. Ltd. and 5 others Suit No. FHC/PH/CS/518/2005
Krishan Kumar v. State of Rajasthan and Ors 1992 AIR 1789
M/s. British Airways Plc. v. Union of India and Others AIR 2002 SC 391
Muhammed Garuba and Others v. Attorney-General of Lagos State Unreported suit no. ID559M/90
Sheikh Bishmillah v. State of Madhya Pradesh and Ors 1994 (0) MPLJ 224
Social and Economic Rights Action Centre and the Centre for Economic and Social Rights v. Nigeria Communication 155/96
Subhash Kumar v. State of Bihar 1991 1 SCC 598
Venkataramana Devaru v. State of Mysore 1958 SCR 895

Web/Online

Black R (2005) Contempt Case for Shell Over Gas. (BBC News, 24 December 2005) http://news.bbc.co.uk/1/hi/sci/tech/4556662.stm
Climate Justice, 'Shell Fails to Obey Court Order to Stop Nigeria Flaring Again'. http://www.climatelaw.org/cases/country/nigeria/media/2007May2/. Accessed 16 January 2015. Also see https://www.foe.co.uk/resource/press_releases/shell_fails_to_obey_gas_fl_02052007
Ako R (2014) Promoting Environmental Justice in Developing Countries: Thinking Beyond Constitutional Environmental Rights at p 7 Paper presented at the 3rd UNITAR-Yale Conference on Environmental Governance and Democracy, available at: http://conference.unitar.org/yale2014/sites/conference.unitar.org.yale2014/files/2014%20UNITAR-Yale%20Conference-Ako_0.pdf

Justiciable Disability Rights and Social Change: A Northern Ireland Case Study

Deborah Magill

1 Introduction

For many decades disability discrimination legislation in the UK has provided justiciable rights for people with a disability. In Northern Ireland discrimination on the grounds of disability in employment, education, access to goods and services, or property tenancy is prohibited by the Disability Discrimination Act 1995 (DDA).[1] Disability rights within the Act are domestically justiciable, with complaints being brought for disability discrimination in employment to an Industrial Tribunal (IT) in Northern Ireland.[2] Whilst the current legislation provides rights to individuals, these justiciable rights have been utilised by organisations seeking to bring about social change for disabled people both individually *and* collectively. This chapter will examine the strategic use of domestically justiciable individual rights by organisations working to secure social change in the area of disability rights in the workplace. In particular it will analyse the differing perspectives, on the utility of justiciable rights in securing social change, of two organisations: Disability Action (DA) and the Equality Commission for Northern Ireland

[1] As modified for application in Northern Ireland by the Disability Discrimination Act 1995, sch 8. Disability discrimination law in Northern Ireland has been extended since the passing of this Act, in particular by the Disability Discrimination (NI) Order 2006. The Disability Discrimination Act 1995 has been repealed in England and Wales and replaced by the Equality Act 2010.

[2] Disability Discrimination Act 1995, s. 8(1). Where the IT finds for the claimant it may make a declaration of rights; order the respondent to pay compensation to the claimant or recommend specific action by the respondent: Disability Discrimination Act 1995, s. 8(2). Where, without reasonable justification, the Respondent does not take action recommended by the IT compensation the IT may make may order compensation or increase the amount of compensation under an existing compensation order see DDA 1995, s 8(5).

D. Magill (✉)
Transitional Justice Institute (TJI), School of Law, Ulster University, Jordanstown, UK
e-mail: dnmagill@gmail.com

A. Diver, J. Miller (eds.), *Justiciability of Human Rights Law in Domestic Jurisdictions*, DOI 10.1007/978-3-319-24016-9_7

(ECNI). An introduction to the origins and objectives of each organisation will be followed by a detailed look at DA's involvement in referring and supporting claimants seeking to litigate and how ECNI has engaged in a litigation strategy throughout the 10 years 2001–2011. The chapter will then explore the role played by litigation and how important it has been for ECNI and DA in their pursuit of social change for disabled workers. It will analyse the reasoning behind each of the organisations' engagement with Industrial Tribunals in Northern Ireland. The empirical data used in this analysis has been drawn from seven case files held by ECNI on completed cases which were examined in detail; interview transcripts from semi-structured interviews with four staff from DA and eight staff from ECNI[3]; DA and ECNI publications. The analysis will benefit from insights drawn from current literature on law and social change.

2 The Origins and Objectives of DA

DA is a voluntary organisation working to secure equal rights for disabled people. It seeks to achieve this by supporting inclusion; raising awareness of disabled people's rights among both disabled and non-disabled people and influencing government policy to facilitate equality and inclusion. Formed in the 1950s it was originally the Belfast Committee for the Handicapped, becoming Disability Action in 1992.[4] It has a head office in Belfast and three regional offices in Derry, Dungannon and Carrickfergus. DA is a pan disability organisation, seeking to support people with various disabilities including physical, mental, sensory, learning and hidden. DA employs approximately 100 staff. The work of DA in equality in employment is carried out by the largest department in the organisation, the Employment and Training Services Department.[5] This department implements the Workable (NI) programme and runs an Employment Advocacy Project. Through these two projects DA aims to achieve social change by making workplaces more inclusive of disabled people. The projects are designed to facilitate long term employment and the professional development of disabled employees.

The Workable (NI) programme is a Department of Employment and Learning (DEL) programme which supports disabled people in or seeking employment and is

[3] In order to safeguard the anonymity of Interviewees job titles have not been used throughout this chapter when referring to interview data. Interviewees have been divided into two groups: team members and managers. Team members are those working directly on litigation or related strategies. Managers are those with influence over strategy selection and/or case selection. Within both organisations there is some overlap between these roles in that managers may also work directly on litigation or related strategies.

[4] A brief history of the organisation is available at: Disability Action, 'Organisation and History', http://www.disabilityaction.org/about/organisation-and-history/.

[5] Twenty-seven DA employees work in this department across all four offices.

fully funded by the Department.[6] In order to be placed on the programme clients must be referred by a Pathways Adviser from the Jobs and Benefits office. Clients on the programme receive support from a DA Employment and Training Officer. This support includes help in finding a job, job coaching, mentoring and advocacy, monitoring reasonable adjustments and liaison with employers to advise on disability issues and where appropriate provide financial assistance.[7] This programme is aimed at facilitating and supporting the employment and retention of individual disabled workers. To gain feedback from disabled employees on the programme DA runs user days which are attended by DEL and give clients the opportunity to discuss ongoing issues and make suggestions about how the programme could be developed.[8]

In response to the high demand for advice and information on employment rights from disabled workers not on the Workable (NI) programme, DA introduced an Employment Advocacy Project in 2011. This project is carried out by a peer advocate, known as an Employment Advocacy Officer, who can be contacted for information by a disabled person experiencing difficulties in employment as a result of their disability. The peer advocate will provide information on workplace rights and may attend meetings with the employer and employee with a view to resolving issues. The main objective of this service is to provide short term support where a disability issue has arisen in employment. It aims to help build and/or maintain good relations between the employee and employer leading to a positive outcome that ensures continued employment in a workplace free from discrimination. The project does not provide legal advice. Where clients on the Workable (NI) programme or the Employment Advocacy Project seek to take a case to an Industrial Tribunal (IT), DA refers them to the Equality Commission for Northern Ireland (ECNI) for legal advice and support.

3 The Origins and Objectives of ECNI

ECNI is a non-departmental government body funded by the Equality and Rights Unit within the Office of the First Minister and Deputy First Minister (OFMDFM). It was established by the Northern Ireland Act 1998.[9] This Act dissolved the existing Fair Employment Commission for Northern Ireland; the Equal

[6] Details of all DA funding sources can be found in: Disability Action, 'Annual Report 2011–12' (Disability Action 2012) available at: http://www.disabilityaction.org/fs/doc/publications/annual-report-2011-to-2012-large-print.pdf.

[7] Financial assistance is assessed on an individual case basis. An employer may be given a lump sum to cover development costs such as the cost of extra supervision or training requirements.

[8] Similar sessions have been organised for employers but there has been very poor uptake of places. Interview D2, Employment and Training Support, Disability Action, (Disability Action) Belfast, Northern Ireland, 15 November 2011.

[9] Northern Ireland Act 1998, s 74.

Opportunities Commission for Northern Ireland; the Commission for Racial Equality for Northern Ireland and the Northern Ireland Disability Council and transferred the functions previously carried out by these commissions to a single commission, the ECNI.[10] The ECNI's overall objectives are to promote equality and eliminate discrimination, on the grounds of age, disability, gender, sexual orientation, race, nationality, ethnicity, religion and political opinion.[11] To achieve these objectives it provides legal advice and advocacy to alleged victims of discrimination; provides equality training to businesses; publishes guidance and codes of practice on equality; seeks to raise public awareness of equality issues through media engagement and advertising; carries out research on equality issues; monitors the effectiveness of current equality legislation; advises government on legislative development and oversees employment composition reporting under the Fair Employment and Treatment (Northern Ireland) Order 1998. It also has power to investigate complaints of a failure by a public authority to comply with its duties under section 75 of the Northern Ireland Act 1998.[12]

The ECNI is made up of four divisions: Advice and Compliance; Legal, Policy and Research; Communication and Promotion; Corporate Services. To promote equality in the workplace the Advice and Compliance Division through its Employment Development Department publishes guidance for employers[13] and provides free equality training for employers including seminars on the Disability Discrimination Act 1995 and 'Managing Disability in the Workplace.' It also runs an enquiry line and email service that allows employers to get advice on their responsibilities under equality legislation. The Strategic Enforcement Department within the Legal, Policy and Research division provides legal advice to members of the public who believe they have been discriminated against in the workplace or in the provision of goods and services. This advice is provided over the phone or clients can arrange to meet with an equality adviser at the ECNI offices in Belfast. Some of these clients will receive free legal advocacy.[14] The outcome of litigation in which the Strategic Enforcement Department has provided such support is passed to the Press Office within the Communication and Promotion division who engage with the media to highlight successes and raise awareness of the issues in the case. The outcome of all ECNI supported cases are published in their annual Decisions and Settlements Review.[15]

---

[10] Ibid.

[11] The functions of the ECNI in relation to disability discrimination are set out in The Equality (Disability, etc) (NI) Order 2000 (Equality Order 2000), art 4.

[12] The ECNI has the power to investigate alleged non-compliance with s 75 under the Northern Ireland Act 1998 sch 9, paras 10 and 11.

[13] Publications available online, see Equality Commission for Northern Ireland, 'Employer Focus' (ECNI) available at: http://www.equalityni.org/sections/default.asp?secid=3.

[14] Assistance in relation to legal proceedings is granted by the ECNI under the Equality Order 2000, art 9(2).

[15] Available to download from the Equality Commission for Northern Ireland, 'General: Commission Supported Cases', (ECNI), available at: http://www.equalityni.org/sections/default.asp?

4 DA Employment Rights Strategy

In the Workable (NI) programme DA focuses on developing the disabled person within a good working environment by putting in place support tailored to their individual needs. A Manager described the goals of DA's work on employment rights as follows:

> Equal inclusion, and having workplace attitudes towards people with disabilities that make it easier for them to be recruited; be comfortable in work and to progress in work. I wouldn't say there is any one of them that is any less important than the other. We had a push on career progression and then we hit recession, and a lot of the work on at the minute is about keeping jobs, it's about keeping people in work so the focus changes depending on what is going on but all of those are still there, recruitment, retention, fair treatment around sick absence, promotion and training.[16]

Sometimes requests to the employer for adjustments or an employer's decision to change or terminate a disabled workers employment can lead to a dispute. In such cases DA will attempt to mediate in the situation in order to reach an agreement. DA also receive calls from disabled workers not on the Workable (NI) programme which, up until 2011, were handled by the Employment and Training Officers responsible for the Workable (NI) programme who offered advice on possible solutions over the phone but referred the caller to the ECNI if legal advice was requested. The problem with this approach was that these DA officers did not have the time to get involved in mediation as they run a full case load of Workable (NI) clients. As a Manager explained this left a lot of disabled workers without support in resolving disputes before they became serious:

> If they go to their Union rep. they may not have expertise. If they go to the Labour Relations Agency they will want them to talk to the Equality Commission because they have the disability rights expertise so they go to the Equality Commission and the Equality Commission will talk to them about time scales for cases, how to go about taking a case and broadly what the DDA means but nobody will actually try and intervene, nobody will actually try to stop things in their tracks before it gets worse.[17]

In 2011 a new scheme was introduced which diverts these calls to a peer advocate employed by DA. This scheme, the Employment Advocacy Project, provides general information and advice to disabled workers over the phone and if necessary the peer advocate attends meetings with the employee and employer with a view to providing short term mediation to resolve disputes. Crucially, from its inception the aim of this programme has always been to facilitate mediation rather than litigation. Speaking at the time when this scheme was just being introduced a manager described the role peer advocates would play as follows:

---

cms=Publications_General_commission%20supported%20cases&cmsid=7_36_983&id=983&secid=8.

[16] Interview D3, Employment and Training Support, Disability Action, (Disability Action) Belfast, Northern Ireland, 15 November 2011.

[17] Ibid.

> They are not going to be legal advocates; they are going to help the person put forward their requests for reasonable adjustment, or to challenge harassment, or to look at why they have been selected for termination or whatever it is that they are going through. Having worked through with the individual what their rights are, they are going to present what their demands are to the employer or what their reasonable adjustment requests are or whatever it is. We would envisage then that they will stay involved for a limited time to make sure that that beds in.[18]

The Workable (NI) programme does not include funding for litigation and DA do not channel any of its own resources into providing legal advocacy for clients on the programme in the event that a dispute arises and an agreement cannot be reached with the employer. The Employment Advocacy Project is funded by DA but no legal advice or advocacy is available through this service. Where it has not been possible to secure agreement between a disabled worker and their employer DA advises clients of the general principles of the Disability Discrimination Act 1995 (DDA) but refers them to the ECNI for legal advice. When asked how DA's approach to litigation would differ if there was no ECNI to provide legal advocacy a manager responded as follows:

> If there was no Equality Commission we would probably be going down the road of seeking funding to have some model of legal advice and support for people with a disability but it is a responsibility we see as sitting with government. We see it as a government role to provide that advice and support.[19]

When referring clients to the ECNI for legal advice DA advises clients that the ECNI only agree to represent at IT a small proportion of the complainants who make an application for legal assistance. DA advises clients that this should not deter them from contacting ECNI because even if ECNI will not provide legal advocacy in their case they will provide legal advice about their case. This will allow the client to make an informed decision about whether to litigate the case themselves.[20] If the ECNI refuse to fund the case and the client does not want to pursue it independently then DA will continue to work to find agreement or refer the client to the Labour Relations Agency (LRA) for assistance through its mediation service.[21] However, in some cases no amount of mediation by LRA or DA can bring agreement between the parties. Some clients in this situation choose to resign rather than take a case to IT so they don't even make an application for support from the ECNI. As a team member explained, 'The formality [of the legal process at IT] puts a lot of people off. It's very stressful... I've seen people resign rather than go to an IT and yet I would have been fairly confident they would have won their case.'[22]

[18] Ibid.

[19] Interview D3 (n 16).

[20] Interview D2 (n 8).

[21] Ibid.

[22] Interview D1, Employment and Training Support, Disability Action, (Disability Action) Belfast, Northern Ireland, 15 November 2011.

DA staff have seen first-hand the stress involved for clients in taking cases but it does not advise clients whether to take a case or not. As a manager explained:

> We have seen people that have thoroughly regretted going down that road. [To IT hearing] We have seen people who have been delighted with their outcomes and glad they went down that road... We certainly wouldn't discourage people from taking a case. It is sometimes the only way to go because their situation is so intolerable but even if we are sitting there thinking it is the only way to go, it's not our choice.[23]

Where clients do apply for legal assistance from ECNI but are refused, it is very unusual for them to take a case independently as legal representation is viewed by them as essential but unaffordable. A team member stated that in her 13 years of experience she had only one client who had taken a case independently and had used a private solicitor, but this was funded by the client's house insurance and settled before hearing.[24] When the ECNI does offer legal advocacy the DA supports its client through this process, provides copies of documents in its case files and DA staff appear as witnesses if required. A team member described her role in supporting one of her clients in litigation as follows:

> It was about him [the client] and I sitting down and going over all the ins and outs of his case and deciding yes, perhaps you have a case, let's now approach the Equality Commission and see what their take is on it. He and I then made all the visits to the Equality Commission. This man was a deaf man so it was making sure he had the communications support... So I supported him right through from the decision making, through meetings with the Equality Commission and at various levels of the employer. He didn't actually get to IT; they resolved it at the door so it was right through to the very end. So practical moral support and organising appointments and attending anything with him and all the paperwork. Making sure everything was produced and recorded and up to date.[25]

DA's approach to litigation is therefore to support the disabled person when they have made an informed decision whether DA believes the case is likely to be successful or not. In some cases DA clients will receive legal assistance from the ECNI but choose not to involve DA in the process or suggest DA as a source of evidence because some information in the case file is detrimental to their case. Although DA client files are confidential and information is only provided to a third party following client consent, employers may have copies of some of the information already, such as Workable (NI) support plans and reviews carried out by DA.[26] As a result some DA evidence can end up being used by the employer as evidence that the claimant is for example asking for more adjustment than was deemed reasonable by DA.

---

[23] Interview D3 (n 16).

[24] Interview D2 (n 8).

[25] Ibid.

[26] Interview D3 (n 16).

5 ECNI's Litigation Strategy

The EC receives requests for legal advice on discrimination law from both employers and employees. It provides general information to employers on discrimination law. It provides legal advice to employees on their specific circumstances and some of these employees will also receive legal advocacy from ECNI. When a claimant applies to the ECNI for legal advocacy they are interviewed by a Legal Officer who will gather information on the case. The Legal Officer relays the information on the case to the Senior Legal officer by filling in a Request for Legal Assistance form. This form is passed to the senior legal officer who reviews the information and then adds a recommendation as to whether assistance should be provided or denied onto the form. This recommendation may include potential problems she foresees and details of the likely cost implications.[27] The form is then passed to the Legal Funding Committee (LFC). The LFC, made up of three Commissioners, meets every 2 weeks to consider all the requests received for legal assistance and determines which cases will be supported by the ECNI.[28] The process of having legal funding approved normally takes about 4 months.[29] Legal Officers advise claimants that they should send a DL 56 questionnaire[30] to the Respondent and fill out an ET1(NI) claim application form[31] to the IT themselves while awaiting the decision of the LFC because delay in doing so might result in missing the claim deadline of 3 months. General advice on completion of these forms is given by the Legal Officer.[32]

When legal assistance has been approved by the LFC, Legal Officers employed by the ECNI do all the preparation to take the case to the IT. This includes taking witness statements, gathering the required evidence for the case; responding to requests from the Respondent; filing documents with the IT and liaising with the

[27] The LFC do not always follow the recommendations of the Senior Legal Officer.

[28] According to the ECNI 1 in 3 applications for free legal assistance are supported and at any one time ECNI are supporting 100 claimants in taking a case. Note this figure relates to complaints across all grounds of discrimination and is not limited to employment cases. See Equality Commission for Northern Ireland, 'Taking a Discrimination Case: A layperson's guide to taking a case of discrimination in employment' (ECNI) available at: http://www.equalityni.org/sections/default.asp?cms=your%20rights_Taking%20a%20discrimination%20case%20-%20a%20guide&cmsid=2_688&id=688&secid=2.

[29] Interview E8, Strategic Enforcement Department, ECNI (ECNI Belfast, Northern Ireland, 16 August 2011).

[30] This is the form used in the questionnaire procedure provided by the DDA 1995, s 56. The form requests information from the Respondent about their treatment of the claimant in order to help the claimant to decide whether to make a claim and to allow them to present that claim fully on their ET1(NI) application form to the IT. Time limits and service requirements relating to the DL56 are contained within the Disability Discrimination (Questions and Replies) Order 2004, s 56.

[31] ET1(NI) is the application form a claimant must complete and send to the Industrial Tribunal in order to initiate an employment law claim.

[32] The ECNI provide a Discrimination Complaint Pack which contains guidance on how to lodge an ET1(NI) form with the Office of Industrial and Fair Employment Tribunals (OIFET).

barrister who will present the case to the IT. Barristers are self-employed and engaged by the ECNI on a case by case basis. The Legal Officer attends the hearing alongside the barrister. The initial decision by the LFC to fund legal assistance covers approval of the cost of early preparation (usually Counsel's opinion) after which funding is reviewed and either the financial limit is increased to take the case forward or funding is discontinued. Further reviews of funding are carried out regularly as the amount approved is allocated.

All claims of disability discrimination in employment are heard by the Industrial Tribunal (IT) in Northern Ireland.[33] This is a formal, adversarial system of adjudication with claims heard in public[34] by a panel consisting of one member from an employer background; one member from an employee background and a chairperson who is an experienced legal professional.[35] At this oral hearing a claimant may present their case to the IT themselves or be represented by a legal professional, a union representative or any other person the claimant chooses.[36] Each party is expected to meet their own legal costs. Legal aid is not available for legal representation however it may be available for initial legal advice.[37] The IT may make an order for costs where a party has 'acted vexatiously, abusively, disruptively or otherwise unreasonably, or the bringing or conducting of the proceedings by the paying party has been misconceived.'[38] Appeal of an IT decision on a point of law is to the Northern Ireland Court of Appeal[39] and must be made within 6 weeks of the IT decision.[40] Most of the cases taken by ECNI are settled before hearing. The few cases that go to hearing are often successful.[41]

The Disability Discrimination Act 1995 (DDA) is the piece of legislation under which disability related claims are brought before the IT.[42] The ECNI issued a code of practice which provides guidance to employers on how to avoid discrimination

---

[33] Jurisdiction for hearing employment claims and rules of procedure for the IT are contained within the Industrial Tribunals (Constitution and Rules of Procedure) Regulations (NI) 2005 (Industrial Tribunals Regulations 2005).

[34] Unless this would disclose information falling within s 16 of the Industrial Tribunals Regulations 2005.

[35] Ibid., s 4(1); The Industrial Tribunals (NI) Order 1996 (IT Order 1996), art 6, allows for the Chairman to sit alone in some cases including where the parties have given their written consent or the Respondent does not contest or ceases to contest the case.

[36] IT Order 1996, art 8.

[37] Provision of legal aid for legal advice depends on the claimant's disposable income and is provided by the Northern Ireland Legal Services Commission.

[38] Industrial Tribunals Regulations 2005, s 40(3).

[39] IT Order 1996, art 22.

[40] The Rules of the Court of Judicature (NI) 1980, order 60B.

[41] For example in 2007/08 a total of 25 disability discrimination IT cases were supported by ECNI; 22 settled before hearing; 1 won; 2 lost.

[42] This Act was amended in 2004 to bring into domestic legislation the requirements relating to disability discrimination of the EU Employment Framework Directive, Council Directive 2000/78/EC of 27 November 2000 establishing a general framework for equal treatment in employment and occupation [2000] OJ L303/16; Disability Discrimination Act 1995 (Amendment) Regulations

under the DDA.[43] Claims may be brought under section 4 of the DDA alleging disability discrimination in the provision of training, promotion, terms of employment or selection for employment. According to section 3A(1)(a) of the DDA an employer discriminates if 'for a reason which relates to the disabled person's disability, he treats him less favourably than he treats or would treat others to whom that reason does not or would not apply.' In some ECNI supported cases the Respondent attempted to defend a claim of disability discrimination by disputing that the claimant was a disabled person as defined by section 1(1) of the DDA. In response to this ECNI organise a medical assessment and report to clarify the issue. The DDA states that 'A person has a disability for the purposes of this Act if he has a physical or mental impairment which has a substantial and long-term adverse effect on his ability to carry out normal day-to-day activities.' The Office of the First Minister and Deputy First Minister (OFMDFM) has issued guidance on matters to be taken into account when considering whether a person falls within this definition.[44] In two of the ECNI case files examined for this research the claimant's disabled status was contested by the Respondent employer but in both these cases this point was conceded by the Respondent prior to hearing.[45]

Many of the cases taken by ECNI contend that the employer has failed to make reasonable adjustments as required by section 4A of the DDA.[46] This provision places a duty on employers to take steps to prevent a disabled person being placed at a substantial disadvantage in their employment, because of their disability, in comparison with employees who are not disabled. This may require an employer to provide training, adapt premises, provide special equipment or adjust working hours.[47] Section 18B(1) of the DDA gives a list of matters to be considered when determining what is reasonable. This list includes consideration of the cost of adjustments to the employer; the practicality of the adjustment; the resources available to the employer to make the adjustment and whether the adjustment would prevent the disadvantage. When preparing a case alleging failure to make reasonable adjustment the ECNI requests from the employer the personnel and

2003. s 17A Disability Discrimination Act 1995 provides for enforcement of the Act by the alleged victim of discrimination.

[43] Equality Commission for Northern Ireland, 'Disability Code of Practice: Employment and Occupation' (ECNI 2005) available at: http://www.equalityni.org/archive/pdf/DisEmploymentCOP05F.pdf which was issued under s 53 DDA 1995.

[44] OFMDFM, 'Disability Discrimination 1995: Guidance on matters to be taken into account when determining questions relating to the definition of disability' (OFMDFM 2008); This guidance is issued under s 3 of the definition of disability under DDA 1995 and is available at: http://www.ofmdfmni.gov.uk/disabilitydiscriminationact1995.pdf. The ECNI have also published a booklet on the definition of disability under the DDA 1995, see Equality Commission for Northern Ireland, 'Definition of Disability: Disability Discrimination Act 1995' (ECNI 2007) available at: http://www.equalityni.org/archive/pdf/DefinitionofDisability07.pdf.

[45] Case Files E4 and E6.

[46] Five of the seven ECNI case files examined for this research involved a claim of failure to make reasonable adjustments.

[47] DDA 1995, s 18B(2).

training records for the claimant, time sheets; risk assessments; reasonable adjustments made and copies of employment policies to determine what steps the employer took to ensure the disabled employee was not placed at a disadvantage because of their disability. Medical records are obtained and expert medical evidence is usually prepared to clarify the specific needs of the disabled person.

It appears from the case files examined and the annually published *Decisions and Settlements Review* published by the ECNI, that the organisation has been very successful in securing positive decisions or settlements for the claimants they have supported to the conclusion of their case.[48] The majority of cases taken settled before a full hearing. Settlement agreements typically contain financial compensation for the claimant; an apology to the claimant; a reaffirmation of the Respondent's commitment to equality and sometimes a donation to a disability support charity nominated by the claimant. The ECNI also insist that an agreement by the Respondent to liaise with the ECNI to develop and review the Respondent's equality policies is included in settlement agreements.[49] ECNI always refuses to include a confidentiality clause within a settlement agreement. Securing payment of awards does not seem to have been problematic for the ECNI as in only one of the seven files examined was it necessary to serve a Civil Bill through the County Court to obtain settlement moneys.[50]

According to one team member, 'Cases that litigate to the full way are usually cases on the margins although some of them are very straight forward cases in which the respondents have no legal representation and they are just 'thran' and they go for it.'[51] In the small number of ECNI cases that do result in a loss at IT very few are appealed by the ECNI. One interviewee explained this reluctance to appeal as follows:

> ...you know costs don't follow the event in the tribunal process, whereas you go somewhere like that, the Appeal Court, you take on enormous risks and particularly for us as a statutory body. With public money you really have to think very long and hard before you go to the Northern Ireland Court of Appeal because you are going to have to pay the other side's cost if you lose.[52]

[48] However, it should be noted that no case files were provided for this research for examination by the ECNI where assistance had been discontinued prior to hearing or settlement.

[49] ECNI clients are made aware at the time of application for legal assistance that ECNI will require this to be included in any settlement terms.

[50] Case file E7.

[51] Interview E1, Strategic Enforcement Department, ECNI (ECNI Belfast, Northern Ireland, 19 October 2011); 'Thran' is a colloquial Northern Irish term used to refer to a person who is stubborn or obstinate. Note the majority of Respondents, including those in the case files examined for this research, do have legal representation.

[52] Interview E4, Strategic Enforcement Department, ECNI (ECNI Belfast, Northern Ireland, 23 August 2011).

6 Objectives of Litigation Strategy: Individual Justice

DA and ECNI have adopted very different approaches to litigation. DA does not provide legal advice. Its strategy in relation to litigation is to refer clients to the ECNI for legal assistance in taking a case, to support the claimant during the process and to provide evidence pertaining to the case to the ECNI. When asked how its litigation strategy would differ if ECNI did not exist, a DA manager stated that they would be forced to commit resources to offering some sort of legal advocacy service to claimants.[53] ECNI has a statutory duty to provide legal advice to disabled people who feel they have been discriminated against and to engage in casework to IT. In carrying out this duty it has adopted a litigation strategy which supports between 60 and 100 cases a year, spread across all grounds of discrimination. The criterion for case selection together with the volume of cases that are concluded by settlement or at first instance reveals a focus on producing numerous, successful outcomes. Despite their differing approaches to, and role in, litigation it is clear from the data collected from both DA and ECNI that they share a common objective of achieving individual justice for claimants through litigation.

6.1 Objective of Litigation: Pursuit of Individual Justice by DA

DA views the tribunal process to be very stressful for disabled people, particularly those with mental health issues, physical conditions that are exacerbated by stress and those with learning difficulties.[54] DA's involvement in supporting clients through the legal process has arisen as a result of their recognition of the difficulty faced by disabled people taking a case to IT. This supporting role is aimed at ensuring access to ECNI advice and a legal remedy for disabled people. However, DA views legal action as the last resort when all other efforts to resolve a dispute between the parties have failed. One team member said, 'I think support and advice and negotiation are always better because at the end of the day when it goes to an IT it has reached the point of no return.'[55] Although some DA clients do decide to pursue a case to IT, in DA's experience most would prefer to come to an agreement with the employer without legal action as one team member explained:

> Most people don't want to take a case; they don't want a judgement; they don't want to rub their employer's nose in it; they don't want it all over the paper. They want the training or they want their employer to back off around their sick absence or they want the promotion

[53] Interview D2 (n 8).

[54] Interview D3 (n 16). DA is not overtly critically of the process which they see as unavoidably legalistic because disability discrimination cases are complex.

[55] Interview D1 (n 22).

> or they don't want to be medically retired or selected for redundancy. They want to continue working or they want to get the job.[56]

DA considers that it would not be financially viable for its organisation to provide legal advocacy in cases that have failed to get ECNI assistance. As a manager explained:

> Actual support to people at IT is a huge undertaking for a voluntary sector organisation to offer. What we would be at risk of doing is you would have the ECNI supporting this percentage of cases; you would have DA supporting an even smaller percentage of cases and you would still have a gap that we just couldn't resource. There is no way we could raise money to meet that demand.[57]

Although DA would like to see all clients who have experienced discrimination and who wish to pursue a legal remedy have the opportunity to do so, it recognises that neither it nor ECNI have the financial resources to accommodate this. DA acknowledges that disabled employees can get justice by taking a case to IT but it doesn't perceive this as the best form of justice as most of its clients would prefer to get justice through negotiation.

6.2 *Objective of Litigation: Pursuit of Individual Justice by ECNI*

Among the criteria which ECNI considers when deciding whether to provide legal advocacy is whether it is unreasonable to expect the complainant to proceed to IT alone. This indicates that, like DA, ECNI places value on ensuring that potential claimants have access to a legal remedy. With legal aid not available for IT cases, ECNI is the only way in which potential claimants can access publicly funded legal assistance to pursue an employment discrimination case. One team member viewed the ECNI's provision of free legal advocacy as a limited form of legal aid.[58] For ECNI, although the disability discrimination legislation gives disabled people rights, it is of no benefit unless disabled people can enforce these in court and the ECNI has a vital role to play in facilitating such enforcement. This aligns with McCann's view that legal norms are not self implementing and therefore their impact may vary depending on the ability of those seeking to rely on them to mobilise.[59] A manager commented that, 'In respect of disability the legislation

[56] Interview D3 (n 16).

[57] Ibid.

[58] Interview E2, Strategic Enforcement Department, ECNI (ECNI Belfast, Northern Ireland, 16 August 2011).

[59] McCann (1994), p. 175.

provides individuals with rights. That's the easy bit. The tough bit is working through the practicalities of actually making those rights real.'[60]

ECNI values the positive results it gets for individual clients. As one team member put it, 'We make a real difference to people's lives. Individuals come in here. They believe they have been treated really unfairly. If we can help them get some redress or some kind of satisfaction out of that; that is fantastic.'[61] Securing the best outcome for the claimant is a priority for Legal Officers when negotiating with the Respondent and advising claimants, as a manager explained: 'We do put the client's best interests at heart and we are very conscious that if you turn down £30,000 for your client and you go in [to a IT hearing] you could lose next week.'[62]

7 Objectives of Litigation: Collective Justice

DA and ECNI share some common ground on how effective litigation can be in achieving individual justice but they have quite contrasting views on how effective a litigation strategy can be in achieving collective justice. DA uses litigation outcomes to a limited extent when seeking to provide employers with a better understanding of their obligations under disability discrimination legislation and to encourage employers to fulfil those obligations in relation to its clients. However, DA is very wary of the potential negative impact litigation outcomes might have on its objective of workplace inclusion for disabled people generally. The ECNI is also aware of this potential for negative impact on collective rights but consider this to be significantly outweighed by the potential benefits of litigation in delivering collective justice.

Collective justice is at the core of the ECNI's litigation strategy. It is used by the ECNI to try and ensure the implementation of disability discrimination in workplaces across Northern Ireland. This is done by using successful outcomes in training and advertising campaigns in order to raise awareness of disability rights among both employers and employees; by gaining settlements that allow the ECNI to influence employer equality policies and practices; and by seeking to influence negotiations between employers and disabled workers by creating what they call a ripple effect as employers become aware of cases that illustrate that non-compliance with legislation carries with it the threat of litigation. The ECNI also believes litigation has the potential to influence the law by gaining favourable interpretations and illustrating where there may be gaps in protection. However, with what they see as good protection already in place under the DDA and a limited

[60] Interview E3, Strategic Enforcement Department, ECNI (ECNI Belfast, Northern Ireland, 19 October 2011).

[61] Interview E1 (n 51).

[62] Interview E3 (n 60).

budget to allocate, it has chosen to favour more straightforward cases with a high probability of success at first instance.

7.1 Objective of Litigation: Pursuit of Collective Justice by DA

DA sees the outcomes in individual cases as having a limited impact on disabled employees collectively by providing a resource that can be used during negotiations with other employers. This very limited view of the potential for using case outcomes has arisen for three key reasons. Firstly DA believes most disputes which arise between employers and disabled employees can be resolved through amicable agreement without the need to become heavy handed and refer to legal obligations. Secondly it believes case outcomes only demonstrate how the legislation operated in the specific facts presented to the IT and factual circumstances vary greatly in disability discrimination cases. Thirdly litigation can lead to the perception by employers that recruiting disabled workers is problematic and risks future litigation. This perception could reduce the likelihood that employers will recruit disabled employees.

DA wants to impress upon employers that adjustments to facilitate the recruitment and ongoing development of a disabled worker are not usually terribly difficult; don't involve huge expense or interfere with business efficiency and that a diverse workforce is a positive thing. As one team member explained 'We would try and approach everything in a very positive way, it's about saying it definitely can work. We try everything we can to make it work and it's only as a last resort then we would fall back on legislation.'[63] When DA does refer to legal obligations they find that often employers do not know what their obligations are under the disability legislation. A team member explained that 'Quite often you would talk to an employer about their legal obligations they will say "oh really gosh I didn't know that I would have to do that. Is that really an obligation?"'[64] In some cases there is knowledge of an employer's obligations within the personnel department of the organisation but the disabled worker is having difficulty with their direct manager who is not aware of the legislation. In such cases it is simply a matter of contacting the personnel department and asking them to get involved in negotiations to bring about a resolution.[65]

Despite focusing on amicable resolutions to disputes DA does consider the DDA to be an important piece of legislation to be able to refer to when negotiations with employers stall. One team member explained how DA would operate in the absence of the DDA: 'We could still negotiate without it. We still are people with skills. We

[63] Interview D2 (n 8).

[64] Interview D1 (n 22).

[65] Interview D3 (n 16).

still are people who would be out there and we did the job long before DDA was ever here, but it has made it easier.'[66] When explaining to an employer their obligations under DDA, DA doesn't usually refer to litigation outcomes. One team member explained how they set out DDA obligations to an employer as follows:

> I don't actually refer much to previous case law. I tell employers what the DDA says and I tell them what I think that means for them. I tell them when I think they need to make adjustments and I tell them they need to be in the form of A, B, C and D. I don't do it from case law and mostly they accept it.[67]

DA appears to separate disability law into *legislation* and *litigation*. It prefers to remind employers of their statutory obligations within the legislation rather than through the application of legislation in cases. This is disingenuous as legislation comes to life by its interpretation in litigation. However this false dichotomy may have arisen as a result of DA concerns over the potential negative impacts of litigation on social change. Referring to litigation may result in employers viewing disabled employees as demanding and as representing a litigation risk (this is discussed further below). Despite mainly relying on the legislation to inform employers of their legal obligations, DA does sometimes refers to specific litigation outcomes in order to explain how the DDA has been interpreted by the IT. Several DA interviewees referred in particular to using the case of *Palmer v Social Security Agency* in cases where sickness absence relating to a disabled worker's disability was causing the worker to have difficulty with their employer.[68] In *Palmer v Social Security Agency*, the portion of Mr Palmer's sick leave which related to his disability had been included in his sick leave accumulation which invoked a disciplinary procedure. The IT held that 'the respondent should have differentiated between the DDA absence and the sinusitis absence in the disciplinary process upon which it embarked.'[69] The claimant was awarded compensation for missing out on a promotion due to the disciplinary procedure and for injury to feelings.[70]

This use of case outcomes by DA is limited as DA views the majority of case outcomes as very individualistic particularly in relation to reasonable adjustments which is the area involved in most disputes. In its view, because the decision as to whether an adjustment is reasonable must take account of the employer's circumstances and the disabled worker's circumstances it is subject to a myriad of factors. Disability itself is a diverse concept and therefore making predictions about what should be considered reasonable on the basis of other cases is not feasible. As a team member explained, 'The concept of reasonable adjustment is so tied to the

---

[66] Interview D1 (n 22).

[67] Interview D2 (n 8).

[68] *Palmer v Social Security Agency* [2008] NIIT131/07IT (11 November 2008); ECNI supported this case to IT.

[69] Ibid., para 21.

[70] The IT calculates the level of award for injury to feeling in line with guidance set down by the Court of Appeal in *Vento v Chief Constable of West Yorkshire Police* (No 2) [2003] IRLR 102.

individual employer's circumstances and the individual disabled person's circumstance. You can get the same employer doing the same thing to different people and it having different outcomes.'[71]

Occasionally DA encounters a situation where pointing out to an employer what their legal obligations are has not been sufficient to achieve compliance. DA believes that sometimes this defiance is based on employers concluding that they can risk taking the financial hit to get rid of what they see as a problem or that an IT is unlikely to result as the disabled worker will probably not want to go through the stress of legal action.[72] For this reason DA believes that there does need to be a flow of meritous cases being brought through the litigation process.[73]

7.2 DA Concerns Over Litigation's Potential Negative Impact on Collective Justice

DA perceives a risk in cases being brought before the IT which would give the impression that disabled employees are demanding and come with a risk of legal dispute. A team member explained its concern over some litigation as follows:

> It can damage the public perception of how demanding a person with a disability is. It can give that perception that people with disabilities are being unreasonable and having very high expectations and wanting everything their way when obviously that's not the case and the majority of people with disabilities would do anything rather than litigate. We have seen a fairly sizeable number of people who have dropped out of employment rather than face the treatment that they were having and that doesn't show in case law, it doesn't come to public attention. So the trivial cases or vexatious cases or cases where the disability is very thin don't do anybody any good.[74]

Although in DA's experience trivial or vexatious cases lose at IT, it still considers these cases to have a damaging impact on how people perceive disabled employees in the workplace. This is therefore seen as detrimental to DA's key objective of bringing about inclusion by encouraging employers to take on more disabled employees. This is similar to Olson's findings in her work on women's' rights litigation in which she notes that activists can be frustrated by individuals outside the movement taking weaker cases independently.[75] ECNI pass cases through a selection process that tests their merits regularly as the litigation progresses which prevents cases without merit going all the way to hearing with ECNI

[71] Interview D3 (n 16).

[72] Interview D1 (n 22) and Interview D4, Employment and Training Support, Disability Action, (Disability Action) Belfast, Northern Ireland, 15 November 2011.

[73] Ibid., Interview D4.

[74] Interview D3 (n 16).

[75] Olson (1995), p. 209.

legal assistance. However, this does not prevent individual claimants taking cases that are without merit.

DA's view of social change is to an extent instrumental under Kostiner's model as they seek to provide a service that enables disabled people to access and maintain employment.[76] In Kostiner's model an social movement organisation (SMO) with an instrumental view of social change will seek to provide a service to the marginalised group in order that this group can secure resources. Within this instrumental schema an SMO will assess the role of law in securing social change by its ability to secure resources for the marginalised group.[77] DA's experience in delivering its support service to disabled workers has resulted in an interesting dichotomy in relation to the role of law in achieving social change. DA considers the disability *legislation* to be significantly important in securing the rights of disabled employees by influencing negotiations. However, DA places a more conservative value on *litigation's* role in delivering both individual and collective justice. It believes some cases do need to be taken to ensure that the legislation remains relevant in negotiations between employers and employees but specific cases are only occasionally relied on in such negotiations. Furthermore taking a case is seen as a last resort in achieving individual justice.

In pursuing amicable resolutions to disputes between employers and employees DA want to bring about social change by transforming how employers view disabled workers. It is hoped that this transformed view will result in more disabled people being employed and adjustments being made to accommodate their needs. This suggests a cultural view of social change within Kostiner's model. According to Kostiner when a cultural view of social change is adopted by an SMO, it results in law being viewed by the organisation as irrelevant because forcing a change in action through the law does not achieve a change in thinking.[78] However this does not align with DA's view of the DDA. DA believes that the law, the DDA, is very relevant and in fact has played a key role in changing how some employers view disabled employees. It is seen by DA to have achieved this by ensuring that disabled people have been integrated into the workforce and, through that integration, employers' views of disabled workers have been altered. A team member explained this as follows:

> If you change the legislation then people start to do things that they might not otherwise have done and discover that actually it wasn't so horrendously awful after all and that in fact we did recruit some disabled workers and it has a positive business benefit; that they did bring something fresh to the organisation; that they weren't off sick every five minutes and we do have a more diverse workforce as a result. I think that the legislation didn't change the mindset but the impact of the legislation over time changed the mindset.[79]

[76] Kostiner (2003), p. 336.

[77] Ibid., p. 349.

[78] Ibid., p. 354.

[79] Interview D3 (n 16).

DA's cultural view of social change has not resulted in law being considered by DA to be irrelevant as Kostiner's model suggests. Instead it has, as with their instrumental view of law in securing individual justice, resulted in a dichotomy. *Legislation* is viewed as having played a central role in transforming how the marginal group is viewed by employers but *litigation* is viewed as potentially detrimental. Whilst separating law into legislation and litigation is disingenuous it is nevertheless how DA perceives law. This segregation has allowed DA to attribute a greater role for legislation and a lesser role for litigation in social change.

DA does not use litigation to secure participation in its projects by disabled people. It refers to being inundated with queries for very simple advice which is usually all the disabled person has needed to resolve whatever the issue it is that they are having with their employer and DA has the staff in place to provide that advice.[80] Support to pursue litigation is not seen as a significant area of need among disabled employees.

7.3 Objective of Litigation: Pursuit of Collective Justice by ECNI

ECNI values the individual justice that its litigation strategy achieves but it also values the potential for litigation to bring about collective justice for disabled workers. As a member of management explained, 'It is about getting a resolution for the individual. But we are very clear that in selecting the cases the strategic value of that case isn't just about the recompense for the individual. It's also about changing behaviours across the board.'[81] A case will not be supported unless it will make a contribution to this collective justice objective. As one manager explained, 'We have to change employer practices or change the level of awareness or change society's understanding of the law. It has to be that, not just the individual but that people will learn something from this case. There has to be a change element.'[82] The criteria which ECNI uses when selecting cases for legal assistance, reveals just how important it considers this collective impact to be as it seeks to eliminate discrimination against disabled employees throughout Northern Ireland. The criteria are made up of the following:

- Does it raise a question of legal uncertainty?
- Does it relate to the strategic objectives of the Commission: potential to improve employment practices; raise public awareness of protection of law; impact on discriminatory practices; potential for follow up by the Commission;

[80] Ibid.

[81] Interview E3 (n 60).

[82] Interview E5, Strategic Enforcement Department, ECNI (ECNI Belfast, Northern Ireland, 23 August 2011).

- Does it raise a question of principle?
- Is it unreasonable to expect applicant to proceed alone?
- What level of complexity is the case
- Are there reasonable grounds for believing discrimination has occurred?
- Is the cost of the case likely to be commensurate with benefit to complainant and generally?
- What are the prospects of success?
- What is the level of cooperation of the claimant?
- Is this a second or subsequent application?
- To what extent has the commission supported similar cases?

When ECNI is choosing a number of cases to support from a list of applications, it tries to spread its case work across all grounds of discrimination including disability. It also tries to spread cases across the geographical area in Northern Ireland; across various industries and across various levels of employee seniority.[83] This ensures that it is raising awareness throughout society as people relate to stories that are local to them or which involve professions or industries they may have a connection to. It continues to take cases involving well established protections that have been the subject of prior litigation. It does this in order to ensure key rights continue to enjoy a high profile. It refers to this practice as profiling.[84]

7.4 ECNI Use of Litigation to Influence What Happens on the Ground

A key focus of ECNI's efforts in relation to disability rights in employment is ensuring that the protection provided by the legislation is enjoyed by disabled people on the ground. One of the ways ECNI does this is by providing training to employers to raise awareness of the obligations legislation places on employers in relation to disabled employees. Litigation outcomes are used extensively in delivering this training. A manager stated, 'Litigation is at the core of explaining to people what rights and responsibilities are actually all about.'[85] The ECNI views disability legislation as complex and therefore it sees a need to support employers in fulfilling their responsibilities under it through training. During this training the ECNI sets out the provisions of the DDA and use IT decisions to provide examples of how these provisions operate in practice. It also uses IT decisions to point out what practices are not compliant with the legislation and give employers guidance on how to avoid being taken to an IT. A manager stated:

[83] Ibid.

[84] Ibid.

[85] Interview E1 (n 51).

> They are difficult issues so it's an unusual situation in respect of disability. It starts with a warm and cuddly feeling, the practicalities are tough and we're there to support and so a lot of things that we would do is from case work. We would roll out case studies from employers – What do you need to do? How do you do it? Those kinds of things and employers are very appreciative of that so I think that it is something that we are very conscious that we have to work with employers on.[86]

ECNI believes working with employers ensures that employers see equality as something that employers should be acting to bring about rather than something the ECNI must deliver. A manager described ECNI's engagement with employers through training as follows:

> It is very much about providing those who have responsibilities under the legislation, employers, service providers, public sector with a top notch service about how to meet their responsibilities because while we may see them in court for cases on the other hand we also do huge amounts of workshops with them, providing guidance notes, give them consultancy, we do all that kind of thing. It is very much about what I will call the agenda of trying to ensure that we no longer say in Northern Ireland equality, the Equality Commission does that, it's nothing to do with the rest of us.[87]

Publicity of positive case outcomes is used to raise both employee and employer awareness of disability rights. Positive case outcomes are forwarded to the media by the ECNI in the hope that they will publish a story around the case. A manager stated that, 'We [ECNI] have very little difficulty selling disability stories to the media... There is very often a real, I suppose what the media people would call a human interest factor around people overcoming specific difficulties relating to disability.'[88] Claimants are required to accept when applying for legal assistance that their case will be publicised by the ECNI. A manager highlighted the importance of publicising case outcomes by saying, 'We [ECNI] are a strategic enforcement agency. The focus for me is how can I publicise this case? How can I use this case to help others? That sounds really crass; it's utilitarian; it's like what can I use this for to get the message out to as many people as possible?'[89] As noted earlier, most cases are concluded before going to a full hearing. ECNI has found a way of maximising the benefit of settlements by always insisting on the inclusion of an undertaking by the Respondent to liaise with the ECNI to review and develop equality policies and procedures. This allows ECNI to influence these policies and ensure they are compliant with equality legislation.

Taking numerous cases that have a high chance of success is considered by ECNI to create what they refer to as the ripple effect of litigation. Galanter calls this effect the shadow of the law.[90] According to Galanter negotiations can be influenced by the perception amongst the parties that a failure to meet demands will result in litigation. ECNI believes this ripple effect is created by running cases

[86] Interview E3 (n 60).

[87] Ibid.

[88] Interview E1 (n 51).

[89] Interview E4 (n 52).

[90] Galanter (1983), pp. 122 and 132.

which can be publicised by presenting a personal account of discrimination and setting out legal reasoning in a manner that non-legally trained members of the public can follow.[91] This informs employers and employees of disability rights and ECNI also believes it impresses upon employers the possibility that disabled employees may take them to an IT if they fail to fulfil their legal obligations. It also reminds employers that the ECNI provides legal assistance to some claimants thus potentially increasing the likelihood that an employee might take a case to IT. Furthermore if ECNI supports the case adverse publicity will follow, identifying their business as one which has discriminated against a disabled person.[92] Even where an employer risks non-compliance, the ECNI believes that when legal assistance is granted this shadow induces a rapid settlement:

> 90 % of our cases settle because employers have seen the publicity, they have seen the awards that can be made against them. Most of our employers and service providers fold; we don't even have to prove discrimination. Now obviously we have the evidence ready if need be to prove discrimination, but we are actually in a very privileged position because of the decades of work that we have done in bringing these cases and proving these cases and getting awards from tribunal over many years.[93]

Despite having built up a body of cases over the years ECNI still feels the need to continue to take cases to ensure the shadow of law endures. A manager explained that 'If individual cases are not pursued, if the punitive aspect of compensation and damages isn't highlighted, people will think they can get away with more.'[94]

ECNI acknowledges that litigation can cast a shadow of law that has a negative impact on how employers act in relation to equality for disabled people by discouraging some employers from recruiting disabled staff. This concern was raised within the ECNI when three cases involving disabled people who were engaged by employers under a work placement scheme applied to the ECNI for assistance with discrimination claims. Although taking these cases carried with it the risk that employers might refuse to take part in the voluntary placement scheme in the future, the LFC decided it was important to send a message to these employers that discrimination was never acceptable, even where the a person was not employed but simply on a placement. However these cases were not published other than in the annual Decisions and Settlement Review as they might have discouraged other employers from getting involved in the placement scheme. This is similar to DA's concerns over the potential negative effect litigation can have on social change.

---

[91] Interview E1 (n 51).

[92] Interview E8 (n 29).

[93] Interview E4 (n 52).

[94] Ibid.

7.5 ECNI Use of Litigation to Influence the Law

The ECNI believes that litigation can be used to clarify the law. However, only a small number of cases are supported in order to do this. Such cases are considered to have less press appeal because they often involve more intricate legal argument. ECNI sees the potential for litigation to expose gaps in current legislative provisions or extend the coverage of legislation to novel situations. However current legislation in relation to disability rights in employment is considered by ECNI to be good. Furthermore cases that have the potential to extend law or highlight any gaps in the legislation are considered by them to be high risk and likely to run through to the Court of Appeal for Northern Ireland and possibly the Supreme Court. Taking cases of this kind requires the commitment of a large portion of its budget and are considered to have less impact on the ground than numerous cases that apply the law as it stands and yield successful outcomes at first instance. A manager described the ECNI perspective on high risk cases by saying:

> You end up putting a lot of money in a very small number of baskets and a lot of people don't even understand what it is you've done...If you lose one or two of those cases, for your money you have nothing to show, whereas we would feel in our cases, through your decisions, your settlements, your publicity from those, you have so much more to show for what money you've spent.[95]

As a result of this perspective ECNI takes very few high risk cases on what it describe as the margins.[96] As a manager explained, 'Our primary goal of being in litigation, it's to operate the law as it presently stands, we are not there on the edges of it.'[97]

In the cases ECNI has taken to extend the law it has achieved a mixed level of success. In *Elizabeth Boyle v SCA Packaging Ltd* the key issue was whether the claimant continued to fall within the definition of disabled under the DDA following surgery on her physical impairment. The ECNI was successful at IT[98]; and in the subsequent appeals to the Court of Appeal for Northern Ireland[99] and the House of Lords.[100] In *Paul Cosgrove v Northern Ireland Ambulance Service* the claimant suffered from psoriasis which caused a facial disfigurement. Having been successful in a recruitment procedure Mr Cosgrove was refused a job because the Respondent contended that his psoriasis presented a potential risk of infection to both the claimant and to patients. The ECNI provided legal assistance to Mr Cosgrove to bring a claim of disability discrimination to IT but it was unsuccessful. The IT held that it was the disfigurement that placed Mr Cosgrove within the statutory definition

[95] Interview E5 (n 82).

[96] Interview E3 (n 60).

[97] Ibid.

[98] *Elizabeth Boyle v SCA Packaging Ltd* [2006] NIIT 3444/01IT (23 May 2006).

[99] *SCA Packaging Ltd v Boyle* [2008] NICA 48.

[100] *SCA Packaging Limited v Boyle* [2009] UKHL 37.

of disability; but the reason for his failure to obtain the post was in no way related to the disfigurement but rather the skin condition. The ECNI unsuccessfully appealed the decision in the Court of Appeal.[101] The ECNI is aware that by losing high risk cases such as that of Mr Cosgrove, litigation can result in a negative impact for disabled employees by creating a precedent that establishes that the law does not extend to cover the situation in the case that is lost. Prior to this case, disabled employees may, when negotiating with employers or prospective employers, have benefited from legal uncertainty as to whether the law covered that particular situation or not.[102]

The ECNI focuses on creating social change by ensuring that disability discrimination is eliminated on the ground suggests it holds an instrumental view of social change within Kostiner's model.[103] As noted earlier, when an SMO adopts this view it assesses the role of law by how well it can secure resources for the marginalised group. Its success in securing positive decisions and settlements in the vast majority of cases has resulted in it viewing litigation as a good method of securing change for the individual claimant. Its extensive use of these positive case outcomes in training, and publicity is evidence of a belief by it that litigation is also an effective way to secure change for disabled people more generally. It is clear that ECNI has made litigation the core strategy for securing social change. One team member summed the ECNI position by saying, 'Everything kind of flows from successful legal outcomes.'[104]

7.6 Litigation as One of a Number of ECNI Strategies

The Strategic Enforcement Department within ECNI is allocated more of the organisation's budget than any other department.[105] Litigation is not the only strategy ECNI uses in its efforts to eliminate disability discrimination but all its other strategies appear to depend heavily on it. As noted earlier, litigation outcomes are passed to the Communications Department where they are used for press releases. A manager noted, 'Our press people have nothing to press unless we give them good stories.'[106] Cases that involve an easily understood legal principle and have what ECNI considers to a good personal interest element are selected for

[101] *Cosgrove v Northern Ireland Ambulance Service* [2006] NICA 44.
[102] Interview E2 (n 58).
[103] Kostiner (2003), p. 349.
[104] Interview E2 (n 58); It is not within the scope of this research to measure how successful the ECNI litigation strategy has been in eliminating disability discrimination in the workplace throughout Northern Ireland.
[105] Interview E3 (n 60).
[106] Ibid.

individual publicity through the press.[107] According to a manager only about 2 cases a month are selected across all grounds of discrimination and ECNI can only hope that the public press run it. Cases are used extensively in training and when giving advice to employers. Settlement agreements are designed to ensure the Employment Development Division of the ECNI can influence policies and procedures. A manager described litigation in this context as providing a foot in the door for other strategies. Litigation outcomes are seen as a key resource to be utilised by other departments. A manager described this resource characteristic as follows:

> People across this commission contact me every day and say "have you got something on" as issues come up or whatever. We are regularly trawling our databases and reports and our collective memories of cases and issues and so on and it would be very, almost every publication, comment, everything that goes out from this commission will relate back to the experience of individuals.[108]

The ECNI seeks to ensure compliance with legislation by carrying out what it calls a twin track strategy, supporting claimants in taking cases and advising employers on their obligations. A manager described this twin track strategy as using both a carrot and stick to eliminate discrimination by showing employers how to be compliant and demonstrating what can happen if they are not. In this analogy however the threat of litigation is the stick and the removal of the threat of litigation is the carrot. Thus litigation is at the heart of both these strategies. The carrot isn't really a reward; it's simply the removal of the punishment. ECNI is however, cautious about appearing as mainly an enforcement body. This caution was explained by a manager as follows:

> I don't think we would want to be known as too much of a litigation organisation, you know, it's only a part of it not the whole... our Employment Development Division would be very keen not to be seen as the enemy... that's why we as the lawyers never go to the employers so we are kept totally out of the loop, it's very separate.[109]

The ECNI seeks to separate its work supporting cases with its work supporting employers so that employers will want to engage with it in building good practice through training and policy development. The data gathered in this research does not provide evidence of whether this division of ECNI departments into 'good cop, bad cop' has been successful in encouraging employers to engage with the ECNI or in maximising compliance with disability legislation. However, according to one ECNI manager employers who avail of the ECNI training course don't see the ECNI as an aggressive policing type body: 'There's lots of employers who we don't sue and who work with our development division and who take training and who attend our courses and who go to all our networks and they don't see us like that.'[110]

---

[107] Ibid.

[108] Interview E5 (n 82).

[109] Ibid.

[110] Ibid.

8 Litigation's Role in Securing Participation for ECNI

To carry out its litigation strategy the ECNI needs to secure the participation of claimants who are prepared to come forward and take a case to the IT. The ECNI wants to maximise the number of applications for legal assistance, not because it wants to take more cases, but rather because it wants to have the widest range of cases to select from. The need for claimants to come forward to carry out its litigation strategy is a result of the enforcement mechanism for employment which only allows cases to be taken by employees alleging discrimination. There is no provision for organisations such as the ECNI to bring independent legal proceedings against an employer for alleged discriminatory practices. All IT cases must be based on a complaint relating to an individual claimant. As a manager put it, 'If we can't get the word out on the street that we are here to take cases, then we may as well close the door.'[111] When money is available the ECNI has used advertising campaigns to inform the public that they can come to the ECNI if they feel they have been discriminated against. The Strategic Enforcement Division conducts outreach clinics which involve ECNI staff going to Citizen Advice Bureaus, Unions and voluntary sector organisations and giving talks on rights and the work of the ECNI in supporting claimants.

The IT sends the ECNI copies of all ET1(NI) applications it receives and as a result the ECNI is very aware that a lot of discrimination cases are lodged with the tribunal without any involvement of the ECNI. This suggests that ECNI efforts to bring in claimants have not been a resounding success. The frustration at this situation is evident from the following statement by one ECNI manager:

> There are so many people lodge forms in the tribunal offices that don't come to us and I would love to know why. Is it because they've never heard of us or they've heard of us and don't know that we assist people or they've some other source of funding you know. Why is it that there's thousands of cases lodged and we only have 3000 that come to us and 300 that apply for assistance so what is it about the cases that go to the tribunal that don't come to us and some of them are good you know and we would like to be involved in them.[112]

To try and get involved in some of the claims it knows are already lodged it gets in touch with the private solicitor representing the claimant. However, in its experience most solicitors hold an unspoken reluctance to refer their client to the ECNI for support as it could result in the loss of client business for them. Clearly the ECNI cannot rely on solicitors to let claimants know that support is available from the ECNI. The ECNI must communicate directly to potential clients.

Publicising positive case outcomes is seen by ECNI as one way in which to illustrate what the ECNI can do to support claimants and encourage more claimants to contact it. Such publication may also encourage employers to come forward for training in order to avoid the IT. The ECNI team members said that in their experience publicity in the press based on a positive case outcome is usually

[111] Interview E4 (n 52).

[112] Interview E5 (n 82).

followed by an increase in queries from potential claimants seeking advice relating to the same area of discrimination as the published case.[113] Potential claimants have been encouraged to contact the ECNI by reading the real life stories of other disabled people who took a case of discrimination and were successful. As one team member explained, 'If you've got a client who they can identify with, who has had similar circumstances; I think that just encourages people to come forward and say 'yeah, that happened to me as well and if that wee woman can do it so can I.'[114] According to Snow et al. amplifying beliefs about the probability of change is one of the frame alignment processes that can be used to secure participation by organisations seeking social change.[115]

Although publication of case outcomes is recognised by ECNI as increasing potential claimant's beliefs about securing change the majority of cases are not selected by ECNI for individual publication through the independent press. This limited approach to individual publication seems to centre round concerns about the public's understanding of the legal principles involved and a judgement by ECNI management that the facts of the case may not make a very interesting human story.[116] The ECNI publishes all its case outcomes in their Decisions and Settlements Review which is available online but this document is unlikely to reach vast swathes of the public.

The ECNI does not seek to create activists through its litigation strategy. In the experience of team members the vast majority of claimants bring a case to IT to secure their own rights and do not have any real ambition that their case will bring about change for other disabled employees.[117] When a claimant's case concludes their contact with the ECNI usually concludes. In a small number of cases claimants may take part in the publicity of their case for a short period.

9 Conclusion

DA and ECNI share the common objective of seeking to eliminate disability discrimination in the workplace but have taken very different approaches to litigation in trying to achieve this social change. DA believes that the best way to increase inclusion of disabled people and eliminate discrimination in the workplace is to engage with individual employees and employers through its Workable (NI) programme and Employment Advocacy Project. DA seeks amicable resolution

[113] An increase in queries from employers or take up of training was not reported during interviews with Strategic Enforcement Staff. No data was gathered on employer training courses or calls to the employer advice service.

[114] Interview E8 (n 29).

[115] Snow et al. (1986), p. 470.

[116] Interview E3 (n 60).

[117] Interview E5 (n 82).

to disputes between employers and disabled employees but when this is not achievable DA will provide moral support and make evidence available to clients who want to take a case to IT. The ECNI provides free legal advocacy to between 60 and a 100 claimants each year across all grounds of discrimination including disability. Cases involving disability discrimination in the workplace are brought to the IT under the DDA. ECNI has been hugely successful in obtaining favourable settlements and decisions for the disabled claimants it has provided legal assistance to.

DA and ECNI have seen firsthand litigation deliver justice for individual claimants. However, DA believes litigation should be the last resort when seeking to achieve justice for clients. Both organisations use litigation outcomes in pursuit of collective justice. However, DA's use of cases is limited in this regard for three reasons. Firstly, it prefers to foster good relations between employers and disabled employees by mediating to bring about an amicable agreement when there is a dispute. Secondly, case outcomes are seen by it as very individualistic and therefore past case outcomes have a limited ability to predict future case outcomes. Thirdly, litigation may discourage employers from recruiting disabled workers in the future. DA does however see a benefit in a small flow of cases with merit going to IT so that the DDA remains relevant in negotiations with employers.

DA displays an instrumental view of social change under Kostiner's model by providing a service to individual disabled employees to help them secure their rights. DA sees legislation as important in achieving change for clients but litigation is only considered to have a very minor role to play. To achieve collective justice DA seeks to change how employers view disabled workers so that they will be more likely to recruit them. This suggests a cultural approach to social change under Kostiner's model which is usually associated with the view by an SMO that law is irrelevant in achieving social change. However, DA sees legislation as having a crucial role in creating, among employers, a positive attitude toward disabled workers. In contrast litigation of cases which are without merit is seen as being potentially detrimental to this.

The ECNI only selects cases for legal assistance if they are going to have an impact on collective justice. It uses litigation to ensure that the rights contained within the DDA are enjoyed on the ground. The ECNI works to bring about collective justice by raising awareness among employers of their obligations under DDA; raising awareness of disability rights among employees; and creating what Galanter has called a shadow of law over negotiations between employers and disabled employees. Each of these strategies relies heavily on litigation outcomes. It is not within the scope of this research to state definitively how effective each of these strategies has been. However, ECNI's experience of employers rapidly agreeing to settlement when faced with an ECNI supported IT case suggests that this shadow of law may have had an impact on settlement negotiations. ECNI uses litigation to only a limited extent in order to influence the law because the current law is considered by it to provide a good level of protection and cases with the potential to develop the law are regarded as high risk and too costly.

The ECNI has adopted an instrumental view of social change within Kostiner's model and views litigation as a very effective way of achieving this change for individual claimants. Litigation outcomes are also seen as a resource which other departments within ECNI can utilise in other strategies. The ECNI uses a twin track approach to maximise compliance with the DDA. Alongside the litigation strategy carried out by its Strategic Enforcement Department, the ECNI provides advice and training to employers through its Employment Development Department. The ECNI has concerns that its work on litigation may cause it to be seen as the enemy of employers, discouraging employer engagement with the ECNI, therefore a conscious effort is made to separate the work of the two departments.

The ECNI's litigation strategy requires the participation of claimants. The publication of case outcomes is one way the ECNI encourages claimants to contact it for advice. Positive decisions and settlements can amplify beliefs about the probability of change as potential claimants identify with successful claimants. The volume of applications made to IT through private solicitors suggests that the ECNI needs to do more to raise awareness among employees about the free advocacy service the ECNI provides. Its heavy reliance on the independent press to publicise case outcomes has perhaps meant it has not cashed in on the potential for good news stories to bring claimants to the ECNI. It could tap into the established network of disability organisations, including DA with whom it does a limited amount of outreach, in order to enhance publication of case outcomes. Tapping into this network to ensure publicity could help to bring more claimants to the ECNI.

References

Galanter, M. (1983). The radiating effects of courts. In K. O. Boyum & L. M. Mather (Eds.), *Empirical theories about courts*. New York: Longman.

Kostiner, I. (2003). Evaluating legality: Towards a cultural approach to the study of law and social change. *Law and Society Review, 37*, 323.

McCann, M. W. (1994). *Rights at work: Pay equity reform and the politics of legal mobilization*. Chicago: University of Chicago Press.

Olson, S. (1995). Comparing women's rights litigation in the Netherlands and the United States. *Polity, 28*, 189.

Snow, D. A., Burke Rochford, E., Jr., Worden, S. K., & Benford, R. D. (1986). Frame alignment processes, micromobilisation and movement participation. *American Sociological Review, 51* (4), 464.

Economic, Social and Cultural Rights in Northern Ireland: Legitimate and Viable Justiciability Mechanisms for a Conflicted Democracy

Katie Boyle

1 Introduction

This chapter proposes justiciability mechanisms for economic, social and cultural (ESC) rights in Northern Ireland. The mechanisms are classified as either underdeveloped or open to future implementation. The chapter examines the existing mechanisms already available in Northern Ireland or the United Kingdom (UK). These mechanisms tend to be underdeveloped, or, may have not yet been categorised as mechanisms relating to ESC justiciability as such (so where rights are adjudicated under the rubric of something else). The chapter then proposes mechanisms for potential implementation in the future in accordance with the particular jurisdictional framework and constitutional settlement in the UK. The mechanisms proposed are measured in terms of their legitimacy—i.e. if their applicability in law is according to, and in compliance with, the rule of law. In this sense, if the of the law renders the rights justiciable then the mechanisms are considered legitimate from a positivist perspective. Viability is also explored in terms of whether there are barriers or democratic gaps in the implementation of the mechanisms, such as for example, jurisdictional gaps, or weak rather than strong ESC protection/fulfillment as a result of procedural rather than substantive mechanisms. The introduction of justiciable mechanisms deepens the review of ESC

The author is grateful to Dr Edel Hughes, Dr Eimear Spain, Laura Donnellan and Navraj Singh Galleigh for comments on previous drafts. All errors remain the responsibility of the author and all views expressed are the author's own.

K. Boyle (✉)
School of Law, Department of Social Sciences, University of Roehampton, London, United Kingdom

Crucible Centre for Human Rights Research, University of Roehampton, London, United Kingdom
e-mail: Katie.Boyle@roehampton.ac.uk

A. Diver, J. Miller (eds.), *Justiciability of Human Rights Law in Domestic Jurisdictions*, DOI 10.1007/978-3-319-24016-9_8

rights beyond a categorisation according to standard of enforcement. This contributes to a more informed discussion on whether ESC justiciability mechanisms can assist in addressing the ESC rights deficit in Northern Ireland as a sub-state transitioning from a protracted conflict that is part of a wider State committed to international human rights norms. There is also a wider contribution to the discussion on ESC justiciability in itself—whereby the mechanisms can be developed and discussed beyond the Northern Ireland context. This assists in clarifying the wider UK position with the potential to unearth potential pitfalls in ESC protection across the UK. This is all the more pertinent in light of broader discussions on the protection of human rights, or the lessening of human rights protections, in the current UK wide Bill of Rights debate. Although not the subject of this chapter, the UK wide debate requires to take account of the particular circumstances of Northern Ireland. In so far as any proposal for a UK Bill of Rights that diminshes the protection of human rights or repeals the Human Rights Act 1998 ought not to diminish rights protection in Northern Ireland. This is as a result of the commitments in the 1998 multi-party peace agreement and 1998 bilateral treaty between the UK and Northern Ireland where the incorporation of the ECHR became part of the foundations of the post-conflict state. The discussion on ESC rights in this chapter should therefore be contextualised within the wider debate but not limited by it. In the same vein the indigenous discussion on ESC rights in Northern Ireland acts as a mechanism to review and consider the ESC deficit across the UK and so adds to the wider UK debate in this sense. There is also the possibility to transfer, where appropriate, the mechanisms identified in this chapter to other jurisdictions beyond the UK context. This is of particular importance given the State's reluctance in this case to acknowledge the legitimacy of ESC rights' justiciability at all. Lessons can be learned from this where other States make claim to similar arguments.

Before outlining the contributions of this chapter in terms of the viable and legitimate justiciability mechanisms for ESC rights in Northern Ireland, it is necessary to first begin by contextualizing the discussion within the confines of subject matter, jurisdiction and legal and academic discipline. First, in terms of subject matter, this chapter addresses the area of human rights, specifically the justiciability of ESC rights. Second, it is important to note the multi-layered jurisdictional context of the case study. Northern Ireland is a devolved legal entity within the United Kingdom (UK). The UK is a Member State of the European Union, a party to the Council of Europe and is committed to a number of international human rights treaties and obligations. The different layers of jurisdiction impose different rights and obligations in connection with human rights. For example, there is a quasi-constitutional recognition of the rights contained in the European Convention of Human Rights 1950[1] (the Convention) at a devolved micro level through the Northern Ireland Act 1998 and at the macro level through

[1] Council of Europe, European Convention for the Protection of Human Rights and Fundamental Freedoms, as amended by Protocols Nos. 11 and 14, 4 November 1950, ETS 5.

the Human Rights Act 1998. Convention rights can therefore be adjudicated upon at the local devolved level, the national level, and the supranational level.[2] However, these protections are limited and do not extend to protection according to the principle of indivisibility[3] leaving the majority of ESC rights unprotected.

There are also obligations emanating from international treaties incumbent on the State and these obligations are at times dealt with at the supranational level, the national level, and the local devolved level to different degrees. The dualist domestic framework of the UK prohibits the domestic application of rights, such as ESC rights, that have not yet been incorporated into domestic law through legislation.[4] It is therefore crucial, whilst considering the domestic constitutional context, to consider also the international context in terms of human rights obligations attached to the domestic State. The reluctance of the State to recognise fundamental constitutional rights and the recommendations of international human rights bodies to rectify the non-binding status of ESC rights across the UK magnifies the current deficit in Northern Ireland. The UK signed the International Covenant on Economic, Social and Cultural Rights (ICESCR)[5] on 16 September 1968 and ratified the Covenant on 20 May 1976. On the matter of justiciability, the UN Committee on Economic Social and Cultural Rights (the body responsible for ensuring compliance with the Covenant) have reaffirmed to the United Kingdom 'that all economic, social and cultural rights are justiciable'[6] and have called on the State to ensure that ICESCR 'is given full legal effect in its domestic law, that the Covenant rights are made justiciable, and that effective remedies are available for victims of all violations of economic, social and cultural rights.'[7]

---

[2] The European Court of Human Rights is the court responsible for adjudicating on Convention rights. These mechanisms predominantly protect civil and political rights. There are also examples of ESC protection in EU Law such as equal pay for equal work. See *Defrenne II*—Case 43/75 [1976] ECR 455. The European Charter of Fundamental Rights also extends protection to economic, social and cultural rights, Charter of Fundamental Rights of the European Union, 26 October 2012, 2012/C 326/02.

[3] The principle of indivisibility recognises the inalienable and interdependent nature of human rights encompassing equal acknowledgement of civil, political, economic, social and cultural rights. See Scott (1989), p. 794; and Alston and Quinn (1987).

[4] For a discussion on the dualist system of incorporation see Aust (2010), pp. 75–76. An example of a non-incorporated treaty dealing with ESC rights is the International Covenant on Economic Social and Cultural Rights, UN General Assembly, 16 December 1966, United Nations, Treaty Series, vol. 993, p. 3.

[5] Ibid.

[6] UN Committee on Economic, Social and Cultural Rights (CESCR): Concluding Observations, United Kingdom of Great Britain and Northern Ireland, 5 June 2002, E/C.12/1/Add.79, para 24.

[7] Consideration of reports submitted by States parties in accordance with articles 16 and 17 of the Covenant: concluding observations of the Committee on Economic, Social and Cultural Rights: United Kingdom of Great Britain and Northern Ireland, the Crown Dependencies and the Overseas Dependent Territories, 12 June 2009, E/C.12/GBR/CO/5, para 13.

The call for justiciable mechanisms in respect of ESC rights is also clearly stipulated in General Comment No. 9[8] of the Committee on Economic, Social and Cultural Rights relating to the domestic application of the Covenant. The Committee recognises the requirement for an effective remedy for those who may be subject to a violation of an economic, social or cultural right and that the most appropriate means of securing this remedy is through judicial mechanisms unless a state can justify otherwise.[9] A blanket refusal to acknowledge the justiciable nature of the rights is considered arbitrary.[10] The capability of vindicating ESC rights before the courts is therefore of paramount importance within the UK domestic context in respect of obligations emanating from international human rights law.

Third, transitional justice is the legal and academic discipline in which conflict or post-conflict societies may address systematic human rights violations committed by a prior regime.[11] Northern Ireland is described as a 'conflicted democracy' within the transitional justice literature.[12] In this sense it is an entity within a wider democratic state that is undergoing incremental transition in order to address historical systemic human rights abuse. The literature has identified that ESC right violations are often left unaddressed in the aftermath of conflict and that this oversight may undermine the transition from war to peace with the vulnerable and marginalized remaining in a state of pre-conflict ESC violation.[13] It is therefore crucial to further contextualize the subject matter of this paper within the transitional justice paradigm as a prism through which the subject matter and jurisdictional context must be viewed.

Finally, the viable and legitimate justiciability mechanisms proposed in this chapter are designed to facilitate the transitional process in accordance with a legal and social mandate for ESC justiciability. They are also proposed in light of the hierarchical jurisdictional context in terms of what is not merely legitimate but legally viable in accordance with the rule of law and the *sui generis* constitutional framework under the jurisdictional hierarchy.[14]

Before proceeding there are some necessary caveats to address. Justiciability of ESC rights is a contentious issue. It is not within the ambit of this chapter to address the legitimacy of justiciability in itself, nonetheless, it is based on the premise that these rights are justiciable if the application of the law renders them

---

[8] UN Committee on Economic, Social and Cultural Rights (CESCR), General Comment No. 9: The domestic application of the Covenant, 3 December 1998, E/C.12/1998/24.

[9] General Comment No. 9, ibid., para 3.

[10] General Comment No. 9, ibid., para 10.

[11] Teitel (2003), pp. 71–72.

[12] Northern Ireland falls within the definition of a conflicted democracy as the State is a liberal democracy committed to international human rights at the macro level however, at the same time, a geographical entity within the State conformed to an illiberal regime subject to systemic human rights violations. For a further discussion on the 'paradigmatic transition' v 'conflicted democracy' see Ní Aoláin and Campbell (2003), p. 193.

[13] Miller (2008) and Rai (2007).

[14] Taking into account the uncodified constitution of the United Kingdom and the doctrine of parliamentary supremacy.

so.[15] Secondly, it is not proposed that justiciability mechanisms are the only model of ESC enforcement available, nor is it proposed that they ought to be. The contribution of the mechanisms outlined in this paper is intended to complement a multifaceted approach to a more stable and democratic society in Northern Ireland. It should also be stated that they are no way intended to displace political dialogue or usurp the requirement for political consensus in Northern Ireland.[16] The justiciability mechanisms are intended to outline the options already available and what options might be explored in the future, with a view to empowering people in Northern Ireland, by offering an informed choice on what is legitimately viable in terms of ESC justiciability. In so doing, the content of this chapter is intended to offer a contribution to the current literature in two respects. First, the legitimate and viable justiciability mechanisms proposed are designed for the particular circumstances of Northern Ireland, however, they may also be applicable beyond Northern Ireland and beyond the transitional justice paradigm. Secondly, hitherto, the literature has tended to examine the area of ESC justiciability on an axis measuring the varying degrees (or the standard) of ESC protection/enforcement through the prism of ongoing jurisprudence. This examination is critical in providing an understanding of how ESC rights can be enforced from negative enforcement (i.e. a duty not to interfere), to minimal enforcement (i.e. a duty to protect a minimum non-derogable core), to substantive enforcement (i.e. a positive duty on the state to ensure substantive fulfilment).[17]

[15] For a full rebuttal of the arguments against justiciability see Nolan et al. (2007). For a discussion on the role of judges in determining human rights see Harvey (2004).

[16] Consensus on how to move forward in respect of human rights in Northern Ireland remains a point of contention at a political level. On unionist dissent see DUP Response to NIO consultation paper, *A Bill of Rights for Northern Ireland: Next Steps, Response by Democratic Unionist Party*, 30 March 2010 and Turner (2010). It should be noted that empirical research demonstrates that there is a larger body of consensus on the enhancement of ESC rights at a local community level on both sides of the polarised divide. In June 2009 polls indicated 83 % were in favour of a Bill of Rights for Northern Ireland at a cross-community level (The Northern Ireland Omnibus Survey, Millward Brown Ulster, June 2009). In 2010 the Human Rights Consortium in conjunction with Millward Brown Ulster Limited published statistics indicating support for a Bill of Rights and for socio-economic inclusion. The figures differed slightly between communities showing 91 % of Catholics and 74 % of Protestants were in favour of a Bill or Rights. When asked more directly on socio-economic issues like 'How important do you think it is to include the right to the highest attainable standard of physical and mental health?' 85 % of Catholics and 80 % of Protestants agreed the inclusion was important (Bill of Rights poll, 44102357 February 2010, prepared for the Human Rights Consortium by Millward Brown Ulster Limited).

[17] Moving on from a misconception based on the positive v negative nature of human rights the Koch (2005) has identified 'waves of duties' applicable to ESC rights. Eide (1989) offers a tripartite typology along the waves of duties spectrum to 'respect, protect and fulfil'. Nolan et al. (2007) identify degrees of enforcement through the tripartite theory to a multitude of varying degrees—from respect, to protect, to fulfil, consideration of progressive realisation and finally non-retrogressive measures. Courtis (2009) has expanded this theory to degrees of standard starting with negative, to procedural, through equality and non-discrimination, minimum core arguments, progressive realisation, and prohibiting retrogression.

The mechanisms proposed in this chapter are based on a categorisation of models (as opposed to standards) of justiciability in response to calls in the literature for how better protection of human rights in Northern Ireland might be achieved.[18] The exploration of justiciability mechanisms therefore deepens the existing review of ESC rights and opens up access to potential remedies for a violation by categorising the point of access (to court) rather than solely focus on the standard of protection (once in court). Whilst it is noted that no one option offers a holistic solution that might apply in any or every circumstance, each of the mechanisms can contribute to the substantive enjoyment of all human rights according to the indivisibility principle through a multifaceted approach. It is therefore argued that, rather than offer a 'one size fits all' approach to ESC justiciability, the mechanisms employed can be explored independently and/or concurrently, with a view to transitioning towards a more accountable and transparent acknowledgment, protection and substantive realisation of ESC rights.

2 Underdeveloped Existing Mechanisms

2.1 A Statutory Framework That Is Subject to Judicial Remedies

Using the legislative process to protect ESC rights is one mechanism through which legitimate justiciable protection can occur in so far as the legislation provides for a judicial remedy for the violation of an ESC right.

ESC rights are protected in some respects through legislation that forms the basis of the Welfare State (enactments relating to education, housing, health, employment rights etc.). The UK Parliament has also enacted legislation to meet ESC rights recognised in international law such as through the Apprenticeships, Skills, Children and Learning Act 2009, which provides for a statutory right to education for detained young offenders in accordance with Article 28 of the UN Convention on the Rights of the Child.[19]

---

[18] Nolan et al. (2007), p. 3 have identified this area as one of paramount importance, 'the questions of how far to go in creating institutional mechanisms for the adjudication and enforcement of social and economic rights, how to demarcate the role of the courts or other bodies in adjudication those rights and how to frame the relationship of institutional mechanisms with the elected branches of government in this area remain real and important'. Dickson and Harvey also recently called for a discussion on how human rights might be better protected in Northern Ireland, Dickson and Harvey (2013).

[19] See also the Welsh example of the Rights of Children and Young Persons Measure (Wales) 2011 which imposes on public bodies to have due regard to the rights contained in the UN Convention on the Rights of the Child, or, the Child Poverty Act 2010 through which the UK Parliament imposed a duty on the Secretary of State to meet the obligations to attain poverty eradication targets. For further discussion on the role of the Joint Committee on Human Rights enhancing Parliament's role in relation to international human rights obligations see Hunt (2010).

The UN Committee on Economic Social and Cultural Rights has recommended that ESC rights ought to be protected in the same manner as civil and political rights at a domestic level.[20] In this regard it would be open to the UK Parliament to extend the protection of rights under the Human Rights Act to ESC rights if it so chooses. The UK Parliament could also incorporate the ICESCR by way of legislation which provides a judicial remedy. Likewise, the Northern Ireland Assembly itself could, according to its legislative competence, enact legislation which observes or implements international obligations, including human rights obligations.[21]

Aside from the constitutional debate on whether it is appropriate to assign sole responsibility to the legislature to protect human right norms,[22] there are also some concerns in relation to applicability under the current legislative measures that undermine the strength in viability of this option. Legislative mechanisms coupled with effective judicial remedies are currently enacted on an incremental basis and so there is no holistic approach to ESC protection. Furthermore, the legislation tends to impose procedural, as opposed to substantive duties, on the State and judicial review is only available to ensure the procedural aspects of the substantive rights are being fulfilled.[23] The duties contained in the current piecemeal legislative approach do not therefore fully encompass all of the duties conferred on the State by international law, nor do they extend to the full jurisdiction of the United Kingdom in every case.[24] Whilst legislative mechanisms are laudable, they do not go far enough to secure the full realisation of ESC rights, nor are they free from future retrogressive measures or repeal, meaning a legislative framework alone is a weak and vulnerable one.

---

[20] General Comment No. 9, *op cit.* n 8, para 7.

[21] Under paragraph 3 of Schedule 2 International relations, including relations with territories outside the United Kingdom, the European Communities (and their institutions) and other international organisations and extradition, and international development assistance and co-operation are excepted matters (i.e. beyond the legislative competence of the NI Assembly). However, an **exemption** to this excepted matter under paragraph 3(c) is the competence to observe and implement international obligations, obligations under the Human Rights Convention and obligations under Community law. Under section 98 of the NI Act 'international obligations' are defined as 'any international obligations of the United Kingdom other than obligations to observe and implement Community law or the Convention rights'.

[22] See for example the arguments posed by King (2012), p. 157 on why majoritarian rule is undermined by the Whip system in Westminster and the practice of lobbying and Wheatley (2003), on how majoritarian rule fails to take into consideration minority groups (often on the receiving end of ESC violations).

[23] The duty to have 'due regard' in the Young Persons Measure (Wales) 2011 does not seek to secure substantive outcomes but imposes a duty on public authorities to take the UN Convention on the Rights of the Child into consideration. Anthony (2005), para 4.27 explores the concept of 'target duties' in relation to Northern Ireland.

[24] Such as section 48 of the Apprenticeships, Skills, Children and Learning Act 2009, the operative section providing for the educational measure for detained young offenders, which only applies to England and Wales.

2.2 A Judicial Remedy for Noncompliance with Equality and Non-discrimination Provisions

The second proposed ESC justiciability mechanism operates through the rubric of equality legislation. The literature demonstrates that equality and non-discrimination measures are used as a vehicle to secure ESC rights.[25] There are examples of both domestic and international case law that affirms this position.[26] McKeever and Ní Aoláin concur that the conflict in Northern Ireland was substantially triggered by the pervasive discrimination and disenfranchisement experienced by the minority Catholic community since the creation of the Northern Ireland sub-state in 1922.[27] Furthermore, relative to the rest of the UK, Northern Ireland was subject to high levels of deprivation, and the polarised communities both suffered economic and social deprivation which exacerbated the conflict.[28] Equality legislation was therefore employed as a tool by the State in an attempt to secure peace both during and after the conflict.

In Northern Ireland equality measures are dealt with under a series of legislative measures and underpinned by the equality provisions found in the Northern Ireland Act 1998.[29] In the rest of the UK, equality provisions have been consolidated into

[25] Nolan et al. (2007). See also McKeever and Ní Aoláin (2004) and Tinta (2007) Equal protection and non-discrimination can also be construed in light of economic, social and cultural rights—including the conditions at work, the right to social security, the right to a healthy environment and the right to have access to basic public services. Tinta also identifies clusters of contentious cases—so most frequently adjudicated case types with ESC rights relate to children, indigenous population, workers rights and vulnerable and disadvantaged groups in Latin American society such as street children, children in institutions, indigenous populations, displaced peoples, migrants, manual workers and prison populations.

[26] Domestic examples: *Harjula v London Borough Council op cit Harjula v London Borough Council* [2011] EWHC 151 (QB); *on the Application of W,M,G & H v Birmingham City Council*, [2011] EWHC 1147 Admin. International examples: *Eldridge v. British Columbia (Attorney General)* [1997] 3 S.C.R.; *Awas Tingi v Nicaragua* Inter-Am Ct HR, August 31 2001; *Shelter Corporation v. Ontario Human Rights Commission* (2001) 143 OAC 54; also *Klickovic Pasalic and Karanovic v Bosnia and Herzegovina, the Federation of Bosnia and Herzegovina and the Republika Sprska*, CH/02/8923, CH/02/8924, CH/02/9364, 10 January 2003; *Khosa v Minister of Social Development*, 2004 (6) SA 505 (CC).

[27] McKeever and Ní Aoláin (2004). See also Ní Aoláin (2000).

[28] McKeever and Ní Aoláin (2004).

[29] Section 75 and Schedule 9 of the Northern Ireland Act provides for the statutory equality framework in Northern Ireland. See also—the Equality Pay Act (NI) (as amended) 1970, which provided equality in employment between men and women; Sex Discrimination (NI) Order (as amended) 1976; Fair Employment Act 1976, which provided equality in employment between those of different religious beliefs; Fair Employment (NI) Act 1989; Disability Act (UK wide) 1995; Race Relations (NI) Order 1997; Fair Employment and Treatment (NI) Order 1998; Police (NI) Act 2000; Equality (Disability etc) (NI) Order 2000; Employment Equality (Sexual Orientation) (NI) Regulations 2003; European Framework Directive on Equal Treatment 2004.

the Equality Act 2010 (which does not extend to Northern Ireland). The provisions in the Equality Act 2010 offer justiciable remedies for ESC rights that are not available under the Northern Ireland legislation.[30]

McKeever and Ní Aoláin have encouraged a move beyond a programmatic protection of socio-economic rights to a more inclusive and substantive enforcement model coupled with judicial remedies in Northern Ireland.[31] For example, they argue that ESC rights protection would be better facilitated in Northern Ireland by amending section 75 of the Northern Ireland Act 1998 to include 'socio-economic status' as part of the procedural duty to have due regard to encouraging equality of opportunity.[32] A previous attempt by the New Labour administration (1997–2010) to codify a socio-economic duty applicable to the rest of the UK through the Equality Act 2010 was rejected by the subsequent administration, the Lib-Dem Conservative Coalition Government, responsible for commencing the legislation. It was described as a 'ridiculous' provision by the then Minister for Equality and Gender, Theresa May, who announced the duty would be 'scrapped' and so the provision was never commenced.[33]

It could be argued that the antipathy towards using legislation in this way fails to recognise the correlation between those who are most marginalised in society and the role poverty plays in further entrenching social exclusion.[34] This is of particular importance in Northern Ireland where poverty and socio-economic status has exacerbated the conflict and communities potentially remain in a state of pre-conflict ESC violation.

Despite the removal of the socio-economic status provision, the Equality Act 2010 has nonetheless transformed the legal landscape in the rest of the UK whereby adjudication on socio-economic rights occurs under the auspice of legislative

[30] Compare the public body duties in s 149 of the Equality Act 2010 with s 75 of the Northern Ireland Act 1998. The Equality Act provides for judicial remedies whilst the Northern Ireland Act provides for administrative remedies through the Equality Commission for Northern Ireland (a non-judicial body). See the case of *Neill's Application* [2006] NICA 5 where the judiciary considered that an alleged breach of an equality provision was best dealt with under the statutory body, the Equality and Human Rights Commission for Northern Ireland, as opposed to being amenable to judicial review. The Equality Act 2010 provides for judicial remedies.

[31] McKeever and Ní Aoláin (2004).

[32] McKeever and Ní Aoláin (2004), p. 172.

[33] Speech delivered by Theresa May, Minister for Women and Equality, on 17 November 2010, available at http://sta.geo.useconnect.co.uk/ministers/speeches-1/equalities_strategy_speech.aspx. Accessed 9 April 2014

[34] For a discussion on the correlation between poverty and social exclusion see for example, 'Poverty and Equality', Scottish Human Rights Commission National Action Plan, Getting it Right? Human Rights in Scotland, 2012, para 2.5.2, available at www.scottishhumanrights.com/actionplan/home. Accessed 10 January 2014 and Oppenheim and Harker (1996).

measures providing for equality. The current equality divide in the UK has been scrutinised at an international level and there have been consistent calls for a consolidated approach to equality for Northern Ireland. It is argued that the same mechanisms for justiciable protection ought to be available for the people in Northern Ireland as is available with those in the rest of the UK under the Equality Act 2010.[35] It is not clear whether it would be open to the Northern Ireland Assembly to enact a consolidated single equality bill with justiciable mechanisms as the area is arguably reserved under the Northern Ireland Act.[36] It would therefore fall to the UK Parliament to ensure legislation is enacted to extend equality provisions to Northern Ireland and facilitate ESC adjudication in line with the rest of the UK. The viability of this option depends upon the reception of the proposal at the UK political level and it would be highly contentious to alter the framework of the existing devolved settlement without consultation and negotiations at the devolved level between the polarised political parties in the consociational power sharing arrangement.

2.3 *The Dynamic Interpretation of Civil and Political Rights*

The third model for legitimate and viable justiciability of ESC rights is adjudication through the ambit of civil and political rights. According to the principle of indivisibility, ESC rights can form an integral part of the realisation of a civil or political right and courts have found that an ESC right can be implied, or derived from, a civil or political right. This approach is referred to as the dynamic, or evolutive, approach to human rights interpretation.[37]

---

[35] Advisory Committee to the Framework Convention for the Protection of National Minorities, FCNM, Third Opinion on the United Kingdom, adopted on 30 June 2011, ACFC/OP/III (2011) 006, para 66; E/C.12/GBR/CO/5, op cit. n 7, paras 16–17; UN Committee on the Elimination of Racial Discrimination (CERD), Concluding Observations, United Kingdom of Great Britain and Northern Ireland, 14 September 2011, CERD/C/GBR/CO/18-20, para 19.

[36] Paragraph 22(f) of Schedule 2 of the Northern Ireland Act 1998 exempts the subject matter of section 75 (the equal opportunity statutory duty on public authorities) from excepted matters under the Act. However, paragraph 42(b) reserves the same to the Parliament of the United Kingdom. There is some discrepancy in a reading of the legislation as to whether it would be within the power of the Northern Ireland Assembly to legislate in respect of the subject matter of this clause (i.e. alter the duty to comply with the duties to mirror those imposed in the rest of the United Kingdom under section 149 of the Equality Act 2010).

[37] Tinta (2007).

The European Court of Human Rights (ECtHR), has taken an arguably teleological approach to interpretation indicative of the principle of indivisibility by deriving ESC rights from civil and political rights,[38]

> While the Convention sets forth what are essentially civil and political rights, many of them have implications of a social or economic nature... [T]he mere fact that an interpretation of the Convention may extend into the sphere of social and economic rights should not be a decisive factor against such an interpretation; there is no water-tight division separating that sphere from the field covered by the Convention.[39]

Apparent in the jurisprudence of the ECtHR is a dynamic approach to interpretation of Article 8 (right to private and family life). This includes acknowledgement of the right to adequate housing respecting cultural dimensions in the case of nomadic travellers[40] and, more broadly, protection from unlawful eviction.[41] In the case of *Yordanova*[42] the ECtHR specifically referred to various international standards,[43] including the standard set by ICESCR in connection with the right to adequate housing and the corollary positive duties incumbent on the state to respect this right.[44]

---

[38] Whilst it is not within the remit of this chapter to examine each of these cases, the following examples indicate the increasing number of cases before the ECtHR expanding the protection and enforcement of ESC rights—indicative of the indivisibility principle; Dybeku v. Albania, Application no. 41153/06, 18 Dec. 2007 *(right to health – prisoners rights);* Khamidov v. Russia, Application no. 72118/01, 2 June 2008 *(housing rights – property rights);* Airey v. Ireland, 32 Eur Ct HR Ser A (1979): [1979] 2 E.H.R.R. 305 *(Economic development and poverty – equality and non-discrimination – women's rights);* Belgian Linguistic Case (Nos. 1 & 2) (No. 1) (1967), Series A, No. 5 (1979–80) 1 EHRR 241 (No. 2) (1968), Series A, No. 6 (1979–80) 1 EHRR 252 *(Education Rights – civil and political rights – equality and non-discrimination);* López Ostra v. Spain, Series A, No 303-C; (1995) 20 EHHR 277 *(Environmental rights – housing rights – positive obligations);* Botta v. Italy *(1998) 26 EHHR 241 (people with disabilities – obligation to provide – positive obligations);* Selçuk and Asker v. Turkey, *(1998) 26 EHRR 477 (Housing rights – property rights – forced evictions – inhuman treatment);* Akkus v. Turkey, App. no. 00019263/92, Judgment 24 June 1997. *(Property rights – compensation).*

[39] *Airey* v. *Ireland* 32 Eur Ct HR Ser A (1979): [1979] 2 E.H.R.R. 305, para 26.

[40] *Connors* v. *United Kingdom*, European Court of Human Rights, Application no. 66746/01, 27 May 2004, para. 95. The Court noted that, 'the eviction of the applicant and his family from the local authority site was not attended by the requisite procedural safeguards, namely the requirement to establish proper justification for the serious interference with his rights and consequently cannot be regarded as justified by a 'pressing social need' or proportionate to the legitimate aim being pursued. There has, accordingly, been a violation of Article 8 of the Convention.'

[41] *Yordanova and Others v Bulgaria,* Application no. 25446/06, 12 April 2012.

[42] Ibid.

[43] The ECtHR referenced "relevant international material" including the European Social Charter; a decision of the European Committee of Social Rights (*European Roma Rights Centre v Bulgaria* Complaint No 31/2005, 25 May 2005); the UN International Covenant on Economic, Social and Cultural Rights, op cit. n 4; and the UN Committee on Economic, Social and Cultural Rights (CESCR), General Comment No. 7: The right to adequate housing (Art. 11.1): forced evictions, 20 May 1997, E/1998/22.

[44] *Yordanova*, op cit. n 41, para 83. For a discussion on the case and the court's approach to interpretation using international ESC standards see Remiche (2012).

In the case of *Watts v UK*,[45] the Court also considered ESC rights arising from Article 2 (right to life), Article 3 (respect from inhumane or degrading treatment), and Article 8 (right to private and family life) in connection with an elderly care resident who was being transferred involuntary between care homes. Whilst the application was deemed inadmissible (on the grounds that the local authority had ensured appropriate safeguards), the Court indicated that inherent within the right to life, and the right to respect of private and family life, are implicit positive obligations on the State to ensure that the related ESC rights are protected.[46]

The dynamic interpretative approach to civil and political rights is also apparent in domestic jurisprudence. In the UK, ESC rights have also to some extent been made justiciable under the ambit of civil and political rights.[47] In the case of *Limbuela,*[48] the House of Lords held that there was a positive duty on the State to ensure those seeking asylum did not fall below a threshold of destitution amounting to inhumane or degrading treatment (relying on Article 3 of the Convention) despite the State's argument that this was a matter of socio-economic policy out with the supervisory jurisdiction of the court.

This is a legitimate and viable option that is currently underdeveloped as the extent to which the wide reaching interpretation of Convention rights in the UK is not yet fully explored. An exploration of the potential adjudication of ESC rights under Articles 2, 3, and 8 in particular could give rise to more comprehensive deliberation on ESC rights in Northern Ireland and the rest of the UK.

2.4 The Common Law Application of (Customary) International Human Rights Obligations

The fourth legitimate and viable justiciability mechanism for ESC rights occurs through the common law implementation of *jus cogen* norms and international obligations arising from treaties.[49] The UK pertains to the dualist framework. The general position in relation to international treaties is that they cannot be enforced

[45] *Watts v UK*, ECtHR, 4 May 2010, Application no. 53586/09.

[46] For a further discussion on the widening scope of Article 2 (the right to life) ECHR, see Brennan (2012).

[47] *Condliff v North Staffordshire Primary Care Trust*, [2011] EWCA Civ 910; *McDonald v Royal Borough of Kensington*, [2011] UKSC 33.

[48] 2005 UKHL 66.

[49] Craven (1995), p. 28 has identified this as a model for the potential legitimate and viable justiciability of the rights contained in the International Covenant on Economic Social and Cultural Rights.

by the judiciary unless they have been incorporated into domestic law through legislation.[50] This is consonant with the doctrine of parliamentary supremacy.

There are indications at the national judicial level that there is scope for an innovative approach to interpretation when dealing with legislation that partially incorporates international law.[51] However, this generally does not filter down to a devolved level in Northern Ireland.[52]

There is perhaps room for further development in the implementation of international human rights obligations through a common law interpretative approach that departs from the strict rule that unincorporated treaties are not applicable at a domestic level. One way of safeguarding the separation of powers argument would be to ensure Parliament has an opportunity to veto accession to a treaty, rather than it solely being the exercise of an executive prerogative power. This would afford the judiciary an opportunity to interpret international obligations through adjudication following endorsement by the legislature. International ESC obligations and standards could thereafter filter down through domestic adjudication (admittedly, this would be somewhat more complex for existing treaty obligations as there would be no retrospective application through this mechanism).

3 Potential Mechanisms for Future Implementation

3.1 An International Complaints Mechanism

The fourth legitimate and viable ESC justiciability mechanism applicable to the particular circumstances of Northern Ireland would be available if the State acceded to an existing international complaints mechanism dealing with ESC rights. The UK is a party to the Council of Europe and the Convention and so is already subject to a supranational complaints mechanism (the ECtHR in Strasbourg) to monitor human rights compliance (namely civil and political rights subject to the evolutive interpretative approach discussed above). Supranational adjudication on ESC rights could be achieved by signing and ratifying the Optional Protocol to ICESCR or through signing and ratifying the Additional Protocol Providing for a System of Collective Complaints to the European Social Charter. The former offers a viable and legitimate ESC justiciability mechanism for individuals and the latter offers the

---

[50] *Re J.H. Rayner (Mincing Lane) Ltd. Appelants v Department of Trade and Industry and Others,* [1989] 3 W.L.R. 969—the general position in relation to international treaties is that they cannot be enforced by the judiciary unless they have been incorporated into domestic law through legislation. This is consonant with the doctrine of parliamentary supremacy.

[51] See, for example, Lady Hale's approach in *ZH Tanzania v SSHD* [2011] UKSC 4.

[52] Contrast the approach taken by the Northern Ireland judiciary in *RE Adams* [2001] NI 1 and *Re Northern Ireland Commissioner for Children and Young People* [2004] NIQB 40.

same to designated collective groups.[53] There is political antipathy towards supranational mechanisms in the UK[54] and so it might be difficult to envisage the development of international scrutiny from other supranational bodies within the current political administration. This antipathy is also reflected in the literature from some corners undermining the viability of the international complaints mechanism as a potential solution. Dennis and Stewart have argued that adjudicating ESC rights through an international complaints mechanisms presents more problems than it solves. In respect of the Optional Protocol to ICESCR they contend that

> much of the arguments in support of an optional protocol merely contends there is no reason not to establish a complaints mechanism, rather than demonstrating good reason to do so – for example, by establishing what tangible benefits would flow therefrom.[55]

They posit that the call for formal, binding case adjudication is an example of

> overreaching legal positivisim, borne of the myth that judicial, or quasi-judicial processes intrinsically produce better, more insightful policy choices than, for example, their legislative counterparts.[56]

Hence, their dismissal of an international complaints mechanism rests on a rejection of the justiciability of ESC rights in itself, rather than a rejection of this particular mechanism. This rejection of the legitimacy of ESC justiciability is, they argue, based on a fear that by empowering a supranational court, such as the ESCR Committee, to adjudicate on ESC rights is a step toward establishing a judicially controlled 'command economy' and that this is fundamentally undemocratic.[57] However, they also recognise, despite not being persuaded, that their vantage point is based in an anti-Kelsenian view.[58] In turn, it is critical to place these arguments within the constitutional paradox particular to the UK and the debate as to whether there should be recognition of fundamental norms acknowledging constitutional human rights. The recognition of fundamental human rights norms (Kelsen's *grundnorm*), would in turn facilitate a Kelsenian based theory of constitutional structure, and this would overcome Dennis and Stewarts' rejection of justiciability on the grounds of illegitimacy. It is arguable that Northern Ireland already sits on a rights-based framework model of constitutionalism given that the 1998 peace agreement contained pre-negotiated norms, one of which was respect

---

[53] For a full discussion of the merits and problems with the ESC Collective Complaints System see Churchill and Khaliq (2004); On the Optional Protocol to ICESCR see Scheinin (2006). For a critical perspective on the Optional Protocol to ICESCR see Dennis and Stewart (2004).

[54] May (2013).

[55] Dennis and Stewart (2004), p. 465.

[56] Ibid., p. 466.

[57] Ibid.

[58] Ibid.

for and protection of international human rights, including a commitment to ESC rights.[59]

Dennis and Stewart also raise important fundamental questions in relation to viability. First, there is a concern that the ESCR Committee would not have the appropriate resources to take on an adjudicative role on top of an already demanding remit in respect of the existing reporting procedure. Second, they argue adjudication at the supranational level could undermine ESC adjudication at the micro level leading to inconsistencies and conflict in interpretation.

These barriers could be addressed in Northern Ireland and the UK through domestic legislation similar to the Human Rights Act and the Ullah principle where the domestic courts ought to have regard to Committee jurisprudence (section 2 of the Human Rights Act). Craven has stipulated that

> the justiciability of a particular issue depends, not on the quality of the decision, but rather on the authority of the body to make the decision. Prima facie then, in so far as the Committee is given the authority to assume a quasi-judicial role over the rights in the Covenant, those rights will be justiciable.[60]

In this respect, if the Parliament of the UK was to legislate for the adjudication of ESC rights through ratification of the Optional Protocol complemented by domestic legislation directing the domestic judiciary as to interpretation, both the concerns over legitimacy and viability would be addressed concurrently.

3.2 A Constitutional Solution

The final option proposed is a constitutional recognition of ESC rights in Northern Ireland and the UK. There is a developing trend towards affording constitutional status to ESC rights in other States.[61] The UK is in a peculiar position because the constitution is uncodified, limiting the way in which ESC rights could be constitutionalised. However, the concept of constitutional transformation in relation to

---

[59] See for example the arguments made by Morison and Lynch that NI does constitute a new constitutional framework at which human rights and equality are the central components and from which neither the legislature nor the judiciary should therefore depart from, Morison and Lynch (2007), p. 142.

[60] Craven (1995), p. 102.

[61] King (2012). See for example the constitutions of Argentina 1853 (reinst. 1983, rev. 1994), Angola (2010), Macedonia 1991 (rev 2011), Bosnia-Herzegovina 1995 (rev. 2009), Cape Verde 1980 (rev. 1992), Croatia 1991 (rev. 2001), Czech Republic 1993 (rev. 2002), Democratic Republic of the Congo 2005 (rev. 2011), East Timor 2002, Eritrea 1997, Ethiopia 1994, Iran 1979 (rev. 1989), Macedonia 1991 (rev. 2011), Montenegro 2007; Mozambique 2004 (rev. 2007); Nepal 2006 (rev. 2010); Nicaragua 1987 (rev. 2005); Portugal 1976 (rev. 2005); Rwanda 2003 (rev. 2010); Sao Tome and Principe 1975 (rev. 1990); Slovakia 1992 (rev. 2001); Surinam 1987 (rev. 1992). Each of which refer to 'economic, social and cultural rights' in their constitutional text.

human rights has been under examination through the consultative process on a UK-wide Bill of Rights.[62] Following a similar indigenous process in Northern Ireland the Northern Ireland Office (the UK Government's executive arm in Northern Ireland) rejected the proposed terms of the Bill of Rights for the particular circumstances of Northern Ireland presented by the Northern Ireland Human Rights Commission.[63] The mandate of the Northern Ireland Human Rights Commission was to advise on a legislative mechanism to provide for rights supplementary to those in the Convention and to reflect the particular circumstances of Northern Ireland drawing on international instruments and treaties.[64] The proposal contained a comprehensive list of ESC rights. The Northern Ireland Office was opposed to this inclusion,

> It is important to emphasise that the Government does not believe the rights listed above [i. e. ESC rights] to be any less significant and important for the people of Northern Ireland than those considered for inclusion in a Bill of Rights for Northern Ireland. But it is the Government's view that the introduction of such rights in Northern Ireland alone would either be unworkable in practice, or could give rise to unjustified inequalities across the UK.[65]

Furthermore, the Commission for a UK-wide Bill of Rights has largely rejected the inclusion of such rights in any future Bill of Rights for the UK,

> [T]he conclusion of a majority of our members, if there were to be a UK Bill of Rights, is that we would be hesitant about it containing socio-economic and environmental rights. Many decisions of this kind that might be regarded as involving rights in practice involve the allocation of scarce resources.[66]

Koch and Vedsted-Hansen argue that adjudication on socio-economic rights need not necessarily require that the judiciary impede on government policy or budgetary decisions of the legislature.[67] They cite the South African example as a

---

[62] Commission on a Bill of Rights, A UK Bill of Rights? The Choice Before Us, December 2012. The consultation on future proposals of a UK Bill of Rights forming part of the conservative manifesto in 2015 is not available at the point of this chapter going to print.

[63] The proposed Bill of Rights was presented by the Northern Ireland Human Rights to the Northern Ireland Office in 2008. The Northern Ireland Office rejected the proposed Bill on 30 November 2009 citing various reasons for the decision, including the perceived controversial inclusion of socio-economic rights, Commission on Northern Ireland Office Consultation Paper, 'A Bill of Rights for Northern Ireland, Next Steps', November 2009.

[64] As per paragraph four of the section entitled 'Rights, Safeguards and Equality of Opportunity' in the peace agreement known as the Belfast Agreement or the Good Friday Agreement. The peace agreement was registered with the UN under a separate bilateral treaty between the Governments of the UK and the Republic of Ireland, Agreement between the Government of the United Kingdom of Great Britain and Northern Ireland and the Government of Ireland (with annexes), Belfast, 10 April 1998, Registration No. 1.36776 UNTS 2114, Treaty series No. 50 (2000) Cm4705.

[65] NIO Next Steps (2009), *op cit.* n 63, para 3.15.

[66] Commission on a Bill of Rights, A UK Bill of Rights? The Choice Before Us, Volume 1, December 2012, para 8.28.

[67] Koch and Vedsted-Hansen (2006).

constitutional deliberative court that decides whether an ESC right has been violated and essentially then defers back to the legislature to reassess the policy in order to remedy the violation.[68] They refer to the meta-right analogy proposed by Amartya Sen that '[a] metaright to something x can be defined as the right to have *policies p(x)*'[69] as a means of addressing ESC policy deficit through justiciable remedies. This would be similar to the statutory obligations imposing procedural duties under the Equality Act 2010 and so would be equally viable in terms of ESC rights in the UK.

Empirical research has highlighted the socio-economic policy deficit that currently exists in Northern Ireland. As part of a qualitative based empirical study conducted by INCORE at the University of Ulster, respondents were asked to identify outstanding challenges hindering the development of 'a shared and better future' for Northern Ireland.[70] One of the key themes emerging was,

> the need to support and encourage socio-economic development as a fundamental priority for the future success of the region and a key element in the delivery of cohesion and integration between and within communities, particularly during periods of economic contraction.[71]

Kelly further notes that the study revealed a need for,

> key social and economic mechanisms that require significant structural or institutional changes, if abstract vision is to take on practical application.[72]

Given the commitments contained in the peace agreement on the continued enhancement of human rights protection in Northern Ireland (beyond the Convention) there is an arguable case that the avoidance of addressing the ESC human rights deficit undermines the transition to substantive peace. Ní Aoláin contends that the reasons for under-enforcement in post-conflict societies are complex and multiple and makes a useful observation in relation to Northern Ireland and what she perceives as an eventual threat to stabilised peace,

> Partial or non-implementation of human rights provisions can be correlated with what a state sees as necessary to achieve conflict resolution in the short term. Undoubtedly, some reform issues are difficult and their resolution has high political costs... Sometimes immediate reform can seem too daunting or too much for a society to bear as it comes to terms with a transforming society. However, I contend that this short-sighted view operates in opposition to the goal of preventing a return to conflict in the long run. This is particularly true of societies where human rights violations have formed the basis for the underlying experience of communal violence in the first place. In those societies, meaningful and sometimes hurtful transformation is a necessary pre-condition to a stable and long-lasting peace.[73]

[68] Koch and Vedsted-Hansen (2006), pp. 17–18.

[69] Sen (1984), p. 70.

[70] Kelly (2012).

[71] Ibid., p. 4.

[72] Ibid., p. 63.

[73] Ní Aoláin (2005), para 45.

The call for a Bill of Rights for Northern Ireland has recently been restated by rights based groups operating in Northern Ireland. In an open letter to the UK Government in May 2013 a group of civil society organisations called for the enactment of a Bill of Rights for Northern Ireland 15 years after the referendum on the peace agreement.[74] In connection with the publication, Fiona McCausland, Chairperson of the Human Rights Consortium, reiterated the importance of fulfilling human rights commitments in the agreement as a prerequisite to lasting peace,

> When the public voted for the agreement 15 years ago today, they voted for all of the agreement, not just part of it. Human rights are part of the normal checks and balances of any healthy democracy. In a society that has come through so much and still remains divided they become all the more important.

It is clear, certainly to civil society actors, that the failure to fully address the commitments in the peace agreement remains a barrier to the full transition in respect of the war v peace antinomy.

It should be noted that, while the procedural policy protection of an ESC right could constitute a mechanism through which ESC justiciability might occur, it is not by any means the only option available. A Bill of Rights that imposes a duty on the State to enact legislation with judicial remedies to protect ESC rights[75] might be a more suitable alternative consonant with the doctrine of parliamentary sovereignty in the UK.

Rather than view judicial supremacy as imposing or usurping the sovereignty of Parliament, the case for a substantive rights-based conception of the rule of law would bind both the legislature and the judiciary to a set of fundamental principles from which neither could derogate. Lord Steyn has proposed that international human rights ought to be considered by the judiciary as *sui generis* from other international obligations.[76] This departs from the view that the constitution cannot impose legal limits on the legislature.[77] The framework model of constitutionalism in Northern Ireland already presents as form of constitutionalism that sits outside of the parameters of the Westminster process model based on parliamentary supremacy—this is evident, for example, in the pre-commitment to human rights and equality in the 1998 peace agreement and international treaty—these normative values arguably displace the absolute authority of legislative supremacy as the rule

[74] Rights NI (2013), signed by Age NI, Amnesty International, Children's Law Centre, Committee on the Administration of Justice (CAJ), Disability Action, Disabled Police Officers Association, Human Rights Consortium, Irish Congress of Trade Unions (ICTU), the National Union of Students-Union of Students in Ireland (NUS-USI), North West Community Network, Northern Ireland Council for Ethnic Minorities (NICEM), Northern Ireland Public Service Alliance (NIPSA), Relatives for Justice, Rural Community Network, Save the Children, UNISON, Unite the Union, WAVE Trauma Centre, Women's Federation Northern Ireland.

[75] Such as the approach under the Constitution of Finland.

[76] Obiter dictum in *Re McKerr* [2004] 1 WLR 807.

[77] For differing views see Ekins (2003); and Waldron (2006), p. 1354.

of law in the transitional constitution affords a foundationalist base to human rights, including ESC rights.[78]

To enact a Bill of Rights for Northern Ireland, or for the rest of the UK for that matter, which includes justiciable remedies for violations of ESC rights would require a paradigmatic shift in the constitution of the UK. It would situate human rights beyond the reach of retrogressive legislation. Perhaps treating fundamental human rights as *sui generis* in nature, in so far as placing a limit on parliamentary sovereignty, might enhance democratic accountability and transparency. If a fundamental (constitutional) right is violated—rather than view the role of the judiciary as an exercise of power usurping the role of the legislature, court adjudication could be viewed as an exercise of accountability, therefore reinforcing the democratic process. It is possible to frame a constitutional settlement that takes into account the separation of powers, the balancing of rights and the limited financial resources of the State. This can be done in a way in which the judiciary play an important role in securing accountability by supervising the exercise of power by other organs of the State.[79] It is crucial that the discussion on the future of human rights protection in Northern Ireland, including justiciable ESC protection, continues. The previous Commission for a UK Bill of Rights reaffirmed the importance of ensuring the indigenous process towards a Bill of Rights for Northern Ireland is not undermined by the UK-wide process because of its importance to the peace process.[80] The UN Committee on Economic, Social and Cultural Rights has also called for the enactment of a Bill of Rights for Northern Ireland, which includes justiciable ESC rights, without delay.[81]

4 Conclusion

This chapter has sought to outline and address the legitimate and viable ESC justiciability mechanisms open to Northern Ireland. It is intended to facilitate and inform the debate on the best way forward for human rights protection in Northern

[78] Feldman sets out what is meant by a framework model of constitutionalism with reference to the *Grundgesetz* or Basic Norm of the 1949 Constitution for the Federal Republic of Germany and the Constitution of Bosnia and Herzegovina, Article X.2 of which provides 'Human Rights and Fundamental Freedoms. No amendment to this Constitution may eliminate or diminish any of the rights and freedoms referred to in Article II of this Constitution or alter the present paragraph' creating a framework in which fundamental human rights norms are foundational, non-derogable and beyond the reach of retrogressive legislative measures. In other words they hold constitutional status. Feldman (2007), pp. 447–453.

[79] For example see the discussion on employing a reasonableness review similar to that employed by the Constitutional Court in South Africa posited by Wesson (2012). See also the arguments posed by King (2012) in the legitimacy of a theory of judicial restraint in securing constitutional social rights.

[80] Commission on a Bill of Rights (2012), *op cit.* n 62, para 75.

[81] CESCR General Comment 9, *op cit.* n 8, para 10.

Ireland. Clearly there are many issues that remain outstanding areas of concern in relation to both the continued polarisation of the divided communities and the failure to fully realise substantive peace. A democratic process that enables a transparent and accountable scrutiny of the actions of the legislature and Government in relation to ESC rights might encourage a shared future and common goals. Of course, human rights are not just for one community or the other, they are for everyone, including those vulnerable and marginalised groups in Northern Ireland that currently have no voice. Access to an effective remedy in the court room is arguably one way of enabling the vulnerable and marginalised an opportunity to participate in the wider democratic process. This need not necessarily be diametrically opposed to the rule of law or the doctrine of parliamentary supremacy. Legitimate and viable ESC justiciability is already underway in the UK both *de jure* and *de facto*—acceptance of this might move the debate on to how it ought to happen in a transparent and democratic manner. In particular, this ought to happen in a way that facilitates the transition to peace in Northern Ireland by ensuring, at the very least, that more substantive human rights protections available elsewhere in the UK are extended to the Northern Ireland jurisdiction without delay.

References

Advisory Committee to the Framework Convention for the Protection of National Minorities, FCNM, Third Opinion on the United Kingdom, adopted on 30 June 2011, ACFC/OP/III (2011) 006.

Alston, P., & Quinn, G. (1987). The nature and scope of states parties' obligations under the International Covenant on Economic, Social and Cultural Rights. *Human Rights Quarterly, 9*, 156.

Anthony, G. (2005). *Judicial review in Northern Ireland.* Oxford, England: Hart.

Aust, A. (2010). *Handbook of international law* (2nd ed.). Cambridge, England: Cambridge University Press.

Brennan, C. (2012). One more step in the expansion of "the right to life", case comment. *Professional Negligence, 28*, 149.

Churchill, R., & Khaliq, U. (2004). The collective complaints system of the European Social Charter: An effective mechanism for ensuring compliance with economic and social rights? *European Journal of International Law, 15*, 417.

Commission on a Bill of Rights '*A UK Bill of Rights? The Choice Before Us*' December 2012.

Commission on Northern Ireland Office Consultation Paper, '*A Bill of Rights for Northern Ireland, Next Steps*', November 2009.

Concluding observations of the Committee on Economic, Social and Cultural Rights: United Kingdom of Great Britain and Northern Ireland, the Crown Dependencies and the Overseas Dependent Territories, 12 June 2009, E/C.12/GBR/CO/5.

Courtis, C. (2009). Standards to make ESC rights justiciable: A summary explanation. *Erasmus Law Review, 2*, 379.

Craven, M. (1995). *The International Covenant on Economic, Social, and Cultural Rights: A perspective on its development.* Oxford, England: Clarendon Press/Oxford University Press.

Dennis, M., & Stewart, D. (2004). Justiciability of Economic, Social and Cultural Rights: Should there be an international complaints mechanism to adjudicate the rights to food, water, housing and health? *The American Journal of International Law, 98*, 462.

Dickson, B., & Harvey, C. (2013, February 22) What do 'you' think is the way forward for human rights in Northern Ireland? *UK Human Rights Blog*. www.ukhumanrightsblog.com/2013/02/22/what-do-you-think-is-the-way-forward-for-human-rights-in-northern-ireland/#more-17350. Accessed 9 Apr 2014

DUP Response to NIO consultation paper, *A Bill of Rights for Northern Ireland: Next Steps, Response by Democratic Unionist Party*, 30 March 2010.

Eide, A. (1989). Realization of social and economic rights and the minimum threshold approach. *Human Rights Law Journal, 10*, 35.

Ekins, R. (2003). Judicial supremacy and the rule of law. *Law Quarterly Review, 119*, 127.

Feldman, D. (2007). Constitutionalism, deliberative democracy and human rights. In J. Morison et al. (Eds.), *Judges, transition and human rights*. Oxford, England: Oxford University Press.

Harvey, C. (2004). Talking about human rights. *European Human Rights Law Review,* 500.

Hunt, M. (2010). Enhancing Parliament's role in relation to economic and social rights. *European Human Rights Law Review, 3*, 242.

Kelly, G. (2012). *Progressing good relations and reconciliation in post-agreement Northern Ireland*. INCORE Research Report, University of Ulster February. http://www.incore.ulst.ac.uk/pdfs/projects/55_Reconciliation_Research_Report.pdf. Accessed 3 Apr 2014.

King, J. (2012). *Judging social rights*. Cambridge, England: Cambridge University Press.

Koch, I. (2005). Dichotomies, trichotomies or waves of duties. *Human Rights Law Review, 5*, 81.

Koch, I. E., & Vedsted-Hansen, J. (2006). International Human Rights and National Legislatures – Conflict or balance? *Nordic Journal of International Law, 75*, 3.

May, T. (2013, March 9). Tories to consider leaving European Convention on Human Rights. *BBC News Online*. www.bbc.co.uk/news/uk-politics-21726612. Accessed 9 Apr 2014.

McKeever, G., & Ní Aoláin, F. (2004). Thinking globally, acting locally: Enforcing socio economic rights in Northern Ireland. *European Human Rights Law Review, 2*, 158.

Miller, Z. (2008). Effects of invisibility: In search of the "Economic" in transitional justice. *International Journal of Transitional Justice, 2*, 266.

Millward Brown Ulster Limited, Bill of Rights Poll, 44102357 February 2010.

Morison, J., & Lynch, M. (2007). Litigating the agreement: Towards a new judicial constitutionalism for the UK from Northern Ireland. In J. Morison et al. (Eds.), *Judges, transition and human rights*. Oxford, England: Oxford University Press.

Ní Aoláin, F. (2005). The Good Friday Agreement, role of human rights in peace agreements. International Council on Human Rights Policy, Review Meeting, Belfast, 7–8 March 2005.

Ní Aoláin, F. (2000). *Politics of force: Conflict management and state violence in Northern Ireland*. Belfast, England: The Blackstaff Press.

Ní Aoláin, F., & Campbell, C. (2003). The paradox of transition in conflicted democracies. *Human Rights Quarterly, 27*, 172.

Nolan, A. et al. (2007). The Justiciability of Social and Economic Rights: An updated appraisal. March 2007 for the Human Rights Consortium. www.chrgj.org/publications/docs/wp/NolanPorterLangford.pdf. Accessed 9 Apr 2014.

Oppenheim, C., & Harker, L. (1996). *Poverty: The facts*. London: Child Poverty Action Group.

Rai, S. M. (2007). Deliberative democracy and the politics of redistribution: The case of the Indian Panchayats. *Hypatia, 22*, 65.

Remiche, A. (2012). Yordanova and Others v Bulgaria: The influence of the social right to adequate housing on the interpretation of the civil right to respect for one's home. *Human Rights Law Review, 12*, 787.

Rights NI. (2013, May 22). Rights from Northern Ireland, '15 Years after the Referendum, UK Gov urged to deliver Bill of Right'. Letter reproduced. http://rightsni.org/2013/05/15-years-after-referendum-uk-gov-urged-to-deliver-bill-of-rights/. Accessed 9 Apr 2014.

Scheinin, M. (2006). The proposed optional protocol to the covenant on economic, social and cultural rights: A blueprint for UN Human Rights Treaty Body reform—Without amending the existing treaties. *Human Rights Law Review, 6*, 131.

Scott, C. (1989). The interdependence and permeability of human rights norms: Towards a partial fusion of the International Covenants on Human Rights. *Osgoode Hall Law Journal, 27*, 769.

Scottish Human Rights Commission 'Poverty and Equality', Scottish Human Rights Commission National Action Plan, Getting it Right? Human Rights in Scotland, 2012. www.scottishhumanrights.com/actionplan/home. Accessed 10 Jan 2014.

Sen, A. (1984). The right not to be hungry. In P. Alston et al. (Eds.), *The right to food*. The Hague, The Netherlands: Martinus Nijhoff.

Teitel, R. (2003). Transitional justice genealogy. *Harvard Human Rights Journal, 16*, 69.

The Northern Ireland Omnibus Survey, Millward Brown Ulster, June 2009.

Tinta, M. F. (2007). Justiciability of Economic, Social, and Cultural Rights in the Inter-American system of protection of human rights: Beyond traditional paradigms and notions. *Human Rights Quarterly, 29*, 431.

Turner, C. (2010). Political representations of law in Northern Ireland. *Public Law*, 451.

UN Committee on Economic, Social and Cultural Rights (CESCR): Concluding Observations, United Kingdom of Great Britain and Northern Ireland, 5 June 2002, E/C.12/1/Add.79.

UN Committee on Economic, Social and Cultural Rights (CESCR), General Comment No. 7: The right to adequate housing (Art. 11.1): forced evictions, 20 May 1997, E/1998/22.

UN Committee on Economic, Social and Cultural Rights (CESCR), General Comment No. 9: The domestic application of the Covenant, 3 December 1998, E/C.12/1998/24.

UN Committee on the Elimination of Racial Discrimination (CERD), Concluding Observations, United Kingdom of Great Britain and Northern Ireland, 14 September 2011, CERD/C/GBR/CO/18-20.

Waldron, J. (2006). The core of the case against judicial review. *Yale Law Journal, 115*, 1346, 1354.

Wesson, M. (2012). Disagreement and the constitutionalisation of social rights. *Human Rights Law Review, 12*, 221.

Wheatley, S. (2003). Deliberative democracies and minorities. *European Journal of International Law, 14*, 507.

Legislation

Sex Discrimination (NI) Order 1976
Fair Employment Act 1976
Fair Employment (NI) Act 1989
Disability Discrimination Act 1995
Race Relations (NI) Order 1997
Fair Employment and Treatment (NI) Order 1998
Police (NI) Act 2000
Employment Equality (Sexual Orientation) (NI) Regulations 2003
European Framework Directive on Equal Treatment 2004
Equal Pay Act (NI) 1970
Rights of Children and Young Persons Measure (Wales) 2011

Case Law

Neill's Application [2006] NICA 5
Watts v UK, ECtHR, 4 May 2010, Application no. 53586/09

Re McKerr [2004] 1 WLR 807.
Re J.H. Rayner (Mincing Lane) Ltd. Appelants v Department of Trade and Industry and Others, [1989] 3 W.L.R. 969
ZH Tanzania v SSHD [2011] UKSC 4
RE Adams [2001] NI 1
Re Northern Ireland Commissioner for Children and Young People [2004] NIQB 40
Condliff v North Staffordshire Primary Care Trust, [2011] EWCA Civ 910;
McDonald v Royal Borough of Kensington, [2011] UKSC 33
Harjula v London Borough Council supra Harjula v London Borough Council [2011] EWHC 151 (QB);
on the Application of W,M,G & H v Birmingham City Council, [2011] EWHC 1147 Admin.
Eldridge v. British Columbia (Attorney General) [1997] 3 S.C.R.*;*
Awas Tingi v Nicaragua Inter-Am Ct HR, August 31 2001*;*
Shelter Corporation v. Ontario Human Rights Commission (2001) 143 OAC 54;
Klickovic Pasalic and Karanovic v Bosnia and Herzegovina, the Federation of Bosnia and Herzegovina and the Republika Sprska, CH/02/8923, CH/02/8924, CH/02/9364, 10 January 2003;
Khosa v Minister of Social Development, 2004 (6) SA 505 (CC)
Dybeku v. Albania, Application no. 41153/06, 18 Dec. 2007
Khamidov v. Russia, Application no. 72118/01, 2 June 2008
Airey v. Ireland, 32 Eur Ct HR Ser A (1979): [1979] 2 E.H.R.R. 305
Belgian Linguistic Case (Nos. 1 & 2) (No. 1) (1967), Series A, No. 5 (1979–80) 1 EHRR 241 (No. 2) (1968), Series A, No. 6 (1979–80) 1 EHRR 252
López Ostra v. Spain, Series A, No 303-C; (1995) 20 EHHR 277
Botta v. Italy (1998) 26 EHHR 241
Selçuk and Asker v. Turkey, (1998) 26 EHRR 477
Akkus v. Turkey, App. no. 00019263/92, Judgment 24 June 1997.
Connors v. *United Kingdom*, European Court of Human Rights, Application no. 66746/01, 27 May 2004,
Yordanova and Others v Bulgaria, Application no. 25446/06, 12 April 2012
European Roma Rights Centre v Bulgaria Complaint No 31/2005, 25 May 2005
Defrenne II – Case 43/75 [1976] ECR 455

Children in Colombia: Discussing the Current Transitional Justice Process Against the Backdrop of the CRC Key Principles

Francesca Capone

1 Introduction: An Overview of the Current Situation in Colombia

Colombia's civilians have been pulled into a five decades long civil war among the government's forces, paramilitary groups and their successors, the Fuerzas Armadas Revolucionarias de Colombia-Ejército del Pueblo ('FARC-EP') and the People's Liberation Army ('ELN').[1] Violence associated with the country's internal armed conflict has forcibly displaced more than 5.7 million Colombians, and upwards of 200,000 persons continue to flee their homes each year, generating the world's second largest population of internally displaced persons ('IDPs').[2] Although the regular armed forces have expanded their military operations throughout the country since 2002, non-state armed groups remain active in most parts of the Colombian territory. In some of the remote areas of the country, guerrilla groups act as the ruling authority, filling the vacuum created by the absence of the state enforcing the law and providing public services. Between 2003 and 2006, the government initiated a process to demobilize the United Self-Defense Forces of Colombia ('AUC'), a right-wing umbrella organisation made up of various para-

[1] The Watchlist on Children and Armed Conflict, '*No one to Trust: Children and Armed Conflict in Colombia*', April 2012, http://www.protectingeducation.org/sites/default/files/documents/no_one_to_trust.pdf (accessed 5 March 2015).

[2] The 2014 Global Report by the Internal Displacement Monitoring Centre (IDMC) placed Colombia as the country with the second highest number of IDPs in the world, http://www.internal-displacement.org/assets/publications/2014/201405-global-overview-2014-en.pdf (accessed 8 March 2015).

F. Capone (✉)
Scuola Superiore Sant'Anna, Piazza Martiri della Libertà 33, Pisa, Italy
e-mail: f.capone@sssup.it

A. Diver, J. Miller (eds.), *Justiciability of Human Rights Law in Domestic Jurisdictions*, DOI 10.1007/978-3-319-24016-9_9

military groups.[3] During President Álvaro Uribe Vélez's administration, legislative action related to the rights of victims of the armed conflict was primarily focused on inducing armed groups to demobilise. The Justice and Peace Law ('JPL' or 'Law 975'), signed by President Uribe on 22 July 2005, seeks to bring peace by facilitating the demobilization and reincorporation into civil society of members of illegal armed groups. In order to achieve its objectives, the JPL has established judicial benefits for members of illegal armed groups who participated in the demobilization process, i.e. access to reintegration programme's incentives and reduced sentences of 5–8 years if they admitted the crimes committed.[4] Law 975 was strongly criticised by international human rights organisations because it unduly limits the legal definition of 'victim' to those individuals who had suffered non-state violence, leaving unpunished the acts perpetrated by state agents.[5] The effect was mainly to protect the paramilitaries (and the state) and neglect the rights of victims. While officially more than 30,000 paramilitaries passed through the program, the government never verified whether all of them had actually demobilised, and it was unable to dismantle the groups' criminal networks and support systems.[6] As a result, some groups or sections of groups have either never demobilised, or re-armed right after the process, forming new groups, the so-called *bandas criminales emergentes* ('BACRIM').[7] Human Rights Watch reported that, as of September 2014, only 37 of the more than 30,000 paramilitaries who officially participated in the demobilisation process had been convicted of crimes under the Justice and Peace Law.[8] The convictions covered only a small portion of the nearly 70,000 crimes confessed to by defendants seeking Law 975 benefits.[9] To remedy, at least partially, the shortcomings of the JPL, on 10 June 2011 President Juan Manuel Santos signed the Victims' and Land Restitution Law ('Victims' Law'). The Victims' Law came into effect on January 2012. It does not replace the existing JPL, but rather supplements it by adding further obligations on the part of the state to provide more extensive reparations programmes.[10] As stated in Articles 1 and

[3] "*Profiles: Colombia's Armed Groups*", BBC News, 29 August 2013, http://www.bbc.co.uk/news/world-latin-america-11400950 (accessed 8 March 2015).

[4] JPL, Arts 24, 29; Report of the Special Rapporteur on extrajudicial, summary or arbitrary executions, Philip Alston, Addendum, Mission to Colombia, 31 March 2010, A/HRC/14/24/Add.2, Appendix C, Justice and Peace Law, para 3.

[5] García-Godos and Lid (2010).

[6] Humphrey (2013), pp. 67–87.

[7] According to OHCHR 53 % of the BACRIM's members are former paramilitaries. See *Annual Report of the United Nations High Commissioner for Human Rights: Addendum: Report on the Situation of Human Rights in Colombia*, 31 January 2012, A/HRC/19/21/Add.3.

[8] Human Rights Watch (2015) World report: Colombia. www.hrw.org/world-report-2015/Colombia (accessed 2 March 2015).

[9] Ibid.

[10] Annual report of the United Nations High Commissioner for Human Rights, Report of the United Nations High Commissioner for Human Rights on the situation of human rights in Colombia, A/HRC/19/21/Add.3, 31 January 2012, para 49.

2 of the Victims' Law, its purpose is to establish judicial, administrative, social, economic, individual and collective measures to benefit victims of violations of international and humanitarian law arising out of the armed conflict in Colombia.[11] The Victims' Law was designed to be a comprehensive set of norms, able to address those victims who were neglected by previous legislative efforts. Notably, the Victim's Law has introduced a number of legal and administrative institutions and programmes to foster victims' access to reparations.[12]

Generally speaking the country is nowadays facing an unprecedented challenge as the attempts to implement the transitional justice process continue in parallel with the peace negotiations, which began officially after the signing of the 'General Agreement for the end of the conflict and the construction of a stable and lasting peace' in August 2012.[13] The talks between the FARC-EP and the Government of Colombia, which are still ongoing in Havana, have achieved so far a number of important results on three issues, namely land reform, the rebels' political participation and the illegal drugs trade.[14] There are still a number of thorny matters which the two sides have to contend with, namely the rights of the victims of the conflict, the disarmament of the rebels and, last but not least, the implementation of all the agreed points. In order to discuss the necessary steps to finally come to terms with the needs and rights of the victims, groups of them have been travelling to Havana to present their views to the negotiators. So far five delegations of victims have been tasked with reporting to the negotiators the views and the proposals collected back home. Over the past 2 years, in fact, a series of regional fora for victims' participation, established upon the request of the negotiators, along with a large number of 'peace roundtables' ('Mesas Regionales de Paz') organised by the Colombian parliament, have been held throughout the country. Several thousand concrete proposals resulting from these consultations have been presented to negotiators.[15] Different categories of victims have participated in the process, including women, indigenous people and children who have been unduly affected by the long lasting armed conflict. According to the UN High Commissioner for Human Rights, 'more so than any other development, the current peace process has the potential to transform Colombia in relation to its level of respect for and

[11] Victims' Law, arts 1–2; see also 'Colombia: Victims Law a Historic Opportunity' *Human Rights Watch*, 10 June 2011, http://www.hrw.org/news/2011/06/10/colombia-victims-law-historic-opportunity (accessed 6 March 2015).

[12] Céspedes-Báez (2012).

[13] International Crisis Group (2012), General Agreement for the Termination of the Conflict and the Construction of a Stable and Lasting Peace, 34.

[14] 'What is at stake in the Colombian peace process?' BBC News, 15 January 2015, http://www.bbc.com/news/world-latin-america-19875363 (accessed 7 March 2015).

[15] "Victims' voice heard in Colombia Peace Talks", Global Justice News and Civil Society Views from the Coalition for the ICC, 16 March 2015, https://ciccglobaljustice.wordpress.com/2015/03/16/victims-voices-heard-in-colombia-peace-talks/ (accessed 8 March 2015).

enjoyment of human rights.'[16] In the context of the ongoing armed conflict, human rights violations have been committed daily, with a disproportionate impact on vulnerable or geographically isolated sectors of the population and on social actors, community leaders and human rights defenders.

2 Child Victims of the Colombian Armed Conflict

In the 2012 report on the situation of human rights in Colombia, the UN High Commissioner for Human Rights registered a disturbingly high number of crimes committed against children in many areas of the country; in particular she referred to cases of 'recruitment and threats of recruitment, deaths and injuries caused by explosive artefacts, occupation of and attacks against schools, displacement, homicide, and injuries.'[17] Despite the official beginning of the peace talks and the progress witnessed since their inception, the 2014 UN Secretary-General's report on children and armed conflict confirmed that several violations have been perpetrated against children by all the parties involved in the ongoing war.[18] The Secretary-General's report stressed that hostilities between FARC-EP, the ELN and the Colombian Armed Forces have even intensified, in particular in the areas of Cauca, Choco, Nariño, Antioquia, Arauca, Santander and Putumayo. Extensive displacement triggered by such hostilities has further increased children's vulnerability, especially those of Afro-Colombian and indigenous origin. At least 110,000 people, including children, suffered from severe mobility restrictions in 2013, mostly as a result of hostilities, but also through confinement, contamination by explosive remnants of war, and security restrictions imposed by armed groups, having an impact on access to humanitarian assistance and basic services.[19] With regards in particular to the violations committed over the last year, the Special Representative on Children and Armed Conflict has reported that the recruitment and use of children has remained a widespread phenomenon, difficult to monitor within Colombia.[20] The UN has verified a total of 81 cases of recruitment and use of children by armed groups in 25 departments and in Bogotá, including 58 children

[16] Annual report of the United Nations High Commissioner for Human Rights, Addendum Report of the United Nations High Commissioner for Human Rights on the situation of human rights in Colombia, 7 January 2013, A/HRC/22/17/Add.3, 3.

[17] Annual Report of the United Nations High Commissioner for Human Rights. Addendum Report of the United Nations High Commissioner for Human Rights on the situation of human rights in Colombia, 31 January 2012, A/HRC/19/21/Add.3, 14.

[18] Children and armed conflict, Report of the Secretary-General, 15 May 2014, A/68/878–S/2014/339.

[19] Ibid., para 35.

[20] The Government of Colombia has voluntarily accepted the monitoring and reporting mechanism pursuant to Security Council resolution 1612 (2005) on the condition that any dialogue between the United Nations and armed groups would take place with its consent.

by FARC-EP and 17 by ELN. In July 2013, eight cases of recruitment of indigenous children by FARC-EP were documented in the department of Cauca. In December, in Antioquia, a 15-year-old boy was recruited by FARC-EP during a declared ceasefire. Furthermore, the Colombian Family Welfare Institute documented 342 children (114 girls and 228 boys) separated from armed groups in 2013, marking a significant increase, compared with the 264 children separated in 2012. Among these children, 261 had been recruited by FARC-EP, 65 by ELN, 15 by armed groups that emerged after the demobilization of the AUC, and 1 by the Ejército Popular de Liberación. At least 43 children were killed and 83 maimed during attacks by armed groups. Four children were killed and 10 maimed in clashes between armed groups or between the national armed forces and armed groups.[21]

The negative impact of the long lasting armed conflict on the youngest sector of the Colombian population is not questionable: the government has adopted new pieces of legislation to enhance the protection and promotion of children's rights, while both the JPL and the Victims' Law have recognised, to differing extents and from diverse perspectives, the need to address violations perpetrated against children. However, the implementation of the existing legal framework has harshly highlighted its shortcomings, for example a comparison between the number of children estimated to have been associated with armed groups, which ranges from 8000 to 18,000,[22] and those actually included in official collective demobilizations, 5417 since 1999,[23] shows that most children did not participate in the processes established through the JPL. In addition to the challenges stemming from the application of the current set of norms, another important aspect concerns the attention, or lack thereof, devoted to child victims during the ongoing peace negotiations. As mentioned above, children were reported to have been taking part in the consultations carried out throughout the country, but the issue of children

[21] Children and armed conflict, Report of the Secretary-General, 15 May 2014, A/68/878–S/2014/339, 35.

[22] The number of children who have been associated with armed groups in Colombia is very difficult to determine; the existing data gathered by NGOs, the UN, local authorities and researchers does not match. According to Springer, the number amounts to 18,000 children. (See Springer 2012, pp. 34–35. According to Human Rights Watch the number of children associated with armed groups is 11,000. (See Human Rights Watch, '*Aprenderás A No Llorar: Niños Combatientes En Colombia*' (2004) Bogotá: Editorial Gente Nueva). Instead the number reported by the el Tribunal Internacional sobre la Infancia Afectada por la Gue- rra y la Pobreza is 8000 children. See Tribunal Internacional sobre la Infancia Afectada por la Guerra y la Pobreza del Comité de Derechos Humanos, Reporte Internacional Anual 2012 sobre la infancia afectada por la guerra. Los dos Congos de la guerra. Colombia y la región de los grandes lagos en África. Dos regiones de muerte para la infancia (Bogotá-Madrid: Tribunal Internacional sobre la Infancia Afectada por la Guerra y la Pobreza del Comité de Derechos Humanos (2012)).

[23] Children and armed conflict, Report of the Secretary-General, 15 May 2014, A/68/878–S/2014/339, 36.

and armed conflict has not been specifically mentioned in the General Agreement. Implicit reference can be found in items 2 and 5 on the agenda, dealing respectively with 'political participation,' which should include also the most vulnerable sectors of the Colombian population, and 'victims', who deserve to have their human rights duly implemented, and access to the truth.[24] Remarkably, on 15 February 2015 the FARC-EP announced that it will 'no longer incorporate, from today on, minors of 17 (and younger) in the guerrilla ranks.'[25] The ban on the recruitment of children under the age of 17 years represents a step towards the FARC-EP's full compliance with international human rights law standards, in particular with the principle enshrined in Article 4 of the Optional Protocol on the Involvement of Children in Armed Conflict, which places an absolute prohibition on the enlistment or conscription of children under 18 years by non-state armed groups, and imposes on governments the obligation to, again, use all feasible measures to prevent such recruitment.[26]

While much attention has been paid to the large number of violations against children which occurred in Colombia over the past 50 years, promptly documented by several IOs and NGOs, very little research has been undertaken to analyse the enhancement of children's rights within the country's national legislation, including the norms adopted as part of the current transitional justice process. To this end the following section will firstly introduce the principle of the best interests of the child and children's right to participation, as they are crucial to the design and development of any decision, law and process which has an impact on children's lives. Then the focus will shift onto Colombia's acceptance of these two key concepts within its legal framework and the ongoing transitional justice process.

3 Children's Best Interests and the Right to Express Their Views as Enshrined in the CRC

Before diving into the Colombian framework dealing with children's rights, it is important to define and analyse the key principles enshrined in the CRC. The first consideration in relation to children, in all legislative efforts and actions that concern them, including the measures, judicial and non-judicial, set up within a

[24] International Crisis Group (2012), General Agreement for the Termination of the Conflict and the Construction of a Stable and Lasting Peace, 35.

[25] The news has been reported by, inter al., Watchlist on Children and Armed Conflict, http://watchlist.org/tag/colombia/ (accessed 12 March 2015).

[26] Optional Protocol to the Convention on the Rights of the Child on the Involvement of Children in Armed Conflict. UNTS Vol. 2173, 222 (entered into force 12 February 2002).

transitional justice process, is what is in their best interests.[27] Article 3, paragraph 1, of the CRC gives the child the right to have his or her best interests assessed and taken into account as a primary concern in all decisions that affect him or her, both in the public and private spheres. The concept of the 'child's best interests' is not a new one, in fact it pre-dates the CRC and was already enshrined in the 1959 Declaration of the Rights of the Child,[28] the Convention on the Elimination of All Forms of Discrimination against Women ('CEDAW'),[29] as well as in regional instruments, many domestic statutes and international law.[30] Despite the significant usage of this concept, the principle of the child's best interests has been properly defined only through the adoption of General Comment 14, in 2013. According to the Committee, the best interests of the child principle is a dynamic concept that encompasses various issues, which are continuously evolving. It should be read as a threefold concept, which entails a substantive right, a fundamental interpretative legal principle and a rule of procedure. With regard to the first, the Committee explains that Article 3(1), which creates an intrinsic obligation for states, is directly applicable (self-executing) and can be invoked before a court. Moreover as a substantive right it should be guaranteed that it will be implemented whenever a decision is to be made concerning a child, a group of identified or unidentified children or children in general.

Secondly the best interests of the child as a fundamental, interpretative legal principle, implies that if a legal provision is open to more than one interpretation, the interpretation which most effectively serves the child's best interests should be the one chosen. Thirdly, as a rule of procedure, the best interests of the child require that whenever a decision is to be made that will affect a specific child, an identified group of children or children in general, the decision-making process must include an evaluation of the possible impact (positive or negative) of the decision on the child or children concerned. In other words the decision must be the result of the assessment and determination of what is the best interests of the child in the specific circumstances.

The notion of the 'child's best interests' is aimed at ensuring both the full and effective enjoyment of all the rights recognized in the CRC and the holistic development of the child, which shall embrace the child's physical, mental, spiri-

---

[27] See Art. 3(1) of the UN Convention on the Rights of the Child. According to this provision: 'In all actions concerning children, whether undertaken by public or private social welfare institutions, courts of law, administrative authorities or legislative bodies, the best interests of the child shall be a primary consideration'.

[28] UN General Assembly, Declaration of the Rights of the Child, 20 November 1959, A/RES/1386 (XIV), para 2.

[29] See CEDAW, arts. 5 (b) and 16, para. 1 (d).

[30] See Committee on the Rights of the Child, General comment No. 14 (2013) on the right of the child to have his or her best interests taken as a primary consideration (art. 3, para. 1), CRC/C/GC/14.

tual, moral, psychological and social development.[31] In one of its General Comments, the Committee on the Rights of the Child has explained that 'an adult's judgment of a child's best interests cannot override the obligation to respect all the child's rights under the Convention.'[32] As within the provisions enshrined in the CRC, there is no hierarchy of rights, all the rights provided for therein are in the 'child's best interests' and no right could be compromised by a negative interpretation of the child's best interests.[33] Significantly the Committee clarifies that the assessment of a child's best interests must include respect for the child's right to express his or her views as stated in Article 12 of the CRC. These two Articles, 3 and 12, appear to be intimately entwined and mutually reinforcing. In particular Article 3(1) cannot be correctly applied if the requirements of Article 12 are not met. Similarly, by facilitating the essential role of children in all decisions affecting their lives, Article 3(1) is crucial for the implementation of Article 12.

Article 12 of the CRC is represented as one of the most innovative of the Convention and it is considered as a unique provision in human rights treaty law.[34] Its scope is to address the legal and social status of children, who, on the one hand lack adults' full autonomy but, on the other hand, are recognized by the CRC as the subjects of rights. Paragraph 1 assures to every child capable of forming his or her own views the right to express those views freely. Paragraph 2 states, in particular, that the child shall be afforded the right to be heard in any judicial or administrative proceedings affecting him or her.[35] As stated above, Article 12 of the Convention establishes the right of every child to freely express her or his views, in all matters affecting her or him, and the subsequent right for those views to be given due weight, according to the child's age and maturity. Article 12 attributes the right to be heard not only to an individual child, but also to a group of children (e.g. the children in a neighbourhood, the children of a given country, children with disabilities, girls, children associated with armed forces or groups). In both cases, i.e. views expressed individually or as a group, due weight should be given in accordance with age and maturity. Article 12 states very clearly that age alone cannot determine the significance of a child's views. In fact, children's levels of understanding are not uniformly linked to their biological age. Research has shown

[31] See Committee on the Rights of the Child, General Comment No. 5 (2003) General Measures of Implementation of the Convention on the Rights of the Child, CRC/GC/2003/5.

[32] See Committee on the Rights of the Child, General Comment No. 13 (2011) The right of the child to freedom from all forms of violence, CRC/C/GC/13, para 61. See also Rodham (1973).

[33] See General Comment No. 14, para 4.

[34] Article 12 of the CRC establishes that: 1. States Parties shall assure to the child who is capable of forming his or her own views the right to express those views freely in all matters affecting the child, the views of the child being given due weight in accordance with the age and maturity of the child. 2. For this purpose the child shall in particular be provided the opportunity to be heard in any judicial and administrative proceedings affecting the child, either directly, or through a representative or an appropriate body, in a manner consistent with the procedural Rules of the national law.

[35] The Committee on the Rights of the Child, General Comment No. 12 (2009), The right of the child to be heard, CRC/C/GC/12, para. 3.

that many factors, such as information, experience, environment, social and cultural expectations, and levels of support, all contribute in different ways to the development of a child's capacities to form his or her view.[36] For this reason, the views of the child have to be assessed on a case-by-case examination. Maturity is mentioned in Article 12 as one of the factors that shall be taken into account when determining the individual capacity of a child. Generally speaking maturity refers to the ability to understand and assess the implications of a particular matter; in the context of Article 12 it can be defined as the capacity of a child to express, in a reasonable and independent manner, her or his views on various issues. As pointed out by the Committee, evaluating the views expressed by the child cannot disregard the impact of the matter *on* the child. In particular it shall be borne in mind that 'a child cannot be heard effectively where the environment is intimidating, hostile, insensitive or inappropriate for her or his age'.[37]

Given the fact that the right enshrined in Article 12 needs to be implemented in accordance with the factors that characterise a specific situation, it is not possible for the Committee to dictate how the child's views should be heard. In its General Comment, whose key findings have been highlighted above, the Committee sets out a number of general principles, according to which, processes in which a child or children are heard and participate, must be: transparent and informative, voluntary, respectful, relevant, child-friendly, inclusive, supported by specific training, safe and sensitive to risk and accountable.[38] In line with the provisions enshrined in Articles 3(1) and 12 of the CRC, the initiatives and measures that have an impact upon children must take all possible steps to minimize the risk of harming them and ensure that their rights are fully respected and duly implemented.

4 Children's Rights Within the Colombian Legal Framework

Under Article 93 of the Colombian Constitution,[39] international human rights treaties, including the CRC,[40] which was adopted under Act No. 12 of 1991, are considered to be part of constitutional law and take precedence over national laws and administrative acts. In addition, Article 44 of the Constitution further details the

[36] See generally UNICEF, 'Inequities in Early Childhood Development: What the Data Say, Evidence from the Multiple Indicator Cluster Surveys', February 2012, http://www.unhcr.org/4566b16b2.pdf (accessed 20 March 2015). See also Bradley and Corwyn (2002).

[37] See General Comment No. 12, para 34.

[38] Ibid., para 134.

[39] The Spanish text of the Colombian Constitution, http://pdba.georgetown.edu/Constitutions/Colombia/vigente.html (accessed 21 March 2015).

[40] UN General Assembly, *Convention on the Rights of the Child*, 20 November 1989, United Nations, Treaty Series, vol. 1577, 3.

rights of children and mandates that these rights be given precedence over the rights of others.[41] The CRC can be directly invoked before the courts and is widely cited and discussed throughout the justice system. Colombia has also ratified the Optional Protocols to the Convention on the Rights of the Child, with the exception of the Optional Protocol on a communications procedure, which entered into force in April 2014.[42] The situation of children's rights in Colombia has drastically changed over the past few years. The Minors' Code, in force until 2006, was designed in accordance with the theory of 'irregular situations,' which conceives the child as a subject of the law, to whom the State must offer protection, provided that he or she has been declared to be in an irregular situation e.g. neglect, lack of family or deviant behaviour. Consistently with this approach, children were assimilated into passive bystanders, in need of care, but unable to exercise the rights enshrined in the CRC. As a result, in the concluding observations issued by the Committee on the Rights of the Child in 2006, Colombia's compliance with the principles of the best interests of the child and the right to participation was commented upon negatively. *In primis* the Committee noted how the 'current legislation and policy fail to take into account the principle of the best interests of the child' and consequently it recommended that 'the State party fully incorporates the principle of the best interests of the child in all programmes, policies, judicial and administrative procedures, and in particular in the reform of the Minors' Code and the development of a National Plan of Action.' With regard to the child's right to participation, the Committee highlighted that 'the views of children are inadequately taken into account in the family, schools and other institutions' and therefore it urged Colombia to set the necessary measures to promote, facilitate and implement in practice, within the family, schools, at community level, in institutions as well as in judicial and administrative procedures, the principle of respect for the views of children and their participation in all matters affecting them, in accordance with article 12 of the Convention.[43]

To redress these shortcomings and advance children's rights implementation, the Colombian government has designed the new Children's and Young Persons' Code

[41] General overview of Colombia's national legal provisions on children's rights, CRIN, 8 December 2011.

[42] Colombia adopted the Optional Protocol on the sale of children, child prostitution and child pornography under Act No. 769 of 2002 and the Optional Protocol on the involvement of children in armed conflict under Act No. 833 of 2003. The Third Optional Protocol to the CRC on a Communications Procedure (OP3 CRC) sets out an international complaints procedure for child rights violations, it entered into force on 14th April 2014. Information about the status of ratification is available at: https://treaties.un.org/pages/ViewDetails.aspx?src=TREATY&mtdsg_no=IV-11-d&chapter=4&lang=en.

[43] *Ibid.*

('CYPC') adopted through Act No. 1098[44] and depicted as a major advancement in the development of specialised legislation on children and young persons.[45] The CRC is an integral part of the CYPC, which has introduced several important changes related, in particular, to safeguarding, protecting, promoting and restoring the rights of children and young persons. The Children's and Young Persons' Code, which fully accepts the concept of comprehensive protection, has significantly departed from the approach followed by the Minors' Code.[46] The principle of comprehensive protection is currently enshrined in Article 7 of the CYPC and encompasses children's recognition as rights holders, the safeguarding and observance of their rights, the prevention of threats to or infringement of those rights and the guarantee of their immediate restoration. These precepts need to be embedded in policies, plans, programmes and activities pursued at the national, departmental, district and municipal levels, with the corresponding allocation of financial, physical and human resources.

With regard in particular to the principles of the best interests of the child and the child's right to express his or her views, the CYPC reflects *in toto* the aim and the moral tenets of the CRC. The concept of the best interests of the child (set forth in article 8 of the Children's and Young Persons' Code as 'the requirement of every individual to guarantee the full and simultaneous enjoyment of all human rights of children and young persons, which are universal, paramount and interdependent') is the guiding principle in society's actions and public policies directed at children and young persons as well as in specific decisions relating to situations where the rights and interests of children and young persons have to be reconciled with those of others.[47] The Colombian Constitutional Court has shed light on this point, by ruling that the concept of the best interests of the child is not an abstract but rather a real and relational principle which can thus only be applied by giving due consideration to the special and unique status of children and young persons.[48] In more detail, the Constitutional Court held that, in order to justify decisions in the best

[44] Ley 1098, 8 November 2006, Còdigo de la Infancia y la Adoloscencia. Article 3 of the Children's and Young Persons' Code defines a child as a human being between the age of 0 and 12 years and a young person as a human being between the age of 12 and 18 years. This distinction does not jeopardise the enjoyment without discrimination of the rights set forth in the Convention on the Rights of the Child, human rights treaties ratified by Colombia, the Constitution and statutory instruments.

[45] Committee on the Rights of the Child, Consideration of reports submitted by States parties under article 44 of the Convention, Fourth and fifth periodic reports of States parties due in 2011, Colombia, 25 October 2013, CRC/C/COL/4-5, p. 8.

[46] In 2006 the Committee on the Rights of the Child stressed the need to proceed with a reform of the Minors' Code in order to provide effective protection of the rights of all children in Colombia. UN Committee on the Rights of the Child (CRC), UN Committee on the Rights of the Child: Concluding Observations, Colombia, 8 June 2006, CRC/C/COL/CO/3.

[47] Committee on the Rights of the Child, Consideration of reports submitted by States parties under article 44 of the Convention, Fourth and fifth periodic reports of States parties due in 2011, Colombia, 25 October 2013, CRC/C/COL/4-5, 31.

[48] Fandino-Barros (2013).

interests of the child, at least four basic conditions must be fulfilled: (a) the interests of the child or young person for whose defence actions are taken have to be real (relationship to his or her particular needs and specific physical and psychological aptitudes); (b) the non-relevance of the arbitrary opinion of others; in other words, the child's or young person's survival and protection are not dependent on the will of parents or of public officials responsible for protecting them; (c) since a relational principle is involved, ensuring protection entails a balance of conflicting interests, the weighing of which must be guided by the safeguarding of this principle; (d) it has to be demonstrated that those interests are conducive to the achievement of a supreme legal good, namely the full and harmonious development of the child's or young person's personality. This rationale is clearly reflected in the above-mentioned Article 44 of the Constitution, which stipulates that the rights of children have primacy over the rights of others by reason of the special level of protection, which children require.[49] The right of children and young persons to be heard is established in Article 26 of the Children's and Young Persons' Code, which provides that, in any judicial or other proceedings in which persons below the age of 18 years are involved, they shall have the right to be heard and to have their views taken into account. The exercise of this right has to be consistent with children's and young persons' freedom of expression, which is guaranteed in Article 34 of the Children's and Young Persons' Code, and their right of participation, which is provided for in Article 30 of the Code.

The Colombian Constitution together with the Children and Young Person's Code represents a sound and comprehensive legal framework. The questions remain as to whether the provisions enshrined in the existing instruments have been duly implemented and to what extent such implementation has resulted in fostering children's rights as well as their involvement in the transitional justice process.

5 Colombia's Implementation of the CRC Key Principles in the Transitional Justice Process

The armed conflict in Colombia continues to have a disproportionate impact on children, who have been the victims of, inter alia, forced recruitment and sexual violence. Over the past decade the government has been striving to improve and increase the legal tools at its disposal to enhance the protection and promotion of children's rights. These efforts have been incorporated into the Colombian legal framework as well as, to some degree, in the specific actions and measures that encompass the current transitional justice process. The JPL and the Victims' Law represent the most challenging and comprehensive attempts to come to terms with

[49] See Corte Constitucional, Sentencia Acción de tutela presentada por Clara contra el Instituto Colombiano de Bienestar Familiar, Centro Zonal Buga (Valle), once (11) de noviembre de dos mil catorce (2014) Magistrado Ponente Maria Victoria Calle Correa. Sentencia T-836/14, para 18.

the long lasting armed conflict and its legacy. Both Laws, although to different extent and from distinct angles, have been designed taking into account also the situation of children.

Through the implementation of the JPL the legislator has tried to purse a manifold goal, namely to achieve demobilisation, disarmament and reintegration of illegal armed groups, to recognize and enforce the rights of the victims to truth, justice and reparation and to conduct criminal proceedings against the leaders of these groups that are responsible for the commission of serious crimes.[50] Despite its ambitious scope and the far-reaching breadth, the JPL has been strongly criticised for prioritising the 'neutralisation' of the state's opponents, over the rights and the needs of victims, including children.[51] Article 64 of the JPL states that 'the handing over of minors by members of outlawed armed groups shall not be ground for losing the benefits referred to in this law and Law 782 of 2002',[52] granting, in other words, *de facto* impunity to those who recruited children to their group's ranks. The choice to put demobilisation above any other possible outcomes has been made despite the fact that Colombian children linked to the parties involved in hostilities have experienced violations of their rights to life, dignity and personal integrity, as well as other violations of their constitutional guarantees.[53]

As stated in the JPL, in order to be eligible for benefits, individual demobilised paramilitary candidates must provide information about the paramilitary organisation, sign a statement of commitment to the government, and turn over all illegally obtained assets which are then collected in the Fondo de Reparación (Reparation Fund).[54] If the candidate fulfils these requirements, judicial proceedings are initiated which involve the following: investigations by a prosecutor; a confessions process, including the delivery of *versiones libres* (voluntary depositions) in which the person provides a list and details of confessed crimes; arraignment following the completion of the prosecutor's investigation; acceptance of charges by the candidate; a public hearing before a Justice and Peace Tribunal to determine whether the acceptance of charges by the individual was free and voluntary; delivery of the verdict; and sentencing.[55] As stressed by several authors, the JPL has been devel-

[50] Review Conference of the Rome Statute, Transitional Justice in Colombia, Justice and Peace Law: An Experience Of Truth, Justice And Reparation, RC/ST/PJ/M.1, 1 June 2010.

[51] See the Report of the Special Rapporteur on extrajudicial, summary or arbitrary executions, Philip Alston, Addendum, Mission to Colombia, 31 March 2010, A/HRC/14/24/Add.2, para 56.

[52] Law 782 of 2002 stated that a child could only be recognized as belonging to an armed group by the spokesperson of the group in question or as a result of evidence provided by the child (Article 53), even though providing such evidence could involve children being used in intelligence work.

[53] Herencia Carrasco (2010).

[54] See JPL, art. 11.

[55] JPL, arts 16–25; see also Report of the Special Rapporteur on extrajudicial, summary or arbitrary executions, Philip Alston, Addendum, Mission to Colombia, 31 March 2010, A/HRC/14/24/Add.2, para 50, Appendix C, Justice and Peace Law, paras 4–6.

oped retaining its core element, namely that of alternative sentences for perpetrators,[56] to the detriment of victims' rights, including their entitlement to participate in the proceedings.[57] As reported by the International Center for Transitional Justice (ICTJ) child victims in Colombia would be keen to play an active role in the trials and share their stories.[58] However the framework established within the JPL does not favour victims' involvement and the lack of a complementary truth-seeking tool, like for example a Truth and Reconciliation Commission, significantly hampers the child's right to express views in relation to the crimes committed in the course of the armed conflict. Concerning the effective results of the JPL's implementation it should be noted that the number of prosecutions for violations against children and information on cases taken up by the Office of the Attorney General remained very limited. While the Colombian Family Welfare Institute attended to at least 5417 children separated since 1999 from armed groups, to date there have been 69 convictions for child recruitment, of which only 5 under the JPL,[59] and 64 by the Human Rights Unit of the Office of the Attorney General.[60] In terms of compliance with the child's best interests it is trivial to observe that this principle was not the primary concern of the JPL's drafters. This strongly emerges from a comparison between the extensive benefits, including the reduced sentences, granted to the demobilised paramilitaries and the scant recognition of the harm suffered by the child victims.

In order to redress, at least to some extent, the shortcomings of the JPL the Colombian government has adopted the Victims' Law, which switched the focus from the perpetrators to the victims of the armed conflict. As stated in Articles 1 and 2 of the Victims' Law, the purpose of the law is to establish judicial, administrative, social, economic, individual and collective measures to benefit victims of violations of international and humanitarian law arising out of the conflict in Colombia.[61] Article 3 of the Victims' Law provides a broader definition of 'victim' than that enshrined in the JPL, thus permitting more persons to participate in the mechanisms and services embedded in the Victims' Law. Unlike the JPL, victims are required to

---

[56] Evans (2012).

[57] Organization of American States Inter-American Commission On Human Rights, Report on the Implementation of the Justice and Peace Law: Initial Stages in The Demobilization of the AUC and First Judicial Proceedings, OEA/Ser.L/V/II. Doc. 3, 2 October 2007, 21.

[58] Aptel and Ladish (2011).

[59] In December 2011, a conviction was obtained against a top AUC commander, Fredy Rendón Herrera, alias El Alemán (the German). He had a direct role in overseeing the illegal recruitment between 1997 and 2002 of 309 children in Chocó and Antioquia, by visiting schools to promote recruitment and authorizing the admission of minors into the group. Fredy Rendon Herrera, Sentencia, Fiscalía 44 Unidad Nacional de Justicia y Paz, Bogota D.C., 16 December 2011, paras 2.3; part 6.

[60] Children and armed conflict, Report of the Secretary-General, 15 May 2014, A/68/878–S/2014/339.

[61] Victims' Law, arts 1–2; "Colombia: Victims Law a Historic Opportunity", *Human Rights Watch*, 10 June 2011, http://www.hrw.org/news/2011/06/10/colombia-victims-law-historic-opportunity (accessed 21 March 2015).

submit a written declaration and supporting evidence of the event and related harm suffered in order to earn the legal status of victim. The Victims' Unit reviews the declaration, verifies the facts provided and decides whether to grant the applicant 'victim status' independent of any proceedings relating to the perpetrator.[62] Once the application is granted, the victim is registered with the Victims' Registry. The Victims' Law states that children and young persons recruited and/or used and also children conceived as a result of rape in armed conflict situations are eligible to obtain victim status, while its Article 13 stipulates that the 'State shall afford special guarantees and measures of protection to groups exposed to increased risk [...] such as women, young persons, children [...]'. Furthermore the Victims' Law focuses its seventh title on children and adolescents, stating that, as victims of the conflict, they are legitimately entitled to obtain truth, justice and reparation.[63] In addition to that, children have the right to be protected from every form of violence or abuse including unlawful recruitment, forced displacement and sexual assault.[64] The Law explicitly recognises children's rights to reparation in general and in Article 182 it specifies children's rights to receive the whole range of reparative measures provided for adult victims. Notably, the broader definition of victim enshrined in Article 3 of the Victims' Law still fails to encompass young adults who are or were members of illegal rebel or paramilitary organisations. Former members of rebel or paramilitary organisations forcibly recruited as children can qualify as a victim *only if* they disassociated from these groups when they were minors,[65] a distinction, strongly criticized by NGOs and international organisations,[66] which certainly does not take into account the best interests of the children currently in the ranks of armed groups who would need to make sure they demobilise before turning 18 years old.

A number of positive aspects of the Victims' Law have been highlighted by the Office of the UN High Commissioner for Human Rights in Colombia. These encompass special provisions for protecting the most vulnerable victims of the armed conflict, including child survivors of human rights abuses, and the recognition of the importance of protection measures for victims returning to lands that are

[62] As noted by Summers (2012), p. 226, "Significantly, the process of acquiring victim status is explicitly divorced from the process of condemning the person responsible for victimization."

[63] 'Title 7: Integral Protection of child-boys, child-girls and adolescents victims.'

[64] See Article 181 et ss.

[65] Victims' Law, arts 3 and 190. In particular Article 190 establishes that until they reach the age of majority girls and boys illegally recruited are entitled to the same reparation regime (whose enforcement has been assigned to the Colombian Institute of Welfare Service) as all the other child victims; once they turn eighteen years old they can be eventually included in the process of reintegration led by the High Council for the Social and Economic Reintegration of the People and Groups who joined the Guerrilla.

[66] See the Report of the Secretary-General on children and armed conflict in Colombia, S/2012/171, 21 March 2012, para 60.

restored to them.[67] However, the UN High Commissioner has made it clear that the Law has both 'strengths and weaknesses'. In particular with regard to the main goal of the Victims' Law, i.e. the restitution of lands, it has been noted that the recognition of victim status is relatively easy for those victims who remained in the areas where their lands are located, whereas those who fled the areas where they lived can face difficulties in being recognized as victims if they have not been previously recognized as forcibly displaced people.[68] Considering the large number of displaced people, including minors, present in the country, this limitation blatantly hinders the effective implementation of the Law.[69] IDPs have been given better access to regular social welfare programmes, but only a small number have so far received the financial reparations outlined by the Victim's Law. The government's response to mass displacements has improved, but immediate assistance for smaller groups of IDPs has often been delayed significantly because local authorities are over-burdened. According to UNCHR more than three million children have received identification cards that prove their status as IDPs and entitle them to acquire services provided by the government, including health benefits and free education.[70] In particular with regard to the latter, since 2012 President Santos has declared primary and secondary education free of tuition fees through the Free Education Policy, allowing 8.6 million Colombian children to finally go to school.[71] Even though the newly established Free Education Policy has formally nothing to do with the measures envisaged by the Victims' Law, within the country there is widespread conceptual and judicial confusion between those social entitlements which citizens should receive as part of public policies, and reparation for victims of the conflict. In terms of children's participation, the drafting of the Victims' Law has not been characterised by a wide involvement of the people, including children, affected by the violations that occurred during the armed conflict.[72] However, in its latest submission to the Committee on the Rights of

[67] UN High Commissioner for Human Rights in Colombia, press release of 7 June 2011.

[68] See Amnesty International, Colombia: The Victims and Land Restitution Law, 2012, 5.

[69] See the Global Report by the Internal Displacement Monitoring Centre, supra n 2. The estimated abandoned or dispossessed land lost by IDPs is, until 2012, calculated to be as high as 6.8 million hectares, AB Colombia "Colombia the Current Panorama: Victims and Land Restitution Law 1448," May 2012: 3.

[70] Højen (2014).

[71] Adriaan. "Colombia implements free primary and secondary education," Colombia Reports, February 2, 2012, http://colombiareports.co/?s=free+education (accessed 13 April 2015). The Free Education Policy has been established following a judgement issued by the Colombian constitutional Court in 2010, in which the Court stated that "the Colombian state has a 36-year-old debt to children in terms of providing education." See Corte Constitucional, Educacion Basica Primaria en Establecimientos Educativos Estatales-Obligatoria y gratuita, diecinueve (19) de mayo de dos mil diez (2010), Magistrado Ponente: Dr. Luis Ernesto Vargas Silva, Sentencia C-376/10.

[72] Committee on the Rights of the Child, Consideration of reports submitted by States parties under article 44 of the Convention, Fourth and fifth periodic reports of States parties due in 2011, Colombia, 25 October 2013, CRC/C/COL/4-5, 31.

the Child, the Colombian Government has highlighted a number of initiatives aimed at fostering minors' involvement as community stakeholders. Various institutions, in fact, have undertaken activities aimed at guaranteeing the effective enjoyment of the child's right to have their views respected, including for example the Counsel-General's Office, the Ministry of Social Protection and the National Institute of Forensic Medicine and Science.

One of the institutional tools to advance the realization of children's right to participation was the 'Facts and Rights Strategy' which enabled children and young persons to speak with departmental governors about a variety of topics on the occasion of the tenth meeting of governors in July 2010. A subsequent initiative, called 'Young persons have their Say Strategy', was set up in July 2011. Such strategy has been implemented with the participation of the International Organization for Migration ('IOM') and the Colombian Family Welfare Institute. As a result of this process, 5374 young persons across the country have been engaged through media initiatives (local radio spots, notices and leaflets) in a bid to motivate them through the opportunity to learn about their right to participation, identity, social skills, participatory mechanisms, communication as a vehicle of social change, public policies on youth, strategic planning, project formulation and youth action.[73] Notably, the Victims' Law and the newly established reparatory framework were not explicitly included in this effort, to the detriment of children's effective involvement in the transitional justice process in place. Moreover, like the JPL, the Victims' Law has fallen short on its objective to seek truth as part of an otherwise comprehensive transitional justice framework.[74] By not including any truth-seeking measures, the Law ends up depriving victims, including children, of a crucial component of the healing and reconciliation process.

6 Conclusion

Introducing the combined third and fourth periodic reports of Colombia on its implementation of the provisions of the Convention on the Rights of the Child, the Director of the Colombian Institute for Family Welfare stressed that the country has been finally taking effective steps towards peace, which due to the current negotiations, has become a real possibility.[75] The Code for Children and Young Persons has duly incorporated CRC obligations and standards, while institutions have been strengthened through the national family welfare system. Investment in childhood and adolescence increased from $1.3 billion in 2011 to $2 billion in 2014

[73] Ibid.

[74] Summers (2012), p. 234.

[75] Committee on the Rights of the Child examines the Report on Colombia, 21 January 2015, http://www.ohchr.org/EN/NewsEvents/Pages/DisplayNews.aspx?NewsID=15499&LangID=E (accessed 14 April 2015).

and education has become free and accessible to many children who previously did not have the opportunity to fully enjoy this crucial rights. Important steps forward have been taken with regards to the promotion of all the rights embedded in the Convention, including the principle of the best interests of the child and the child's right to have his/her views taken into account. Nonetheless, the ongoing armed conflict and its profound consequences are not easy to overcome. The transitional justice process has been launched prioritising the demobilisation of non-state armed groups' members in lieu of the victims of forced recruitment, displacement and several other forms of violence. This approach has been partially corrected along the way due to the adoption of the Victims' Law, but the road to reconciliation and justice is still arduous and many challenges need to be addressed. Despite its attempt to comply with international standards by establishing a solid legal framework, the Colombia government has a long journey ahead if it truly wants to implement in a meaningful way the key principles enshrined in the CRC. In particular, internally displaced children face significant hurdles to enjoy the rights to which they are entitled, the disarmament process has produced limited results in terms of minors involved and both the Justice and Peace Law and the Victims' Law have neglected the importance of truth-seeking initiatives which would have provided the population, including children, with a powerful tool to finally express themselves.

References

Amnesty International (2012). 'Colombia: The Victims and Land Restitution Law'.

Aptel, C., & Ladish, V. (2011). Through a new lens: A child-sensitive approach to transitional justice. *ICTJ,* 12.

Bradley, R. H., & Corwyn, R. F. (2002). Socioeconomic status and child development. *Annual Review of Psychology, 53*, 371–399.

Céspedes-Báez, L. (2012). Colombia's victims law and the liability of corporations for human rights violations. *Estudios Socio-Jurídicos, Bogotá (Colombia), 14*(1), 180.

Evans, C. (2012). *The right to reparation in international law for victims of armed conflict.* Cambridge, England: Cambridge University Press.

Fandino-Barros, Y. (2013). The best interest of the child in the Colombian constitutional jurisprudence. *Advocatus Edición Especial, 21*, 271–282.

García-Godos, J., & Lid, K. A. O. (2010). Transitional justice and victims' rights before the end of a conflict: The unusual case of Colombia. *Journal of Latin American Studies, 42*, 487–516.

Herencia Carrasco, S. (2010). *Transitional justice and the situation of children in Colombia and Peru* (Innocenti Working Paper No. 2010-16). UNICEF Innocenti Research Centre, 21, Florence.

Højen, L. (2014). *Colombia's 'Invisible Crisis': Internally displaced persons.* COHA.

Human Rights Watch 'World report: Colombia' (2015).

Humphrey, M. (2013). The individualising and universalising discourse of law: Victims. In T. Bonacker & C. Safferling (Eds.), *Truth commissions and trials' in victims of international crimes: An interdisciplinary discourse.* The Hague, the Netherlands: T.M.C. Asser Institute.

IDMC. (2014). The 2014 Global Report by the Internal Displacement Monitoring Centre.

International Crisis Group. (2012, September 25). *Colombia: Peace at last? Crisis group Latin America Report* (No 45).

Springer, N. (2012). *Como lobo entre corderos. Del uso y reclutamiento de niños, niñas y adolescentes en el marco del conflicto armado y la criminalidad en Colombia* (pp. 34–35). Bogotá, Colombia: Springer Consulting Services.

Summers, N. (2012). Colombia's victims' law: Transitional justice in a time of violent conflict? *Harvard Human Rights Journal, 25*, 219–235.

The Watchlist on Children and Armed Conflict, 'No one to Trust: Children and Armed Conflict in Colombia'.

Prosecuting International Core Crimes Under Libya's Transitional Justice: The Case of Saif Al-Islam Gaddafi and Abdullah Al-Senussi

Hilmi M. Zawati

1 Introduction

Reacting to the former Libyan government forces' deadly repression of peaceful demonstrations in Benghazi following the detention of a human rights lawyer in late January 2011, and in response to the expansion of protests to other Libyan cities in mid-February 2011, the UN Security Council unanimously adopted Resolution 1970 on 26 February 2011, referring the situation in Libya to the prosecutor of the ICC under Chapter VII of the Charter of the United Nations. One week later, protestors resorted to armed resistance using different kinds of weapons seized from government caches of heavy artillery. By 21 February 2011, the protests had evolved into a full-fledged revolutionary movement, and insurgents took control of Benghazi, while the Libyan government's security forces and pro-Gaddafi paramilitaries continued their brutal and systematic attacks on civilian populations in the protesting cities.[1]

However, pursuant to the above Security Council resolution, the prosecutor of the ICC announced on 3 March 2011 his decision to investigate the situation in Libya. On 16 May 2011, he sought warrants of arrest from the PTCI.[2] Subsequently, the latter issued three warrants of arrest on 27 June 2011 for Muammar Gaddafi, Saif Al-Islam Gaddafi, and Abdullah Al-Senussi for crimes against humanity, namely murder and persecution, allegedly committed by government security forces against Libyan civilians across Libya between 15 and at least 28 February 2011.[3] Pursuant to the killing of Muammar Gaddafi on 20 October 2011,

[1] Shenkman (2012), pp. 1229–1230.

[2] ICC (2011a), para. 2.

[3] Bishop (2013), p. 401.

H.M. Zawati (✉)
International Centre for Legal Accountability and Justice (ICLAJ), Montreal, QC, Canada
e-mail: hilmi.zawati@mail.mcgill.ca

A. Diver, J. Miller (eds.), *Justiciability of Human Rights Law in Domestic Jurisdictions*, DOI 10.1007/978-3-319-24016-9_10

the PTCI formally terminated the case against him on 22 November 2011. By that time, Saif Al-Islam had been captured by the Zintan insurgents' brigade on 19 November 2011, while Al-Senussi was still at large.[4]

Despite its incompetent judicial system and lack of sufficient political stability to prosecute international core crimes or serious breaches of international criminal law, not to mention its apparent inability to restore post-conflict justice and accountability, Libya has challenged the admissibility of both cases against Saif Al-Islam and Al-Senussi,[5] emphasizing its ability and willingness to prosecute the prisoners and provide them and other senior members of the Gaddafi regime with fair and public trials.

As was mentioned in an earlier work, a continuous legal tug of war has ensued between the various Libyan transitional governments and the ICC on the admissibility of the cases against Saif Al-Islam and Al-Senussi.[6] While Libya has made every effort to emphasize its right to prosecute and try Saif Al-Islam and Al-Senussi in Libyan courts and before Libyan Judges, the ICC continues to assert its jurisdiction over their trial pursuant to the UN Security Council's Resolution 1970 (2011), which was adopted under Chapter VII of the Charter of the United Nations (UN 2011).

Nevertheless, pursuant to Article 19(2)(b) of the Rome Statute, the government of Libya formally challenged the admissibility of the case against Saif Al-Islam on 1 May 2012, asking the Court to declare the case inadmissible and reverse the surrender request.[7] On 31 May 2013, the PTCI rejected Libya's challenge and requested the latter to meet its obligations under the UN Security Council's Resolution 1970 (2011) and to surrender the suspect to the ICC.[8] Consequently, Libya appealed the PTCI's decision on 7 June 2013.[9] Finally, the Appeals Chamber endorsed the PTCI's decision on 21 May 2014, and asked Libya to capitulate and send Saif Al-Islam to the Court in The Hague.[10]

By contrast, in response to Libya's challenge of the admissibility of the case against Al-Senussi, filed on 2 April 2013, the PTCI decided on 11 October 2013 that the case is inadmissible under Article 17(1)(a) of the Rome Statute, and that it is subject to domestic proceedings conducted by the competent Libyan authorities. The PTCI Judges added that Libya is willing and able genuinely to prosecute and investigate this case. They asserted that their decision had been taken in accordance with the principle of complementarity enshrined in the Rome Statute.[11] Consequently, an appeal was filed against the PTCI's decision by the defence team on

[4] Al-Senussi was extradited from Mauritania to Libya on 5 September 2012.

[5] Kersten (2014), p. 188.

[6] Zawati (2014b), p. 81.

[7] ICC (2012b), para. 23.

[8] ICC (2013f).

[9] ICC (2013g).

[10] ICC (2014b).

[11] ICC (2013r), para. 311.

17 October 2013, pursuant to articles 19(6), 82(1)(a), 82(3), 83(2)(a), of the Rome Statute, Rules 154(1) and 156 of the Rules of Procedure and Evidence, and Regulations 33(1)(d) and 64 of the Regulations of the Court.[12] On 24 July 2014, the Appeals Chamber unanimously confirmed the PTCI's decision, which had declared the case against Abdullah Al-Senussi inadmissible before the ICC.[13]

Based on the above discussion, this chapter explores whether the post-Gaddafi Libyan criminal justice system is the proper judicial mechanism to undertake the prosecution of Saif Al-Islam and Al-Senussi for international core crimes, and particularly for the widespread and systematic violence allegedly committed by the former Libyan government's agents against the country's civilian population. To provide a legal framework for addressing the question, this analysis is divided into three inter-related sections. Section 2 examines the horizons of prosecuting international core crimes under Libya's transitional justice. It starts by shedding some light on the basis of the prosecution of international core crimes—as defined in the Rome Statute—in national courts. From there, it proceeds to review Libya's criminal justice system by looking into the provisions of the Libyan Penal Code, as well as into the Libyan laws of the transitional period. Section 3 brings to light four major challenges to prosecuting international core crimes under Libya's post-Gaddafi, transitional justice system, including legal impunity and lawlessness; the rule of militia justice vs. rule of law; the failure to provide standard, fair trials; and the lack of criminal justice reform. Section 4 considers the complementarity regime of the ICC and the admissibility of Libya's cases against Saif Al-Islam and Al-Senussi. It offers some reflections on the complementarity principle enshrined in the provisions of the Rome Statute, reviews Libya's challenge to the admissibility of the cases against Saif Al-Islam and Al-Senussi, and finally, underlines the ICC's inconsistent decisions on the admissibility of the above cases.

Finally, this work concludes by elucidating the findings of the above overlapping themes and tries to answer the legitimate question of whether the emerging Libyan transitional justice system is genuinely able to investigate and prosecute international core crimes, allegedly committed by government armed forces against Libyan civilians during the ongoing civil war, which broke out in protest against the repressive Gaddafi regime in February 2011.

2 International Core Crimes and Libya's Transitional Justice

This section focuses on the prospects of prosecuting international core crimes under Libya's transitional justice system. To address this issue with the attention that it warrants, it starts by examining the obligation of states to prosecute international

[12] ICC (2013s).

[13] ICC (2014e).

core crimes, as defined in the Rome Statute and enshrined in international law—both customary and conventional—in national courts. Then it proceeds to review Libya's criminal justice system by looking into the provisions of the Libyan Penal Code, as well as into the Libyan laws of the transitional period, to explore the extent to which the norms of these laws conform to the provisions of international criminal law.

2.1 *Prosecuting Core Crimes in National Judicial Bodies*

Prior to the adoption and entry into force of the Rome Statute on 1 July 2002,[14] international core crimes, namely genocide, crimes against humanity, and war crimes, were governed exclusively by customary international law, and investigated and prosecuted under national criminal jurisdiction in domestic courts. States were, and still are, reluctant to relinquish their jurisdiction over prosecuting these crimes, particularly those committed on their soil, to international criminal judicial bodies, arguing that such an act would diminish their national sovereignty.[15] However, the Preamble of the Rome Statute has addressed the sovereignty concerns of States by stressing that the Court "established under this Statute shall be complementary to national criminal jurisdictions."[16] In other words, the Complementarity principle, which will be the focus of the next section of this chapter, implies that the court can only exercise its jurisdiction over the core crimes when states are unwilling or unable genuinely to carry out the investigation or prosecution.[17]

Nonetheless, a closer look at the provisions of different international humanitarian and human rights instruments reveals that States Parties are requested to incorporate international core crimes into their national criminal legislation, and exercise their jurisdiction over these crimes.[18] This is in addition to the fact that the prevention of international core crimes has come to be considered a norm of customary international law with *jus cogens* standing, with the result that states are obliged to investigate and prosecute these crimes whether they are signatories or not to the treaties constituting the applicable law to these crimes. For example, the *Convention on the Prevention and Punishment of the Crime of Genocide* ('Genocide Convention'),[19] the law that applies to the core crime of genocide, provides in Article I that "[t]he Contracting Parties confirm that genocide, whether committed

---

[14] Treaties (1998).

[15] Kleffner (2008), p. 18.

[16] Treaties (1998).

[17] Treaties (1998), Article 17.

[18] Kleffner (2008), p. 10. See for example: Articles 49–51 of Geneva Convention I; Articles 50–52 of Geneva II; Articles 129–131 of Geneva III; Articles 146–148 of Geneva IV.

[19] Treaties (1948a); Acceded by Libya on 16th May 1989.

in time of peace or in time of war, is a crime under international law which they undertake to prevent and to punish."[20] Moreover, Article V of the same Convention provides that "[t]the Contracting Parties undertake to enact, in accordance with their respective Constitutions, the necessary legislation to give effect to the provisions of the present Convention."[21] Similarly Article VI stresses that "[p]ersons charged with genocide or any of the other acts enumerated in article III shall be tried by a competent tribunal of the State in the territory of which the act was committed, or by such international penal tribunal as may have jurisdiction with respect to those Contracting Parties which shall have accepted its jurisdiction."[22]

Before the adoption of the Rome Statute, the norms of customary international law had also governed crimes against humanity, committed as part of a widespread or systematic attack perpetrated against a civilian population. The laws that applied to these crimes, enshrined in the norms of several international treaties, encompassed provisions requesting States Parties to adopt adequate legislative measures to suppress such crimes. For example, Article 5 of the *International Convention on the Elimination of All Forms of Racial Discrimination*[23] ('CERD') imposes fundamental obligations on States Parties to "undertake to prohibit and to eliminate racial discrimination in all its forms and to guarantee the right of everyone, without distinction as to race, colour, or national or ethnic origin, to equality before the law."[24] Moreover, Article 9 of the same convention demands that States Parties "submit to the Secretary-General of the United Nations, for consideration by the Committee, a report on the legislative, judicial, administrative or other measures which they have adopted and which give effect to the provisions of this Convention."

By the same token, Article 2(1) of *Convention against Torture and Other Cruel, Inhuman or Degrading Treatment or Punishment* ('CAT')[25] provides that "[e]ach State Party shall take effective legislative, administrative, judicial or other measures to prevent acts of torture in any territory under its jurisdiction". Similarly, Article 1 of the *Supplementary Convention on the Abolition of Slavery, the Slave Trade, and Institutions and Practices Similar to Slavery* ('Supplementary Convention')[26] stipulates that each of the States Parties to the Convention shall take all practicable and necessary legislative measures to abolish and abandon all kinds of slavery practices. Furthermore, Article 3(1) of the same convention demands of State Parties that "[t]he act of conveying or attempting to convey slaves from one country to another by whatever means of transport, or of being accessory thereto, shall be a criminal offence under the laws of the States Parties to this Convention

[20] Treaties (1948a), Article 1.

[21] Treaties (1948a), Article V.

[22] Treaties (1948a), Article VI.

[23] Acceded by Libya on 3 July 1968.

[24] Treaties (1965).

[25] Acceded by Libya on 16 May 1989.

[26] Acceded by Libya on 16 May 1989.

and persons convicted thereof shall be liable to very severe penalties". On the other hand, Article 1(1) of the *Convention Concerning Forced or Compulsory Labour*[27] provides that each State Party should undertake to suppress the use of forced or compulsory labour in all its forms within the shortest possible period. Moreover, Article 25 of this convention requires that "[t]he illegal exaction of forced or compulsory labour shall be punishable as a penal offence, and it shall be an obligation on any Member ratifying this Convention to ensure that the penalties imposed by law are really adequate and are strictly enforced."

Finally, war crimes, incorporated in Article 8 of the Rome Statute, have been traditionally governed by the rules of customary international law that are included in different treaties of international humanitarian law and in other laws of armed conflict, including but not limited to: the *Convention for the Amelioration of the Condition of the Wounded and Sick in Armed Forces in the Field* (Geneva I);[28] the *Convention for the Amelioration of the Condition of Wounded, Sick and Shipwrecked Members of Armed Forces at Sea* (Geneva II);[29] the *Convention Relative to the Treatment of Prisoners of War* (Geneva III);[30] the *Convention Relative to the Protection of Civilian Persons in Time of War* (Geneva IV);[31] the *Protocol Additional to the Geneva Conventions of 12 August 1949, and Relating to the Protection of Victims of International Armed Conflicts*, (Protocol I);[32] and the *Protocol Additional to the Geneva Conventions of 12 August 1949, and Relating to the Protection of Victims of Non-International Armed Conflicts*, (Protocol II).[33]

Several articles in the Geneva Conventions—particularly Articles 49–51 of *Geneva I*; Articles 50–52 of *Geneva II*; Articles 129–131 of *Geneva II*; and Articles 146–148 of *Geneva IV*—emphasize respectively that: (a) the High Contracting Parties should take serious steps to enact legislation to impose penal sanctions for persons committing, or ordering others to commit any of the grave breaches listed in the present convention; (b) each High Contracting Party is obligated to search for persons who allegedly committed, or ordered others to commit, grave breaches, and bring them before its own courts, regardless of their nationality; and (c) each High Contracting Party should suppress all acts contrary to the provisions of the present convention other than the grave breaches.

In view of the above accounts, Libya, as a State Party to several concerned international instruments and as a member of the international community, is clearly expected to investigate and prosecute international core crimes committed on its soil since the eruption of the civil war in late February 2011.[34]

[27] Ratified by Libya on 13 June 1961.

[28] Ratified/Acceded by Libya on 22 May 1956.

[29] Ratified/Acceded by Libya on 22 May 1956.

[30] Ratified/Acceded by Libya on 22 May 1956.

[31] Ratified/Acceded by Libya on 22 May 1956.

[32] Ratified/Acceded by Libya on 7 June 1978.

[33] Ratified/Acceded by Libya on 7 June 1978.

[34] Zawati (2014b), p. 63.

2.2 Libya's Criminal Justice System

The endemic weakness of the rule of law and the lack of judicial independence are among the most deeply-rooted problems in the Libyan justice system. A closer look at the judicial system since the independence of Libya in 1951 reveals that it had endured several problems that have impeded its efficiency. For example, during the monarchy, Libya's judicial system suffered from a shortage of national actors in the criminal justice system. The shortage was so great that judges and other judicial staff were contributed by neighbouring Arab countries,[35] particularly Tunisia and Egypt.[36] Despite the substantial contribution of these judges in building Libya's judicial system, particularly in training Libyan judges, some of them were receiving instructions from the governments that had sent them.[37]

However, the military coup of 1 September 1969 shifted Libya's judicial system from bad to worse. After the adoption of the Jamahiriya system pursuant to the declaration of the Peoples' Authority in 1977, the judicial system suffered interference that badly affected its integrity and independence.[38] The Jamahiriya executive authorities systematically violated judicial independence and made unequivocal interferences in the judicial system. The authorities infringed the principles of fundamental justice by creating unlawful investigating bodies parallel to the Public Prosecutor's Office and by setting up special courts that never followed the Libyan judicial system, e.g., the People's Court, established pursuant to a resolution passed by the Revolutionary Command Council on 26 October 1969 to try Libyans connected to the former royal elite.[39] Even worse, the judgements of this parallel court, which never adhered to the provisions of the Libyan Penal code or the Code of Criminal Procedure, were final and could not be appealed.[40] Moreover, judges of this court, which sentenced tens of the regime's political opponents to death,[41] came from non-judicial backgrounds and never held any legal qualifications.[42]

Finally, since the collapse of the Gaddafi regime, Libya has been confronting the dilemma of building an effective judicial system that is coherent with the international measures.[43] Although the Constitutional Declaration, adopted by the NTC on 3 August 2011, explicitly provides for the supremacy of the law, judicial independence, and separation of powers,[44] Justice Mustafa Abdul Jalil, the NTC Chairman,

[35] Report (2013b), p. 9.

[36] Report (2012c), p. 73.

[37] Ben-Halim (1992), pp. 62–63.

[38] Report (2012c), p. 75.

[39] Report (2012c), p. 77. In an attempt to take steps to gradually reform the judicial system under pressure made by international human rights groups, the regime abolished this court in 2005. Two years later, the regime established the State Security Court and Prosecution in 2007.

[40] Report (2013b), p. 12.

[41] Report (2013b), p. 12.

[42] Report (2012c), pp. 77–78.

[43] Mancini (2012), p. 104.

[44] Libyan Laws (2011).

violated the later when he made a statement abolishing certain laws and declaring Islamic law as the source legislation.[45] Moreover, the NTC adopted the disappointing Law No. 38 on 2 May 2011, which grants blanket amnesty for crimes committed during the February 17th revolution by insurgents. Article 4 of the same law, which is in conflict with the norms of international criminal law, provides that "there shall be no penalty for military, security, or civil actions dictated by the February 17th Revolution that were performed by revolutionaries with the goal of promoting or protecting the revolution."[46]

In the following sections we examine Libya's criminal justice system by looking into the provisions of the Libyan Penal Code, as well as into the Libyan laws passed during the transitional period, and at the same time explore whether Libya, as a State Party, has implemented the norms on international core crimes in the provisions of its criminal legislation.

2.2.1 Libyan Penal Code

Historically speaking, The Libyan Penal Code was adopted by a royal decree on 28 November 1953.[47] The code, which contains 507 articles, was largely influenced by the Italian Penal Code, and was subjected to 22 amendments, the most worthy of note being two substantive amendments in 1956[48] and 1975, respectively. The latter amended 32 articles in the section entitled "crimes against the public interest," to include 21 articles providing for the death penalty for crimes against the interests of the State.[49]

When the Penal Code was adopted in 1953, only a few international humanitarian and human rights treaties had been adopted, including: the *United Nations Charter*, 1945;[50] the *Universal Declaration of Human Rights*, 1948; (Treaties 1948b) the Four Geneva Conventions, 1949; the *European Convention for the Protection of Human Rights and Fundamental Freedoms*, 1950;[51] and the *Convention on the Prevention and Punishment of the Crime of Genocide*, 1948.[52] However, despite the several amendments made over the past 60 years, it is an unfortunate fact that none of the above agreements' norms came to be reflected in the provisions of the Libyan Penal Code.

---

[45] Report (2012c), p. 82.

[46] Libyan Laws (2012d).

[47] Libyan Laws (1953).

[48] Law No. 48 of 23 September 1956, which provided for the cancellation of 9 articles, adding 20 articles, and modifying 213 articles.

[49] Zawati (2014b), p. 58; under Law No. 38 of 1975.

[50] Treaties (1945). Libya was admitted to the United Nations on 14 December 1955.

[51] Treaties (1950). It was not signed by Libya.

[52] Treaties (1948a).

Nonetheless, pursuant to Articles 19 and 50 of the Rome Statute, Libya filed on 28 May 2012 a compilation of the provisions of Libyan law,[53] which it referred to in its application to challenge the admissibility of the cases concerning Saif Al-Islam and Al-Senussi before the ICC. The compilation also includes another document, entitled "National Transitional Council Decree recognizing the applicability of international crimes within Libyan law".[54] However, this latter decree, which emphasizes Libya's recognition of all international humanitarian and human rights obligations arising from the above-mentioned conventions and suggests the reproduction of international core crimes—incorporated in Articles 6–8 of the Rome Statute—in the Libyan Penal Code, is merely a draft decree proposed by Ahmed El-Gehani, Libya's coordinator for the ICC, to the NTC on 10 April 2012. This was explicitly mentioned in Mostafa Lindi's letter of response to El-Gehani,[55] informing him that his proposal had been submitted to the specialized legal committee within the NTC for examination. It is unfortunate that the proposed decree has never been adopted, neither by the NTC nor by the General National Council (GNC), its elected successor.

In short, after 4 years of instability, during which Libya has had two parliaments, two governments, two proclaimed national armies, and dozens of warring factions, Libyan legislators have utterly failed during this long period of time to incorporate international crimes into the Libyan Penal Code or to take steps to domesticate war crimes and crimes against humanity embodied in the Rome Statute.

2.2.2 Libyan Laws of the Transitional Period

As has already been mentioned, since the toppling of the Gaddafi regime in the fall of 2011, the unsettled situation in many parts of Libya has impeded any serious attempts at legislation reform.[56] Consequently, Article 35 of the Constitutional Declaration provides that all the provisions prescribed in existing legislation—i.e., laws enacted before the uprising of 17 February 2011—shall continue to be valid so long as they are not in conflict with the provisions of this Declaration or unless they are amended or revoked.[57]

Notwithstanding the aforesaid limitation, the NTC—from its establishment on 27 February 2011 until the handing over of power to the elected General National Congress on 8 August 2012—has adopted a number of laws and decisions although none of them has explicitly condemned any of the international core crimes.[58] Examples include: Law No. 17 on the *Establishment of Rules of National*

[53] ICC (2012c), Annexes A & B.

[54] ICC (2012d), Annex J.

[55] ICC (2012e), Annex K.

[56] Report (2014a), p. 10.

[57] Libyan Laws (2011).

[58] Zawati (2014b), p. 58.

Reconciliation and Transitional Justice,[59] Law No. 26 on the *Higher Body for Implementation of the Criteria of Integrity and Transparency*,[60] Law No. 35 On an *Amnesty for Some Crimes*,[61] and Law No. 38 regarding Some *Procedures Relating to the Transitional Period*.[62]

Taking a closer look at the provisions of the above laws, it seems clear that they all fall short of harmony with the norms of several of the international humanitarian and human rights treaties to which Libya is a signatory State. For example, Law No. 35 addresses only violations of human rights by former government agents between 1 September 1969 and 15 February 2011. In other words, it fails to consider violations committed individually or collectively by the insurgents or the transitional government's agents. In addition, this law excludes from amnesty Qadhafi's wife, children (biological and adopted), brothers, sisters, sons and daughters in-law, and assistants. The latter category is open to interpretation depending on personal interests and political orientation.[63]

By the same token, Law No. 26 prohibits a large segment of the Libyan population listed in Article 8(B) "General Regulations"—up to 60 %, falling into 16 categories of people who held leading positions in the former Libyan government over the past 35 years—from holding 18 leading positions, listed in Article 9, in the political, economic, military, diplomatic, and educational domains.

Finally, Law No. 38 is regrettable and promotes the culture of impunity. For instance, Article 4, which places rebels above the law, provides that "there shall be no penalty for military, security, or civil actions dictated by the February 17th Revolution that were performed by revolutionaries with the goal of promoting or protecting the revolution." Earlier reports suggested that this amnesty law was drafted in order to appease Libya's tribal leaders who apparently fear that anti-Qadhafi rebels will be held accountable for human rights violations they committed during the uprising. Moreover, Article 5 of the same code abolishes the right of individuals who were arbitrarily detained by rebels to pursue the government or its agents in the courts. It states that even if a court acquits a person who was detained by militia, that person has no right to initiate a criminal or civil complaint against the state or the militia, unless the detention was based on fabricated or mendacious allegations.[64]

On the other hand, the GNC has adopted a number of pertinent laws, including: Law No. 10 (2013) on the *Criminalization of Torture, Forced Disappearance, and Discrimination*[65]; Law No. 13 (2013) on *Political and Administrative Isolation*[66];

[59] Libyan Laws (2012a).

[60] Libyan Laws (2012b).

[61] Libyan Laws (2012c).

[62] Libyan Laws (2012d).

[63] Zawati (2014b), pp. 54–55.

[64] Ibid., p. 56.

[65] Libyan Laws (2013a).

[66] Libyan Laws (2013b).

and Law No. 29 (2013) on *Transitional Justice*.[67] Nevertheless, despite the fine-sounding norms of Law No. 10, there is deep concern over its conjunction with the provisions of the *UN Convention Against Torture and Other Cruel, Inhuman or Degrading Treatment or Punishment* (CAT).[68] Moreover, it lacks an accurate description of the crimes of "Torture," "Discrimination," and "Enforced Disappearance," a substantial requirement to apply the law in the courtroom.[69] The failure of the Libyan legislator to provide an accurate description of these crimes infringes the principle of legality, *nullum crimen sine lege*, embodied in Article 22 (2) of the Rome Statute, which provides that: "[t]he definition of a crime shall be strictly construed and shall not be extended by analogy. In case of ambiguity, the definition shall be interpreted in favour of the person being investigated, prosecuted or convicted".[70] Furthermore, the abstractness of the above crimes violates the principle of fair labelling, leads to inconsistent verdicts and punishments, and constitutes a barrier to justice.[71] The principle of fair labelling requires that offences be categorized and labelled in a way that reflects different degrees of wrongdoing and, accordingly, entails distinctive levels of punishment consistent with the gravity of the offence.[72] This deliberate ambiguity leaves much room to the Libyan judges' discretion, thus creating the risk that they will choose a narrow and regressive understanding of the law.

Moreover, this law has proved in practice to be a paper construction rather than a practical reality. A report by the United Nations Support Mission in Libya ('UNSMIL') reveals that torture and ill-treatment of detainees in detention facilities across Libya are systematic and widespread. That many of the detention centres are out of the government's control and under the authority of armed warring factions, emerged during the February 2011 uprising. The UNSMIL recorded 27 cases of deaths in custody as a result of torture up to and including October 2013, with 11 of them killed in 2013 alone.[73] Cases of abductions and enforced disappearances at the hands of militias and armed brigades have frequently occurred, and with impunity.[74] The Libyan government, has, unsurprisingly, failed to properly investigate and prosecute any of these cases.[75]

Another recent piece of legislation is Law No. 13 of 2013 on *Political and Administrative Isolation*, passed on 5 May 2013 and put into force on 5 June 2014, aims at the prevention of Gaddafi-era officials, comprising 22 categories listed in Article 1, from holding public office. This prevention encompasses also those who

---

[67] Libyan Laws (2013c).

[68] Treaties (1984).

[69] Amnesty (2011a), p. 25.

[70] Treaties (1998).

[71] Zawati (2014a), p. 3.

[72] Ibid., p. 27.

[73] UN (2013), p. 8.

[74] Report (2014a), p. 11.

[75] Report (2014b), p. 11.

defected from the Gaddafi regime and played a prominent role in the 17 February 2011 uprising, including Mahmoud Jibril, Mustafa Abdul-Jalil, Mohammad al-Muqarief, and other leading figures.[76] However, this law has been seen by legal scholars and commentators as problematic. They argue that it was adopted under enormous pressure exerted by armed militias—when voices across Libya were in favour of getting rid of any one who served under Gaddafi regime—and that it fails to conform with international human rights standards, particularly the provisions of the *International Covenant on Civil and Political Rights* ('ICCPR'), to which Libya is a State Party.[77] The *Political and Administrative Isolation* law may also violate Libyan citizens' civil and political right to elect their representatives under Article 25(b) of the ICCPR.[78] Recently, on 2 February 2015, Libya's rival parliament (House of Representatives) in Tubruk voted in favour of suspending this controversial law,[79] asserting that all Libyans are equal, and should not be deprived of the right to participate in politics except when found guilty of wrongdoing.[80]

Finally, Law No. 29 on *Transitional Justice*, which was adopted by the GNC on 22 September 2013, has replaced Law No. 17 on the *Establishment of Rules of National Reconciliation and Transitional Justice*, adopted by the NTC on 26 February 2012.[81] The purpose of this law, as stipulated in Article 1, is to address serious and systematic violations of the fundamental rights of liberties of the Libyan people committed by the former regime's government agents. This will be achieved through legislative, judicial, social, and administrative measures with the purpose of revealing the truth, holding perpetrators accountable, reforming institutions, preserving the national memory, and seeking reparations for victims.[82] Like Law No. 10 on the *Criminalization of Torture, Forced Disappearance, and Discrimination*, this law has never been implemented in practice. Indeed, the existence of two contradictory governments, two opposing parliaments, and the domination of the armed militias and warring groups over large parts of Libya have obstructed judicial reform and hindered the implementation of transitional justice.[83]

---

[76] Libyan Laws (2013b).

[77] Libyan Laws (2013b). Acceded by Libya on 15 May 1970.

[78] Treaties (1966).

[79] Following the legislative elections held in Libya on 25 June 2014 for the Council of Deputies, where nationalist and liberal factions won the majority of seats, the Supreme Court has annulled the elections on 6 November 2014, determining that the constitutional amendment made in March 2014 to allow the elections to take place was illegal. Accordingly, it ruled that the elections held in June were unconstitutional and that the parliament and government which resulted from that vote should be dissolved. This ruling, which has deepened political disputes amongst Libyans, has left the country with two rival parliaments and governments, resulted in the killing of hundreds of Libyans, and displaced thousands of citizens in war-torn areas.

[80] Supreme Court (2014).

[81] HR Watch (2014), p. 42.

[82] Libyan Laws (2013c), Article 1.

[83] Report (2014a), p. 13.

3 Challenges for Prosecuting International Core Crimes Under Libya's Transitional Justice

Combating impunity and ensuring accountability for international core crimes, committed by both government forces and insurgents during the February 2011 uprising and in the ongoing civil war, is key to the Libyan government's task of restoring justice and achieving peace and security in Libya.[84] Since the ouster of Gaddafi's regime in the fall of 2011, successive Libyan transitional governments did less than nothing to reform the Libyan judicial system, while militias and armed groups have proliferated, gaining control over many different Libyan cities, and operating above the law with impunity.[85]

Despite the fact that Articles 32 and 33 of the NTC's Constitutional Declaration unambiguously provide for the independence of the judicial authority, prohibit the establishment of exceptional courts, and emphasize the peoples' right of resorting to the judiciary, nothing has come into practice. The successive transitional governments have continued the legacy of the former regime's interference in the judicial system and its failure to incorporate international standards for fair trials and imprisonment. Recent human rights reports document arbitrary detention, unauthorised interrogations, coerced confessions and torture to death.[86]

Due furthermore to the lack of security, the government has been unable to bring many conflict-related detainees to justice without undue delay. Moreover, in many parts of Libya, people have little chances to resort to judicial bodies, as many primary courts have closed their doors, preventing people from gaining access to judicial process.[87] Furthermore, prosecutors have utterly failed to prosecute suspects related to armed groups because judges are scared of vengeance.[88] This lawlessness, which is paralyzing the entire judicial process, has resulted in severe challenges to prosecuting international core crimes under Libya's transitional justice. We will underline a number of the challenges below.

3.1 Legal Impunity and Lawlessness

The controversial laws of the transitional period, in addition to the crisis of the proliferation of weapons and the government's inability to gain control over independent armed groups, have triggered lawlessness and obstructed the NTC's endeavour to restore justice and combat the culture of impunity.[89] The challenge of

---

[84] Mancini (2012), p. 104.

[85] HR Watch (2015b).

[86] Ibid.

[87] Report (2014a), p. 16.

[88] Report (2015).

[89] Amnesty (2012c), p. 32.

holding insurgents accountable for crimes they allegedly committed during and in the aftermath of the February 2011 uprising has created lasting frustration.[90] The government's overwhelming failure to investigate and prosecute the extrajudicial executions by militias and armed groups of hundreds of Gaddafi soldiers—after they surrendered or were captured—including alleged "African mercenaries" and suspected loyalists to the former regime, creates a state of lawlessness and promotes the culture of impunity.[91]

A closer look at the Libyan transitional laws, adopted by both the NTC and GNC, reveals that these laws are retributive rather than constructive. They gave legal sanction to impunity by conferring legal status on the above crimes. The legal immunity awarded to the members of armed groups encouraged them to operate above the law, and thwarted any attempt to prosecute them for their wrongdoings.[92] As indicated earlier, Article 4 of Law No. 38 provides blanket immunity for persons who carried out the task of toppling the Gaddafi regime, approving the status of lawlessness.[93] Moreover, in contrast to Article 12 of the Libyan Constitution,[94] which stresses that all Libyans shall be treated equally before the law, Law No. 17 regarding the establishment of rules of national reconciliation and transitional justice limits the cases to be addressed by the Fact-Finding and Reconciliation Commission to crimes allegedly associated with the former regime between 1 September 1969 and 23 October 2011, while crimes committed by insurgents, armed groups, and transitional government's agents remain unconsidered.[95]

By allowing a significant number of people who allegedly committed international core crimes to walk free simply because they are members of one of the insurgents' armed groups, indicates that the provisions of Laws No. 38 and No. 17 preserve a culture of selective justice and promote a culture of impunity—a culture that, ironically, gave rise to the 17th of February uprising against the Gaddafi regime.[96] This posture of lawlessness was clearly reflected in the failure of the judicial authorities to allow access to thousands of the former regime's loyalists in the militias' detention centres across the country, their continued illegal denial of defence lawyers to detainees, and their neglect of the principle of bringing prisoners to justice in a reasonable time.[97] Furthermore, lawlessness has hindered practitioners of criminal justice—fearful of armed groups' attacks and retribution—from carrying out justice procedures against insurgents, and obliged them to refrain from

[90] Amnesty (2012c), p. 39.

[91] Bassiouni (2013), pp. 516–517.

[92] Report (2013b), p. 29.

[93] Heller (2013). Early reports suggest that this amnesty law was drafted in order to address the tribal leaders' concerns of holding members of relative rebel forces accountable for human rights violations allegedly committed during and after the uprising.

[94] Libyan Laws (1951).

[95] Libyan Laws (2012a).

[96] HR Watch (2012a).

[97] Amnesty (2012c), p. 38.

taking serious steps to bring those who have allegedly committed core crimes to justice.[98]

A case in point: the NTC announced investigations into the killings of Abdul Fattah Younes al-Obeidi, former Secretary of the General Peoples' Committee for Public Security in the Gaddafi era (Minister of Interior), who was captured by protestors in Benghazi in February 2011, and then defected to the insurgents. On 27 July 2011, al-Obeidi was recalled for questioning. He was taken together with two of his assistants by a group of insurgents and executed. Similarly, Muammar Gaddafi and his son Mu'tasim were extra-judicially executed by insurgents shortly after being captured on 20 October 2011. Despite the formation of independent investigating committees into these killings, no findings have yet been made public. Likewise, no investigation was made into the killing of 65 people found dead on the grounds of the Mahari Hotel in Sirte on 23 October 2011, 3 days after the execution of Muammar Gaddafi and his son.[99]

Looking more closely into the post-Gaddafi judicial system, one finds that many judicial police members, investigators, and prosecutors haven't the proper training to deal with international core crimes. For example, a Libyan judge has suspended the trial of Buzeid Dorda, a senior former intelligence officer, who was charged with killing civilians and inciting civil war, over the failure of the prosecutor's office to follow the court's rules and procedures. This laxity on the part of the judicial authorities makes any judicial reform, which is a high priority for the transitional justice process, likely to fail.[100]

3.2 *Rule of the Gun v. Rule of Law*

Since the fall of the Gaddafi regime, Libya has endured an incomprehensible transitional period, marked by the collapse of the security apparatus and judicial institutions. Despite the transitional government's exertions to bring stability and establish the rule of law, the ongoing power struggle among different militias and armed brigades, has substantially undermined the government's efforts to extend its control over the state's institutions.[101]

Indeed, one of the most serious challenges facing the current transitional government is the immediate need to gain control over hundreds of armed groups and disarm them.[102] Militant groups are affecting most aspects of Libyans' lives—including

[98] Report (2013b), p. 37.

[99] Amnesty (2012c), p. 39.

[100] ICC (2012a), paras. 75–76.

[101] UN (2014), p. 3.

[102] Amnesty (2012c), p. 32.

security and justice[103]—and multiplying the number of *de facto* authorities within the Libyan state.[104] They take on the roles of police, prosecutors, judges and prison guards; they establish investigation and arrest units;[105] they draft lists of wanted people; and they proceed to hunt them through checkpoints or by raiding their homes.[106]

Thousands of Libyans were, and still are, vulnerable to kidnapping by rebel militias.[107] Many citizens are held in different detention facilities outside the jurisdiction of Libya's justice system, while others have been subjected to extrajudicial killing, or assassination in mysterious circumstances.[108] During and in the aftermath of the 2011 conflict, militias arrested and arbitrary detained thousands of people suspected of having belonged to the security forces of the former regime, Gaddafi loyalists, or alleged foreign mercenaries.[109] They continue to hold many of these in secret detention facilities without indictment or trial and in inhuman conditions, subjecting many of them to humiliation, torture, sexual torture, mutilation and torture leading to death.[110]

Moreover, acts of violence have been extended to the legal community. Attacks and retaliation against actors in the judicial system have increased—a development that constitutes a great threat to restoring the rule of law. In this respect, human rights groups working in Libya have documented a number of attacks on judges and lawyers, including the assassination of judges Mohammed Naguib Huwaidi from Bayda, Murad Alarouby in Tripoli, and Gumma Aljawi in Benghazi. In another incident, Misrata lawyer and human rights activist Hanan Al-Newaisery was assaulted and beaten up together with her father in front of Misrata's Zarouk courthouse. She had previously informed Libyan authorities of threats made to her, including threats of rape, but the authorities had turned a blind eye and no action was taken.[111]

Another case in point is the arbitrary detention of four staff members of the ICC's Office of Public Counsel for the Defence ('OPCD') on June 7, 2012, during their authorized visit to Saif Al-Islam who has been held in a detention facility run by the Zintan brigade since he was captured. Despite the immunity of the Court's team as prescribed in Article 48 of the Rome Statute, the Zintan militia detained the

[103] The general prosecutor in al-Zawiya, 50 km to the west of Tripoli, told Amnesty International that the judicial system is functioning in difficult and tense circumstances as armed militias control most aspects of life in the city. He added that a group of armed men once stormed the court room and threatened one of the judges as they thought he had imposed a light sentence on an alleged Qadhafi supporter. In another similar incident, a group of armed men abducted a public prosecutor in al-Zawiya, held him for several hours and dragged him to the prosecution's office demanding that he must be punished for ordering the release of a detainee they accused of committing crimes.

[104] Amnesty (2012a).

[105] Amnesty (2014c), p. 15.

[106] Report (2013b), p. 22.

[107] Amnesty (2012b), p. 24.

[108] Zawati (2014b), p. 68.

[109] HR Watch (2015a).

[110] Amnesty (2014c), pp. 19–20.

[111] Report (2013a).

staff for nearly 1 month without bringing them before a judge.[112] Zintan militia accused Melinda Taylor, Saif al-Islam's defence lawyer, of smuggling spying devices and a coded letter to Saif Al-Islam from his special assistant, Mohammad Ismaili, who is also wanted by the Libyan authorities.[113] Alajmi Ali al-Atiri, commander of the Zintan brigade considered the above letter to be a suspicious document constituting a direct threat to Libyan national security.[114] The arbitrary detention of the staff, however, reflects the failure of the Libyan authorities to control the armed groups active throughout Libya, and to fulfil its obligations to comply with the UN Security Council's Resolution 1970, which referred the Libyan situation to the ICC under chapter VII of the UN Charter, and requires Libya to abide fully by the rules of the Court.[115] Moreover, the above cases demonstrate Libya's devastating failure to adhere to the rules of the law, nationally and internationally, thereby justifying the ICC's demand to surrender Saif Al-Islam to The Hague.[116]

3.3 *Failure to Ensure Due Process and Fair Trial Standards*

Fair trial standards embodied in the provisions of legally binding treaties of international human rights law[117] imply that anyone in custody should enjoy certain pre-trial, at trial, and post-trial rights, including:[118] the right to be informed of any charges; the right to legal counsel and to choose a lawyer; the right to have access to the outside world, including family visits; the right to be brought before a judge promptly and to be triad without undue delay; the right to humane detention conditions and freedom from torture and ill-treatment; the right to equality before the law and courts; the right to trial by a competent, independent, and impartial judicial body established by law; the right to the presumption of innocence; the right to a fair and public hearing; the right to remain silent and not to be compelled to incriminate oneself; the prohibition of retroactive application of criminal law and of double jeopardy; the right to be present at trial and appeal and to call and examine witnesses; and the right to appeal a conviction before a higher tribunal.[119] While the competence of any judicial body depends on its capacity to deliver justice

---

[112] Fry (2013), p. 224.

[113] Akande (2012).

[114] Kersten (2014), pp. 195–196.

[115] HR Watch (2012b).

[116] Goldstone (2012).

[117] Particularly, the International Covenant on Civil and Political Rights (ICCPR), adopted by the UN General Assembly in 1966 and entered into force in 1976.

[118] Amnesty (2014a).

[119] Report (2012a).

in a timely, efficient, and impartial way, nevertheless, the current Libyan judicial system has shown itself incapable, thus far, of meeting the above standards.

Indeed, the perilous security situation and the weakness of the state's control over governmental institutions constitute one of the major obstacles to establishing an independent Libyan judicial system. In the absence of the rule of law and with the failure of the Libyan authorities to demilitarize heavily armed militants, the arbitrary detention, torture and ill-treatment of detainees,[120] enforced disappearances and assassinations, assaults on the state's institutions and abductions of state officials, including the prime minister[121] and foreign diplomats[122] have become regular occurrences in Libyan daily life.[123]

Although Article 26 of Law No. 29 (2013) on Transitional Justice requires the ministries of Justice, the Interior and Defence to adopt all necessary measures to end the detention of those associated with the previous regime, either by referring them to the public prosecutor or by releasing them,[124] there are approximately 8000 detainees still held in inhumane conditions without due process, since the eruption of the civil war in February 2011.[125] More importantly, most of these detainees have been denied the right to a fair trial as many of them have not yet been brought before a judge, have not had access to lawyers, and have not been allowed to contact the outside world, including having family visits.[126]

In addition to the above violations, there are serious concerns about the capability of the Libyan judicial system to provide fair trials for the detainees. The phenomenon of bomb attacks against courts in different Libyan cities and constant threats of violence against judges and lawyers by armed groups, have resulted in the

---

[120] Report (2013b), p. 31.

[121] Cockburn (2013). Following the US Secretary of State's confirmation of the Libyan government's role in the US kidnap of Abu Anas al-Libi from Libya, a militant group, known as the Operations Room of Libya's Revolutionaries, kidnapped the Libyan Prime Minister Ali Zeidan at gunpoint from a Tripoli hotel on 10 October 2013. He was escorted by 150 armed rebels in a convoy of waiting cars to an unknown location and only later freed when members of another militia group stormed the site where he was being held.

[122] Jordanian Ambassador (2014). On 15 April 2014, Fawaz al-Aitan, Jordan's ambassador to Libya, was kidnapped in Tripoli by masked armed men who attacked his car and shot his driver. The kidnappers had demanded the release of Mohamed Dersi, a Libyan jailed for life in 2007 in Jordan for plotting to blow up the Queen Alia International Airport in Amman. In January 2014, five Egyptian diplomats, the secretary of Tunisia's ambassador to Libya and a South Korean trade official were abducted. These events were overshadowed by the 2012 incident in which the American ambassador Chris Stevens and three officials were killed when the US consulate in Benghazi was overrun.

[123] Stephen (2013). After she had served a 10-month prison sentence for entering the country with a fake passport in October 2012 to visit her jailed father, Anoud Abdullah al-Senussi was snatched on 2 September 2013 by heavily armed gunmen while the judiciary police were escorting her to Tripoli Airport. She was freed one week later.

[124] Libyan Laws (2013c).

[125] Amnesty (2011b), p. 14.

[126] Amnesty (2014d), p. 6.

assassination of eight judges as of the time of writing. A significant proportion of Libya's population will not allow actors in the judicial system to conduct investigations or deliver consistent and impartial trials.[127]

By way of example, both Saif al-Islam—denied the opportunity to attend the hearings of the Indictment Chamber in violation of his right to be present at his trial in Tripoli (the Zintan brigade locked him in a secret place, and refused to hand him over to the Libyan transitional governments)—and Abdullah Al-Senussi who is currently being held in solitary confinement, have been denied the right of having access to legal counsel or to be represented by a lawyer. It may be argued that, on paper, Article 53 of the Libyan Prisons Law No. 47 asserts the right of detainees to have access to their lawyers,[128] but it is a sad fact that the latter have refrained from visiting their clients, fearing revenge or retaliation from prison guards or militant groups controlling different parts of the country. Furthermore, in contrast to Article 106 of the Libyan Code of Criminal Procedure,[129] neither of the above defendants nor any other detained members of the overthrown Gaddafi regime was interrogated in the presence of his lawyer.[130] This is an outrageous violation of the detainees' right to a fair trial, and clear proof of the incompetence of the Libyan judicial system as it stands today.[131]

3.4 Lack of Criminal Justice Reform

The Libyan penal code, the code of criminal procedure, and much other legislation enacted post-February 2011 conflict contain provisions that are inconsistent with the main principles of international criminal law. For example, the Libyan penal code does not explicitly or implicitly criminalize international core crimes, namely genocide, war crimes or crimes against humanity. Furthermore, the penalty of capital punishment is imposed for a broad range of offences, including offences which do not meet the threshold of "most serious crimes," prescribed in Article 6(2) of the *International Covenant on Civil and Political Rights*.[132]

To achieve conflict resolution and peace-building, Libya needs a comprehensive criminal justice reform,[133] including the establishment of an independent judicial system that responds adequately to conflict-related crimes and provides impartial and fair trials to defendants.[134] The inability of the Libyan authorities to ensure fair

[127] Ibid., p. 4.

[128] Libyan Laws (1975).

[129] Libyan Laws (1999).

[130] Amnesty (2014d), p. 7.

[131] Zawati (2014b), p. 69.

[132] UN (2014), p. 15.

[133] Report (2013b), p. 39.

[134] Zawati (2014b), p. 45.

trials to conflict-related detainees highlights the urgent need to reform the judicial system. Despite the NTC's and the successive transitional governments' promises to reform both security and judiciary systems, they have failed to do so in practice.[135] For example, the NTC was unable to adopt the abovementioned proposal by Gehani to incorporate international core crimes in the provisions of the Libyan Penal Code under the influence of the Court's complementarity regime, which controls the norms of due process when the Court decides on the admissibility of a case under Article 17 or Article 20(3) of the Rome Statute.[136] It goes without saying that the failure of Libyan lawmakers to incorporate crimes listed in the Rome Statute into the Libyan penal code has weakened the state's governance and resulted in a fragile judicial system that retains the legacies of the past. It remains a tool of repression and consequently puts fair trials out of reach.[137]

To help Libya reform its criminal justice system in conformity with the norms of the Rome Statute and the provisions of international humanitarian human rights law instruments, the UNSMIL and the United Nations Development Program ('UNDP') have worked hard with the Supreme Judicial Council, Libya's highest judicial authority, to setup a judicial reform strategy over the past 4 years. To this end, and in collaboration with the High Judicial Institute in Libya, the Tripoli Bar Association, and No Peace Without Justice ('NPWJ'), several meetings and workshops were organized in Europe and Libya to train actors in the Libyan judicial system, including judges and prosecutors, and to remind them of Libya's obligations under international humanitarian and human rights law to provide fair trials in line with international standards.[138]

Regrettably, these efforts have been severely undermined due to the lack of security in Libya and the absence there of the rule of law. The pervasive ambiance of fearfulness and panic among judiciary staff left a defeatist impact on the performance of judges and prosecutors, who were, and still are, vulnerable to all kinds of attacks, including kidnapping, serious threats, physical assaults, and murder by armed groups. In post-Gaddafi Libya, threats against professionals in the justice system have been common while the real number of attacks is far greater than what has been reported.[139] Also, any reform to the Libyan penal code and legislation should be preceded by Libya's ratification of relevant international treaties, including the Rome Statute, the *Optional Protocol to the Convention against Torture and other Cruel, Inhuman or Degrading Treatment or Punishment* (Optional Protocol to the CAT)[140], and the *International Convention on the Protection of All Persons from Enforced Disappearances* ('CPED').[141] Furthermore,

[135] Amnesty (2014b), p. 1.

[136] ICC (2012f), Annexes J & K.

[137] Homes (2012).

[138] Report (2014a), pp. 20–21.

[139] Mangan and Murtaugh (2014).

[140] Treaties (2002).

[141] Treaties (2006).

reigning in armed groups, on the one hand, and introducing international human rights standards into the provisions of the new Libyan constitution and international core crimes into the Libyan penal code, on the other, are the fundamental steps that must be taken to restore peace and justice in Libya.[142]

4 The Complementarity Regime of the ICC and the Admissibility of Libya's Cases

In response to Libya's admissibility challenges of the cases of Saif Al-Islam[143] and Al-Senussi[144], the Court issued two differing decisions. On 31 May 2013, the PTCI confirmed the Court's jurisdiction over the case against Saif Al-Islam and rejected Libya's admissibility challenge, asserting that Libya has failed to demonstrate its ability to conduct meticulously its investigation of the alleged crimes.[145] On the other hand, the PTCI issued its diverging decision on 11 October 2013, declaring that the case against Al-Senussi is subject to domestic proceedings to be conducted by the Libyan competent authorities and that Libya is willing and able genuinely to carry out such investigation. Accordingly, the PTCI concluded that the latter case is inadmissible before the Court, in conformity with the principle of complementarity contemplated in both paragraph 10 of the Preamble and Article 1 of the Rome Statute.[146]

Nonetheless, while both decisions acknowledged—in different degrees—Libya's due process guarantees, many commentators and legal scholars, including the author, argue that the current Libyan judicial system is incompetent and would not guarantee due process rights to the defendant, the matter that makes Libya far away from conducting fair and impartial trials.[147] The Court's assessment of the admissibility of a case in transitional societies should give further weight to the guarantee of international standards of due process rights to the defendant than to the willingness of a state to investigate and prosecute the alleged crimes.[148]

This section therefore considers the complementarity regime of the ICC in light of the admissibility of the above Libyan cases. It starts by offering some reflections on the complementarity principle embodied in the provisions of the Rome Statute, reviews Libya's challenges to the admissibility of the cases against Saif Al-Islam and Al-Senussi, and finally, underlines the ICC's inconsistent decisions on the admissibility of the above cases.

---

[142] Amnesty (2011c).
[143] ICC (2012b).
[144] ICC (2013d).
[145] ICC (2013f).
[146] ICC (2013r).
[147] Bishop (2013), p. 398.
[148] Walker (2014), p. 307.

4.1 The Complementarity Regime of the ICC and the Admissibility Principle

The complementarity principle was generally developed in the norms of different international treaties following the end of World War I, and was recently crystallized in the provisions of the Rome Statute.[149] Despite the failure of the drafters to define it or to provide any legal relationship between the Court and the States' criminal jurisdiction, as embodied in paragraph 10 of the Preamble and in Article 1 of the Rome Statute,[150] complementarity has been considered as the cornerstone of this treaty.[151] In this respect, Schabas argues that the Rome Statute could not have been adopted without the existence of the principle of complementarity.[152]

Article 17 of the Rome Statute addresses the concerns of States Parties by introducing complementarity as a basis for admissibility and asserting that the jurisdiction of the Court shall be complementary to national criminal jurisdiction.[153] In other words, the Court shall declare the inadmissibility of any case which is being or has been investigated or prosecuted by a State, which has jurisdiction over it, unless that state is unwilling or unable genuinely to carry out the investigation or prosecution.[154] Moreover, Article 17 clearly demonstrates how the complementarity procedure strikes a balance between the Court's need to emphasize its effectiveness and jurisdiction over international core crimes and the States' right to preserve their sovereignty and to exercise their national criminal jurisprudence over crimes committed on their soil.[155]

Article 17 furthermore explicitly regulates the principle of complementarity and stipulates four situations that constitute the Court's framework for determining a case's admissibility. Article 17(1) provides that—taking into consideration paragraph 10 of the Preamble and Article 1—the Court should consider a case inadmissible where:

> (a) The case is being investigated or prosecuted by a State which has jurisdiction over it, unless the State is unwilling or unable genuinely to carry out the investigation or prosecution;
> (b) The case has been investigated by a State which has jurisdiction over it and the State has decided not to prosecute the person concerned, unless the decision resulted from the unwillingness or inability of the State genuinely to prosecute;
> (c) The person concerned has already been tried for conduct which is the subject of the complaint, and a trial by the Court is not permitted under article 20, paragraph 3; and
> (d) The case is not of sufficient gravity to justify further action by the Court. (Treaties 1998, Article 17(2))

---

[149] El Zeidy (2008), p. 11.
[150] Hobbs (2012–2013), p. 28.
[151] Bo (2014), p. 506.
[152] Schabas (2010), p. 506.
[153] Bishop (2013), p. 392.
[154] Dumbryte (2014), p. 3.
[155] Stigen (2008), p. 87.

The above provisions affirm the aim of the principle of complementarity, which stresses the State's right to priority in conducting legal proceedings against perpetrators of international core crimes which occur within their jurisdiction, unless they are unwilling or unable genuinely to investigate and prosecute them.[156] Moreover, Article 17(2) underlines the principles of due process recognized by international law when it comes to determining the concept of "unwillingness" referred to in Article 17(1)(a) & (b). Notwithstanding the lack of a clear definition of the due process principle in Article 17(2), one may understand it to refer the rights and rules of a fair trial, including the right of the accused to be brought before a judge without undue delay, and to be tried by a competent, independent, and impartial court. Taking this point into consideration, Article 17(2) provides that the Court shall determine the unwillingness of a State in a particular case with reference to the existence of one or more of the following situations. In other words, the failure of a State to guarantee an accused's due process rights in a certain case, lies under the jurisdiction of the Court, would render that case admissible under Article 17.[157] These situations are:

(a) The proceedings were or are being undertaken or the national decision was made for the purpose of shielding the person concerned from criminal responsibility for crimes within the jurisdiction of the Court referred to in article 5;
(b) There has been an unjustified delay in the proceedings which in the circumstances is inconsistent with an intent to bring the person concerned to justice; and
(c) The proceedings were not or are not being conducted independently or impartially, and they were or are being conducted in a manner which, in the circumstances, is inconsistent with an intent to bring the person concerned to justice.

However, in addition to unwillingness, Article 17(3) introduces inability as another rationale to disprove the admissibility of a case. For example, in certain cases a State may in good faith be willing to investigate and prosecute a person accused or suspected of committing international core crimes under its jurisdiction, and yet at the same time lacks the ability to adequately carry out the proceedings in a reasonable timeframe.[158] To clarify this point, this article provides:

> In order to determine inability in a particular case, the Court shall consider whether, due to a total or substantial collapse or unavailability of its national judicial system, the State is unable to obtain the accused or the necessary evidence and testimony or otherwise unable to carry out its proceedings.

A closer look at the above article reveals that the concept of inability involves one or more of the following situations: (a) the State's total or substantial collapse or the unavailability of its national judicial system; (b) the State is unable to lay its hands on the accused or obtain the necessary evidence and testimony; or (c) the State is otherwise unable to carry out its proceedings. A case in point is the Trial Chamber's III decision on the admissibility and abuse of process challenges in the

[156] Hobbs (2012–2013), p. 28.

[157] Fry (2012), p. 41; Nouri (2013), p. 22.

[158] Gordon (2011), p. 750; Stigen (2008), p. 326.

case of Jean-Pierre Bemba Gombo of the Central African Republic (CAR). The Trial Chamber ruled that the fact that "the CAR national judicial system is unable to investigate effectively or try the accused leads inevitably to the conclusion that for the purposes of Article 17(3) of the Statute, the national judicial system of the CAR is 'unavailable,' because it does not have the capacity to handle these proceedings".[159]

On the basis of the above discussion, therefore, it is clear that if commentators regard complementarity as the cornerstone of the Rome Statute, effectiveness should be seen as the foundation of complementarity. In other words, admissibility should be determined on the grounds of whether a State's national justice system can fully ensure the effective and adequate investigation, protection and prosecution of a person accused of international core crimes.[160]

4.2 Libya's Challenge to the Admissibility of the Case Against Saif Al-Islam

As has already been noted, pursuant to the United Nations Security Council Resolution 1970 (2011) referring the situation in Libya to the Prosecutor of the ICC, the PTCI issued arrest warrants for Saif Al-Islam[161] and Al-Senussi[162] on 27 June 2011 for their alleged criminal responsibility as indirect co-perpetrators on two counts of crimes against humanity—murder under Article 7(1)(a) and persecution under Article 7 (1)(h) of the Rome Statute—committed in Benghazi and other Libyan cities by members of the armed forces under their control during the uprising between 15 and 28 February 2011.[163]

In response, Libya brought admissibility challenges against both decisions before the Court in accordance with Article 19(2)(b) of the Rome Statute.[164] On 1 May 2012, the NTC challenged the admissibility of the case against Saif Al-Islam before the ICC. Basing its challenge on Article 17(1)(a) of the Rome Statute and claiming its willingness and ability genuinely to carry out the investigation and prosecution of Saif Al-Islam, Libya asserted that its national judicial system was

[159] ICC (2010), para. 246.

[160] Kleffner (2008), p. 161.

[161] ICC (2011b).

[162] ICC (2011c).

[163] The court has never referred to the situation in Libya as an armed conflict or to alleged war crimes although many commentators have described the conflict during the last week of February 2011 as a civil war. This fact was also confirmed by the Court's Prosecutor when he noted that his allegations did not include war crimes committed during the armed conflict that erupted at the end of February 2011. Accordingly, one may argue that the warrants of arrest should be amended to include war crime committed at a later time, including gender-based crimes mentioned in the Prosecutor's third report on Libya.

[164] ICC (2012b).

actively investigating the suspect for his alleged criminal responsibility for acts of murder and persecution amounting to crimes against humanity, committed as a part of a widespread or systematic attack against Libyan civilians in Tripoli, Benghazi, and Misrata in February 2011.[165]

Moreover, Libya offered other facts that would demonstrate the above claim, including the fact that it had requested the assistance of the UN High Commissioner for Human Rights ('UNHCHR') and other organizations to help in training judges and prosecutors with a particular focus on litigation related to transitional justice.[166] At the same time, Libya warned the court at the outset of its admissibility motion that denying the Libyan people the historic opportunity to eradicate the country's long-standing culture of impunity by investigating and prosecuting Saif Al-Islam would be inconsistent with the principle of complementarity enshrined in the provisions of the Rome Statute, which assigns great importance to the national judicial system.[167]

The Libyan application also pointed out that, even in other post-conflict situations far more difficult than the one prevailing in Libya, there had been no rush to conclude that the national judicial system was incapable of dealing with the cases before it. To illustrate this point, Libya referred to the case law of the Court, particularly its jurisdiction on the *Lubanga case*, where the PTCI concluded—after certain changes were made to the national judicial system of the Democratic Republic of Congo ('DRC')—that the Prosecution's argument (i.e., that the DRC's national judicial system was dysfunctional in light of Articles 17(1) & (3) of the Rome Statute) no longer held.[168] Accordingly, Libya petitioned the Court to postpone the order for the surrender of Saif Al-Islam, pursuant to Article 85 of the Rome Statute, and requested under Article 19 that the Court declare the case against him inadmissible and invalidate his surrender request.[169]

In response to Libya's challenge, as outlined above, the Prosecutor raised a central question regarding Libya's ability to adequately investigate and prosecute Saif Al-Islam who has been kept in the custody of the Zintan Brigade, a powerful armed group operating outside the control of the NTC.[170] He also indirectly touched upon the international due process rights of the accused by indicating that Libya had not yet either appointed an attorney for him or demonstrated its ability to actually investigate and prosecute Saif Al-Islam.[171] The OPCD basically raised the same concerns as before and underlined the NTC's lack of qualified judges and prosecutors to investigate and prosecute the suspect.[172] Moreover, the

[165] ICC (2012b).

[166] ICC (2012b), para. 97.

[167] Ibid., para. 2.

[168] ICC (2006a), para. 37.

[169] ICC (2012b), paras. 107–108.

[170] ICC (2012g), para. 8.

[171] Ibid., paras. 8 and 41.

[172] ICC (2012h), paras. 369–381.

OPCD argued that Libya also lacked the power to protect the actors in the criminal justice system, as well as the witnesses, from deadly attacks launched by different armed groups.[173] As well, the NTC had no authority to execute the orders of judges made with respect to this case.[174]

After 2 days of admissibility hearings held on 9 & 10 October 2012,[175] in which the OTP and the OPCD expressed their concerns about the ability of Libya to provide a fair trial to Saif Al-Islam, followed by Libya's submission of further information in support of its admissibility challenge,[176] the PTCI rendered its decision on 31 May 2013, rejecting Libya's admissibility challenge, determining that the case against Saif Al-Islam is admissible, and reminding Libya of its obligation to surrender Saif Al-Islam to the Court.[177] In the course of the admissibility hearings, the OPCD had issued a number of issues to be addressed by Libya's representative team, including the lack of security in the country and the absence there of the rule of law,[178] the failure of the judicial system to bring Saif Al-Islam and other detainees before a judge without undue delay,[179] and the capability of the judicial system to deliver justice to Saif Al-Islam when it has completely failed to provide him with due process rights, such as to be brought before a judge, to have legal counselling, and to have a suitable time and facilities to prepare his defence.[180] This was in spite of the position adopted by the OTP however, which has endorsed Libya's assertions and supported its admissibility challenge, believing that Libya was investigating the case against Saif Al-Islam properly and in keeping with the Court's standards, and arguing that trying Saif Al-Islam in a Libyan court would eradicate the culture of impunity that has prevailed there for the past four decades.[181]

In the aftermath of the hearings, and at the request of the Court, Libya submitted additional information on 23 January 2013, including 23 public and confidential annexes, addressing critical issues raised during the hearing sessions and related to its admissibility challenge.[182] To demonstrate the efficiency of its judicial system, Libya advised the Court that on 23 December 2012, the Supreme Court of Libya had abolished the procedure of the People's Court used in the case of Buzeid Dorda, unanimously declaring it to be unconstitutional.[183] Further, it added that Saif Al-Islam would be tried as a Libyan public officer in view of his unofficial position

[173] Ibid., paras. 382–404.
[174] Ibid., paras. 405–408.
[175] ICC (2012i).
[176] ICC (2012a).
[177] ICC (2013f), para. 220.
[178] ICC (2012j), para. 4.
[179] Ibid., para. 10.
[180] ICC (2012k), para. 18.
[181] ICC (2012j), para. 58.
[182] ICC (2012a).
[183] Ibid., paras. 75–76.

as a *de facto* prime minister.[184] Libya also elaborated upon assistance received from the international community, particularly the UNSMIL, in terms of improving its criminal justice system.[185]

Additional support for the Libyan position came when the OTP submitted its response to Libya's submissions on 12 February 2013,[186] revealing, *inter alia*, that the case against Saif Al-Islam had progressed and that Libyan legislation permitted trial *in absentia*.[187] In other words, the OTP reinforced its position regarding the ability of Libya to try Saif Al-Islam on a fair basis, on the one hand, and contradicted the OPCD's claim regarding Libya's ability to prosecute Saif Al-Islam *in absentia*, on the other.

Soon after this, the OPCD identified still further issues in its response of 18 February 2013 to Libya's submissions, including: the failure of the Libyan judicial system to carry out in practice the decision of the Libyan Supreme Court, which had annulled the People's Court procedures;[188] Libya's ambiguity over its adoption of the controversial "Isolation Law", which requires the dismissal of judges and other actors in the judicial system who served under the former regime's administration—a decision that could affect the independence and impartiality of the Libyan judicial system;[189] and Libya's failure to provide concrete answers to the PTCI's inquiry regarding witness protection and security.[190]

Finally, the PTCI delivered its decision on 31 May 2013, confirming the admissibility of the case against Saif Al-Islam and requesting Libya that surrender him to the Court.[191] The PTCI grounded its ruling on materials placed before it, which revealed that Libya was neither actively investigating the same case as that before the Court[192] nor pursuing the defendant for the conduct that formed the object of the ICC's proceedings.[193] In this respect, the PTCI recalled its ruling in the *Lubanga* case, emphasizing that for a case to be inadmissible before the Court, the State's judicial proceedings should "encompass both person and the conduct which is the subject of the case before the Court".[194]

As further reinforcement of its decision on the admissibility of the case against Saif Al-Islam, the PTCI also cited the Appeals Chamber's interpretation of Article 17(1)(a) of the Rome Statute in its judgement on the appeal of *Katanga* against the decision of the Trial Chamber II of 12 June 2009. In considering an admissibility

[184] Ibid., para. 85.
[185] Ibid.
[186] ICC (2013a).
[187] ICC (2013c), para. 3.
[188] ICC (2013b), para. 169.
[189] Ibid., paras. 170–173.
[190] Ibid., paras. 222–257.
[191] ICC (2013f).
[192] Ibid., paras. 134–135.
[193] Ibid., para. 70.
[194] ICC (2006b), para. 31.

challenge, the Appeals Chamber provided that the above article proposes a two-step test, which shall address in turn two questions: the first is whether the State with jurisdiction, at the time of the proceedings in respect of an admissibility challenge, is investigating and prosecuting the same case that is before the ICC, and the second is, should the answer to the first question be in the affirmative, whether the state is unwilling or simply unable to carry out such investigation or prosecution.[195]

In addressing the first question, the PTCI focussed on whether Libya was investigating and prosecuting the same person—Saif Al-Islam—for substantially the same conduct attributed to him in the warrant of arrest issued by the same chamber on 27 June 2011.[196] In this conduct-based interpretation of the same case test, carried out on the basis of the available materials, the PTCI found that Libya's investigation covered only "certain discrete aspects" of the case before the ICC,[197] and, accordingly, determined that the same conduct test had not been met.

In addressing the second part of the admissibility test—i.e., to decide whether Libya was genuinely able to investigate and prosecute Saif Al-Islam—the PTCI determined that Libya was clearly unable to genuinely carry out the proceedings against him, and, therefore, found that there was no need to address the alternative requirement of willingness.[198] The PTCI maintained that Libya continued to face persistent challenges that compromised its ability to exercise its judicial powers fully across the country.[199] These difficulties include, *inter alia*: Libya's inability to secure the transfer of Saif Al-Islam from Zintan militia custody into the Libyan government's authority,[200] a situation that would prevent national proceedings from taking place, particularly as *in absentia* trials are not permitted under Libyan law when the accused is present on Libyan territories;[201] the inability of the Libyan judicial system to obtain the necessary testimony due to the lack of control by governmental authorities and the failure of the latter to provide adequate witness protection;[202] and finally, the failure of the Libyan authorities either to ensure that Saif Al-Islam have access to his own choice of legal counsel or at the very least to appoint a lawyer to represent him.[203] For the above reasons, the PTCI ruled that Libya was unable to carry out national proceedings against Saif Al-Islam in the light of the provisions of Article 17(3) of the Rome Statute.[204]

In response to the PTCI's decision, the government of Libya filed its appeal against the latter on 7 June 2013. Pursuant to Articles 19(6), 82(1)(a) and 82(2) of

---

[195] ICC (2009), paras. 1 and 75–79.
[196] ICC (2013f), paras. 77–78.
[197] Ibid., para. 134.
[198] Ibid., para. 216.
[199] Ibid., para. 205.
[200] Ibid., para. 206.
[201] Ibid., para. 208.
[202] Ibid., para. 209.
[203] Ibid., para. 209.
[204] Ibid., para. 205.

the Rome Statute, Libya asked the Appeals Chamber to revoke the PTCI's decision on the admissibility of the case against Saif Al-Islam, and to determine that the case against him is inadmissible. Moreover, pursuant to Article 82(3) of the Rome Statute, it requested that the Appeals Chamber suspend the order for the surrender of the accused pending determination of the appeal.[205] It is worth mentioning here that Libya had established its appeal on the basis of four grounds, i.e.: (a) that the PTCI had erred in law by holding that the Libyan authorities had failed to satisfy the "same conduct" test under article 17(1)(a) of the Rome Statute; (b) that it had erred in finding that Libya has not proven that its national investigation encompasses the same case as that before the Court; (c) that it had erred by failing to "take appropriate measures for the proper conduct of the procedure", thus depriving Libya of the ability to rely upon highly relevant evidence in support of its admissibility challenge; and (d) that it was wrong in considering that Libya had fallen short of obtaining custody of Saif Al-Islam, and that accordingly it was unable to carry out its proceedings, pursuant to article 17(3) of the Rome Statute.[206]

On 18 July 2013, the Appeals Chamber delivered its decision on the request of Libya to suspend the surrender of Saif Al-Islam to the Court, and on other related issues. It turned down the Libyan government's request and its application for leave to file a consolidated reply to the defence response to Libya's request for suspension effect, while the final decision on the admissibility challenge is pending.[207]

Already in this respect, the OPCD had requested on 7 June 2013 that the PTCI's judges make a finding of non-compliance with regards to the failure of the government of Libya to immediately surrender Saif Al-Islam to Court.[208] Then on 23 July 2013, the OPCD filed a motion before the PTCI requesting it find: (a) that the government of Libya had repeatedly failed to carry out the PTCI's orders to surrender Saif Al-Islam to the Court; (b) that it had failed, pursuant to Article 97 of the Rome Statute, to consult with the Court without delay with regard to compliance with the surrender request; and (c) that Libya be referred to the UN Security Council for non-compliance with the Court's orders to turn over Saif Al-Islam to the Hague.[209] Still later, on 9 December 2013, the OPCD submitted an urgent request to the PTCI to issue an immediate ruling on the above decisions.[210] In the light of the absence of a ruling from the PTCI, the OPCD submitted a request for leave to Appeal in relation to whether the PTCI had erred in failing to issue a decision on the OPCD's above requests.[211]

Ultimately, on 21 May 2014, the Appeals Chamber handed down its judgment on the appeal of Libya against the decision of the PTCI of 31 May 2013 regarding

[205] ICC (2013g), paras. 11–12.
[206] ICC (2014b), para. 45.
[207] ICC (2013k), paras. 23 and 27.
[208] ICC (2013h), para. 10.
[209] ICC (2013l), para. 17.
[210] ICC (2013t), para. 10.
[211] ICC (2014a), para. 88.

the admissibility of the case against Saif Al-Islam. The judgement, which dismissed Libya's plea to prosecute Saif Al-Islam on its own soil and reinforced its overdue obligation to relinquish him to the Court, was adopted by a majority, with a separate concurring opinion by Judge Sang-Hyun Song, and a dissenting opinion by Judge Anita Ušacka. The Appeals Chamber thus confirmed the PTCI's decision to reject Libya's request to investigate and prosecute the accused in Libya. It also held that Libya had fallen short of providing enough evidence to establish that it was investigating the same case as that before the Court.[212] Furthermore, it rejected Libya's allegations that the PTCI had made procedural errors when delivering its decision on the admissibility of the case against Saif Al-Islam.[213]

Justice Song however added a separate opinion to the judgement, arguing that Libya was indeed investigating the case against Saif Al-Islam. He nevertheless concluded by confirming that he could find no clear error or unreasonableness in the PTCI's decision on the admissibility of the case, as Libya was unable to obtain custody over the accused.[214] By contrast, Justice Ušacka's dissenting opinion maintained that the PTCI's decision on the admissibility of the case against Saif Al-Islam was based on an erroneous interpretation of the first limb of Article (17)(1)(a) of the Rome Statute, as well as on its application as a result.[215] For this reason, she suggested that the Impugned Decision of the PTCI should be reversed and sent back to the Chamber for new consideration.[216] As a final point, it should be noted that the above Appeals Chamber decision was final and that no further appeal will be possible.

4.3 Libya's Challenge to the Admissibility of the Case Against Al-Senussi

Pursuant to Article 19 of the Rome Statute, the government of Libya filed a challenge to the admissibility of the case against Al-Senussi on 2 April 2013. It requested of the PTCI that it declare the case relating to Al-Senussi inadmissible, and quash the surrender order pertaining to him.[217] Libya grounded its application on several arguments: (a) that, based on the extensive evidence annexed in support of its application, it had carried out concrete and specific investigative steps in relation to the case of Al-Senussi, who was being actively investigated by the Libyan national judicial system since 9 April 2012 for the same charges as those before the ICC;[218] (b) that the range of the Libyan investigation of Al-Senussi was

[212] ICC (2014b), para. 213.

[213] Ibid., para. 146.

[214] ICC (2014c), para. 36.

[215] ICC (2014d), para. 46.

[216] Ibid., para. 66.

[217] ICC (2013d), para. 206.

[218] Ibid., para. 36.

significantly broader than the Court's investigation, for while the Court's investigation is limited to alleged crimes committed between 15 and 18 February 2011, the Libyan national judicial system has been investigating him for crimes committed during the revolution until the fall of the Gaddafi regime, as well as other serious crimes committed before the revolution (including the Abu Selim prison massacre, which took place on 27 June 1996, where 1270 prisoners were brutally murdered);[219] (c) that Libya emphasized how its investigation of the case against Al-Senussi was not in any way vitiated by "unwillingness" or "inability" on its part;[220] (d) that the investigation of Al-Senussi conducted by the national judicial system demonstrated that Libya had no reason to shield Al-Senussi from accountability;[221] and (e) that Libya stressed how there was no evidence or well-founded reason to establish that it was either unable or unwilling to carry out a genuine investigation into the Al-Senussi case.[222]

However, Libya's admissibility challenge application was subsequently followed by written submissions filed by parties and participants to the proceedings. On 24 April 2013, the OPCD filed a response on behalf of Al-Senussi to Libya's request for postponement of the surrender of Al-Senussi to the Court. The OPCD asked the PTCI to reject Libya's demand to postpone the surrender request of Al-Senussi pursuant to Article 95 of the Rome Statute, and to emphasize its order to hand him over to the ICC.[223] The PTCI issued a twofold decision, replying to Libya's request to postpone the surrender of Al-Senussi pursuant to Article 95 of the Rome Statute, and to the OPCD's demand to refer Libya to the UN Security Council. The PTCI decided that Libya might postpone the execution of the surrender request issued by the PTCI on 4 July 2011, until the determination on the admissibility challenge.[224] Moreover, The PTCI found the OPCD's request to refer Libya to the UN Security Council on account of its failure to surrender Al-Senussi to the ICC to be unwarranted and of no benefit. Accordingly, it rejected the OPCD's request to make a finding of non-cooperation by Libya and refer the matter to the UN Security Council.[225]

Consequently, the OPCD filed an application on 9 August 2013, on behalf of Al-Senussi to refer Libya to the UN Security Council with confidential *Ex Parte* Annex 1. The OPCD requested that the PTCI find, pursuant to Articles 87(5) & (7), that Libya was in non-compliance with the PTCI's order of 6 February 2013, and to refer it to the UN Security Council.[226] Moreover, the OPCD submitted on

[219] ICC (2013d), para. 160.
[220] Ibid., para. 36.
[221] Ibid., para. 195.
[222] Ibid., para. 39.
[223] ICC (2013e), para. 63.
[224] ICC (2013i), para. 42.
[225] Ibid., para. 44.
[226] ICC (2013o), para. 27.

9 September 2013 its appeal to the Appeals Chamber on behalf of Al-Senussi against the PTCI's decision on Libya's postponement of execution of the request for arrest and surrender of Al-Senussi pursuant to Article 95 of the Rome Statute, and related the OPCD's request to refer Libya to the UN Security Council. The OPCD submitted a double-barrelled appeal: (a) it was at odds with the PTCI's decision finding that Libya had not unduly failed to file its challenge of admissibility in a timely manner "at the earliest opportunity," in violation of Article 19(5) of the Rome Statute;[227] and (b) the OPCD stated that the PTCI had erred in rejecting its arguments that Libya took custody of Al-Senussi from Mauritania in violation of the ICC's orders to surrender him to the Court; that Libya had formed the explicit intention to try him in Libya regardless of the ICC's decision; and that Libya had violated Al-Senussi's due process rights, including not having allowed him access to legal counsel.[228]

The Prosecution submitted its response to the Appeals Chamber on 20 September 2013, asserting that the OPCD's above arguments were groundless, and that its appeal should be dismissed.[229] The Prosecution provided that the OPCD had failed to demonstrate how the PTCI abused its discretion and erred when it found that Libya's admissibility challenge was not belated, with reference to Article 19(5) of the Rome Statute. The Prosecution emphasized that the PTCI was correct when decided that Libya's admissibility challenge was submitted at the earliest opportunity within the terms of the above article, and that it had also correctly disregarded the OPCD's submissions on Libya's taking custody of Al-Senussi, following his extradition from Mauritania, in violation of the Court's orders.[230]

Notwithstanding Libya's violations of Al-Senussi's due process rights—including depriving him the right to appear before a judge without undue delay;[231] the failure to provide him with legal representation;[232] the lack of independence and impartiality of the Libyan judicial system;[233] Libya's lack of control over detention facilities;[234] and the lack of security and witness protection impeding testimonies in the case of Al-Senussi,[235] the PTCI concluded in its decision of 11 October 2013 that Libya was not unwilling or unable genuinely to carry out its proceedings in relation to the case against Al-Senussi. Accordingly, it declared this case inadmissible before the ICC, pursuant to Article 17(1)(a) of the Rome Statute, and to be subject to domestic proceedings conducted by the Libyan competent authorities.[236]

[227] ICC (2013p), para. 12.
[228] Ibid., para. 45.
[229] ICC (2013q), para. 14.
[230] Ibid., para. 27.
[231] ICC (2013j), para. 163.
[232] Ibid., para. 144.
[233] Ibid., para. 244.
[234] Ibid., para. 93.
[235] Ibid., para. 72.
[236] ICC (2013r), para. 311.

Moreover, the PTCI recalled Article (19)(10) of the Rome Statute, which provides that

> [i]f the Court has decided that a case is inadmissible under article 17, the Prosecutor may submit a request for review of the decision when he or she is fully satisfied that new facts have arisen which negate the basis on which the case had previously been found inadmissible under article 17.[237]

In challenging the PTCI's decision, the OPCD filed an appeal on 17 October 2013, pursuant to Articles (19)(6), 82(1)(9), 82(3) and 83(2)(a) of the Rome Statute, as well as to Rules 154(1) & (156) of the Rules of Procedure and Evidence, and to Regulations 33(1)(d) & 64 of the regulations of the Court.[238] The OPCD requested the Appeals Chamber to reserve the PTCI's admissibility decision of 11 October 2013 and determine that the case against Al-Senussi is admissible before the Court.[239] It also asked the Appeals Chamber that this appeal have suspensive effect on the PTCI's decision of 11 October 2013, so that Libya should not try Al-Senussi until the Appeals Chamber would have rendered its final judgement on the admissibility of the case.[240]

After examining the three grounds of the OPCD's appeal submitted on 17 October 2013, the Appeals Chamber handed down its judgement on 24 July 2014.[241] It found no errors in the findings of the PTCI that Libya was not unwilling or unable to genuinely prosecute Al-Senussi. Accordingly, it dismissed the OPCD's appeal and unanimously confirmed the PTCI's decision, which declared the case against Al-Senussi inadmissible before the Court.[242] Despite their agreement with the majority of the Appeals Chamber that the impugned decision of the PTCI be confirmed and the OPCD's appeal rejected, Judge Sang-Hung Song and Judge Anita Ušacka appended separate opinions to the judgement. Judge Song disagreed with the conclusion of the majority that

> the Pre-Trial Chamber found that, as a matter of law, the specific incidents alleged against Mr. Al-Senussi did not form part of the comparator in deciding on whether Libya is investigating the same case. The Appeals Chamber recalls that this is not in line with the jurisprudence of the Appeals Chamber just cited, which considers such incidents to play a central role in this comparison.[243]

For her part, Judge Ušacka recalled her dissenting opinion to the Appeals Chamber's judgement on Libya's appeal against the PTCI's decision—finding the case against Saif Al-Islam to be admissible—where she addressed the interpretation of the term "same case" in Article 17(1) of the Rome Statute.[244] In the light of that

---

[237] ICC (2013r), para. 312.

[238] ICC (2013s), para. 1.

[239] Ibid., para. 11.

[240] Ibid., para. 19.

[241] ICC (2014e), para. 66.

[242] Ibid., para. 196.

[243] ICC (2013m), para. 1.

[244] ICC (2014d), paras. 47–59 and 63–65.

interpretation, she disagreed with the interpretation and application of the "same person/same conduct" test, as set out in section IV.A.2.(c)(ii) of the majority judgement.[245] Moreover, she offered dissenting remarks on the majority judgement regarding aspects of the interpretation of Article 17(1)(a) of the Rome Statute, as well as on the notions of "unwillingness" and "inability" enshrined in Article 17(2) and (3) of the Rome Statute.[246]

4.4 *Were the Court's Decisions on the Admissibility of the Cases Against Saif Al-Islam and Al-Senussi Consistent?*

The theoretical understandings of the complementarity regime, enshrined within the provisions of the Rome Statute, do seem to be at odds with the practical interpretations developed in the Court's decisions—outlined above—on the admissibility of the cases against Saif Al-Islam and Al-Senussi. These contradictory decisions[247] have raised unprecedented questions regarding the impact of the violations of a defendant's due process rights on the Court's ruling on the admissibility of a case before it. While many commentators emphasize the conventional explanation of Article 17 of the Rome Statute—by arguing in favour of declaring the admissibility of a case when a State fails to guarantee a defendant's due process rights,[248] others argue that the admissibility of a case should be determined on the basis of the competence of national criminal system to convict a defendant and deter impunity, regardless of fair trial violations.[249]

245 ICC (2013n), para. 6.

246 Ibid., paras. 8–16.

247 Svaček (2013), p. 18. One may argue that the PTCI had failed to recognize inconsistency between its ruling on the admissibility of the case against Al-Senussi and its own earlier verdict on the admissibility of the case against Saif Al-Islam, delivered on 31 May 2013. In the latter decision, the PTCI rejected Libya's admissibility challenge due to the lack of legal representation, which factor it basically ignored in arriving at its decision on the admissibility of the case against Al-Senussi. A recent Chatham House report, entitled "The International Criminal Court and Libya: Complementarity in Conflict," elucidates three different elements that played a significant role in the adoption of the Court's divergent decisions: (a) differences in the amount and quality of evidence and testimony required in each case, since the investigation into the case of Saif Al-Islam is broader than Al-Senussi's (in Saif Al-Islam's case, the evidence covers Benghazi and other cities, while in Al-Senussi it covers Benghazi alone); (b) the suspects are detained in two different detention facilities, Al-Senussi in a government-controlled prison in Tripoli, and Saif Al-Islam in the custody of a militia in Zintan outside the control of the Libyan authorities; and (c) and the prosecution's differing opinions regarding the admissibility challenges submitted by the government of Libya. While the Prosecutor endorsed Libya's request to declare Al-Senussi's case inadmissible before the Court, he opposed Libya's admissibility challenge of the case against Saif Al-Islam.

248 Walker (2014), p. 315.

249 Mégret and Samson (2013), p. 573.

On the basis of the above discussion, one can ask whether the failure of a State to provide a defendant with due process rights should require the Court to step in and declare the case admissible under Article 20(3), and determine that this failure constitutes inability or unwillingness to investigate or prosecute under Article 17(2) & (3) of the Rome Statute, or *par contre*, defer to the State as long as it has the intent to bring the accused to justice regardless of the unfairness of the proceedings.[250]

In their interpretations of the above articles, many scholars support the first part of the inquiry, arguing that a State's failure to assure a defendant due process rights shall make a case admissible under Article 17, which stresses the quality of justice from the perspective of both procedural and substantive fairness.[251] By contrast, some scholars argue that considering a State "unable" under Article 17 if it fails to provide a fair trial to a defendant is unreasonable. Kevin Jon Heller, for example, argues that it is difficult to declare a functioning national judicial system unavailable or collapsed because it cannot deliver perfect due process.[252] Even Luis Moreno-Ocampo, the former Prosecutor of the ICC, went further than that in a press conference during his visit to Libya, on 22 November 2011, in the aftermath of the capture of Saif Al-Islam by the Zintan brigade on 19 November 2011. He explicitly provided that the ICC is not a court of human rights, but is interested primarily in the genuineness of the proceedings rather than the fairness of the trial.[253] On the other hand, Elinor Fry proposed a moderate explanation of this issue, which provides that the lack of basic due process rights for an accused—not the lack of complete compliance with the international due process standards—is a realistic standard for regarding a State as "unable" under the provisions of Article 17.[254]

According to the above arguments, a case could be declared inadmissible—regardless of the failure of a State to provide the defendant with sufficient due process rights, although it leads to an unfair trial—if the State demonstrates that it is willing to bring the defendant to justice.[255] So, the case against Al-Senussi will remain inadmissible since Libya has expressed its willingness to investigate and prosecute him under its criminal judicial system on the one hand, and not to allow him to enjoy impunity or to carry out the investigation and prosecution of him with the intent to shield him from justice.[256]

Nonetheless, regardless of these distinct arguments, Article 17(3) clearly provides that in order to determine the inability of a State in a particular case, the Court should consider the availability of the following measures: (a) the total or

[250] Fry (2012), p. 40.

[251] Heller (2006), p. 259.

[252] ICC (2003), p. 42.

[253] O'Donohue and Rigney (2012), p. 2.

[254] Fry (2012), p. 42.

[255] Fry (2012), p. 44; Bishop (2013), p. 406.

[256] ICC (2013d), para. 102.

substantial collapse or unavailability of the State's national judicial system; (b) the failure of a State to obtain the accused; (c) the State's inability to obtain the necessary evidence and testimony; or (d) the State's inability to carry out its proceedings.[257]

5 Conclusion

This chapter argued that the post-Gaddafi Libyan criminal justice system is not the proper judicial mechanism to undertake the prosecutions of Saif Al-Islam Gaddafi and Abdullah Al-Senussi for international core crimes allegedly committed by former Libyan government agents against the civilian population across Libya during the February 2011 popular uprising. In pursuing this analysis, this chapter first examined the prospects of prosecuting international core crimes under Libya's transitional justice. It started by shedding some light on the basis of the prosecution of international core crimes, defined in the Rome Statute and in national courts. Then it proceeded to review Libya's criminal justice system by looking into the provisions of the Libyan Penal Code, as well as into the Libyan laws of the transitional period. Second, it brought to light four major challenges to the prosecution of international core crimes under Libya's transitional justice, namely: legal impunity and lawlessness; the rule of militias' justice vs. rule of law; the failure to provide standard fair trials; and the lack of criminal justice reform. Finally, it considered the complementarity regime of the ICC and the admissibility of Libya's cases against Saif Al-Islam and Al-Senussi. It offered some reflections on the complementarity principle enshrined in the provisions of the Rome Statute, reviewed Libya's challenge to the admissibility of the cases against both Saif Al-Islam and Al-Senussi, and finally, underlined the ICC's inconsistent decisions on the admissibility of the above cases.

Moreover, this chapter maintained that the Court's decision on the inadmissibility of the case of Al-Senussi offends the principles of fundamental justice, particularly the right to life, as Libya has made it clear that Al-Senussi could be sentenced to death if convicted in Libya. It also infringes other legal principles and concepts, including the offender's right to be tried without undue delay, as well as the right to fair trial and sentencing. The incompetence of the current Libyan transitional justice system, manifested in: the failure to incorporate international core crimes and international human rights law into the provisions of Libya's penal law; the lack of the rule of law vs. militia justice; legal impunity and lawlessness; the absence of security and public order; and the lack of trained judicial actors

[257] Treaties (1998). In contrast with the principle of legality, which is enshrined in Article 22 of the Rome Statute, this article makes no mention of the failure of a State to incorporate international core crimes into its national criminal code as a valid reason to consider it "unable" to investigate and prosecute these crimes.

would impede access to justice for Al-Senussi and leave Libyans' peace-building process open to the danger of collapse.

The continuous escalation in violence in Tripoli and across the country between rival militias has increased threats and physical attacks on actors in the Libyan judicial system, including judges, prosecutors, and lawyers, and has consequently put Libya's fragile transition at risk. The sharp decline in the country's security situation and the failure of the Libyan authorities to rein in militias has thrown Libya into increasing chaos, impairing thereby the government's power to gain control over detainees in militia-run detention centres, to conduct independent investigations and prosecutions, and to provide them with basic due process rights. These violations include not having access to lawyers of their choice, lack of legal counselling during interrogation sessions, and the lack of judicial review of their cases. The security vacuum has placed the country on the horns of a dilemma and has challenged the Libyan judicial system to guarantee something that it cannot deliver, i.e., that Saif Al-Islam and Al-Senussi, as well as other 35 officials of the former regime, will receive fair trials at Libyan Courts. The failure of the Libyan government to provide them with basic due process rights is incongruous with its pledge to provide them with justice, and the evidence shows that Libya is unable to prosecute them at the present time.

In sum, this inquiry reveals that Libya has no criminal jurisdiction over international core crimes committed on Libyan soil since the toppling of the former regime in the fall of 2011, and accordingly, it should surrender Saif Al-Islam to The Hague and make self-referral of Al- Senussi's case to the ICC under Article 14 of the Rome Statute. To support peace and justice in Libya, therefore, it is recommended that the prosecutor of the ICC request the Court to review the inadmissibility decision of the case against Al-Senussi under Article 19(10) of the Rome Statute, on the one hand, and to refer Libya to the UN Security Council under Article 87—which permits the Court to issue a finding of non-compliance—to oblige the Libyan Government to surrender Saif Al-Islam to the ICC, on the other.

Post Scriptum

On July 28, 2015, while this work was in print, the Appeals Court of Tripoli delivered its judgment in the case No. 630/2012 against 37 prominent officials of the former Libyan regime. As anticipated by this chapter, the Court sentenced Saif Al-Islam, Abdullah Al-Senussi, and seven other former high-ranking regime officials to death by firing squad. It also gave sentences ranging from five years to life imprisonment to 23 other former officials; acquitted four defendants, and referred one for medical treatment. The trial, which was critically undermined by serious due process violations, has underlined the failure of the Libyan transitional judicial system to offer fair trials to defendants and to deliver justice in the post-Gaddafi era.

References

Secondary Sources

Akande, D. (2012, June 18). The immunity of the ICC Lawyers and staff detained in Libya. Blog of the *European Journal of International Law*. http://www.ejiltalk.org/the-immunity-of-the-icc-lawyers-and-staff-detained-in-libya/. Accessed 31 May 2015.

Amnesty. (2011a, September). *The battle for Libya: Killings, disappearances and torture*. Amnesty International. Index: MDE 19/025/2011.

Amnesty. (2011b, October). *Detention abuses staining the new Libya*. Index: MDE 19/036/2011.

Amnesty. (2011c, September). *Libya: Human rights agenda for change*. Index: MDE 19/028/2011.

Amnesty. (2012a, 7 September). *Fair trials still out of reach in Libya*. Amnesty International Canada.

Amnesty. (2012b, 5 July). *Libya: Rule of law or rule of militias*? Amnesty International. Index: MDE 19/012/2012.

Amnesty. (2012c, February). *Militias threaten hopes for new Libya*. Amnesty International. Index: MDE 19/002/2012.

Amnesty. (2014a). *Fair trial manual* (2nd ed.). London: Amnesty International Publications.

Amnesty. (2014b, March). *Libya: Fair trial rights for Saadi al-Gaddafi must be respected*. Index: MDE 19/002/20147.

Amnesty. (2014c, October), *Rule of the gun: Abductions, torture and other militia abuses in Western Libya*. Index: MDE 19/009/2014.

Amnesty. (2014d, April). *Trial of former Libyan officials including Saif Al-Islam Al-Gaddafi and Abdullah al-Senussi*. Index: MDE19/003/2014.

Bassiouni, M. C. (Ed.). (2013). *Libya from repression to revolution: A record of armed conflict and international law violations, 2011–2013*. Leiden, the Netherlands: Martinus Nijhoff.

Ben-Halim, M. A. (1992). *Forgotten pages from Libya's political history*. London.

Bishop, A. (2013). Failure of complementarity: The future of the International Criminal Court following the Libyan admissibility challenge. *Minnesota Journal of International Law, 22*, 388–421.

Bo, M. (2014). The situation in Libya and the ICC understands of complementarity in the context of UNSC-referred cases. *Criminal Law Forum, 25*(3–4), 505–540.

Cockburn, P. (2013, 10 October). Libya: Ali Zeidan's abduction perfectly illustrates failure of the post-Gaddafi State. *The Independent*. http://www.independent.co.uk/voices/comment/libya-ali-zeidans-abduction-perfectly-illustrates-failure-of-the-postgaddafi-state-8871516.html. Accessed 23 Mar 2015.

Dumbryte, A. (2014). Assessing ability and willingness of states what can the ICC learn from International Refugee Law? *Journal of International Criminal Justice, 12*(5), 997–1017.

El Zeidy, M. M. (2008). *The principle of complementarity in International Criminal Law: Origin, development and practice*. Leiden, the Netherlands: Martinus Nijhoff.

Fry, E. (2012). Between show trials and sham prosecutions: The Rome Statute's potential effect on domestic due process protections. *Criminal Law Forum, 23*(1–3), 35–62.

Fry, E. (2013). International Criminal Court. *Netherlands Quarterly of Human Rights, 31*(2), 217–226.

Goldstone, R. (2012, 22 June). ICC's Libyan crisis shows Saif Gaddafi should be tried in The Hague. *The Guardian*. http://www.theguardian.com/law/2012/jun/22/icc-libya-crisis-saif-gaddafi-hague. Accessed 23 Mar 2015.

Gordon, G. (2011). Complementarity and alternative forms of justice: A new test for ICC admissibility. In C. Stahn & M. M. El Zeidy (Eds.), *The International Criminal Court and complementarity: From theory to practice* (pp. 745–806). New York: Cambridge University Press.

Heller, K. J. (2006). The shadow side of complementarity: The effect of Article 17 of the Rome Statute on national due process. *Criminal Law Forum, 17*(3–4), 255–280.

Heller, K. J. (2013). The International Commission of inquiry on Libya: A critical analysis. In J. Meierhenrich (Ed.), *International Commissions: The role of commissions of inquiry in the investigation of international crimes*. Available at SSRN: http://ssrn.com/abstract=2123782.

Hobbs, H. O. (2012–2013). The security council and the complementary regime of the International Criminal Court: Lessons from Libya. *Eyes on the ICC, 9*(1), 19–51.

Homes, H. (2012, 7 September). Fair trials still out of reach in Libya. *Global Public Square*. http://globalpublicsquare.blogs.cnn.com/2012/09/07/fair-trials-still-out-of-reach-in-libya. Accessed 30 May 2015.

HR Watch. (2012a, 11 May). Libya: Amend new special procedures law. *Human Rights Watch*.

HR Watch. (2012b, 3 July). Libya: ICC staff detentions raise justice concerns – Incident undermines lawyers' independence. *Human Rights Watch*.

HR Watch. (2014). *Priorities for legislative reform: A human rights roadmap for a new Libya*. New York: Human Rights Watch.

HR Watch. (2015a, 30 September). Hanan Salah, "Lawlessness in Libya." *Human Rights Watch*. http://www.hrw.org/news/2013/09/30/lawlessness-libya. Accessed 30 May 2015.

HR Watch. (2015b, 14 April). Hanan Salah, "Libya's Justice Pandemonium." *Human Rights Watch*. http://www.hrw.org/news/2014/04/14/libyas-justice-pandemonium. Accessed 30 May 2015.

Jordanian Ambassador. (2014, 15 April). Jordanian Ambassador to tripoli abducted by gunmen. *The Guardian*. http://www.theguardian.com/world/2014/apr/15/libya-jordanian-ambassador-tripoli-abducted-gunmen. Accessed 23 Mar 2015.

Kersten, M. (2014). Justice after the war: The International Criminal Court and post-Gaddafi Libya. In K. J. Fisher & R. S. Abingdon (Eds.), *Transitional justice and the Arab Spring* (pp. 188–207). New York: Routledge.

Kleffner, J. K. (2008). *Complementarity in the Rome Statute and national criminal jurisdictions*. New York: Oxford University Press.

Mancini, M. (2012). The day after: Prosecuting international crimes committed in Libya. *Italian Yearbook of International Law*, 85–109.

Mangan, F., & Murtaugh, C. (2014). *Security and justice in post-revolution Libya: Where to turn?* Washington, DC: United States Institute of Peace.

Mégret, F., & Samson, M. G. (2013). Holding the line on complementarity in Libya: The case for tolerating flawed domestic trials. *Journal of International Criminal Justice, 11*(3), 571–589.

Nouri, A. (2013). *The principle of complementarity and Libya challenge to the admissibility before the International Criminal Court*. LL.M., Lund University.

O'Donohue, J., & Rigney, S. (2012, 8 June). The ICC must consider fair trial concerns in determining Libya's application to prosecute Saif al-Islam Gaddafi nationally. Blog of the *European Journal of International Law*. http://www.ejiltalk.org/the-icc-must-consider-fair-trial-concerns-in-determining-libyas-application-to-prosecute-saif-al-islam-gaddafi-nationally/. Accessed 2 June 2015.

Schabas, W. A. (2010). *The International Criminal Court: A commentary on the Rome Statute*. Oxford, England: Oxford University Press.

Shenkman, C. (2012). Catalyzing national judicial capacity: The ICC's first crimes against humanity outside armed conflict. *New York University Law Review, 87*, 1210–1248.

Stephen, C. (2013, 5 September). Libyan police unit admits kidnapping ex-spy chief's daughter. *The Guardian*. http://www.theguardian.com/world/2013/sep/05/libyan-police-kidnap-senussi-daughter. Accessed 23 Mar 2015.

Stigen, J. (2008). *The relationship between the International Criminal Court and national jurisdictions: The principle of complementarity*. Leiden, the Netherlands: Martinus Nijhoff.

Supreme Court. (2014, 6 November). Libya Supreme Court rules anti-Islamist Parliament unlawful. *The Guardian*. http://www.theguardian.com/world/2014/nov/06/libya-court-tripoli-rules-anti-islamist-parliament-unlawful. Accessed 2 June 2015.

Svaček, O. (2013). Review of the International Criminal Court's case-law 2013. *International and Comparative Law Review, 13*(2), 5–24.
Walker, A. (2014). The ICC versus Libya: How to end the cycle of impunity for atrocity crimes by protecting due process. *UCLA Journal of International Law and Foreign Affairs, 18*, 303–354.
Zawati, H. M. (2014a). *Fair labelling and the dilemma of prosecuting gender-based crimes at the International Criminal Tribunals*. New York: Oxford University Press.
Zawati, H. M. (2014b). The challenge of prosecuting conflict-related gender-based crimes under Libyan transitional justice. *Journal of International Law and International Relations, 10*, 44–91.

Legislation

Libyan Laws (2013a), *Law No. (10)) for the Year* 2013 *on the Criminalization of Torture, Forced Disappearance, and Discrimination*, General National Congress, Libya, 14 April 2013.
Libyan Laws (2013b), *Law No. (13) for the Year* 2013 on *Political and Administrative Isolation*, General National Congress, Libya, 5 May 2013.
Libyan Laws (2013c), *Law No. (29) for the Year 2013 on Transitional Justice*, General National Congress, Libya, 2 December 2013.
Libyan Laws (2012a), *Law No. (17) for the Year 2012 on Establishing the Rules of National Reconciliation and Transitional Justice*, National Transitional Council, Libya, 26 February 2012.
Libyan Laws (2012b), *Law No. (26) for the Year 2012 on the High Commission for the Application of National Standards and Integrity*, National Transitional Council, Libya, 4 April 2012.
Libyan Laws (2012c), *Law No. (35) for the Year 2012 on Amnesty for Some Crimes*, National Transitional Council, Libya, 2 May 2012.
Libyan Laws (2012d), *Law No. (38) for the Year 2012 on Some Special Measures Regarding the Transitional Period*, National Transitional Council, Libya, 2 May 2012.
Libyan Laws (2011), *The Constitutional Declaration*, National Transitional Council, Libya, 3 August 2011.
Libyan Laws (1999), Libyan Arab Jamahiriya, *Libyan Code of Criminal Procedure for Armed Personnel* (1999).
Libyan Laws (1975), *Prisons Law No. (47) for the Year 1975*, Al-Jarida Al-Rasmiyya, 1975-23-06, Vol. 13, No. 30, pp. 1-914-939, Libya, Adopted on 23 June 1975.
Libyan Laws (1953), *Libyan Penal Code*, 28 November 1953.
Libyan Laws (1951), *The Constitution of Libya*, Contained 213 articles, was promulgated by the National Constituent Assembly on 7th October 1951 and abolished by a military *coup d'etat* on 1st September 1969. Available online at http://www.libyanconstitutionalunion.net/constitution%20of%20libya.htm (Accessed on: 21 May 2015).

UN Documents

UN (2014), United Nations High Commissioner for Human Rights, *Technical Assistance for Libya in the Field of Human Rights*, UN Doc. A/HRC/25/42 (13 January 2014).
UN (2013), United Nations Support Mission in Libya, Office of the United Nations High Commissioner for Human Rights, *Torture and Deaths in Detention in Libya*, (October 2013).
UN (2011), UN Security Council's Resolution 1970 (2011), *Situation Referred to International Criminal Court* (26 February 2011), UN Doc. S/RES/1970 (2011).

International Treaties

Treaties (2006), *International Convention for the Protection of All Persons from Enforced Disappearance*, G.A. res. 61/177, U.N. Doc. A/RES/61/177 (2006), (Adopted on 20 December 2006).

Treaties (2002), *Optional Protocol to the Convention against Torture and other Cruel, Inhuman or Degrading Treatment or Punishment*, G.A. res. A/RES/57/199, Adopted on 18 December 2002 at the fifty-seventh session of the General Assembly of the United Nations by Resolution A/RES/57/199, *Reprinted in* 42 I.L.M. 26 (2003. (Entered into force on 22 June 2006).

Treaties (1998), *Rome Statute of the International Criminal Court*, UN Doc. A/CONF.183/9 (17 July 1998), 37 I.L.M. 999–1069 (Entered into force on 1 July 2002).

Treaties (1984), *Convention against Torture and Other Cruel, Inhuman or Degrading Treatment or Punishment*, G.A. res. 39/46, [Annex, 39 U.N. GAOR Supp. (No. 51) at 197, U.N. Doc. A/39/51 (1984)], (Entered into force on 26 June 1987).

Treaties (1978a), *Protocol Additional to the Geneva Conventions of 12 August 1949, and Relating to the Protection of Victims of International Armed Conflicts*, (Protocol I), Opened for signature on 12 December 1977, 1125 U.N.T.S. 3 (Entered into force on 7 December 1978).

Treaties (1978b), *Protocol Additional to the Geneva Conventions of 12 August 1949, and Relating to the Protection of Victims of Non-International Armed Conflicts*, (Protocol II), Opened for signature on 12 December 1977, 1125 U.N.T.S. 609 (Entered into force on 7 December 1978).

Treaties (1966), *International Covenant on Civil and Political Rights*, (1966), GA Rex. 2200 (XXI), 21 UN GAOR, Supp. (No. 16) at 52, UN Doc. A/6316 (1966), 999 U.N.T.S. 302, 1976 Can. T.S. No. 47 (1966). (Entered into force on 23 March 1976).

Treaties (1965), *International Convention on the Elimination of All Forms of Racial Discrimination*, (1965), GA Res. 2106A (XX), 20 UN GAOR, Supp. (No. 14) at 47, UN Doc. A/6014 (1965), 660 U.N.T.S. 195, 1970 Can. T.S., No. 28 (1965). (Entered into force on 4 January 1969).

Treaties (1957), *Supplementary Convention on the Abolition of Slavery, the Slave Trade, and Institutions and Practices Similar to Slavery*, 226 U.N.T.S. 3, (Entered into force on 30 April 1957).

Treaties (1950), European Convention for the Protection of Human Rights and Fundamental Freedoms, (ETS No. 5), 213 U.N.T.S. 222, Entered into force on 3 September 1953, as amended by Protocols Nos. 3, 5, 8, and 11.

Treaties (1949a), *Convention for the Amelioration of the Condition of the Wounded and Sick in Armed Forces in the Field (Geneva I), Opened* for signature 12 August 1949, 6 U.S.T. 3114, T. I.A.S. No. 3362, 75 U.N.T.S. 31 (Entered into force on 21 October 1950).

Treaties (1949b), *Convention for the Amelioration of the Condition of Wounded, Sick and Shipwrecked Members of Armed Forces at Sea (Geneva II)*, 75 U.N.T.S. 85 (Entered into force on 21 October 1950).

Treaties (1949c), *Convention Relative to the Treatment of Prisoners of War (Geneva III), Opened* for signature 12 August 1949, 6 U.S.T. 3316, T.I.A.S. No. 3364, 75 U.N.T.S. 135 (Entered into force on 21 October 1950).

Treaties (1949d), *Convention Relative to the Protection of Civilian Persons in Time of War (Geneva IV)*, Opened for signature 12 August 1949, 6 U.S.T. 3516, T.I.A.S. No. 3365, 75 U.N.T.S. 287 (Entered into force on 21 October 1950).

Treaties (1948a), *Convention on the Prevention and Punishment of the Crime of Genocide*, 9 December 1948, GA Res. 260A (III), 3 UN GAOR at 174, UN Doc. A/810 (1948).

Treaties (1948b), *Universal Declaration of Human Rights*, Adopted on 10 December 1948, GA Res. 217A (III), 3 UN GAOR (Resolutions, part 1) at 71, UN Doc. A/810 (1948); Reprinted in 43 American Journal of International Law Supp. 127 (1949).

Treaties (1945), *United Nations Charter*, (1945), Signed at San Francisco, 26 June 1945. 59 Stat. 1031, T.S. 993, 3 Bevans 1153, (Entered into force on 24 October 1945).

Treaties (1932), *Convention Concerning Forced or Compulsory Labour* (ILO No. 29), 39 U.N.T. S. 55, (Entered into force on 1 May, 1932).

ICC Documents

ICC (2014a), *Prosecutor* v. *Saif Al-Islam Gaddafi & Abdullah Al-Senussi*, Public redacted version of "Request for Leave to Appeal the Pre-Trial Chamber's Failure to Issue a Decision," Pre-Trial Chamber I, Case No.: ICC-01/11-01/11 (10 March 2014).

ICC (2014b), *Prosecutor* v. *Saif Al-Islam Gaddafi & Abdullah Al-Senussi,* Judgment on the Appeal of Libya against the Decision of Pre-Trial Chamber I of 31 May 2013 entitled "Decision on the Admissibility of the Case against Saif Al-Islam Gaddafi," the Appeals Chamber, Case No.: ICC-01/11-01/11 OA 4 (21 May 2014).

ICC (2014c), *Prosecutor* v. *Saif Al-Islam Gaddafi & Abdullah Al-Senussi,* Separate Opinion of Judge Sang-Hyun Song: Judgment on the Appeal of Libya against the Decision of Pre-Trial Chamber I of 31 May 2013 entitled "Decision on the Admissibility of the Case against Saif Al-Islam Gaddafi," the Appeals Chamber, Case No.: ICC-01/11-01/11 OA 4 (21 May 2014).

ICC (2014d), *Prosecutor* v. *Saif Al-Islam Gaddafi & Abdullah Al-Senussi,* Dissenting Opinion of Judge Anita Ušacka: Judgment on the Appeal of Libya against the Decision of Pre-Trial Chamber I of 31 May 2013 entitled "Decision on the Admissibility of the Case against Saif Al-Islam Gaddafi," the Appeals Chamber, Case No.: ICC-01/11-01/11 OA 4 (21 May 2014).

ICC (2014e), *Prosecutor v. Saif Al-Islam Gaddafi & Abdullah Al-Senussi*, Judgment on the Appeal of Mr Abdullah Al-Senussi against the Decision of Pre-Trial Chamber I of 11 October 2013 Entitled "Decision on the Admissibility of the Case against Abdullah Al-Senussi," the Appeals Chamber, Case No.: ICC-OI/II-OI/IIOA6 (24 July 2014).

ICC (2013a), *Prosecutor* v. *Saif Al-Islam Gaddafi & Abdullah Al-Senussi*, Prosecution's Response to "Libyan Government's Further Submissions on the Issues Related to the Admissibility of the Case against Saif al-Islam Gaddafi," Pre-Trial Chamber, Case No.: ICC-01/11-01/11 (12 February 2013).

ICC (2013b), *Prosecutor* v. *Saif Al-Islam Gaddafi & Abdullah Al-Senussi*, Public Redacted Version of the "Response to the Libyan Government's Further Submissions on Issues Related to Admissibility of the Case against Saif Al-Islam Gaddafi," Pre-Trial Chamber, Case No.: ICC-01/11-01/11 (18 February 2013).

ICC (2013c), *Prosecutor* v. *Saif Al-Islam Gaddafi & Abdullah Al-Senussi*, Prosecution's Notice of Withdrawal Regarding a Reference in its "Prosecution's Response to Libyan Government's Further Submissions on Issues Related to the Admissibility of the Case against Saif al-Islam Gaddafi," (ICC-01/11-02/22-276-Red 2), Pre-Trial Chamber, Case No.: ICC-01/11-01/11 (19 February 2013).

ICC (2013d), *Prosecutor* v. *Saif Al-Islam Gaddafi & Abdullah Al-Senussi*, Application on Behalf of the Government of Libya Relating to Abdullah Al-Senussi Pursuant to Article 19 of the ICC Statute, Pre-Trial Chamber I, Case No.: ICC-01/11-01/11 (2 April 2013).

ICC (2013e), *Prosecutor* v. *Saif Al-Islam Gaddafi & Abdullah Al-Senussi*, Response on Behalf of Abdullah Al-Senussi to the Submission of the Government of Libya for Postponement of the Surrender Request for Mr. Al-Senussi, Pre-Trial Chamber I, Case No.: ICC-01/11-01/11 (24 April 2013).

ICC (2013f), *Prosecutor* v. *Saif Al-Islam Gaddafi & Abdullah Al-Senussi,* Decision on the Admissibility of the Case against Saif Al-Islam Gaddafi, Pre-Trial Chamber I, Case No.: ICC-01/11-01/11 (31 May 2013).

ICC (2013g), *Prosecutor* v. *Saif Al-Islam Gaddafi & Abdullah Al-Senussi,* The Government of Libya's Appeal against Pre-Trial Chamber I's "Decision on the Admissibility of the Case

against Saif Al-Islam Gaddafi," the Appeals Chamber, Case No.: ICC-01/11-01/11 (7 June 2013).
ICC (2013h), *Prosecutor* v. *Saif Al-Islam Gaddafi & Abdullah Al-Senussi*, Request for Finding of Non-Compliance, Pre-Trial Chamber I, Case No.: ICC-01/11-01/11 (7 June 2013).
ICC (2013i), *Prosecutor* v. *Saif Al-Islam Gaddafi & Abdullah Al-Senussi*, Decision on Libya's Postponement of the Execution of the Request for Arrest and Surrender of Abdullah Al-Senussi Pursuant to Article 95 of the Rome Statute and Related Defence Request to Refer Libya to the UN Security Council, Pre-Trial Chamber I, Case No.: ICC-01/11-01/11 (14 June 2013).
ICC (2013j), *Prosecutor* v. *Saif Al-Islam Gaddafi & Abdullah Al-Senussi*, Defence Response on Behalf of Mr. Abdullah Al-Senussi to "Application on Behalf of the Government of Libya Relating to Abdullah Al-Senussi Pursuant to Article 19 of the ICC Statute," Pre-Trial Chamber I, Case No.: ICC-01/11-01/11 (14 June 2013).
ICC (2013k), *Prosecutor* v. *Saif Al-Islam Gaddafi & Abdullah Al-Senussi*, Decision on the Request for Suspensive Effect and Related Issues, The Appeals Chamber, Case No.: ICC-01/11-01/11 OA 4 (18 July 2013).
ICC (2013l), *Prosecutor* v. *Saif Al-Islam Gaddafi & Abdullah Al-Senussi*, Request for Finding of Non-Compliance and Referral to United Nations Security Council, Pre-Trial Chamber I, Case No.: ICC-01/11-01/11 (23 July 2013).
ICC (2013m), *Prosecutor* v. *Saif Al-Islam Gaddafi & Abdullah Al-Senussi*, Separate Opinion of Judge Sang-Hyun Song: Judgment on the Appeal of Mr Abdullah Al-Senussi against the Decision of Pre-Trial Chamber I of 11 October 2013 Entitled "Decision on the Admissibility of the Case against Abdullah Al-Senussi," the Appeals Chamber, Case No.: ICC-OI/II-OI/IIOA6 (24 July 2013).
ICC (2013n), *Prosecutor* v. *Saif Al-Islam Gaddafi & Abdullah Al-Senussi*, Separate Opinion of Judge Anita Ušacka: Judgment on the Appeal of Mr Abdullah Al-Senussi against the Decision of Pre-Trial Chamber I of 11 October 2013 Entitled "Decision on the Admissibility of the Case against Abdullah Al-Senussi," the Appeals Chamber, Case No.: ICC-OI/II-OI/IIOA6 (24 July 2013).
ICC (2013o), *Prosecutor* v. *Saif Al-Islam Gaddafi & Abdullah Al-Senussi*, Defence Application on behalf of Mr. Abdullah Al-Senussi to refer Libya to the Security Council with Confidential *Ex Parte* (Chamber only) Annex 1, Pre-Trial Chamber I, Case No.: ICC-01/11-01/11 (9 August 2013).
ICC (2013p), *Prosecutor* v. *Saif Al-Islam Gaddafi & Abdullah Al-Senussi*, Appeal on behalf of Mr. Abdullah Al-Senussi against the "Decision on Libya's Postponement of the Execution of the Request for Arrest and Surrender of Abdullah Al- Senussi Pursuant to Article 95 of the Rome Statute and Related Defence Request to Refer Libya to the UN Security Council," Pre-Trial Chamber I, Case No.: ICC-01/11-01/11 (9 September 2013).
ICC (2013q), *Prosecutor* v. *Saif Al-Islam Gaddafi & Abdullah Al-Senussi*, Prosecution's Response to the "Appeal on behalf of Mr. Abdullah Al-Senussi against the "Decision on Libya's Postponement of the Execution of the Request for Arrest and Surrender of Abdullah Al-Senussi Pursuant to Article 95 of the Rome Statute and Related Defence Request to Refer Libya to the UN Security Council," Pre-Trial Chamber I, Case No.: ICC-01/11-01/11 (20 September 2013).
ICC (2013r), *Prosecutor* v. *Saif Al-Islam Gaddafi & Abdullah Al-Senussi,* Decision on the Admissibility of the Case against Abdullah Al-Senussi, Pre-Trial Chamber I, Case No.: ICC-01/11-01/11 (11 October 2013).
ICC (2013s), *Prosecutor* v. *Saif Al-Islam Gaddafi & Abdullah Al-Senussi*, Appeal on Behalf of Abdullah Al-Senussi against Pre-Trial Chamber I's "Decision on the Admissibility of the Case against Abdullah Al-Senussi," and Request for Suspensive Effect, the Appeals Chamber, Case No.: ICC-01/11-01/11 (17 October 2013).
ICC (2013t), *Prosecutor* v. *Saif Al-Islam Gaddafi & Abdullah Al-Senussi*, Urgent Request for Ruling on Requests for Finding of Non-Compliance, Pre-Trial Chamber I, Case No.: ICC-01/11-01/11 (9 December 2013).

ICC (2012a), *Prosecutor* v. *Saif Al-Islam Gaddafi & Abdullah Al-Senussi*, Libyan Government's Further Submissions on Issues Related to the Admissibility of the Case Against Saif al-Islam Gaddafi, Pre-Trial Chamber, Case No.: ICC-01/11-01/11 (23 January 2012).

ICC (2012b), *Prosecutor* v. *Saif Al-Islam Gaddafi & Abdullah Al-Senussi*, Application on Behalf of the Government of Libya Pursuant to Article 19 of the ICC Statute, Pre-Trial Chamber I, Case No.: ICC-01/11-01/11 (1 May 2012).

ICC (2012c), *Prosecutor* v. *Saif Al-Islam Gaddafi & Abdullah Al-Senussi*, Libyan Government's Filing of Compilation of Libyan Law Referred to in its Admissibility Challenge, Pre-Trial Chamber I, Case No.: ICC-01/11-01/11 (28 May 2012).

ICC (2012d), *Prosecutor* v. *Saif Al-Islam Gaddafi & Abdullah Al-Senussi*, Libyan Government's Filing of Compilation of Libyan Law Referred to in its Admissibility Challenge, Pre-Trial Chamber I, Case No.: ICC-01/11-01/11 (28 May 2012).

ICC (2012e), *Prosecutor* v. *Saif Al-Islam Gaddafi & Abdullah Al-Senussi*, Libyan Government's Filing of Compilation of Libyan Law Referred to in its Admissibility Challenge, Pre-Trial Chamber I, Case No.: ICC-01/11-01/11 (28 May 2012).

ICC (2012f), *Prosecutor* v. *Saif Al-Islam Gaddafi & Abdullah Al-Senussi*, Libyan Government's Filing of Compilation of Libyan Law Referred to in its Admissibility Challenge, Pre-Trial Chamber I, Case No.: ICC-01/11-01/11 (28 May 2012).

ICC (2012g), *Prosecutor* v. *Saif Al-Islam Gaddafi & Abdullah Al-Senussi*, Prosecution Response to Application on Behalf of the Government of Libya Pursuant to Article 19 of the ICC Statute, Pre-Trial Chamber, Case No.: ICC-01/11-01/11 (5 June 2012).

ICC (2012h), *Prosecutor* v. *Saif Al-Islam Gaddafi & Abdullah Al-Senussi*, Defense Response to the Application on Behalf of the Government of Libya Pursuant to Article 19 of the ICC Statute, Pre-Trial Chamber, Case No.: ICC-01/11-01/11 (31 July 2012).

ICC (2012i), *Prosecutor* v. *Saif Al-Islam Gaddafi & Abdullah Al-Senussi*, Hearing on the Admissibility Challenge, Pre-Trial Chamber, Case No.: ICC-01/11-01/11 (9 October 2012).

ICC (2012j), *Prosecutor* v. *Saif Al-Islam Gaddafi & Abdullah Al-Senussi*, Hearing on the Admissibility Challenge, First Day Transcript, Pre-Trial Chamber, Case No.: ICC-01/11-01/11 (9 October 2012).

ICC (2012k), *Prosecutor* v. *Saif Al-Islam Gaddafi & Abdullah Al-Senussi*, Hearing on the Admissibility Challenge, Second Day Transcript, Pre-Trial Chamber, Case No.: ICC-01/11-01/11 (10 October 2012).

ICC (2011a), Prosecutor's Application Pursuant to Article 58 as to Muammar Mohammed Abu Minyar Gaddafi, Saif Al-Islam Gaddafi and Abdullah Al-Senussi, Pre-Trial Chamber I, Case No.: ICC-01/11 (16 May 2011).

ICC (2011b), Warrant of Arrest for Saif al-Islam Qadhafi, ICC Pre-Trial Chamber I, No. ICC-01/11 (27 June 2011).

ICC (2011c), Warrant of Arrest for Abdullah Al-Senussi, ICC Pre-Trial Chamber I, No. ICC-01/11 (27 June 2011).

ICC (2010), *Prosecutor* v. *Jean-Pierre Bemba Gombo*, Decision on the Admissibility and Abuse of Process Challenges, Trial Chamber III, Case No.: ICC-01/05-01/08 (24 June 2010) para. 246.

ICC (2009), *Prosecutor* v. *Germain Katanga and Mathieu Ngudjolo Chui*, Judgment on the Appeal of Mr. Germain Katanga against the Oral Decision of Trial Chamber II of 12 June 2009 on the Admissibility of the Case, The Appeals Chamber, Case No.: ICC-01/04-01/07 OA 8 (25 September 2009).

ICC (2006a), *Prosecutor* v. *Lubanga*, Decision on the Prosecutor's Application for a Warrant of Arrest, Article 58, Case No.: ICC- 01/04- 01/07, Pre-Trial Chamber 1 (10 February 2006).

ICC (2006b), *Prosecutor* v. *Thomas Lubanga Dyilo*, Decision Concerning Pre-Trial Chamber I's Decision of 10 February 2006 and the Incorporation of Documents into the Record of the Case against Mr Thomas Lubanga Dyilo, ICC-01/04-01/06-8-Corr. (24 February 2006).

ICC (2003), "An Informal Expert Paper: The Principle of Complementarity in Practice," Online: Office of the Prosecutor, the International Criminal Court (2003) http://www.icc-cpi.int/iccdocs/doc/doc654724.pdf (Accessed on: 13 June 2015), at 8–9.

Reports

Report (2015). *Corporate Report: Libya – Country of Concern*, in Human Rights and Democracy Report 2013, Online: Foreign & Commonwealth Office, UK, Updated on (21 January 2015) https://www.gov.uk/government/publications/libya-country-of-concern/libya-country-of-concern#access-to-justice-and-the-rule-of-law. (Accessed on: 12 June 2015).

Report (2014a). *Libya: Judiciary and Security Sector*, Office of the Commissioner General for Refugees and Stateless Persons, UK (19 December 2014).

Report (2014b). *Libya: Two Victims of Enforced Disappearance Reappear and Describe the Conditions of Detention and the Torture Practiced in Libyan Prisons*, Online: Alkarama (26 June 2014) http://www.pressreleasepoint.com/libya-two-victims-enforced-disappearance-reappear-and-describe-conditions-detention-and-torture-prac. Accessed on: 12 June 2015).

Report (2013a). *Lawyers for Justice in Libya Concerned by Attacks on Judges and Lawyers in Libya*, Online: Lawyers for Justice in Libya (LFJL), (19 June 2013) http://www.libyanjustice.org/news/news/post/92-lawyers-for-justice-in-libya-concerned-of-attacks-on-judges-and-lawyers-in-libya (Accessed on: 12 June 2015).

Report (2013b). *Trial by Error: Justice in Post-Qadhafi Libya*, International Crisis Group, Middle East/North Africa Report No. 140 (17 April 2013).

Report (2012a). *Legal Digest of International Fair Trial Rights* (Warsaw, Poland: Published by the OSCE Office for Democratic Institutions and Human Rights (ODIHR), 2012).

Report (2012b). "Milestones in International Criminal Justice: Victims' Rights and Complementarity," by Online: Chatham House (28 February 2012) https://www.chathamhouse.org/sites/files/chathamhouse/public/Research/International%20Law/280212summary.pdf. Accessed on: 2 June 2015).

Report (2012c). *The Reform of Judiciaries in the Wake of the Arab Spring*: *Proceedings of the Seminar, 11–12 February 2012, Rabat*, Euro-Mediterranean Human Rights Network (May 2012).

DNA Evidence Under the Microscope: Why the Presumption of Innocence Is Under Threat in Ireland

Michelle-Thérèse Stevenson

1 Introduction

A miniscule molecule has transformed criminal investigations during the past three decades. Since the discovery of DNA (deoxyribonucleic acid) profiling in 1984, the power of this tiny molecule has become so great that it has already usurped the atom as the new 'scientific icon' of the twenty-first century.[1] In fact, DNA evidence is often feted as a 'gold standard' of forensic evidence, capable of transcending subjectivity and bias.[2] However, although the DNA molecule has achieved this level of recognition due to its capacity to exonerate the innocent, it has more recently started to accrue a degree of notoriety for its role in inculpating the innocent. In truth, what actually lies beneath its gilded exterior is a warning that criminal justice systems are failing to differentiate between misleading DNA evidence and powerful DNA evidence.[3]

In order to scrutinise how these issues may affect the presumption of innocence in the Irish jurisdiction, the chapter is divided into four sections. The first section provides an analysis of how DNA evidence works. The second section investigates why the interpretation of certain DNA evidence continues to pose problems for science and consequently the courts. The third section of the chapter turns to an analysis of the presumption of innocence and its current status in the Irish jurisdiction. The concluding section of the chapter discusses recent case law surrounding DNA evidence in Ireland and evaluates the potential impact of the Criminal Justice (Forensic Evidence and Database System) Act 2014 on the presumption of

[1] Kaye (2010).

[2] Dror and Hampikian (2011), pp. 204–208.

[3] Thompson et al. (2003a, b), pp. 16–25 and 47–54.

M.-T. Stevenson (✉)
Centre for Crime, Justice and Victim Studies, University of Limerick, Limerick, Ireland
e-mail: Michelle.stevenson@ul.ie

A. Diver, J. Miller (eds.), *Justiciability of Human Rights Law in Domestic Jurisdictions*, DOI 10.1007/978-3-319-24016-9_11

innocence in the jurisdiction, drawing on the findings outlined in the three preceding sections of the chapter.

2 A Brief Outline of Some Problems with DNA Evidence

It is a relatively simple matter to *exclude* someone as the contributor of forensic evidence. The potential pitfalls lie in determining who may have been the contributor of evidence found at a crime scene.[4] Masked by DNA's iconic status there lies a simple and frequently overlooked truth. From the taking of forensic samples until its presentation in court, DNA evidence is completely reliant on fallible and subjective human interaction which may also be subject to bias. The interpretation of mixed DNA profiles is a potential casualty of these fallibilities. A mixed DNA profile is made up of samples from more than one contributor and is therefore quite commonplace at crime scenes. However, for some time the scientific community has been warning that there are a number of problems surrounding the interpretation of these mixed samples. These concerns may not only pose problems for the courts, they also raise a number of human rights concerns. To be specific, they may pose a number of threats to the presumption of innocence.

The presumption of innocence is a fair trial right at the heart of a democracy. It is also a fundamental human right set out in Article 6.2 of the European Convention of Human Rights ('ECHR') ratified by Ireland in 2003. DNA evidence, often vital in securing convictions, is becoming increasingly relied upon in the Irish jurisdiction and this is highlighted by the introduction of The Criminal Justice (Forensic Evidence and Database System) Act 2014. In order to explore the impact of these potential problems surrounding mixed DNA interpretation on the presumption of innocence in the jurisdiction, it is first of all essential to understand how DNA biotechnology actually works.

2.1 *Back to Basics: What Is DNA?*

Forensic genetics works on the fundamental principle that—apart from identical twins—every one of us is unique.[5] Half of our genome (our genetic makeup in other words) is inherited from our mother and the other half comes from our father.[6] This genetic material is found in the DNA molecule in the 'form of chromosomes.'[7] Our chromosomes are in turn found in the nucleus of all of our cells with the exception

[4] Wayne (2011).
[5] Butler (2010).
[6] Swanson et al. (2010).
[7] Aronson (2007).

of the red blood cells, which do not have a nucleus. It is important to note here that chromosomes have coding and non-coding regions. The coding regions determine a person's physical traits; however, the non-coding regions are the focus of this chapter because they exhibit more variation than the coding regions.[8]

The DNA molecule that is tightly packed within these chromosomes comprises two spiralling strands which are sometimes referred to as the double helix. These strands are linked together in a ladder-like structure by four nucleotide bases called adenine, thymine, guanine and cytosine—abbreviated to A, T, G and C. These nucleotide bases bind together in strict pairs and in a regular pattern: bases A and T always bind together and similarly, bases G and C always bind together.[9]

2.2 *The Double Helix*

See Fig. 1.

2.3 *Development of DNA Profiling and DNA Databases*

In 1984, the geneticist Sir Alec Jeffreys, publisher of the first DNA profile, discovered quite by chance that the repeating patterns of these base pairs of DNA sequences occur next to each other.[10] What became more relevant to criminal justice systems, however, was his discovery that these patterns vary from person to person. To put it another way, by developing a technique to examine these DNA pattern variations, Alec Jeffreys had in fact discovered the means of distinguishing one person from another.[11] It was this discovery that led to the genesis of DNA fingerprinting (or DNA profiling as it is more commonly labelled today). In criminal investigations, an equally crucial stepping stone in the rapid expansion of the use of DNA evidence has been the development of government databases for storing DNA profiles and this is more fully explored in Sect. 4. Briefly, these databases allow the police to compare a suspect's DNA profile with those held on a database.

[8] Puch-Solis et al. (2012).

[9] *Ibid.*

[10] Butler (2010).

[11] *Ibid.*

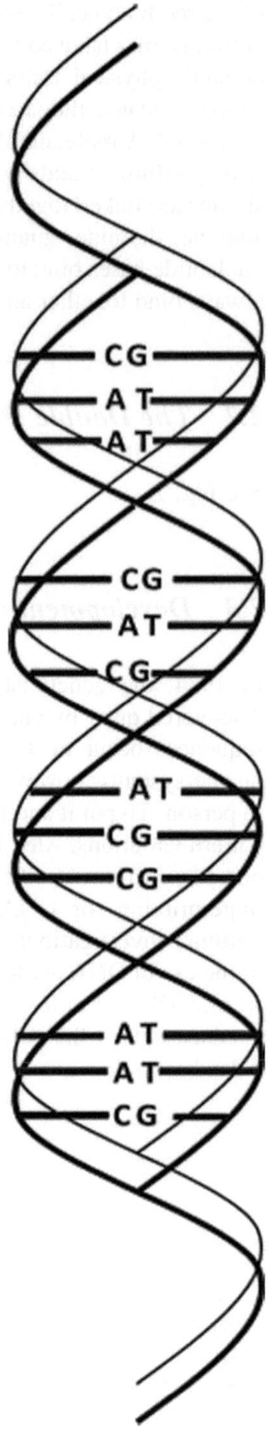

Fig. 1 Shows the ladder-like structure of the DNA molecule—the double helix—comprising nucleotide base pairs of cytosine and guanine (*CG*) and adenine and thymine (*AT*). These base pairs produce the repeating sequences that occur next to each other. The discovery that these patterns vary from one person to another led to the birth of DNA profiling

2.4 *DNA Profiles and DNA Profiling Today*

A DNA profile is basically a chart (which may be stored on a database) which has a graphic display of genetic information located at a number of regions called *loci* within the human genome.[12] DNA profiling on the other hand, works by sampling a number of these *loci*. In criminal justice investigations, an individual's DNA profile is compared against a DNA profile taken from either the suspect or the victim and then compared with that of a sample found at a crime scene.[13] However, forensic profiling does not require the reconstruction of a person's entire DNA sequence to do this.[14] The most common profiling method used today is short tandem repeat analysis (generally abbreviated to STR analysis). These STRs contain the short repeating DNA sequences that vary from one person to another. Otherwise put, DNA profiling involves the analysis of a small, selected number of these STRs. The number of STRs examined in a DNA profile varies between jurisdictions. In Ireland, for example, 10 regions (that is, STRs) of DNA are examined by the national forensic science laboratory, Forensic Science Ireland (formerly the Forensic Science Laboratory).[15]

In short, a DNA profile can provide the measurements for these STRs and it can express the short sequences of the base pairs (AT and CG) which are repeated multiple times: these measurements are called *alleles* and they appear as peaks on a DNA profile.[16] So, the two *allelelic* peaks represent the genetic material inherited from each parent.

3 Presenting DNA Evidence in Court

The presentation of DNA evidence in court generally relies on the comparison of an individual's DNA profile with that of a sample population. Traditionally, the prosecution has tended to rely on swaying juror opinion with almost vanishingly tiny and/or massive numbers that stretch far beyond every day experience and comprehension. In terms of forensic genetics, it is noted that a sample population is defined as a group of people who share a common ancestry.[17] It has also been noted that the probative value of a DNA match is presented to fact finders in the form of frequency statistics that illustrate how common a DNA profile is in this sample population.[18] In other words,

---

[12] Thompson et al. (2003b).

[13] Heffernan and Ní Raifeartaigh (2014).

[14] Puch-Solis et al. (2012).

[15] The Law Reform Commission (2005).

[16] Puch-Solis et al. (2012).

[17] Goodwin et al. (2007).

[18] Koehler (2001), pp. 1275–1305.

> a DNA match statistic of, say, one in one million means that approximately one person out of every one million will match that DNA profile. An equivalent way to say this is that the chance that a randomly selected person will match this DNA profile is one in one million....it is (therefore) unlikely that the match between a suspect and a recovered crime scene sample is purely coincidental.[19]

However, probability analysis is not always this straight-forward. It often requires very much more complex statistical reasoning from the fact finder and it has, on occasion, presented the courts with a number of challenges that have led to a number of miscarriages of justice. Clearly, this raises a number of human rights concerns in relation to the safeguarding of suspects' rights in relation to the presumption of innocence.

3.1 Fallacious Statistical Reasoning

One clear problem identified by research is that not only jurors but also judges may have a tendency to view DNA evidence as infallible.[20] As a result of this inclination, it is said that problematic calculations of random match probabilities that are confidently presented by the prosecution in court may go unchallenged by the fact finder and automatically taken as fact.[21] Indeed, the prosecutor's fallacy, which refers to fallacious statistical reasoning relating to the assessment of guilt or innocence of a suspect, was labelled by Thompson and Schumann in 1987.[22] It not only accounts for a number of miscarriages of justice, it also graphically illustrates the potentially serious consequences of any failure on behalf of the fact finder or defence to challenge complex and confidently presented (albeit erroneous) statistical information. The Irish Law Reform Commission (LRC) has noted the potential dangers posed by this fallacious reasoning, observing that the error might be made not only by an expert witness or counsel—but also by a judge in his or her summing up.[23] As the error could also be made by the jury, the LRC has stressed the importance that judges and counsel remain on their guard against it in cases reliant on DNA evidence.

---

[19] *Ibid.*

[20] Briody (2004), pp. 231–252.

[21] Prainsack (2010), pp. 15–39.

[22] Thompson and Schumann (1987), pp. 167–187.

[23] The Law Reform Commission (2005).

3.2 *Is DNA Profiling Really Infallible?*

Irrespective of these issues, the use of this impressive biotechnology has grown exponentially during the past two decades: there have also been substantial improvements in the speed of laboratory analysis.[24] This period has also seen the emergence of a new cultural phenomenon which is generally acknowledged to account for the tendency to view DNA evidence as infallible. This phenomenon, labelled the *CSI effect,* refers to the ubiquitous television series *CSI: Crime Scene Investigation.* In this television show, forensic science and DNA have actually taken centre stage as the heroes of the show—promoting the mind-set that forensic DNA is wholly objective.[25] As previously stated, it has been demonstrated that jurors and even judges may not be immune to this perception. It is also argued that the 'rhetoric of infallibility' that surrounds DNA is also accountable for the rapid development of government DNA databases in jurisdictions.[26]

The very real dangers that this misconception may prompt were in fact manifested in 2008 in a rape case in Australia, *R v Jama,*[27] which involved the collection and contamination of DNA samples. The Vincent Inquiry that conducted the investigation into this miscarriage of justice concluded that the universally popular belief in the infallibility of DNA evidence led to forensic samples being regarded with 'an almost mystical infallibility that enabled [their] surroundings to be disregarded. The outcome was, in the circumstances, patently absurd.'[28]

Shortly after *Jama*, the extent to which the roles of subjectivity and human bias may play in the laboratory—and which co-exist alongside the issues raised over the dangers of viewing DNA evidence as infallible—were unveiled in a groundbreaking experimental study. These are now evaluated in the second section of the chapter.

4 DNA, Subjectivity and Human Bias in the Laboratory

The scientific community has been 'embarrassed' by fundamental problems with DNA testing for some time.[29] These problems clearly challenge the perception that DNA evidence is wholly objective and capable of providing criminal justice systems with consistently unassailable and truthful evidence.[30] Research into

[24] Butler (2010).

[25] Prainsack (2010).

[26] Thompson (2008).

[27] *R v Jama* (Unreported, Supreme Court of Victoria – Court of Appeal, Warren CJ and Redlich and Bongiorno JJA, 7 December 2009).

[28] Vincent (2010).

[29] Aronson (2007).

[30] Prainsack (2010).

DNA mixture interpretation demonstrates that—contrary to popular perception—forensic analysis is not always objective, rather that it is potentially blighted by subjective elements which may also be subject to bias.[31] This first ever experimental study into the role of bias in DNA mixture interpretation, conducted by Dror and Hampikian, exposed that the results of DNA mixture analyses from 17 independent examiners varied. These expert DNA examiners produced inconsistent interpretations for a mixed DNA sample when they were asked for their interpretations of an adjudicated criminal case.[32] This study not only calls for further empirical research into mixed DNA interpretation, but also for a cessation to the misconception that all aspects of DNA testing represent a 'gold standard.'[33] Indeed, Peter Gill (who co-published the first DNA profile with Alec Jeffreys) is also quoted as echoing these findings: 'If you show ten colleagues a [DNA] mixture, you will probably end up with ten different answers.'[34]

Clearly, this empirical research could have a potentially huge impact on criminal justice investigations—and the presumption of innocence—because DNA mixtures are prevalent at crime scenes. But it also raises a number of salient questions: why and where is there any scope for this sort of subjectivity in the laboratory? Even more pertinently, how might this affect the law?

4.1 Observer Effect (Examiner Bias) and Context Effect

The most basic requirement of any forensic analyst is a detachment from external influences that may cloud his or her judgement when examining and judging data.[35] However, all human beings are subject to innate cognitive biases of which they may well be unaware. These biases represent a tangible menace to analysts during DNA mixture interpretation. Crucially, there are two types of bias which are the potential enemies of any forensic scientist: the first of these is the confirmation bias (in which the/examiner bias has its roots) and the second is contextual bias.[36]

The confirmation bias is based on the fact that when conducting any investigation, *all* human beings have an intuitive tendency toward information that confirms their preconceptions, rather than to seek out evidence that disproves their hunches.[37] In fact it was this bias that was largely accountable for the miscarriage of justice in *Jama*. Commenting on *Jama*, Gill observes, '[s]cience and the law are supposed to rest on logic, but it seems that the entire legal process

[31] Dror and Hampikian (2011).

[32] *Ibid.*

[33] *Ibid.*

[34] *Ibid.*

[35] Dror et al. (2006), pp. 74–78.

[36] Budowle et al. (2009), pp. 810–821.

[37] Myers (2008).

can itself be 'contaminated' by the *CSI effect* and confirmation bias.'[38] Next, the contextual bias, which could possibly pose just as much of a threat to an analyst's objectivity, refers to his or her potential to use:

> information or consistency to reinforce a position. In other words, contextual bias is where the forensic scientist uses other evidence to believe that the specific evidence being analysed is related to a particular reference sample(s).[39]

What is significant is that while the *CSI effect* has been gaining momentum and nurturing the belief in the infallibility of DNA evidence, it has been noted that empirical cognitive research into these biases in the laboratory has effectively been neglected—even ignored.[40] Even more startling is the fact that criminal justice systems are still clinging to the belief that expert interpretation of evidence is still reasonably objective.[41]

4.2 *Subjective Judgements When Interpreting* Alleles *in Mixed DNA Samples*

When and why is there scope for a laboratory analyst to use subjective judgement when interpreting mixed DNA samples? It will be recalled that there may be two *alleles*—one from each parent—at a *locus* in one person's DNA profile. If there are more than two *alleles* present at several *loci* on a DNA profile, however, the DNA evidence is generally classified as a mixture that is, mixed DNA.[42] Research has demonstrated the exact scope of interpreting these DNA mixtures. To be specific, there are 'more than one million ways to interpret a mixture of two contributors.'[43]

What is important to bear in mind at this juncture is that DNA from a crime scene may contain the mixture of more than two contributors. These samples may in turn be in various stages of degradation and they may vary greatly. A laboratory analyst's subjective judgement is therefore called upon to determine exactly how many contributors there are in any mixed DNA sample: unsurprisingly, this is notoriously difficult.[44] There are a number of reasons for this.

---

[38] Gill (2014).

[39] Budowle et al. (2009).

[40] Dror et al. (2006).

[41] *Ibid.*

[42] Buckleton and Curran (2008), pp. 343–348.

[43] Jamieson (2008), pp. 1031–1046.

[44] Paoletti et al. (2012), pp. 113–122.

4.3 *Shared* Alleles *in Mixed DNA Profiles*

In an ideal world, it might be logical to assume that a two person DNA mixture would generate a DNA profile with four *alleles* at some of the *loci* and a three person mixture with six *alleles* and so on. However, crime scenes are complex and far from ideal. In certain mixed DNA evidence, for example, one of the problems is that two of the contributors to the mixture may well share a number of *alleles* making it difficult to interpret exactly how many contributors there are to the sample.[45] These ambiguities can massively impact the statistical weight attached to DNA samples that are used in evidence.[46]

Research illustrates what this could mean in practical terms: in certain 'worst case' analyses of mixed DNA, around 3 % of three-person mixtures would be mischaracterised as two-person mixtures.[47] What is a great deal more significant, however, is that in the case of four-person mixed DNA samples, in excess of 70 % of these samples 'would be mischaracterised as two- or three-person mixtures using only the maximum number of *alleles* observed at any tested *locus*.'[48]

4.4 *Partial DNA and* Allelic *Dropout*

A laboratory analyst may also be called to use subjective judgement in the cases when samples from scenes of crime have yielded diminutive amounts of biological material. These are referred to as partial or incomplete DNA samples. As samples age, it is noted that the DNA may begin to break down which means that the heights of some of the peaks on the chart (the *alleles* in other words) are indistinguishable—and they might even totally disappear.[49] In fact, the number of DNA samples removed from crime scenes containing partial DNA samples may be as high as 50 %.[50]

The risk that an STR test is able to detect only one of two possible *alleles* from a contributor from a degraded sample is known as *allelic* drop-out. This

> complicates the process of interpretation because **analysts** must decide whether a mismatch between two profiles reflects a true genetic difference or simply the failure of the test to detect all of the *alleles* in one of the samples.[51]

---

[45] *Ibid.*

[46] *Ibid.*

[47] Paoletti et al. (2005), pp. 1361–1366.

[48] *Ibid.*

[49] Thompson et al. (2003b).

[50] Naughton and Tan (2011), pp. 245–257.

[51] Thompson et al. (2003b).

Simply put, in cases of ambiguity such as this and when the analyst needs to make a judgement call as to whether or not to disregard information, there is a risk that an individual who was present at a crime scene may go undetected. Or, as Thompson *et al.* put it more succinctly, the police may have arrested the wrong person.[52]

4.5 *Major-Minor DNA Mixtures*

In addition to this, the laboratory analyst may also be faced with the problems of a technical artefact which is known as a stutter and which may actually mask an *allele*.[53] STR interpretation also demands that analysts use their subjective judgement to distinguish between these false peaks that do not contain DNA.[54]

Yet the complexities do not end here. There are problems surrounding the safety of separating certain DNA mixtures.[55] Once different *alleles* from different sources are mixed, it is impossible to identify which *allele* came from which contributor.[56] One exception to this is in cases where there are major-minor DNA mixes—that is, when a large amount of DNA from one person is mixed with a smaller amount of DNA from another.[57] However, it is said that there are no experimental studies to determine what constitutes a *safe* level for the analyst to follow when separating a major-minor mix. So, yet again, the interpretation boils down to the analyst's subjective judgement.[58]

4.6 *The False Positive Fallacy*

Mixed DNA profiles have even been misinterpreted by laboratories as single source DNA profiles—an error that has also led to false convictions. In 1993 in the US, for example, an Oklahoma jury convicted Timothy Durham of rape. However, this conviction was as a result of a misinterpretation of his DNA test results which produced what is known as a false positive—that is, 'when a laboratory erroneously reports a DNA match between two samples that actually have different profiles.'[59] In the Durham case,

[52] *Ibid.*

[53] Gill et al. (2006), pp. 90–101.

[54] Thompson et al. (2003b).

[55] Jamieson (2008).

[56] *Ibid.*

[57] *Ibid.*

[58] *Ibid.*

[59] Thompson et al. (2003b).

> [t]he victim's *alleles,* when combined with those of the true rapist, produced an apparent genotype that matched Durham's. The laboratory mistook this mixed profile for a single source result, and thereby falsely incriminated an innocent man.[60]

4.7 Analysts' Subjective Judgement and Arbitrary Cut-Off Values

Running concurrently with the call for more research into biases in the laboratory, is a warning from the scientific community which draws attention to the 'significant need' for more research into the problems surrounding the interpretation of mixed DNA samples.[61] The most troubling fact surrounding all of these problems, though, is the extent to which the interpretation is reliant upon the laboratory analyst's subjective judgement. This is disquieting on a number of counts not least of which is as a result of the threats posed by bias. The manner in which laboratories compute statistical estimates in cases of mixed DNA analysis is a case in point. There is a warning that these calculations should be treated with caution as they are often based on dubious assumptions—which invariably favour the prosecution.[62] Perhaps the most outstanding point of all, however, is that there is still no definitive frame of reference for analysts to follow when interpreting data regarding DNA mixtures. In fact, different laboratories use different 'cut-off values,' some of which are arbitrary.[63]

To increase these potential problems further, it is also argued that it has traditionally been the prosecution (rather than the generally resource-challenged defence) that instigates the taking of forensic samples.[64] Concerns over the validity of testimony surrounding forensic samples produced for the prosecution in the US have also raised alarm bells more recently. Recent research has demonstrated, for example, that forensic analysts called by the prosecution in the US actually provided invalid testimony at trial. In the trials of innocent defendants,

> 60 % (of) forensic analysts called by the prosecution provided invalid testimony at trial. .... This was not the testimony of a mere handful of analysts: this set of trials included invalid testimony by 72 forensic analysts called by the prosecution and employed by 52 laboratories, practices or hospitals from 25 states.[65]

---

[60] *Ibid.*

[61] Gill et al. (2006).

[62] Thompson et al. (2003b).

[63] *Ibid.*

[64] Wayne (2011).

[65] Garrett and Neufeld (2009), pp. 1–97.

5 A Culture of Science or a Culture of Law Enforcement?

In spite of its reputation as a forensic shibboleth, there can now be little doubt that DNA evidence should be treated with caution.[66] It is therefore hardly surprising that the US National Association of Defense Lawyers is calling attention to the dangers of forensic facilities—be it consciously or unconsciously—replacing a culture of science with a culture of law enforcement.[67] Consequently, to militate against the biases and fallibilities which research demonstrates imperil the objectivity of forensic sampling, the Association is urging that forensic laboratories remain separate not only from law enforcement but also from the prosecution.[68] In the laboratory, it has been demonstrated that when faced with uncertainty over the analysis of DNA mixtures, analysts will generally take a view that supports the prosecution's theory.[69] The most obvious explanation for this is as a result of the effect of contextual bias and the fact that the scientist may be influenced by knowledge of the profiles in the samples he or she is interpreting.[70]

In the court, it has been argued that defence lawyers still do not generally have sufficient expertise and knowledge of this biotechnology to enable them to ask sufficiently probing questions in order to defend their clients when DNA evidence is presented by expert witnesses and in the event that any ambiguities should arise.[71] To what extent might these issues imperil the presumption of innocence in Ireland?

5.1 The Status of the Presumption of Innocence in Ireland

In theory, the presumption of innocence underscores the criminal justice system in the Irish jurisdiction. In practice, its status is by no means as clear cut. It is noted that the presumption of innocence is recognised as a constitutionally protected right which flows from Article 38.1 of the Constitution.[72] It was endorsed by the courts in *People (AG) v O'Callaghan* in 1966 when O'Dálaigh CJ referred to '[t]he requirement that a man shall be considered innocent until he is found guilty.'[73] The right to be presumed innocent was also clearly stated in the joint appeals of *DPP v Gormley and DPP v White* in 2014 in the Supreme Court.[74] In addition, it is said that the right

---

[66] Naughton and Tan (2011).

[67] Wayne (2011).

[68] *Ibid.*

[69] Thompson et al. (2003b).

[70] Jamieson (2008).

[71] Yttri Dahl (2010), pp. 197–217.

[72] Ryan (2012).

[73] *People (AG) v O'Callaghan* [1966] IR 501.

[74] *DPP v Gormley, DPP v White* [2014] IESC 17.

to be presumed innocent was incorporated into Irish law by the European Convention on Human Rights Act which provides that judges in Irish courts must take 'judicial notice' of the Convention which was ratified by Ireland in 2003.[75]

5.2 *The Theory Underpinning the Presumption of Innocence*

On the 25th anniversary of his landmark discovery of DNA profiling in 2009, Alec Jeffreys issued a warning. He called for changes in the law surrounding DNA databases stating that 'innocent people do not belong on that database.'[76] There have also been warnings surrounding the taking of DNA samples, notably that it is complete anathema to the presumption of innocence.[77] It is important to call to mind the fundamental principle underlying the presumption of innocence in order to examine these warnings.

Underpinning the presumption of innocence is the theory that a wrongful conviction is a deep social injustice resulting in fundamental moral harm. It is generally acknowledged that the injurious effects of convicting an innocent person prompt a far greater sense of moral outrage than acquitting someone who is guilty. This is why the presumption of innocence should be at the heart of any democracy. Article 6 (2) of the ECHR is unequivocal: 'Everyone charged with a criminal offence shall be presumed innocent until proved guilty according to law.'

It is also important to bear in mind that the DNA molecule has reached its iconic status in only very recent times—and very quickly. The presumption of innocence on the other hand is an enduring icon of ancient standing that captures not only the spirit of the law, but also the spirit of a democracy. As Lord Sankey famously noted in *Woolmington v DPP* in 1935, 'Throughout the web of the English law one golden thread is always to be seen, that it is the duty of the prosecution to prove the prisoner's guilt.'[78] What Lord Sankey could not have anticipated of course, were the complex challenges that technology and biotechnology would pose, potentially straining the 'golden thread' and human rights to the limits today.

5.3 *Is the Presumption of Innocence Working* Against *the Innocent?*

Although the presumption of innocence is almost universally recognised, it is surprising how difficult it is to define the concept.[79] One of the main reasons for

[75] Ryan (2012).

[76] BBC News (2009).

[77] Corns (1992).

[78] *Woolmington v DPP* [1935] 1 AC 462, [1935] AC 462, [1935] UKHL 1, (1936) 25 Cr App R 72.

[79] Schwikkard (1998).

this difficulty is because this ancient legal precept embraces the polar opposites of guilt and innocence. What commentators do seem to be able to agree upon, therefore, is that the presumption of innocence comprises two core components. These are first, the burden of proof on the prosecution to prove guilt beyond reasonable doubt and second, the element which provides protection against punishment for the innocent. Although it has been noted that these are a logical extension of each other, both components must be perfectly balanced if suspects' rights are to be upheld and the innocent protected.[80]

There is also the consideration that the first of these two components—the burden of proof on the prosecution—is relatively easy to define.[81] As a result, there is a weighty amount of research into the mechanical rules surrounding this burden placed on the prosecution to prove guilt. In addition to this, for some time, a great deal of attention has gone into rationalising the burden of proof as a mathematical concept using probability calculus.

It is when trying to define the second more abstract component which provides the protection against punishment for the innocent that gives rise to more difficulties. It is argued that this lack of clear definition allied to the fact that there is scant research on the abstract shield against punishment in its own right, means that it is in danger of being eclipsed by the more easily definable burden of proof.[82] Certainly, there are a number of fair trial rights including the right to silence and right of access to a lawyer which have been identified as being associated with the presumption of innocence. However, translating this second, abstract component of the presumption of innocence into consistent and coherent legislation that adequately balances the burden on the prosecution is proving a serious challenge across a number of jurisdictions. It is also argued that if an undue burden rests on the prosecution, what this could mean in practical terms is that the presumption of innocence may actually work *against* those who might be innocent:

> This is because the 'presumption', in effect, renders suspects of crime passive and generally inactive whilst the 'burden' places pressure on the police and prosecution to chip away at the presumed innocent status and construct cases that might obtain a conviction, rendering innocent victims vulnerable to wrongful convictions.[83]

5.4 *Presumption of Guilt During Pre-trial*

During the pre-trial stage, suspect vulnerability is arguably at its greatest. Yet in addition to what may be an undue burden resting on the prosecution, there is also

[80] Quintard-Morénas (2010).

[81] Stumer (2010).

[82] Quintard-Morénas (2010).

[83] Naughton (2011).

the same threat posed by the confirmation bias as noted above to all actors in the criminal justice system—of which they may or may not be aware. The threat of this bias has also not received very much attention from criminal justice systems.[84] This is clearly a recurring theme. As previously outlined, the threats that are potentially posed by the confirmation and contextual biases in the laboratory have also gone ignored.[85]

What is known, however, is that if police officers or investigators conduct their investigations with a presumption that the suspect is guilty, due to a lack of awareness in the confirmation bias, they are at risk of conducting their enquiries by actively seeking out information that confirms this hypothesis.[86] To put it bluntly, they are every bit as much at risk of the confirmation bias as laboratory analysts who may have to interpret ambiguities in a mixed DNA sample.

It has also been established that a presumption of guilt in investigators sets up a cascade reaction which influences not only the interrogator's behaviour, but also that of the suspect and ultimately the judgements of neutral observers.[87] In fact, Kassin *et al.'s* survey into the interviewing techniques of 631 police investigators revealed some alarming statistics, In the US, investigators admitted eliciting self-incriminating statements from 68 % of suspects, 4.78 % of whom were innocent.[88] The rights to silence and access to a lawyer therefore provide an essential counter-balancing mechanism not only to this bias, but also to the heavy burden placed on the prosecution. Are there sufficient safeguards and consistent legislative provisions in place in Ireland to uphold these rights—and therefore the presumption of innocence—in order to mitigate these concerns?

5.5 The Right of Access to a Lawyer Prior to the Taking of Forensic Samples

Before the decision handed down by the Supreme Court in *Gormley,*[89] it was noted that the Irish legislature had interpreted the ECtHR jurisprudence as being limited to allowing a consultation with a lawyer prior to questioning.[90] In *Gormley,* the Supreme Court upheld a suspect's right of access to a lawyer prior to interrogation in order to mitigate what were identified by the court as 'the complexities of criminal procedure'—especially for vulnerable suspects. But *Gormley* has also raised some complex challenges. In the judgement, the Supreme Court made a

[84] Hill et al. (2008).
[85] Dror et al. (2006).
[86] Hill et al. (2008).
[87] Meissner and Kassin (2004), pp. 85–106.
[88] Kassin et al. (2007).
[89] *DPP v Gormley, DPP v White* [2014] IESC 17.
[90] Ryan (2012).

clear cut distinction between the provision of access to a lawyer prior to suspect interrogation and the right to see a lawyer before the taking of 'objective forensic samples'—which was *not* upheld. In fact, repeated reference was made to 'objective' forensic samples in the judgement. The Court's reasoning focuses on the perceived objectivity of forensic samples. Indeed, this thinking is based on the presupposition that forensic testing is objective. The Court held that 'it must be acknowledged that the results of forensic testing are objective' and, additionally, that 'if there is truly any question about the reliability of any form of objective testing adopted, then any such issues can be fully explored at the trial.'[91] But this is problematic on a number of counts.

First, do defence lawyers always have enough expertise of DNA technology (and often incomprehensibly presented statistics) to 'explore' potential issues when confidently presented by expert witnesses at trial? The fact is this: research has demonstrated that serious mistakes have occurred in a number of cases when expert witnesses have gone unchallenged. The acknowledged culturally embedded belief in the objectivity of DNA evidence may also mean that there is still a danger of defence lawyers accepting

> lab reports at face value without looking behind them to see whether the actual test results fully support the laboratory's conclusions.[92]

Second, it is vital to remember that contrary to the perception that DNA evidence is infallible, 'objective' samples are wholly reliant on subjective and fallible human interaction (not to mention the threats also posed by bias). This concern co-exists with the worries surrounding the reliability of forensic evidence called by the prosecution as illustrated by Garrett and Neufeld's recent study.[93]

Third, there is a potential problem raised regarding the re-testing of DNA samples should reliability concerns be raised at trial. It has been demonstrated by research that some DNA tests cannot always be repeated if errors are detected: this is because it may not always be possible to re-test critical samples which may have been exhausted by the first test.[94]

Although *Gormley* has clearly made some inroads to changing the criminal justice system in Ireland, it is the introduction of the Criminal Justice (Forensic Evidence and DNA Database System) Act 2014 in Ireland that will provide the jurisdiction with its most significant change, however. This complex piece of legislation not only predicts a major upswing in the use of DNA evidence in the courts, it also makes provision for the establishment of a DNA database for use by the Garda Síochána in criminal investigations which will herald an increase in the use of DNA evidence. The potential shortfalls and impact of this legislation on the

[91] *DPP v Gormley, DPP v White* [2014] IESC 17.

[92] Thompson et al. (2003b).

[93] Garrett and Neufeld (2009).

[94] Thompson et al. (2003b).

presumption of innocence are therefore analysed in the concluding section of the chapter, alongside relevant case law surrounding DNA evidence.

6 Early Development of DNA Evidence in Ireland

The growth of DNA evidence in Ireland has evolved insidiously since the early 1990s due to the fact that there has only been a small number of reported cases featuring this type of forensic evidence.[95] Initially, the testing of DNA samples removed from crime scenes in the Irish jurisdiction took place in English laboratories. Certainly this was the case until 1994, when the Forensic Science Laboratory in Ireland (now Forensic Science Ireland) largely took over the analysis of DNA samples for criminal investigations.[96] The first occasion in which DNA profiling technology was used in Ireland was in a case of sexual assault and murder in 1995, *People (DPP) v Lawlor*.[97] In this case, the validity of DNA profiling was accepted—and the evidence was permitted to go to the jury. In fact, *Lawlor* is one of only a small flurry of cases in the Irish courts which have challenged the scientific validity of DNA evidence in more recent times. These cases have however, generally involved single contributor DNA samples as opposed to mixed DNA samples. In *Lawlor,* the admissibility of evidence was challenged and then upheld. Similarly, a second challenge was raised in the subsequent *People (DPP) v Horgan*.[98] In *Horgan*, the scientific validity of DNA evidence was yet again challenged—but the reliability of the DNA evidence was once again upheld by the court. It is important to bear in mind at this point that there is still no formal test that an Irish court can use to determine whether—or not—expert evidence is reliable.[99]

6.1 Criminal Justice (Forensic Evidence and DNA Database System) Act 2014

The most recent piece of legislation surrounding DNA evidence in Ireland, the Criminal Justice (Forensic Evidence and DNA Database System) Act 2014, replaces the existing statutory and common law measures surrounding the taking of forensic samples from suspects. Significantly, it also makes provision for the

[95] Heffernan and Ní Raifeartaigh (2014).

[96] *Ibid.*

[97] *People (DPP) v Lawlor* Central Criminal Court (2 Dec 1995) (Court of Appeal Feb 2001, unreported).

[98] *People (DPP) v Horgan* (reported Irish Examiner 25 June 2002).

[99] Law Reform Commission Consultation Paper: Expert Evidence (2008).

establishment of a DNA database system for use by An Garda Síochána in criminal investigations. Prior to the introduction of the 2014 Act, fingerprints and bodily samples could be taken from suspects—with, or without, their consent.[100] Although there were a number of statutory provisions in place for this, the most significant of which was the Criminal Justice (Forensic Evidence) Act 1990, they were subsequently repealed by the 2014 Act.

6.2 The DNA Database in Ireland

One of the most notable aspects of the 2014 Act is the provision in Section 8 which provides for the establishment and operation of Ireland's national database. To be specific, the database system comprises two divisions. These are the investigation division (which includes the crime scene index) and the identification division. The identification division contains the missing persons' index. This section of the 2014 Act also makes the provision for the operation of the database to be conducted by Forensic Science Ireland (formerly the Forensic Science Laboratory). Contrary to the concept of separating forensic science laboratories and law enforcement facilities as a safeguard against the threat of confirmation or contextual bias, Forensic Science Ireland is based in the Garda Headquarters in Dublin, a situation typical in many jurisdictions.

6.3 Human Rights Concerns

The 2014 Act has, however, attracted a great deal of scrutiny and debate. A particular concern surrounds the taking of samples from people in custody. Section 11 (1) raises a number of human rights and ethical issues in this regard and makes provision for the arbitrary taking of forensic samples. Of note, it provides that any member of the Garda (not below the rank of sergeant) can take a non-intimate forensic sample from a detained person, not for the investigation of a particular offence, but simply to generate a DNA profile which may be held on a database. What this effectively means is that an innocent person could find that their DNA profile is held on the database. The Irish Human Rights Commission (IHRC), noting the decision in *S and Marper v United Kingdom*[101] by the ECtHR, have focused their attention on the potential threats to the right to privacy that this provision may pose.[102] In *Marper*, the ECtHR held that the retention of DNA

[100] Conway et al. (2010).

[101] *S and Marper v United Kingdom* [2008] ECHR 1581, (2009) 48 EHRR 50, 25 BHRC 557, 48 EHRR 50, [2009] Crim LR 355.

[102] Irish Human Rights Commission (2013).

samples of people who are arrested but subsequently acquitted is a breach of the right to privacy. However, imposing this provision of the 2014 Act on a vulnerable suspect who has not been allowed access to a lawyer is also impossible to reconcile with the presumption of innocence. Far more worrying is Section 11 (3) (c). This provision allows reasonable force to be used if the person refuses to allow the taking of such a sample.

6.4 Consent Concerns

There are also human rights concerns regarding consent over the taking of intimate samples of the 2014 Act. Section 12 (1), for example, makes a provision for the taking of an intimate sample from a detained person which may also be used to generate a DNA profile for entry into the DNA database. Although reasonable force may not be used to take an intimate sample, the detainee's consent must be obtained in writing under Section 12 (2) (b). The presumption of innocence is under threat on two specific counts here. Before requesting the taking of such a sample, under Section 12 (3) (b) the member of the Garda Síochána must have reasonable grounds 'for believing that the sample will tend to confirm or disprove the involvement of that person in the commission of the offence concerned.' The first problem here is that a detained person who has not been allowed access to a lawyer is at risk from the known tendency to view suspects with a presumption of guilt, rather than innocence.[103] The second is this: as there is an acknowledged inequality of arms in Garda custody, how truly voluntary is such consent? (McInerney 2010).

6.5 Adverse Inferences Provision: Another Blow for the Presumption of Innocence

The provisions that allow adverse inferences to be drawn are also problematic, notably Section 19 (1) (b) which allows adverse inferences to be drawn if consent to provide an intimate sample is denied:

> the court (or, subject to the judge's directions, the jury), in determining whether the accused is guilty of the offence charged (or of any other offence of which he or she could lawfully be convicted on that charge), may draw such inferences from the refusal or withdrawal, as the case may be, as appear proper;

Although, in theory, Section 19 (2) (b) makes provision for a detained person to be made aware of the right to consult a solicitor before refusing consent, this may lead to a particularly troubling question for defence lawyers in the Irish jurisdiction:

[103] Kassin et al. (2003).

what constitutes best practice in the light of this adverse inferences provision? Yet again, this is impossible to balance with the presumption of innocence. Contrary to Alec Jeffrey's warning that innocent people do not belong on a database, innocent suspects could possibly find that their DNA profile is placed on the database.

6.6 Section 13 of the Criminal Justice (Forensic Evidence and DNA Database System) Act 2014

However, it is perhaps Section 13 (1) of the 2014 Act that poses one of the greatest threats to the presumption of innocence that the Irish jurisdiction has seen to date. This section makes a provision for the taking of non-intimate samples from a detained person for the purposes of investigation of an offence—and possibly to generate a DNA profile *without* his or her consent. In addition to this, Section 13 (5) (d) makes the provision that reasonable force may be used without prior access to a lawyer. Again, these provisions are totally anathema to the fundamental human right to be presumed innocent.

6.7 Problems with Mixed DNA Evidence in Court

The problems surrounding mixed DNA evidence have not been a focus for the Irish courts prior to the introduction of this legislation. However, the fallibility of mixed DNA evidence was examined by the courts in what has been—so far—an uncommon case in 2013, *DPP v O'Callaghan.*[104] In *O'Callaghan*, the Appeal Court had to examine some of the typical problems potentially posed by the interpretation of mixed DNA. Specifically, this case involved the correct identification of the number of contributors to a mixed DNA profile and also the interpretation of a major-minor mix. It will be recalled that there are no experimental studies to determine what constitutes a *safe* level when separating a major-minor mix.[105]

O'Callaghan involved the armed robbery of a post office in Cork by two masked raiders which led to the conviction of Michael O'Callaghan, who was sentenced to a 10 year jail sentence in 2009. A forensic scientist from the Forensic Science Laboratory (now Forensic Science Ireland) gave evidence that a DNA sample lifted from a balaclava (and which a witness claimed had been thrown into a canal by one of the post office raiders) indicated the presence of 'more than two people.' The analyst went on to explain that the 'mixture consisted of a major male component and a minor component.' She also gave evidence that the 'major profile matched the profile of the applicant.' Additionally, the expert witness estimated that 'the chance

[104] *DPP v O'Callaghan* [2013] IECCA 46 (31 July 2013).

[105] Jamieson (2008).

that an unrelated person chosen at random would have this same DNA profile is considerably less than one in one thousand million.' In the appeal, the Court found that there was nothing in the forensic evidence 'which would entitle the jury to differentiate between the various people who had been in contact at some point with the balaclava.' The conviction was therefore seen to be unsafe and was subsequently quashed.

This is not the first occasion in which the Irish courts have concluded that the forensic evidence was unsafe. In *People (DPP) v Allen* (2003)[106] the Court of Criminal Appeal overturned a conviction as the statistical DNA evidence put before the jury was incomplete. So far though, appellate challenges in Ireland have tended to focus on the manner in which DNA evidence is presented at trial, or they have concentrated on the absence of DNA evidence.[107] However, the enactment of the 2014 Act undoubtedly anticipates a reversal of this trend and the Irish courts will doubtless have to face cases that rely on mixed DNA evidence in the near future.

The currently unresolved problems and complexities surrounding the interpretation of DNA mixtures, allied to the complexities of the 2014 Act, co-exist within a nexus of inconsistent legislation which surrounds the right of access to a lawyer. Consequently, there are currently insufficient safeguards in place to uphold a suspect's basic human right to be presumed innocent in Ireland. As the number of cases surrounding mixed DNA evidence inevitably increases following the enactment of this legislation, not only the 'golden thread' but also constitutional boundaries are set to be strained way beyond their limits in the Irish jurisdiction during the coming years.

7 Conclusion

No matter how impressive the technology that supports it, science is ultimately a completely human activity. So is the law. Yet there is still a surprisingly tacit expectation that both science and the law can remain grounded solely in logic and reason—able to operate free from human fallibility and bias. Research unequivocally demonstrates they cannot on both counts. Indeed, a recurring theme echoes throughout science and reverberates back through the law. It calls for more research into the riddles that still surround the interpretation of DNA mixtures. Commentators are also calling for more empirical studies into the role of cognitive bias in the laboratory and in criminal investigations. Yet there is still a scarcity of research in these areas. In the meantime, the courts continue to interact with laboratories that are not bound by a universally-accepted frame of reference for interpreting DNA mixtures. Clear guidelines are yet to be established. The ancient presumption of

[106] *People (DPP) v Allen* [2003] IR 295.

[107] Heffernan and Ní Raifeartaigh (2014).

innocence is a casualty of the dramatically sudden increase in the use of this biotechnology, despite being explicitly spelt out in Article 6.2 of the ECHR.

In Ireland, the Criminal Justice (Forensic Evidence and DNA Database System) Act 2014 signals future increases in the use of DNA evidence by the prosecution. As a result of the prevalence of DNA mixtures lifted from crime scenes, it is highly likely that the number of cases relying on mixed DNA evidence is set to rise, clearly raising a number of human rights issues. To be specific, the legislative provision allowing specified Gardaí arbitrarily to take a non-intimate forensic sample from a detained person—simply to generate a DNA profile that may be held on the newly established DNA database—means that an innocent person could well find that their DNA profile is retained. Again, there is no way that this can be reconciled with the presumption of innocence.

Until the scientific community can resolve the problems surrounding the interpretation of DNA mixtures, Irish courts—alongside other EU Member States—will have to rely on the fallible and subjective interpretation of DNA mixtures. This will continue in an environment in which there are no definitive guidelines for laboratories during the analysis of mixed DNA and in which laboratory cut-off points may, similarly, also be arbitrary. Is there now a risk that a presumption of guilt—rather than innocence—could now be the default setting in the Irish jurisdiction?

References

Aronson, J. (2007). *Genetic witness: Science, law and controversy in the making of DNA profiling*. New Brunswick, NJ: Rutgers University Press.

BBC News. (2009). *DNA fingerprinting 25 years old*. http://news.bbc.co.uk/2/hi/uk/8247641.stm. Accessed 15 Feb 2015.

Briody, M. (2004). The effects of DNA evidence on homicide cases in court. *Australian and New Zealand Journal of Criminology, 37*, 231–252.

Buckleton, J., & Curran, J. (2008). A discussion of the merits of random man not excluded and likelihood ratios. *Forensic Science International: Genetics, 2*(4), 343–348.

Budowle, B., Onorato, A., Callaghan, T., Della Mann, A., Gross, A., Guerrieri, R., et al. (2009). Mixture interpretation: Defining the relevant features for guidelines for the assessment of mixed DNA profiles in forensic casework. *Journal of Forensic Sciences, 54*(4), 810–821.

Butler, J. (2010). *Fundamentals of forensic DNA typing*. London: Elsevier.

Conway, V., Daly, Y., & Schweppe, J. (2010). *Irish criminal justice: Theory, process and procedure*. Dublin, Ireland: Clarus Press.

Corns, C. (1992). The science of justice and the justice in science. *Law in Context, 10*(2), 7.

Dror, I., Charlton, D., & Péron, A. (2006). Contextual information renders experts vulnerable to making erroneous identifications. *Forensic Science International, 156*, 74–78.

Dror, I., & Hampikian, G. (2011). Subjectivity and bias in forensic DNA mixture interpretation. *Science and Justice, 51*, 204–208.

Garrett, B., & Neufeld, P. (2009). Invalid forensic science testimony and wrongful convictions. *Virginia Law Review, 95*(1), 1–97.

Gill, P. (2014). *Misleading DNA evidence: Reasons for miscarriages of justice*. London: Elsevier.

Gill, P., Brenner, C. H., Buckleton, J. S., Carracedo, A., Krawczak, M., Mayr, W. R., et al. (2006). DNA Commission of the International Society of Forensic Genetics: Recommendations on the interpretation of mixtures. *Forensic Science International, 160*, 90–101.

Goodwin, W., Linacre, A., & Hadi, S. (2007). *An introduction to forensic genetics*. Chichester, England: Wiley.
Heffernan, L., & Ní Raifeartaigh, Ú. (2014). *Evidence in criminal trials*. Dublin, Ireland: Bloomsbury Professional.
Hill, C., Memon, A., & McGeorge, P. (2008). The role of confirmation bias in suspect interviews: A systematic evaluation. *Legal and Criminological Psychology, 13*, 357–371.
Irish Human Rights Commission, Observations on the Criminal Justice (Forensic Evidence and DNA Database System) Bill 2013. http://www.ihrec.ie/download/pdf/final_obs_on_the_dna_crim_justice_bill_2013_doc_ff.pdf. Accessed 15 Dec 2014.
Jamieson, A. (2008). The philosophy of forensic scientific identification. *Hastings Law Journal, 59*, 1031–1046.
Kassin, S., Richard, M., Leo, A., Meissner, C. A., Richman, K. D., Colwell, L. H., et al. (2007). Police interviewing and interrogation: A self-report survey of police practices and beliefs. *Law and Human Behaviour, 31*, 381–400.
Kassin, S. M., Goldstein, C. C., & Savitsky, K. (2003). Behavioural confirmation in the interrogation room: On the dangers of presuming guilt. *Law and Human Behaviour, 27*(2), 186–203.
Kaye, D. (2010). *The double helix and the law of evidence*. Cambridge, MA: Harvard University Press.
Koehler, J. (2001). The psychology of numbers in the courtroom: How to make DNA match statistics seem impressive or insufficient. *Southern California Law Review, 74*, 1275–1305.
Law Reform Commission Consultation Paper: *Expert Evidence* (2008) http://www.lawreform.ie/_fileupload/consultation%20papers/cpexpertevidence.pdf
McInerney, P. (2010). "Equality of Arms" between the suspect interrogated in Garda custody and the Gardai. *Judicial Studies Institute Journal*.
Meissner, C., & Kassin, S. (2004). You're guilty, so just confess! Cognitive and behavioural confirmation biases in the interrogation room. In G. D. Lassiter (Ed.), *Interrogations, confession and entrapment* (pp. 85–106). New York: Kluwer.
Myers, D. (2008). *Social psychology*. New York: McGraw Hill.
Naughton, M. (2011). How the presumption of innocence renders the innocent vulnerable to wrongful convictions. *Irish Journal of Legal Studies, 2*, 40–54.
Naughton, M., & Tan, G. (2011). The need for caution in the use of DNA evidence to avoid convicting the innocent. *The International Journal of Evidence and Proof, 15*, 245–257.
Paoletti, D., Doom, T., Krane, C., Raymer, M., & Krane, D. (2005). Empirical analysis of the STR profiles resulting from conceptual mixtures. *Journal of Forensic Sciences, 50*(6), 1361–1366.
Paoletti, D., Krane, D., Raymer, M., & Doom, T. (2012). Inferring the number of contributors to mixed DNA profiles. *IEE/ACM Transactions on Computational Biology and Bioinformatics, 9*(1), 113–122.
Prainsack, B. (2010). Key issues in DNA profiling and databasing: Implications for governance. In R. Hindmarsh & B. Prainsack (Eds.), *Genetic suspects: Global governance of forensic DNA profiling and databasing* (pp. 15–39). Cambridge, England: Cambridge University Press.
Puch-Solis, R., Roberts, P., Pope, S., & Aitken, C. (2012). *Assessing the probative value of DNA evidence: Guidance for judges, lawyers, forensic scientists and expert witnesses*. London: Royal Statistical Society.
Quintard-Morénas, F. (2010). The presumption of innocence in the French and Anglo-American legal traditions. *American Journal of Comparative Law, 58*, 107–151.
Ryan, A. (2012). Ireland. In K. Ligeti (Ed.), *Toward a prosecutor for the European Union Volume 1: A comparative analysis*. Oxford, England: Hart.
Schwikkard, P. J. (1998). The presumption of innocence: What is it? *South African Journal of Criminal Justice*, 396–409.
Stumer, A. (2010). *The presumption of innocence, evidential and human rights perspectives*. Oxford, England: Hart.
Swanson, T., Kim, S., & Glucksman, M. (2010). *Biochemistry, molecular biology and genetics*. Philadelphia: Lippincott Williams & Wilkins.

The Law Reform Commission. (2005). *The establishment of a DNA database*. http://www.lawreform.ie/_fileupload/reports/rdnadatabase.pdf

Thompson, W. (2008). *The potential for error in forensic DNA testing and how that complicates the use of DNA databases for criminal identification*. http://www.councilforresponsiblegenetics.org/pageDocuments/H4T5EOYUZI.pdf. Accessed 01.06.15.

Thompson, W., Ford, S., Doom, T., Raymer, M., & Krane, D. (2003a). Evaluating forensic evidence: Essential elements of a competent defense review. *The Champion, 27*, 16–25.

Thompson, W., & Schumann, E. (1987). Interpretation of statistical evidence in criminal trials: The prosecutor's fallacy and the defense attorney's fallacy. *Law and Human Behaviour, 11*, 167–187.

Thompson, W., Taroni, F., & Aitken, C. (2003b). How the probability of a false positive affects the value of DNA evidence. *Journal of Forensic Sciences, 48*(1), 47–54.

Vincent, The Honourable F.H.R. (2010). *Inquiry into the circumstances that led to the conviction of Mr. Farah Abdulkadir Jama*. Victorian Government Printer. http://assets.justice.vic.gov.au/justice/resources/4cd228fd-f61d-4449-b655-ad98323c4ccc/vincentreportfinal6may2010.pdf. Accessed 03.12.14.

Wayne, L. (2011). *Turning the investigation on the science of forensics. NACDL statement to Senate Science Committee*. http://www.nacdl.org/WorkArea/DownloadAsset.aspx?id=23226. Accessed 20.02.15.

Yttri Dahl, J. (2010). DNA the Nor-way: Black-boxing the evidence and monopolising the key. In R. Hindmarsh & B. Prainsack (Eds.), *Genetic suspects: Global governance of forensic DNA profiling and databasing* (pp. 197–217). Cambridge, England: Cambridge University Press.

List of Cases

DPP v Gormley, DPP v White [2014] IESC 17

DPP v O'Callaghan [2013] IECCA 46 (31 July 2013)

People (AG) v O'Callaghan [1996] IR 501

People (DPP) v Lawlor (Central Criminal Court 2 Dec 1995); (Court of Appeal Feb 2001) unreported

People (DPP) v Allen [2003] IR 295

R v Jama (Unreported, Supreme Court of Victoria — Court of Appeal, Warren CJ, Redlich and Bongiorno JJA, 7 December 2009)

S and Marper v United Kingdon (2009) 48 EHRR 50.

State v. Timothy Edward Durham, No. CF-91-4922 (Okla. Dist. Ct. Mar. 9, 1993)

People (DPP) V Horgan Irish Examiner 25 June 2002

Surveillance and the Right to Privacy: Is an 'Effective Remedy' Possible?

Maria Helen Murphy

1 Introduction

Privacy—the right most directly implicated in any discussion of surveillance—is often identified solely as a benefit to the individual, weighing against general social goods such as security.[1] The imperceptibility of both the concept of privacy and the value of 'national security' favours the security side of the equation, as the threats of terrorism and organised crime loom large as omnipresent fears in a security conscious society. Recognising these challenges, recourse to an external—yet, legitimate—source of privacy protection is an attractive option. Accordingly, the European Convention on Human Rights (ECHR) is a crucial instrument of human rights protection in the area of surveillance. While Ireland has avoided direct scrutiny of its surveillance regime from the ECtHR, the jurisprudence of the Strasbourg Court has played a clear role in the formulation of Irish surveillance legislation. In spite of this influence, there is cause to suspect that the legislative reforms may not add up to effective protection of the right to respect for private life as guaranteed by Article 8 of the Convention. While Article 8 is the substantive article most relevant in the surveillance context, the right to an effective remedy, as provided for in Article 13, must also be considered. The specific function of Article 13 is to ensure the 'availability at national level of a remedy to enforce the substance of the Convention rights and freedoms'.[2] The inherently secretive nature of surveillance presents a considerable obstacle to the justiciability of Article 8 rights in the surveillance context. This chapter considers how the challenges to providing an effective remedy in the surveillance context can be resolved and uses

[1] See for example, Solove (2008), p. 10.

[2] *Rotaru v Romania* [2000] ECHR 192, 67.

M.H. Murphy (✉)
Department of Law, Maynooth University, Co. Kildare, Ireland
e-mail: maria.murphy@nuim.ie

A. Diver, J. Miller (eds.), *Justiciability of Human Rights Law in Domestic Jurisdictions*, DOI 10.1007/978-3-319-24016-9_12

the Criminal Justice (Surveillance) Act 2009 (Surveillance Act) as a case study in order to evaluate how the Oireachtas has attempted to meet the standard for an effective remedy in this complex context.

2 The Importance of Remedies

According to the former President of the European Court of Human Rights (ECtHR), Luzius Wildhaber, '[t]he Convention is all about remedies. In a sense, the existence of effective remedies is more important than the wording of the Convention itself'.[3] While the right of individual petition to the Strasbourg Court under Article 25 of the ECHR provides an avenue for redress at the supra-national level and offers the potential for 'just satisfaction',[4] the drafters of the Convention recognised the need to provide for a system of remedies at the national level with the inclusion of Article 13. Buergenthal contended in 1966 that the 'real significance of the Convention' derives from the acceptance by the signatory States of the two interrelated obligations of implementing the Convention in their domestic law and providing a domestic remedy to individuals who wish to enforce their rights under the Convention.[5]

The ECtHR has stated clearly that the Party States 'assumed the obligation to secure to everyone within its jurisdiction the rights and freedoms defined in Section 1 of the Convention' when they signed the ECHR.[6] The ECtHR has gone so far as to claim that the States have accepted a 'general obligation to solve the problems that have led to the Court finding a violation of the Convention'.[7] If violations still occur, mechanisms must be established at the domestic level that provide for effective redress of violations of the rights of the ECHR.[8] In line with the principle of subsidiarity, the ECtHR gives discretion to the States 'as to the manner in which they conform to their obligations' under Article 13.[9] Accordingly, Article 13 guarantees the availability of a remedy at the national level to enforce Convention rights in whatever form they may happen to be secured in the domestic legal order.[10] Thus, the provision of a domestic remedy should allow the national

[3] Wildhaber (2005), p. 9. Available at: http://www.echr.coe.int/NR/rdonlyres/82597AB6-124F-48D5-8BBB-792899EB0C6A/0/AmeliorationsRecours_EN.pdf.

[4] Article 41 ECHR.

[5] Buergenthal (1966), p. 59.

[6] *Lukenda v Slovenia* [2005] ECHR 682, 94–95 [hereinafter, *Lukenda*].

[7] *Lukenda*, 94–95.

[8] *Lukenda*, 94–95.

[9] *Chahal v The United Kingdom* (1996) 23 EHRR 413, 145 [hereinafter, *Chahal*]. See *Vilvarajah v The United Kingdom* (1991) 14 EHRR 248, 122 [hereinafter, *Vilvarajah*].

[10] For example, *Khan v The United Kingdom* (2000) 31 EHRR 45, 44.

authority both to deal with the substance of the Convention complaint and to grant appropriate relief.[11]

3 'Effective Remedy' and Implications in the Surveillance Context

A key concept in the Convention jurisprudence on Article 13 is the requirement that a remedy must be '"effective" in practice as well as in law'.[12] According to the ECtHR, 'effective' means that the remedy must be 'adequate and accessible'.[13] Shelton has summarised the attributes of an effective remedy as including 'institutional independence of the remedial body for the authority responsible for the violation'; the 'ability to invoke the Convention guarantees in question'; the ability of the remedial body to provide redress; and 'effectiveness in fact'.[14] While such criteria are instructive, the context of the violation is important when determining what effectiveness means. According to the ECtHR, the nature of the complaint affects the scope of the obligations of the State under Article 13.[15]

Plainly, context plays a particularly important role in surveillance cases. The ECtHR has regularly repeated that an effective remedy 'must mean a remedy that is as effective as can be having regard to the restricted scope for recourse inherent in any system of secret surveillance'.[16] Therefore—even though the ECtHR admitted in *Klass v. Germany* that the German system of remedies had limited effectiveness—the Court decided that it would be 'hard to conceive of more effective remedies being possible' in the circumstances of the case.[17]

The ECtHR recognises that judicial remedies 'furnish strong guarantees of independence, access for the victim and family, and enforceability of awards in compliance with the requirements of Article 13'.[18] The importance of safeguards like impartiality and independence of remedial bodies have been recognised by the

---

[11] *Smith and Grady v The United Kingdom* [1999] ECHR 72, 135.

[12] *McFarlane v Ireland* [2010] ECHR 1272, 108 [hereinafter, *McFarlane*]; *Ihan v Turkey* [2000] ECHR 354, 97. The ECtHR has also called for this effectiveness in practice requirement in the national security context. *Al Nashif v Bulgaria* [2002] ECHR 502, 136.

[13] *McFarlane*, 108; *Paulino Tomás v Portugal* [2003] 58698/00 ECHR.

[14] Shelton (1999), p. 23.

[15] *McFarlane*, 108.

[16] *Klass v Germany* (1979–80) 2 EHRR 214, 69 [hereinafter, *Klass*]. Referenced in *Leander v Sweden* (1987) 9 EHRR 433, 78 [hereinafter, *Leander*]; *Mersch v Luxembourg* [1985] 10439/83, 10440/83, 10441/83, 10452/83, 10452/83, 10512/83 and 10513/83 (joined) 34, 118 [hereinafter, *Mersch*]; *Ekimdzhiev v Bulgaria* [2007] ECHR 533, 99 [hereinafter, *Ekimdzhiev*].

[17] *Klass*, 70.

[18] *Z v The United Kingdom* (2002) 34 EHRR 97, 110.

ECtHR in the surveillance context as early as the *Klass* decision.[19] The ECtHR has, however, maintained a flexible conception of how these characteristics can be achieved.[20] The ECtHR has stated that 'the authority referred to in Article 13 may not necessarily in all instances be a judicial authority in the strict sense'.[21] To be effective the remedial institution must be 'sufficiently independent' of the relevant authority.[22] Van Dijk and van Hoof submit that 'independence' goes beyond the notion of 'the mere absence of hierarchical or institutional connection' and should mean 'practical independence', as this bolsters 'the objective nature of inquiries and the public confidence in their legitimacy'.[23] Following arguments that a 'national authority' as mentioned in Article 13 must 'at least be composed of members who are impartial and who enjoy the safeguards of judicial independence', the ECtHR stated that while 'national authority' does not necessarily mean judicial authority, the 'powers and procedural guarantees an authority possesses are relevant' when determining effectiveness.[24]

In some circumstances, the ECtHR has 'strictly examined the powers, procedures and independence of non-judicial bodies when evaluating if they provide effective remedies under Article 13'.[25] Harris has pointed out that, while the ECtHR is prepared to be flexible in 'special cases' such as *Klass* and *Leander v. Sweden*—both cases involved the secretive activities of security agencies—the judicial model is influential in determining the effectiveness of the remedy.[26] It is important to note, however, that the national security type issues that mark *Klass* and *Leander* as 'special' tend to be common, almost ubiquitous, in surveillance cases. When evaluating the effectiveness of remedies, the ECtHR looks for certain practical and logical features. The ECtHR has shown that it will look for evidence of adequate jurisdiction to hear the Convention complaint, the ability to grant binding decisions, powers of enforcement, and independence.[27]

---

[19] According to the Court: 'The rule of law implies, inter alia, that an interference by the executive authorities with an individual's rights should be subject to an effective control which should normally be assured by the judiciary, at least in the last resort, judicial control offering the best guarantees of independence, impartiality and a proper procedure'. *Klass*, 55, 67.

[20] *Klass*, 67.

[21] *Klass*, 67.

[22] Harris et al. (2009), p. 565. According to the Committee of Ministers, while Article 13 does not necessitate that the remedy is administered by a court of law, the relevant authority must be 'identified and composed of members who are impartial and who enjoy safeguards of independence'. Committee of Ministers of the Council of Europe, Recommendation R (98) 13 (18 September 1998). See Eckes (2009), p. 182.

[23] van Dijk et al. (2006), p. 1007; Mowbray (2004), pp. 32–33.

[24] *Klass*, 67.

[25] Mowbray (2004), p. 207, as cited in Helfer (2008), pp. 125–159.

[26] Harris et al. (2009), p. 565.

[27] *Silver v The United Kingdom* [1983] ECHR 5; *PG and JH v The United Kingdom* [2001] ECHR 550.

4 The Relationship of Notification to Remedies

The inherently secretive nature of surveillance presents a considerable obstacle to those entitled to a remedy for violations of their Article 8 rights. As the ECtHR has accepted that subjecting an individual to surveillance constitutes an interference with the right to respect for private life, compulsory notification of surveillance would seem to be a natural corollary of the entitlement to an effective remedy. As succinctly stated by Cameron, '[w]ithout notification, the individual's fundamental right to obtain redress for a possibly unlawful act is meaningless'.[28] The ECtHR has recognised that there is 'little scope for recourse to the courts' unless an individual is notified of his or her subjection to surveillance measures.[29]

The special nature of surveillance cannot be ignored and there are several justifications for not notifying a surveillance subject.[30] The ECtHR clearly appreciates the difficulties and risks of notification, but there is a tension between this understanding and the desire of the Court to facilitate effective access to remedies at the domestic level. On the one hand, when considering the application of Article 13 in *Klass*, the ECtHR recognised the obstacles that a surveillance target must overcome if he or she is to successfully 'seek any remedy of his own accord, particularly while surveillance is in progress'.[31] On the other hand, the ECtHR admitted—'albeit to its regret'—that secret surveillance is sometimes necessary in a modern-day democratic society.[32] The ECtHR has affirmed that while surveillance is underway no notification of the target is possible, as notification would jeopardise the investigation.[33] The ECtHR has gone so far as to say that this conclusion is 'obvious'.[34] This assertion rests on the argument that individuals should be 'deprived of the possibility to challenge specific measures ordered or implemented against them' out of 'necessity'.[35]

The ECtHR takes a more robust line with regard to notification following the termination of surveillance measures. Twenty-five years ago, the Council of Europe issued a recommendation requiring the notification of individuals once the surveillance measures had ceased, and to some extent this approach has been reflected in

---

28 Cameron (2000), p. 162.

29 *Klass*, 57.

30 *Klass*, 58.

31 *Klass*, 68.

32 Ibid.

33 *Ekimdzhiev*, 100.

34 Ibid.

35 Ibid. This does not, of course, mean that it is impossible to provide a limited remedy at this stage. An example of a possible limited remedy is provided in *Klass*, where individuals believing themselves to be under surveillance could complain to the commission overseeing the system of secret surveillance and apply to the German Federal Constitutional Court in exceptional cases. See *Klass*, 79.

the case law of the ECtHR.[36] The Article 13 discussion of notification in *Klass* has been interpreted as requiring notification 'where continued secrecy was not essential'.[37] Following the decision in *Klass*, it was clear that the German notification provisions were considered to amount to 'adequate' protection under the ECHR; however, the ECtHR had not delivered a clear statement as to whether the notification procedures 'were actually *necessitated*'.[38] Accordingly, whether provision for subsequent notification of surveillance was a minimum requirement under the ECHR—or whether it was simply one of several options available to Party States when constructing a Convention compatible regime—remained an open question.

A key case on the question of subsequent notification is *Ekimdzhiev v. Bulgaria*, where the Bulgarian system was found to be in violation of both Article 8 and Article 13.[39] In *Ekimdzhiev*, the Court found that the absence of a notification system in Bulgaria contributed to the lack of safeguards under the Article 8 inquiry and the criticisms made in the Article 8 section of the opinion were reflected in the Article 13 reasoning.[40] The ECtHR condemned the Bulgarian practice of not providing for the notification of targets at any point under any circumstances.[41] Contrasting the Bulgarian situation unfavourably to the legislation considered in *Klass* and *Weber and Saravia v. Germany*, the ECtHR pointed out that unless criminal proceedings were initiated or unless there was an information leak

> a person is never and under no circumstances apprised of the fact that his or her communications have been monitored. The result of this lack of information is that those concerned are unable to seek any redress in respect of the use of secret surveillance measures against them.[42]

The ECtHR in *Ekimdzhiev* went on to criticise the lack of information on remedies available to any individual who discovered that they had been targeted[43] and the Court concluded that the Bulgarian law did not provide an effective remedy.[44] The case of *Ekimdzhiev* represents an important point in the case law

[36] Committee of Ministers of the Council of Europe, Recommendation R (87) 15 (17 September 1987). See de Hert and Boehm (2012), p. 20.

[37] Burke (1981), p. 1113 citing *Klass*, 69, 71.

[38] Collins (1993), p. 31.

[39] As part of an overall assessment of the safeguards provided under Article 8, the Court concluded that insufficient guarantees against abuse were provided for in the Bulgarian legislation *Ekimdzhiev*, 93. Under the Article 13 analysis, the Court concluded that the Bulgarian law did not provide an effective remedy. *Ekimdzhiev*, 102–103.

[40] Cameron has pointed out that there is 'a considerable degree of overlap between the adequacy of the system of safeguards and the adequacy of the grievance procedure provided for the individual'. Cameron (1986), p. 143. Consideration of notification under Article 8 has been defended on the grounds that the Article 8 safeguard of judicial control is also '[i]nextricably linked' to the issue of subsequent notification. *Klass*, 57. In *Ekimdzhiev*, the ECtHR considered the question of notification under both Article 8 and Article 13.

[41] *Ekimdzhiev*, 101.

[42] Ibid.

[43] No information was provided to individuals on applications for a declaratory judgment or an action for damages.

[44] *Ekimdzhiev*, 102–103.

of the ECtHR concerning the issue of notification. While the ECtHR had previously endorsed the notification requirements provided for in the domestic regimes examined in *Klass* and *Weber and Saravia*, it was in the case of *Ekimdzhiev* that the ECtHR directly required notification following the termination of surveillance for the first time.[45] De Hert and Boehm highlight the significance of the decision by pointing out that while the ECtHR was 'satisfied' by the notification requirements detailed in the two German cases, it was in *Ekimdzhiev* that the Court explicitly called for the provision of a notification instrument.[46] This was a major development in the use of Article 13 in surveillance cases, and is an approach that could greatly enhance the transparency of surveillance systems. In turn, this enhanced transparency has the potential to lead to greater protection of the right to private life.

Scepticism regarding the practical stringency of this development must be expressed, however. In the surveillance context, the ECtHR tends to avoid a full consideration of Article 13. Accordingly, the ECtHR has previously found surveillance regimes that provide no subsequent notification, such as the regime examined in *Kennedy*, to be compatible with the Convention. Following the finding in *Kennedy* that the variety of safeguards detailed in the Regulation of Investigatory Powers Act 2000 (RIPA) provided adequate control under Article 8, the ECtHR found no violation of Article 13 regarding the complaint directed against the alleged actual interception of Mr. Kennedy's communications. Rather than engaging in a discussion of the compliance of the UK system under Article 13, the ECtHR decided to take 'regard' of its conclusions on Articles 8 and 6 and concluded that the Investigatory Powers Tribunal (IPT) provided an effective remedy against the alleged interception.[47]

In considering the compatibility of the system with Article 8, the Court found that the jurisdiction of the IPT to examine any allegation brought by an individual who believed that they had been subjected to wrongful surveillance provided an effective remedy.[48] The ECtHR praised the fact that—unlike many other systems in Europe[49]—any person who suspects that his or her communications have been or are being intercepted may apply to the UK complaints mechanism. Drawing from this, the ECtHR asserted that the effectiveness of the tribunal did not depend on notification of the interception subject.[50] This conclusion appears to disregard the

[45] Notification was required 'as soon as notification can be made without jeopardising the purpose of the measure'.

[46] de Hert and Boehm (2012), p. 30.

[47] *Kennedy v The United Kingdom* [2010] ECHR 682, 196. De Hert suggests that the remedial system examined in *Kennedy* provided an alternative means to an effective remedy in lieu of subsequent notification. de Hert and Boehm (2012), p. 32.

[48] *Kennedy*, 75. The ECtHR also noted the various powers of the IPT including access to relevant information, the power to annul interception orders, require destruction of secret material and order compensation. *Kennedy*, 167.

[49] Including those discussed in *Klass*.

[50] *Kennedy*, 167.

reality that innocent people subjected to surveillance are highly unlikely to suspect that they have been targeted.[51]

The case of *Kennedy* illustrates how reliance by the ECtHR on a cumulative analysis of multiple safeguards can result in the right to an effective remedy being lost in the deluge of protective measures. The ECtHR in *Kennedy* analysed the system for redress under Article 8[52] and it is suggested that if the ECtHR had undertaken a fuller analysis under Article 13 there may have been a different result. A better approach for the ECtHR would be to engage in a genuine dual examination of the overlapping issues in both their Article 8 and Article 13 contexts. By declining to engage in an in-depth consideration of the Article 13 issues and instead concentrating its focus on the Article 8 analysis of RIPA,[53] the ECtHR invites States to appease the Court with a 'battery of controls' in an effort to avoid evaluation of effective remedies.[54]

The Article 13 analysis in *Ekimdzhiev* is the most complete analysis in the case law of the ECtHR regarding the issue of subsequent notification. If, however, the ECtHR opts to follow the example set in *Kennedy* in cases where the domestic system under review provides numerous safeguards that contribute to the Article 8 analysis, further application of the notification requirements of *Ekimdzhiev* may be rare and readily avoided by States.

An additional factor, which may hinder attempts to strengthen the requirement of subsequent notification, is the limited circumstances where it is likely to be enforced. The German system of subsequent notification, endorsed by the ECtHR, required notification only where notification could be made 'without jeopardising the purpose of the restriction'.[55] Considering the nontrivial risks of notification, executive authorities and domestic oversight bodies are likely to be amenable to arguments supporting the operative value of secrecy in this area in the majority of cases.

5 Case Study: Criminal Justice (Surveillance) Act 2009

In 2000, the ECtHR confirmed that the use of covert surveillance devices by government authorities can constitute a breach of the right to respect for private life as protected under Article 8.[56] The Surveillance Act provides the legal basis for

[51] Ferguson and Wadham (2000), p. 106.

[52] Having determined that the extensive jurisdiction of the IPT compensated for the lack of notification, the ECtHR then chose to take regard of this conclusion in its Article 13 analysis, and declined to engage in an in-depth consideration of the Article 13 issues. *Kennedy*, 167, 196.

[53] *Kennedy*, 167.

[54] Cameron (2000), p. 38.

[55] *Klass*, 71.

[56] *Khan v The United Kingdom* [2000] Crim LR 684, 24.

the government use of such devices in Irish law. Under the Surveillance Act, An Garda Síochána, the Defence Forces, and the Revenue Commissioners are given a legal basis to carry out covert surveillance in order to combat serious criminal, subversive, or terrorist activity. While the Surveillance Act has a broad title, a formative decision was made in the drafting process to devise a narrow definition of surveillance. Accordingly, the Surveillance Act applies only where a 'surveillance device' as defined under the Act[57] is used to monitor, observe, listen to, or record a person, place, or thing.[58]

Dermot Ahern (the then Minister for Justice, Equality and Law Reform) described the primary purpose of the legislation as facilitating the use in evidence of material gained by means of secret surveillance in criminal proceedings. The ability to use surveillance information as evidence in court was represented as crucial in the fight against organised crime and terrorism. The Explanatory Memorandum to the Criminal Justice (Surveillance) Bill 2009 (Surveillance Bill) explained how the introduction of the Surveillance Act would ensure that 'any possible legal obstacles to the admissibility of such material in criminal trials are removed in cases involving arrestable offences'.[59] While this a legitimate aim, such surveillance also has clear potential for abuse and misuse. Accordingly, in light of the case law discussed previously in this chapter, it is necessary to consider whether the Surveillance Act provides effective remedies for those who wish to vindicate their Article 8 rights at the domestic level.

The Surveillance Act operates under the general principle that a 'Superior Officer'[60] of either An Garda Síochána, the Defence Forces, or the Revenue Commissioners must make an application to a District Court judge for an authorisation before using a surveillance device in an investigation.[61] When the judge of

[57] A 'surveillance device' is 'an apparatus designed or adapted for use in surveillance, but does not include—(*a*) an apparatus designed to enhance visual acuity or night vision, to the extent to which it is not used to make a recording of any person who, or any place or thing that, is being monitored or observed, (*b*) a CCTV within the meaning of section 38 of An Garda Síochána Act 2005, or (*c*) a camera, to the extent to which it is used to take photographs.' Surveillance Act, s. 1.

[58] Surveillance Act, s. 1.

[59] Explanatory memorandum, *Criminal Justice (Surveillance) Bill, 2009.*

[60] A 'superior officer' is '(*a*) in the case of the Garda Síochána, a member of the Garda Síochána not below the rank of superintendent; (*b*) in the case of the Defence Forces, a member of the Defence Forces not below the rank of colonel; and (*c*) in the case of the Revenue Commissioners, an officer of the Revenue Commissioners not below the rank of principal officer.' Surveillance Act, s. 1.

[61] Surveillance Act, s. 4(1)(2)(3). Section 4 of the Surveillance Act describes three categories of circumstances sufficient to justify an application for judicial authorisation. The first category is where the Superior Officer of An Garda Síochána, the Defence Forces, or Revenue Commissioners has reasonable grounds for believing that such surveillance is necessary for determining whether, or under what circumstances, an arrestable offence has been committed, or for obtaining evidence for the purposes of court proceedings in relation to the offence. Surveillance Act, s. 4(a). The second category is where the surveillance in question is necessary for the prevention of an arrestable offence. Surveillance Act, s. 4(b). The third category permits authorisation on the grounds that the surveillance is necessary for the maintenance of the security of the State. Gillane

the District Court is satisfied that the proposed surveillance meets the necessary conditions[62] the judge shall authorise the surveillance.[63] The judge must produce a written authorisation specifying the particulars of the surveillance device that is authorised to be used; the person, place, or thing that is to be the subject of the surveillance; the name of the superior officer to whom the authorisation is issued; any conditions subject to which the authorisation is issued; and the expiration date of the authorisation.[64] Due to the secretive and sensitive context of the surveillance, the authorisation procedure is *ex parte* and heard otherwise than in public.[65]

The Surveillance Act restricts the maximum period of a surveillance authorisation to 3 months, although the length of a surveillance measure may be extended where a Superior Officer applies for a renewal to the authorising judge and provides satisfactory information under oath justifying the continued use of surveillance devices.[66] When examining the availability of remedies under the Surveillance Act, two key sections of the Act are most relevant: Section 11 provides for the complaint procedure under the Act and Section 12 establishes the review process.

6 The Availability of Remedies Under the Surveillance Act

The Surveillance Act complaints system is based on the procedure established under the Interception of Postal Packets and Telecommunications Messages (Regulation) Act 1993 (Interception Act).[67] The Surveillance Act expands the role of the 'Complaints Referee'—as established under the Interception Act—by also bringing complaints made under the Surveillance Act under his or her remit.[68] The 'Complaints Referee' is an individual who must be either a Circuit or District Court judge or a practising barrister or solicitor of not less than 10 years' standing.[69] The Taoiseach appoints the Complaints Referee for a renewable term of 5 years.[70]

criticised the general application, pointing out that arrestable 'essentially means just about any offence beyond very minor public order matters and offences of that class.' Gillane (2009). Available at: http://www.dppireland.ie/filestore/documents/10th_ANPC_-_Sean_Gillane_BL_-_Paper.pdf.

[62] As attested to by the Superior Officer under oath. The Garda who applies must believe on reasonable grounds that the surveillance is part of an investigation or prevention of an arrestable offence or is necessary for national security reasons. Surveillance Act, s. 4(1)(a)(b)(c). The Revenue Commissioners equivalent is described in Surveillance Act, s. 4(3)(a)(b).

[63] In cases of urgency, surveillance will be possible without judicial authorisation for a period of up to 72 h, subject to some conditions.

[64] Surveillance Act, s. 5(6).

[65] Surveillance Act, s. 5(1)(a).

[66] Surveillance Act, s. 5(8); Surveillance Act, s. 6(1).

[67] Interception Act, s. 9. Dáil Debates 29th April 2009 col 338.

[68] Surveillance Act, s. 11(12).

[69] LRC (1996) 130. Interception Act, s. 9(2)(a)(b).

[70] Interception Act, s. 9(2)(c).

If a person believes that they may be subject to surveillance they may apply to the Complaints Referee to request an investigation.[71] Unless the Complaints Referee considers the application 'frivolous or vexatious', he or she will investigate the matter and determine if a contravention of the Surveillance Act has occurred.[72] If the Complaints Referee finds a contravention he or she will notify the people affected in writing and prepare a report of his or her findings to the Taoiseach.[73] If the discovered contravention is material,[74] and the Complaints Referee believes that such action is justified, he or she has the power to direct the quashing of the authorisation, recommend compensation (not exceeding €5000), and report the matter to the 'Designated Judge'.[75] However, if the Complaints Referee believes the provision of any of these remedies would be against the public interest, he or she shall decline to utilise them.[76] If the Complaints Referee finds no relevant contravention, he or she shall write to the complainant stating this fact. The decision of the Complaints Referee is final.[77]

As discussed earlier, while the ECtHR takes the view that it is not essential that remedial institutions be composed of members of the judiciary, the 'powers and procedural guarantees and authority possessed' are relevant when determining effectiveness.[78] When the ECtHR is evaluating remedial institutions, the Court tends to look for evidence of adequate jurisdiction to hear the Convention complaint, the ability to grant binding decisions, powers of enforcement, and independence. However, the ECtHR does not view the existence of each of these features as contingent for compliance and instead has adopted an 'aggregation of remedies' approach. By viewing a collection of remedies in the aggregate, the ECtHR is able to avoid a strict application of these requirements. Unlike the situation criticised by the ECtHR in *Ekimdzhiev*—where the Bulgarian legislation failed to provide any information regarding the form of remedies available[79]—the Surveillance Act clearly grants the Complaints Referee the power to grant remedies,[80] and also grants the Complaints Referee the power to order the Minister for Justice to implement any recommendation for compensation.[81] Similar powers to award compensation were praised by the ECtHR in *Segerstedt-Wiberg v. Sweden*.[82]

[71] Surveillance Act, s. 11(1).

[72] Surveillance Act, s. 11(3).

[73] Surveillance Act, s. 11(4).

[74] 'Material' is undefined in the Act.

[75] Surveillance Act, s. 11 (5)(a)(b)(d). The Designated Judge is discussed further in the following section.

[76] Surveillance Act, s. 11(6).

[77] Surveillance Act, s. 11(7)(8).

[78] *Klass*, 67.

[79] *Ekimdzhiev*, 102.

[80] Interception Act, s. 9(5)(c).

[81] Interception Act, s. 9(12).

[82] In *Segerstedt-Wiberg*, the ECtHR praised the power granted to the Chancellor of Justice to award compensation *Segerstedt-Wiberg v Sweden* [2006] ECHR 597, 118. The ECtHR did not

In spite of these positive points, significant concerns arise about the effectiveness of the Surveillance Act procedure. Connected with the requirement of adequate jurisdiction is the issue of notification. As noted earlier, the ECtHR has stated on several occasions that 'as soon as notification can be made without jeopardising the purpose of the surveillance after its termination, information should be provided to the persons concerned'.[83] In order for an individual to be notified that he or she has been the subject of surveillance, the individual must first suspect they have been the subject of an authorisation or approval. In the report on the Surveillance Act published by the Irish Human Rights Commission (IHRC), the IHRC recommended a watered-down subsequent notification requirement that would only require notification where the 'report of the Designated Judge reveals a case in which an individual has been the subject of surveillance in contravention of the legislation'.[84] The IHRC believed that such a mechanism would enable individuals to 'exercise any further causes of action or remedies available to them' and that it would be particularly important to inform affected individuals of the complaints system.[85] Unfortunately, however, the legislature rejected a notification requirement in any form.

Surveillance is an inherently secretive activity. Until a person is aware that their rights have been infringed, their right to an effective remedy under Article 13 cannot be realised. It follows, therefore, that to ensure a genuine system of effective remedies, a system of notification should be required. Practically speaking, it is those most likely to be innocent of any relevant offence that are least likely to suspect that they are being monitored illegally, thereby reducing the chances that they would even consider making an application to the Complaints Referee. A situation where this could be particularly problematic is in the instance of an innocent third party who happens to communicate with a person under surveillance.

It is clear that the ECHR protects the rights of third parties from interception.[86] In *Lambert v. France* the ECtHR reasoned that depriving a large number of people of 'effective control' would 'in practice render the protective machinery largely devoid of substance'.[87] This logic can be extended to the realities of the Surveillance Act—where an innocent individual is highly unlikely to seek the attention of the Complaints Referee. In line with this reasoning, it is contended that if the other safeguards are to provide protection of substance they must be supported by a

---

find, however, that the flaws in the system of remedies were sufficiently offset by the potential for seeking compensation. *Segerstedt-Wiberg*, 121.

[83] *Ekimdzhiev*, 90; *Klass*, 58; *Leander*, 66.

[84] Irish Human Rights Commission (2009), p. 9. Available at: http://www.ihrc.ie/legislationandpolicy/legislativeobse.html.

[85] *Ibid.*

[86] *Lambert v France* [1998] ECHR 75. An individual is entitled to respect for their private life—and to challenge interferences with their rights—irrespective of whether the interception was carried out on the phone line of a different person. *Lambert*, 21, 34.

[87] *Lambert*, 38.

system of subsequent notification. While the absence of a notification requirement under the Surveillance Act has been described as 'bizarre',[88] it is important to note that there is a distinct possibility that the ECtHR would be satisfied with the procedures as the ECtHR has previously held that the right of any person who suspected that his or her communications had been intercepted to complain to the UK's remedial body obviated the necessity for notification.[89]

The problems with the provision made for remedies in the Surveillance Act do not end with the lack of a notification requirement. Even if an individual correctly suspects that he or she has been subjected to surveillance, the individual can only have this fact confirmed if the Complaints Referee decides there has been a contravention and also believes it is not against the public interest to inform the individual. This discretion given to the Complaints Referee is potentially harmful, particularly as there is no appeal system and his or her determination is final. Similar problems exist in the RIPA system, where information on interceptions is limited to a statement that either a determination has been made in favour of the complainant,[90] or that no determination has been made in favour of the complainant.[91] Accordingly, if the reasoning in *Kennedy* was followed in a Strasbourg examination of the Surveillance Act, this issue may not be found to be problematic. In spite of this, it is contended that the acceptance by the ECtHR of the UK complaints procedure is questionable. A system of protection needs to be interlinked and self-supporting. The willingness of the ECtHR to accept the array of safeguards detailed in RIPA in place of demonstrably effective protection represents a significant defect in its approach.

In addition to providing for a complaints system, the Surveillance Act also provides for the post hoc review of surveillance operations conducted under the Act. In the covert surveillance context, the provision of such review has an important role to play in the protection of privacy rights. Where there is a significant imbalance of knowledge, individual complaints are much less likely to be made. This reality increases the importance of the public watchdog role to even greater significance. By requiring review of the surveillance system, the authorities are subjected to increased scrutiny that should encourage the following of procedures and deter the abusive exercise of surveillance powers. Crucially, a reporting requirement provides insight to interested parties and accordingly facilitates the pursuit of remedies.

[88] Whelan (2010), p. 4. Whelan criticises the fact that the complaints 'allows you to find out if a disclosure request has been made about you only by making a request (if you first believe that you might be the subject of an authorisation or approval!) but you will only be told if an approval or authorisation was made if it turns out that there has been a contravention and the Referee decides it does not offend the public interest to tell you.'

[89] *Kennedy*, 167. In *Kennedy*, the issue of where notification was primarily considered as an issue under the Article 8 analysis.

[90] RIPA, s. 68(4)(a).

[91] RIPA, s. 68(4)(b). The IPT is also governed by the Investigatory Powers Tribunal Rules, 2000.

Under Section 12 of the Surveillance Act a 'Designated Judge' is appointed. The Designated Judge for the Surveillance Act may investigate any case where a District Court judge authorises or renews surveillance and any case where approval is granted for the use of tracking devices or the emergency use of a surveillance device.[92] The Designated Judge is obliged to report to the Taoiseach from 'time to time' and at least once every 12 months.[93]

Concerns have been raised regarding the effectiveness of the review procedure provided under the Surveillance Act. Whelan, for example, is critical of the system and is sceptical of the protection provided by requiring just one annual report.[94] Gillespie is apprehensive about the ability of the supervising judge to adequately manage the work load that would be involved.[95] The Designated Judge is a full-time High Court judge who assumes the review responsibilities under the Surveillance Act as an additional role that he or she must manage.[96] Another shortcoming of the Surveillance Act is the lack of provision for specific resources or staff that would enable the Designated Judge to carry out his or her duties more effectively.

Four reports have been compiled concerning the Surveillance Act to date.[97] Previous reports have provided a description of the systems for record keeping in the three bodies authorised to carry out surveillance and the manner in which the relevant records had been made available. The reports illustrate how these systems operate. For example, the reports point out how the centralised system that operates within An Garda Síochána results in applications being reviewed by senior officers trained in the operation of the Act; this helps to ensure that the procedures and record keeping rules are maintained on the ground.[98]

While a notification requirement, as discussed above, has the potential to offer very valuable protection and transparency, a related—perhaps, more achievable—requirement to report and publish surveillance statistics could serve as a more realisable, albeit more limited, alternative. It is submitted that the publication of statistics achieves some of the goals of effective remedies in the complex context of surveillance. As human rights violations have effects beyond the individual victim, remedies exist not merely 'as private redress but public policy as an important means of promoting compliance with the human rights norm'.[99] Providing for

[92] Surveillance Act, s. 12(4); The Designated Judge under the Surveillance Act is also granted extensive access to official documents Surveillance Act, s. 8(2)(b) 8(5).

[93] Surveillance Act, s. 12.

[94] Whelan (2010), p. 4. One annual report is the minimum requirement under the Surveillance Act.

[95] Gillespie (2009), p. 75.

[96] Surveillance Act, s. 12(1).

[97] The first three reports were delivered by the late Mr Justice Kevin Feeney. The current Designated Judge is Michael Peart.

[98] Report of the Designated Judge pursuant to Section 12 of the Criminal Justice (Surveillance) Act 2009 (2009/2010) 12. Available at: http://www.scribd.com/doc/98008526/Covert-Surveillance-Report-2009-2010; Report of the Designated Judge pursuant to Section 12 of the Criminal Justice (Surveillance) Act 2009 (2010/2011) 10. Available at: http://www.scribd.com/doc/98008741/Covert-Surveillance-Report-2010-2011.

[99] Shelton (1999), p. 52.

greater transparency of surveillance practices aids this function and progresses one of the goals of a system of remedies by acting as a deterrent to abusive action. With knowledge of the restraints the ECtHR has placed on the notification requirement, a call for an obligation on States to publish official statistics of their surveillance practices might be the most pragmatic, yet still beneficial step. While the publication of statistics reporting the levels and types of surveillance carried out by government authorities is likely to contain some gaps,[100] if the limitations and the processes behind the collection, compilation, and publication of surveillance statistics are transparent, statistics can be a useful tool for interested parties to keep the actions of their governments under scrutiny from year to year.[101]

In each of the reports made to date under the Surveillance Act, the Designated Judge has provided an indication of the levels of surveillance that had been carried out in the reporting period. While the numbers in the reports are kept vague, they are indicative and have the potential to be useful when examining trends or significant spikes in usage.[102] In the Surveillance Act Report 2009/2010, the former Designated Judge, Mr Justice Kevin Feeney, reported that the Defence Forces had used the provisions of the Act on less than ten occasions and accordingly he was able to review every use of the Surveillance Act by this body. In the 2010/2011 report he noted that there had been a 'marginal increase' in the use of the Act by the Defence Forces.[103] According to the 2010/2011 report, District Court authorisations granted to An Garda Síochána were in the small double figures.[104] In the 2009/2010 review, the Designated Judge reported that the number of approved applications for the use of tracking devices granted to the Revenue Commissioners was in the small double figures.[105] While the number of approved applications for the use of tracking devices granted to An Garda Síochána in the 2009/2010 period was substantial, the number of such approvals was less than 100.[106] There was a slight increase reported in the 2010/2011 report, but the figure

[100] Schwartz (2003–2004), p. 1252.

[101] See EPIC (2009).

[102] 2010/2011 Report.

[103] 2009/2010 Report, 26. Each Defence Force request had gone through the general District Court authorisation procedure and each application had been successful.

[104] 2010/2011 Report, 16. He noted that there had been a 'small increase'. In the 2009/2010 Report, the Designated Judge reviewed one third of An Garda Síochána authorisations on a random basis. 2009/2010 Report, 15. The Designated Judge found that the cases reviewed had involved appropriate uses of the Surveillance Act and had been used in such matters as the delivery of controlled drugs and investigations of crimes of serious violence against organised criminal or subversive groups. 2009/2010 Report, 15. In the 2010/2011 review, the Designated Judge adopted a different approach and discussed each case with senior officers from An Garda Síochána. The Designated Judge found that the documentation confirmed all the requirements. 2010/2011 Report, 16.

[105] 2009/2010 Report, 20. In the 2010/2011 Report, the Designated Judge merely stated that there was 'a number' of tracking device approvals granted.

[106] 2009/2010 Report, 17.

remained lower than 100.[107] Since assuming the role of Designated Judge, Mr. Justice Michael Peart has continued in a similar vein. He reported in 2014 that the District Court had granted 'less than 50 authorisations' for the police deployment of a surveillance device and reported that there had been 17 approvals for the use of a tracking device in Revenue investigations.[108]

While the provision of these approximate numbers is to be welcomed, it would be preferable if the provision of more complete statistics were mandated as the publication of statistics serves the crucial function of enhancing democratic accountability and transparency. The subjective nature of the descriptors in the Surveillance Act reports—such as 'small double-figures'—are clearly open to broad interpretation and fail to provide a sufficiently detailed picture of the current level of surveillance practices that a more complete and precise disclosure of statistics would provide. There seems to be little justification for not taking the further step of replacing vague reporting with precision; statistics reported in an anonymised manner pose little threat to operational effectiveness, offer greater transparency, and should increase public trust in the system.

7 Conclusion

While Reid has described Article 13 as a 'technical provision' whose role has been 'whittled away by interpretations and not given its proper prominence',[109] this assessment appears outdated when some developments under the Article are considered. Commentators have commended the ECtHR for expanding this formerly 'obscure' Article and encouraging States to 'augment existing domestic remedies and create new ones tailored to the violation of different civil and political liberties'.[110] Certain areas have seen developments beyond the early limited application of the Article. For example, in cases involving the right to a hearing within a reasonable time, the ECtHR has moved past its reluctance to indicate a specific 'form or type' of effective remedy and has become more prescriptive.[111]

It has been remarked that, at times, the ECtHR has 'carefully analysed domestic remedies, often in excruciating detail'.[112] Regrettably, such claims can appear exaggerated in the surveillance context, where the ECtHR is confronted by considerations of national interest and the importance of secrecy. As one of the primary goals of the Convention is to reach a stage where rights are realised without

[107] 2009/2010 Report, 19.

[108] The Report of the Designated Judge pursuant to Section 12 of the Criminal Justice (Surveillance) Act 2009 (2013/2014) 5 and 13.

[109] Reid (2011), p. 712.

[110] Helfer (2008), p. 144.

[111] For example, *Scordino v Germany* (2007) 45 EHRR 7, 183.

[112] Helfer (2008), p. 146.

recourse to Strasbourg, consistently requiring an 'effective and embracing' scheme of national remedies would seem to be good policy for the ECtHR.[113]

Nonetheless, it appears that in more recent years there is an increased willingness on the part of the ECtHR to deal with the issue of Article 13. While the ECtHR has tended to deem it unnecessary to rule on the issue of remedies following a finding of a breach under Article 8, in the case of *Ekimdzhiev* the ECtHR showed appreciation of the importance of considering the Article 13 issues. Notwithstanding the fact that the ECtHR had already found a breach under Article 8, the Court chose to proceed and consider Article 13—even though neither party to the case had made a submission on the Article 13 point.[114]

In light of these developments, it does appear that the ECtHR is altering its attitude towards Article 13, even in the complex context of surveillance cases. This is a positive development that suggests that national governments will need to pay increased attention to such issues in future. However, it is important to remember that these changes are incremental and several issues remain regarding the application of Article 13 in surveillance cases.

While the special requirements of secrecy and sensitivity that pertain to surveillance systems appear to rationalise a flexible approach to Article 13, the 'inherent secrecy' of some control systems can render the right to respect for private life especially vulnerable.[115] It is clear that the failure of the Surveillance Act to provide for notification is a pernicious flaw that serves as a serious hindrance to effective remedies. While the ECtHR is unlikely to require such a provision in light of the open jurisdiction of the Complaints Referee, it is maintained that without notification, access to an effective remedy under the Surveillance Act is fatally undermined. Where individual notification is unfeasible, the provision of detailed and accurate surveillance statistics has the potential to achieve some of the goals of notification. While previous reports of the Designated Judge have included some approximate description of surveillance levels, it is maintained the Surveillance Act should be amended to mandate more precise and granular statistics.

References

Buergenthal, T. (1966). The domestic status of the European Convention on Human Rights: A second look. *Journal of the ICJ, 7*, 55.

Burke, K. (1981). Secret surveillance. *Stanford Law Review, 33*, 1113–1140.

[113] Harris et al. (2009), p. 575.

[114] *Ekimdzhiev*, 93–94. In respect of the requirement for particular remedies to address specific wrongs, in *Segerstedt-Wiberg* the ECtHR both praised the Swedish system for the provision of compensation and potential judicial appeal, and severely criticised the system for the absence of any remedies offering the opportunity to rectify or erase the stored data. *Segerstedt-Wiberg*, 119–122.

[115] Dissenting opinion of Judge Ryssdal in *Leander*, 5.

Cameron, I. (1986). Telephone Tapping and the Interception of Communications Act 1985. *Northern Ireland Legal Quarterly, 37*(2), 126.
Cameron, I. (2000). *National security and the European Convention on Human Rights*. The Hague, the Netherlands: Kluwer Law International.
Collins, M. (1993). Telephone tapping and the law in Ireland. *ICLJ, 3*(1), 31.
Committee of Ministers of the Council of Europe. (1987). Recommendation R (87) 15.
Committee of Ministers of the Council of Europe. (1998). Recommendation R (98) 13.
de Hert, P., & Boehm, F. (2012). The rights of notification after surveillance is over: Ready for recognition? In J. Bus, M. Crompton, M. Hildebrandt, & G. Metakides (Eds.), *Digital enlightenment yearbook* (p. 20). Amsterdam: Ios Press.
Eckes, C. (2009). *EU counter-terrorist policies and fundamental rights: The case of individual sanctions*. Oxford, England: OUP.
EPIC. (2009). FBI reporting concerning pen register/trap and trace statistics [letter to Senator Patrick Leahy]. Retrieved from http://epic.org/privacy/wiretap/ltr_pen_trap_leahy_final.pdf.
Ferguson, G., & Wadham, J. (2000). Privacy and surveillance: A review of the Regulation of the Investigatory Powers Act 2000. *EHRLR, 101*.
Gillane, S. (2009). *Criminal Justice (Surveillance) Bill 2009*. Paper presented at the Annual National Prosecutors Conference, Dublin, 23 May 2009. Retrieved from http://www.dppireland.ie/filestore/documents/10th_ANPC_-_Sean_Gillane_BL_-_Paper.pdf.
Gillespie, A. (2009). Covert surveillance, human rights and the law. *ICLJ, 19*(3), 71.
Harris, D., O'Boyle, M., Bates, E., & Buckley, C. (2009). *Law of the European Convention on Human Rights*. Oxford, England: OUP.
Helfer, L. (2008). Redesigning the European Court of Human Rights: Embeddedness as a deep structural principle of the European human rights regime. *EJIL, 19*(1), 125.
Irish Human Rights Commission. (2009, May). Observations on the Criminal Justice (Surveillance) Bill 2009. Retrieved from http://www.ihrc.ie/legislationandpolicy/legislativeobse.html.
Mowbray, A. (2004). *The development of positive obligations under the European Convention on Human Rights by the European Court of Human Rights*. Oxford, England: Hart.
Reid, K. (2011). *A practitioner's guide to the ECHR*. London: Sweet & Maxwell.
Schwartz, P. (2003–2004). Evaluating telecommunications surveillance in Germany: The lessons of the Max Planck Institute's Study. *The George Washington Law Review, 72*, 1244.
Shelton, D. (1999). *Remedies in international human rights law*. Oxford, England: Oxford University Press.
Solove, D. (2008). *Understanding privacy*. Cambridge, MA: Harvard University Press.
van Dijk, P., van Hoof, F., van Rijn, A., & Zwaak, L. (Eds.). (2006). *Theory and practice of the European Convention on Human Rights*. Antwerp, Belgium: Martinus Nijhoff.
Whelan, A. (2010). Are they watching you? The Criminal Justice (Surveillance) Act 2009. *BR, 15*(1), 1.
Wildhaber, L. (2005). Applying and supervising the ECHR: The improvement of domestic remedies with particular emphasis on cases of unreasonable length of proceedings. Paper presented at a workshop held at the initiative of the Polish Chairmanship of the Council of Europe's Committee of Ministers, Strasbourg, 28 April 2005, 9. Retrieved from http://www.echr.coe.int/NR/rdonlyres/82597AB6-124F-48D5-8BBB-792899EB0C6A/0/AmeliorationsRecours_EN.pdf.

The 'Contractual Enforcement' of Human Rights in Europe

Roberto Cippitani

1 Introduction

The notion of the contract was established to achieve patrimonial objectives (i.e. property protection) not least in relation to the transfer of key rights between individuals. However today domestic and transnational legislation, as well as case law, does generally recognise the importance, and the impacts, of human rights law, as it relates to contractual matters, especially in respect of the following areas: social services, public administration, informed consent to health treatments and research activities, and the protection of privacy. This chapter looks specifically at changing legal perceptions of 'the contract' in relation to the protection of human rights in Europe, and argues that the blurring of the various distinctions between the fields of public and private law has enabled domestic judges to actively embed more fully fundamental human rights protections.

2 The Function of Contracts in Traditional Civil Law

Private law traditionally concerns 'patrimony,' in other words, those sets of civil obligations and property rights which can be measured in monetary terms.[1] This approach was formalised by European continental civil codes in the nineteenth and twentieth centuries, based upon the work of the Pandectist scholars who 'recovered' Roman law and founded modern private law.[2] Within this context, contract law,

[1] See *Relazione al Re* to the Italian Civil Code (para 23).

[2] See for example Savigny (1840), Windscheid (1900), Domat (1689), and Pothier (1819).

R. Cippitani (✉)
Università degli Studi di Perugia, Perugia, Italy
e-mail: roberto.cippitani@unipg.it

A. Diver, J. Miller (eds.), *Justiciability of Human Rights Law in Domestic Jurisdictions*, DOI 10.1007/978-3-319-24016-9_13

together with the notion of legal succession, provided the main legal frameworks for the regulation of property circulation.[3] The parties in such relationships were considered to be formally equal with domestic laws and customs on contract generally being underpinned by the notion of bi-lateral exchange.[4] Whatever the national law might be, the notion of 'the contract' is clearly based upon this concept of *exchange*, which can be expressed in various ways: for example as '*corrispettività*' and '*onerosità*' in the Italian *Codice Civile*[5]; '*bilateralité*' and '*onerosité*' under French Law,[6] or as bilateral contracts in accordance with the common law. The function of other types of obligation (e.g. tort, delict, unjust enrichment, *negotiorum gestio*[7]) is to ensure and maintain patrimonial equilibrium between those involved in a legal relationship, for example via indemnity and liability for compensation. This may be achieved through the use of such concepts as rights in *rem,* tortious liability, unjust enrichment or *negotiorum gestio*. The difference between contractual and non-contractual obligations is largely to do with the free will of the individuals concerned: obligations arising from contracts are based on presumed agreement between the parties, whilst non-contractual obligations tend to arise from 'non-legal' conduct such as a wilfully reckless act or

[3] Caprioli (2008) and Halperin (1992).

[4] As Portalis (1891) argued on the draft of the Napoleonic Civil Code, '*Les contrats et les successions sont les grands moyens d'acquérir ce qu'on n'a point encore.*' ('Contracts and successions are the main means of acquiring what one has not yet'). On this ground, according to Article 1101 of Code Civil: '*Le contrat est une convention par laquelle une ou plusieurs personnes s'obligent, envers une ou plusieurs autres, à donner, à faire ou à ne pas faire quelques chose'*. ('The contract is an agreement by which one or more persons undertake, as regards one or more others, to give, to do or not to do something'). Similarly, the Italian Codice Civile defines contracts as agreements aimed at establishing, modifying or ending patrimonial relationships (see Article 1321 Codice Civile). Article 1254 of the Spanish Código Civil states that: '*El contrato existe desde que una o varias personas consienten en obligarse, respecto de otra u otras, a dar alguna cosa o prestar algun servicio.*' ('The contract exists where one or more persons agree to be bound, for another or others, to give something or provide some service').

[5] Both concepts considered in the Italian Civil Code refer to exchange, but from two differing viewpoints. The *corrispettività* means an exchange of performances between parties to the same contract. A lack of *corrispettività* (e.g. in case of breach, force majeure or hardship) leads to termination of the contract. *Onerosità* however, refers to patrimonial equilibrium between two parties, which can be achieved via *corrispettività* (exchange of performances) or through a series of contracts which, considered together, achieve patrimonial equilibrium. Lack of *onerosità* may class an act or relationship as gratuitous. Gratuitous acts, including donations, may amount to patrimonial disequilibrium between parties, prejudicing creditors, or decreasing the patrimony of the debtor (see Article 809 of the Italian Civil Code).

[6] According to the French Civil Code '*bilateralité*' is an exchange not of performances, but of obligations. The concept of *onerosité* is similar to that of *onerosità* within the Italian Civil Code.

[7] '*Negotiourm gestio*' refers to non-contractual obligations, 'arising out of an act performed without due authority in connection with the affairs of another person' (See further Article 11 Regulation (EC) No 864/2007 of the European Parliament and of the Council of 11 July 2007, OJ 2007 L 199/40) for example where one 'interferes in the business transaction of another person in that person's absence, done without authority but out of concern or friendship.' Under *negotiorum gestio* the actor is entitled to be reimbursed for any expenses incurred.

negligence, or from some event which results in unjust enrichment of one of the parties.[8]

3 National and International Constitutionalism

From the second half of the nineteenth century, the social and ideological context of private law changed significantly. Under Catholic doctrine,[9] the notion of charity moved towards the social or public sphere, through such concepts as 'social solidarity,'[10] which began to appear in the discourses of various human sciences, such as sociology and economics.[11] Especially relevant were the theories of those French 'solidarists'[12] who adopted, with some significant changes, the ideas of the Revolution, inspired by affirmations of individualism and equality. Solidarism thus influenced thinking on social rights as they emerged from Catholic and socialist co-operativist theories, with political, ideological, religious, and scientific debates then being reflected in legal discourse. The first field of application for the concept of solidarity was within administrative law, to develop tools for enabling early social insurance schemes and other forms of public protection. Civil law began to be considered from a social rights perspective: as authors such as Menger and Renner observed, highlighting the social functions of private law.[13] Menger, during the debate on the new German Civil Code, demonstrated how much private law in Germany and Austria favoured the interests of the wealthy, and argued the need to draft a civil code, which would maintain societal peace.[14] Moreover two other factors changed the fate of private law: constitutionalisation and European integration. Constitutions embedded the fundamental rights of all persons, and endorsed the rule of law,[15] underscoring the State's legal obligations to actively protect

[8] See further Jansen (2010). For a critical overview of the topic see Jhering (1972) on how contract law, rather than simply amounting to an expression of egoism, might more accurately be seen as representing a 'wonder of humankind' by allowing for individualised self-interests to be re-organised into common goals, which should ultimately satisfy the needs or interests of all concerned.

[9] See the encyclical Rerum Novarum of Leo XIII of 15 May 1891.

[10] See the encyclical *Mater et Magistra* of John XXIII in 1961, which refers explicitly for the first time to the term 'solidarity'; see further http://w2.vatican.va/content/john-xxiii/en/encyclicals/documents/hf_j-xxiii_enc_15051961_mater.html (accessed 06.06.15).

[11] See for example the work of economists of the *Verein für Socialpolitik* (the Association of Social Policy).

[12] See for example Bourgeois (1911, 1919) and Duguit (1908).

[13] See Renner (1929) and Menger (1908).

[14] Ibid.

[15] Sepúlveda Iguíniz (2013), pp. 239–244.

political, civil and social rights, through solidarity and substantive equality.[16] Constitutions thus attribute 'social' character to the State,[17] with the protection of individual rights furthered through international law principles, and the establishment of 'global constitutionalism;'[18] this in turn promotes further development of national constitutions.[19] Several international law conventions are especially relevant: the UN Charter of 1945, for example, aimed 'to save succeeding generations from the scourge of war, which twice in our lifetime has brought untold sorrow to mankind,' stressing the need 'to reaffirm faith in fundamental human rights, in the dignity and worth of the human person, in the equal rights of men and women' in order 'to promote social progress and better standards of life.'[20]

Regional protections also exist in respect of Europe and America, via transnational Courts, whilst the process of European integration particularly detracts from the argument that private law is only truly concerned with domestic relationships. The community 'market,' as an area without borders, and in which there is free movement of persons, goods, services and capital, is recognised and protected. This market is not merely economic in nature, but also gives rise to a legal system,[21] which provides precedent relevant to civil matters, including those arising under the laws of contract and obligations. Civil matters thus serve as a sort of cornerstone,[22] with European integration having a profound impact on traditional notions of the contractual relationship. This occurs via legislative intervention (regulating directly

[16] See Cippitani (2013), pp. 642–649; Cippitani (2010); Pérez Luño (1991), p. 19; Rawls (1980), pp. 4–7.

[17] See for example Article 1 of the French Constitution of 1958, which provides that 'France shall be an indivisible, secular, democratic and social Republic.' (available at http://www.conseil-constitutionnel.fr/conseil-constitutionnel/english/constitution/constitution-of-4-october-1958.25742.html, accessed 06.06.15); Article 20 (1) of the German Grundgesetz, setting out that 'Mindful also of its responsibility toward future generations, the state shall protect the natural foundations of life and animals by legislation and, in accordance with law and justice, by executive and judicial action, all within the framework of the constitutional order.' (available http://www.gesetze-im-internet.de/englisch_gg/englisch_gg.html#p0079, accessed 06.06.15); Article 1 (3) of the Romanian Constitution ('Romania is a democratic and social state, governed by the rule of law, in which human dignity, the citizens' rights and freedoms, the free development of human personality, justice and political pluralism represent supreme values, in the spirit of the democratic traditions of the Romanian people and the ideals of the Revolution of December 1989, and shall be guaranteed'(available http://www.cdep.ro/pls/dic/site.page?den=act2_2&par1=1#t1c0s0sba1, accessed 06.06.15); Article 2 of the Constitution of Slovenia: 'Slovenia is a state governed by the rule of law and a social state' (available http://www.us-rs.si/en/about-the-court/legal-basis/, accessed 06.06.15).

[18] See Bobbio (1984) and Espinoza de los Monteros Sánchez (2010).

[19] See Pernice (1999), p. 703; Häberle (2002), p. 455; Cardone (2011).

[20] Charter of the United Nations: Preamble (available at http://www.un.org/en/documents/charter/, accessed 06.06.15).

[21] ECJ, Case 26/62 *Van Gend en Loos* ECR [1963] *ECR* 1, p. 3; ECJ, Case 6/64 *Costa* [1964] *ECR* 585; ECJ, Case 155/79 *AM & S Limited* [1982] *ECR* 1575, para 18.

[22] See Chapter VII of the Presidency Conclusions of the Tampere European Council 15 and 16 October 1999.

such matters as contracts between professionals and consumers; agreements between enterprises; public procurements) and non-legislative actions through the elaboration of common principles, for example, those provided in the Draft of the Common Frame of Reference ('DCFR').[23] European Union law also includes among its primary objectives the protection of human rights,[24] especially in the wake of the Lisbon Treaty, which constitutionalised the Charter of Fundamental Rights ('EU Charter'). The Communication of the European Commission, accompanying the Charter of Fundamental Rights, provided that all legislative and other proposals of the Commission would have to be assessed, taking into account their compliance with the EU Charter.[25]

4 The Impact of Human Rights Law on the Law of Contract

When the various Constitutions entered into force, they had a profound impact on contract law. Initially such 'direct effect' was denied,[26] with any reference to fundamental rights only really applying to public acts carried out by the State;[27] provisions relating to constitutional rights, whether social, political, or economic, were not viewed as having immediate effect,[28] nor were they regarded as enforceable in court.[29] The situation began to change post-Weimar Constitution,[30] when a general rule of 'good faith'[31] was argued (on the basis of constitutional principles) to protect employee salaries against inflation. Since the 1960s, the tendency to interpret traditional civil laws, especially those enshrined in Civil Codes, using a fundamental rights perspective has gradually become accepted. This is not only so in respect of family law, which was the initial field of application for constitutional principles, but also in relation to patrimonial relationships.[32] Equating a right to property with having absolute power over the goods in question (as occurs for example in Article 832 of the Italian Civil Code) had implications for the principles

---

[23] See in particular von Bar et al. (2009). For an overview of the DCFR, see Fuchs (2008), pp. S1–S6; Clive (2008), pp. S13–S31.

[24] See ECJ, Case 29/69 *Stauder* [1969] *ECR* 419.

[25] See Rodotà (2005), pp. 21 ff.

[26] Ost (1990), p. 161.

[27] Crisafulli (1952), p. 135; Barettoni Arleri (1975), pp. 410 ff.

[28] Calamandrei (1950), pp. 28 ff.; Lucifredi (1952), p. 275.

[29] See Lega (1952, 1969); Chiarelli (1957), p. 10.

[30] Costa (2002), Vol. IV; Mortati (1946).

[31] See section 242 BGB (Performance in good faith): "An obligor has a duty to perform according to the requirements of good faith, taking customary practice into consideration" (available at http://www.gesetze-im-internet.de/englisch_bgb, accessed 06.06.15).

[32] Rodotà (1990).

of social utility,[33] especially in relation to such key common interests as environmental protection.[34]

---

[33] See Article 151 Weimer Constitution (1919) which, although it granted economic freedom, also provided that economic relationships had to respect fundamental rights principles and grant dignity. Common interest was also key, under Article 153 (see http://germanhistorydocs.ghi-dc.org/sub_document.cfm?document_id=3937, accessed 06.06.15) See also Article 33(1) Spanish Constitution, which refers to the social function of property and which places limitations on the ground of the social utility; see also the social aims of economic relationships outlined in Article 80 of the Portuguese Constitution, and Article 74 of the Slovenian Constitution which provides that trade enterprises cannot be carried out in opposition to public interests. (See also Spanish Constitution (1978) at http://www.congreso.es/portal/page/portal/Congreso/Congreso/Hist_Normas/Norm/const_espa_texto_ingles_0.pdf, accessed 06.06.15). The German *Grundgesetz* S.14 (2) implicitly quotes the Weimar Constitution '*Eigentum verpflichtet. Sein Gebrauch soll zugleich dem Wohle der Allgemeinheit dienen*' ('Property entails obligations. Its use shall also serve the public good' available http://www.gesetze-im-internet.de/englisch_gg, accessed 06.06.15) Article 43 (1) of the Irish Constitution similarly states that 'The State acknowledges that man, in virtue of his rational being, has the natural right, antecedent to positive law, to the private ownership of external goods.' 43(2) notes that 'The State accordingly guarantees to pass no law attempting to abolish the right of private ownership or the general right to transfer, bequeath, and inherit property.' (The principles of social justice are also referred to, as is the common good.). (See http://www.irishstatutebook.ie/en/constitution, accessed 06.06.15). Article 9 of the Preamble to the French Constitution (1946) further states '*Tout bien, toute entreprise, dont l'exploitation a ou acquiert les caractères d'un service public national ou d'un monopole de fait, doit devenir la propriété de la collectivité.*' ('All goods, any company whose operation has or acquires the character of a national public service or a monopoly in fact must become the property of the community.') See http://www.conseil-constitutionnel.fr/conseil-constitutionnel/francais/la-constitution/les-constitutions-de-la-france/constitution-de-1946-ive-republique.5109.html (accessed 06.06.15). Article 11 (2) of the Charter of the Fundamental Rights and Fundamental Freedoms of the Czech Republic establishes also that law must frame legal ownership with respect to the needs of society as a whole (see http://www.usoud.cz/en/charter-of-fundamental-rights-and-freedoms, accessed 06.06.15).

[34] See the French *Charte de l'Environnement* (2004) Article 6 '*Les politiques publiques doivent promouvoir un développement durable. A cet effet, elles concilient la protection et la mise en valeur de l'environnement, le développement économique et le progrès social*' ('Public policies shall promote sustainable development. To this end they shall reconcile the protection and enhancement of the environment, economic development and social progress') http://www.legifrance.gouv.fr/Droit-francais/Constitution/Charte-de-l-environnement-de-2004, accessed 06.06.15); Article 9 (2) of the Italian Constitution (1948) '*Tutela il paesaggio e il patrimonio storico e artistico della Nazione*' ('It [the Italian Republic]safeguards the landscape and the historical and artistic heritage of the Nation') (http://www.governo.it/Governo/Costituzione/principi.html, accessed 06.06.15); Article 37 of the European Charter of Human Rights (on environmental protection) establishes that 'A high level of environmental protection and the improvement of the quality of the environment must be integrated into the policies of the Union and ensured in accordance with the principle of sustainable development.' (http://www.europarl.europa.eu/charter/pdf/text_en.pdf, accessed 06.06.15). Article 23 of Belgium's Constitution also sets out 'le droit à la protection d'un environnement sain' ('the right to protection of a healthy environment' http://www.senate.be/doc/const_fr.html, accessed 06.06.15) See also Article 21 of the Constitution of The Netherlands (stating that 'It shall be the concern of the authorities to keep the country habitable and to protect and improve the environment.' http://www.government.nl/documents-and-publications/regulations/2012/10/18/the-constitution-of-the-kingdom-of-the-netherlands-2008.htm, accessed 06.06.15) and Article 20 of Finland's Constitution, on how 'Nature

Legal systems shaped by Constitutions are thus no longer focused only on the regulation of patrimonial issues.[35] Fundamental rights, as recognised and protected by Constitutions, are applied to vertical relationships (between citizens and public authorities) and to horizontal relationships (between individuals). Particular attention has however been devoted to the constitutional interpretation of contract law.[36] The first field of application for fundamental rights was within employment contracts, where the rights of the worker were not limited to the payment of a salary, but also included such non-patrimonial issues as the right to strike.[37] Other particularly relevant issues include equality between the contracting parties, and the concept of respect.

4.1 *Substantive Equality of Contracting Parties*

Whether parties to contracts are always on an equal footing remains doubtful. Weaker parties often require protection, as *Berliner Verkehrsbetriebe* (BVG) [1993][38] established. Although individual autonomy is recognised by the German constitution, the court observed that contracts could create significant power imbalances: judicial oversight might be needed to investigate the existence of such disparities, and perhaps provide redress for these. At the supranational level, the European Court of Justice, via the *Courage* judgement,[39] pointed out how one party may be in a situation of 'serious inferiority' through contractual limitations, and a lack of information. That said, a general right *to be informed* is provided under Article 11 of the EU Charter.[40] Several directives foresaw the need to offer a wide range of pre-contractual information. In addition to the information required by

---

and its biodiversity, the environment and the national heritage are the responsibility of everyone. The public authorities shall endeavour to guarantee for everyone the right to a healthy environment and for everyone the possibility to influence the decisions that concern their own living environment' at https://www.finlex.fi/fi/laki/kaannokset/1999/en19990731.pdf, accessed 06.06.15).

[35] Carbonnier (2004), p. 97 on solidarity in private relationships.

[36] Cédras (2003) available at https://www.courdecassation.fr/publications_26/rapport_annuel_36/rapport_2003_37/deuxieme_partie_tudes_documents_40/tudes_diverses_43/doctrine_devant_6260.html (accessed 6.6.15).

[37] See Article L. 120-2 of the French Code du travail. See also, for example, the judgments of the *Cour de Cassation*, Soc., 13 March 2001, in Bull. 2001, V, no 87, p. 66; Soc., 28 May 2003, no 02-40.273, concerning the unfairness of the dismissal in case of violation of fundamental rights.

[38] Berliner Verkehrsbetriebe (BVG) [1993], judg. in *Foro Italiano,* 1995, IV, 88 ff., with the commentary of Barenghi.

[39] ECJ, Case C-453/99 *Courage Ltd.* [2001] *ECR* I-6297.

[40] Article 11 (1) of the Charter of Fundamental Rights (Freedom of expression and information) provides that 'Everyone has the right to freedom of expression'. The right includes 'freedom to hold opinions and to receive and impart information and ideas without interference by public authority and regardless of frontiers.' See http://www.europarl.europa.eu/charter/pdf/text_en.pdf (accessed 06.6.2015).

consumer contracts, Directive 97/5/EC on cross-border bank transfers included the obligation to provide information on execution times and transaction expenses.[41] Directive 2000/31/EC (on electronic commerce) requires the communication of information regarding the different technical steps needed to conclude the contract, storage information systems, languages in which the contract can be concluded, as well as the possible presence of codes of conduct.[42] Directive 87/344/EEC (on legal protections in the insurance sector) requires insurers to inform customers of their right to request arbitration,[43] whilst Article 4 (2) of Directive 90/314/EEC (on package travel) sets out that the text of the contract has to include specific information.[44]

Under Directive 92/96/EEC Article 31 (2) and Annex II (on life insurance) insurers must provide the insured with updated information on their insurance company and the policy conditions.[45] Similarly, Directive 87/102/EEC Article 6 (2) (on consumer credit) requires that the consumer must be informed of any change in the annual rate of interest and other applicable charges.[46] Directive 97/5/EC Article 4 (on cross border bank transfers) provides that after payment, the bank is obliged to provide the customer with the necessary information to identify the transaction, the initial amount, the fees and expenses.[47] Article 12 of Directive 86/653/EEC (on self-employed commercial agents) requires that the commercial agent be supplied with a statement of the commissions earned, along with the essential elements upon which the calculation was based. Such 'formalism' also serves to verify whether or not a contract has met its legal obligations. As Jannarelli argued, formalism here also performs the same function as a product label, showing the characteristics of the contract.[48]

---

[41] See Article 3 (Prior information on conditions) of Directive 97/5/EC of the European Parliament and of the Council of 27 January 1997 on cross-border credit transfers, OJ 1997, L 043, p. 25.

[42] See in particular Article 10 (Information to be provided), paras 1 and 2 of Directive 2000/31/EC of the European Parliament and of the Council of 8 June 2000 on certain legal aspects of information society services, in particular electronic commerce, in the Internal Market ('Directive on electronic commerce'), OJ 2000, L 178, p. 1.

[43] See the text of Council Directive 87/344/EEC of 22 June 1987 on the coordination of laws, regulations and administrative provisions relating to legal expenses insurance, OJ 1987, L 185, p. 77.

[44] See Council Directive 90/314/EEC of 13 June 1990 on package travel, package holidays and package tours, OJ 1990, L 158, p. 59.

[45] See Council Directive 92/96/EEC of 10 November 1992 on the coordination of laws, regulations and administrative provisions relating to direct life assurance and amending Directives 79/267/EEC and 90/619/EEC (third life assurance Directive), OJ 1992, L 360, p. 1.

[46] Council Directive 87/102/EEC of 22 December 1986 for the approximation of the laws, regulations and administrative provisions of the Member States concerning consumer credit, OJ 1987, L 042, p. 48.

[47] See Directive 97/5/EC of the European Parliament and of the Council of 27 January 1997 on cross-border credit transfers, OJ 1997, L 043, p. 25.

[48] Jannarelli (2002). This approach is also evident in the DCFR where a list is provided of pre-contractual information that the parties should exchange *inter se*, either in general, or with

4.2 The Obligation to Respect Fundamental Rights

In sum, private law relationships can claim fundamental rights protections. As the German Constitutional Court (*Bundesverfassungsgericht*) confirmed in the case of *Parabolantenne* (interpreting the § 242 of the BGB in the light of § 5 (1) Basic Law), the right to freedom of information prevented a landlord from refusing a tenant permission to install a satellite antenna.[49] Another example is provided by EU law, according to which, grants provided by the European Commission have to comply with environmental protection rights and equality between women and men.[50] Perhaps most significantly, contractual relationships must also protect human dignity, a concept which is core to fundamental human rights.[51] As highlighted by the Advocate General Christine Stix-Hackl in the *Omega* case,[52] 'human dignity' is an expression of the respect to be attributed to each human being on account of his or her humanity. It is concerned with protection of the essence or nature of the human being *per se*—that is to say, the 'substance' of mankind. Mankind itself is therefore reflected in the concept of human dignity; it is what distinguishes him from other creatures. However, this substance of human dignity is ultimately determined by a particular 'conception of man.'[53] Thus dignity is considered to be a sort of 'concept-matrix' needed to protect humanity, not least those who are most vulnerable to suffering rights violations.[54]

In accordance with the Article 1 of the EU Charter (see also Section 1 of German *Grundgesetz*), human dignity has to be not only respected, but also actively protected by States and indeed by international and supranational organizations.[55] For that reason, public administrations are entitled to intervene if private relationships might affect human dignity or infringe fundamental rights, as affirmed within

reference to particular contracts such as those concerning consumers, or those between professionals (Articles 14–29 DCFR). The consequence of violating obligation of information is compensation not only for loss of interest, but also for having concluded the contract on differing terms to those that were accepted (Article 30 DCFR).

[49] BVerfG 9 February 1994, BVerfGE 90, 27 (Parabolantenne).

[50] ECJ, Case C-44/96 *Mannesmann Anlagenbau Austria AG et oth v Strohal Rotationsdruck GesmbH* [1998] *ECR* I-73.

[51] See the Preamble to the Charter of Fundamental Rights of the European Union and Article 16 French Civil Code. On the concept of dignity within the EU Charter, see also Jones (2012); for dignity in bioethics see Andorno (2009).

[52] See the opinions of Advocate General Christine Stix-Hackl, submitted 18 March 2004 and concerning ECJ, Case C-36/02, *Omega Spielhallen- und Automatenaufstellungs-GmbH/ Oberbürgermeisterin der Bundesstadt Bonn* [2004] *ECR* I-9609.

[53] Ibid., para 75.

[54] Mislawski (2010).

[55] Sanz Caballero (2013), pp. 466–474. See also the case-law of the Court of Justice of the European Union affirming the need for states to respect fundamental rights: ECJ, Case C-2/92, *Bostock* [1994] *ECR* I-955, para 16; ECJ, Case C-292/97, *Karlsson et oth.* [2000] *ECR* I-2737, para 37; ECJ, Case C-442/00 *Rodríguez Caballero* [2002] *ECR* I-11915, para 30.

Omega by the Court of Justice.[56] The autonomy of parties to a contract cannot be pleaded to justify violations of fundamental human rights, as recognized also by the Committee on the International Covenant on the Civil and Political Rights ('ICCPR').[57]

This rights-led perspective, with respect to traditional private law fields, is particularly evident within the DCFR.[58] Article I.-1:102 provides that the rules contained therein must be interpreted and applied in the light of fundamental rights and freedoms. The DCFR has also 'privatised' fundamental rights, recognising the 'overriding nature' of such principles as solidarity and the promotion of social responsibility, the preservation of cultural and linguistic diversity, and the protection and promotion of welfare within domestic markets.[59]

4.3 The Consequences of Non-compliance with Human Rights

The violation of human rights in relation to contracts leads to nullity of the agreement, as national case law has confirmed, for example, in relation to discrimination on grounds of nationality or ethnicity.[60] In particular, Article VI.-2: 203 states that

> loss caused to a natural person as a result of infringement of his or her right to respect for his or her dignity, such as the rights to liberty and privacy, and the injury as such are legally relevant damage.

The violation of these rights carries sanctions under civil law: Article II.-7: 301 of the DCFR also states that

> a contract is void to the extent that: (a) it infringes a principle recognised as fundamental in the laws of the Member States of the European Union; and (b) nullity is required to give effect to that principle.

Compensation does not refer only to patrimonial rights damages, as established for example by the Court of Justice in *Leitner,* in relation to Article 5 of the Directive on package travel.[61] The consequences of non-compliance with

---

56 ECJ, Case C-36/02, *Omega* [2004] *op cit.* n 52.

57 See Communication No. 854/1999: France. 26/07/2002. CCPR/C/75/D/854/1999, especially para 7.(4) in respect of the ban by the French authorities of the activity known as 'dwarf throwing'. See also Wilkinson (2003), p. 42; Millins (1996), pp. 375 ff.

58 Cherednychenko (2010), p. 42; see also Hesselink (2003), p. 119; Colombi Ciacchi (2006), p. 167.

59 See von Bar et al. (2009), paras 14–17.

60 See Tribunal of Padua, order of 19 May 2005 '*Giurisprudenza italiana*' (2006), p. 5, with the commentary of Maffeis. Furthermore the relevance of human rights to contract law is evident within the DCFR, books II and III, and in some of the provisions of Book VI (on torts.).

61 ECJ, Case C-168/00 *Leitner v TUI Deutschland* [2002] *ECR* I-2631.

fundamental rights principles may also be relevant to grant agreements, for example in respect of the Horizon 2020 Programme, which is the main instrument of the European Union for funding scientific research.[62] In EU research grants, any violation of ethical principles results in termination of the agreement between the Commission and the beneficiaries.[63]

4.4 'General Clauses' as Expressions of Fundamental Rights Principles

In contrast to domestic Civil Codes (which aim to avoid references to the more vague notions found in some contracts, i.e. 'good faith,' 'equity,' and 'correctness'), case law may frequently look to generally wording.[64] 'Good faith' is considered to be the main and most general expression of the duty of solidarity within private law[65] as shown by the Italian *Corte di Cassazione*,[66] in relation to Article 2 of the Constitution.[67] The Court's approach to such issues as unlimited liability in performance bonds ('fideiussione *omnibus*'[68]), unfair penalty clauses,[69] failure to honour contractual obligations,[70] and arbitrary withdrawal,[71] bears this out. At a wider level, the DCFR also refers to such general concepts as 'reasonableness' (Article I-1: 104) and 'basic principles infringing contracts' (Article II.-7: 301). The concept of 'good faith' is also seen in Directive 1986/653 in respect of fulfilling

---

[62] See the paragraph 29 of the Preamble of the Regulation (EU) 1291/2013 of the European Parliament and of the Council of 11 December 2013, establishing the Programme Horizon 2020, OJ 2013, L347, p. 104. See also Articles 14 (2), Article 18 (6) and Article 23(9) of Regulation (EU) 1290/2013 of the European Parliament and of the Council of 11 December 2013, providing the rules of participation to the Programme Horizon 2020, OJ 2013, L 347, p. 81.

[63] See Article 34 of the Model Grant Agreement of Horizon 2020, available at http://ec.europa.eu/research/participants/data/ref/h2020/mga/gga/h2020-mga-gga-multi_en.pdf (accessed 06.06.15).

[64] Rodotà (1991).

[65] See Natoli (1974); Rodotà (2004), p. 168; Siccherio (1993), pp. 2132 ff.

[66] See in particular the judgments of the Italian *Cassazione* as follows: 11 February 2005, n. 2855 '*Responsabilità civile*' (2005), p. 881; 9 July 2004, no. 12685 '*Foro italiano*' (2005), 1, c. 3429; 24 February 2004, no. 3610 '*Guida al diritto*' (2004), 16, p. 50; 5 November 1999, n. 12310 '*Massimario Giurisprudenza italiana*' (1999).

[67] See *Cassazione* of 30 July 2004, no. 14605 '*Massimario Giurisprudenza italiana*' (2004).

[68] Before the Italian legislation established limitation of the performance bond (in accordance with the law 17 February 1992, no. 154), see *Cassazione*, judg. 18 July 1989, no. 3362; *Cassazione*, judg. 15 March 1991, no. 2790.

[69] See especially *Cassazione* (United Sections), judg. 13 September 2005, no. 18128, in *Obbligazioni e contratti*, 2005, 2, p. 103; see also *Cassazione* 24 September 1999, no. 10511, '*Foro italiano*' (2000), I, c. 1929.

[70] *Cassazione*, judg. 4 March 2003, no. 3185, '*Giurisprudenza italiana*' (2005) II, p. 958.

[71] *Cassazione*, judg. 6 August 2008, n. 21250, in www.leggiditaliaprofessionale.it (accessed 06.06.15).

obligations as an agent or employer. The notion of good faith is also taken into consideration where unfair clauses agreed to by the parties might lead to a power imbalance, even where the clause was itself initially drafted in good faith.[72] Within EU law, the principle of good faith is more widely seen than in national law,[73] not only with respect to the various legal systems of continental law, but also in relation to common law, where the concept was perhaps more traditionally 'avoided.'[74]

Another important principle is that of 'equity', seen for example in Article 8 of Directive 87/102 (on consumer credit) which establishes the right to an equitable reduction in the total cost of credit, if the consumer exercises his right of early redemption. Under Article 6 of Directive 1986/653 (18 December 1986), in the absence of agreements, standards or customs, an agent shall be entitled to 'reasonable remuneration;' Article 3 (3) of the Directive on Late Payments (Directive 2000/35/EC) also provides for compensation for damages in the case of delayed payments. This principle is widely seen in the case-law of the Court of Justice[75]; it generally serves to 'adapt' the rules to the case in question, as occurred in medieval courts, based on the '*aequitas singularis*' (application of justice to individual cases).[76]

5 The Contract as a Protector of Human Rights

5.1 Implementation of Public Policies

Arguably, contract law, and the law of obligations, may be considered key to the implementation and protection of human rights. Today, the contract is a key instrument in implementing public policies aimed at protecting personal and

---

[72] See for example Article 3 (1) of Council Directive 93/13/EEC of 5 April 1993 on unfair terms in consumer contracts, OJ 1993, L 095, p. 29. Also see De Nova (1994), pp. 693 ff.; Rizzo (1996).

[73] ECFI, Case T-115/94 *Opel Austria v Conseil* [1997] ECR II-39. The EU Judge normally elaborates upon the notion of 'good faith', making reference to international law. See the case-law of the International Court of Justice, the judgment of 25 May 1926, *Intérêts allemands en Haute-Silésie polanaise*, CPJI, series A, n. 7, pp. 30, 39, afterwards included in the Wiener Convention on the International Treaties of 1969.

[74] See the decision of the *House of Lords*, *Director General of Fair Trading vs. First National Bank* [2001] UKHL 52 (25th October 2001) on the application of Directive 93/13/EEC *op cit.* n 72 in the English legal system. On the application of the principle of good faith in European Countries, see also Whittaker and Zimmermann (2000).

[75] See ECJ, Case C-446/93 *SEIM* [1996] *ECR* I-73, para 41; ECJ, Case C-58/86, *Coopérative agricole d'approvisionnement des Avirons*, [1987] *ECR* 1525, para 22; ECJ, Case C-283/82, *Schoellershammer/Commission*, [1983] *ECR* 4219, para 7; ECFI, Case T-239/00 *SCI UK/Commission* [2002] *ECR* II-2957, paras 44 and 50.

[76] See Sassi (2005).

collective rights and interests.[77] For example, at the supranational level (according to the White Paper on *European Governance*[78]), the EU should adopt 'a less top-down approach... complementing its policy tools more effectively with non-legislative instruments.'[79] In fields concerning fundamental rights (e.g. privacy, research on humans) domestic legislation usually provides for the establishment of several types of codes of conduct,[80] and agreements that complete or implement supranational or national policy.[81] Codes of conduct and other negotiated instruments (e.g. the opinions of ethical committees) provide scope for some degree of fairness in cases where conflicts between constitutional interests might occur, for example where economic and scientific activities may impact upon individual rights or the protection of the environment. Education policies provide another example: the Bologna Process and the EU's higher education policy led to the Higher Education Area, establishing joint degrees and recognising training periods,[82] and putting in place opportunities for technology transfer between universities, research institutions and enterprises.[83] Agreements between local public authorities may also be significant, with European law controlling agreements between sub-regional or local authorities and municipalities, regions or other kinds of administrative bodies, depending on the structure of the each State. In respect of local authorities, the White Paper of the Committee of European Regions on Multilevel Governance ('Building Europe in partnership' of 17 June 2009) affirms that:

> By recognising the contribution of territorial governance and decentralised co-operation, international and European institutions have in recent years strengthened the role of local and regional authorities in global governance.[84]

Collaboration between transnational non-state entities has constitutional relevance, via the principle of subsidiarity and the implementation of the cohesion policy (e.g. Article 174 of the TFEU). The main means of implementing policies on economic, social and territorial cohesion may be via the Structural and Cohesion Funds.[85] One area where such collaboration is very significant is that of cross-border

[77] Lipari (1987).

[78] Communication of the Commission, *European Governance*, COM (2001) 428 final/2, of 5 August 2001.

[79] Ibid., p. 4.

[80] Galgano (2001), p. 215.

[81] Zagreblesky (1992), pp. 45 ff.

[82] Cippitani and Gatt (2009), pp. 85–397.

[83] Commission Recommendation of 10 April 2008 on the management of intellectual property in knowledge transfer activities and Code of Practice for universities and other public research organizations (notified under document number C (2008) 1329).

[84] See para 1.3. See also the Communication of the European Commission, Local Authorities: Actors for development, (SEC (2008) 2570).

[85] Armstrong (1995); Barro and Sala-I-Martin (1991), pp. 107–182; De La Fuente and Domenéch (1999); López-Bazo et al. (1999), pp. 257–370.

co-operation, enabled by liaison between the local authorities of different states, especially in relation to border territories.[86,87]

5.2 Social Services

Constitutions have clearly acknowledged socio-economic rights[88] especially the right to receive social services (which characterises the welfare State[89]) both at national and supranational levels.[90] From a traditional patrimonial viewpoint, social rights would not however be considered truly enforceable: that argument is contradicted however by the fact that many Constitutional provisions and domestic statutes include reference to 'rights' or similar. In Spanish Law for example the above mentioned Law no. 39/2006 article 1 provides that citizens have a 'subjective right [. . .] to promote the personal autonomy and care for people in situations of dependency.' In the French *Code de l'action sociale et des familles,*[91] the first chapter of Title I is entitled '*Droit à l'aide sociale*'. In other provisions of this Code the word '*droit*' or some equivalent is used.[92] Under Italian law, Article 2 (2) of Law 328/2000 ('Diritto alle prestazioni', i.e. right to social services)[93] concerns an integrated system of social services by the State, the Regions and local authorities. At the supranational level, Article 34 of the EU Charter also clearly recognises the right of access to social security benefits. In particular, paragraph 2 provides that 'Everyone residing and moving legally within the European Union is entitled to social security benefits and social advantages in accordance with Community law and national laws and practices' while paragraph 3 sets out 'the right to social and

[86] Perkmann (2003), pp. 153–171.

[87] Council of Europe, *Practical Guide to Transfrontier Co-operation*, (2006) 3 available at http://www.espaces-transfrontaliers.org/fileadmin/user_upload/documents/Documents_MOT/Etudes_Publications_MOT/Practical_guide_COE_MOT_EN.pdf, accessed 28/6/2015. In Europe, cross-border co-operation arose spontaneously after World War II, especially through twinning agreements between towns and other local authorities. In the 1980s, those forms of collaboration were recognised by the Council of Europe, through the European Outline Convention on Transfrontier Co-operation between Territorial Communities or Authorities ('Madrid Agreement' of 21 May 1980, see at http://conventions.coe.int/Treaty/EN/Treaties/Html/106.htm).

[88] Mazziotti (1964), vol. XII.

[89] Marshall (1998).

[90] See European Commission, *White Paper on Services of General Interest*, COM (2004) 374 of 12 Mary 2004.

[91] The *Code de l'action sociale et des familles* ('Code of Social Action and Families') is available at http://www.legifrance.gouv.fr/affichCode.do?cidTexte=LEGITEXT000006074069.

[92] See, for example, Article L114-1 and L114-1-1 of the Code de l'action sociale et des familles.

[93] Available at http://www.normattiva.it/uri-res/N2Ls?urn:nir:stato:legge:2000-11-08;328, accessed 05.05.15.

housing assistance so as to ensure a decent existence for all those who lack sufficient resources.'[94]

The enforceability of social rights is also clearly endorsed by supranational judges.[95] Such rights may be the subject of contractual relationships and can thus also be protected in domestic, civil law courts.[96] In other words, socio-economic rights may be implemented via contracts, for example for the provision of social services: EU law regards them as protecting services of general economic interest (Article 36 Charter of Fundamental Rights).[97] Article 6 (1) of the European Convention gives the Strasbourg court ('ECtHR') jurisdiction over such 'civil law' disputes, that is to say those which may affect the socio-economic rights and interests of the recipients of such services,[98] as seen in *Mennitto v Italy* (2000) which concerned services provided by the Region of Campania for the families of disabled children. According to the Court, those social services fit perfectly into the arena of 'private law human rights.'[99] The protection of such rights via private or civil law is clearly not excluded just because they are provided for by public authorities.[100]

5.3 *Informed Consent*

Via contracts, individuals may give consent to participate in activities which might affect his/her personal integrity or private life. Article 32 of The Italian *Costituzione* (1948) established an obligation to seek consent to medical treatment;[101] other Constitutions, directly or indirectly, also provide for this. For example, Article 7 of the Constitution of Finland, and paragraph 2 (2) of the German Constitution, both recognise the right to personal liberty.[102] More recently, consent has also been required for involving an individual in scientific research. Symbolically, the first such document in the field of research was adopted by the medical/scientific community in Nuremberg; the 'Nuremberg Code' concerning 'Permissible Medical Experiments' sets out as absolutely essential for medical experimentation, the

[94] Available http://www.europarl.europa.eu/charter/pdf/text_en.pdf (accessed 07.06.15).

[95] Sayn (2005).

[96] Peces-Barba Martínez (1986), p. 13; Álvarez Ledesma (1998), pp. 1 ff.

[97] ECJ, Case C-158/96, *Raymond Kohll*, [1998] *ECR* 1998 I-1931; ECJ, Case C-120/95, *Nicolas Decker* [1998] *ECR* I-1831; ECJ, Case C-67/96, *Albany International BV* [1999] *ECR* I-5751.

[98] Colcelli (2010).

[99] See among others *Salesi v. Italy* (App. No. 13023/87) [1993] ECHR 14, para 19.

[100] *Schuler-Zagraggen* v *Swistzterland* (App No. 14518/89) (1993) 16 EHRR 405.

[101] See Corte Costituzionale, 23 December 2008, No 438, in *Foro Italiano*, No 5, parte I, Bologna, 2009, p. 1.328.

[102] Nys et al. (2002).

voluntary consent of the person concerned.[103] However, the issue of informed consent has not been explicitly tied to scientific activity. Only the most recent, or recently modified, Constitutional charters take into consideration the issue of consent in the specific field of scientific research. This is a development that depends on cultural and legal sensitivity in respect of the importance and risks of techno-science (i.e. science impacting upon the world through technology). Thus, under the Swiss Constitution (Article 118b, entered into force 2010), informed consent is necessary for research involving humans.[104] The Constitutions of Bulgaria of 1991 (Article 29),[105] Slovenia (Article 18),[106] Hungary (Article III, para. 2)[107] and Croatia (Article 23)[108] also prohibit medical or scientific experimentation without the consent of the person concerned. Otherwise, at the level of national law, consent is covered by ordinary legislation or policy.

Amongst national legislation, French law devotes several provisions to the concept of consent in the scientific and health sectors. In particular, several laws have been approved in the field of bioethics, which has in turn modified the Civil Code.[109] In respect of the field of biomedicine, the French Code requires individual consent for all treatments (under Article 16-3, paragraph 2), for the collection of genetic information (under Articles 16-10, 16-11, 16-12 Civil Code) and brain imaging techniques (Civil Code Article 16-14).[110] The issue of informed consent is considered a pivotal aspect of European society[111] as shown by the EU Charter, which acts as a sort of a 'bioethics constitution' taking into consideration the need to protect fundamental rights interests within the framework of economic,

---

[103] Available http://www.hhs.gov/ohrp/archive/nurcode.html (accessed 06.06.15).

[104] See the translation in English of the Federal Constitution at https://www.admin.ch/ch/e/rs/1/101.en.pdf (accessed 06.06.15).

[105] See http://www.parliament.bg/en/const (accessed 06.06.15).

[106] See http://www.us-rs.si/en/about-the-court/legal-basis/ (accessed 06.06.15).

[107] For the translation of the Constitution of 2011 in English, see http://www.kormany.hu/download/e/02/00000/The%20New%20Fundamental%20Law%20of%20Hungary.pdf.

[108] Scc http://www.sabor.hr/Default.aspx?art=2405.

[109] French laws concerning bioethics include Law 94-548 of 1 July 1994 concerning 'traitement des données nominatives ayant pour fin la recherche dans le domaine de la santé'; Law no. 94-653 of 29 July 1994 related to the "respect du corps humain"; Law no. 94-654 also od the 29 July 1994 "don et à l'utilisation des éléments et produits du corps humain, à l'assistance médicale à la procréation et au diagnostic prénatal"; Law no. 2004-800 of 6 August 2004 concerning bioethics; the Law no. 2011-814 of 7 July 2011), modified the Civil Code, introducing in Book I 'Des personnes' Title I (De civils droits) the Chapter II 'Du respect du corps humain' (Articles 16 to 16-9), the chapter III 'De l'examination des caractéristiques Génétiques d'une personne et de l'identification d'une personne par ses empreintes Génétiques' (Article 16-10 to 16-13), and chapter IV 'De l'utilization des techniques d'imagerie cérébrale '(Article 16-14). With respect to the French legislation concerning bioethics see further Cippitani (2012a), pp. 1836–1865.

[110] For the Netherlands see the Civil Code, see Article 7:450.

[111] Sassi (2013), pp. 70–77.

therapeutic and scientific activities.[112] In particular, Article 3 of the EU Charter sets out that human dignity has to be respected in medicine and biology, noting especially that in such activities the free and informed consent of the person concerned is required, in the manner defined by domestic law. Informed consent is not directly controlled by the Convention of Rome, but the ECtHR looks for guidance to Article 8 ECHR (the right to respect for home, family and private life).

The Council of Europe has also set out a specific regional convention concerning biomedicine, namely the 'Convention for the Protection of Human Rights and Dignity of the Human Being with regard to the Application of Biology and Medicine: Convention on Human Rights and Biomedicine' ('Oviedo Convention'[113]). The Institutions of the Council of Europe, such as the Committee of Ministers and the Parliamentary Assembly, also adopt instruments of 'soft law' such as recommendations and resolutions relating to the Oviedo Convention and its Additional Protocols. The Oviedo Convention in particular states the 'general rule' according to which 'an intervention in the health field may only be carried out after the person concerned has given free and informed consent to it.' (Article 5). The need for consent is also provided for in respect of all matters regulated by the Oviedo Convention, such as scientific research (Article 15) and the donation of human organs or tissues (Article 19).[114]

Under European law, informed consent is not only a key consideration in biomedical fields; the protection of personal data also requires (for the lawful processing of such data) the consent of the persons concerned, in accordance with Article 8 (2) of the EU Charter, and Directive 95/46/EC of the European Parliament and Council (24th of October 1995) on the protection of individuals with regards to the treatment of personal data and the free movement of such data. Generally speaking, persons have the right to withhold consent in any situation where human activity might affect individual rights to health, integrity, and privacy.

[112] The European Union, in the last two decades, has developed the notion of a 'knowledge-based society' i.e. a society in which research and technology play a key role (see further Cippitani 2012b). EU law also addresses both the opportunities and risks of a society of based on research and technology.

[113] See http://conventions.coe.int/treaty/en/Treaties/Html/164.htm, accessed 6.6.15. The Convention was supplemented by additional protocols on specific topics: the additional Protocol concerning organ transplantation and tissues of human origin (Strasbourg, 24 January 2002); the additional Protocol concerning biomedical research (Strasbourg, 25 January 2005); the additional Protocol concerning genetic testing for health purposes (Strasbourg, 27 November 2008).

[114] Moreover, with regards to scientific research into bioethics, it is important to mention the Additional Protocol of 2005, particularly Article 13.

5.4 'Liability' as an Instrument to Protect Human Rights

Contracts and obligations may ensure that public authorities act consistently, in ways which respect the rights of individuals. Civil liability on the part of States is the result of a process of external and internal control over the concept of sovereignty: where there has been a failure to fulfil obligations (positive or negative) under EU law, for example, the Court of Justice will recognise state liability, irrespective of which organs of the state have caused such failure.[115] This is so whether action or inaction has led to liability, even when they are constitutionally independent,[116] for example, as local authorities or as the judiciary. As the EU Court stated in *Francovich:*

> It follows that the principle whereby a State must be liable for loss and damage caused to individuals as a result of breaches of Community law for which the State can be held responsible is inherent in the system of the Treaty.[117]

The ECtHR also usually elaborates within its case-law on state liability under Article 41 ECHR, which provides that

> If the Court finds that there has been a violation of the Convention or the Protocols thereto, and if the internal law of the High Contracting Party concerned allows only partial reparation to be made, the Court shall, if necessary, afford just satisfaction to the injured party.

Compensation is decided in order to enforce respect for human rights, even if these are not necessarily connected to the patrimonial sphere.[118] The ECtHR often makes reference to the protection of patrimonial rights, especially the right to not be deprived of one's property as recognised by Article 1 of First Protocol to the Convention. ('A1P1') In *Maurice v France* (2005)[119] the ECtHR found that French law no. 2002-203 (also known as '*loi anti-Perruche*'[120] which limits liability in medical negligence in the event of misdiagnosis of foetal malformation) offended against A1P1: the parents' right to sue therefore amounted to a valuable possession.

---

[115] See for example ECJ, Case C-34/89 *Italy v Commission* [1990] *ECR* I-3613, on EU grants.

[116] ECJ, Case C-129/2000 *Commission v Italy* [2003] *ECR* I-14672.

[117] ECJ, Case C-6/90 and C-9/90, *Francovich and Bonifaci v Italy*, [1991] *ECR* I-5357, paras 35 ff.

[118] See *Mennesson v. France* (App. No. 65192/11), judgement 26 Jun 2014, concerning the violation of the right to respect of family life (Article 8 ECHR) in relation to surrogacy.

[119] (App. No. 11810/03), (2006) 42 EHRR 42.

[120] See further the decision of the *Cour de Cassation* of the 17 November 2000, on indemnity where severe foetal abnormality is not detected during pregnancy, lack of information, and damages reflecting the costs involved in raising a child with a grave disability. See also Aynès (2001), pp. 492–496; '*Code civil Dalloz*' (2008) bibl., p. 1594.

6 Application of the Rules on Contracts

If human rights can impact upon contract law, and contract law can afford protection to human rights, this gives rise to legal issues which might never be fully resolved. Generally speaking, it has to be asked whether contract law, which had its origins in regulating patrimonial property interests and relationships, might be applied to situations where fundamental human rights are involved. A number of traditional rules within the laws of contract and obligations appear inconsistent with the furtherance of individual human rights. The concept of contractual capacity and the right to withdraw, are useful examples.

6.1 Capacity vs. Competence

Under most Civil Codes only persons above a specified age (usually 18 years) and who have not been declared incapable by the courts (via a severe mental disability or some penal sanction) may act as parties to a contract. Arguably, this mirrors to some extent the legal 'incapability' referred to in the International Ethical Guidelines for Biomedical Research Involving Human Subjects (2002) which excludes '*those who are relatively (or absolutely) incapable of protecting their own interests*.'[121] Such rules, if applied strictly, would lead to violation of key constitutional principles. Article 12 (2) of the UN Convention on the Rights of Persons with Disabilities establishes different rules, namely that 'persons with disabilities enjoy legal capacity on an equal basis with others in all aspects of life.' This also applies to such issues as informed consent. The same provision stipulates (at paragraph 4) that the obligation of the State is to 'take appropriate measures to provide access for persons with disabilities to the support they may require in exercising their legal capacity' and that 'such safeguards shall ensure that measures relating to the exercise of legal capacity respect the rights, will and preferences of the person.'[122] European systems of protection for human rights provide that such persons must be guaranteed the highest possible level of autonomy[123] and that any restrictions upon autonomy must be strictly necessary,[124] and respect the

[121] Council for International Organizations of Medical Sciences, http://www.cioms.ch/publications/layout_guide2002.pdf (accessed 06.06.15).

[122] In the European regional law in particular this principle is stated with regard to people with psychological disabilities. See the recommendations provide to the Commissioner of Human Rights of the Council of Europe in 'Who gets to decide? Right to legal capacity for persons with intellectual and psychosocial disabilities' of 20 February 2012 (at https://wcd.coe.int/ViewDoc.jsp?id=1908555) on consenting to therapeutic treatments.

[123] *Stanev v. Bulgaria* (App. No. 36760/06) (2012) ECHR 46.

[124] *Shtukaturov v. Russia* (App. No. 44009/05) [2008] ECHR 223, paras 90 and 93–95.

principle of proportionality.[125] Therefore, therapeutic treatments or other invasive practices cannot be carried out without the consent of the person, as in for example, *Shtukaturov v. Russia* (2008) where the Strasbourg Court declared unlawful the practice of coercive hospitalization.[126] In this context, a formal definition of capacity involves an objective approach based upon two substantial and dynamic notions: vulnerability and competence. Vulnerability serves to identify people in need of special protection[127] due to a situation of 'dependency'. Dependency is defined by the Committee of Ministers of the Council of Europe as the state in which those in need of help or assistance to perform activities of daily living, lack autonomy.[128] Dependency can be caused by various factors, for example 'arising from age, illness or disability, and linked to a lack or loss of physical, mental, intellectual or sensory autonomy.'[129] People who are in a vulnerable situation still have the right to withhold consent.

In relation to dependency, competence[130] is a key issue e.g. to understand relevant information and to give true consent. Competence can be defined as an ability 'to understand relevant information, to evaluate that information and make a reasoned decision, to decide without undue influence, and to communicate consent or refusal.'[131] Competence may be 'contextually relative' (where it relates to types of interests) or 'complexity-relative,'[132] for example, where a person may have competence in respect of decisions on their health, yet still be unable to take care of their patrimonial interests. It may also be considered 'risk-relative' depending on the type of risk which might arise as a result of an intervention.[133] Therefore, according to the accepted definitions of competence, traditional notions of capacity are not necessarily appropriate.[134]

---

125 *Salontaji-Drobnjak v. Serbia* (App. No. 36500/05) [2009] ECHR 1526.

126 *Shtukaturov v. Russia, op cit,* n. 124.

127 Schroeder and Gefenas (2009); Macklin (2003); Goodin(1985), p. 110.

128 Committee of the Ministers of Council of Europe, Recommendation no. R 98(9) concerning dependency, Annex of 18 September 1998, available at https://wcd.coe.int/com.instranet.InstraServlet?command=com.instranet.CmdBlobGet&InstranetImage=532369&SecMode=1&DocId=486242&Usage=2 (accessed 06.06.15).

129 See Article 2, n. 2 Spanish Law no. 39/2006, of December 14 of the Promotion of Personal Autonomy and Care (Ley 39/2006, de 14 de diciembre, de Promoción de la Autonomía Personal y Atención a las personas en situación de dependencia, available at http://www.boe.es/buscar/doc.php?id=BOE-A-2006-21990) (accessed 6.6.15).

130 On competence' see Beauchamp and Childress (2009); Buchanan and Brock (1990); Culver and Gert (1990); Drane (1985); Jonas (2007), pp. 255–262.

131 European Commission '*European Textbook on Ethics in Research*', Brussels, European Union (2010), p. 55.

132 Buller (2001).

133 Wilks (1997).

134 This observation can also be applied to those agreements needed to implement fundamental rights. The legal literature and the case-law affirms that it is not acceptable to deny legal capacity to minors (especially adolescents) when participating in a contract to use ITC technologies. See in particular Palazzo (2013).

6.2 The Right to Withdraw Consent

Furthermore, the agreements used to protect fundamental rights may derogate from other traditional principles such as the rules on initially agreed terms as set out by the parties to the contracts. The principle of *pacta sunt servanda* is affirmed at both international and national levels: see for example Article 1372 of the Italian Civil Code on how contracts 'have the force of the law between the parties'. In cases where a contract is being used to protect personal rights however, such an absolute form of agreement cannot be accepted. Consent to a therapeutic or other intervention (intruding on the personal sphere of an individual) may be allowed by the person, but only up until the point where the person concerned no longer wants the intervention. Indeed, consent may at any time be freely withdrawn by a person, under Article 5 of the Oviedo Convention.[135] An example of such a revocation can be found in *Evans v. UK* (2007) where a woman suffering from ovarian cancer decided upon in vitro fertilization with her partner. The embryos were cryopreserved. When the couple's relationship ended, her partner sought destruction of the embryos.

7 Conclusion: Contracts and Obligations as Instruments for the Implementation of Human Rights

In sum, contract law, originally devised to regulate patrimonial relationships between individuals, on the basis of formal parity, has changed significantly in terms of content and function. Human rights, as well as those principles established by domestic Constitutions to protect them (such as 'solidarity') are able to integrate with the rules of contract law. Today it would be difficult to argue that the definition of contract as provided by the various European civil codes can cover all such aspects of an agreement. Notions such as the formal equality of contracting parties, assumed contractual capacity, or the immutable nature of agreements, no longer hold the same level of influence. Current legal systems, both national and transnational, ensure that agreements are not aimed simply at enabling patrimonial exchanges: they are now facilitating governance and the implementation of public policies; regulating consent to medical treatments and participation in research activities. They regulate other activities which may engage human rights, not least those concerned with privacy and dignity: the gifting of organs and human tissue or the provision of social services. A blurring of the lines may thus arise between the different disciplines of public and private law;[136] as Savigny has

[135] See also Article 13 (3), Additional Protocol of biomedical research to the Convention of Oviedo; Article 9 (2), of the Additional Protocol to the Oviedo Convention on genetic testing for health purposes, 2008.

[136] Guettier (2008), pp. 33 ff.

argued, at the centre of public law there are societal public aims, with individuals sometimes left in the background. On the other hand, private law *is* focused on individuals, and the relationships between them. The jurisprudence referred to in this chapter suggests however an emergence of new hybrid models, and a lessening of the strict disciplinary distinctions between private and public law.[137] Several academics have proposed theoretical approaches aimed at overcoming lingering divisions,[138] using formulations which are much more comprehensive, such as, for example, a 'private law of public administration.'[139] Private relationships are strongly influenced by collective social interests (fundamental rights, economics) and yet the implementation of many public policies no longer relies solely upon unilateral instruments but looks to achieve meaningful agreement and satisfy 'good conscience' obligations.

Public law emphasizes the doctrinal, higher role of fundamental interests in legal relationships; private law is no longer beyond the reach of human rights law. And yet, private law increasingly provides a useful means of embedding in domestic legal systems, in an efficient, flexible and pervasive manner, meaningful protections for key elements of human rights law. Definitions of fundamental rights are no longer a matter solely for political decision-makers, but may be influenced by domestic jurists. This is not surprising given the nature of private law, not least its ability to adapt to the new and unexpected demands of society and the economy.[140] Its traditional function was to provide logical, legal tools, such as contracts and trusts, to solve those difficult problems that tend to arise within the realm of 'human relationships,' irrespective of whether parties are private or public entities, or indeed the state itself.[141]

References

Álvarez Ledesma, M. I. (1998). *Acerca Del Concepto De Derechos Humanos*. México: McGraw-Hill.

Andorno, R. (2009). Human dignity and human rights as a common ground for a global bioethics. *Journal of Medicine and Philosophy, 34*, 223–240.

Armstrong, H. W. (1995). Convergence among regions of the European Union 1950–1990. *Papers in Regional Science, 74*(2), 143–152.

Aynès, L. (2001). Préjudice de l'enfant né handicapé: la plainte de Job devant la Cour de cassation. *Dalloz*, 492–496.

[137] Terneyre (2000), pp. 575 ff.

[138] Within the French doctrine the debate is always live: see, for example, Gaudemet (1999), p. 626; Drago (1990), pp. 110 ff.; Jossaud (2002), pp. 1483 ff. Lichére (2005), pp. 79 ff.

[139] Saporito (2006).

[140] Pennasilico (2005), p. 432.

[141] Roman Law utilised the ancient scheme of agreement in order to cover the new needs which were emerging, through a 'reproductive imitation (*dicis causa*)'. See Betti (1935), pp. 279 ff.; Treggiari (2006).

Barettoni Arleri, A. (1975). L'assistenza nell'attuale momento normativo e interpretativo. *Rivista degli infortuni e delle malattie professionali, 2*, 410.

Barro, R. J., & Sala-I-Martin, X. (1991). Convergence across states and regions. *Brookings Papers on Economic Activity, 2*, 107–182.

Beauchamp, T. L., & Childress, J. F. (2009). *Principles of biomedical ethics*. Oxford, England: Oxford University Press.

Betti, E. (1935). *Diritto romano* (Vol. I). Padova: Cedam.

Bobbio, N. (1984). *Il problema della guerra e le vie della pace*. Bologna: Il Mulino.

Bourgeois, L. (1911). *La politique de la Prévoyance sociale. La doctrine et la méthode*. Paris.

Bourgeois, L. (1919). *La politique de la Prévoyance sociale. L'action*. Paris.

Buchanan, A. E., & Brock, D. W. (1990). *Deciding for others: The ethics of surrogate decision making*. Cambridge, England: Cambridge University Press.

Buller, T. (2001). Competence and risk-relativity. *Bioethics, 15*(2), 93–109.

Calamandrei, P. (1950). *La Illegittimità Costituzionale Delle Leggi Nel Processo Civile*. Padova: Cedam.

Caprioli, S. (2008). *Il Codice Civile. Struttura e Vicende*. Milano: Giuffrè.

Carbonnier, J. (2004). *Droit civil* (vol. I). Paris: PUF.

Cardone, A. (2011). *'Diritti fondamentali (tutela multilivello dei)' Enciclopedia del diritto. Annali, IV*. Milano: Giuffrè.

Cédras, M. J. (2003). Le solidarisme contractuel en doctrine et devant la Cour de cassation. Available at https://www.courdecassation.fr/publications_26/rapport_annuel_36/rapport_2003_37/deuxieme_partie_tudes_documents_40/tudes_diverses_43/doctrine_devant_6260.html. Accessed 06.06.15.

Cherednychenko, O. (2010). Fundamental rights, policy issues and the Draft Common Frame of Reference for European private law. *European Review of Contract Law, 6*(1), 39–65.

Chiarelli, G. (1957). Lo Stato E L'assistenza Sanitaria. Feder. med.

Cippitani, R. (2010). *La Solidarietà Giuridica Tra Pubblico E Privato*. Roma-Perugia-México: ISEG.

Cippitani, R. (2012a). Principi e metodo nella revisione della normativa francese relativa alla bioetica. In *Diritto di famiglia e delle persone*. Roma-Perugia-México: ISEG.

Cippitani, R. (2012b). *El Derecho de la Sociedad del Conocimiento*. Roma-Perugia-México: ISEG.

Cippitani, R. (2013). Solidaridad. In M. I. Álvarez Ledesma & R. Cippitani (Eds.), *Diccionario analítico de Derechos humanos e integración jurídica* (pp. 642–649). Roma-Perugia-México: ISEG.

Cippitani, R., & Gatt, S. (2009). Legal developments and problems of the Bologna process within the European higher education area and European integration. *Higher Education in Europe, 34* (3), 385–397.

Clive, E. (2008). An introduction to the academic Draft Common Frame of Reference. *Era Forum, 9*, 13–31.

Colcelli, V. (2010). *Le situazioni giuridiche soggettive nel sistema CEDU*. Roma-Perugia: ISEG.

Colombi Ciacchi, A. (2006). The constitutionalization of European contract law: Judicial convergence and social justice. *European Review of Contract Law, 2*, 167.

Costa, P. (2002). *Civitas. Storia della cittadinanza in Europa* (vol. IV). L'Età dei totalitarismi e della democrazia. Roma-Bari: La Terza.

Crisafulli, V. (1952). Costituzione e protezione sociale. In *La Costituzione e le sue disposizioni di principio*. Milano: Giuffrè.

Culver, C. M., & Gert, B. (1990). The inadequacy of incompetence. *Milbank Quarterly, 68*, 619–643.

De La Fuente, A., & Domenéch, R. (1999). *The redistributive effects of the EU budget: An analysis and some reflections on the Agenda 2000 negotiations*. CERP Discussion Paper 2113.

De Nova, G. (1994). Criteri generali di determinazione dell'abusività delle clausole ed elenco di clausole abusive. *Rivista trimestrale di diritto e procedura civile*, 693 ff.

Domat, J. (1689). *Traité des lois civiles prises dans leur ordre naturel*. Paris.
Drago, R. (1990). Le contrat administratif aujourd'hui. *Droits, 12*, 110.
Drane, J. F. (1985). The many faces of competency. *Hastings Centre Report, 15*(2), 17–21.
Duguit, L. (1908). *Le droit social, le droit individuel et la transformation de l'État*. Paris.
Fuchs, A. (2008). A plea a Europe-wide discussion of Draft Common Frame of Reference. *Era Forum, 9*, S1–S6.
Galgano, F. (2001). *Lex mercatoria*. Bologna: Il Mulino.
Gaudemet, Y. (1999). Prolégomenès pour un théorie des obligations en droit administratif français. In *Mélanges En hommage a Jean Gaudemet*. Paris: PUF.
Goodin, R. E. (1985). *Protecting the vulnerable: A re-analysis of our social responsibilities*. London: University of Chicago Press.
Guettier, C. (2008). *Droit de contrats administratifs*. Paris: Presses Universitaires de France.
Häberle, P. (2002). Dallo Stato nazionale all'Unione europea: evoluzioni dello Stato costituzionale. *Diritto pubblico comparato europeo*.
Halperin, J. L. (1992). *L'impossible Code Civil. Paris*. Paris: PUF.
Hesselink, M. (2003). The horizontal effect of social rights in European contract law. In M. Hesselink et al. (Eds.), *Privaatrecht tussen autonomie en solidariteit*. Den Haag, the Netherlands: Boom Juridische Uitgevers.
Jannarelli, A. (2002). La disciplina dell'atto e dell'attività: i contratti tra imprese e tra imprese e consumatori. In N. Lipari (Ed.), *Trattato di diritto privato europeo* (vol. III). L'attività e il contratto. Padova: Cedam.
Jansen, N. (2010). The concept of non-contractual obligations: Rethinking the divisions of tort, unjustified enrichment, and contract law. *Journal of European Tort Law, 1*, 16–47.
Jhering, R. (1972). *Lo Scopo Del Diritto* (Italian transl. of Losano MG). Torino: Einaudi.
Jonas, M. F. (2007). Competence to consent. In R. E. Ashcroft, A. Dawson, H. Draper, & J. R. McMillan (Eds.), *Principles of health care ethics* (pp. 255–262). Chichester, England: Wiley.
Jones, J. (2012). Human dignity in the EU charter of fundamental rights and its interpretation before the European Court of Justice. *Liverpool Law Review, 33*, 281–300.
Jossaud, A. (2002). Pour un droit public des marchés. *AJDA*, 1483.
Lega, C. (1952). *Il diritto alla salute in un sistema di sicurezza sociale*. Roma: Istituto di Medicina Sociale.
Lega, C. (1969). *Il rapporto giuridico di previdenza sociale*. Milano: Giuffrè.
Lichére, F. (2005). *Droit des contrats pubblics*. Paris: Dalloz.
Lipari, N. (1987). La formazione negoziale del diritto. *Rivista di diritto civile*, I.
López-Bazo, E., Vayá, E., Mora, A. J., & Suriñac, J. (1999). Regional economic dynamics and convergence in the European Union. *Annals of Regional Science, 33*, 257–370.
Lucifredi, R. (1952). *La nuova Costituzione italiana raffrontata con lo Statuto albertino e vista nel primo triennio di sua applicazione*. Milano: Giuffrè.
Macklin, R. (2003). Bioethics, vulnerability and protection. *Bioethics, 17*(5–6), 472–486.
Marshall, T. H. (1998). Ciudadanía y clase social. In T. Bottomore & T. H. Marshall (Eds.), *Ciudadanía y clase social*. Madrid: Alianza.
Mazziotti, M. (1964). Diriti sociali. In *Enciclopedia del diritto* (vol. XII). Milano: Giuffrè.
Menger, A. (1908). *Das bürgerliche Recht und die besitzlosen Volksklassen. Eine Kritik des Entwurfes eines Bürgerlichen Gesetzbuch für das Deutsche Reich*. Tübingen: H. Laupp.
Millins, S. (1996). Dwarf-throwing and human dignity: A French perspective. *Journal of Social Welfare and Family Law, 18*(3), 375.
Mislawski, R. (2010). Dignité, autonomie, vulenrabilité: aproche juridique. In E. Hirsch (Ed.), *Traité de bioétique* (vol. I) Fondements, principles, repéres. Toulouse: Érés.
Espinoza de los Monteros Sánchez, J. E. (2010). Contitucionalismo global. In *Diccionario Histórico Judicial de México, Ideas e Instituciones*. Tomo I. México: Suprema Corte de Justicia de la Nación de México.
Mortati, C. (1946). *La Costituzione di Weimar*. Firenze: Sansoni.
Natoli, U. (1974). *L'attuazione del rapporto obbligatorio*. Milano: Giuffrè.

Nys, H., Dreezen, I., Vinck, I., Dierickx, K., Dequeker, E., & Cassiman, J.-J. (2002). 'Genetic Testing Patients' rights, insurance and employment. A survey of regulations in the European Union. Luxembourg' (2002), Brussels: Office for Official Publications of the European Communities.

Ost, F. (1990). Droit et intérêt. In *Entre droit et non-droit: l'intérêt* (vol. II). Bruxelles, Belgium: Publications des Facultés universitaires Saint-Louis.

Palazzo, A. (2013). *La filiazione*. Padova, Italy: Cedam.

Peces-Barba Martínez, G. (1986). *Derechos fundamentales*. Madrid, Spain: Universidad Complutense, Facultad de Derecho.

Pennasilico, M. (2005). L'interpretazione dei contratti della pubblica amministrazione tra conservazione e stabilità degli effetti. *Rassegna di Diritto civile, 2*, 432.

Pérez Luño, A. E. (1991). *Los derechos fundamentals*. Madrid: Tecnos.

Perkmann, M. (2003). Cross border regions in Europe. Significance and drivers of regional cross-border cooperation. *European Urban and Regional Studies, 10*, 153–171.

Pernice, I. (1999). Multilevel constitutionalism and the treaty of Amsterdam: European constitution making revisited. *Common Market Law Review*, 703.

Portalis, J. M. E. (1891). *Discours préliminaire du premier projet de Code civil*. Paris.

Pothier, R. G. (1819). *Pandectae Justinianae in novum ordinem digestae*. Paris: ex typis Dondey-Dupré.

Rawls, J. (1980). *A theory of justice*. Cambridge, MA: The Belknap Press of Harvard University.

Renner, K. (1929). *Die Rechtsinstitute des Privatrechts und ihre soziale Funktion*. Tübingen.

Rizzo, V. (1996). Il significativo squilibrio 'malgrado' la buona fede nella clausola generale dell'art. 1469 bis c.c.: un collegamento ambiguo da chiarire. *Rassegna di diritto civile*.

Rodotà, S. (1990). *Il terribile diritto. Studi sulla proprietà privata*. Bologna: Zanichelli.

Rodotà, S. (1991). Le clausole generali. In G. Alpa & M. Bessone (Eds.), *Giurisprudenza sistematica di diritto civile e commerciale. I contratti in generale*. Torino: Utet.

Rodotà, S. (2004). Buona fede e correttezza nel quadro dell'integrazione. In *Le fonti d'integrazione del contratto*. Milano: Giuffrè.

Rodotà, S. (2005). Il Codice civile e il processo costituente europeo. *Rivista Critica di Diritto privato*, 21.

Sanz Caballero, S. (2013). Obligaciones positivas del Estado. In M. I. Álvarez Ledesma & R. Cippitani (Eds.), *Diccionario analítico de Derechos humanos e integración jurídica* (pp. 466–474). Roma-Perugia-México: ISEG.

Saporito, L. (2006). I vizi della volontà della Pubblica Amministrazione. In P. Stanzione & A. Saturno (Eds.), *Il diritto privato della Pubblica Amministrazione*. Padova: Cedam.

Sassi, A. (2005). Equità e buona fede oggettiva nel diritto interno ed 'europeo'. In T. Sediari (Ed.), *Cultura dell'integrazione europea*. Torino: Giappichelli.

Sassi, A. (2013). Consentimiento informado. In M. I. Álvarez Ledesma & R. Cippitani (Eds.), *Diccionario analítico de Derechos humanos e integración jurídica* (pp. 70–77). Roma-Perugia-México: ISEG.

Savigny, F. K. (1840). *System des heutigen römischen Rechts*. Berlin: Veit.

Sayn, I. (2005). *Le contentieux de la protection sociale: procédures comparées (Allemagne, Angleterre, Belgique, France)*. Saint'Ètienne, France: Publication de l'Université de Saint-Etienne.

Schroeder, D., & Gefenas, E. (2009). Vulnerability: Too vague and too broad. *Cambridge Quarterly of Healthcare Ethics, 18*, 113–121.

Sepúlveda Iguíniz, R. (2013). Estado de Derechos. In M. I. Álvarez Ledesma & R. Cippitani (Eds.), *Diccionario analítico de Derechos humanos e integración jurídica* (pp. 239–244). Roma-Perugia-México: ISEG.

Siccherio, G. (1993). Appunti sul fondamento costituzionale del principio di buona fede. *Giurisprudenza italiana, I*(1), 2132.

Terneyre, P. (2000). Le montages contractuels complexes. *AJDA*, 575.

Treggiari, F. (2006). Fiducialitas. Tecniche e tutele della fiducia nel diritto intermedio. In M. Lupoi (Ed.), *Le situazioni affidanti*. Torino: Giappichelli.

von Bar, C., Clive, E., Schulte-Nölke, H., Beale, H., Herre, J., Huet, J., et al. (2009). *Principles, definitions and model rules of European private law Draft Common Frame of Reference (DCFR) outline edition.* Prepared by the Study Group on a European Civil Code and the Research Group on EC Private Law (Acquis Group). Munich: Sellier.

Whittaker, S., & Zimmermann, R. (2000). Good faith in European contract law: Surveying the legal landscape. In R. Zimmermann & S. Whittaker (Coord.), Good faith in European contract law (Vol. 44, pp. 7 ff.). Cambridge: Cambridge University Press.

Wilkinson, S. (2003). *Bodies for sale: Ethics and exploitation in the human body trade*. London: Routledge.

Wilks, I. (1997). The debate over risk-related standards of competence. *Bioethics, 11*(5), 413–426.

Windscheid, B. (1900). *Lehrbuch des Pandektenrechts*. Frankfurt: Rütten & Loening.

Zagreblesky, G. (1992). *Il diritto mite*. Torino: Einaudi.

Case Law

European Court of Human Rights

Maurice v France (App. No. 11810/03), (2006) 42 EHRR 42.

Mennesson v. France (App. No. 65192/11), judgement 26 Jun 2014.

Salesi v. Italy (App. No. 13023/87) [1993] ECHR 14.

Salontaji-Drobnjak v. Serbia (App. No. 36500/05) [2009] ECHR 1526.

Schuler-Zagraggen v *Swistzterland* (App No. 14518/89) (1993) 16 EHRR 405.

Shtukaturov v. Russia (App. No. 44009/05) [2008] ECHR 223.

Stanev v. Bulgaria (App. No. 36760/06) (2012) ECHR 46.

European Union Case Law

Case 26/62 *Van Gend en Loos* [1963] *ECR* 1.

Case 29/69 *Stauder* [1969] *ECR* 419.

Case 6/64 *Costa v ENEL* [1964] *ECR* 585.

Case 155/79 *AM & S Limited* [1982] *ECR* 1575.

Case C-283/82, *Schoellershammer/Commission*, [1983] *ECR* 4219.

Case C-58/86, *Coopérative agricole d'approvisionnement des Avirons*, [1987] *ECR* 1525.

Case C-34/89 *Italy v Commission* [1990] *ECR* I-3613.

Case C-6/90 and C-9/90, *Francovich and Bonifaci v Italy*, [1991] *ECR* I-5357.

Case C-2/92, *Bostock* [1994] *ECR* I-955.

Case C-446/93 *SEIM* [1996] *ECR* I-73.

Case C-120/95, *Nicolas Decker* [1998] *ECR* I-1831.

C-44/96 *Mannesmann Anlagenbau Austria AG et oth v Strohal Rotationsdruck GesmbH* [1998] *ECR* I-73.

Case C-67/96, *Albany International BV* [1999] *ECR* I-5751.

Case C-158/96, *Raymond Kohll*, [1998] *ECR* 1998 I-1931.

Case C-292/97, *Karlsson et oth.* [2000] *ECR* I-2737.

Case C-453/99 *Courage Ltd.* [2001] *ECR* I-6297.

Case C-168/00 *Leitner/TUI Deutschland* [2002] *ECR* I-2631.

Case C-442/00 *Rodríguez Caballero* [2002] *ECR* I-11915.

Case C-129/2000 *Commission v Italy* [2003] *ECR* I-14672.

Case C-36/02, *Omega Spielhallen- und Automatenaufstellungs-GmbH v Oberbürgermeisterin der Bundesstadt Bonn* [2004] *ECR* I-9609.

Case T-115/94 *Opel Austria v Conseil* [1997] ECR II-39.

Case T-239/00 *SCI UK/Commission* [2002] *ECR* II-2957.

Putting Dignity to Bed? The Taxing Question of the UK's Housing Rights 'Relapse'

Alice Diver

1 Introduction

> The lack of affordable housing especially places poor people in the impossible position of having to choose between the most basic of human necessities: housing or food, housing or health care, housing or clothing, and so on.[1]

Despite being 'wrapped up in . . .ideological discourse,'[2] the UK's recent statutory cap on Housing Benefit (a form of welfare payment aimed at helping unemployed or low-paid tenants pay their rent[3]) has significantly affected the lives of 'some of the most vulnerable members' of society.[4] Recent domestic case law has examined a range of rights-relevant issues, such as the legal definition of justifiable discrimination, equality, the nature of the overlap between fundamental rights, and the fluid scope of judicial deference and the margin of appreciation as these apply to human rights issues, especially those which are underpinned (or, perhaps more accurately, undermined) by socio-economic decision-making.[5] Taken together the decisions provide fairly detailed guidance, if only very limited hope, for anyone

---

[1] Gomez and Thiele (2005).

[2] Gibb (2015), p. 2.

[3] See s. 134 of the Social Security Administration Act 1992. In the private rented sector, Housing Benefit is paid by way of a rent allowance. In Northern Ireland, at the time of writing, the cap on Housing Benefit applies only to the private rented sector, pending welfare reform in the region. See further http://www.niassembly.gov.uk/assembly-business/legislation/primary-legislation-current-bills/welfare-reform-bill/ (accessed 10.03.15).

[4] See Rolnik (2014) available http://www.ohchr.org/EN/NewsEvents/Pages/DisplayNews.aspx?NewsID=13707&LangID=E (accessed 01.02.15); See Rolnik (2009).

[5] See Costa (2013).

A. Diver (✉)
Dept. of Law and Criminology, Edge Hill University, Ormskrik, Lancs, UK
e-mail: divera@edgehill.ac.uk

A. Diver, J. Miller (eds.), *Justiciability of Human Rights Law in Domestic Jurisdictions*, DOI 10.1007/978-3-319-24016-9_14

seeking to argue that the various impacts of harsh austerity measures might amount to unlawful human rights infringements at national level. There is little sign that a meaningfully juridical right to adequate housing is being embedded in domestic law here, with judicial concern over preserving finite, scarce resources generally serving to 'trump' the various arguments put forward by housing rights advocates. As Grant has argued however,

> one of the most basic human needs which millions of the poorest people around the world lack, is housing. Implementation of the right to housing is therefore a fundamental requirement of a human rights approach to poverty eradication.[6]

The UN Special Rapporteur on adequate housing did stress in 2012 that there was an urgent need for a general 'paradigm shift from housing policies based on the financialization of housing, to a human rights-based approach to housing policies.'[7] A year later, she warned specifically of a clear 'regression' in respect of the right to adequate housing within the UK stressing how a clear 'deterioration in the enjoyment of the right' was becoming increasingly evident.[8] The introduction of the 'bedroom tax' was largely to blame for this, with its underpinning policy aims strongly suggesting a government commitment to prioritising and privileging home-ownership over other modes of tenure, namely the leasehold interest.[9] Arguably, a wider political agenda exists, which seeks to limit the role of the state generally in acting as a provider of social housing.[10] This is so despite the UK having had a 'long history of providing affordable and good quality housing [and] having placed this human right at the centre of its policy priorities.'[11]

---

[6] Grant (2007), p. 2. See also however Hohmann (2013) on the 'primary importance' of a right to housing, and the 'vexed questions' that accompany its realization.

[7] Rolnik (2014) on how the 'ruling paradigm of housing policies… focus(es) on housing finance as the main means of promoting home ownership..' She argues that 'full realization of the right to adequate housing, without discrimination, cannot be promoted solely by financial mechanisms and requires broader and more holistic housing policies and State interventions.' (Available http://www.ohchr.org/Documents/Issues/Housing/A-67-286.pdf, accessed 12.02.15).

[8] Rolnik (2014). She also cited the cumulative effect of various socio-economic policies, which have served to gradually 'erode one of the world's finest systems of affordable housing.'

[9] *Ibid.*

[10] See also the domestic case law on homelessness and eviction proceedings, for example *Kay v. Lambeth Borough Council*; *Price v. Leeds County Council*, 8 March 2006, [2006] UKHL 10, where the House of Lords revisited *Qazi v. London Borough of Harrow* [2003] UKHL 43; *Sheffield City Council v. Smart* [2002] EWCA Civ 4 in the wake of the decision in *Connors v. the United Kingdom*, no. 66746/01, 81–84, (27 May 2004). The Court held that the decision in *Connors* was not incompatible with the majority view in *Qazi* i.e. that there was no need for a County Court review of Article 8 (2) (of the European Convention) issues in tenancy possession cases where legislation had clearly addressed the issue. A tenant might however still be able to rely upon Article 8 in exceptional cases where, as in *Connors*, domestic law was incompatible with Article 8 rights, or where it was possible to challenge a social landlord on public law grounds e.g. as an abuse of state power.

[11] Rolnik (2014). 'For generations, being poor in the UK didn't necessarily equate to being homeless, or to living badly housed and in permanent threat of eviction.'

The question of whether some form of positive obligation (or even a minimum threshold) now exists, to underpin meaningful, rights-led safeguards (against poverty, ill-health, eviction and homelessness) is not fully answered by recent, domestic judicial discourses on such issues as bedroom tax and welfare caps. Courtroom arguments citing inequality or discrimination are prone to a swift rebuttal, on the grounds that these are essentially lawful (under statute or policy) or justified on the basis of scarce resources. Judicial deference is also a factor, with domestic courts not especially keen to take on the mantle of law-maker in such contexts. The concept of human dignity, not least as it relates to an adequate standard of living, is thus perhaps particularly relevant to advocates seeking to highlight the harsh inequities of such systems. As Gomez and Thièle have observed,

> access to adequate housing directly affects other human rights. Without it, employment is difficult to secure and maintain, health is threatened, education is impeded, violence is more easily perpetrated, privacy is impaired, and social relationships are frequently strained.[12]

This chapter will analyse the small but significant body of domestic case law which continues to emerge over issues of housing and welfare within the UK. It will argue that the rights-language of such judicial discourses is relevant to gauging whether a meaningfully safeguarded entitlement to 'adequate housing' might ever be brought into existence. Arguably, where recession-led, discretion-based decision-making can so easily hinder the impact and scope of human rights law, then this perhaps sends a message relevant to other rights areas: if public funds are needed for the realisation of such basic entitlements as decent housing or health, then these rights might be more accurately described as a social privileges. Put bluntly, if human dignity can be easily tied to purse strings, in a state as prosperous and rights-rich as the UK, then what message does this send to rights-advocates in regions emerging from poverty or conflict? If a 'duty' to preserve finite state resources is an acceptable 'get out clause' for jurists and legislators (to infringe basic rights), then there is no guarantee that similar reasoning might not apply to cases involving civil or political rights issues. Economic austerities should not bring to mind political atrocities: where benefit caps lead directly to food-banks, evictions and squalor, it can be argued that the concept of a human dignity baseline has been ill-served by those tasked with ring-fencing meaningful protections for human rights.

2 The 'Bedroom Tax': Capping Social Welfare, Re-defining Vulnerability?

> The meaning of home is brought into sharp relief by the threat of losing the roof overhead...the most recent housing market crisis, with all its adverse economic

[12] Gomez and Thiele (2005), p. 2.

consequences, has underlined the universal significance of home meanings and their significance for law and housing policy.[13]

The chief catalyst for the housing 'rights-relapse' within the United Kingdom was the introduction of 'austerity measures' legislation: the Housing Benefit and Universal Credit ('Size Criteria') Regulations (2013) ('Regulation B13')[14] were part of a wider policy of welfare reform, apparently aimed at preserving finite state resources by targeting help at those most in need of financial support.[15] As a 'de facto compulsory levy'[16] this 'bedroom tax' is a key component of the wider austerity measures introduced by the UK's Coalition Government since their election in 2010. As Gibb argues, many of these welfare reforms have impacted profoundly upon the very 'poorest in society.'[17] An additional policy aim was that such reductions would however actively encourage unemployed people to find work, rather than have them remain over-reliant upon social security benefits.[18] In other words, the legislation's chief aim was to 'incentivize . . .households to occupy property of the appropriate size or face a financial penalty.'[19] Persons in receipt of Housing Benefit have been particularly affected, across both the private and social rented housing sectors. Termed the scourge of the 'spare room subsidy' by its supporters, Regulation B13 is referred to as 'the bedroom tax' by its critics. Put simply, the new rules on claiming Housing Benefit have limited the amount of welfare payments which can be received by tenants. Often this is on the basis of room usage or room size: where for example a single person is living in a two-bedroom apartment, or a family with two young children are living in a three-bedroomed house, this will be deemed as under-occupation, and the amount of Housing Benefit paid to the claimant by the state will be capped. Where benefits are then reduced on this basis, the tenant is expected to perhaps take in a lodger, move to smaller accommodation with fewer bedrooms (which might well require finding more costly private-sector landlord accommodation) or make up the shortfall in rent themselves, out of any savings or other 'income.' Given that claimants generally tend to be unemployed or in low-income employment, or are perhaps also claiming other welfare benefits (e.g. on the basis of caring their commitments,

---

[13] Fox-O'Mahony (2013), p. 157.

[14] Available at http://www.legislation.gov.uk/uksi/2013/2828/made (accessed 12.01.15).

[15] See also The Welfare Reform Act 2012 (available http://www.legislation.gov.uk/ukpga/2012/5/contents/enacted (accessed 14.01.15) which also introduced a more general 'benefit cap' limiting the level of welfare benefit payments for any family with children to £500 a week irrespective of family size.

[16] Gibb (2015), p. 2.

[17] *Ibid.*, p. 8. As Gibb further notes, disabled persons are 'massively over-represented in those affected by the bedroom tax.' p. 10.

[18] See The 2013 Policy Guidance (available at https://www.gov.uk/government/publications/hb-circular-a172013-discretionary-housing-payments, accessed 23.03.15).

[19] Gibb (2015), p. 1. As Gibb observes, the policy has been given several other titles, by its opponents and supporters respectively. These include the 'social sector size criteria' and the 'under-occupation charge.' (p. 2).

disability or illness) their options for simply finding this extra money to pay their rent are often limited. Taking in a lodger may well breach the terms of their original lease (in the private sector) or serve to prevent familial contact visits: dipping into savings, or quickly finding employment may not be a realistic option, especially where a claimant has disability or health issues, as much of the case law in this area clearly confirms. Tenants in such a position can apply for state support however, which, if awarded, will take the form of a discretionary housing payment ('DHP'). Funding for these is finite, and often varies between the local authorities tasked with running the scheme.

A number of cases have recently been brought by disappointed applicants, with varying degrees of success. In *Burnip v Birmingham City Council* (2012)[20] for example the Court of Appeal noted that 'disability can be expensive. It can give rise to needs which do not attach to the able-bodied.'[21] In this private rented sector case, a key issue was that of 'unlawful discrimination'[22] in the sense of there being no justification in law for the distinctions made between claimants. The Court also found that the legislative criteria for the receipt of Housing Benefit were unlawfully discriminatory in relation to disabled children (who were unable to share a bedroom as a result of their respective conditions) and against severely disabled adults in need of overnight care (whose carers were not classed as eligible 'occupiers' under the Regulations). As such, the statute was found to have offended against the non-discrimination principle enshrined in Article 14 of the European Convention on Human Rights ('ECHR').[23] The case is noteworthy for confirming that Housing Benefit can fit within the relatively protective remit of Article 1 Protocol 1 of the ECHR as a 'possession'.[24] As such, it was not necessary for the Court of Appeal to consider here whether there had been an infringement of the applicants' Article 8 right to respect for their home, family and private life (so as to underpin a claim of Article 14 discrimination).[25] Citing *Stec v United Kingdom* (2006)[26] it was noted that 'difference in treatment' is

[20] *Burnip v Birmingham City Council & Anor* [2012] EWCA Civ 629 (15 May 2012).

[21] *Ibid.*, per Kay LJ, para 1.

[22] The Housing Benefit Regulations 2006 focused upon the number of 'occupiers' present, defining them under Regulation 13 D (12) as: "the persons whom the relevant authority is satisfied occupy as their home the dwelling to which the claim or award relates except for any joint tenant who is not a member of the claimant's household." Regulation 13D (3) allowed one bedroom each for couples, a person who was not a child, two children of the same sex; two children under 10 year, or a child.

[23] Article 14 of the ECHR provides that: "The enjoyment of the rights and freedoms set forth in the Convention shall be secured without discrimination on any ground such as sex, race, colour, language, religion, political or other opinion, national or social origin, association with a national minority, property, birth or other status."

[24] Article 1 of Protocol 1 of the ECHR states that: 'Every natural or legal person is entitled to the peaceful enjoyment of his possessions. No one shall be deprived of his possessions except in the public interest and subject to the conditions provided for by law and by the general principles of international law.' See further *REG (RJM) v Secretary of State for Work and Pensions* [2009] 1 AC 311.

[25] *Burnip* [2012] *Op cit.*, n 20, para 8.

[26] *Stec v United Kingdom* (2006) 43 EHRR 47.

> discriminatory if it has no objective and reasonable justification; in other words, if it does not pursue a legitimate aim or if there is not a reasonable relationship of proportionality between the means employed and the aim sought to be realised.[27]

The claimants here also looked to the positive state duties that had been highlighted in *Thlimmenos v Greece* (2001) in respect of indirect discrimination via non-differential treatment which had stressed that

> the right not to be discriminated against in the enjoyment of the rights guaranteed under the Convention is also violated when States without an objective and reasonable justification fail to treat differently persons whose situations are significantly different.[28]

In sum, there was clearly a state obligation to actively 'make provision to cater for the significant difference.'[29] The court conceded that few cases in the wake of *Thlimmenos* had truly managed to embed meaningfully the concept of a positive, juridical state obligation to fairly allocate scarce public resources. A cautious approach on the part of domestic jurists was therefore needed here, with careful consideration having to be given to the state's explanation for the discrimination. It was noted that such scrutiny should also occur at a later stage of the proceedings (i.e. when the question of lawful justification was being considered) rather than at the earlier point of determining whether any discrimination had actually occurred.[30]

In addition to the procedural aspects of such decision-making processes, the Court also touched upon issues of substantive law. While the Equality and Human Rights Commission sought to rely upon the United Nations Convention on the Rights of Persons with Disabilities ('the CRPD') the state argued that its provisions were not relevant to determining the remit of Article 14.[31] Looking to *AH v West London MHT* [2011] (an Upper Tribunal case) for guidance however, it was noted that the CRPD clearly prohibited discrimination against people with disabilities, and promoted their fundamental rights on an equal basis with others.[32] Significantly, Kay LJ also stressed that the CRPD provided a clear framework for signatory states; as a 'legally binding international treaty' it also gave rise to 'corresponding obligations.'[33]

---

[27] *Ibid.,* para 51. Equally, 'The Contracting State enjoys a margin of appreciation in assessing whether and to what extent differences in otherwise similar situations justify a different treatment.'

[28] *Thlimmenos v Greece* (2001) 31 EHRR, para 44.

[29] *Burnip* [2012] *op cit.,* n 20, para 15.

[30] Para 18 per Kay LJ who added (citing Baroness Hale in *AL (Serbia) v Secretary of State for the Home Department* [2008] 1 WLR 1434 (paras 20–25) that such a methodology would offend against the spirit of Article 14, given the need 'to concentrate on the reasons for the difference in treatment and whether they amount to an objective and reasonable justification.'

[31] Relying on the *obiter* opinion of Sales J in *Reg (NM) v London Borough of Islington* [2012] EWHC 414 (Admin), para 99.

[32] (2011) UKUT 74 (AAC) per Carnwath LJ, para 15.

[33] At para 19. The CRPD was adopted by the General Assembly on 13 December 2006, ratified by the United Kingdom on 7 August 2009 and by the European Union on 23 December 2010.

Although welfare benefits are not specifically provided for, the provisions were still highly relevant to the case at hand. Strasbourg jurisprudence was also cited, in respect of the European's Court of Human Rights' use of international law provisions to assist it in its interpretation of the European Convention. ('ECHR'). In *Demir and Baykara v Turkey* (2009)[34] for example, the Grand Chamber had declared the need to

> take into account elements of international law other than the [ECHR], the interpretation of such elements by competent organs and the practice of European States reflecting their common values.[35]

Similarly, *Opuz v Turkey* (2010) had seen the Court stress that

> in addition to the more general meaning of discrimination as determined in its case-law ... the Court has to have regard to provisions of more specialised legal instruments and the decisions of international legal bodies.[36]

In sum, no 'objective and reasonable justification for the discriminatory effect of the statutory criteria' had been established here. Given however that amending Regulations had subsequently been put in place (to remove the discriminatory elements of earlier legislation) the Court granted the claimants declaratory relief, rather than any monetary compensation.[37] In his judgment, Henderson LJ looked particularly at the issue of justification, confirming that the correct test to apply here was the one which had been set out in *Stec*, namely that the Secretary of State must

> establish that there was at the material time objective and reasonable justification for the discriminatory effect of the relevant HB criteria as they applied to the particular circumstances of the appellants.[38]

He added that the UK's scheme of Housing Benefit *as a whole* did not need to be justified, nor did the general policy on calculating it. The focus had to be on the *difference in treatment* which had resulted from applying those specific statutory criteria which had infringed Article 14 of the European Convention.[39] On the more difficult issue of the margin of appreciation, he again cited *Stec*, stressing that its apparently fluid remit would 'vary according to the circumstances, the subject-matter and the background'[40] of any given case. In any event, 'very weighty

---

[34] (2009) 48 EHRR 54.

[35] The Grand Chamber was construing Article 11 ('Freedom of Association') of the ECHR via reference to the International Labour Organisation ('ILO') Conventions and the European Social Charter ('ESC') (para 85).

[36] (2010) 50 EHRR 28, para 185 on the issue of considering the definition and scope of discrimination against women (and violence against them). He added that 'It seems to me that [The CRPD] has the potential to illuminate our approach to both discrimination and justification.' (para 22).

[37] Following *Francis v Secretary of State for Work and Pensions* [2006] 1 WLR 3202.

[38] Para 26.

[39] See *A v Secretary of State for the Home Department* [2004] UKHL 56, [2005] 2 AC 68, para 68 (per Lord Bingham) and *AL (Serbia) v Home Secretary* [2008] UKHL 42, [2008] 1 WLR 1434, para 38 (per Baroness Hale).

[40] Para 52.

reasons' would be needed to justify a difference in treatment based upon an individual characteristic e.g. race or, as here, gender. Where economic or social policies were at issue however, states were much more likely to be afforded a wide margin of appreciation by the European Court on the basis that domestic authorities are best placed to decision-make on such key matters of public interest. Unless policies were found to be 'manifestly without reasonable foundation' they would not be classed as infringing European Convention rights. In respect of distinguishing between direct and indirect forms of discrimination, there was

> no good reason to impose a similarly high standard in cases of indirect discrimination, or cases where the discrimination lies in the failure to make an exception from a policy or criterion of general application, especially where questions of social policy are in issue.[41]

The review of proportionality required here did not therefore demand a higher, 'enhanced' standard; the 'function, operation and interaction' of the various social security benefits which were available to the appellants were however relevant to the question of whether or not justification had been achieved.[42] In respect of Mr Burnip, the variety and amounts of benefit received by him were directly relevant to this issue: the sums received from his student loan and Incapacity Benefit were set out in detail, as was his Disability Living Allowance, despite the fact that this benefit ('DLA') was not meant to be included in calculations for determining Housing Benefit levels.[43] Henderson LJ further observed that a distinction could be drawn between those welfare benefits which were received to enable subsistence, and those benefits which might be claimed in relation only to housing costs. Benefits received in connection with incapacity and disability were clearly 'not intended to help with his housing needs.'[44] This was underpinned by the fact that discrete, separate rules attached to the Housing Benefit system.

Moreover, the appellant had an 'objectively verifiable need' for two bedroom accommodation because of his condition; the fact that the shortfall brought about by the deduction to his Housing Benefit might be made up via a discretionary, unpredictable welfare payment, did not offer a 'complete or satisfactory answer' to his long-term difficulties.[45] As such, the discriminatory effects of the policy were not justified. Given also the 'long term commitment' that tended to attach to housing, and the difficulties that severely disabled persons often faced in finding a suitable home (for example, in relation to disabled adaptations) it seemed that no

[41] Para 28.

[42] Para 29.

[43] On whether local authorities should take into account the care component of the Disability Living Allowance benefit, see the recent High Court decision in *R (Hardy) v Sandwell Metropolitan Borough Council* [2015] EWHC 890 (Admin).

[44] Para 45.

[45] *Ibid.* The payments were purely discretionary in nature; their duration was unpredictable; they were payable from a capped fund; and their amount, if they were paid at all, could not be relied upon to cover even the difference between the one and two bedroom rates of LHA, and still less the full amount of the shortfall.

'reasonable degree of reassurance' would be achieved via a fund-capped, discretionary payments system, which required claimants to be very frequently re-assessed (e.g. every 12 weeks).[46] The purpose of Housing Benefit was, after all, to 'help people to meet their basic human need for accommodation of an acceptable standard.'[47] Equally, the exception sought here was not one which would apply to disabled persons generally: only 'a very limited category of claimants' could probably be covered, namely those with a disability which was 'so severe' that an extra bedroom would be required for their nocturnal carer, or for their disabled children to sleep in. As such cases were not likely to be very great in number, they would not be as easily 'open to abuse,' nor would they tend to be subject to future change or need 'regular monitoring.' Given that a need to protect public funds had provided the catalyst for the reforms, it made sense to keep claimants in their own homes rather than have them move into more costly residential accommodation as a result of cutting their Housing Benefit. The law had also since been amended: it seemed therefore likely that the government had acknowledged both 'the justice of such claims and the proportionate cost and nature of the remedy.'[48] As such, the discrimination here was found to be unjustified.

Unfortunately the remit of the *Burnip* reasoning was not extended to disabled adult couples who were unable to share a bedroom, as *MA and others* v *The Secretary Of State For Work And Pensions* (2014) subsequently established.[49] Here the claimant had spina bifida, hydrocephalus, was doubly incontinent, and suffered from recurring pressure sores. Her husband cared for her full-time in their two-bedroom flat. Her condition required a hospital-type single bed, electronic pressure mattress, in-bed toileting equipment, medical sheets and incontinence pads. The bedroom was not large enough for a second bed, nor could the couple share her single hospital bed. Under the Regulations, their Housing Benefit was reduced by 14 % for 'under-occupation' on the basis that co-habiting couples were expected to share a bedroom. The Court of Appeal did at least concede that bedroom tax

> if read in isolation... plainly discriminates against those disabled persons who have need for an additional bedroom by reason of their disability as compared with otherwise comparable non-disabled persons who do not have such a need.[50]

The core issue however was again whether or not such discrimination might be deemed justifiable. Looking to the Supreme Court's decision in *Humphreys* (2012) for guidance, the key question was whether the discrimination was 'manifestly without reasonable foundation.'[51] Given that the legislative reforms had been

---

[46] Para 47.

[47] Para 64.

[48] Para 64.

[49] [2014] EWCA Civ 13.

[50] Para 39.

[51] *Humphreys v Revenue and Customs Commissioners* [2012] UKSC 18, [2012] 1 WLR 1545.

introduced to specifically address the nation's economic crisis (by reducing a 'culture of welfare dependency' among sections of the population) this standard had clearly not been met. A system of support, albeit a discretion-based one, clearly existed at the level of local authority decision-making; extensive parliamentary debate had also preceded the introduction of the reforms. It could thus be said that the new Regulations were *not* lacking in reasonable foundation. The Court further noted that a clear decision to treat disabled adults and children differently was open to objective and reasonable justification, on the basis that there was for example an over-arching duty under the Children's Convention to consider and protect the best interests of the child. Thus, as the state had argued,

> There are differences between disabled couples and disabled children. Couples are expected to share a bedroom. Further, adults are able to exercise choice in all aspects of their lives.[52]

The Public Sector Equality Duty ('PSED') was also considered here, insofar as it obliges public authorities to have 'due regard' to the need to 'eliminate discrimination, harassment, victimisation and any other conduct that is prohibited by or under' the Equality Act 2010. The positive obligation to 'advance equality of opportunity between persons who share a relevant protected characteristic and persons who do not share it'[53] meant that public authorities should seek to 'remove or minimise disadvantages suffered by persons who share a relevant protected characteristic that are connected to that characteristic' and also 'take steps to meet the needs of persons who share a relevant protected characteristic that are different from the needs of persons who do not share it.'[54]

The wider policy behind the legislative reforms was again key however, particularly in relation to the state-sanctioned need for a de-centralisation of governance via 'a fundamental shift of power from Westminster to people.'[55] Reduction of the UK's budget deficit was a clear priority; cutting and capping social security spending was also a necessary consequence of 'accurately target[ing] support'[56] at those most in need of financial help. 'Hard cases' such as this one had been identified by critics at an early stage of the law-making process; legislators were

---

[52] Para 77. 'Choice' was apparently evidenced by their ability to 'enter living arrangements knowing that they may have to compromise to accommodate their needs. As well as making applications for benefits and DHPs, they are also able to negotiate with landlords and [local authorities], take proactive steps to find more suitable accommodation of the right size, take in a lodger, find work or increase hours of work.' para 77.

[53] See The Equality Act 2010 in particular s 149 (1) (c) which creates a duty to 'foster good relations between persons who share a relevant protected characteristic and persons who do not share it.'

[54] See s 149(7)—disability is classed as a protected characteristic.

[55] Para 16 (citing the then-newly elected Government's *Coalition Agreement* 2010; They also promised to 'promote decentralisation and democratic engagement, and [to] end the era of top-down government by giving new powers to local councils, communities, neighbourhoods and individuals.')

[56] Para 21.

reluctant however to define what exactly 'significantly adapted accommodation' might amount to, so as to not automatically exempt such dwellings from the statute's remit.[57] They did opt for 'localism' however, delegating difficult decisions (and state accountability) on the allocation of shortfall-meeting DHPs to local authorities. State concerns over protecting taxpayers were addressed 'by offering a limited funding pot rather than an exemption of which the potential scale would be quite uncertain.'[58]

Meaningful consultations with local stakeholders (e.g. local councils and housing associations) had been carried out. Although such a discretion-based system could lead to uncertainty and controversy it still had several advantages: local authorities would be tasked with providing help directly to those in need, and with targeting finite resources rather than having these go to those who were able to make up benefit shortfalls out of their own income or assets.[59] On the discriminatory aspect of the new legislation, the Court was unequivocal;

> The bedroom criteria define under-occupation by reference to the objective needs of non-disabled households, but not by reference to the objective needs of at least some disabled households. This demonstrates that on any view Regulation 13B discriminates on the ground of disability.[60]

Given however that the regulation was 'part of a package for dealing with the problem of under-occupation' and that recognition had been given in respect of those who merited exemption, the core question was whether the scheme *as a whole* discriminated against disabled persons. The claimants argued that a non-disability related need for additional accommodation (e.g. family size) entitled applicants to sufficient, automatic Housing Benefit to meet their rent payment. Needs which arose by virtue of disability however (and which did not fall under the exemptions e.g. for disabled children) gave rise only to a right to *apply* for discretionary assistance, which still might not meet their housing costs in full. Similarly, a right of appeal existed in respect of Housing Benefit refusals, but legal challenges to discretionary payment refusals were possible only via judicial review, which is not an appeal process, but focuses on procedural aspects of decision-making, legal error and public law principles, rather than on matters of fact. In terms of disproportionate effect, it was argued that disabled persons often depended more upon community ties and/or adaptations to their dwelling than their able-bodied counterparts. The type of discrimination was not however deemed to be particularly important

[57] 'Such an exemption would be difficult and expensive to deliver effectively, especially when Universal Credit was introduced. It would either be too broad brush or leave out many other equally deserving hard cases.' para 23.

[58] Para 26.

[59] Impact Assessment and Equality Impact Assessments had also been carried out and these confirmed that approximately 660,000 Housing Benefit claimants were living in the social housing rented sector; of these, around 420,000 were disabled persons. With no ring-fencing of funding, local authorities were tasked with deciding which applicants should be afforded priority.

[60] Para 39.

given that the Strasbourg jurisprudence did not tend to make such a clear distinction:

> when analysing the extent of justification required, it is the substance of the discrimination which matters, not its form. I doubt whether it matters whether the discrimination is properly to be characterised as direct, indirect or *Thlimennos.*[61]

The key issue to be determined was, again, whether the discrimination had occurred, but whether it had been justified. In terms of the standard to which the state must justify a discriminatory provision, it was held that the correct test was whether or not it had been made "manifestly without reasonable foundation." Citing Henderson J's dicta in *Burnip* it was decided that whilst

> weighty reasons may well be needed in a case of positive discrimination... there is no good reason to impose a similarly high standard in cases of indirect discrimination, or cases where the discrimination lies in the failure to make an exception from a policy or criterion of general application, especially where questions of social policy are in issue.[62]

Applying *Stec,* the scope of the margin of appreciation was found to fluctuate 'according to the circumstances, the subject matter and the background.'[63] If 'general measures of economic or social strategy' were at issue, a wide margin would be applied. Again a central question was whether the discrimination amounted to a 'proportionate means of meeting a legitimate aim.' The Regulations were a key component of a 'high policy decision' involving important public policy choices; the Court was still however required to conduct 'careful scrutiny' of such provisions, whilst bearing in mind that Parliament had already debated and approved of the measures.[64]

Burnip was distinguished here on the basis that the scheme had since been changed: further Guidance had been issued by the Government, and more resources had been allocated to the discretionary payment funds. The discrimination had been justified, in the sense that 'differential treatment of adults and children was not irrational' given that the best interests of children were a primary consideration.[65] The "manifestly without reasonable foundation" test was a stringent one, but it did not require the state to actually demonstrate that such a policy was not irrational. Again, the key issue was whether the discrimination complained of had 'an objective and reasonable justification.' The court's role was one of careful scrutiny of the justification put forward by the state. Where a scheme had 'some flaws' or state justification was 'not particularly convincing' this was not enough to satisfy the high standard of the 'manifestly without reasonable foundation' test. Rather, a

[61] Para 46. Lady Hale had previously noted in *Humphreys v Revenue and Customs Commissioners* [2012] UKSC 18 (1) WLR 1545, para 19 that in a benefits case the test for justification would be the same irrespective of how discrimination might be characterised.)

[62] Para 49.

[63] Para 50.

[64] See further *Bank Mellat v HM Treasury* [2013] 3 WLR 179, para 44 per Lord Sumpton and *Black v Wilkinson* [2013] EWCA Civ 820, [2013] 1 WLR 2490.

[65] Para 60.

'serious flaw' in the scheme, which produced an 'unreasonable discriminatory effect' had to be present.[66]

The underlying policy purposes were presumably sound: some cases were better dealt with via the discretionary, local authority system than by the Housing Benefit scheme, there was a need to instil a sense of 'greater financial responsibility' amongst welfare claimants, and a fair balance had to be struck between 'the rights of the individual and the interests of the community.'[67] Administrative workability was a further factor for policy-makers, so that a refusal to expand the categories of exempted claimants was neither unfair nor irrational. As the Court put it, 'tighter definition would have resulted in an administratively intensive and costly process involving outside agencies as well as local authority staff.'[68] This was especially so where a claimant's housing needs or disability might change, although it is difficult to see how this could be applied to such severely disabled persons as the tenant in question. The rights of disabled children have perhaps to some extent been ring-fenced here, given how the Court accepted the state's argument that,

> This policy supports wider Government strategy on the rights of the child, supports family life and helps make families make the best choices for the welfare and development of all the children in their care. In addition, it acknowledges that there is an implicit vulnerability in childhood.[69]

While further embedding of the rights of the child is clearly to be welcomed, it could be argued that adults with a severe disability often have a similarly inherent vulnerability. In this case the claimant's conditions and situation were such that her care needs were not entirely dissimilar to those of a child. Similarly, had her carer not been her resident spouse, but say a lodger or friend, then presumably their second bedroom could potentially have been framed as essential to her needs and not deemed surplus to requirements. Arguably the chief consideration in relation to justifying discrimination in this context is how to best preserve scarce resources.

Subsequent case law has increasingly emphasised the finite nature of the 'public purse.' In *R (Rutherford) v SSWP* (2014)[70] for example, the High Court (for England and Wales) referred to 'extreme national financial austerity'[71] at the close of the case and to 'acute financial stringency'[72] at its outset. Here, the child affected by the benefit cap was aged 14 and suffered from a rare genetic condition known as Potoki-Shaffer Syndrome. He required constant care by at least two people, in this case his maternal grandmother and step-grandfather, both of whom

---

[66] Para 80.

[67] Para 68.

[68] Para 73.

[69] Para 77.

[70] [2014] EWHC 1631 (Admin).

[71] Para 61.

[72] Para 4. The term 'bedroom tax' was described as a colloquialism, and the *MA* case praised for its careful detailing of the 'political and legislative background' which had led to the need for welfare reform.

were also in poor health. Respite care was provided by overnight carers, twice weekly, without which it was quite likely that the child would have had to be placed in residential care. Under the Regulations, a disabled child requiring overnight care was not specifically exempted from the scheme, as disabled adults had been. His grandparents thus had to seek a discretionary payment to make up their Housing Benefit shortfall.

They sought to argue unlawful discrimination and that the Regulations should be interpreted to include disabled children as entitled to an extra bedroom for an overnight carer. In relation to justification, in the wake of the decision in *MA* a number of 'propositions and principles' now existed however: the scheme needed to be looked at in its entirety; the state must justify such differences in treatment; justification would not be proven if the court, after careful scrutiny, found it to be "manifestly without reasonable foundation." A discriminatory difference in treatment will lack the requisite objective and reasonable justification if a legitimate aim is not pursued, or if there is no 'reasonable relationship of proportionality' between method and policy aim. Parliamentary approval (especially where it has come via affirmative resolution in both Houses) was a key factor, and strongly suggestive of lawfulness.[73] Most significantly, a wide margin of appreciation attaches to issues of social or economic policy, not least where welfare benefits are concerned; flaws in the scheme must therefore be 'serious flaws' which have led to an *unreasonable* form of discrimination.[74]

Although *Burnip* had created binding precedent, the High Court described it as a 'fact sensitive decision' on an earlier, different scheme.[75] It was capable of being distinguished from the current case given the potentially greater numbers of persons affected in this context, the increased scope for abuse of the system, and the need for careful monitoring. In respect of European Convention rights, it should be remembered that 'substantial rather than theoretical breaches' are needed. With no 'substantial detriment' found here, the scheme seemed unlikely to be in breach. Parliament's role as law-maker must also be respected;

> the democratic process is liable to be subverted if, on a question of moral and political judgment, opponents of the Act achieve through the courts what they could not achieve in Parliament.[76]

That said, The Human Rights Act 1998 placed a clear burden upon judges in relation to primary legislation, beyond that of basic interpretation. The effects of such statutes in terms of infringing Convention rights must be considered and a declaration of incompatibility made if necessary. Comparison should be made between the effect of the legislation and of the Convention right itself; the policy

---

[73] Para 35. Dyson MR had stressed that "the effect of the 2012 Regulations (as amended) in conjunction with the DHP scheme on the position of disabled persons was well understood by Parliament." (see *MA*, para 57).

[74] *MA* Ibid., para 80.

[75] Para 21.

[76] Para 38, citing Lord Bingham in *R (Countryside Alliance) v AG* [2008] AC 719 (para 45).

aims of both are relevant. In terms of gauging the practical effect of the domestic statute, the court can however look beyond it to the 'underlying social purpose sought to be achieved.' In respect of proportionality, a "value judgment" may also be made, to take into account any wider societal circumstances.[77] Although the central question in *MA* differed slightly to the one raised here,[78] both cases essentially turned upon the same issue—that the decision to address the needs of some disabled tenants automatically under the Regulation and others via the DHP discretionary scheme was a justified, proportionate approach.

Taking *Burnip* and *MA* together, the High Court concluded that the DHP scheme would not be justified if it failed to 'provide suitable assurance of present and future payment in appropriate circumstances.'[79] Flaws in the scheme would however again need to be serious in nature, causing an 'unreasonable discriminatory effect.'[80] Though discretion-based, the 2013 Guidance particularly identified health problems as an important factor in restricting tenants' choices over housing; they therefore merited consideration.[81] The claimants in question had not suffered true detriment, given that the DHP had made up their benefit shortfall. A lack of assurance over future payments was essentially dismissed by the court, on the basis that funding had been forthcoming previously and that their circumstances were unlikely to change. It was noted that any assumption that non-resident carers (giving respite care) would not require a bedroom was unjustified and in this case, incorrect. Taken on its own or as part of the larger 'structurally reasonable'[82] scheme however, this did not amount to irrationality or to an unlawful form of discrimination which was manifestly without reasonable foundation. Rather it was down to the fact that children tended not to live alone. There was therefore some 'logical justification for treating the two groups differently even if it would have been possible to draft further provisions so that they were treated the same.'[83]

That the claimants had found the discretionary process both 'time consuming and stressful' was not enough to amount to a 'serious flaw in the scheme which produces an unreasonable discriminatory effect.'[84] Instead this was an error on the part of the local authority who had initially refused to fund their shortfall, but later reversed their decision. The court did not take into account a Papworth Trust report

---

[77] Para 39 citing Lord Nicholls in *Wilson v First County (No 2)* [2004] 1 AC 816 (para 61).

[78] Para 47 '... the question being answered in *MA* was not the same as the question in the present case. As formulated by the Court of Appeal, the question in *MA* was whether the different treatment of the need for additional accommodation of disabled and non-disabled persons was justified. Here the question posed by the Claimants is whether the different treatment of able bodied persons with an ascertained need for an additional bedroom and a disabled child with the same ascertained need is justified.'

[79] Ibid., para 50.

[80] Ibid.

[81] Ibid., para 51.

[82] Ibid., para 57.

[83] Ibid., para 57.

[84] Ibid., para 59.

(February 2014) on DHPs, stating that this was not relevant to the case in hand and that its correct place was in a wider political or legal debate.[85] The backdrop of 'considerable financial stringency,' was again stressed *R (D) v Worcestershire County Council* (2013).[86] Although this case was concerned with the provision of adult community care, a central issue was whether the claimant could remain living in his own home in the wake of 'reduced public funding of services.'[87] Here, the local council had introduced a '*Policy for Determining the Usual Maximum Expenditure for Non-Residential Care Packages*' (November 2012) which capped its maximum weekly expenditure on community care for adults under 65.[88] The affected claimant was due to turn 18 the following year: his mother, who was also his carer, had herself been diagnosed with cancer and was concerned that his needs (which arose directly from his various disabilities[89]) would not be fully met under the local authority's revised policy. No substantive legal challenge to the policy was made however, with the focus instead being placed upon the 'unlawfulness' of the consultation process used (i.e. the lack of information provided to consultees) and on its apparent failure to comply with the PSED under s. 149 of the 2010 Equality Act.

Put simply, the claimant was essentially being given the choice of going into residential care or remaining at home in his community with a potentially reduced level of care. The local authority had assessed his future needs as not falling within a high level of need. The High Court referred to the relevant legislation[90] and to an almost disturbingly long list of policy documents[91] which highlighted a number of

[85] Ibid., para 60. The report was based upon survey responses from 222 councils in England and Wales, and showed that Disability Living Allowance was wrongly being included in calculations on household income and that 59 % of disabled claimants had been successful in applying for a DHP, compared with 67 % of non-disabled people.

[86] [2013] EWHC 2490 (Admin), para 1.

[87] Ibid., para 1.

[88] It had already capped community care for those aged over 65, in 2008.

[89] These included a learning disability, attention deficit hyperactivity disorder, auditory processing difficulties and epilepsy.

[90] S. 29 of the National Assistance Act 1948 (which obliges local authorities to make arrangements for promoting the welfare of 'permanently handicapped' individuals); S. 2(1)(a) of the Chronically Sick and Disabled Persons Act 1970 extended this to include 'provision of practical assistance for that person in his home' where necessary to meet their needs; S. 47 of the National Health Service and Community Care Act 1990 requires local authorities to assess needs, and then decide upon service provision. See also s. 57 of the Health and Social Care Act 2001 on direct payments.

[91] See: '*Fair Access To Care Services: Guidance On Eligibility Criteria For Adult Care*' (2003) (FACS) which set out four categories of need (critical, substantial, moderate and low) and the criteria for 'severity'; its 2007 successor '*Putting People First: A Shared Vision And Commitment To The Transformation Of Adult Social Care*' ("Putting People First") aimed at promoting individualised budgeting for care and direct payments, and the revised 2010 Guidance '*Prioritising Need In The Context Of Putting People First: A Whole System Approach To Eligibility For Social Care – Guidance On Eligibility Criteria For Adult Social Care*' ("Prioritising Need"). See also '*Valuing People Now: A New Three-Year Strategy For Learning Disabilities*' (2009) on the importance of personalised programmes, choice and control for persons with learning difficulties,

'policy strands' on the use of finite state resources. Fairness and transparency were key concerns, as were the concepts of informed choice for disabled tenants and individualised control over one's finances within the context of 'strong and supportive communities.'[92] The court did refer specifically to Article 19 of the CRPD which, although not directly applicable within the UK, still sets out useful norms in terms of community living: states should for example 'take effective and appropriate measures' in relation to 'full inclusion and participation in the community' by disabled persons. Having an element of choice over one's place of residence, and access to support services to prevent isolation or segregation, for example, were hailed as significant aspects of the rights contained therein. As such, co-operation and discussion between local authorities and individuals (or their carers) was crucial. The process was likely to amount however to a 'sophisticated and often challenging exercise, balancing all material factors.'[93]

Resource allocation as ever remained significant.[94] It was noted that 'the public purse is not bottomless'[95] and that a wide degree of discretion attached to the allocation of resources for those deemed to be in need. The fact that there was an 'increasingly pressing need to make savings'[96] could (as one pressure group had stressed in their own formal report) result in a 'fettering' of funder discretion, unmet need and 'coercive institutionalism.'[97] As with the bedroom tax, where the costs (of care) might well exceed the amounts allowed to be claimed under the new policy, individuals were expected either to make up the shortfall themselves out of their income or savings or to opt for an alternative e.g. residential care.

In exceptional circumstances, exemptions could be made however, for example to avoid family breakdown or to take into account cultural factors. In any event, local authorities had to undertake a 'sophisticated balancing exercise' between enabling individual preferences and saving on costs; this would become much 'more difficult when public money is short; but it is the sort of exercise that public decision-makers have to perform every day. It is their job.'[98] Although the court

---

especially in respect of 'own home' accommodation. See in particular '*Personalisation Reform and Efficiencies in Adult Social Care*' (2010) which posits that individuals can find 'innovative, creative and cost-effective arrangements to meet their own assessed needs.'

[92] *Ibid.*

[93] Para 17.

[94] See *R v Gloucestershire County Council ex parte Mahfood* (1997) 1 CCLR 7, *R v Gloucestershire County Council ex parte Barry* [1997] AC 584, *Savva v Royal London Borough of Kensington and Chelsea* [2010] EWCA Civ 1209, *R (JG and MB) v Lancashire County Council* [2011] EWHC 2295 (Admin); [2012] 15 CCLR 167 and *R (KM) v Cambridgeshire County Council* [2012] UKSC 23; [2012] PTSR 1189.

[95] Para 19.

[96] Para 25.

[97] '*WeareSpartacus*' responded to the local government consultation on the proposed policy reforms with a highly critical 2012 report ('*Past Caring*') which warned that benefit shortfalls could compel many disabled persons into moving into residential care. (The court described this as 'dramatic pessimism'—para 87).

[98] Para 77.

expressed sympathy 'for those with real needs' and noted that reductions in state welfare may well lower their 'quality of life,' it did not find the adoption of the policy to be illegal, given the consultation process and also that the PSED had been satisfied.[99] Arguably, had the claimant contended that the actual *substance* of the policy was discriminatory and unjustified (rather than seeking to establish that the process of consultation which had surrounded its introduction was flawed) the court might have had to consider in more detail those human rights issues that tend to flow from a loss of social security and which in turn can impact profoundly upon the right to respect for home, family or private life.

Recently the High Court examined these issues in the context of a challenge to a council decision on calculating a DHP. In *R (Hardy) v Sandwell* (2015)[100] a retired, disabled claimant sought a judicial review of his local council's decision to include the care component of his Disability Living Allowance in their calculations of his DHP-eligibility, arguing that this contravened the government's own 2013 Guidance, and also placed an 'unlawful fetter' on the exercise of their discretion, amounting to unlawful discrimination, contrary to Article 14 of the European Convention. It was further argued that the PSED had not been discharged and that no reasonable adjustments had been made as required under s. 29(7) of the 2010 Equality Act. Such behaviour therefore constituted discrimination in the exercise of a public function (contrary to sections 15, 19 and 29(6) of the 2010 Act) with the inclusion of DLA in the calculations amounting to an irrational act.

The background to the case was that the claimant's wife was also disabled, and they together often provided overnight care for her elderly mother, who suffered from dementia. They were ineligible for a one bedroom council property, so were destined to 'over-occupy' in any event, even if some suitable alternative to their three-bedroom, substantially disability-adapted house were to be found. The court considered the recent judicial challenges to the scheme and looked to the 2013 Guidance on DHPs, which stated that local authorities might 'decide how to treat any income or expenditure, taking into consideration the purpose of the income where appropriate.'[101] Income from disability related benefits could be disregarded, given that these were designed to help pay for the extra costs of living generally associated with having a disability (e.g. adaptations to one's dwelling, as was the case here). Similarly, 'in all cases [they] should consider what is reasonable and not create a process that is too onerous for the claimant.'[102]

Where, as here, a rented home had been subject to significant disabled adaptations, local authorities were urged to consider making awards of DHP sufficient to allow people to remain in their adapted houses. Sandwell's own Policy (2013–2014) allowed them to 'give consideration' to the DHP Guidance, but to

[99] Para 106.

[100] [2015] EWHC 890 (Admin).

[101] See s 3.8 of the 2013 Guidance.

[102] Para 30.

also look at the 'individual merits' of each case. The council's blanket policy took into account *all* of an applicant's income, apart from the mobility component of DLA (the benefit also has a care component and is graded according to the level of care an individual needs.)[103] By including the care component of DLA in its calculations, the council had not grasped the meaning of the DHP Guidance and thus had failed to give it 'proper consideration.' It had not exercised its discretion 'properly or at all.'[104] They had also erred by basing their policy on the judgment in *R (Turner) v London Borough of Barnet Housing Benefit Review Board* [2001][105] which had dealt with a decision pre-dating the of the Human Rights Act 1998.[106] The failure to take the 2013 Guidance into account also meant that both their policy and their decision in respect of Mr Hardy's case were both clearly unlawful.

In relation to the issue of whether such decisions on DHPs engaged Article 14 non-discrimination rights, *Burnip* and *MA* were cited to confirm that there was 'no dispute' over this; Housing Benefit fell firmly within the remit of Article 1 of Protocol 1 of the European Convention ('A1P1') as a 'possession.'[107] Whether DHPs might also fall under the protections of A1P1, was a less straightforward question.[108] If they were looked at as a key element of the HB size criteria scheme as a whole,[109] on the basis that this had been done previously (e.g. in *Rutherford*) then they clearly also fell holistically within A1P1's ambit.[110] It was suggested also that Article 14 ECHR rights arose in connection with Article 8 rights (respect for private and family life, home and correspondence) which was a legal point left unanswered in *Burnip*. Although such rights did not extend to an obligation to actually house someone,[111] the issue of potential eviction or homelessness should not simply be overlooked. As *R (JS) v Secretary of State for Work and Pensions* [2014][112] has since decided, a capping of social security could lead to the loss of one's residence, which would clearly engage Article 8 rights.

Under Strasbourg case law (namely *Petrovic v Austria* (2001)[113] and *Okpisz v Germany* (2006)[114]) Article 14 may even be relevant where state actions have *not* directly engaged a Convention right, provided that they are tied to another right that

[103] See s 71(1) of the Social Security Contributions and Benefits Act 1992; See further The Discretionary Financial Assistance Regulations 2001.

[104] Para 41.

[105] EWHC 204 (Admin).

[106] Para 42.

[107] Para 46. See: *R (RJM) v Secretary of State for Work and Pensions* [2009] 1 AC 311.

[108] See per Sedley LJ, para 74 *Langely v Bradford Metropolitan District Council* [2006] QB 380.

[109] Lord Dyson MR in *MA*, paras 39–40, stressed that the HB size criteria were essentially a 'package' and that DHPs were an important part of these.

[110] Para 48.

[111] *Anufrijeva v London Borough of Southwark* [2004] QB 1124.

[112] PTSR 643.

[113] 33 EHRR 14.

[114] 42 HRR 32.

is protected e.g. a welfare benefit that might 'demonstrate the State's respect for family life within the meaning of Article 8.'[115] In other words, decisions on the allocation of DHPs to disabled applicants are relevant to those rights which are protected by Article 8; Article 14 rights are therefore engaged. These payments were clearly made to 'protect the private and family life of disabled applicants, in particular their recognised need to keep their existing home.'[116] A decision to reduce a tenant's payments to the extent that a rent shortfall is created may thus have a 'direct impact'[117] upon the very interests that Article 8 is meant to protect and promote.

Phillips J added that this case was an example either of indirect or *Thlimmenos* discrimination; claimants with a disability were dealt with no differently to those who were not disabled, thus giving rise to 'unfavourable treatment.'[118] The expenses associated with disability may be considerable, and are often subject to fluctuation; the notion of a 'windfall' for disabled persons (via their DLA benefits) was thus not an accurate one. The key question was again whether or not this discrimination was justified i.e. if it had 'an objective and reasonable justification'[119] and was (under s. 15 of the 2010 Act) 'a proportionate means of achieving a legitimate aim.' As the scheme in general had been justified on the basis that DHPs were provided by the state to prevent rent shortfall, it was very difficult to justify this form of discrimination.

Including the care component of DLA in the calculations *was* discriminatory, contrary to Article 14, and in breach of s. 29 (6) of the 2010 Act. The case is also of interest in respect of offering some measure of guidance as to how local authorities should monitor the way in which their discretion is being exercised, not least in its impact upon disabled tenants. Rather than simply 'ticking boxes' councils should be undertaking some form of 'substantive consideration.'[120] Arguably, such reasoning could perhaps also be applied to other cases which involve the loss or reduction of social security, or the denial of access to services which in turn might impact adversely upon human rights. Irrespective of the numbers of tenants affected, if eviction, poverty, homelessness or woefully inadequate housing can arise in the wake of money-saving domestic reforms, then decision-makers must ask themselves whether such laws and policies are truly compliant with the fundamental provisions of human rights law. Judicial discourse on the core rights concepts of human dignity, a decent standard of living, and the equitable

---

[115] Para 51. See further *R (Chester) v Secretary of State for Justice* [2014] AC 271 SC where it was held that as a "*general principle of Strasburg law under article 14 of the Convention. . .additional rights falling within the general scope of any Convention right for which the state has voluntarily decided to provide must in that event be provided without discrimination. . .*" per Lord Manse JSC, para 63.

[116] Para 52.

[117] Ibid.

[118] Para 58.

[119] As set out in *MA* per Lord Dyson MR, para 80.

[120] Para 67.

distribution of resources could do much to enlighten and inform future debates on the meaning and nature of welfare reform.

3 Adequate Housing as Meaningfully Juridical Right?

> Inhuman and degrading treatment is an important baseline. But it is an "on/off switch" focusing on extreme misery, where policy and resources lose any relevance. Social rights have a different virtue.[121]

It is difficult to argue that a 'right' to adequate housing is a truly juridical one within the UK, given the brick wall mantras of 'available resources' and 'benefit dependency,' and the finite nature of the public purse. As Remiche has further argued in relation to the loss of the home, a civil right to have one's home life respected frequently has to rely upon the less robust socio-economic right to actually be adequately housed.[122] The case law in this area does at least look fairly regularly to the provisions of international human rights law for some degree of guidance, even if the margin of appreciation almost always then proves to be impenetrable. Domestic decision-makers are also at least being reminded of such important rights concepts as the child's best interests and of the relevance of such instruments as the CRPD. As the Court of Appeal clearly stated in *Burnip*, 'by ratifying a Convention, a state undertakes that wherever possible its laws will conform to the norms and values that the Convention enshrines.'[123] Those tasked with amending or crafting social welfare policies, and indeed with monitoring their adverse effects upon vulnerable persons, could do worse than look to Article 4 of the CRPD which obliges signatory states to:

> take all appropriate measures, including legislation, to modify or abolish existing laws, regulations, customs or practices that constitute discrimination against persons with disabilities.

Article 5(3) also usefully provides that:

> in order to promote equality and eliminate discrimination, State Parties shall take all appropriate steps to ensure that reasonable accommodation is provided.

Article 19 similarly calls for recognition of 'the equal right of all persons with disabilities to live in the community, with choices equal to others.' This in turn is likely to be grounded upon 'the opportunity to choose their place of residence and where and with whom they live on an equal basis with others' so that they are not simply 'obliged to live in a particular living arrangement.' Other relevant provisions include Article 11 (1) of the International Covenant on Economic, Social and Cultural Rights ('ICESCR') which highlights the need for 'adequate food,

[121] Fordham (2013), p. 386.
[122] Remiche (2012), p. 793.
[123] LJ Kay in *Burnip* (2012), para 19.

clothing and housing and the continuous improvement of living conditions.' Article 2 (1) provides a sort of 'get out clause' via its proviso on 'maximum available resources' which goes some way towards enabling a defence of justification in cases involving discretionary, economic decision-making. The ICESCR General Comment 3 (5th session, 1990) (on the Nature of States Parties Obligations) remains particularly relevant however, highlighting the need for 'a minimum core obligation to ensure the satisfaction of, at the very least, minimum essential levels of each of the rights' contained therein.' Thus where

> any significant number of individuals is deprived of essential foodstuffs, of essential primary health care, of basic shelter and housing.. ...[the state] is, prima facie, failing to discharge its obligations under the Covenant.[124]

Although 'resource constraints' and the limits of 'maximum available resources' are regularly cited as reasons for failing to meet basic standards, states should still visibly

> demonstrate that every effort has been made to use all resources that are at its disposition in an effort to satisfy, as a matter of priority, those minimum obligations.[125]

As Fordham has observed, the Charter of Fundamental Rights of the European Union 2000 ('CFREU') perhaps has the potential to be 'a game-changer. Like the UDHR and African Charter, it includes as fundamental rights economic and social rights.'[126] Whether or not this will translate into a 'direct justiciability of social rights'[127] is still unclear. In relation to social rights,

> human rights advocates in the UK have made 'next to nothing' of the rights associated with achieving an adequate standard of living. And yet access to such basic resources as 'food, shelter and healthcare [are] paradigm examples of social rights...They are not new.[128]

Much more effort has gone into complying with those civil and political rights that have been enshrined in the European Convention. And yet, small victories of domestic justiciability for socio-economic rights remain possible. As he notes in relation to *Secretary of State for the Home Department v Limbuela & Ors* [2005][129];

> British politicians and legislators decided to make arrangements forcing asylum seekers into destitution, they fought the rule of law, and the rule of law won. In the end, vindication

[124] Available http://www.bayefsky.com/themes/adequate_general_general-comments.pdf, accessed 21.03.15. See also General Comment 4: The Right to Adequate Housing (1991).

[125] Ibid. See also Leckie (1989), p. 525 for a detailed analysis of how a right to housing 'occupies a permanent place on legal agendas from international to local levels' yet still often struggles for meaningful 'global realization.'

[126] Fordham (2013), p. 381. As Article 34(3) states; 'In order to combat social exclusion and poverty, the Union recognises and respects the right to social and housing assistance so as to ensure a decent existence for all those who lack sufficient resources, in accordance with the rules laid down by Community law and national laws and practices.'

[127] Ibid.

[128] Ibid.

[129] UKHL 66.

> came because massed ranks of conscientious solicitors besieged the High Court with emergency injunction applications, many granted by brave judges, undeterred by restrictive Court of Appeal authority. Rescue came at the hands of the absolute human right of freedom from inhuman and degrading treatment.[130]

Whether hindsight will eventually say the same about those lawyers and activists who struggle to advocate for the rights of people affected by such austerity measures as 'bedroom tax,' remains to be seen. The plight of the displaced refugee may lend itself more easily to human rights arguments grounded in the need for human dignity, decent standards of living and the state's duty to prevent degradation. The social housing tenant who must find extra cash to offset a reduction in their Housing Benefit does not quite carry the same weight in terms of framing their daily economic hardships as high level civil or political rights violations. Statute-heavy case law focusing on detailed policies on the dimensions of a 'spare' room, to determine whether or not it might be classed or used as a bedroom, rarely seems to attract the attention of human rights scholars keen to prevent global poverty or advance the rights of the oppressed. Domestic laws attaching to property ownership, leasehold tenure and social security benefits fit very comfortably into the category of mundane, 'black letter' private law matters; as such they may be destined to sit forever beyond the scope of those international law provisions aimed at addressing emergency situations or effecting humanitarian relief.

And yet as Steinberg argued, there is a 'direct correlation between substandard housing and other evil social conditions.'[131] With the need for food banks becoming increasingly commonplace within the UK, the work of housing lawyers and anti-poverty activists should not be framed as a minor domestic law matter. In terms of property rights being infringed, a tenant facing a forced 'eviction' (via lease surrender on the grounds of 'under-occupation' or through inability to pay their rent) may not be in an entirely dissimilar rights-position to others finding themselves dispossessed of home life or 'displaced' from their community. As Fox-O'Mahony puts it,

> The challenge for scholarship is to build the bridges that can make the reality of home's meanings count where it matters most: in the governance of the real issues and challenges of property law and housing.[132]

Recent Strasbourg case law on a 'right' to housing has to some extent at least acknowledged the importance of 'the home'[133] as a key component of Article 8 rights, with some measure of judicial consensus evident on the need for signatory states to provide their citizens with some base level protection against

[130] Fordham (2013), p. 385.

[131] Steinberg (1975–1976), pp. 64–79.

[132] Fox-O'Mahony (2013), p. 158.

[133] See for example *McCann v. The United Kingdom* – 19009/04 [2008] ECHR 385 (13 May 2008); *Marzari v Italy* [1999] 28 EHRR CD 175; See however *Bah v. The United Kingdom* – 56328/07 [2011] ECHR 1448 (27 September 2011). See further Buyse (2006); See also Remiche (2012) on the 'factual approach' of the Strasbourg Court to the concept of the home, p. 795.

homelessness. As Remiche has observed however in relation to *Yordanova v Bulgaria*[134] (a case concerned with forced evictions) any 'proportionality analysis is a contextual one and ought to be anchored in the circumstances of the case.'[135] Here, several factors were key to assessing whether the Article 8 (2) requirement of proportionality had been complied with at domestic level: the presence, not to mention the loss, of 'community life,' the failure of local building plans to materialize and the 'socially disadvantaged position of the applicants' were all deemed relevant.[136] The issue of absent or insufficient procedural safeguards was also important, given that there was an onus upon domestic authorities to examine the relevant Article 8 issues raised by applicants, with a view to providing adequate reasoning as to why their infringement was justified.[137] In respect of potential consequences, the risk of homelessness should not simply be disregarded, especially where members of a socially disadvantaged group were involved. Thus, a procedural and substantive analysis of what might be necessary in a democratic society was required here, with the state's clear 'lack of procedural safeguards. . .sufficient to found a violation of Article 8.'[138] As Nield and Hopkins have argued (albeit in respect of mortgage repossessions) there is a 'stark logic' in property law, so that occupiers who lack real property rights are particularly vulnerable and often tend to become 'invisible.'[139] The 'language of home'[140] seems to be absent from much of the case law in this area, so that it is perhaps not surprising that

> our highest courts have struggled to come to terms with the impact of Article 8 [ECHR] upon repossession proceedings of rented public sector housing.[141]

Procedural safeguards are therefore essential given that the loss of one's home represents a severe infringement of the right to respect for home (and family) life.[142] Vulnerability is perhaps the single most important factor, which domestic courts must not disregard in cases involving the loss of the home, irrespective of whether the premises are owned, mortgaged or rented.

---

[134] See for example *Yordanova and Others v Bulgaria* [2012] 25446/06.

[135] Remiche (2012), p. 791.

[136] Ibid. These in turn underpinned the concept of a justified rights interference under Article 8 (2).

[137] Ibid.

[138] Ibid., p. 793.

[139] Nield and Hopkins (2013), p. 431.

[140] Ibid.

[141] Ibid., p. 442.

[142] Ibid., p. 443. Justification also differs between A1P1 and Article 8, with the former requiring only that 'public interest' be satisfied and the latter demanding that the rights-infringement in question be 'necessary' to 'address a pressing social need.'

4 Conclusion

> To the naked eye, these look like human rights built on sand.[143]

It may be argued that the 'absence of property rights does not mean the absence of rights to respect for the home,'[144] but it is equally true that respect for one's home life may be very far-removed from a juridical right to access adequate housing. As Rolnik has stressed, housing's role is a central one; thus 'displacements, evictions, threats on security of tenure of urban dwellers, [and] the right to be an integral part of the decision-making process'[145] all share common links, not least in relation to how they tie in to the concepts of human dignity, adequate standards of living and equitable distributions of scarce resources. Rights violations in the field of housing do occur in relation to the loss of security of tenure, and a failure to safeguard the dignity of vulnerable persons.[146] Whether any 'single monitoring body [can] in isolation, ensure compliance with housing rights'[147] on a global or indeed national scale remains to be seen. What does seem clear is that the use of discretionary payment systems as a means of protecting basic rights or establishing minimum standards thresholds is an issue that merits continued judicial scrutiny and fuller analysis by human rights scholars. The wide 'margins of appreciation' which seem to attach to socio-economic rights (and in particular to localised decision-making) will perhaps always serve to defeat those rights claims which are seen as founded upon quite fragile entitlements e.g. social security benefits, health and adequate housing, even where these are meant to be underpinned by norms of human dignity or a basic, decent standard of living. As Leijten has argued, there is still a need for

> either A1 P1 or a different Convention Article [to] provide... the necessary 'safety net' in cases that because of their severity deserve fundamental rights protection.[148]

Where property rights are concerned, a 'crucial question' may still be whether or not welfare benefits are truly viewed as 'possessions.' For such fragile rights to be meaningfully justiciable (for example, under A1 P1) they should either be tied to a right already in existence or linked to some 'legitimate expectation.' Unless this is so, it seems that 'a right to acquire property is not a truly juridical one.'[149] Similarly, if rights depend entirely upon national budgets or discretionary decision-making for their realization, then arguably they might be better framed

[143] Fordham (2013), p. 386.

[144] Nield and Hopkins (2013), p. 454.

[145] Rolnik (2014), p. 294.

[146] *Ibid.*, p. 298.

[147] Leckie (1989), p. 560.

[148] Leijten (2013), p. 311.

[149] *Ibid.*, p. 315. She further argues that almost all social security issues seem now to be protected as rights-bearing claims. This has in turn led to a fairly wide margin of appreciation, which (when taken together with the complicated, sensitive nature of many such cases) perhaps underscores the difficulties of enforcing such rights via a supra-national court system (*Ibid.*, p. 349).

as mere social privileges. If the focus of judicial discourses were however to shift more towards the issue of actually defining adequacy of housing or living standards, especially in the context of socially vulnerable or disabled tenants, this might provide useful guidance for those other areas of human rights law (e.g. access to health care) which also seem to regularly fall foul of non-justiciability parameters. By the same token, if 'purse-strings' must be factored into the question of whether or not domestic decision-makers have failed in their human rights law obligations, this perhaps in turn challenges the 'indivisibility' of human rights generally.[150] It is difficult to frame such key resource-dependant rights (to property, social security or adequate living standards) as anything other than blatantly secondary to those civil or political rights involving not dissimilar issues (land seizures, displacement, degrading treatment).

To class rights as juridical on the basis that domestic law and policy-makers, or indeed the courts, have simply given due regard to the issue of justifying their infringement on the basis of 'the greater good' surely does a disservice to the wider notion of the 'social right.'[151] As Wolf has argued, promoting and enabling civil and political 'participation by stakeholders in decision-making processes'[152] may yet be the best way of embedding meaningful housing rights. Those 'whose interests are most at stake' tend to be best placed to 'bridge the gap between justiciability and enforcement.'[153] A steady stream of domestic litigation at least highlights just how severely vulnerable individuals may be affected by those laws and policies which are underpinned by purse strings reasoning. As King has further noted, even where constitutions or bills of social rights have been drafted to protect specific socio-economic rights, there may be little obvious 'reduction in inequality.'[154] Although a 'myriad of progressive laws and policies' might well exist at local level, 'enforcement is the most vital facet.'[155] As such, 'judicial oversight is crucial' to embedding such rights, especially given that 'housing means a lot more than a roof over one's head.'[156] Using the notion of justified discrimination to draw a sort of veil of legality over essentially unjust allocations (or, more accurately, over ineffective re-allocations) of state resources does little to promote meaningful models of social justice or of human rights aspirations. As Spano has observed in respect of judicial deference;

> the whole point of judicial review, whether national or international, is to provide a check on democratic decision-making as it may disproportionately restrict individual human rights.[157]

---

[150] Spano (2014), p. 2.

[151] See further King (2012), p. 2.

[152] Wolf (2006–2007), p. 270.

[153] *Ibid.*, p. 294.

[154] King (2012), p. 2.

[155] Chenwi (2008), p. 137.

[156] *Ibid.*

[157] Spano (2014), p. 2.

Judicial adjudication must therefore continue to play a 'substantial supporting role'[158] in embedding and monitoring fundamental yet fragile rights, not least in respect of those which are aimed at providing some base level, definitional thresholds for human dignity.[159] Meaningfully adequate standards of living are unlikely to be achieved unless the higher ideals of international human rights law are not just aspired to, but actually adhered to, by those tasked with equitably allocating scarce resources.

References

Buyse, A. (2006). Strings attached: The concept of home in the case law of the ECHR. *European Human Rights Law Review, 11*, 294.

Chenwi, L. (2008). Putting flesh on the skeleton: South African judicial enforcement of the right to adequate housing of those subject to evictions. *Human Rights Law Review, 8*(1), 105–137.

Costa, J. P. (2013). The relationship between the European Court of Human Rights and the National Courts. *European Human Rights Law Review, 3*, 264–274.

Fordham, M. (2013). Social rights. *Judicial Review, 18*(4), 379–387.

Fox-O'Mahony, L. (2013). The meaning of home: From theory to practice. *International Journal of Law in the Built Environment, 5*(2), 156–171.

Gibb, K. (2015). The multiple policy failures of the UK bedroom tax. *International Journal of Housing Policy, 15*, 148–166.

Gomez, M., & Thiele, B. (2005). Housing rights are human rights. *Human Rights, 32*, 2.

Grant, E. (2007). Enforcing social and economic rights: The right to adequate housing in South Africa. *African Journal of International and Comparative Law, 15*, 1–28.

Hohmann, J. (2013). *The right to housing: Law, concepts, possibilities*. London: Hart.

King, J. (2012). *Judging social rights*. Cambridge, England: Cambridge University Press.

Leckie, S. (1989). The UN Committee on economic, social and cultural rights and the right to adequate housing: Towards as appropriate approach. *Human Rights Quarterly, 11*, 522–560.

Leijten, I. (2013). From *Stec* to *Valkov*: Possessions and margins in the social security case law of the European Court of Human Rights. *Human Rights Law Review, 13*(2), 309–349.

Nield, S., & Hopkins, N. (2013). Human rights and mortgage repossession: Beyond property law using article 8. *Legal Studies, 33*(3), 431–454.

Remiche, A. (2012). Yordanova and Others v Bulgaria: The influence of the social right to housing on the interpretation of the civil right to respect for one's home. *Human Rights Law Review, 12* (4), 787–800.

Rolnik, R. (2009). *The promotion and protection of all human rights, civil, political, economic, social and cultural rights, including the right to development: Report of the special rapporteur on adequate housing as a component of the right to an adequate standard of living, and on the right to non-discrimination in this context* (Distr. GENERAL A/HRC/10/7 4 February 2009).

Rolnik, R. (2014). Place, inhabitance and citizenship: The right to housing and the right to the city in the contemporary urban world. *International Journal of Housing Policy, 14*(3), 293 300.

Spano, R. (2014). Universality or diversity of human rights? Strasbourg in the age of subsidiarity. *Human Rights Law Review, 14*, 487–502.

[158] King (2012), p. 2.

[159] See further http://just-fair.co.uk/uploads/The_Right_to_Housing_FINAL_27.07.15_.pdf (accessed 01.06.15).

Steinberg, M. I. (1975–1976). Adequate housing for all: Myth or reality? *The University of Pittsburgh Law Review*, 37.
Wolf, R. (2006–2007). Participation in the right of access to adequate housing. *Tulsa Journal of Comparative and International Law*, *14*, 269–294.

Legislation

Chronically Sick and Disabled Persons Act 1970
Discretionary Financial Assistance Regulations 2001
Equality Act 2010
Health and Social Care Act 2001
Housing Benefit Regulations 2006
National Assistance Act 1948
National Health Service and Community Care Act 1990
Social Security Administration Act 1992
Social Security Contributions and Benefits Act 1992
Welfare Reform Act 2012

Strasbourg Case Law

Bah v. The United Kingdom – 56328/07 [2011] ECHR 1448 (27 September 2011)
Connors v. the United Kingdom, no. 66746/01, 81–84, (27 May 2004)
Demir and Baykara v Turkey (2009) 48 EHRR 54
Marzari v Italy [1999] 28 EHRR CD 175
McCann v. The United Kingdom – 19009/04 [2008] ECHR 385 (13 May 2008)
Okpisz v Germany (2006) 42 HRR 32
Opuz v Turkey (2010) 50 EHRR 28
Petrovic v Austria (2001) and 33 EHRR 14
Stec v United Kingdom (2006) 43 EHRR 47
Thlimmenos v Greece (2001) 31 EHRR 44
Yordanova and Others v Bulgaria [2012] 25446/06

UK Case Law

A v Secretary of State for the Home Department [2004] UKHL 56, [2005] 2 AC 68
AH v West London MHT (2011) UKUT 74 (AAC)
AL (Serbia) v Secretary of State for the Home Department [2008] 1 WLR 1434
Anufrijeva v London Borough of Southwark [2004] QB 1124
Bank Mellat v HM Treasury [2013] 3 WLR 179
Black v Wilkinson [2013] EWCA Civ 820, [2013] 1 WLR 2490
Burnip v Birmingham City Council & Anor [2012] EWCA Civ 629 (15 May 2012)
Francis v Secretary of State for Work and Pensions [2006] 1 WLR 3202
Humphreys v Revenue and Customs Commissioners [2012] UKSC 18, [2012] 1 WLR 1545
Kay v. Lambeth Borough Council; Price v. Leeds County Council, 8 March 2006 [2006] UKHL 10

Langely v Bradford Metropolitan District Council [2006] QB 380
MA and others v *The Secretary Of State For Work And Pensions* [2014] EWCA Civ 13
Qazi v. London Borough of Harrow [2003] UKHL 43
R (Chester) v Secretary of State for Justice [2014] AC 271 SC
R (Countryside Alliance) v AG [2008] AC 719
R (D) v Worcestershire County Council [2013] EWHC 2490 (Admin)
R (Hardy) v Sandwell Metropolitan Borough Council [2015] EWHC 890 (Admin)
R (JG and MB) v Lancashire County Council [2011] EWHC 2295 (Admin); [2012] 15 CCLR 167
R (JS) v Secretary of State for Work and Pensions [2014] PTSR 643
R (KM) v Cambridgeshire County Council [2012] UKSC 23; [2012] PTSR 1189
R (RJM) v Secretary of State for Work and Pensions [2009] 1 AC 311
R (Rutherford) v SSWP [2014] EWHC 1631 (Admin)
R (Turner) v London Borough of Barnet Housing Benefit Review Board [2001] EWHC 204 (Admin)
R v Gloucestershire County Council ex parte Barry [1997] AC 584
R v Gloucestershire County Council ex parte Mahfood (1997) 1 CCLR 7
Reg (NM) v London Borough of Islington [2012] EWHC 414 (Admin)
REG (RJM) v Secretary of State for Work and Pensions [2009] 1 AC 311
Savva v Royal London Borough of Kensington and Chelsea [2010] EWCA Civ 1209
Secretary of State for the Home Department v Limbuela & Ors (2005) UKHL 66
Sheffield City Council v. Smart [2002] EWCA Civ 4
Wilson v First County (No 2) [2004] 1 AC 816

Justiciable Property Rights and Postcolonial Land Reform: A Case Study of Zimbabwe

Khanyisela Moyo

1 Introduction

> Land reform is a contested terrain in Africa and it impedes consensus (on human rights) between the north and the south.[1]

Legal justification for land reform can be found in both regional and international human rights conventions.[2] In particular, land reform is an intrinsic component of the right to an adequate standard of living, in that landlessness amounts to an abrogation of the obligation to fulfill this right as outlined in the International Covenant on Economic, Social, and Cultural Rights (ICESR) and the Universal Declaration of Human Rights (UDHR).[3] Also, access to land is a basic component

---

[1] Moyo (2009), p. 613.

[2] The human rights norms that are of relevance to agrarian reform include, *inter alia*,

- the right to adequate standard of living, provided for in Article 11 (1) International Covenant on Economic, Social, and Cultural Rights, (1966) 993 U.N.T.S. 3 (hereinafter ICESCR);
- the right to self-determination stipulated in Common Article 1(2) of the International Covenant on Civil and Political Rights, (1966) 999 U.N.T.S. 171 (hereinafter ICCPR) and the ICESCR and Article 2(3) of the United Nations Declaration on the Right to Development, G. A. Res. 41/128, Annex 41 U.N. GAOR Supp (No 53) at 186, U. N Doc. A/41/53 (1986) (hereinafter Declaration);
- the right to property found in *Article 17* of the *Universal Declaration of Human Rights*, G.A Rees 217A (111), U.N. Doc, A/810 (1948), (hereinafter UDHR) and Articles 14 and 21 of the African Charter on Human and Peoples' Rights, adopted June 27, 1981, OAU Doc. CAB/LEG/ 67/3 rev. 5, 21 I.L.M. 58 (1982), *entered into force* Oct. 21, 1986 (hereinafter The Charter).

[3] The content of the right to an adequate standard of living implies ensuring the availability and accessibility of the means that ensure livelihood. See also Ssenyonjo (2013), pp. 3–25.

K. Moyo (✉)
Transitional Justice Institute/School of Law, Ulster University, Magee, UK
e-mail: k.moyo@ulster.ac.uk

A. Diver, J. Miller (eds.), *Justiciability of Human Rights Law in Domestic Jurisdictions*, DOI 10.1007/978-3-319-24016-9_15

of the right to adequate food.[4] Further, the World Bank has stated that the emphasis of land reform in developing countries ought to be on improving property rights.[5] Yet, land reform programs also involve the modification of prevailing property rights in a manner that can be construed to infringe on the right to property.

This chapter scrutinises the tension between a justiciable right to property and a state-led agrarian land reform program in a postcolonial context by examining Zimbabwean Constitutional law. The Zimbabwean experience is very pertinent as it was the craving for land and resources that impelled the colonisation of most African societies. In Zimbabwe, this was achieved through military conquest and validated by both legislation and colonial jurisprudence.[6]

A dualistic land tenure system was maintained whereby white settlers, who totalled approximately 5 % of the populace, had the best land. This inequity was further bolstered by good infrastructure, state subsidies, loans and various tax incentives. Huge investments were established to help the settlers create international markets, thus ensuring that their farming was export oriented.[7] The same kind of assistance was not accorded to the majority black farming communities, who were pushed into reserves that received less rainfall and had poor soil quality. Consequently, black agricultural output was either subsistence or aimed at local markets.[8] These policies had the effect of both marginalizing the agricultural production of the indigenous population and ensuring that the black majority remained at the perpetual servitude of the settlers.[9]

This skewed and inequitable land structure, which was a rallying concern for the struggle for independence in Zimbabwe, was further exacerbated by the guerrilla war and the international isolation created by the United Nations sanctions against Southern Rhodesia.[10] Trade embargos prompted white commercial farmers to shift from export oriented farming to local markets to the further detriment of peasant production. By the time of the country's independence in 1980, white farmers produced approximately 90 % of the country's marketed food needs.[11]

Against this background, land reform was therefore a crucial component in Zimbabwe's transition from the racist colonial past to majority rule and justice. The major aims of this reform were to transfer land from whites to blacks so as to

---

[4] Ziegler (2002), paras 24 and 30. See also Debucquois (2014).

[5] World Bank (1975).

[6] *See* Hansungule (2000); Asmal (2013), pp. xx–xx1. See also In *Re Southern Rhodesia* 1919 AC 211 CD (whereas an English court approved the appropriation of land from Africans, maintaining that the land that they lived on and cultivated was now vested in the Crown). To the court, the natives' estimation of rights was: 'so low in the scale of social organization that their usage's and conception of rights and duties are not to be reconciled with the institutions or the legal ideals of civilized society'. Id.

[7] De Villiers (2003).

[8] Ibid.

[9] Ng'ong'ola (1992); and Ng'ong'ola (2013), pp. 154–183.

[10] For a discussion of the origins of the Zimbabwean land crisis, *see* Mitchell (2001); *See also* Moyo (1987), Nading (2002) and Ng'ong'ola (1992).

[11] De Villiers (2003).

foster peace, to empower the landless and war veterans, to reduce overpopulation in communal areas, to maintain and if possible increase existing levels of agricultural production, and to improve standards of living.[12]

Cognisant of the economic importance of the white farmers and also of the experience of Mozambique, where their departure resulted in economic collapse, the country's independence negotiations that took place at Lancaster House in London, struck a balance between two competing policy objectives, namely to redress the historical economic inequalities and to promote economic growth.[13] These concerns were reflected in the declaration of rights enshrined in the country's independence Constitution, which incorporated a right to property clause that provided the basis for state action.[14]

This chapter is divided into three sections. Section 2 outlines the conceptual framework that underlines the nexus between land reform, the right to property and justiciability. Section 3 is a discussion of the various land reform policies adopted by the government of Zimbabwe from 1980 to 2013, focusing on the relevant constitutional and legislative arrangements. Section 4 concludes by analyzing these constitutional and legislative frameworks and outlines the implications for human rights justiciability.

2 The Nexus Between a Justiciable Constitutional Property Right and Land Reform in a Post-colonial Context

The right to property has a somehow uneasy place in international human rights law. At an international level, protection for individual and collective property rights can only be found in the UDHR. This right cannot be said to be an absolute since it can be discerned from the wording of the UDHR that property deprivations that are not arbitrary are permissible.[15] Since ideological differences in the 1960s precluded this right from being included in both the ICESCR and the International Covenant on Civil and Political Rights (hereinafter ICCPR), the UDHR provision remains the international legal guideline on the right to property.[16] It can therefore be implied that a land reform program implemented through a constitutional amendment and a legislative act cannot be said to be a violation of the international human right to property.

[12] *See* Bratton (1990). Note that in Zimbabwe, the term war veteran is popularly used to refer to those men and women who fought in the war of liberation from colonial rule.

[13] De Villiers (2003).

[14] Article 16 of the former Constitution of Zimbabwe (S.1 1979/1600 of the United Kingdom) as amended to (No. 19) Act, 2009 (Hereinafter Lancaster House Constitution).

[15] Article 17 of UDHR (note 17) states '(1) everyone has the right to own property alone as well as in association with others. (2) No one shall be arbitrarily deprived of his property.'

[16] Bugge (1998).

At regional level the right to property is articulated differently in several regional human rights charters.[17] For the purposes of this chapter, the relevant regional instrument is the African Charter on Human and Peoples' Rights (The Charter),[18] in particular Articles 14 and 21. Article 14 states that:

> The right to property shall be guaranteed. It may only be encroached upon in the interest of public need or in the general interest of the community and in accordance with the provisions of appropriate laws.[19]

In an apparent support for land reform in postcolonial Africa, where natural resources were exploited by the colonial powers, Article 21(2) of the Charter states that "in case of spoliation the dispossessed people shall have the right to the lawful recovery of its property as well as to an adequate compensation."

It is arguable from the reading of the two provisions that the Charter is more concerned with the lawful recovery of historically exploited African resources than protection of the right to property of the beneficiaries of the colonial era.[20] In the African context, when it comes to the quest for economic self-determination, national law usually supersedes the provisions of the Charter. This differs from conventional expectations that regional instruments embody obligations that member states have to their citizens. The Charter has an ambitious expectation that former colonial powers are to compensate the historically dispossessed natives for spoliation.[21] While imposing an obligation on the spoliators, the Charter could be said to be weak in that it does not prescribe any accountability mechanism in this regard.[22] The Zimbabwean experience to be discussed below is a good illustration of these shortcomings.

2.1 *Zimbabwe Land Reform: Implementation and Obstacles*

The following land related clauses that were inserted in Zimbabwe's Lancaster House Constitution were the outcome of the Lancaster house decolonisation deliberations in 1980:

---

[17] For example The American Convention on Human Rights (generally known as the San Jose Pact) states that; (1) everyone has the right to the use and enjoyment of his property. The law may subordinate such use and enjoyment to the interest of society (2) No one shall be deprived of his property except upon payment of just compensation, for reasons of public utility or social interest, and in the cases and according to the forms established by law. (3) Usury and any other form of exploitation of man by man shall be prohibited by law.

[18] African [Banjul] Charter on Human and Peoples' Rights, adopted June 27, 1981, OAU Doc. CAB/LEG/67/3 rev. 5, 21 I.L.M. 58 (1982), entered into force Oct. 21, 1986 (Hereinafter The Charter).

[19] Ibid. Article 15.

[20] For a similar viewpoint *see* Shirley (2004), p. 162.

[21] Article 14 of The Charter, *op cit.* n 18. *See also* Shirley (2004).

[22] For a comprehensive critique of the Charter *see* Ebow Bondzie (1988).

- A 10-year moratorium was put on the constitutional guarantees to the right to property. Any changes before 1990 had to be made with the approval of a unanimous vote of all the Parliamentarians.
- Property was constitutionally enshrined as a fundamental right. The state could only acquire underutilised land. Any property was to be expropriated only on a willing buyer–willing seller basis at its market value.
- Before farmers could sell land on the open market, the Zimbabwean government was given the right of first refusal.
- In the event of an expropriation, "adequate" and "prompt payment" was to be effected in currencies preferred by the seller.
- The state was required to give the landowners (farmers) proper notification before acquiring a farmer's land.
- The British government made an undertaking to assist in the land reform process on condition that the Zimbabwean government matched this funding.[23]

Two crucial issues from the clauses highlighted above are worth noting. First, contrary to global uncertainty on the existence of a right to property, at Lancaster House the property clause was linked with the notion of human rights.[24] The constitutional entrenchments sought to show that this was a fundamental right, thus implying that the post-colonial state had a legal obligation to abide by it. Notwithstanding the history of appropriation and obvious economic disparities that had a racial basis, according to the law, all Zimbabweans were now equal and their rights to private property had to be secured from unlawful governmental encroachment.[25]

Second, in common with other agreements that the United Kingdom entered into with its colonies, the Lancaster House land terms were binding on Zimbabwe, the postcolonial state, and not binding on Britain, the colonial master.[26] Britain merely verbally pledged to offer financial contributions. Interestingly, this pledge was couched in the language of "aid" and not reparations for colonial injustices.[27] With regard to Zimbabwe, Britain did not exhibit the same inclination to pay off those white farmers who wanted to dispose of their land, as it did in Kenya.[28] Perhaps, this difference could be explained by the unique decolonisation history of Zimbabwe. By 1979, at the time of the Lancaster House talks, Britain had successfully claimed the moral high ground and was working with the black majority

[23] De Villiers (2003).

[24] This is a common feature of most independence agreements that Britain entered into with former colonies. *See* Ng'ong'ola (1992).

[25] Sachikonye (2004), p. 7.

[26] Musamirapamwe (1982). Musamirapamwe has asked whether in light of the unequal relationship between the colonizer and the colonized people, these agreements, including, the Lancaster House agreement, could be set aside on the basis that there were unequal treaties in terms of Article 53 of the Vienna Convention of the Law of Treaties.

[27] Moyo (1995).

[28] Ibid. *see also* De Villiers (2003).

against the government of Ian Smith.[29] This may serve as an explanation as to why Britain assumed the role of arbitrator, rather than party to, the proceedings of the Lancaster House talks.

2.2 Execution of the Lancaster House Land Clauses: 1980–1990

As indicated above, the Lancaster House outcome was tilted towards an aspiration of economic growth that entailed giving assurances to white Zimbabweans who, at independence, were responsible for 90 % of domestic market food needs, that they would not lose all their privileges in the advent of black majority rule.[30] This, however, is not to say that the postcolonial leadership was oblivious to the sensitive nature of the land question. From the onset, the government clearly enunciated that one of the major aims of its land reform programme was to assign the land possessed by whites to blacks so as to abate civil conflict.[31]

For the first 10 years, the government religiously adhered to the Lancaster House clauses relating to land reform. Land was mainly acquired in three different ways. The first method was through the "Normal Intensive Resettlement" programme, where the government purchased the land that the landowners offered for sale. The land thus acquired was redistributed to those identified by district officials as being suitable beneficiaries. Second, the state also purchased land acquired through the "Accelerated Land Resettlement Programme", at market rates. In this situation, land-hungry peasants who "illegally squatted" on underutilised and abandoned land, identified the land to be acquired. Finally, black Zimbabweans who could afford to do so, purchased farms from willing sellers at market rates.[32]

It is worth noting that in cases of land purchased by the state, the state was the legal beneficiary of the land reform process, since all title to purchased land was vested in it. To the new farmers, the concern over tenure did not just create insecurity, but also affected their credit worthiness for farming purposes.[33]

During this period, the National Land Policy consisted of four schemes of land allocation. The first one, Model A, involved the allocation of 5–6 ha plots, and a share to communal grazing areas, to black individual households. Approximately 80 % of resettlement between 1980 and 1990 formed part of this program. Model B involved the establishment of co-operatives in commercial farms for new

[29] *See* Metthres (1990).

[30] Riddell (1980), p. 12. Note that by the time of the Lancaster House Conference white commercial farmers had turned to domestic markets as a result of the international isolation resulting from sanctions imposed on the UDI regime. Ranger (1978), p. 119.

[31] *See* Bratton (1990).

[32] Moyo (2004).

[33] De Villiers (2003).

farmers. Model C was a scheme whereby commercial estates with individual smallholdings were established. Finally, pastoral grazing areas were also created under Model D.[34]

The land reform program embarked upon during this era was internationally acclaimed for being one of the more advanced land schemes amongst African postcolonial states. The production of small black farmers was impressive. Significantly, at least 300 black farmers, of whom approximately 10 were Cabinet Ministers, joined the previously all white Commercial Farmers Union (CFU). With the emergence of a black elite in commercial farming, the CFU's influence and ability to lobby the government was strengthened, thus dispelling any insecurities that the commercial farmers might have had in the transition from a minority regime to majority rule.[35]

Despite these positive outcomes, the land that was actually distributed was merely a third of the government's target of "nine million hectares or the resettlement of 162 000 households."[36] The failure to meet these targets could be mainly attributed to the Zimbabwean government's lack of resources and capacity.[37] Even though there was much land to be acquired, the available land was not necessarily of good quality, and it was not evenly distributed throughout the whole country. The requirement for adequate and prompt payment also precluded the government from meeting its target, more so given the Lancaster House bilateral agreement that the government had to match whatever was provided by Britain on a pound by pound basis. The grant of £33 million provided by the United Kingdom was not enough for the land reform process that was envisaged. While the USAID, World Bank, The Overseas Development Institute, various think tanks, NGOs, and the EU had shown an interest in funding the land reform program, limited contributions were made.[38] The failure to meet targets could also be explained by the fact that the government's focus during that time was not confined to the mere distribution of land; there were also efforts to improve other socio-economic needs of the population. Thus education, health and housing became of primary importance during the first decade.[39]

One of the criticisms made of the land reform process during this time was that the resettlement of people was not combined with programs for financial, technical, educational, and infrastructural support.[40] In the rural areas where the return of refugees had led to an increase in population, alleviation of overpopulation was minimal through the land reform process. A major critique of the land reform

[34] Ibid.

[35] Ibid.

[36] Moyo (2004) and Sachikonye (2004).

[37] De Villiers (2003).

[38] Ibid.

[39] Ibid.

[40] Ibid.

exercise in the first decade was therefore that its high cost was not justified by the outcome.[41]

2.3 Early Manifestations of Ideological Crisis: 1990–1999

While the land reform program embarked on in the first 10 years of Zimbabwe's independence can clearly be described as "state centred but market based", the program adopted between 1990 and 1999 marked an ideological crisis. This period saw an attempt to combine free market dictates with social justice notions.

Soon after the expiration of the constitutional moratorium on the right to property, Section 16 of the Constitution was amended in tandem with the enactment of the Land Acquisition Act of 1992 (the Act).[42] This new legal order repealed three key Lancaster house provisions on land, namely, that property could only be expropriated on a "willing seller, willing buyer" basis; that in the event of an acquisition of land, payment had to be promptly made; and the stipulation that payment was to be effected on any currency preferred by the seller.[43] According to the new law, the market could no longer determine compensation, and Parliament was now mandated to enact laws that would stipulate principles for calculating compensation for expropriated land and the duration of payment.[44] The Lancaster House provision of "prompt payment" in the event of acquisition was replaced by Section 19(5) of The Act, which stipulated the terms for payment within a 'reasonable' time after acquisition.[45]

A critical point worth noting is that landowners no longer led the land purchasing process; the responsible minister was now empowered to designate certain pieces of land for acquisition. The legal position was that the service of notice of acquisition on the titleholder of the land designated precluded such landowner from selling, leasing or otherwise disposing of the property.[46] Pursuant to the Act, 83 white owned farms were designated for acquisition between 1992 and 1993.[47] In *Davies*

[41] Ibid.

[42] *See* Constitution of Zimbabwe Amendment (No. 11) Act, 1990, Act No. 30/1990 and Constitution of Zimbabwe Amendment (No. 12) Act, 1993, Act 4/1993.

[43] The implementation of the land reform process was now through "The Land Acquisition Act of 1992," which laid down the procedures for the compulsory acquisition of rural land.

[44] Section 1 of the Act provided for the creation of a Compensation Committee which had the mandate to determine the value of the property acquired taking into consideration its size, soil type, improvements affected on it infrastructure and other relevant factors. Section 23 of the Act further provided that disputes on the Compensation Committee's findings had to be handled by the administrative court. Land Acquisition Act of 1992.

[45] The first half was to be paid within a reasonable time following the compensation, thereafter, half of the balance had to be paid in the 2 years of the acquisition, and the rest within 5 years after acquisition.

[46] Land Acquisition Act 1992, § 14.

[47] Dancaescu (2003).

and others v. The Minister of Land, Agriculture and Water Development,[48] five commercial farmers whose farms had been slated for acquisition, challenged the constitutionality of the 1992 Act. They contended that the Ministerial designation of land was tantamount to expropriation, as it restricted the owners' rights to dispose of the land. They also intimated that the designation of their land would reduce its market value. The court, however, rejected their arguments on the basis that designation could not be held to be unconstitutional, as it did not result in the transfer of the right to dispose of the property from the landowner to the state.[49]

During this decade, both the land acquisition and transfer process were increasingly plagued by controversy and criticism. It was held that the process was open to political abuse, as, for example, where a farm owned by a black opposition leader, Reverend Ndabaningi Sithole, was also designated for compulsory acquisition.[50] A second criticism of the program was that instead of complying with the 1992 National Land Policy's objective of establishing "a just, democratic, and efficient land economy", nepotism was rife in land distribution.[51]

In spite of the relaxation in the legal order, less than 25,000 peasant households benefited from the land reform process between 1990 and 1997, making the total number of resettled households from 1980 to 1997 approximately 71,000, which was far below the government's target of 162,000 households.[52] The government's failure to meet its targets has been largely attributed to successful court challenges of the procedural aspects of acquisition by white commercial farmers.[53]

Notwithstanding the low numbers of resettled households, the land reform program embarked upon during this period was orderly and peaceful. It is also remarkable to note that by 1997 at least 500 black commercial farmers had emerged.[54] In 1997 the government launched its second phase of the land Reform and Resettlement Program, the objective of which was to resettle 150,000 households within a period of 5 years. Instead of achieving the stated objectives, the period 1997–2000 marked a transition from a nonbelligerent and organized land reform process, to a belligerent and haphazard one, termed by the government and

---

[48] *Davies v. Min. of Land Agriculture and Water Development*, 1996 SACLR LEXIS 29.

[49] For an elaborate discussion of this case *see* Ford (2001).

[50] See, Stiles (1994). The government's rational for designating Reverend Ndabaningi's Sithole's farm for acquisition was that the ZANU (Ndonga) party leader's turning his farm into a peri-urban settlement was an illegal act which could well pose a public health risk. *See also* Hlatshwayo (1994).

[51] *See* Hansungule (2000). For example, in 1994, 20 farms acquired purportedly for land hungry peasants were allocated to government officials. It is also alleged that in 1998 forty-seven government officials were beneficiaries of the 24 farms.

[52] Sachikonye (2004).

[53] Moyo (2004). For a discussion on how commercial farmers challenged the land acquisition process *see* McCandless (2001).

[54] Sachikonye (2004).

its supporters as 'The third Chimurenga/Umvukela' (the third Liberation struggle).[55]

Several reasons can best explain this policy volte-face. The first of these is related to the conditions in the country at that time. The 1990s saw a huge population increase that made the demand for land acute. This was compounded by job losses and a decline in the standard of living, that many commentators have linked to the government's capitulation to the World Bank's demands for the introduction of the liberal Economic Structural Adjustment Program (ESAP).[56] The drought of 1992 and 1993 rendered it impossible for the rural areas to continue subsidizing the cities. Kanyeze sees a nexus between the worsening living conditions in the rural areas and the determination of the government to adopt a much more robust land reform process.[57]

The second issue that catapulted the policy change in land reform was the strain in the relations between the government of Zimbabwe and the international community. Unlike Kenya, where 95 % of the funding for land reform came from foreign donors, many within the international community saw the Zimbabwean land issue as a bilateral dispute between Zimbabwe and the United Kingdom.[58] Similarly, the new Labour Party's blunt assertions that their new government had no obligation to fund the Zimbabwean land reform exercise, were not well received by the Robert Mugabe regime. In a letter dated November 5, 1997, and addressed to the Zimbabwean Minister of Agriculture and Land, Clare Short, the then British minister for overseas development, stated thus:

> I should make it clear that we do not accept that Britain has a special responsibility to meet the costs of land purchase in Zimbabwe. We are a new government from diverse backgrounds without links to former colonial interests. My own origins are Irish and as you know we were colonized not colonizers.[59]

The British government, which saw its contributions to the Zimbabwean land reform program as aid, typically saw the funding as contingent on good governance and poverty eradication.[60] Irked by the Labour government's attitude and pressured by the war veterans, in 1997, the Zimbabwean government slated 1,471 farms for acquisition, but with full compensation.[61] However, approximately 40 % of these farms were de-listed, after commercial farmers successfully challenged the

[55] Ibid. Also see Moyo (2004) and De Villiers (2003).

[56] *See* for example Kanyenze (2004).

[57] Ironically, ESAP was introduced in tandem with the 1992 land reform legislation which made the impression that the government was departing from the notion of a market based economy. For an analysis Stiles (1994).

[58] Moyo (2004) and De Villiers (2003) For the United Kingdom's official position (then) on the Zimbabwean land reform *see* United Kingdom Select Committee on Foreign Affairs Minutes of Evidence (2015).

[59] For a full copy of Clare Short's letter see Ankomah (2015). *See also* Moyo (2004).

[60] Moyo (2004).

[61] Ibid.

acquisition process in the courts.[62] Since European Union (EU) citizens largely owned the land occupied and expropriated, EU embassies became involved in the delisting process. The engagement of the EU embassies in the farm delisting process, might have confirmed the Mugabe regime's concern that the latter's intervention in Zimbabwe's affairs was motivated by the need to preserve the interests of their citizens.[63]

In 1998 at a conference in Harare attended by 48 countries and international organisations, the Zimbabwean government attempted to reach an agreement with the donor community. At the conference the Zimbabwean administration introduced Phase Two of its land reform process to the donors. An interest in funding the program was expressed by the donors, albeit, with many in the international community expressing the view that they were only in favour of a less costly market-dictated land reform. The donors thus endorsed the land reform policy presented, on condition that the notions of good governance, poverty reduction, free market, rule of law and sustainable economic policy were taken into consideration in the implementation process.[64]

In the wake of the donor conference of 1998, the phenomenon of invading white owned farms increased.[65] Court orders mandating the police to evict the squatters were largely ignored, with the tacit support of the executive.[66] As a result of the invasions and the state's response, the international community suspended payouts of the money pledged at the donor conference.[67] The United Kingdom's official explanation for this default is that the illegal farm invasions were not compatible with the agreements entered into between the government of Zimbabwe and the donors in 1998.[68]

As dissatisfaction grew in both government and landowner's circles, the former appointed a constitutional commission to draft a Constitution with a clause empowering the state to compulsorily acquire land, with compensation only for improvements effected on the land, and not for the full value of the property.[69] The opposition, and the white commercial farmers, who interpreted the constitutional reform process as a cynical ploy by an increasingly unpopular regime to maintain its hold on power, vehemently opposed the draft Constitution produced. At a referendum held in February 2000, the electorate rejected the draft.[70]

[62] Ibid. In 1999, the court further struck off the 847 remaining farms from the expropriation list on the basis that the authorities had not properly complied with the necessary legal and administrative procedures.

[63] Ibid.

[64] Ibid.

[65] Ibid.

[66] Ibid.

[67] *See* Bruce (2000).

[68] *See* United Kingdom Select Committee on Foreign Affairs Minutes of Evidence (2015).

[69] The Redress Trust (2005).

[70] Ibid.

Therefore, the third possible explanation for the radicalisation of land reform could be simply one of political survival.[71] It was the ruling party's reaction to the emergence of a new, well-funded opposition party, the Movement for Democratic Change (MDC), a party that was openly allied to white commercial farmers.[72] President Robert Mugabe explained away the rejection of the draft Constitution as an international community regime change tactic. He thus used land reform to garner support from the landless Zimbabweans, gaining sympathy from developing countries in the process.

2.4 Radical Land Reform Program and Property Rights in the Current Zimbabwean Constitutional Scheme

In 2000 both the Lancaster House Constitution and the Land Acquisition Act were amended to legalize the proposed radical land reform program.[73] These amendments legitimated the government's decision to expropriate land from commercial farmers with compensation only for improvements effected on the land, and not full market value compensation. Invoking the history of dispossession of native land by the settlers during the colonial era, the constitutional amendment obliged Britain, the former colonial master, to establish an adequate fund to compensate the owners for agricultural land acquired for resettlement purposes.[74]

In variance with the 1992 Land Acquisition Act, the 2000 amendments stipulated that only one quarter of the compensation was to be paid at the time of acquisition. Another quarter would be payable within 2 years and the balance was to be paid in a 5 year period.[75] The Compensation Committee's appellate mandate was also restricted to cases involving non-compliance with the provisions of the Land Acquisition Act, and it could not adjudicate on complaints that the compensation was not fair.[76]

This radical program for land acquisition, which was referred to as "fast track", was officially launched in July 2000.[77] It consisted of two methods, namely, the A1 model aimed at giving land to the landless poor, and the A2 model, which entailed

[71] For this viewpoint *see* Sachikonye (2004).

[72] Ibid.

[73] Constitution of Zimbabwe Amendment (No. 16) Act, 2000, (Act 5 of 2000), commenced on 20th April 2000. *See also* Coldham (2001).

[74] S. 16 A(1) of the Constitution added by Constitution of Zimbabwe Amendment (No. 16) Act, Ibid.

[75] *See* De Villiers (2003).

[76] Constitution of Zimbabwe Amendment (No. 16) Act, 2000, (Act 5 of 2000), commenced on 20th April 2000 and Land Acquisition Amendment Act, 2000 (No. 15) Official Gazette, 2000, No. 15, pp. 309–322. *See also* Coldham (2001).

[77] Amnesty International (2004).

the creation of black large scale commercial farms.[78] In 2000, the legislature also enacted the Rural Land Occupiers (Protection from Eviction) Act.[79] This law protected farm occupiers from eviction from land designated for settlement.

In December 2000, at the instigation of the Commercial Farmers Union, the Zimbabwean Supreme Court had occasion to deliberate on the legality of the fast track resettlement program. It held that the fast track land reform program was haphazard and unlawful. It saw the exercise as a serious disregard for the rule of law as the farm workers and the farmers had been deprived of the protection of the law.[80] The reaction of government officials, war veterans, traditional chiefs and others, including President Mugabe, to this decision, was to verbally attack the judiciary.[81]

In addition to verbal attacks, war veterans invaded the Supreme Court on 24 May 2000, asking for the resignation of the judges, especially Chief Justice Antony Gubbay. No prosecution of the perpetrators ensued.[82] The general feeling of those who hurled attacks on mostly white judges, was that they were allied to big business and the commercial farmers, sectors that were under the control of Zimbabwean whites and Western countries perceived to be opposed to the economic empowerment and advancement of blacks.[83] For example, in rationalizing his non-compliance with court orders the Commissioner of Police stated thus:

> These are not disputed but suffice to point out that the rule of law which is divorced from justice and just laws becomes a hollow concept. Enforcement of unjust and iniquitous ethically land ownership structure, through the application of brutal state power, such as demanded by the respondent, is not promotive of the rule of law.[84]

Even the judiciary did not escape politicization. For example, Judge Godfrey Chidyausiku stated publicly that Chief Justice Antony Gubbay favored commercial farmers, and had given white farmers assurances that if they approached the court on matters relating to land reform, they would be successful.[85]

Following intimidation and pressure from the government, the Chief Justice and other judges took early retirement.[86] Exclusively black appointments were thereafter made, with Judge Godfrey Chidyausiku assuming the position of Chief Justice of the Supreme Court.[87] Sitting with three other new appointees, the new bench

---

[78] *See* Moyo (2004).

[79] Rural Land Occupiers (Protection from Eviction) Act (Chapter 20:26), as amended in § 4(a)(iii) by § 30 of the General Laws Amendment Act 2002, February 4, 2002.

[80] *Commercial Farmers Union v. Minister of Lands, Agriculture and Resettlement,* Const. Application no 262/2000.

[81] International Bar Association (2001).

[82] Ibid.

[83] Goredema (2004), p. 115.

[84] International Bar Association (2001).

[85] Ibid.

[86] Ibid.

[87] Goredema (2004), p. 104.

overturned Judge Gubbay's Supreme Court's ruling on the legality of the land reform process.[88] To them the land reform process was "not strictly speaking a legal issue", but a matter of "social justice."[89] The court also held that by legalizing illegal occupations, the Rural Land Occupiers (Protection from Eviction) Act had re-established the rule of law.[90]

There was a public concern that the judiciary was now compromised. These concerns were exacerbated by revelations that the appointees, including the Judge President and the Chief Justice, had acquired farms under the new fast track land reform process.[91] In September 2005, after increasing domestic and international calls for the restoration of the rule of law, the Zimbabwean government passed the Constitutional Amendment (No. 17) Act.[92] This amendment nationalized all farmland and also ousted the jurisdiction of the Zimbabwean Courts to decide on the merits, or any other issue relating to land acquisition. It also permitted the retrospective application of the law as it concerned the acquisition and vesting of full title of the acquired land to the state.[93]

One of the effects of this amendment was a protracted and vicious legal battle between the government of Zimbabwe and Mike Campbell (Pvt) Ltd.[94] While the Southern African Development Community (SADC) tribunal decisions provide a unique case study for evaluating the nexus between land reform, human rights and state sovereignty, this essay's remit is restricted to the domestic Constitutional provisions and related jurisprudence.

Noteworthy is the Zimbabwean Supreme Court (ZSC)'s decision in *Mike Campbell (Pvt) Ltd v Minister of National Security Responsible for Land, Land Reform and Resettlement & Others.*[95] The ZSC held that the ousting of the jurisdiction of the legislature was lawful. According to the ZSC

> The question what protection an individual should be afforded under the Constitution in the use and enjoyment of private property is a question of a political and legislative character. In other words, what property should be acquired and in what manner is not a judicial

[88] *Minister of Lands, Resettlement v. Commercial Farmers Union* S -111-01 (2001).

[89] Ibid.

[90] *Minister of Lands, Resettlement.* See also *Igudu Farm (Pvt) Ltd v. Commissioner of Police & Ors.*, HH-143-2001; *Trustees of Roper Trust v. District Administrator, Hurungwe*, (1) HH-192-2001; *Trustees of Roper Trust v. District Administrator, Hurungwe*, (2) HH-200-2001; *Trustees of Roper Trust v. District Administrator, Hurungwe*, (1) HH-192-2001.

[91] Goredema (2004).

[92] Constitution of Zimbabwe Amendment (No. 17) Act, 2005 (Act No. 5 of 2005).

[93] S16B of the Lancaster House Constitution.

[94] *Mike Campbell (Pvt) LTD and Others v The Republic of Zimbabwe* SADC (T) 11/2008, SADC (T) 02/2007; SADC (T) 02/08, SADC (T) 03/2008, and SADC (T) 06/2008 as read with *Gideon Stephanus Theron and Others v the Republic of Zimbabwe* SADC (T) 02/2008. See the discussion in Naldi (2009), pp. 305–320; and Moyo (2009).

[95] *Mike Campbell (Pvt) Ltd. and Another v Minister of National Security Responsible for Land, Land Reform and Resettlement* (124/06), available at http://www.zimlii.org/zw/judgment/supreme-court/2008/1 (accessed 12 June 2015).

> question. .... It is clear from the wording of s 16B (3) of the Constitution that the intention of the Legislature is that the acquisition of agricultural land in terms of s 16B (2) (a) must not be put in the category of justiciable controversies.[96]

This legal position was maintained in the new Constitution of 2013 which oust the court's jurisdiction on issues related to compensation for compulsory acquired agricultural land.[97] In contrast to the position taken by the SADC tribunal in 2008, the 2013 Constitution further states that an appropriation may not be contested on the basis that it is discriminatory.[98] Moreover, the Constitution refers to the country's history and imposes a duty on the former colonial power to establish an adequate fund for paying compensation.[99]

3 Analysis

> Since the native is subhuman the declaration of human rights does not apply to him; inversely, since he has no rights, he is abandoned without protection to inhuman forces brought in with the colonialists praxis, engendered every moment by the colonialist apparatus and sustained by relations of production that define two sorts of individuals – one for who privilege and humanity are one, who becomes a human being through exercising his rights; and the other for whom a denial of rights sanctions misery, chronic hunger, or in general subhumanity.[100]

In short, land reform in Zimbabwe has been implemented in accordance with the country's Constitutions and enabling legislation.[101] Over the years this legal framework has been repeatedly amended: firstly, to facilitate a willing-seller, willing-buyer market driven program; secondly, to introduce a "fair compensation" social justice driven land redistribution program; and thirdly, to give effect to a revolutionary social justice driven fast-track land reform process.[102]

As explained in '*Mimicry, Transitional Justice and the Land Question in Racially divided former Settler Colonies*'[103] Zimbabwe's experience with land

[96] Ibid.

[97] 'except for compensation for improvements effected on the land before its acquisition' See S72 (3) Constitution of Zimbabwe Amendment (No 20) 2013 (Hereinafter 2013 Constitution).

[98] S72 (3) (C) 2013 Constitution.

[99] S72(7) and (8) 2013 Constitution.

[100] Sarte (2013), pp. 20–21.

[101] S16 of the Constitution of Zimbabwe (S.1 1979/1600 of the United Kingdom) as amended to (No. 19) Act, 2009 (Hereinafter Lancaster House Constitution). As read with Sections 71 and 72 of the Constitution of Zimbabwe Amendment Act (No 20) Act, 2013.

[102] *See* De Villiers (2003) For all the relevant amendments see: See also Crozier (2014).

[103] Moyo (2015).

reform reveals a tension between the North and South over compensation for land acquired from white commercial farmers. As I aptly put it:

> Western governments recognize three limitations on a state's entitlement to expropriate property within its borders: expropriation must be done for a public purpose, the process should not be discriminatory and it should be combined with full compensation, which according to Peter Malanczuk is 'often expressed as prompt, adequate and effective compensation.' However, postcolonial states do not agree on these limitations.[104]

Zimbabwe's insertion of a clause which ousted the jurisdiction of the courts in issues of compensation and the insertion of an implicit clause which calls upon the former colonial master to establish an appropriate fund can be read as the South's position on a postcolonial state's right to expropriate property within its borders. These provisions convey the message that issues of compensation for agricultural land can be impeded by a justiciable property right and that land reform in former settler colonies is a struggle for reparations for the colonial past.[105] However, the idea of holding former colonial powers accountable for colonial wrongs by the use of a national Constitution is itself problematic as it raises issues of enforceability.

Notwithstanding the reparations issue, a land reform program can be seen as a program for the progressive realization of the right to an adequate standard of living. The primary instrument that protects the right to an adequate standard of living is article 11(1) of the ICESCR. In its 29th session, the Committee on Economic, Social and Cultural rights (The Committee) intimated that this right not only covers the expressly stipulated rights to food, clothing and housing, but other categories of guarantees, including the right to water.[106]

In terms of Article 2 of the ICESCR, the principal obligation of states is to *progressively act* towards realizing the right to an adequate standard of living.[107] Violations of the right will occur when the state fails to ensure the satisfaction of, at the very least, the minimum essential levels. The Committee draws a distinction between the unwillingness and inability of a state to take action. A state that attributes its failure to fulfill its obligations to reasons beyond its control, has to demonstrate that it has done everything in its power, including appealing to the international community for support.

International assistance in the progressive realization of the right to an adequate standard of living, as prescribed in the ICESR, could by implication be interpreted

---

[104] Ibid., p. 6.

[105] For a similar analysis see Moyo and Chambati (2013).

[106] CESCR General Comment 15, The right to water (29th session, 2003), U.N. Doc. E/C.12/2002/11 (2002), reprinted in Compilation of General Comments and General Recommendations Adopted by Human Rights Treaty Bodies, U.N. Doc. HRI/GEN/1/Rev.6 at 105 (2003).

[107] See Article 2(1) ICESCR as interpreted in CESCR General Comment 3, The nature of States parties' obligations (Fifth session, 1990), U.N. Doc. E/1991/23, annex III at 86 (1991), reprinted in Compilation of General Comments and General Recommendations Adopted by Human Rights Treaty Bodies, U.N. Doc. HRI/GEN/1/Rev.6 at 14 (2003).

as obliging rich countries to finance relevant programs, including land reform, in resource–poor countries.[108]

The content of the right implies ensuring the availability and *accessibility* of the means that ensure livelihood. In respect to the right to food the Committee has stated that:

> Availability refers to the possibilities either for feeding oneself directly from productive land or other natural resources, or for well functioning distribution, processing and market systems that can move food from the site of production to where it is needed in accordance with demand.[109]

This implies that access to land is a basic component of the right to adequate food. Based on this understanding, the Special Rapporteur on the right to food has affirmed that, '[A]ccess to land and agrarian reform must form a key part of the right to food.'[110]

According to the Committee, the right to an adequate standard of living imposes three levels of obligations on state parties. Firstly there is an obligation to *respect the right,* which requires that the state must desist from adopting policies that would adversely affect an individual's right to an adequate standard of living. Secondly, there is an obligation to *protect the right,* which requires states to put in place measures that will ensure that individuals and enterprises do not deprive anyone the right to an adequate standard of living. Thirdly, there is an obligation to *fulfill the right,* which postulates that states must pro-actively engage in activities intended to strengthen people's access to, and the utilization of, both resources and means to ensure and facilitate their livelihoods.[111]

Due to the nexus between the right to food and access to land, the Special Rapporteur on the right to food has implied that the three levels of obligation also apply to access to land. States therefore have an obligation to "*respect, protect* and *fulfill* an individual's access to land".[112]

ICESCR General Comment No. 12 as read with the Food and Agriculture Organization (FAO)'s 'Voluntary Guidelines to Support the Progressive Realization of the Right to Adequate Food in the Context of National Food Security'[113] recommends that governments adopt a national strategy for the progressive reali-

[108] Ibid. General Comment 3, paras 10–14.

[109] CESCR General Comment 12, Right to adequate food (20th session, 1999), U.N. Doc. E/C.12/1999/5 (1999), reprinted in Compilation of General Comments and General Recommendations Adopted by Human Rights Treaty Bodies, U.N. Doc. HRI/GEN/1/Rev.6 at 62 (2003) (emphasis added).

[110] Ziegler (2002), paras 24 and 30.

[111] Ibid. Para 15. It is only when individuals are for reasons beyond their control unable to enjoy their livelihood rights that the state has an obligation to *(fulfill)* provide that right directly.

[112] *See* Suarez (2006).

[113] "Voluntary Guidelines to Support the Progressive Realization of the Right to Adequate Food in the Context of National Food Security," Adopted by the 127th Session of the FAO Council November 2004, *available at* http://www.fao.org/docrep/009/y7937e/y7937e00.htm (accessed 07 June 2015).

zation of the right to adequate food.[114] Land reform policies have been identified as being a crucial part of these domestic food security programs.[115]

Although the right to an adequate standard of living was not constitutionally enshrined in Zimbabwe in the Lancaster House Constitution, the government was still bound by its international and regional obligations to respect, protect and fulfill this right. Internationally, Zimbabwe is a state party to the ICESR and the ICRC,[116] and at a regional level, to the African Charter on Human and Peoples' Rights (hereinafter The Charter) and the African Charter on the Rights and Welfare of the Child.[117] The international covenants expressly bind the government to *respect, protect* and *fulfill* the right to an adequate standard of living. The government is also expressly called upon to take appropriate measures to the maximum extent of its resources to guarantee the progressive realization of this right. In a country like Zimbabwe, where land has played an integral part in inter-racial economic relations, it could hardly be expected that the right to an adequate standard of living be implemented without land reform.[118]

Even though the right to an adequate standard of living is not incorporated in the Charter, the African Commission on Human and Peoples' Rights (the Commission) has found this right to be implicit in the instrument, in provisions on the right to life, right to health and the right to economic, social and cultural development.[119] With respect to the right to food, the Commission has stated that a state is obliged to:

> Protect and improve existing food sources and to ensure access to adequate food for all its citizens.[120]

A land reform program could well be a means of ensuring access to adequate food. Notwithstanding the fact that Zimbabwe had been involved in a land reform process since its founding in 1980, global attention to this process only began in 2000. This followed the abandonment of market driven acquisition for a radical land reform exercise, which the ruling party referred to by euphemism 'third chimurenga/umvukela wesithathu', or third revolution. Early academic writings and civic society reports on this fast track land reform process focused on its

---

[114] Suarez (2006).

[115] Ziegler (2002), para 22.

[116] Zimbabwe acceded to the ICESR on May 13, 1991 and ratified CRC on September 11, 1990. *See* Office of High Commissioner for Human Rights, http://www.unhchr.ch/ (Accessed 14 June 2015).

[117] Zimbabwe ratified The Charter on May 30, 1986 and the African Charter on the Rights and Welfare of the Child (OAU Doc. CAB/LEG/24.9/49 (1990), entered into force Nov. 29, 1999) (hereinafter Children's Charter) on January 19, 1995.

[118] For the pivotal role of the land question in Zimbabwe *see* McCandless (2001).

[119] In *Social and Economic Rights Action Centre (SERAC) v. Nigeria*, 2001 AHRLR 60 (ACHPR 2001), the Commission found that a right to food (which is a component of the right to an adequate standard of living) to be implicit in such rights as the right to life (Article 4); the right to health (Article 6); and the right to economic, social and cultural development (Article 22); which are incorporated in the Charter.

[120] *Social and Economic Rights Action Centre (SERAC) v. Nigeria,* para 64.

implementation. In particular, the emphasis was on how that program not only impacted badly on white commercial farming interests, but also resulted in discrimination and human rights violations against workers, women and the intended beneficiaries.[121]

Why did interested parties, including the Zimbabwean landless and farm workers, not invoke a rights based approach in their quest for land? Was it, as has been articulated in mainstream literature, because the government of Zimbabwe embarked on land reform only for reasons of political expediency and that the landless lacked access to the courts? Or was it rather that those human rights norms do not have a relevant framework for repairing historic injustices?[122]

The issue of the application of human rights norms has been addressed by Hellum and Derman, who have argued that international human rights instruments provide a framework for balancing property rights and social justice.[123] Their analysis focuses on the implementation of the post 2000 fast track land reform strategy, highlighting how this program violated the livelihood rights of farm workers, their families and women. However they disregard the fact that Zimbabwean land reform was a post-colonial democratic project that was partly geared towards redressing the colonial legacy of using black indigenous labor for predominately white capitalist production.[124] It is worth noting the assertions of Jonathan Shirley who has looked at the inadequacy of international human rights law in remedying the property rights of white commercial farmers.[125] His work has not however, gone further to ascertain whether it was feasible for the landless people of Zimbabwe to invoke this rights based approach.

4 Conclusion

This chapter has demonstrated that agrarian reform is a crucial component of the right to an adequate standard of living, and that a land reform program implemented in accordance with a Constitution and its enabling legislation cannot *prima facie* be said to be a violation of the right to property. It has also pointed out that the declaration of rights enshrined in the Zimbabwe's first Constitution only incorporated civil and political rights and the controversial right to property. The incorporation of economic, social and cultural rights in the 2013 domestic Constitution is thus progressive. This is in line with both contemporary opinion on the

[121] *See, e.g., Zimbabwe Power and Hunger—Violations of the Right to Food* (London: Amnesty International, International Secretariat, 2004). *Available at* http://www.amnesty.ie/reports/zimbabwe-power-and-hunger-%E2%80%93-violations-right-food (accessed 14 June 2015). *See also* Hellum and Derman (2004) and Human Rights Watch (2002).

[122] For these viewpoints *see* Nading (2002), Shaw (2003) and Hellum and Derman (2004).

[123] Hellum and Derman (2004).

[124] Sachikonye (2004).

[125] Shirley (2004).

interdependence and indivisibility of human rights, and the Zimbabwean government's commitment to *respect, protect* and *fulfill* the livelihood rights of its citizens by ratification of the ICESR.[126]

Nonetheless, notwithstanding the guarantees enshrined in international and regional human rights instruments, as well as in domestic Constitutions, there are implicit domestic and international obstacles to land reform in postcolonial contexts. This conundrum is further complicated by the fact that whilst there is no overarching right to property in international human rights law, in Constitutions of British former colonies the right to property was incorporated as a fundamental right.[127] This is in contrast to the language of the Charter, where this right is inferior to the public interest.[128] Thus, domestically, the hindrance may be a judiciary that is unwilling to interpret a justiciable property right in a manner that would contradict business interests.[129] In Zimbabwe, this concern led to the forced resignation of mostly white judges.[130]

The state's leading role in the Zimbabwean land reform process presented challenges to the use of human rights language in land reform.[131] This is against the backdrop of a paradigmatic state-centric human rights perspective that sees the nation state as the principal violator of human rights. A major criticism of this state-centric perspective has been that it assumes that all states are equal, and that such a perspective does not take issues of moral responsibility into cognizance.[132] In the case of Zimbabwe, it could be said that the traditional human rights approach does not take into cognizance the role of colonization in the creation of a racially skewed and inequitable land structure.

Internationally, even though United Nations human rights committees might progressively interpret the rights enshrined in the core human rights treaties, enforcing the obligations of other states and non-state actors may not be feasible. The Zimbabwean land debacle is at best an illustration of this difficulty, in particular as it relates to the United Kingdom's and possibly other Western states', financial obligations to compensate Zimbabwean commercial farmers for the land appropriated.

This raises doubts as to the effectiveness of both the Constitution of Zimbabwe and the Charter as vehicles for social change. The relevant property rights clauses which were incorporated in both the new and former Constitution of Zimbabwe depart from the traditional expectation that it is the state that is duty-bound *to*

[126] *See also* Vienna Declaration and Programme of Action G.A A/CONF.157/23, July 12, 1993, adopted in Vienna on 14–25 June 14–25, 1993, ¶ 1.5.

[127] Hansungule (2000), p. 335.

[128] African Charter on Human and Peoples' Rights.

[129] This was the concern for example in India. *See* Patil Kolse (2004).

[130] See International Bar Association (2001).

[131] For a distinction between land reform from below and state led land reform see Via Campesina Issue Paper #5 (2015).

[132] Ibid.

respect protect and fulfill the rights of its citizens. Rather, the former colonial master is identified as being primarily responsible for paying full market value for the land acquired for resettlement. Similarly, Article 21 of the Charter can be interpreted to mean that the beneficiaries of the colonial era ought to restore the property unlawfully taken from Africa and also compensate Africans. Since current human rights discourse has not conceptualized the role of colonization in the violations of human rights in Africa,[133] there is no accountability mechanism for holding a former colonial power responsible in the international human rights machinery.

Against this backdrop, a national constitution and human rights norms may not realistically address the issue of land reform in a postcolonial situation such as Zimbabwe. Rather, the solution lies in a combination of constitutionalism, human rights norms and international diplomacy.

References

Amnesty International. (2004). Zimbabwe: Power and hunger—Violations of the right to food. AI Index: AFR 46/026/2004. Available at http://web.amnesty.org/ (accessed 14 June 2015).

Ankomah, B. (2015). Zimbabwe: The Spark...Claire Short's letter of November 1997. SWANS available at http://www.swans.com/library/art9/ankomah5.html (accessed 14 June 2015).

Asmal, K. (2013). Foreword. In B. Chigara (Ed.), Re-conceiving property rights in the new millennium: Towards a new sustainable land relations policy (pp. 3–25). London: Routledge.

Bratton, M. (1990). Ten years after: Land redistribution in Zimbabwe, 1980–90. In R. L. Oysterman (Ed.), *Agrarian reform and grassroots development.* Boulder, CO: Lynne Rienner.

Bruce, J. W. (2000). Land reform in Zimbabwe? *Land Tenure Centre Newsletter* 79. Available at http://www.ies.wisc.edu (accessed 14 June 2015).

Bugge, H. C. (1998). Human rights and resource management—An overview. In E. Berge & N. C. Stenseth (Eds.), *Law and governance of renewable resources.* Oakland, CA: ICS Press.

Coldham, S. (2001). Statute note: Land Acquisition Amendment Act, 2000 (Zimbabwe). *Journal of African Law, 45*(2), 227–229.

Crozier, B. D. (2014). Constitutional history of Zimbabwe. *UZ Student Journal Law Review, 2*(1), 1–8.

Dancaescu, N. (2003). Land reform in Zimbabwe. *FJIL, 15*, 616–644.

De Villiers, B. (2003). *Land reform: Issues and challenges; A comparative overview of experiences in Zimbabwe, Namibia, South Africa and Australia.* Johannesburg, South Africa: Konrad-Adenauer-Stiftung.

Debucquois, C. (2014). Access to land and the right to food. New York: Springer.

Ebow Bondzie-S. (1988). A critique of the African Charter on Human and People's Rights. *Howard Law Journal, 31*, 643–666.

Ford, R. (2001). Law, history, and the colonial discourse: *Davies v. Commissioner* and Zimbabwe as a colonialist case study. *Howard Law Journal, 45*, 213–246.

Goredema, C. (2004). Whither judicial independence in Zimbabwe. In B. Raftopoulos & T. Savage (Eds.), *Institute for Justice & Reconciliation: Cape Town* 106.

[133] A similar viewpoint is also raised in Shivji (1989).

Hansungule, M. (2000). Who owns land in Zimbabwe? In Africa? *International Journal on Minority and Group Rights, 7*(4), 332.
Hellum, A., & Derman, B. (2004). Land reform and human rights in contemporary Zimbabwe: Balancing individual and social justice through an integrated human rights framework. *World Development, 32*(10), 1785–1180.
Hlatshwayo, B. (1994). Churu and Ellsworth farm designations: Fighting illegality with illegality. *Legal Forum, 6*, 11.
Human Rights Watch. (2002). Zimbabwe: Fast track land reform program. http://www.hrw.org/reports/2002/03/08/fast-track-land-reform-zimbabwe (accessed 7 June 2015).
International Bar Association. (2001). Report highlighting the critical situation faced by judges and lawyers in Zimbabwe, as read with International Bar Association (2011)' Zimbabwe: time for a new approach. http://www.ibanet.org/Human_Rights_Institute/HRI_Publications/Country_reports.aspx (accessed 14 June 2015).
Kanyenze, G. (2004). Economic Structural Adjustment Program (ESAP): Precursor to fast track resettlement? In M. Masiiwa (Ed.), *Post-independence land reform in Zimbabwe*. Harare, Zimbabwe: Friedrich Ebert Stiftung.
McCandles, E. (2001). The case of land in Zimbabwe; Cause of conflict, Foundation of Sustained Peace. In M. Abu-Nimer (Ed.), *Reconciliation, justice, and peace in interethnic conflict.* Oxford, England: Rowman and Littlefield.
Metthres, R. O. (1990). From Rhodesia to Zimbabwe: Prerequisites of a settlement. *International Law Journal, 45*, 292–233.
Mitchell, T. (2001). The land crisis in Zimbabwe: Getting beyond the myopic focus upon black & white. *Indiana University International and Comparative Law Review, 11*, 587–603.
Moyo, A. (2009). Defending human rights and the rule of law by the SADC tribunal: Campbell and beyond: Recent developments. *AHRLJ, 9*(2), 590–614.
Moyo, K. (2015). Mimicry, transitional justice and the land question in racially divided former settler colonies. *International Journal of Transitional Justice, 9*(1), 70–89.
Moyo, S. (1987). The land question. In I. Mandaza (Ed.), *Zimbabwe: The political economy in transition, 1980–1986*. Harare, Zimbabwe: Jongwe Press.
Moyo, S. (1995). *The land question in Zimbabwe*. Harare, Zimbabwe: Sapes Books.
Moyo, S. (2004). *The land and agrarian question in Zimbabwe*. Paper presented at the Conference on The Agrarian Constraint on Poverty Reduction: Macroeconomic Lessons for Africa, Addis Ababa, Ethiopia, 17–18 December 2004. http://www.sarpn.org/documents/d0001097/P1211-Moyo_Dec2004.pdf (accessed 14 June 2015).
Moyo, S., & Chambati, W. (2013). *Land and agrarian reform in Zimbabwe. Beyond white-settler capitalism.* London: Codesria Publications.
Musamirapamwe, O. N. (1982). The Evian Agreements on Algeria and the Lancaster Agreements on Zimbabwe: A comparative analysis. *The Georgia Journal of International and Comparative Law, 12*, 153–170.
Nading, J. M. (2002). Note, property under siege: The legality of land reform in Zimbabwe. *Emory International Law Review, 16.*
Naldi, G. J. (2009). Mike Campbell (Pvt) Ltd et al v The Republic of Zimbabwe: Zimbabwe's land reform programme held in breach of the SADC Treaty. *Journal African Law, 53*, 305–320.
Ng'ong'ola, C. (1992). The post-colonial era in relation to land expropriation laws in Botswana, Malawi, Zambia and Zimbabwe. *International and Comparative Law Quarterly, 41*, 118.
Ng'ong'ola, C. (2013). Property guarantees in old and new southern African constitutions. In B. Chigara (Ed.), *Re-conceiving property rights in the new millennium: Towards a new sustainable land relations policy* (pp. 3–25 and 154–183). London: Routledge.
Patil Kolse, B. G. (2004). Class-bound judiciary. *India National Magazine* 14(25). Available at http://www.hinduonnet.com/flin/ (last accessed 14 June 2015).
Ranger, T. (1978). Growing from the roots: Reflections on peasant research in central and southern Africa. *Journal of South African Studies, 5*, 99–133.

Riddell, R. (1980). Zimbabwe land problem: The central issue. In W. H. Morris-Jones (Ed.), *From Rhodesia to Zimbabwe: Behind and beyond Lancaster House*. Totowa, NJ: Frank Cass.
Sachikonye, L. (2004). The promised land: From expropriation to reconciliation and Jambanja. In B. Raftopoulos & S. Tyrone (Eds.), *Zimbabwe: Injustice and reconciliation*. Cape Town, South Africa: Institute for Justice and Reconciliation.
Sarte, J.-P. (2013). Introduction. In A. Memmi (Ed.), *The colonizer and the colonized*. London: Routledge.
Shaw, W. H. (2003). They stole our land: Debating the expropriation of white farms in Zimbabwe. *Journal of Modern African Studies, 41*(1), 75–89.
Shirley, J. (2004). The role of international human rights and the law of diplomatic protection in resolving Zimbabwe's land crisis. *Boston College International & Comparative Law Review, 27*, 161–171.
Shivji, I. G. (1989). *The concept of human rights in Africa*. London: Codesria Book Series.
Ssenyonjo, M. (2013). Land ownership and economic, social and cultural rights in the Southern African Development Community (SADC). In B. Chigara (Ed.), *Re-conceiving property rights in the new millennium: Towards a new sustainable land relations policy* (pp. 3–25). London: Routledge
Stiles, M. (1994). Zimbabwe land reform: What's going on? *Southern African Report* 9, 48. Available at http://www.africafiles.org/article.asp?ID=3997 (accessed 14 June 2015).
Suarez, S. M. (2006). Access to land and productive resources—Towards a systematic interpretation of the FAO voluntary guidelines on the right to food. http://www.escr-net.org/sites/default/files/FIAN_Accesstoland_print_0.pdf (accessed 14 June 2015).
The Redress Trust. (2005, June 17). Torture in Zimbabwe, past and present: Prevention, punishment, and reparation? A survey of law and practice. Available at http://www.redress.org/downloads/publications/Amani2005.pdf (accessed 14 June 2015).
United Kingdom Select Committee on Foreign Affairs Minutes of Evidence. (2015). Zimbabwe: UK approach to land reform. http://www.publications.parliament.uk/pa/cm200203/cmselect/cmfaff/339/3032509.htm (accessed 14 June 2015).
Via Campesina Issue Paper #5. (2015). Agrarian reform in the context of food sovereignty, the right to food and cultural diversity. Available at http://nyeleni.org/spip.php? (accessed 14 June 2015).
World Bank. (1975). Land reform: Sector policy paper. http://r1.ufrrj.br/geac/portal/wp-content/uploads/2012/03/BIRD-Land-reform1975.pdf (accessed 13 June 2015).
Ziegler, J. (2002, February 15). *Report of the special rapporteur of the Commission on Human Rights on the Right to Food*. U.N. Doc. A/57/356.

Legislation

Domestic (Zimbabwe)

Constitution of Zimbabwe (S.1 1979/1600 of the United Kingdom) as amended to (No. 19) Act, 2009
Constitution of Zimbabwe Amendment (No. 20) Act 2013
Land Acquisition Act 1992.
Land Acquisition Amendment Act, 2000 (No. 15) Official Gazette, 2000, No. 15, pp. 309–322.
Rural Land Occupiers (Protection from Eviction) Act (Chapter 20:26), as amended in § 4(a)(iii) by § 30 of the General Laws Amendment Act 2002, February 4, 2002.

International Standards and Guidelines

ICESCR General Comment 15, The right to water (29th session, 2003), U.N. Doc. E/C.12/2002/11 (2002), reprinted in Compilation of General Comments and General Recommendations Adopted by Human Rights Treaty Bodies, U.N. Doc. HRI/GEN/1/Rev.6 at 105 (2003).
ICESCR General Comment 3, The nature of States parties' obligations (Fifth session, 1990), U.N. Doc. E/1991/23, annex III at 86 (1991), reprinted in Compilation of General Comments and General Recommendations Adopted by Human Rights Treaty Bodies, U.N. Doc. HRI/GEN/1/Rev.6 at 14 (2003).
ICESCR General Comment 12, Right to adequate food (20th session, 1999), U.N. Doc. E/C.12/1999/5 (1999), reprinted in Compilation of General Comments and General Recommendations Adopted by Human Rights Treaty Bodies, U.N. Doc. HRI/GEN/1/Rev.6 at 62 (2003)
International Covenant on Economic, Social and Cultural Rights (1966) 993 U.N.T.S 3.
International Covenant on Civil and Political Rights, (1966) 999 U.N.T.S. 171
United Nations Declaration on the Right to Development, G. A. Res. 41/128, Annex 41 U.N
GAOR Supp (No 53) at 186, U. N Doc. A/41/53 (1986)
Universal Declaration of Human Rights, G.A Rees 217A (111), U.N Doc, A/810 (1948)
Vienna Declaration and Programme of Action G.A A/CONF.157/23, July 12, 1993, adopted in Vienna on 14–25 June 14–25, 1993
Voluntary Guidelines to Support the Progressive Realization of the Right to Adequate Food in the Context of National Food Security, Adopted by the 127th Session of the FAO Council November 2004, *available at* http://www.fao.org/docrep/009/y7937e/y7937e00.htm (accessed June 07, 2015).

Regional Standards

African [Banjul] Charter on Human and Peoples' Rights, adopted June 27, 1981, OAU Doc. CAB/LEG/67/3 rev. 5, 21 I.L.M. 58 (1982), entered into force Oct. 21, 1986.
African Charter on the Rights and Welfare of the Child, (OAU Doc. CAB/LEG/24.9/49 (1990), entered into force Nov. 29, 1999)

Case Law

Commercial Farmers Union v. Minister of Lands, Agriculture and Resettlement, Const. Application no 262/2000
Davies v. Min. of Land Agriculture and Water Development, 1996 SACLR LEXIS 29
Gideon Stephanus Theron and Others v the Republic of Zimbabwe SADC (T) 02/2008.
Igudu Farm (Pvt) Ltd v. Commissioner of Police & Ors., HH—143-2001
InRe Southern Rhodesia, 1919 AC 211 CD
Mike Campbell (Pvt) LTD and Others v The Republic of Zimbabwe SADC (T) 11/2008, SADC (T) 02/2007; SADC (T) 02/08, SADC (T) 03/2008, and SADC (T) 06/2008.
Mike Campbell (Pvt) Ltd. and Another v Minister of National Security Responsible for Land, Land Reform and Resettlement (124/06), available at <http://www.zimlii.org/zw/judgment/supreme-court/2008/1> (accessed 12 June 2015).

Minister of Lands, Resettlement v. Commercial Farmers Union S-111-01 (2001).
In *Social and Economic Rights Action Centre (SERAC) v. Nigeria*, 2001 AHRLR 60 (ACHPR 2001
Trustees of Roper Trust v. District Administrator, Hurungwe, (1) HH-192-2001
Trustees of Roper Trust v. District Administrator, Hurungwe, (2) HH-200-2001
Trustees of Roper Trust v. District Administrator, Hurungwe, (1) HH-192-2001

Women's Land Rights and Customary Law Reform in South Africa: Towards a Gendered Perspective

Vinodh Jaichand

1 Introduction

For obvious reasons, land is arguably the most contentious subject in South Africa today. Racially discriminatory laws under apartheid ensured that a disproportionately large size of the total land in the country is concentrated in the hands of White minority while the majority of Blacks struggle to access land.[1] The negative consequences of this history currently manifests in evictions, homelessness, pervasive unemployment amongst Blacks and entrenched poverty. After the transition to multiracial democracy in 1994, government immediately took steps to address this problem but the land reforms processes so far have been slow and the majority of landless Blacks are increasingly impatient.[2] Proponents of appropriation of land without compensation are becoming more vocal. The land question therefore permeates all aspects of social, economic and political discourse in South Africa and the government faces the challenge to initiate land reform policies that reflect the socio-economic realities and at the same time survive tests of constitutionality.

Based upon a paper prepared for presentation at the 2014 *World Bank Conference On Land And Poverty*, The World Bank—Washington DC, March 24–27, 2014. The financial assistance of the National Research Foundation of South Africa towards this research is acknowledged. Opinions expressed and conclusions arrived at are those of the author and are not necessarily to be attributed to the National Research Foundation.

[1] Under Apartheid, 87 % of the total land in the Republic of South Africa was reserved for Whites and only 13 % was allocated to Blacks. See PLAAS. See also Jaichand (2013), pp 445–487.

[2] South African land reform policy basically follows three main trajectories: land restitution, land redistribution, and land tenure reform. See Department of Land Affairs (1997); Polity. See also Cousins (2005), p. 488.

V. Jaichand (✉)
School of Law, University of the Witwatersrand, Johannesburg, South Africa
e-mail: Vinodh.Jaichand@wits.ac.za

A. Diver, J. Miller (eds.), *Justiciability of Human Rights Law in Domestic Jurisdictions*, DOI 10.1007/978-3-319-24016-9_16

One such challenge is how to give meaning to the constitutional rights guaranteed to women in respect of access to land on the basis of equality.[3]

In South Africa, as in other parts of Africa, the nature of land rights is such that they spring from social relations and 'exist relative to the claims and needs of others'.[4] Therefore, the norms and values that are implicated in the management, control, negotiation and resolution of land disputes in local communities are 'historically specific'.[5] It is also within the context of such historic specificity that institutions and frameworks designed to reform land tenure system must be sought and that the norms, values and institutions that evolved from this context be taken into account as useful in addressing the problems of land reform especially in respect of settlement of land disputes.[6] This is even more so in the case of women's access to land because 'the forum in which land rights are negotiated and disputes resolved have a direct impact on security of tenure [and] the processes and institutions that negotiate land rights determine who gets land and who is able to retain it in the face of competing claims.'[7]

Thus the structures of land allocation, administration, and the framework for land dispute resolution are important in the implementation of any land tenure reform policy to guarantee access to land and security of tenure for marginalised groups such as women. The Restitution of Land Rights Act, the Communal Land Rights Act (CLARA), the Land Claims Commission, the Land Claims Court are only a few of the structural changes intended by government to address the land question in South Africa.[8] As pointed out above, and given the context-specific

---

[3] See Cousins and Claassens (2006), p. 2. Generally, under African customary law, women's land rights are often limited and tied to inheritance, marriage or gift. See also Cousins (2008a), pp. 109–37 at 111; See generally, Bank and Southall (1996). A woman is not viewed as an enduring member of her natal family because under some customary norms she is expected to get married and leave her parent's home for her husband's. See Bennett (2004), pp. 344–345. At the same time, she is not also regarded as a perpetual member of her husband's family and as such may not inherit from his estate at his death. This is particularly so in respect of land which in most African societies is based on the principle of primogeniture. However, progress in human rights and the opening of the political space for female participation has the potential to introduce changes to some of these customary practices. Many African countries have ratified international human rights treaties to protect the rights of women and have domestic legislation aimed at giving effect to these treaty obligations. Yet, there remain many areas of tension between customary practices and certain values and institutions that underpin a constitutional democracy like South Africa. The principle of equality and non-discrimination, not only on grounds of gender, amongst others, is one of the most fundamental values for the free, open and democratic society contemplated by the South African Constitution. One area in which this tension is manifest is the roles and functions of tribal authorities especially with reference to the allocation and administration of land, and the dispensation of justice.

[4] Claassens and Ngubane (2008), pp. 154–183 at p. 173.

[5] See Yngstrom (2002), p. 34.

[6] *Ibid.*

[7] Claassens and Ngubane (2008), p. 173.

[8] See Communal Land Rights Act No 11 of 2004, Government Gazette 20 July 2004. The CLARA was declared unconstitutional by the Constitutional Court in *Tongoane v National Minister for*

nature of the land problem, the process of negotiation and the customary law and practices of the group concerned are implicated. Hence, legislation such as the Traditional Leadership and Governance Framework Act (TLGFA) and the Traditional Courts Bill (TCB)—though primarily aimed at customary law reform—also have implications for access to land and security of tenure because of the scope of authority they confer. The TLGFA is the fundamental legislation underpinning customary law reform in South Africa and provides the framework for subsequent legislation such as the CLARA and TCB.

The TLGFA and TCB raise the challenge of how to reconcile inconsistencies between customary practices and constitutional principles of equality and non-discrimination on grounds of gender, especially in respect of women's land rights. Critics see the TCB as the resurgence of traditionalists trying to roll back the gains made in the advancement of women's right to land since 1994 and the Constitutional Court's decisions in several landmark judgments.[9] This research aims to provide an analytic framework for re-framing the discourse—a proposition of a shift from the 'Constitution *versus* customary law' approach which has dominated the mainstream discourse on the subject. As empirical evidence suggest, significant social changes are taking place across the erstwhile homelands that challenge traditional notions of the limitations on the rights of women to access land.[10] The idea is that when these changes are taken into account in the process of reconciling the apparent contradiction between the equality principle and custom, the tension reduces and the constitutional values could actually be useful instruments in reforming customary law to accommodate the rights guaranteed to women under the Constitution. To achieve this, it is not necessary to question customary law norms and institutions espoused in legislation like the TLGFA and TCB. Nor is it necessary to subscribe to the view that resolving the conflict will necessarily have to take place outside the constitutional framework.[11] It is possible to reach that

---

Agriculture and Land Affairs 2010 (6) SA 214 (CC). Section 1 of CLARA defines 'communal land' as 'land ... occupied by members of a community subject to the rules or custom of that community', while 'community' is defined as 'a group of persons whose rights to land are derived from shared rules determining access to land held in common by such group'.

[9] See for example, *Ex Parte Chairperson of the Constitutional Assembly: In re Certification of the Republic of South Africa* 1996 (4) SA 744 (CC); *Alexkor Ltd & Another v Richtersveld Community & Others* 2004 (5) SA 460 (CC); *Bhe & Others v Magistrate Khayelitsha & Others* 2005 (1) SA 580 (CC); *Doctors for Life International v Speaker of the National Assembly & Others* 2006 (6) SA 416; *Matatiele & Others v President of the Republic of South Africa & Others* 2006 (5) SA 47 (CC); and more recently, *Shilubana & Others v Nwamitwa* 2009 (2) SA 66 (CC); *Tongoane & Others v Minister of Agriculture and Land Affairs and Others* 2010 (6) SA 214 (CC).

[10] See for example Claassens (2013), p. 71; Budlender et al. (2011), pp. 118–140.

[11] Bennett (2004) had proposed that '[i]n the circumstances, the solution to a conflict between customary law and gender equality will have to be sought outside the parameters of the Constitution. Both the social implications of specific conflicts and their legal origins would be relevant. Once problems are fully contextualized, certain issues will be revealed as more urgent than others, and certain techniques for solving them will appear more appropriate than others.' It is possible to avoid the 'thorough purge of customary law' by the gender equality clause that Bennett warned

point if only policy makers would allow empirical evidence of the social changes taking place at grassroots and rural community levels to shape the institutional and legal frameworks necessary to give effect to a 'living customary law'. As custom is not stagnant the officials in such institutions would have to distinguish 'official customary law' from the 'living' one. Therefore training is essential to avoid the risk of being overturned on review, when legislation permits the adjudication of land disputes. The recent decision by the government to shelve the TCB has been welcomed by civil society groups although the Deputy Minister of Justice has been reported as saying there will be a traditional court in the future.[12] It is unlikely that the TCB can be reintroduced in same the form again.

The chapter is divided into five main sections. Section 1 gives an introduction and provides a contextual background. It discusses the questions to be interrogated, what the chapter seeks to achieve and how. Since customary courts are a part of the plan for access to justice in rural areas, the TCB may be an inevitable part of the justice sector reform and transformation in justice delivery efforts, probably not in the form proposed in the withdrawn TCB. The challenge is how to craft it in a way that does not violate the Constitution but secures and promotes women's land rights. Hence in this section, the question asked is how best do we secure and protect the land rights of women in the context of customary law and the Constitution? Secondly, what legal and institutional frameworks best facilitate this objective and how should government go about putting such structure in place in the context of the TCB? Thirdly, what are the implications of, and how should policy makers approach the conundrum of the power relations and contested authority of tribal authorities and institutions in the control, allocation and administration of land especially with regard to women's land rights, and what would the role of any TCB be in this regard? In Sect. 2, a brief historical account of women's land rights vis-à-vis customary law in South Africa is provided and is situated in the context of post-1994 developments in the country in order to highlight some of the problems now raised by the TLGFA and TCB. In Sect. 3, the salient provisions of the TCB are unpacked and how a similar Bill could undermine women's land rights by impeding their access to traditional justice system and other challenges the implementation of the TCB might face in practice are outlined. In Sect. 4, an alternative analytic framework for understanding traditional justice system while mainstreaming gender and the protection of women's land rights and security of tenure is provided. Section 5 ends by making recommendations on how to improve future notions on a TCB both as an instrument for the promotion of access to justice and protection of women's land rights and security of tenure. The final section provides some concluding remarks.

---

about, and at the same time protect and promote the values of equality in an open and democratic society envisaged by the Constitution.

[12] Legal Brief, Today *"Traditional Courts Bill to be 'resuscitated' after elections"* Monday 3 March 2014, Issue number 3464.

2 Women's Land Rights Under Customary Law in South Africa: A Brief Overview

In pre-colonial South Africa, land rights and access to land basically depended on group membership, though rights could also be gained through marriage, migration and formal transfer.[13] Land was vested in the lineage, tribe, chiefdom or other group, and though a member could claim and exercise his right to land as long as he complied with the group's ethical standards, such a right was also limited by obligations to the group and the rights and duties of group members inter se.[14] It was a "system of complementary interests held simultaneously' where both individual and community had interests in the land, not in the manner of Western understanding of property ownership but in a uniquely African system deriving, as it were, from 'locally legitimate landholding rather than the law'.[15] Every male had access to land to support his family but this soon changed as the population grew and land became scarcer.[16] Though men were at the apex in the hierarchy, they were also under obligation to utilize inherited property for the benefit of family members and had to consult their wives and children before alienating family property.[17] Women's land rights were 'socially embedded' within a family context that imposed rights and duties on members.[18] Married women could easily take up fields on communal land to cultivate on their own without limitation on size providing they did not encroach on the fields of others.[19] Women were not excluded from accessing land and they enjoyed a certain degree of security of tenure.[20] Colonialism, and subsequently, apartheid changed all of these. According to van der Merwe,

> [n]ot content to gain access to, and ultimately control over, land and other natural resources, they [colonists] sought, and achieved, sovereignty over the indigenes. They reinforced their *imperium* by a process of land allocation, distribution and utilisation that eventually ensured the sort of political and economic emasculation of the Africans that presently disfigures South African society.[21]

---

[13] Cousins (2008a), p. 111.

[14] Cousins (2005), p. 490.

[15] Cousins (2008a), pp. 111–113.

[16] *Ibid.*, p. 116.

[17] *Ibid.*, p. 119.

[18] *Ibid.*

[19] *Ibid.*, p. 120.

[20] For a good description of the system of land allocation and administration under indigenous law, see Okoth-Ogendo (2008), pp. 95–108.

[21] Van Der Merwe (1989), p. 664.

Through a series of legislation, the character of customary land tenure and the position of women in that equation changed.[22] First, efforts were made to codify customary law by reducing it to writing, but the interpretation given to customary norms, values and practices in the process were very different to what actually obtained in practice and this became known as 'official customary law' which is now widely seen as discredited.[23] As Cousins puts it,

> [i]n southern Africa, the interpretation of 'customary' law by colonial administrators and magistrates served to strengthen, not weaken, patriarchal controls over women and to freeze a level of subordination to male kin (father, husband, brother-in-law, son) that was unknown in pre-colonial societies . . . this project involved not simply the imposition of Eurocentric views and prejudices on the part of colonisers, but also the collusion of male patriarchs within African society, who were anxious to shore up their diminishing control over female reproductive and productive power.[24]

Legislation such as the Black Administration Act, documents such as Permission to Occupy (which were only granted to men), and other forms of policies that redefined the power relations between men and women, introduced a rigid form of primogeniture and entrenched patriarchal system by weakening women's right to land and tenure security.[25] These policies were also reflected in the structures and institutions responsible for land administration during apartheid. Tribal authorities were responsible for the allocation of land within their jurisdictions which were delineated by the State.[26] It is important to emphasise that these territorial boundaries and their demarcations were done arbitrarily with the sole aim of fully implementing the state's spatial racial segregation policy.[27] Thus, as people were forcibly removed and dumped in other jurisdictions under the control of different Chiefs, the hitherto existing communal land tenure systems were distorted and the consequences remain to this day. Some of these people contest the authority of these Chiefs just as the original inhabitants challenge the land rights and claims of

---

[22] Some of this legislation included The Native Lands Act of 1913, The Released Areas Act of 1936, Black Administration Act of 1927, and Bantu Authorities Act of 1951 amongst others. For a historical account of land administration in South Africa prior to 1994, see Van Der Merwe (1989).

[23] 'Official customary law' means the version of customary rules created by the state and legal profession while 'living customary law' refers to those rules 'actually observed by those people who created it'. See Bennett (2008), pp. 138–153 at p 144. According to Bennett, 'The "official" version applied by state courts and the administrative bureaucracy is especially suspect. Because it is presented in the forms of legislation or precedent, it is most likely to have distorted the actual social practice in order to serve some ulterior purpose.' See also Bennett (2004), p. 7; In *Alexkor Ltd & Another v Richtersveld Community & Others* 2004 (5) SA 460 (CC), para 54, the Constitutional Court held that books and old authorities on customary law should be used with caution because of their tendencies to give conflicting statements of what the relevant customary law is on the subject. See also *Bhe & Others v Magistrate Khayelitsha & Others* 2005 (1) SA 580 (CC), 2005 (1) BCLR 1, para 152; Cousins (2008b), pp. 3–31 at p. 10

[24] See Cousins (2008a), p. 120.

[25] Ibid. See also Meer (1997), pp. 1–14 at p. 1.

[26] See Ntsebeza (2005), p. 14.

[27] See Walker (2008), p. 2; Van der Merwe and Pienaar (1997), pp. 334–380 at p. 338.

those forcefully relocated to their territories by the apartheid government.[28] How to deal with the pattern of customary land tenure administered by the apartheid state-backed Chiefs that emerged during this period are some of the major challenges confronting the CLARA, the TFLGA and the erstwhile TCB.

Given the centrality of land, the question of where authority for the allocation and administration of land is located is critical to the success of any land reform policy.[29] Should authority be vested in tribal chiefs and what should be the role and function of traditional leaders and customary law in land administration?[30] Chiefs and tribal authorities have been accused of abuse of power and corruption which led to many anti-chiefs protests in the past.[31] In particular, chiefs have used the distorted 'official customary law' to discriminate against women, and chieftaincy being an undemocratic institution, is seen as unaccountable and so cannot be vested with powers for land administration.[32] Discrimination against women on account of gender is still pervasive in rural areas, but despite that more single women can access land.[33] In the event of a divorce, the woman is expected to return to her parental home where male relatives are unlikely to allow her access to land.[34] Widows are sometimes evicted from their husbands' lands if they have no sons to inherit the land.[35] Tribal institutions are usually patriarchal in organisation and membership, and women are discriminated against during proceedings.[36] Right from the commencement of the constitutional negotiation process for a democratic South Africa, the position of customary law and institutions vis-à-vis elected officials and democratic values and norms underpinning the new constitutional democracy on the one hand, and the status of women under customary law and how

[28] For an account of the socio-economic impacts of these removals on contemporary land relations in South Africa, see Van der Walt (2009).

[29] See the White Paper on South African Land Policy 1997.

[30] Cousins (2008b), pp. 3–31 at p 10.

[31] See Ntsebeza (2008), pp. 238–258 at pp. 239 and 246. See also Bank and Southall (1996), p. 418.

[32] See Claassens (2008), pp. 355–382 at p. 355. In a series of surveys conducted by the Institute for Poverty, Land and Agrarian Studies (PLAAS), it was discovered that whereas the majority of rural dwellers lamented the abuse of power and corruption of traditional leaders, at the same time, most of these same respondents still preferred that traditional leaders be the central authority in land allocation and administration and demonstrated unwavering loyalty and respect for the resilience and strength of their traditional leaders and institutions. See Ntsebeza (1999); Claassens (2001); Cousins (2008a), p. 126. Another research study by the University of Pretoria also found that notwithstanding the criticisms of traditional authorities, most rural dwellers were satisfied with the communal land administration system and regarded traditional leaders and headmen as the proper institutions for the administration of communal land. See Machethe (2009), pp. 131–146 at p. 145.

[33] Budlender et al. (2011).

[34] Cousins (2008a), pp. 109–137 at p. 120.

[35] *Ibid.*

[36] *Ibid.*

to reconcile them, had always been a difficult one to balance.[37] As with most countries in post-colonial Africa, the role of traditional institutions and the basis of their legitimacy under the supreme constitution remain unclear.[38] This question is particularly acute in relation to the land rights of women under the Constitution on the one hand and under customary law and practices on the other hand, notwithstanding the supremacy of the former.

As mentioned above, given the provision in Section 9(3) of the Constitution, women now have the opportunity of asserting their land rights by relying on this equality clause.[39] However, the constitution also recognises customary law and as Bennett puts it,

> [b]y implicitly recognizing customary law, and at the same time prohibiting gender discrimination, the Constitution has brought about a head-on confrontation between two opposed cultures – admittedly a confrontation that has long been gathering force.[40]

This "clash of cultures", to use Bennett's words, came to the fore in the TLGFA, CLARA and the TCB, all purportedly were aimed at aligning customary practices and institutions with the Constitution. The view that this was undertaken to bolster chiefly power also exists. The Constitutional Court has declared the CLARA unconstitutional for failing to follow the proper parliamentary procedures for its enactment.[41] However, reference to its provisions here is necessary because there is an intersection amongst the three pieces of legislation—TLGFA, CLARA and the TCB—relevant to understanding the issue of women's land rights and how they might yet inform some future land reform legislation. Besides, just like the TCB which had been introduced twice before in Parliament—first in 2008, and then in 2012 in exactly the same form—it is more than likely that the CLARA will find its way back to Parliament in the near future whether tinkered with or not.[42]

2.1 Women's Constitutional Land Rights and Customary Law Reform

Section 25(6) of the Constitution provides that '[a] person or community whose tenure of land is legally insecure as a result of past racially discriminatory laws or

---

[37] See *Ex Parte Chairperson of the Constitutional Assembly: In re Certification of the Constitution of the Republic of South Africa*, para 200.

[38] There are different proposals on how this problem could be approached. See the collection of essays in Claassens and Cousins (2008).

[39] See The Constitution of Republic of South Africa Act No 108 of 1996. See also Bennett (1994).

[40] *Ibid.*, p. 123.

[41] See *Tongoane & Others v National Minister for Agriculture and Land Affairs& Others* 2010 (6) SA 214 (CC), para 133 (c) (i) and (ii).

[42] The TCB was referred back to the Provinces and was not on the list of legislation slated to be passed before the 2014 general elections. See Joubert (2014), p. 6.

practices is entitled, to the extent provided by an Act of Parliament, either to tenure which is legally secure or to comparable redress'. Similarly, Section 25(9) provides that 'Parliament must enact the legislation referred to in subsection (6).' A combined reading of these legislation means that Parliament is under obligation to enact laws such as CLARA intended to give effect to the provisions in S. 25(6).[43] CLARA was intended to reform communal land tenure and the promoting of conditional use rights.[44] Together with the TLGFA and TCB, they provide the legal and institutional frameworks for customary law reform with implications for different aspects and subject matter of indigenous law, including land rights and access to land by women. As the Constitutional Court stated,

> statutes do not ordinarily deal with indigenous law in the abstract. They do so in the context of specific subject matter of indigenous law, such as matrimonial property, intestate succession, or the occupation and use of communal land, as CLARA does. Therefore any legislation with regard to indigenous law will ordinarily and indeed, almost invariably, also be legislation with regard to the underlying subject-matter of the indigenous law in question. The mere fact that a statute that repeals, replaces or amends indigenous law might have a different subject-matter of its own, does not detract from the fact that it also falls within the functional area of indigenous law.[45]

It is not surprising therefore, that all three legislations have implications for women's land rights and have been criticised for undermining those rights.[46] In *Tongoane*, although the Constitutional Court eventually declared CLARA

---

[43] It is important to read these provisions with the equality provisions in the Constitution: S.9

(1) Everyone is equal before the law and has the right to equal protection and benefit of the law.
(2) Equality includes the full and equal enjoyment of all rights and freedoms. To promote the achievement of equality, legislative and other measures designed to protect or advance persons, or categories of persons, disadvantaged by unfair discrimination may be taken.
(3) The state may not unfairly discriminate directly or indirectly against anyone on one or more grounds, including race, gender, sex, pregnancy, marital status, ethnic or social origin, colour, sexual orientation, age, disability, religion, conscience, belief, culture, language and birth.
(4) No person may unfairly discriminate directly or indirectly against anyone on one or more grounds in terms of subsection (3). National legislation must be enacted to prevent or prohibit unfair discrimination.
(5) Discrimination on one or more of the grounds listed in subsection (3) is unfair unless it is established that the discrimination is fair.

[44] See Communal Land Rights Act No 11 of 2004. (Available at http://www.ruraldevelopoment.gov.za/phocadownload/Acts/communal%20land%20land%20rights%20act%2011%20%20of%202004.pdf accessed 27.12.13).

[45] See *Tongoane & Others v Minister for Agriculture and Land Affairs & Others* 2010 6 SA 214 (CC), para 74.

[46] For a critical review of the CLARA, see Smith (2008), pp. 35–71.

unconstitutional for not following proper procedure in its enactment it did not go into the constitutionality of its substantive provisions and answer the question whether they discriminated against women,[47] it is important to underscore that it was argued that the Bill discriminated against women and would undermine women's land rights rather than enhance them.[48] Hence, the challenge of land reform and the frequent resulting conflict of norms between constitutionally guaranteed rights and customary law remains and resonate in the former TCB, which focused on reform of traditional justice system. The importance of the TCB in securing and protecting women's land rights lay in how issues of women's land rights and land-related disputes would be mediated and settled within the traditional dispute resolution institutional mechanisms of the TCB and the broader constitutional framework.

2.2 *Women's Land Rights and Traditional Justice System Reform*

It is important to stress that the customary justice system is an inescapable reality of the Africa. To deny it is to obfuscate the reality of African societies. The result is that written law would be largely ignored while the people carry on with their lives according to the norms and values of customary law and practice deriving from their history and culture.[49] Considering past vilification and efforts to discredit it, customary law in general and traditional justice system in particular has proved itself so resilient in Africa that it is almost practically impossible to supplant or completely obliterate it.[50] The same applies to customary land tenure.

The attempts to abolish customary law through systematic replacement with Western-style legal system has now been jettisoned and we have seen the renaissance of African traditional justice systems, as most African states try to contend with the challenges of a 'dual legal system' bequeathed by colonialism and apartheid. The legacy of colonialism in Africa means that postcolonial African countries have had to grapple with the impact of the interface of Western constructs of individual legal rights and duties and Africa's conception of such rights that emphasise family and community especially with reference to land.[51] Consequently, understanding the unique character of African land tenure system and the workings of its complex processes, as distinct from a Eurocentric conception of

[47] It was tagged and passed as a S. 75 Bill which does not affect the provinces, rather than as a S. 76 Bill which does. See *Tongoane & Others v Minister for Agriculture and Land Affairs & Others* 2010 6 SA 214 (CC), para 4, 45.

[48] See Claassens (2008), p. 355.

[49] See Okoth-Ogendo (2008), p. 99.

[50] See Clarke (2011), p. 16.

[51] See Bennett (2004), p. 6. See also Cousins and Claassens (2006), p. 2. See Allott (1965), pp. 366–368.

individual property right, has proved difficult.[52] In respect of land tenure in Africa, one of the most vocal proponents of the inability of African customary law and traditional justice systems to provide the legal basis for effective market-oriented property relations was the World Bank.[53] Throughout the 1970s and 1980s, the World Bank was vociferous in claiming that because of the emphasis on 'communal' interest and lack of 'ownership' paradigm in the sense of Western economic model, African land tenure systems were incapable of supporting a market economy and thus fostering economic development.[54] However, this has since been disproved by extensive research and more recently the World Bank itself has had to admit that these conclusions had been based on faulty assumptions.[55]

First, not only can the African land tenure system sustain a market economy, although distinct from Western conception of 'property ownership', there is evidence to support the conclusion that African traditional systems are not alien to the notion of individual property ownership.[56] Secondly, after decades, the World Bank had to admit that just as colonialism could not diminish it, customary law had once again proved itself a resilient system that has so far outlived all attempts to abolish or replace it—not the least because the proposed alternative of individual titling do not necessarily result in security of tenure or increased economic development, as evidenced by the customary law substitution policy pursued by many African countries after independence and the justice sector reform programmes vigorously promoted by international donor institutions, multilateral and development partners and agencies of African countries.[57] This is what necessitated a policy reappraisal and the return to the traditional justice systems that we have witnessed across Africa (with the support of former sceptics) in recent times. The challenge therefore, is how to tap the benefits of the traditional justice system while minimizing its effects especially where this negatively impact on women's land rights.[58] Since stakeholders now accept that traditional justice systems will continue to be relevant in African societies especially rural communities, the question then is how should a country like South Africa pursuing traditional justice reform in the former TCB ensure that such legislation secures and protect women's land rights in the context of traditional justice systems and the Constitution? The next section reviews essential provisions of the TCB and the implications for women's land rights.

[52] See Cousins (2005), p. 489. See generally Van Maanen and Van der Walt (1996) discussing some of these conceptual and theoretical issues.

[53] See Clarke (2011), p. 4.

[54] See World Bank (1989).

[55] See Yngstrom (2002), p. 23.

[56] See Okoth-Ogendo (2008), pp. 99–101.

[57] See Deininger (2003), p. 39.

[58] Section 1 of the TCB defines traditional justice system as a 'system of law which is based on customary law and customs'. Emphasis added. S 1 defines a 'traditional court' as a 'court established as part of the traditional justice system' headed by a king, queen, headman or headwoman, and which functions in accordance with 'customary law and custom'.

3 The Erstwhile Traditional Courts Bill (TCB): An Overview

Section 211(1) of the Constitution recognises traditional leadership and customary law and provides that '[t]he courts must apply customary law when that law is applicable, subject to the Constitution and any legislation that specifically deals with customary law.'.[59] It would not be possible to undertake a wholesale analysis of the TCB in a chapter of this nature, hence what is sought here is to unpack the essential parts of the TCB and how it impacts women's land rights directly or indirectly. The long title of the Bill makes clear its objectives:

> [t]o *affirm the recognition of the traditional justice system and its values, based on restorative justice and reconciliation*; to provide for the structure and functioning of traditional courts *in line with constitutional imperatives and values*; to enhance customary law and the customs of communities observing a system of customary law; and to provide for matters connected therewith.[60]

Even from the objects of the TCB as contained in S. 2(a), (b)(i), it is clear that there would be normative clash between the system the Constitution seeks to establish on the one hand, and the traditional justice system also recognised by the Constitution on the other hand. Procedurally, if not in substance, both systems pursue justice as an end but differ, not just in the meaning and content of justice, but also in the approach to doing justice. Whereas the court system listed by the Constitution in section 166(a)–(d) contemplates retributive justice, African traditional justice systems, which is apparently contemplated in section 166(e) of the Constitution, and which the TCB now seeks to 'affirm and recognise', by its very nature is restorative and reconciliatory.[61] The norms and values underpinning both systems are radically different too. The one draws heavily on flexible customary rules, traditional religious beliefs and practices for its operation and legitimacy, while the other relies on concepts and facts, evidence and a rigid system of rules.[62] Whereas the primary objective of the one is restorative, reconciliation and promotion of familial ties, social cohesion and community harmony, the other is basically retributive and promotes individualism. It therefore seems that both will continue to be relevant in rural communities where the majority of South Africans still live under traditional justice systems and the Constitution which make it mandatory for such courts to function subject to the Bill of Rights. So, whether women's land rights can be secured and protected under traditional justice systems will largely be a function of how much traditional institutions are amenable to reform to reflect

[59] See S 211(3) of the Constitution.

[60] Emphasis added.

[61] See section 166(e). Some maintain that traditional courts are created under Section 34 of the Constitution. See PMG Report. See however, Mnisi Weeks (2011), p. 34.

[62] See Mnisi Weeks (2011) *ibid,* arguing that traditional courts are not the type of impartial tribunals contemplated under Section 34 of the Constitution (although we do not necessarily agree with the author's view that traditional courts are not impartial).

constitutional values, and to what extent Parliament is willing to push the boundaries when legislating to provide the type of framework contemplated in the former TCB. Since it is impossible to abolish traditional courts, it is imperative to make sure that they function in accordance with constitutional values while acknowledging the procedural uniqueness of the courts in that they do not necessarily have to be evaluated through the prism of Western legal tradition.[63]

3.1 Composition of Traditional Courts and Women's Land Rights

In terms of S.1 of the former TCB, a traditional court is 'a court established as part of the traditional justice system, which—

> *(a)* functions in terms of customary law and custom; and
> *(b)* is presided over by a king, queen, senior traditional leader, headman, headwoman or a member of a royal family who has been designated as a presiding officer of a traditional court by the Minister in terms of section 4, and which includes a forum of community elders who meet to resolve any dispute which has arisen, referred to in the different languages ...'

The above excerpt implies that there shall be a presiding officer who would be the decision-maker. It has been argued that this centralises power in the hands of one individual contrary to the actual participatory and consensual character of traditional justice systems in rural communities.[64] In this respect, the TCB is not a true reflection of customary practices but an iteration of distortions introduced by official customary law legislation such as the Black Authorities Act and the Black Administration Act.[65] In customary courts, though a *head* may exist *de jure*, there is actually no *de facto* 'presiding judge' per se, as the former TCB seeks to create in the fashion of western legal tradition with a single independent decision-maker.[66] Rather, the court represents a public space for community consultations where members freely and actively engage in the 'hearing, questioning, deliberation and decision-making' process of the court.[67]

> Anyone can ask questions and there is no unseemly hurry; ... Then the smaller fry among the men of the lekhotla give their opinion, the more important people next, and finally the

---

[63] See *Alexkor Ltd & Another v Richtersveld Community & Others*, para 54.

[64] Community members, councils and other relevant groups play important roles in the traditional justice systems and traditional leaders do not ordinarily preside over traditional courts let alone being sole decision-makers as assumed by the drafters of the Bill. See Shirinda (2012). See also Institute for Poverty and Land and Agrarian Studies (2010). See Mnisi Weeks and Claassens (2011), p. 844.

[65] See Mnisi Weeks (2011), p. 32.

[66] Ibid., p. 33.

[67] Ibid., p. 32.

> headman gives his decision, which is generally the summing up of the views of the majority. In theory, he can give any decision he likes, but in practice, . . . the final verdict is really the general opinion of all present.[68]

In theory, the former TCB provides that there could be a female presiding over a customary court.[69] However, the participation of women in the proceedings of customary courts is uneven and few preside in such courts.[70] Women litigants are often forbidden from representing themselves and have to be represented by male relatives.[71] It is argued that given the male-dominated composition of these courts, women litigants would face discrimination where the other party is a male because these courts are likely to favour male litigants.[72] This is more particularly so if the subject matter of the dispute is land or land rights. During the parliamentary hearing on the Bill, one of the women made comments relating her ordeal in a customary court where the other party was a man.[73]

It is important to note that whereas a piece of legislation may stipulate gender equality in the composition of a traditional body, that does not guarantee that this would be socially realisable and could in fact be undermined in practice through a wide process of social arrangements, dialogues and interaction and other patrilineal 'socially embedded' organisation.[74] So, mere provision for the inclusion of women in the composition of traditional courts, without more, is unlikely to be successful in addressing the challenge of women's marginalisation, unless it pays close attention to the dynamics and fluid nature of patriarchal organisation of rural communities and the underlying normative values.[75] As Mnisi puts it 'by failing to specifically provide for women in the constitution and operation of customary courts (except as litigants, and even then without the protections they need), the TCB reinforces the problem that women were and are excluded from involvement in the decision making of customary courts.'[76]

---

[68] See Mnisi Weeks (2011) citing Dutton (1923), pp. 59–60.

[69] See section 1 of the TCB. In family disputes involving male and female parties (and in some cases this would involve dispute over land), customary courts are accused of being biased in favour of male parties; and by providing for a forum of community leaders in which women are hardly members, the TCB continues the marginalisation of women. See Alliance for Rural Democracy (2012), pp. 1–3.

[70] See Mnisi Weeks and Claassens (2011), p. 64.

[71] See Alliance for Rural Democracy (2012).

[72] See Claassens and Ngubane (2008), pp. 156, 163, and 166–167.

[73] The story of Stombi Hlombe was one of the oral presentations made by the victim before the Select Committee on Security and Constitutional Development during parliamentary public hearing on the TCB. "I was born with ten fingers. Now, I don't have ten fingers because the traditional leader stood by and did nothing to protect me because I am a woman." A male member of the Amahlubi Traditional Council was so upset that she had been elected to the traditional council in KwaZulu-Natal that he bit off one of her fingers so badly that it had to be amputated. See Joubert (2012).

[74] See Curran and Bonthuys (2005).

[75] See Polity.

[76] Mnisi Weeks (2011), p. 34.

In reality, and as emerging changes suggest, whether in the allocation of land or the settlement of disputes relating to land under customary law, the system is one of nested authorities and power: something in the nature of a pyramid involving the family, the headman, the ward, and the village.[77] Through this participatory process, members of the community develop, advance and adapt customary law and practices to reflect the interpretations and assessments of the people in accordance with their changing circumstances.[78] Through this process, women were able to articulate, negotiate and extend their land rights under customary law and custom.[79] However, it appears that the former TCB had eroded this important space because it only recognised the tribal chief as constituted in official customary law and implicitly confers on him the power to expound customary law. This ignores the 'living customary law' emphasised by the Constitutional Court because in reality, the bulk of disputes are resolved at the headmen's courts at the village level where participation is more broad-based.[80]

3.2 Subject-Matter Jurisdiction of Traditional Courts and Women's Land Rights

The civil jurisdiction of customary courts is contained in S. 5(1) which provides

> 5. (1) A traditional court may, subject to subsection (2), hear and determine civil disputes arising out of customary law and custom brought before the court where the act or omission which gave rise to the civil dispute occurred within the area of jurisdiction of the traditional court in question.
>
> (2) A traditional court may not under this section or any other law hear and determine—
>
> (e) any matter arising out of customary law and custom where the claim or the value of the property in dispute exceeds the amount determined by the Minister from time to time by notice in the Gazette; or
>
> (f) any matter arising out of customary law and custom relating to any category of property determined by the Minister from time to time by notice in the Gazette.[81]

From the above provisions, a chief's court would have subject-matter jurisdiction over property and since the Bill does not define 'property', one could infer that this would include movable and immovable property and so the traditional courts would have jurisdiction over land. The only proviso to the exercise of this jurisdiction by a traditional court in relation to land would be that the value of the land in question does not exceed the jurisdictional limit set by the Minister. It also means that the Minister could raise or lower the bar on the value of land over which a

[77] See Okoth-Ogendo (2008), p. 101.

[78] See Shirinda (2012), p. 64.

[79] See Mnisi Weeks and Claassens (2011), pp. 829–836.

[80] See Alliance for Rural Democracy (2012), p. 2.

[81] See section 6 of the TCB for the criminal jurisdiction of traditional courts.

traditional court could exercise jurisdiction from time to time. Therefore vesting jurisdiction over land dispute in traditional courts will be antithetical to this individualisation of land rights because land rights in these areas are, by default, communal. It will also have implications for women because their land rights matters will be heard by traditional courts which many believe to be skewed in favour of men. A woman may not be the one to institute an action in a traditional court, but where a man brings a land-related dispute before the traditional court and the defendant is a woman, the woman has no choice but to submit to the jurisdiction of the court even though she might have serious doubts about the impartiality of the court.[82]

Although the Bill forbids jurisdiction to the court in matrimonial cases and administration of estate, it is not clear how the court will deal with causes that might have overlapping issues. It is possible for the cause of action in a suit to arise from land but also raise legal issues bordering on matrimonial or testamentary law. Will the traditional courts have the requisite technical ability to delineate such technical matters and draw the thin lines between complex mix of often hazy and grey legal issues sometimes involved in a single subject matter suit such as land? It is easy to demarcate the subject matter jurisdiction of traditional courts but it will probably prove more difficult to exercise this jurisdiction in practice without acting *ultra vires* the powers of the courts.

3.3 Territorial Jurisdiction of Traditional Courts and Women's Land Rights

Even in pre-colonial times, traditional South African societies were not monolithic in social and political organisation.[83] One view was that various tribes were organised around a leadership of a tribal chief.[84] However, as already stated above, this system was changed through different legislation under apartheid. In order to realise the racial spatial segregation policy of the government, it was necessary to modify this pattern of traditional geographical demographics. The policy of forced removals meant that members of one community and tribe under one traditional leader found themselves being removed and placed in another territory under the leadership of a different traditional leader.[85] Herein lies one of the major obstacles to customary law reform in South Africa, especially in relation to land. Because, customary law is not uniform across the country, it follows that members of a particular tribe with a particular custom now live in a territory created

[82] Section 20(c) of the TCB makes it a crime not to appear before a traditional court, and arguably, implies that it is also criminal for anyone to refuse to submit to the jurisdiction of the court.

[83] See generally Bennett (2004).

[84] *Ibid.*

[85] See The Star (2012).

by apartheid under the leadership of another tribal leader whose legitimacy they sometimes challenge.[86] Section 4(1) of the former TCB provides that

> [t]he Minister may, in the prescribed manner, after consultation with the Premier of the province in question, designate a senior traditional leader recognised as such by the Premier, as is contemplated in the Traditional Leadership and Governance Framework Act, as presiding officer of a traditional court for the *area of jurisdiction in respect of which such senior traditional leader has jurisdiction.*[87]

So, by seeking to formally recognise the contested authority of such traditional leaders over the making, ascertainment, and interpretation of customary law practices in such territories, the former TCB entrenches these arbitrary territorial demarcations and is bound to open a floodgate of contestations.[88]

Furthermore, S.5 (1) provides that a traditional court has jurisdiction to hear a matter if the dispute arose from the *area of jurisdiction of the court in question.* It only takes a look at the differences in the attitudes of some communal practices in relation to women to understand how this territorial jurisdiction of the traditional courts will impact women's land rights. Since the 1980s, members of some communities have contested the authority and legitimacy of their traditional leaders.[89] Whereas some communities have been more progressive and transformative in granting access to land to women by allocating land to single women, divorcees and widows in their own rights, others have been less adaptive and responsive to the social and political transformations envisaged by the Constitution.[90] Therefore, the implication of the above provision is that a woman who lives in a jurisdiction which does not encourage the allocation of land to women will have no choice but to submit to the jurisdiction of the traditional court there to decide questions affecting her land rights. This will place such women in a disadvantaged position and further undermine their ability to access land.

3.4 *Procedural Frameworks of Traditional Courts and Women's Land Rights*

Section 9 of the former TCB set out a number of procedural safeguards aimed at ensuring fair hearing.[91] The proceedings of the court must meet the standards set

---

[86] See Alliance for Rural Democracy (2012), p. 1.

[87] Emphasis added.

[88] See Polity (2012)

[89] See Shirinda (2012); Mnisi Weeks (2012) (available at http://www.lrg.uct.ac/za/research/focus/tcb/ accessed 15.01.14). Section 9(4) covers situations where the applicable customary law is disputed between the parties.

[90] See the extensive case study conducted by Budlender et al. (2011) showing emerging differences in practices relating to women's land rights in several different rural communities.

[91] See S. 9 (2)(b)(i) and (ii) of the TCB stipulating that proceedings must comply with principles of natural justice.

out in the Bill of Rights of the Constitution especially in relation to women who are to be 'afforded full and equal participation'.[92] In terms of section 9(3)(b), a woman can represent her husband at a traditional court proceedings "according to customary law". *Prima facie* this provision appears to address the exclusion of women from participation in the proceedings of the courts. In fact there is no such customary law. It has also been pointed out that there is no express provision for women to be appointed as presiding officers.[93]

But more importantly, section 3(a) provides that '[n]o party to any proceedings before a traditional court may be represented by a legal representative'. Again, this is another controversial provision of the former TCB which flies in the face of sections 2(a) and (c), 3(a), (2)(a)(i) and (iii) of the TCB all of which purport to reflect the minimum procedural standards set by the Constitution for court trials. For this reason, the former TCB has been roundly criticised. Significantly, in what seems an attempt to justify this provision, the former TCB provides that the application of the Bill should be guided by the rule that the principles

> underlying the traditional justice system are not, in all respects, the same as in the context of *due process, as applied or understood in the retributive justice system.*[94]

If the exclusion of legal representation was intended to facilitate the main objective of the Bill which is the 'enhancing access to justice by providing a *speedier, less formal and less expensive resolution* of disputes',[95] then the legislature must find a way to achieve this without violating the right to legal representation enshrined in the Constitution, because the former TCB in its current form denies the right to be represented by counsel of one's choice to parties attending customary courts.[96] In addition, the former TCB recognises Chiefs' courts at the expense of other courts down the ladder such as family, clan and headmen's courts that actually undertake the bulk of dispute resolution at grassroots level.[97]

3.5 Sanctions of Traditional Courts and Women's Land Rights

The nature of punishment and sanction system of traditional courts as proposed in the TCB seems to pose the greatest threat to women's land rights. According to section 10(2)(*i*) of the former TCB, a traditional court could give an order 'depriving the accused person or defendant of any benefits that accrue in terms of

[92] See S. 9 (2)(a) of the TCB.

[93] Mnisi Weeks (2011), pp. 34–35.

[94] See section 3(2)(d). Emphasis added.

[95] See S. 2(b) (ii) of the TCB.

[96] See section 9(3)(a) of the TCB, *Cf.* section 35(3)(f) of the Constitution.

[97] See Mnisi Weeks (2011), p. 33.

customary law and custom'. Section 9(1)(b) further provides that 'the manner of execution of any sanction imposed by a traditional court, must be in accordance with customary law and custom, except in so far as the Minister prescribes otherwise under section 21(2)(a).'[98] The concern here is that deprivation of 'benefits that accrue in terms of customary law and custom' is wide enough to include deprivation of land rights for women as litigants before the court; and for a group that already suffers marginalisation in accessing land, this sort of punishment will further limit their land rights, undermine their tenure security and increase existing gender inequality in access to land.[99]

3.6 Appellate Jurisdiction of Traditional Courts and Women's Land Rights

Every system of sanctions should have a review mechanism in order to avert miscarriage of justice. Section 13(1) of the former TCB provides that

> [a] party to a civil or criminal dispute in a traditional court may, in the prescribed manner and period, appeal to the magistrate's court having jurisdiction against an order of a traditional court, as contemplated in section 10(2)*(a)*, *(b)*, *(h)* or *(i)*, as well as section 10 (2)*(k)*, to the extent that the order in terms of section 10(2)*(k)* relates to an order contemplated in section 10(2)*(a)*, *(b)*, *(h)* or *(i)*.

Furthermore, section 14(1) provides that

> [a] party to any proceedings in a traditional court may, in the prescribed manner and period, take such proceedings on review before a magistrate's court in whose area of jurisdiction the traditional court sits on any of the following grounds ...[100]

Notwithstanding the above provision for appeal from traditional courts to magistrates' courts in the Bill, many of the critics argue that the former TCB does not have a provision for appeal and as such there is no mechanism for women to challenge decisions of traditional courts where it undermines or infringes a woman's land rights.[101] The Bill lists the grounds for review to include where a traditional court exercised its powers *ultra vires* the TCB; where it lacks jurisdiction; procedural irregularities, bias, conflict of interest, or where it implicates corrupt practices.[102] Section 14(2) specifically recognises the powers of the magistrate court to review the decisions of traditional courts notwithstanding the

[98] Section 21(2) (a) gives the Minister power to make regulations regarding the procedures of customary court proceedings and the methods of executing their sanctions.

[99] See SHRC.

[100] See sections 13 and 14 of the TCB respectively.

[101] See for example, Submission of the Joint-Monitoring Committee on the Status of Women on the Communal Land Rights Act, pp. 3–4.

[102] See Section 14(1) (a)–(d) of the TCB.

provision in section 12 of the TCB which makes the decision of a traditional court final. In terms of section 13(3) of the TCB, a magistrate court could confirm, amend, vary, substitute or dismiss an order of a traditional court. It is therefore incorrect to suggest that the TCB has no provision for appeals, except that the grounds are limited. It is unclear, as stated earlier, whether the presiding officers would be trained in the 'living customary law' or not.

In general, however, it is apparent that there are many shortcomings in the former TCB as it affects women's land rights, ranging from the centralisation of power in the hands of chiefs, lack of accountability by these chiefs and tribal authorities, the challenge of ascertainment of customary law, exclusion of women from active roles whether as litigants or officials of customary courts, undemocratic governance process, and how all of these could further undermine rural development initiatives as far as access to land for women is crucial to such programmes. This makes it imperative to examine the jurisprudence of the Constitutional Court in an attempt to address the challenge posed by reconciling customary law and custom with constitutional values particularly the promotion of the rights of women and all other aspects of gender equality. The section that follows draws on the jurisprudence of the Constitutional Court and three major criteria developed in those cases as parameters for gauging how customary law and custom should articulate with constitutional imperatives.

4 A Gendered Perspective to Customary Law Reform to Improve Women's Land Rights Through Constitutional Court Jurisprudence

Before examining how some of the important principles developed by the Constitutional Court could be used to address the challenges arising from the former TCB, some conceptual clarifications would be in order. One way of looking at the problem of customary law reform and alignment with constitutional values is to not see customary law and the formal legal systems as mutually exclusive as is often done. Rather they should be viewed as mutually reinforcing systems working in harmony to accomplish the objectives of our Constitutional transformative enterprise. The principle of the 'living customary law' can be useful in this regard to the extent that it reflects the series of adaptations customary law and practices undergo as the people change their life patterns.

Friction is often exacerbated when well-intentioned legal and policy reform initiatives ignore or fail to capture these adaptations in their different manifestations. First, it is necessary to stop looking at traditional justice systems through the formal legal systems. The very essence of customary law and its most fundamental characterisation are often viewed as antithetical to the principles of law commonly associated with Western legal tradition. For example, in criminal law, it is a fundamental principle of criminal justice system that no one shall be punished for an act which at the time it was committed did not constitute a crime defined in a written law, and for which punishment is prescribed. Customary criminal law is never written and that is one of its basic features.

Secondly, it is also an important aspect of the administration of criminal justice in the Western legal tradition that an accused be represented by a legal counsel of her choice and where she cannot afford it, at the expense of the state. But by the very nature of customary law, legal representation (which is more an element of accusatorial or adversarial system) is in contrast with the reconciliatory foundational principle of customary justice system. So, to call for legal representation in traditional courts would undermine one of the most important elements of traditional justice system—restitution and reconciliation. But not to allow legal representation would also result in a contravention of S.35 (3)(f) of the Constitution. The way out, it seems is to provide an 'opt out' clause which might resolve all the inconsistencies and conflict with Constitutional values. The focus should not be how to make traditional justice systems conform to Western legal traditions, but how to adapt it to incorporate constitutional values such as gender equality. Since flexibility is one of the veritable characteristics of customary law, this affords us the opportunity to accomplish this task with minimum friction and disruption to existing traditional institutions and values.

5 Clarifying a Complex Legal System: Traditional Justice Systems *v*. Formal Legal System

Gender inequality in access to land and security of tenure, to varying degrees, have always characterised customary law and practices in South Africa and Africa.[103] The three pieces of legislation aimed at customary law reform in South Africa: TLGFA, CLARA and the former TCB underscore the resilience and resurgence of customary law, just like in other parts of Africa. However, this resurgence has not been preceded by a thorough conceptual interrogation or debate of the complexities of underlying issues.[104] One of the questions is how 'two legal systems with radically different traditions, form and operation are to function together, reinforce the other and promote the rule of law'.[105] The CLARA and TCB in particular, have often been vilified using the 'right' *versus* 'culture' paradigm but with little examination of the theoretical debates underpinning them or proposals for viable alternatives.[106]

[103] Cousins (2008b), p. 19.

[104] See Clarke (2011)

[105] *Ibid.*, p. 2.

[106] See for example, Claassens and Cousins (2008). Several newspaper articles and editorials have criticised the TCB.

For its part, this neglect of a sound theoretical framework to underpin the reform of customary law prior to the TLGFA, CLARA and TCB enactment has raised constitutional challenges and thus undermined government's intentions and the problems the legislation were designed to address. For any government policy on reform of customary law to be legitimate and viable, it must reflect the practice of the people that live by it, and for any such practice to be tenable in a constitutional democracy such as South Africa's, it must be in consonance with constitutional values. These are some of the challenges the former TCB allude to when it, on the one hand, declares its objectives to be inter alia, to 'affirm the values of the traditional justice system, based on restorative justice and reconciliation and to align them with the Constitution'[107]; and on the other hand, asserts that the implementation of the TCB shall be guided by 'principles underlying the traditional justice system [which] are not, in all respects, the same as in the context of due process, as applied or understood in the retributive justice system'.[108] A rigorous conceptual analysis and theoretical debate of this issue should therefore engage the attention of researchers and policy makers and presage any customary law reform policy of the government. Luckily, the Constitutional Court has pointed the way in this respect.

The Constitutional Court's decisions have shown that it is not impossible for customary law to adapt itself to the values of the Constitution and those traditional institutions and dispute resolution mechanisms need not necessarily be opposed to these values, deriving though from different legal traditions. Indeed, the chief's courts and the institutions of state can function harmoniously to realise women's land rights. The Constitutional Court developed three principles that could be useful in this regard: firstly, the recognition of customary law as part of an overarching South African legal system whose validity is based on and superintended by the Constitution.[109] Secondly, customary law should be seen as referring to the 'living customary law' 'which is an acknowledgement of the rules that are adapted to fit with changed circumstances' as contrasted with colonial and apartheid-era 'official customary law'.[110] Thirdly, the principle of gender balance and equality should be consciously factored in and integrated into customary law as part of the processes of social change occurring in communities since the inception of the Constitution.[111] These principles should therefore shape the customary law reform discourse in general and inform any implementation of traditional courts in particular to promote access to land for women and secure women's land rights. Once this is understood, then it would be acknowledged by both supporters and opponents of the former TCB that it is fruitless engaging in polemical arguments to discredit the

[107] See section 2(a) of the TCB.

[108] See section 3(2)(d) of the TCB.

[109] See *Alexkor Ltd & Another v Richtersveld Community & Others* 2004 (5) SA 460 (CC), para 51.

[110] See *Bhe & Others v Magistrate Khayelitsha & Others* 2005 (1) SA 580 (CC), para 87.

[111] See *Shilubana & Others v Nwamitwa* 2009 (2) SA 66 (CC).

customary justice system as one that sets up an 'inferior parallel justice system' for rural South Africans.[112] Neither is it possible, in view of countervailing constitutional values for the former TCB to operate in a way that infringe the land rights of women. The task therefore is to infuse customary law reform with constitutional values and make them work for the protection of women's land rights through the TCB in particular and the traditional justice system in general.

5.1 A Dual but Connected Legal System?

The first principle implies that customary law and legal system is an 'independent source of norms' and forms part of South African legal system deserving of respect 'in its own right' though it must function in line with constitutional values.[113] The Constitutional Court crafted some criteria that should help in resolving some of the controversies surrounding the former TCB as is demonstrated below.[114]

Apparently, in practice, there is likely to be a conflict in the implementation of the provisions of the former TCB. For example, the objects of the former TCB outlined in S.2(b)(iii); the Guidelines for the implementation of the former TCB outlined in S.3(1)(a)(ii) and (iii); S.3(2)(a)(i),(ii), S.3(2)(b), all provide that traditional courts are to function in accordance with customary law and practices. Yet, in S. 9(1)(a)(b), the former TCB provides that the courts shall operate, taking into account the particular provisions of the Bill of Rights in the Constitution and with particular reference to the equal participation of women. While this makes perfect sense, it will be difficult to see how traditional courts will function and ensure equal participation of women, if it is to operate in 'accordance with customary law and practices' because, as we all know, customary law and practices are fundamentally patriarchal and marginalise women.

Does it mean that the courts will have to modify those aspects of customary law that marginalise women in order to comply with these provisions? If the answer is yes, it is not clear how the courts would go about doing this since some of these values are deeply entrenched in rural areas and even though custom evolves, it takes a long time for customary norms to form and once they emerge, it also takes a long and slow process to bring about modification or eradication. In recognition of this, the Constitutional Court has preferred not to leave the customary law on certain subject matter such as succession to the process of customary law development

[112] See Hartley (2012)

[113] See *Shilubana & Others v Nwamitwa* 2009 (2) SA 66 (CC), para 43.

[114] In ascertaining customary law, a court must (a) consider the traditions, history, past and current practices of the community in question relying on the paradigmatic settings of the particular community rather that of the common law; (b) respect the rights of communities living by the customary law to develop their own law; (c) strive to balance flexibility and development against the need for certainty of legal rules while paying respecting protection constitutional rights. See *Shilubana & Others v Nwamitwa* 2009 (2) SA 66 (CC), para 44-7.

because it would result in inadequate protection for the rights of women and children.[115] Similarly, not every element of traditional courts should be left to customary law development.

Where the practice of traditional courts would result in injustice, both the provisions in section 39(2) of the Constitution and section 9 of the former TCB actually impose a legal duty and provide the means for traditional courts to avoid such injustice by prioritising the constitutional rights of parties. Thus, a traditional court confronted with a case involving a woman's land rights is under a duty both under the Constitution and the former TCB to adjudicate such matter in a way that does not infringe the rights of such party. Some of the criticism of the former TCB is that it vests power to 'determine and make customary law' in the hands of traditional chiefs to the exclusion of other community institutions and participants in the process.[116] To the extent that the former TCB and the traditional courts allow the participation of community members in the determination and development of customary law, no one is better suited to ascertain and develop customary law norms than these traditional courts and the traditional communities in which they operate. In the Shilubana case, the Constitutional Court emphasised the need to consider the customary practices of the relevant community when ascertaining the contents of a customary law norm.[117] In particular, the Court stated that '[t]he right of communities under section 211(2) includes the right of traditional authorities to amend and repeal their own customs.'[118]

The Court stressed the need for the rights of communities regulating their lives by customary law to be respected and left to develop their own law bearing in mind the character of the law in question, how it was brought about, the implications for rights guaranteed in the Constitution, and the impact on vulnerable persons.[119] One of the arguments against the former TCB has been whether the chiefs presiding in traditional courts (who are usually men and so beneficiaries of the status quo) would not become despotic with such immense power. This is one of the areas the training sessions contemplated in Section 4 of the former TCB should address. The contents of customary law have always been expressed through the practices of those who live by it, including members of the traditional courts in the particular community. It is therefore unhelpful, to try to prescribe the trajectory of development in customary law using paradigms designed by common law and the formal legal system in the sense of division of powers between legislature, executive and judiciary. Traditional justice system knows no such division. The TCB should therefore focus on encouraging active participation of community members in the

[115] *Bhe & Others v Magistrate Khayelitsha & Others* 2005 (1) SA 580 (CC), para 110-ff.

[116] See Legal Resource Centre (2011) 'The Traditional Courts Bill must start with Women's Rights' (available at http://www.lrc.org.za/index.php/papers/images/stories/Newsletters/June_2011_The _LRC_Brief.pdf accessed 27.12.13).

[117] See *Shilubana & Others v Nwamitwa* 2009 (2) SA 66 (CC), para 46.

[118] Ibid., para 45.

[119] *Shilubana & Others v Nwamitwa* 2009 (2) SA 66 (CC), para 47.

courts in order to address this problem. The incongruity in some of the suggestions based on the common law paradigm is apparent when the question of legal representation in traditional courts—a major criticism of the former TCB—is considered.

Clearly, the purpose of Section 9 (3) which forbids legal representation is to avoid the technicalities, high cost of legal services, long delays occasioned by lawyers, the hostility, retributive and antagonistic bad blood often bred and that characterize common law and the formal legal system which all stand in contrast to the quick, cheap, accessible, reconciliatory and restorative purpose of traditional courts. It goes without saying that the aim of the TCB would hardly be realisable if it were to begin by importing the exact same procedural requirements that clog the conventional courts and make them so protracted, expensive, and causing disaffection in communities and making justice inaccessible to the poor in rural areas, to traditional courts. The argument that prohibition of legal representation in traditional courts makes traditional justice system an 'inferior justice system' disregards the fact that a person may elect not to exercise this right by rejecting legal representation and choosing to defend himself.

Therefore, this issue in the former TCB could be fixed by inserting an opt-out clause whereby a party is allowed to choose whether to submit to the jurisdiction of a traditional court and so be deemed to have waived his right to legal representation, or to go to conventional courts and exercise his right to be represented by a counsel.[120] However, a further problem will arise where a complainant in a land dispute before a traditional court insists on the matter being decided by the traditional court while the defendant, say, a woman who fears the court will be biased in favour of a male complainant, insists on the magistrates' court. It would seem that one way out in such a case would be to allow the party exercising a constitutional right—in this case the defendant—to prevail.

Another possibility would be to provide that, in such a case, the defendant must submit to the jurisdiction of the traditional court 'under protest' through some sort of preliminary objections, and when the matter is decided and he is dissatisfied, he could then go to the magistrates' court under S.13 or 14 of the former TCB. This option will serve to maintain the integrity of the traditional courts and prevent them from falling into disrepute through frequent disobedience of its summons. In the final analysis, if traditional justice system reform is to be effective, it must avoid the technicalities and other pitfalls otherwise, it will amount a replication of the conventional.

[120] See Mnisi Weeks (2011), p. 35.

5.2 The 'Living Customary Law' as a Guardian Angel

In *Tongoane & Others v National Minister for Agriculture and Land Affairs & Others*, the Constitutional Court declared the CLARA unconstitutional because it failed to comply with the requirements of section 76 of the Constitution before the Bill was passed into law—lack of broad consultations.[121] One of the criticisms of the TCB is the failure to consult with stakeholders—particularly women and women's groups in rural communities who are most likely to be affected by the Bill—other than the National House of Traditional Leaders.[122]

First, such consultations would provide the opportunity for the legislative process to take full cognisance of the varying degree of social changes and customary practices on the ground and so incorporate them in the formulation of any TCB. This is one way of engaging the 'living customary law' principle developed in Constitutional Court jurisprudence. In terms of women's land rights for example, it would be found that in several communities though to varying degrees, changes are beginning to occur on the ground in relation to how different categories of women access land.[123] An eloquent testimony to how 'living customary law' captures changing community practices through what Mnisi Weeks and Aninka Claassens call 'vernacular values'[124] is stated in a research conducted by the Community Agency for Social Enquiry (CASE) in several communities that:

> in the past there were very few requests from single women to have access to land because it was assumed that their acquisition of land would come through marriage. These days, it was reported that there has been a decline in marriage. The pressure to get married is no longer strong and this has made it easier for women to have access to land. It has, in particular, become easier for women with children to be given a site. Indeed, in some cases a woman having children was the motive behind her family wanting her to get her own site because they consider her to be troublesome.[125]

One of the recommendations of this chapter therefore, is that in formulating the law on this subject, it would be useful that the legislative process be guided by the 'living customary law' as generated from broad consultations and with inputs from the different categories of persons any traditional courts bill is intended to regulate including women. This would require the empowerment of rural women, of women's groups and capacity-building initiatives for women's groups in order to be able to articulate the social changes taking place in these communities and how it is bringing about shifts in customary practices in respect of women's land rights, so

---

[121] See *Tongoane & Others v National Minister for Agriculture and Land Affairs& Others* 2010 (6) SA 214 (CC), para 133 (c) (i) and (ii).

[122] See Institute for Poverty, Land and Agrarian Studies (PLAAS) (2014) 'Reintroducing the Contentious Traditional Courts Bill' (available at http://www.plaas.org.za/sites/default/files/publications-pdf/UW%2014.pdf accessed 14.01.14).

[123] See generally, Claassens (2013).

[124] See Mnisi Weeks and Claassens (2011), p. 823.

[125] See Budlender et al. (2011), p. 55.

that the legislature could better capture this rather than reflecting the preferences of just a section of the community. This can bring about the necessary policy shift without the government necessarily having to throw its weight behind one group or the other.

Secondly, it is the failure of the former TCB to reflect the 'living customary law' as being expressed in on-going changes regarding women's land rights in rural communities across South Africa that creates the apprehension about the potential impact of traditional courts on women's land rights. Traditional courts already appear to be needed in these communities and represent the local communities currently access justice. However, as a law intended to strengthen the operations of these courts, there is disconnect between some provisions of the former Bill and changing customary practices on the ground. For example, had the drafters of the Bill reckoned with the fact that there are now female members of councils, following the *Shilubana Case*, a female traditional leader, the drafters of the former TCB would have had no reservations in expressly providing for women to be officials in traditional courts.

As Claassens rightly asserts, whereas Constitutional Court jurisprudence point to the direction of a 'living customary law' formation process that is inclusive, participatory and democratic in its own unique way and producing norms and rules that are flexible and dynamic, Parliament keeps introducing legislation that work in the opposite direction by concentrating power in the hands of chiefs.[126] Although land allocation had always followed the patrilineal paradigm in order to preserve land for the children of sons of the community and prevent outside men from gaining access to community land through marriage to daughters of the community, there is evidence of customary practices gradually changing and adapting to some of these changes as more and more single women are setting up their own homes, a decline in marriages amongst women and increasing demands from women lobby groups.[127] Thus, Claassens and Ngubane argue that

> current practices do indeed reflect the patriarchal nature of tribal structures and systems, the changes currently taking place [in KwaZulu-Natal where land is gradually being allocated to single mothers] draw attention to the capacity of customary systems to adapt and respond to the broader social and political context in which they function.[128]

While there may still be uncertainty about the extent and trajectories of these changes in respect of how women's land rights and access to land are changing and being impacted, Claassens observes that

> [t]he scale and pace of single women obtaining residential sites varies between areas and from province to province, but is taking place throughout the 'communal areas' of South Africa. *It was not precipitated by a particular new law or land reform measure.*

[126] See Claassens (2013), p. 72.

[127] *Ibid.*, p. 171.

[128] Ibid., p. 170.

> *Instead, it appears to be the outcome of spontaneous local negotiations between women and land authorities, which began around 1994 and have since gathered momentum.*[129]

It is this element of dynamism and flexibility underpinned by the 'vernacular values' mentioned earlier that the Constitutional Court has emphasised in the capacity of 'living customary law' to meet the needs of peoples as their life patterns change over time, and this is what the former TCB should reflect in other to strengthen and bring the operations of traditional courts in alignment with the constitution. If this is done, it will go a long way in securing women's land rights because the traditional courts will then reflect the social changes taking place on the ground which have seen more and more women of various categories being able to access land.

5.3 Access to Courts for Gender Equality and Land Rights

By its very nature, land rights in South African customary law stems

> from social relations and exist relative to the claims and needs of others, the forum in which land rights are negotiated and disputes resolved has a direct impact on security of tenure. The processes and institutions that negotiate land rights determine who gets land and who is able to retain it in the face of competing claims.[130]

Women's access to land and their security of tenure are shaped by the prevailing local customary law and practices irrespective of any existing national legislation.[131] Such customary practices as pervades a local community would include its marriage systems, land allocation system, dispute resolution systems and dispute resolution mechanisms. This is the first reason for it being counter-productive to attempt to provide a uniform traditional court system across the country because there are variations in customary law and custom from one community to another. Another reason it might be unworkable is when there is an attempt to centralise the jurisdiction of chiefs without resolving underlying issues of contested authority due to apartheid-created arbitrary territorial base.

If legislation attempts to replace a 'socially embedded' customary practice or institution without so much as acknowledging such practice and the necessary process of evolution, the people simply ignore such legislation and continue to live according to such practice.[132] For example, merely providing that wives can represent their husbands at traditional courts would not protect a widow's land rights because it apparently ignores the practical difficulties of implementing such provision and bringing about necessary shifts in deeply entrenched discriminatory

[129] Id. (emphasis added).

[130] Ibid., p. 173.

[131] See Curran and Bonthuys (2005), p. 607.

[132] See Okoth-Ogendo (2008), p. 99.

customary practices. As we have seen, notwithstanding the decision in *Gumede v President of the Republic of South Africa*,[133] *Bhe v Magistrate, Khayalitsha, Shilubana & Others v Nwamitwa* and other cases, studies suggest that social practices do not necessarily comply with these legal changes and views in relation to protection of women's land rights through allocation of land to single women which bear witness to little changes in communities.[134] This supports the conclusion that the social context and processes in which women's land rights are defined and articulated are also critical to their protection and tenure security.[135]

Statutes may empower women, but customary law and social practices may not necessarily reflect these changes and we could have a situation where 'official law and social practice are not always reinforcing and, in some instances, may in fact clash with one another'.[136] This is where the Constitutional Court drew the distinction between 'official customary law' and 'living customary law' as necessary in reconciling customary law and constitutional values. In fact, this particular provision is capable of having unintended consequences. The fact that the former TCB allows parties to be represented by relatives could actually be used to justify and provide a legal basis for the current practice of male relatives representing women, for exclusion of women from customary courts' proceedings and widows being gagged in spaces considered sacred in traditional courts.[137] Hypothetically, nothing will abridge a widow's access to land and land rights more than bringing a land dispute with a male brother-in-law before a predominantly male court only for her to be represented by the same male relative challenging her right to her deceased husband's land.[138]

The character and composition of institutional arrangements such as traditional courts, and the power relations within which questions of land rights are settled shape the outcomes and determine who is able to access land and who is not. So, if as is currently the practice, women cannot participate in these courts, and are not members of these courts, it is difficult to expect that such system would meet the standards of constitutional values of equality.[139] Practices such as women not being allowed to speak in the courts; widows in mourning clothes must stand outside the and pass their message through male relatives, elderly male members of the court sympathise with the causes of men in court and women who approach the court on land disputes are frowned at and labelled as niggling.[140]

---

[133] 2009 3 SA 152 (CC).

[134] See Budlender et al. (2011).

[135] See Mnisi Weeks and Claassens (2011), p. 831.

[136] See Curran and Bonthuys (2005), p. 607.

[137] See Alliance for Rural Democracy (2012), p. 1.

[138] See Van der Westhuizen (2012).

[139] See Human and Science Research Council (2006).

[140] See Oomen (2005), p. 86; Claassens and Ngubane (2008), pp. 173–174.

6 Conclusion

The criticisms of the erstwhile TCB are that it entrenched patriarchy and apartheid-era discrimination and sought to consolidate the existing difficult environment in which women's access to justice and land rights are shaped and negotiated.

The reform of traditional justice system institutions such as customary courts can draw on the transformative agenda of the Constitution by extending equal rights to women as it does to men in access, participation and representation in land disputes in traditional courts.[141] To achieve this, any traditional courts bill should do more than granting women *locus standi* before the courts. It must take cognisance of the underlying socio-economic inequalities and traditional institutional norms that make discrimination against women in land allocation possible and seek to engage them in a transformative manner.[142]

The debates on the former TCB often ignore the fact that even current state legal institutions have focused more on the weakness of the Bill and less on how best the Bill could bring access to justice to women recognising that millions of women meant to be served by customary courts are distant from current justice structures of the state. The dominant narrative is that law-making, interpretation and implementation are state functions and must be vested in different arms of government. This is the 'rule of law orthodoxy' that inherently contradicts the former TCB that gives presiding officers in a chief's court the power to determine and apply customary law.

One commentator however sees this as an opportunity:

> After decades of marginalizing customary justice systems in justice sector reform and efforts to improve access to justice, engaging with customary law and its related institutions is gaining more prominence on the policy agenda. This commendable development has arisen from governments in the developing world and aid agencies recognizing what the rural poor have always known: the formal justice system represents only a fraction of the normative framework and justice services on which citizens rely.[143]

Should the erstwhile Traditional Courts Bill resurface in the future, not necessarily in its previous incarnation, perhaps these ideas might guide it to a better outcome.

References

Albertyn, C. (2011). Gender transformation in South African jurisprudence: Poor women and the constitutional court. *Stellenbosch Law Review, 3*, 591.

[141] See Albertyn (2011), p. 598.
[142] Ibid., p. 600.
[143] See Clarke (2011), p. 2.

Alliance for Rural Democracy. (2012). Fact sheet: The traditional courts bill. Available at http://www.lrg.uct.ac.za/usr/lrg/doc/TCB/2012/ARD_factsheet_final.pdf

Allott, A. N. (1965). Towards the unification of laws in Africa. *The International & Comparative Law Quarterly, 14*(2), 366.

Bank, L., & Southall, R. (1996). Traditional leaders in South Africa's new democracy. *Journal of Legal Pluralism,* 37–38, 407.

Bennett, T. W. (1994). The equality clause and customary law. *South African Journal of Human Rights, 10*, 122.

Bennett, T. W. (2004). *Customary law in South Africa.* Lansdowne, India: Juta & Company Ltd.

Bennett, T. (2008). "Official" vs "Living" customary law: Dilemmas of description and recognition. In A. Claassens & B. Cousins (Eds.), *Land, power and custom: Controversies generated by South Africa's Communal Land Rights Act* (pp. 138–153). Cape Town, South Africa: Juta & Company Ltd.

Budlender, D., Mgweba, S., Motsepe, K., & Williams, L. (2011). *Women, land and customary law.* Johannesburg, South Africa: Community Agency for Social Enquiry (CASE).

Claassens, A. (2001, October). *It's not easy to challenge a chief: Lessons from Rakgwadi* (Research Report No 9). Institute for Poverty, Land and Agrarian Studies (PLAAS).

Claassens, A. (2008). Customary law and zones of chiefly sovereignty: The impact of government policy on whose voices prevail in the making and changing of customary law. In A. Claassens & B. Cousins (Eds.), *Land, power and custom: Controversies generated by South Africa's Communal Land Rights Act* (pp. 355–382). Cape Town, South Africa: Juta & Company Ltd.

Claassens, A. (2013). Recent changes in women's land rights and contested customary law in South Africa. *Journal of Agrarian Change, 13*(1), 71.

Claassens, A., & Cousins, B. (Eds.). (2008). *Land, power and custom: Controversies generated by South Africa's Communal Land Rights Act.* Cape Town, South Africa: Juta & Company Ltd.

Claassens, A., & Ngubane, S. (2008). Women, land and power: The impact of the Communal Land Rights Act. In A. Claassens & B. Cousins (Eds.), *Land, power and custom: Controversies generated by South Africa's Communal Land Rights Act* (pp. 154–183). Cape Town, South Africa: Juta & Company Ltd.

Clarke, R. (2011). Customary legal empowerment: Towards a more critical Approach. In *Traditional justice: Practitioners' perspectives.* International Development Law Organisation Working Papers Series No. 4.

Cousins, B. (2005). "Embeddedness" versus titling: African land tenure systems and the potential impacts of the Communal Land Rights Act 11 of 2004. *Stellenbosch Law Review, 3*, 488.

Cousins, B. (2008a). Contextualising the controversies: Dilemmas of communal tenure reform in post-apartheid South Africa. In A. Claassens & B. Cousins (Eds.), *Land, power & custom controversies generated by South Africa's Communal Land Rights Act* (pp. 3–31). Cape Town, South Africa: Juta & Company Ltd.

Cousins, B. (2008b). Characterising "Communal" tenure: Nested systems and flexible boundaries. In A. Claassens & B. Cousins (Eds.), *Land, power and custom: Controversies generated by South Africa's Communal Land Rights Act* (pp. 109–137). Cape Town, South Africa: Juta & Company Ltd.

Cousins, B., & Claassens, A. (2006). More than simply "Socially Embedded": Recognising the distinctiveness of African Land Rights. *Keynote Address at the International Symposium on at the Frontier of Land Issues: Social Embeddedness of Rights and Public Policy held at Montpellier*, 17–19 May 2006. Available at http://wwwmokoro.co.uk/files/13/lria/African_land_rights_distinctiveness.pdf (accessed 02.12.13)

Curran, E., & Bonthuys, E. (2005, October). Customary law and domestic violence in rural South African communities. Centre for the Study of Violence and Reconciliation. *South African Journal on Human Rights, 21*, 607.

Deininger, K. (2003). *Land policies for growth and poverty reduction.* World Bank/Oxford University Press.

Department of Land Affairs. (1997, April 30). White Paper on South African Land Policy. Available at http://www.ruraldevelopoment.gov.za/phocadownload/White-papers/whitepaperlandreform.pdf

Dutton, E. (1923). *The Basuto of Basutoland.* London: Jonathan Cape.

Hartley, W. (2012, September 20). New chief's bill creates parallel justice system for rural people. *Business Day Live.* Available at http://www.bdlive.co.za/national/law/2013/09/20/new-chiefs-bill-creates-parallel-justice-system-for-rural-people

Human and Science Research Council. (2006). Longitudinal study: The effect of the legislated powers of traditional authorities on rural women in South Africa.

Institute for Poverty, Land and Agrarian Studies. (2010). Reconciling living customary law and democratic decentralisation to ensure women's land rights security. *Policy Brief.*

Jaichand, V. (2013). Finding common ground: Rights arising from land reform in South Africa. In O. Vilhena, U. Baxi, & F. Viljoen (Eds.), *Transformative constitutionalism: Comparing the Apex Courts of Brazil, India and South Africa.* Available at http://www.pulp.up.ac.za/pdf/2013_12/Chapter21_IBSA.pdf (accessed 01.06.15).

Joubert, P. (2012, September 22). Women's minister whacks chiefs bill. *City Press.* Available at http://www.citypress.co.za/news/womens-minister-whacks-chiefs-bill-201220922

Joubert, J. J. (2014, February 2). Women force rethink on traditional courts bill. *Sunday Times.*

Machethe, C. (2009). The Communal Land Rights Act (CLaRA) baseline study in three South African Provinces: Free State, Mpumalanga and North West. In *Land reform in South Africa: Constructive aims and positive outcomes: Reflecting on experiences on the way to 2014* (pp. 131–146). Johannesburg, South Africa: Konrad-Adenauer-Stiftung.

Meer, S. (1997). Introduction. In S. Meer (Ed.), *Land, women and authority: Perspective from South Africa* (pp. 1–14). Cape Town, South Africa: National Land Committee.

Mnisi Weeks, S. (2011). Beyond the traditional courts bill: Regulating customary courts in line with living customary law and the constitution. *South African Crime Quarterly, 35*, 31.

Mnisi Weeks, S. (2012, February 20). Traditional leaders. Available at http://www.lrg.uct.ac/za/research/focus/tcb/

Mnisi Weeks, S., & Claassens, A. (2011). Tensions between vernacular values that prioritise basic needs and state versions of customary law that contradict them: We love these fields that feed us, but not at the expense of a person. *Stellenbosch Law Review, 3*, 823.

Ntsebeza, L. (1999). *Land tenure reform, traditional authorities and rural local government in post-apartheid South Africa* (Research Report 3). Institute for Poverty, Land and Agrarian Studies (PLAAS).

Ntsebeza, L. (2005). *Democracy compromised: Chiefs and the politics of the land in South Africa.* Leiden, the Netherlands: Brill.

Ntsebeza, L. (2008). Chiefs and the ANC in South Africa: The reconstruction of tradition. In A. Claassens & B. Cousins (Eds.), *Land, power and custom: Controversies generated by South Africa's Communal Land Rights Act* (pp. 238–258). Cape Town, South Africa: Juta & Company Ltd.

Okoth-Ogendo, H. W. O. (2008). The nature of land rights under indigenous law in Africa. In A. Claassens & B. Cousins (Eds.), *Land, power and custom: Controversies generated by South Africa's Communal Land Rights Act* (pp. 95–108). Cape Town, South Africa: Juta & Company Ltd.

Oomen, B. (2005). *Chiefs in South Africa: Law, power and culture in the post-apartheid era.* New York: Palgrave.

PLAAS. *The distribution of land in South Africa: An overview* (Fact Check No. 1). Institute for Poverty, Land and Agrarian Studies. Available at http://www.plaas.org.za/sites/default/files/publications-pdf/No1%20Fact%20check%20web.pdf (accessed 01.05.15)

PMG Report. Available at http://www.pmg.org.za/report/20090901-department-justice-constitutionaldevelopment-traditional-courts-bill.

Polity. (2012, November 29). Controversial traditional courts bill withdrawn. Available at http://www.polity.org.za/article/controversial-traditional-courts-bill-withdrawn-2012-11-29

Polity. Official customary law and the disruption of patriarchal power: The case of Msinga. Available at http://www.polity.org.za/article/official-customary-law-and-the-disruption-of-patriarchal-power-the-case-of-msinga-2013-09-26

Restitution of Land Rights Act No. 22 of 1994.

Shirinda, S. (2012). Traditional courts bill must start with women's rights. *The Star*. Available at http://www.mg.co.za/article/2012-06-07-the-bill-must-start-with-womens-rights

SAHRC. Submission by the South African Human Rights Commission on the TCB. Available at http://www.sahrcc.org.za/home/21/files/SAHRC%20Submission%20Traditional%20Courts%20Bill%20NCOP%2015%202%2012.pdf

Smith, H. (2008). An overview of the Communal Land Rights Act 11 of 2004. In A. Claassens & B. Cousins (Eds.), *Land, power and custom: Controversies generated by South Africa's Communal Land Rights Act* (pp. 35–71). Cape Town, South Africa: Juta & Company Ltd.

Submission of the Joint-Monitoring Committee on the Status of Women on the Communal Land Rights Act.

The Star. (2012, November 7). Bill promotes inequality, injustice. Available at http://www.iol.co.za/the-star/bill-promotes-inequality-injustice-1.1418781#.Uv3haNFDHzA

Van Der Merwe, D. (1989). Land tenure in South Africa: A brief history and some reform proposals. *Journal of South African Law,* 663.

Van Der Merwe, G., & Pienaar, J. M. (1997). Land reform in South Africa. In P. Jackson & D. C. Wild (Eds.), *The reform of property law* (pp. 334–380). Aldershot, England: Ashgate.

Van der Walt, A. J. (2009). *Property in the margins*. Oxford, England: Hart.

Van der Westhuizen, C. (2012, March 7). Traditional courts bill throwback to the past. *Cape Times*.

Van Maanen, G. E., & van der Walt, A. J. (1996). *Property law on the threshold of the 21st century*. Antwerp, Belgium: Maklu Uitgevers.

Walker, C. (2008). *Landmarked: Land claims and land restitution in South Africa*. Athens, Greece: Ohio University Press.

World Bank. (1989). *Sub-Saharan Africa: From crisis to sustainable growth: A long term perspective*. Washington, DC: The World Bank.

Yngstrom, I. (2002). Women, wives and land rights in Africa: Situating gender beyond the household in the debates over land policy and changing tenure systems. *Oxford Development Studies, 30*(1), 21.

Case Law

Alexkor Ltd & Another v Richtersveld Community & Others 2004 (5) SA 460 (CC).

Bhe & Others v Magistrate Khayelitsha & Others 2005 (1) SA 580 (CC).

Doctors for Life International v Speaker of the National Assembly & Others 2006 (6) SA 416.

Ex Parte Chairperson of the Constitutional Assembly: In re Certification of the Republic of South Africa 1996 (4) SA 744 (CC).

Matatiele & Others v President of the Republic of South Africa & Others 2006 (5) SA 47 (CC).

Shilubana & Others v Nwamitwa 2009 (2) SA 66 (CC)

Tongoane & Others v Minister of Agriculture and Land Affairs and Others 2010 (6) SA 214 (CC).

Legislation

Bantu Authorities Act of 1951.
Black Administration Act of 1927.
Communal Land Rights Act No 11 of 2004, Government Gazette 20 July, 2004.
Constitution of Republic of South Africa Act No 108 of 1996.
The Native Lands Act of 1913
The Released Areas Act of 1936.
White Paper on South African Land Policy 1997

MIX
Papier aus verantwortungsvollen Quellen
Paper from responsible sources
FSC® C105338

If you have any concerns about our products,
you can contact us on
ProductSafety@springernature.com

In case Publisher is established outside the EU,
the EU authorized representative is:
Springer Nature Customer Service Center GmbH
Europaplatz 3, 69115 Heidelberg, Germany

Printed by Libri Plureos GmbH
in Hamburg, Germany